Don't Tell Dad

Don't Tell Dad

a memoir

Peter Fonda

NEW YORK

The author gratefully acknowledges permission to reprint excerpts from the following lyrics:

The Dance by Tony Arata copyright © 1989 Morganactive Song, Inc. and Pookie Bear Music. All rights outside USA and Canada administered by WB Music Corp. All rights reserved. Used by permission of Warner Bros. Publications, Inc.

Buckets of Rain copyright © 1974, 1975 by Ram's Horn Music. *It's Alright Ma (I'm Only Bleeding)* copyright © 1965 by Warner Bros., Inc., renewed 1993 by Special Rider Music. *Shelter from the Storm* copyright © 1974, 1975 by Ram's Horn Music. All rights reserved. International copyright secured. Reprinted by permission.

Ballad of Easy Rider by Roger McGuinn, copyright © 1969 EMI Blackwood Music and Last Minute Music. All rights controlled and administered by EMI Blackwood Music Inc. All rights reserved. International copyright secured. Used by permission.

Colours by Donovan, copyright © 1965 by Donovan (Music) Ltd. Administered by Southern Music Publishing Co. Inc. Copyright renewed. International copyright secured. Used by permission.

Library of Congress Cataloging-in-Publication Data

Fonda, Peter.
    Don't tell dad: a memoir/Peter Fonda.—1st ed.
      p.   cm.
    ISBN 0-7868-6111-8
    1. Fonda, Peter, 1940– . 2. Motion picture actors and actresses—United States—Biography. I. Title.
PN2287.F57A3   1998
791.43'028'092—dc21
[b]   97-36543
             CIP

Book design by Nicholas A. Bernini

FIRST EDITION

10 9 8 7 6 5 4 3 2 1

*For
Jane*

$\mathcal{A}$cknowledgments

I would like to thank Bob Miller and Leslie Wells for their patience, Jamie Harrison for her understanding, wit, and humor, and my wife and family, and the pups.

Preface

In my memoir, I speak often of the different illegal drugs I've tried. I speak of them in the context of the times they were being used. I speak of them casually, but I know of their casualties. Do not misunderstand me. I know their "casual use" has pushed many of my friends over the big edge. There are people who can have just one marijuana cigarette and fall into the abyss of abuse. One "acid trip" from which some have never come back. I was lucky. I don't have an addictive personality. Many people do. You may lose it all.

PF

Don't Tell Dad

In the fall of 1986 I visited my sister, Jane, for a few days at her house in Santa Monica before I went off to shoot a motion picture. Jane's daughter, Vanessa, and son, Troy, were there one evening, too, and we gathered in the kitchen while Jane prepared chicken, rice, and a salad for supper.

"What are you up to, aside from this movie?" she asked.

"Well . . ." I stalled for a thought. "Actually, I have an offer to write my memoir."

"Your memoir?"

"Yeah. I've been courted a lot about doing a bio, and now the courting has become *verrry* real. Doubleday has offered one point two mil, and that's just too good to ignore."

She began to lose a bit of color in her face. Her long beautiful fingers started to twitch, just a little.

"Well, I, ah . . ."

"I've got a pretty good title, and—"

"Ah . . . Peter"—a long pause with more twitching—"I . . ."

Jane wasn't usually at a loss for speech. I tried to reassure her.

"Listen, check out the title, it's—"

"No, no, Peter—"

"Jane, you gotta check—"

"Listen, Peter,—"

"Jane! Jane, you've got to . . ."

"*Peter*—"

". . . check out this title. You know they want to really sell the book, so there'll be a huge 'PETER FONDA,' and just under it will be a small 'a happy man.' Then, under that will be a huge 'CONFES-SIONS,' and under *that* will be a very small 'of a drug-crazed, child-abused, runaway Hollywood brat as told to Chuck Barris.' "

"Chuck Barris? Peter, what the—"

"Jane. Jane . . . That's just the—"

"No! Peter, you can't—"

"Just the title. Chuck Barris isn't a part of the book, just the title!"

"But what . . . oh shit, Peter . . . I mean . . ." Jane was experiencing a sudden loss of cabin pressure, and no yellow masks were dropping from the ceiling to aid her.

"What am I going to say about you?"

"Well, yes." She was having some trouble with the chicken.

"You *are* my sister. And we've seen the battle from the same fox-hole. You are a big part of the life."

"Yeah, but I mean what are . . ."

"I *am* going to dedicate a special chapter to you. You are a major player."

"Oh God! Peter—"

"No, listen."

"Peter, stop talking! You—"

"Jane, listen, this is the title of the chapter: *Don't Tell Dad.*"

Her color was gone, her movements stuttered. A piece of chicken dropped to the floor. Troy and Vanessa stared at her.

"But, Peter, you promised *never* to tell!" Her voice was dry and cracking.

"Shit, Jane. That's just the title of one of the chapters! You'll see that title on a chapter page, and then, when you turn the page, there'll be nothing. Blank. Turn the next page, and it's blank, too, and so on, for three or four pages, until you finally turn a page and read, "I never told Dad a fucking thing!"

"Oh! You mean it's going to be a *funny* book?"

My poor sister. I didn't have a book deal.

*W*ho Packed the Bags

My mother, Frances Ford Seymour, was born at the General Hospital in Brockville, Ontario, in 1908. Her family lived on a farm in Morrisburg, Ontario.

The Seymour family came to Hartford, Connecticut, in 1639. They beat the Fondas to the New World by twelve years. Richard Seymour—"the Settler"—was related to Lady Jane Seymour, Henry VIII's third wife. With a background like that, it might be easy to assume my mother was a socialite, and so she was called in 1936, when she married my father. But she was born as much a farm girl as my dad was a farm boy. She was blond, very beautiful, with aquamarine eyes and fabulous cheekbones.

When she married George Brokaw, recently divorced from Clare Boothe Luce, my mother married into society, and she fit in very well. She had been a teller at the Guaranty Trust Company of New York, but after her marriage to George, she became a vice president of the bank. Nine months from the day of her first marriage, my half-sister, Pan, was born. A few years later, George Brokaw died. George was from Old Money. He had sailed the world in his 178-foot sailing-steam ship *Blackwatch*. Pan showed me photos of some of his journeys that I am sure fueled my dreams. And we *are* related to Tom Brokaw by many twists and turns. I like the idea. George was a terrible alcoholic. As was her father, Eugene Ford Seymour.

My father, Henry Jaynes Fonda, was born in Grand Island, Nebraska. When he was six months old, his family moved to Omaha, where his father started a printing business. A few years after Mother was born, her family moved to Fairfield, Connecticut, where her father became a superior court judge. She met my father on a luxury liner bound for England. She was on her way to a European vacation; he was on his way to work. She arranged to be on the same ship as my father on his return to the United States. By the time the ship arrived in New York, she had sent a telegram to her mother saying that she was going to announce her engagement to Henry Fonda. He saw the telegram before she sent it and tacitly agreed with the statement. When he left her, to fight in the Pacific in 1943, my mother's farm and financial experience prepared her well to provide for the family.

The Fondas came to the New World in 1651 from Amsterdam. The Fonda family had lived in the Netherlands for two hundred years, after having been exiled from their native land in northern Italy, where they can be traced as a family to the early thirteenth century. By the time the Fondas hit the beaches of the New World, they were a Dutch family, members of the Dutch Reform Church. Richard "the Settler" was Episcopalian, and very English, when he hit the shores of Connecticut. Anglo-Saxon to the max, both families. But just enough Italian in my father's family to put some music into the mix.

. . .

While considering my life, I've reflected often, as have many people, about what I might do differently had I the chance to do it over. Each time, without exception, I have reached the same conclusion. I don't want to relive or redo any part of the boogie. I have no desire to be eighteen or any other age again. This has nothing to do with the quality of my life at any given time or the circumstances, such as the birth of my children. I am quite pleased with the lives my children decided to make for themselves. If I have made any mistakes in fatherhood, I accept them fully as mine. Lord knows I was never a perfect father nor a perfect husband. Few things have been perfect in my life. But there is no way I would desire to "do it over." Other than recalling the past for the purpose of writing this book, I would prefer to never again even think of the dark parts of my past.

My desires, naturally, have little effect on the actual living of my life. I am cursed, instead, with a detailed memory that unfolds itself constantly on the plate of my past. This plate, unwanted by me, is continually placed in front of me as each new secret is revealed from

my occluded past. Although some have accused me of living in two
time zones, the reader will begin to see, by example, how an event
that happened in 1985 revealed an incredible incident in 1946. And
again in 1990 another trauma that brought me smashing back into
1946. And so on.

For the past few years I have had the benefit of a special therapy.
Until I started this program, there were very few nights since 1946
during which I had a peaceful sleep. I can remember the last
night—or rather the last morning—when I awakened as a child and
could not or did not want to continue sleeping. This is the kind of
sleep that happens to youth, when something about the new day
demands immediate investigation or attention, a time when nothing
in the dream world could be more captivating than the discovery of
the new day, the experience of the newborn over the darkness of the
dream. I had little comfort in the dream world after the age of six. In
awakening, the terror of my dream world's special little nightmare
became a part of the new day, and the certain terror of the next sleep
would keep me awake at all costs. This destructive pattern continues
today, but with the therapy it is less ruinous. My dreams, uncomfortable and scary, were determined by actions that left no room for
youthful discovery, and I didn't understand them. Years later I discovered the source of these constant, insistent nightmares, and with this
discovery, I became very angry with my mother and father.

After coming eye-level with the reality of my youth, I learned that
there was no real or good reason to ever respect anyone who pro-
fessed authority over my life—parents, teachers, cops, corporate
heads, government. To this day I can find no reason to invest authority in any person other than myself. Nothing since childhood has per-
suaded me to change my mind.

So many people have written about the Fondas. So many crass
writers have made a lot of money "detailing" the "history" of my life
and the lives of my sister, father, mother, and daughter. These plagia-
rists and poachers have been given a free hand in attacking and trivi-
alizing our lives by the Supreme Court, and I will in turn count on the
First Amendment to give me full rights in exposing these minor assholes for the yellow journalists that they are. But their versions of our
history remain out there in the public conscience as "truth," and there
is very little I can do to defend us. I certainly don't want to spend
much time answering their distortions, as it would leave little room

for my own story. Even so, their stories are, at times, the "reason" for my stories. Even more disturbing are the number of critics who have strengthened these distortions by acclaiming them and giving them intelligence, affirming their half-truths or outright lies. It's a very frustrating thing to have no recourse in these matters, but I don't want to use this book to address this stuff. Although I was delighted when the *New York Times* called Peter Collier's book, *The Fondas, A Hollywood Dynasty,* "psychobabble."

Some members of my family might not like what they will read, but few will dispute it. As for my friends, I have changed some of the chronology and some of the names to keep their privacy. For the most part, though, the details, dialogues—the facts—are accurate, and the words you will read come from my fingertips to your eyeballs.

After I achieved my initial success, I was asked, many times, "Are you *the* Peter Fonda?" My usual reply was, "Well, I'm fucked if I'm not." In 1982, I was shopping for a shirt in Los Angeles and was asked the above question, to which I gave the above reply. The very nice salesman who was handling my purchase did not drop a beat. "Hold on!" he said, as he went to the store's filing terminal. And what do you know, he found two *other* Peter Fondas, Peter M. and Peter D. Fonda. Can you imagine what *they* go through in their life identities?

Just because I am writing a memoir at this hopefully early point in my life does not mean that I feel that my "job" on this planet is finished, or that I have nothing left to do or think that is interesting. It does mean that I have a song to sing and I want to sing it now. I will hopefully have another song to sing later in my life and a voice with which to sing it.

On my fiftieth birthday, my sister, Jane, wrote a poem about the event. It was the first poem she had written, and it is absolutely beautiful. In it she advised me to think of my life as a glass, half full instead of half empty. I have thought about or read the poem many times, and each time I read or think about that advice, I am filled with hope and enthusiasm, for my life is and has been an overflowing cup whose mess on the tablecloth is as priceless to me as any Picasso. Even the part of the mess that can never be cleaned up.

chapter *One*

I was born in New York City on the twenty-third of February, 1940, at twelve o'clock noon on a Friday. Friday's child is loving and giving. I was delivered by caesarean section. My mother moved to the Pierre Hotel as soon as she was able. There were no complications with the birth, and I would have loved to have gone to the Pierre with her, but Friday's child stayed at the Le Roy Sanitarium for more than seven weeks, the only baby in the hospital, before flying to California with his father. I *was* brought to the Pierre a few times for a photo-op with Mother, but the Le Roy was my main crib. Dad had to change me just outside Kansas City.

An announcement of my birth in the *New York Times* ran with a photo of my mother and stated that I was a nine-pound baby. My father ran around the set of the movie he was making, *The Return of Frank James*, yelling, "Boy, I've got a fullback!" My father's version of my birth weight was later revised to almost ten pounds, but according to the delivering doctor's records, I weighed eight pounds, six ounces. I was "almost ten pounds" until I was almost twenty—not the best stats for a fullback. The weight factor would play an important role during the next few decades.

According to many different silver cups and a birth spoon, I was named Peter Hilton Fonda, Henry Pieter Ten Eyck Fonda and Henry Pieter Ten Eyck Hilton Fonda. On the twenty-third of June, 1940, I was christened Peter Henry Fonda, and my sister was christened Lady Jane Seymour Fonda and called "Lady" until she was eight, though I have always called her Jane. Our half-sister from our mother's first marriage, Frances de Villers Brokaw, has always been called Pan.

My father and I flew home to a house in Brentwood (a Los Angeles suburb in those days), on Chadbourne Avenue. Some of my memories, including a constant sense of searching for my parents as I learned to crawl, then walk, are very specific. I remember the brass upholstery tacks that studded the leather chair in Mother's little office, off the back right end of the living room. I remember our nursery, where Dad had painted likenesses of the Oz characters and several children's rhymes on the ceiling and walls; the bricked patio where I would skin my knees happily escaping the always prohibitive grasp of a governess as I crawled like a maniac toward an impossible freedom. But I also remember riding my push-scooter out of the Chadbourne gate and onto the street, scooting down the street to our grandmother's house or up the street to Mrs. Asparagus's house (not her real name, but that is what Jane and I called her, for reasons we've since forgotten).

My parents were building a house at 600 Tigertail Road, in the Santa Monica Mountains, and they went to the property as often as possible. We picnicked all over the nine acres, finding the site for the house, and moved in increments from 1942 to 1944.

We had a long driveway that wound up from Tigertail Road. First it passed the lower orchards and the barn where Pan, seven years older than Jane, kept her five-gaited gelding, My Boy, and where Jane and I later kept our burros. Farther up on the right was our playground, with a jungle gym, swings, two circus horses my mother had found in Greenwich Village in lower Manhattan from an old merry-go-round, a sandbox, and the playhouse, a miniature two-story structure with a little play kitchen, upstairs bedrooms, a bathroom, and a living room–dining room. It was far enough away from the main house so that nothing the children might be doing would disturb the grown-ups.

Just above the playhouse were the rabbit hutches and henhouse, an incinerator, and an ingenious compost pit my father had designed and built; then, farther up was the vegetable garden. There were nine huge oak trees on the property, refuges from the governesses-of-the-moment, none of whom wanted to climb. The main house lay at the end of the driveway, which circled around the garage, passing under a roof that connected the main house to the garage, with servants' quarters on the second story. A supper bell sat in a little cupola in the middle of the roof between the two buildings.

I think that Mom and Dad got the idea for the playhouse from Maggie and Leland Hayward, but Maggie (my father's first wife, Margaret Sullavan) and Leland took the "special house for the children" to a literal place. They had a separate house built for Brooke, Bridget, and Bill and that was where the children lived, slept, and ate. Jane and I always felt that the three Hayward children had a much tougher life with their parents than we ever had. They, of course, felt that *we* had a much tougher time. It was the antithesis of "the grass is greener." In the end, we all lost.

Although we lived in a way few other Los Angeles families did in the forties, we lived in the manner of many ordinary families across the United States. We had pets, dogs and cats, and Pan had a pet king snake. We had a Victory Garden—ours was more like a small truck farm. We used gas rations. We recycled all metals and newspaper. Mother made preserves, putting up every kind of fruit and vegetable we grew. Grapes, kumquats, oranges, apples, grapefruit, strawberries, raspberries, peaches, apricots, and tomatoes all found their way into the mason jars that lined the shelves in cabinets built along the back of the three-car garage. The henhouse had a wing of cages in which the laying hens were kept. The hens laid their eggs, and the eggs rolled gently out into a wire trough from which they were gathered each day. Whatever was not used in the cooking or eating process—except meat and dairy products—was put into the compost pile. All else was burned in our incinerator; the ashes left over were then added to the compost. In other words, we left no trash unused. It was not just a response to the war effort, it was our way of life. I knew not to fool around in the garden.

. . .

By the time of my birth, when he was thirty-five, my father had already found a place in the collective consciousness of the country as Tom Joad, Young Mr. Lincoln, and Frank James. But my first distinct memory is of him leaving, in 1943, for the war. After boot camp, he went to an officer candidate school—or OCS—in Quonset, Rhode

Island, and trained as a Naval Air Combat Intelligence officer. We were at Tigertail by then, and the night he left he spent some time with Jane in her room before he came in to see me. He caught me out of bed and carried me back. Mom was with him. I remember the smell of his skin, his rough, unshaven face rubbing mine, as he hugged me good-bye. He sat on the edge of my bed and sang a little rhyme: "My doggie's name is guess, my doggie's name is guess, he wags his tail for no and shakes his head for yes." For many years I have puzzled over the meaning of the rhyme at that special moment. Perhaps it had no hidden meaning, or perhaps it was his "Rosebud." Nevertheless, he was off to save the country. Between the time of my birth and his departure for the war in 1943 he made ten movies, and it's no wonder that we saw so little of him and weren't always sure of what he looked like.

Mother was a brave war wife and carried on with the details of living. She helped prepare the meals. She was the one who butchered the rabbits and wrung the chickens' necks and plucked them. I learned a great deal about the killing of things in order to have food on the table and understood that the killing of the chickens and rabbits was as necessary as the harvesting of the carrots and other vegetables. It was not heartless, it was the process of life. We never named the rabbits.

For a while, an artist in need of a place to stay bunked out in the playhouse. He drew pictures for me and taught me to play the harmonica. The first song I learned to play was "Old Black Joe."

I'm comin', I'm comin', though my head is hangin' low,
I hear those gentle voices callin', "old black Joe."

I think my mother had an affair with him. I hope she did. I remember one night, after a mountain lion had been raiding our chickens and rabbits, Mother had Jane and me stay with her in that little house while she waited for the big cat. She had a shotgun, and she was determined to drive the cat off. I was very excited by this notion and stayed awake to see the action.

When the action did come, it was so dark and there was so much noise from the chickens, the mountain lion, and Mother, I didn't have any idea what was really happening until the boom from the shotgun cleared my sleepy mind. The cat never came back. And I never wanted to sleep overnight in the playhouse again.

I asked about the things of life as any child would, and, I suppose, as any child would, believed what I was told. I *truly* believed. I trusted. How does one catch a bird? Put salt on its tail. Hours were spent crawling on my belly on the grass at Tigertail with a saltshaker in my hand, followed by many nights of punishment for leaving the silver shaker in the grass. Several doors in the Tigertail house had strange opaque, swirled panes of glass. What is that? I asked. Hurricane glass. What's a hurricane? Someone explained, reminding me of a hurricane I'd seen on a Castle Films Newsreel.

Then one day, one afternoon, sometime, somewhen, the Santa Ana winds bashed the house. The doors that had the odd glass panes began to howl. And I became afraid and ran around the house crying in fear. I was certain that the house was going to blow away. I did not understand that the tiny space between the door and the frame was the source of the howling, as I was too afraid to get close to them. Dad was always disgusted by my fright, but why else would someone have hurricane glass in a door if not for a possible hurricane? It was years before I learned the name came from the design, from the swirls that looked like hurricane clouds in the glass.

I learned not to ask too many questions. Dad would become annoyed, but Mother would answer, "put salt on its . . ." I spent years silently thinking about the salt and the bird line, trying to process the explanation into real action. Finally deciding that I was lied to, and finally understanding: if I could get close enough to put salt on a bird's tail, I could easily catch it.

. . .

When I was three or four I saw a movie called *Chad Hanna*, in which my father played the part of a man who runs away with the circus. I had been told that he was fighting in World War II against the Japanese, but what I saw on the movie screen wasn't war. It was a circus, and my father had run away with Linda Darnell. I was upset to see this, as no one had explained to me yet that my father was an actor, or that movies weren't real life. I most likely wouldn't have understood the difference at that age. I watched, confused but patient, until Dad had to go into a lion's cage to clean it. He didn't realize that the lion was in the cage with him, but I did, and I was certain that he was going to be eaten by the lion. I mean, the man on the screen looked like the photos I had seen of my dad, and there he was walking around looking and sounding like Dad, but he was about to be eaten by this very large lion, and I couldn't understand why Jane and Pan weren't saying anything. So I ran up to the screen, screaming out warnings. Our mother had to take me out of the screening room and finally calmed me down by explaining that it wasn't Dad; it was someone who looked like Dad, but it wasn't him. I decided that there was a man walking around the world who looked and sounded just like my father but who was called Chad Hanna, and I did calm down. I certainly wasn't going to worry about some stupid man named Chad Hanna who wasn't smart enough to see if the lion was still in the cage before he went to clean it.

Dad came home on leave twice. The first time, a few months after the movie, I was at the Brentwood Town and Country School. I was walking down the school's driveway when I noticed the big black Buick sedan-limo that was the "special" family car. And out of the car stepped Chad Hanna. I ran and hid in the bushes that lined the driveway to the school. It took a lot of coaxing to get me out of the bushes. I held on to the branches and screamed. I would never go anywhere with someone called Chad Hanna. I'm sure Dad was very angry with me for not coming to him happily, but he had no way of knowing that I was certain he was Chad, a man who had been eaten by a lion and had come back from the dead to haul me away. None of the rest of the family knew that I had tiptoed around the house looking at every photograph of the man who looked like my father and decided they were photos of Chad Hanna. I never asked what the hell Chad was doing in all the family photos. I felt it was better to leave it alone; Jane had made enough fun of me already. I still couldn't comprehend my father's job, or the nature of movies. The things that I had seen on the screen at our home were cartoons, Castle Films Newsreels, and family home movies. I did wonder, though, how Chad had managed to appear in so many of our home movies.

Years later, sitting with Dad in his study in the New York town house, stripping off reels of 16mm film while we made three sets of all the family home movies (one set for Pan, one for Jane, and one for me), I would say things like, "Look at Chad Hanna flying a kite," or, "Look at Chad trying to drown Jane." Dad peered at me as if there were several loose screws in my head. I had long before stopped trying to explain my nonwelcome at school that day. I think Dad never got over my total rejection of him while he was home on a short leave.

There we were in New York, as I stripped the film off the reels, checking the footage and telling Dad what each reel contained, while he made notes for how to edit them in a smooth way.

One particular reel made no sense to me. "I've got one here of Josh just sitting in a chair." Josh Logan was an actor and director and a dear friend of my father's from the early years with The University Players, on Cape Cod.

"What's he doing?" Dad asked.

"Just sitting in the chair pretending to read something."

"Oh, God, it's Josh killing babies! Let me see it."

He told me about working in the theater in Baltimore in the early thirties with Josh Logan and the gang, riding the train back to his cold-water flat in New York City every night. Everyone was so very tired, but there always seemed to be a baby on the train whose crying kept the actors awake. So they began to invent ways of killing the baby, but they had to do it silently. My father, thirty years later in New York, did the pantomimes for me perfectly, very subtly. We were both in hysterics as I watched an incredible variety of pantomimed murder. I loved it when I could watch Dad laugh out loud and, in this case, totally out of control. It was a rare thing.

.   .   .

Our father came home one more time before the war ended. Jane and I sat on the steps at the top of the staircase waiting for him, studying photographs so we would recognize him. I was still suspicious about Chad, but Jane very carefully and kindly explained what it was all about. When he arrived we gathered in the living room and asked many things, listened to many stories. After a while, I wandered off to his dressing room to look at the little things that were his "personals." I often did this with both my parents' keepsakes and jewelry. I would touch them and try to imagine where they had been with Mom and Dad. I wondered about the world my parents would go to, all dressed up and carrying these talismans down the driveway in the dark.

That night, after looking at his watch and dog tags, I reached up into a large bowl that was full of pennies and little candies—mostly licorice—and took a candy and went back to the living room. I climbed onto the couch next to him, and he noticed I was sucking on the candy. He asked me where I got the candy, but the look on his face and the tone in his voice were terrifying. He was asking me a simple question, probably unaware of his demeanor, but it was as if God were asking me why I had the apple in my mouth. I told him I had just found it. He bellowed that I was a liar. I jumped off the couch and ran for my life, with Dad in hot pursuit. I made it upstairs and into my bathroom, locking the door. The antique early-American fixture held for a second, and then Dad kicked the door in. He picked me up by my small, terrified neck and carried me into my bedroom, giving me the spanking of my life with what had to be the largest hairbrush in the world.

I'd always liked to search through drawers and hiding places. I found a little wooden box in the governess's room, hidden in the closet, one day. I liked the look of the bills that were stashed in the box. I had never had any paper money of my own, and these had large numbers printed on them. The room, after all, didn't belong to the governess; it was part of our house. So I took the box and put it in *my* closet and forgot about it. I don't remember how long it took for my theft to be discovered, but I remember the day, exactly. Tiger-tail was being photographed for *House Beautiful,* and as soon as the shoot was finished, the shit hit the fan. I don't remember the punishment, but I did learn the lesson: don't take someone else's things. It's called stealing.

· · ·

If one were to believe the standard, tawdry biographies of our family history, Jane and I never had any unsupervised time. Quite to the contrary, after Dad came home from the war, we were on our own many times and explored everything, crawling through thick brush, searching caves, climbing on the roof (that one really freaked Mom out). We were oblivious to the possibility of rattlesnakes and cave-ins, and snuck around nearby houses, spying on the occupants. Dad didn't take the place of the governesses, as he was away filming most of the time. I think he just banished them for a while, deciding that we should be raised by our parents. He forgot that he was away, and forgot or didn't know that our mother increasingly spent time in her bedroom with the curtains drawn. Her physical health was not great, but there was, obviously, more to it than that. Something was happening to the family, but I wasn't sure what or why. Jane and I pulled together, more or less successfully.

During the war years, we had blackout curtains throughout the house. When there were air-raid warnings, Mother and the governess would quickly put up the black drapes and put blankets over a table in our nursery. Pan, Jane, and I would lie under the table as Mother read stories to us by the light of a small lamp until the all-clear sirens.

Both Jane and I had nightmares about the war. I saw everything burning in some, and had another, recurring dream that was quite fantastic. I dreamed that I was flying over our house on an Electrolux vacuum cleaner, a long cylindrical tube with runners like a sled. In real time, I remember sitting on the thing and riding around the rooms while the housekeeper was vacuuming. I wonder now what happened to her lower back in her later years, but I was so delighted by the activity that towing me around probably made everyone's life easier.

I don't remember what Jane dreamt. She walked in her sleep often in the early years at 600 Tigertail. I could hear her through the wall that separated our rooms. Most of the time, she would move as much furniture—bureaus, chairs, big things—as she could over to her windows and then return to her bed. She piled them all at the window we both used to get out on the roof, just the place where someone could get into her room. She said she didn't remember doing it, and I believed her. Later, when we were old enough to look back, she decided she'd blockaded the room to keep the Japanese away. Sounds right to me.

We began to carve holes in the wall between our rooms so we could talk at night. We tapped loudly on the wall to each other, and when we were positive about the position of each other's tapping spot, Jane dug away from her side, and I drilled from mine. After weeks of doing this, we knew we were close to the big breakthrough. We had (still have) our very secret word that we would whisper into our little holes. Eventually, we both claimed to hear each other say the secret word. More than likely, we were whispering so loudly we could be heard by the governess and Pan, and maybe by the entire house. I can imagine a party in the living room, all the adults suddenly quieting as they listened to this mad whispering of a meaningless word between Jane and myself. We never made it through the wall, but we were sure that we had only an inch to go.

Jane, who claims to have tortured me regularly during childhood, was given to many of the temptations of the average older sister, and hid under my bed one night. After the lights were turned out, and I was alone in the dark, she rose up from under the bed like a monster and roared as deeply as she could. It took only one of those tricks to put me into the "monsters everywhere" belief mode.

Another time, after I had excitedly run into Jane's room to show a loosening tooth, she and Pan tied it with dental floss and attached the other end to Jane's bedroom doorknob. I was a willing subject, thinking about the dime I'd find under my pillow the next morning. There was a slight hitch; the tooth wasn't really ready to come out. Maybe in two weeks, but . . . *slam*! Lots of screaming, mostly from me, and lots of blood, all from me. Mother was not amused. I can't remember if or how my sisters were punished, but we didn't try that one again.

. . .

Dad bought us two burros when the war was over, Pancho and Pedro. He bought himself a treat, too, a Ford tractor to mow the large fields of clover, field grass, and mustard weed. He was seriously into making the best and the most compost in the greater Los Angeles area. The Ford with a side-sickle bar was the major toy for him that summer.

The tractor was brought to 600 Tigertail in the bed of a large truck. The idea was to drive the thing off the truck on planks. I was hanging around to see the blessed event and be with a bunch of men—in the house, it was five (counting the governess and our housekeeper, Katie) to one when Dad was away. Anyway, young Newton could see at once what was to become of the *heavy* tractor as it was being driven off the truck on *little* planks. Faw down go boom, right on Daddy, who insisted that he be given the privilege of doing the "launch" himself.

I threw a complete shit fit. There was no way I could be silenced. My father was going to be killed, and I couldn't allow it. I ran around crying and yelling, throwing rocks at the men. My father grabbed me, very embarrassed by my tantrum and tears, and tried to muffle me. But when he let go of me to get up on the tractor I went bananas again, and it was decided that one of the other men would off-load the tractor. I kept quiet. The tractor fell off the planks, almost crushing the man. Almost.

Years later, Marlon Brando, while riding on the back of my Triumph Bonneville motorcycle, asked me if I hated my father. I may have been very angry with Dad for one thing or another over the years, but when I remember that day with the tractor, I know I loved my father. Nothing was said to me after the screwup, not one word. It didn't matter. Dad was alive.

Dad did do some pretty funny things to me, or should I say with me. As I have said, though I was a chubby little baby, I was a skinny little boy, and would be one for many years. It embarrassed Dad, and therefore it embarrassed me. He did everything he could think of to help me put on weight. When I was being tutored, I was home more than most children and therefore had the chance to be with my father more than I would have under normal schooling conditions. Because of his long absences this was especially a treat for me, even though he was a very difficult man.

My mother and father read some insane book to put together a weight-gain program for me. I was allowed—*ha!*—to drink goat's milk. Dad made a special time for us to have lunch together almost every day while Jane and Pan were at school, which beat the egg yolk and ice-cream drinks I'd sometimes share with my mother in her darkened bedroom. We ate sandwiches and drank large beers. I was seven, and having beers with my father was the absolute best, something none of my friends ever got to do with their dads. The idea behind the beer was that it might help me gain weight. Dad was very serious that I understand the goal, that I not think it was all right for me to have a beer at any time other than those weight-gain lunches. The beers were unimportant to me; Dad giving them to me was.

Dad loved flying kites, but for Dad regular kites weren't exciting enough. He came home one day with the largest kite I had ever seen. It was a target kite for gunnery practice on board naval ships. Dad had cut down one of his deep-sea fishing rods so that only the first ferrule remained. He had his largest reel rigged up on the rod, and he fastened the line to the kite. I was allowed to help by holding the kite up. It was twice as tall as I was and very hard to hold on to in the wind. I let the kite go when Dad yelled, just when I was losing strength, and it raced upward. Dad almost forgot to release the brake on the reel, and the force of the kite pulled him forward, even as he dug his heels in. He released the brake and the kite zoomed higher and away, stripping line off the reel rapidly until the spool was almost empty, while Dad laughed like mad. It was all he could do to keep himself on the ground. He looked like a cowboy trying to hold on to a bull at the end of a rope. He skidded around laughing, yelling, and whooping. It was wonderful.

He did have to take it down, though. Grinding in the kite was more difficult than reeling in a marlin, and he was exhausted when he finally got the kite back on the ground. He couldn't get the huge grin off his face.

Dad and Jimmy Stewart, his best friend, loved to build model airplanes. Several times these models were being built "for Peter." I sensed some mythical bonding. I had no way to articulate it, but I spent time watching them sit together, building and gluing and painting. These two great men of the theater spent hours building an enormous glider without speaking more than three or four words. The silence was more than religious.

Dad put in three times the amount of work on the eight-foot glider than Jimmy, and many more hours were spent in "tuning" the glider. He took it up to the "north forty" and made five or six running launches, which meant running with the glider in hand and letting it loose, without thrusting, right at the moment the wings got lift. The glider thereby would reveal its "in-flight" characteristics, and Dad would add clay to the forward or aft part of the main body according to the way the model dipped or flew evenly.

Launch day came, the great event. It was special to me, as it involved the kite and the glider and my dad. During our kite flying, I had learned the little trick called "sending a note to the pilot." Dad showed me how to tear a small piece of stiff paper, put it on the string, and let the wind make it spin as it twirled up the string to the harness of the kite. This time he'd rigged the kite with a special clasp, and the "note" would be the glider. After the liftoff of the kite, I had to fasten the glider, huge yet light, to the clasp. During the many flight trials, I was allowed to run to where the glider had landed and very carefully bring it back to Dad. But this time the task was too much for me.

Dad gave me the chopped-off fishing rod and took charge of rigging the glider. I was immediately pulled to the ground and dragged along by the kite. Dad caught me and helped me to dig my feet into the ground. I hung on to the rod with all my strength as Dad rigged the glider. He grabbed the rod just as I was running out of strength. I scrambled away and watched as the glider was pulled up the line. When this offering of balsa wood, paper, clay, and rubber bands reached the harness, Dad took the rod and yanked it, fiercely. The glider, several hundred feet above us, bounced off the rig, swirled around out of control, then suddenly caught the wind and began to soar.

Dad had driven the station wagon up and we jumped in it, taking off after the glider. I had never been in a car that was driven as fast as Dad was going. We stopped many times, and Dad jumped out, watching the glider fly toward the coast. The glider, of course, wasn't following any road, so Dad raced along to the next ridge. He was agitated by the fact that he had to drive down to Sunset Boulevard to reach the next ridge. Finally, he stopped along the last ridge and watched as the graceful glider soared away to the ocean. My heart was racing. I was thrilled by the sight of the glider soaring to the horizon, but worried about my father's mood as his prize flew away. He was delighted by the entire adventure. I realized, much later, that the glider did exactly what he wanted it to do—it flew away over the horizon. As we drove back to 600, he kept saying, "How about that, son, how about that?" With that grin, that same grin. I can close my eyes now, and see his face just as it was that late afternoon. He was magnificent when he was happy.

• • •

Dad and his friends loved to fish for swordfish and marlin in the Catalina Channel, and, from time to time, the children were invited along. I got to hang with the "men," always a special event. Sometimes we'd charter a yacht and join his friends at the Emerald Bay Yacht Club. These were usually peaceful days, everyone happy at the same time.

On one trip to the Channel Islands aboard Dana Andrews's 127-foot schooner, I was allowed to bring a friend, as were Jane and Pan. I had a grand time with Danny Pyzel, the son of a close friend of my mother. It was the first sailing vessel I had been on, and as we motored along to the islands, Danny and I had a ball climbing in the

rigging and hanging in the bowsprit net. We explored the wilds of
Catalina Island, where there were still wild boar and buffalo. We visited director John Ford's yacht, *Araner,* and fished with the Duke on
Ward Bond's cabin cruiser, *Bandy.* But a couple of days later, on a
fine, windy day, Dad decided to actually sail the schooner. As soon
as the sails filled and the ship began to move by the power of the
wind, which was considerable that day, I freaked out. The dynamics
of sailing had never been explained to me, and I was certain that we
were going to tip over at any moment. Tears of fright flowed, all to
the embarrassment of Dad, whose angry face and voice frightened
me even more. After we stopped trying to tip the ship over and turned
the engines back on, I was fine, which made Dad even madder. In
1973 Dad came on board my yacht *Tatoosh*, in Hanalei Bay, Kaui, and
I took him for the sail of his life.

Though we had everything we needed at 600 Tigertail, Mother
often took us to the beach and other interesting places—circuses, the
Pony Park, the La Brea tar pits. I recall one day at the ocean when we
looked back at the inland hills and saw an enormous column of
smoke from the late summer fires that have always been a part of the
Southern California environment. Everyone at the beach was worrying about the fire, though I never really worried about the fires because Dad never seemed to worry about them. On two occasions, I
"helped" the men (including Jimmy Stewart, John Wayne, Ward
Bond, and Randolph Scott) clear some of the thick brush down by
the horse stables and corrals. They piled it up and burned it very
carefully in an exhilarating bonfire, me dancing around, helping them
control any stray flames. Dad always did one special thing—he would
take some of our potatoes and, just at the right moment, put them in
the hot ashes. After a specific amount of time, he removed the potatoes from the hot ashes and peeled off the burnt skin, and we would
all eat the best-tasting baked potatoes ever. No butter, no salt, just
fresh, hot potatoes. A bit of magic.

Anyway, I never worried about the fires until one very bad afternoon. Bill Hayward and I were having a rock fight in the north forty
at Tigertail. Dad had put up two little log huts for the kids to play in,
and we pretended they were forts and bombarded each other with
rocks. This particular afternoon the rock fight lost its appeal early, so
we built a campfire, and it quickly got out of control. We ran to the
pool, which was nearby, filled tennis ball cans with water, and rushed

back and forth to the fire, trying our best to control it. Fat chance. The
north forty was soon a dangerous fire, and the fire department
showed up. They doused it, but one of the firefighters was bitten by
a rattler.

Bill and I used every lie we could think of to escape disaster, but,
at the bottom of it all, we were playing with matches. We were mortified and waited for our punishment. Dad, to our eternal shock, said
that we must have learned an important lesson by our carelessness,
and that our agony during the firefighters' rescue of the fields above
the pool and courts was punishment enough. I was amazed. The
candy was door-breaking time. The fire that could have wiped out a
healthy chunk of Santa Monica . . .

. . .

Sometime in the summer of 1946, I went with my sisters to the
beach one sunny day. Pan, who'd just gotten her driver's license,
drove us in her wonderful black Mercury convertible. I loved being
with my sisters, alone, away from our parents. We sailed to Will Rog-
ers State Beach, unloaded our little picnic, and climbed carefully over
the huge rocks to the beach. There was a fisherman out on the rocks
surf-casting, but otherwise we were alone. Pan and Jane put out the
beach towels and laid rocks on the corners to keep them straight. I
found an old Wildroot Cream hair oil bottle washed up in the sand.
Everyone knew the jingle: "Wildroot Cream Oil, in the unbreakable
bottle!" This one had survived the surf and rocks.

Jane and I played catch. We tossed the bottle to each other over
our shoulders, between our legs. If we missed the bottle, no problem.
It was unbreakable, and it bounced in the sand. Even Pan knew it
was unbreakable. The whole English-speaking world knew it was
unbreakable, as far as I was concerned. And it broke right in the
middle of my forehead. Within a few seconds, blood was pulsing out
of my forehead like a Niagara Falls rivulet, scaring the shit out of all
of us. Pan quickly got the help of the fisherman to carry me up over
the rocks to the Pacific Coast Highway. He suggested that we press a
towel tightly on the wound to stop the heavy bleeding, we did so
before speeding off to the nearest hospital. As we shot down the road,
I became calmer and curious. The wound wasn't hurting me, so I
looked in the rearview mirror and took the towel away. A nanosec-

ond, and then, spurt, spurt . . . Blood shot out of the wound and all over the dash, and we all began to scream. I quickly pressed the towel back on the wound.

We got to St. Johns Hospital in Santa Monica, Pan called home, and we waited for Mom and Dad. A parent or legal guardian had to okay the stitching-up process. It was the first time I had to have stitches, and I was just a little bit scared. When Dad arrived, the process began at once. I was worried the stitching would be painful, and began to cry, and Dad got quite angry with me. I was only six, and the tears that followed my fright were not unexpected. The doctor explained this to Dad, but he was insisting on being embarrassed by my lack of bravery. I felt terrible about making him feel embarrassed, but I was still frightened. He got angry with Jane, too, but it wasn't like she had purposely hit me with the bottle. In the end the stitching didn't hurt a bit, and I calmed down at once, but it was still a silent, angry drive back home with Dad. I wanted desperately to be in the black Merc with my sisters instead.

"Boy, I hope you've learned your lesson!" he snapped.

That one puzzled me for a long time. What lesson? Unbreakable bottles do break? Don't trust my sisters? Don't cry? Ah, yes, that must have been the lesson. I can't remember if this happened before the tractor falling, or after, but I knew that my reaction was a very normal happening. The lesson was that dads don't always get it right.

· · ·

Jane and Pan and I went to a semiprogressive private school—I was in kindergarten—the Brentwood Town and Country School. The school day began with the entire student body gathering together and reciting the Salutation to the Dawn, the Pledge of Allegiance, and the school song, sung to the tune of "Anchors Aweigh," and ended with "The Brentwood Town and Country School, Hooray!" Actually, it was a good experience. We were there with Brooke, Bridget, and Bill Hayward, film director Henry Hathaway's son, Jack, Hoagy Carmichael, Jr., and several other sons and daughters of Hollywood guns.

After my kindergarten year, in the fall of 1946 when I was six and a half, I was sent to a boarding school. The plan, though no one spelled it out to me, was that outdoor activities in a Boys Town type of school would make a man out of me, and, in the process, help me gain weight.

My parents came up with the Barton School for Boys, in the upper part of Topanga Canyon. In later life I was told it was a school for "difficult boys." Although I believe my sister, Jane, that I was a total brat, I somehow can't imagine being such a brat that the Barton School for Boys was the correct punishment for a first-grader. Nevertheless, I was stranded at this purgatory along with Danny Pyzel.

Barton was basically a farm school, and it had many acres spread out along the canyon slope, with a little creek flowing slowly through tall eucalyptus groves. Often, to escape the pressure and abuse that the older boys doled out to us, Danny and I would hide up in the groves and devise ways to catch the crawfish that skittered about in the shallow water. After classes, we were pretty much free to roam. It took us a while to learn that roaming was the best thing we could do.

For the first few weeks, I would go out to the courtyard during class breaks, and try to "socialize" with the other boys. These clever little assholes had a neat game they would run on the new boys, Scissors-Paper-Rock-Candle. Most people have suffered through it at some point in their lives—the loser of this multiple finger exercise had to extend his forearm and allow the winner to whack his wrist with two fingers. One can imagine what became of little "Petey Boy." After the first session of this social event, Petey Boy's wrist was two or three times its normal size, and I looked like I had elephantiasis in my right wrist. In my mind, it was a badge of honor. In reality, it was the mark of a fool. Two days into it, I realized this was not a normal experience but the badge of a boy who wanted to fit in but would never make it.

During the first few weeks, Danny Pyzel and I found our beds short-sheeted and filled with sand. It was a miserable time for both of us, and we finally went to the wife of the principal and told her of the sand in our beds and the short-sheeting. I had big tears rolling down my cheeks, and I was embarrassed that I was crying and not being a brave boy. My friend Danny stood by me though with fewer tears, and the wife of the principal was very angry and maintained that sort of thing was not allowed or tolerated in the school. She and her husband made the entire school assemble and stated that this "special" treatment was a disgrace and if it continued, they would severely punish all the older boys.

Danny and I felt vindicated, but we soon learned that the older punks considered us crybabies and found even more elaborate punishments for ratting on them. We never gave names, but they had it out for us anyway. And we still had to remake our beds to empty out the sand each night. Most nights, as I cried myself to sleep as quietly as possible, I wondered what I had done that was so bad that I was sent to this semireform school.

Out in front of the main buildings there were many large oak trees, old ones with long branches almost a foot and a half wide. Young boys could run along those branches like little monkeys. Climbing the oaks around the house on Tigertail had made me an experienced tree boy. With the older boys in constant pursuit, I quickly learned that up in the higher branches, the ones that were smaller and more likely to break, I could escape their punches and kicks. The first asshole who tried to get me down from those higher branches outweighed me by thirty or forty pounds, and he broke the limbs and fell to the ground with screams and tears. It was quickly reported that I had kicked him out of the tree, and I was promptly punished for such unfair behavior. Mind you, I weighed little more than twenty-five pounds, and I would have loved to have been the one who "kicked" the little idiot out of the tree. Instead, I was punished for antisocial behavior and made to stay inside for three days, which meant three days of respite from the Storm Troopers.

After figuring out the smaller branch theory, I reckoned that absence from the area was a better defense and took to roaming off to the eucalyptus groves and the stream. I'd plan my escape in this isolation, but occasionally I made the mistake of wandering back toward the crowd.

There was a barn in the complex with a lower room full of the farming tools and an upper loft full of hay. Up in the hayloft, there was a rope that was used to bring up the bales. It was a place to play, and we would go up there and swing on the rope. The older boys would take the kittens that were constantly born at this farm school and drop them out of the upper barn doors to see if the old adage that cats "always landed on their feet" was true. It wasn't.

One afternoon, once again trying to be one of the guys, I ventured up to the loft and began swinging on the rope. The older boys were "helping" the younger ones swing by pushing them when they were swinging. I stood by the open hayloft doors and watched the bigger boys swing around the loft. They would almost swing out through the open doors. For a moment, I looked down at the ground where the kittens fell, many of them to their deaths. In that moment, one of the boys swung out toward the doors and pushed me out with his feet.

I vividly recall the front of the barn as it zipped past my face. I can see the hay forks and big rakes that were hanging on the outside of the barn rush past me. I looked up just as I augured in, slamming into the ground fifteen feet below right on my chin with the palms of my hands out, trying to break the fall. I remember lying on the ground crying and being very scared, then nothing.

I woke up in the dingy infirmary with my head bandaged up. I was told that I had chipped my chin and broken my jaw, and remained in the infirmary for more than two weeks, being fed through a small hole in the bandages. I was only six years old and wished that someone, anyone from my family would visit me while I was strapped to the bed and explain what was going on, comfort me. In hindsight I believe the school, terrified of a lawsuit, probably never called my parents.

Soon after the bandages and castlike head gear were removed, I was allowed to resume "playing" with the other boys. I had no desire to do anything with the other boys, who had told the principal that I had jumped out the window on my own to show I wasn't a scaredy-cat. How logical—jump out of a window, head first, fifteen feet to the hard ground. Thirty-nine years later, while being x-rayed after a bad motorcycle accident, the doctors and radiologists asked me if I had had any kind of trauma to my head when I was six or seven. Many lights flashed in my mind. They told me I had broken my neck, badly, and were amazed that I didn't know. They asked me what my parents had done about it. What parents?

A month or so after the incident my father's sister, Harriet Peacock, who lived in Nebraska, came to visit me at the school from hell, the first person from my family to check out the place. She went back to my mother and father and read them the riot act. She was absolutely astounded that I was sent off to a boarding school ("with its dirt floors," she would say later); a six-year-old surely didn't deserve such punishment, and six years old was too young to be sent away. My mother and father said they thought it would make me gain weight and become tougher. Aunt Harriet told them that they should have their heads examined, and forced them to take me out of the school.

A couple of weeks later, my mother decided to take me on a trip with her, a fun trip to the East Coast to visit Pan at her boarding school. I was going to fly in an airplane for the second time in my life. Just going to the airport was an adventure. We boarded a DC-4, a four-engine plane with berths in the back, like a railroad sleeper. I was very excited and had a hard time sitting still in my seat. I wanted to explore the entire place. Cross-country trips by air took an amazingly long time in those days. We went from day to night to day, landing several times. Mother had the flight attendants pull down the upper berth for me and told me to look carefully out the window and maybe I could see the curvature of the earth. After she explained what that meant, I wouldn't come down from the berth, spending all my time peering out a little oval window looking for the curve on the horizon, dozing off from time to time. When it was night, I made out many tiny lights, and wondered about the people who lived where those lights were, wondered if they could see the lights of my plane. Before the berth was prepared, I was allowed to peek into the cockpit, and I carried that dreamlike vision of the gauges with their unknown tales back to the berth with me.

Through the many takeoffs and landings, the pressurizing and depressurizing, the noises in the cabin and the rumble of the motors, my memory banks opened like the great white gates of our first house on Chadbourne, slowly and majestically revealing the grounds of my crawling and walking days. It wasn't articulate memory, but sense memory.

Years later, I asked my father about our trip out from the East Coast when I was an infant, but he didn't want to discuss it. I told him that I had cried when he put me down in the window seat with my head facing inward, to the darkness of the cabin. But when he turned me so I could see the window, I was silent.

He snapped at me. "Somebody told you that, boy!"

"Who else was with us, Dad?"

"You can't possibly remember any of that!"

"Who could have told me? You don't talk, so it wasn't you."

"Your mother made it all up."

"Nope."

"Horseshit!"

"We're *all* up to our necks in that, Dad."

Many takeoffs and landings later, many tiny lights like beacons pointing the way, a sunrise, a noon, and candy to suck on and we were on the East Coast. Actually we were in Baltimore, although I didn't know it was Baltimore until years later. I had never been in a taxi, and I was intrigued. A ride in an airplane, the curvature of the earth, and a taxi. This surely was a magical journey. In those days, I said "maggage" for magic and "Yew Nork" for New York. To this day when I speak the city's name I wonder if I've said "Yew Nork" by mistake.

The taxi stopped in front of a big brick building. I thought that it was a fancy hotel. I had never stayed at a hotel and tried to summon up all the images I had of hotels, though none came close to this impressive brick building. Mother and I stepped from the taxi with our luggage and climbed the front stairs. Mother was wearing a black dress with a sable stole and black hat and shoes. I can see her as clearly now as I did on that special day. But once inside the brickness, things began to come unsnapped. Mother separated our bags and went to the left without saying a word. I can still hear the sound of her shoes, clicking away down the long lobby. I was brought along with my bag to the right, up a few stairs, and then on an elevator. Moments later I was left in a large room with two beds and no pictures on the walls. Nothing was familiar, but there were several toys on a strange-looking metal table that could swing over the bed. The only time I had seen these metal beds and tables was when I had my tonsils removed two years earlier. They didn't frighten me, and I wondered if Dad would be proud of me for not being afraid. I didn't know where I was; I was alone and yet not afraid.

That evening, a woman in a uniform brought in a tray of food. "Now, you don't have to eat all of the food, but you must drink all this liquid." I was flabbergasted. These were "maggage" words. I'd always been punished for not eating, and here was a person of some authority telling me that I didn't have to eat all the food on the tray. I was beginning to like this hotel. I wasn't allowed out of the room, but I didn't have to finish the meal. The food was not very good.

Everything at our place in California was homegrown and fresh. This food was awful. I drank all the liquid and poked at the plate. When the person dressed in a uniform returned, she was delighted that I had finished the drink, and never said a word about the uneaten food.

"After you have gone to the potty, you will have to put away the toys and go to sleep." This was familiar talk. Nothing out of the ordinary. However, within an hour, going to the potty took on a whole new meaning. I felt the urge, and went into the little bathroom. I think I was there for an hour, but it was probably only a half hour. The woman came to my room and called out to me, asking if I was "doing my business." I yelled from the potty that I was. Shit, I was pissing out my ass.

When I finally *was* finished, I was literally drained. I had never had that experience before, but I was assured by the wonderful woman who hadn't made me finish all the food that it was very normal and was the result of all the liquid. I fell asleep quickly, but I was worried that I would go to the bathroom in my bed.

The next morning, several older people came to get me up. There was no breakfast, and I was perfectly happy not to ask about it. But I was becoming uneasy, aware that this was not a normal place. A bed on wheels was brought into the room, and I was placed on it and rolled out of the room. I had been on a bed like that the past summer, when my forehead was stitched up after the beach accident. This place was looking more and more like a hospital, and I didn't have a cut anywhere.

I was wheeled into a room with large lights hanging from the ceiling. "This is just like having your temperature taken," said one voice, and I suddenly felt something being shoved up my ass. I was terrified and managed to get off the table and run for the door, but the adults quickly subdued me, held me down on the table, and started to push a long flexible thing way up my ass. I screamed and yelled and cried and struggled, but they only gripped me harder and became angry with me, like my father. But my father never pushed five or six feet of flexible wire up my ass. All I could do was cry and scream. I was being raped and no one came to help me. After that moment, I have no memory, no anything.

Years later, Eulalia Chapin, my mother's closest friend, explained to Susan Brewer, my first wife, what had gone down. She said that Mother and Dad had been very concerned by my skinniness. Mother had decided to have a hysterectomy. She had called Eulalia and asked her if she wanted to come and have one, too, as if she were suggest-

ing cocktails. And while she was at Johns Hopkins, she was going to
have me checked for a tapeworm. *A tapeworm?* I was raped for a
tapeworm at Johns Hopkins? I had forty-four years of painful, terrifying nightmares of anal abuse, not one night without them, except
when I was on my sailing ship.

. . .

The next thing I remember, I was out of the hospital and with my
sister Pan at her school, Garrison Forest. Whatever had happened at
Johns Hopkins was buried deep in the old brain. I felt that I was safer
with my sister, who was also my godmother. She took me around the
school and showed me all the places where she studied. When we
got to the biology lab, she and her classmates gave me a little white
mouse. That mouse was a great comfort to me, and I kept it in one of
my pockets when Mother and I flew from Baltimore to Aunt Harriet's
house in Omaha. I no longer looked for the curvature of the earth, or
the tiny lights, way below, but the little mouse was my friend, and
would crawl out of whichever pocket and sit on my shoulder. I didn't
even want to leave my seat. Something had scared me so much that I
had lost interest in airplanes and flying and simply dreaded whatever
might happen next. Nothing would ever be the same in my life, but I
didn't quite understand what had gone wrong.

When Mother and I arrived at Harriet's house in Omaha, I felt a
little more protected. There was a family at her house, and people
actually spoke to each other. No one was angry with me, and I wasn't
punished for being so skinny. Things were very different, there.

After a while it was time for us to return to Los Angeles, and Harriet
joined us on the trip. She later told me she was astonished that I was
allowed to run free on the train. I was afraid to go to sleep at night,
and afraid to wake up in the morning, so I would stay up as long as I
could, running from the front of the train to the rear, running until I
was so exhausted that I would fall asleep in any empty seat. I invented situations that needed my attention at all times. I had to report
to the engineer about the condition of each car, and communicated
with a secret device that only I could operate, a corncob pipe for a
microphone and a yo-yo as an earpiece. I made it to Los Angeles after
only one instance of my brand-new nightmare.

Dad and Jane were waiting at the terminal when we arrived. Forty-one years later, Jane asked me to spend five days with her, to talk about our childhood. She said that she needed to put the fractured pieces together, and I remembered so much of the detail that she had forgotten, and if "something" happened to me she would never . . . she began to cry. We sat in her library, holding on to one another while we both cried. It was the first time she had ever let it go quite like that, and it moved me tremendously. She said, among other things, that she needed to know where we would go each time I went away alone with our mother as it made her feel abandoned. Except for several day trips up the coast, I can only remember one time that I went anywhere with our mother alone, and I have just told you all about that.

· · ·

After the Barton debacle I was tutored privately for more than a year. I would have preferred Brentwood, but I liked my tutor. When I asked a question for which she had no answer, we would turn to books and both learn. Therefore, though I wasn't spending enough time on math and English, I was understanding the learning process and was turned on to learning for the rest of my life.

But I wasn't able to be with my pals or other kids my own age, and it upset me. Only when the Haywards and other friends would come home with Jane was I able to hang with people my own age, and this wasn't necessarily a good thing for the other kids.

While I was being tutored, when I was seven or so, my mother took me to a movie, though I don't recall which one, that had a small part of a parking-lot attendant. I was absolutely fascinated by the character sitting under an umbrella for some shade while waiting for his next customer and smoking a cigarette.

After the movie, and as soon as I was back at Tigertail, I found an umbrella and a small chair, and, with my red wagon, I sat out in the gravel parking area off the side of the three-car garage waiting to park anyone who happened to come by. After a few minutes, I realized I didn't have a cigarette. No problem. I went into the house, found a few butts in an ashtray, and returned to my important post. A few minutes after that, I got some matches and fired up one of the butts. I had never smoked a cigarette, never even held one in my mouth, and it tasted awful. I coughed like a maniac, though I hadn't inhaled anything. I didn't know how. I certainly didn't know it was something I should not be doing. No one had told me a thing about it, and both my parents smoked, as did all their friends. The thing tasted so bad just touching my lips, I made a third trip to the house for some of my mother's cigarette holders. They were made of stiff paper and plastic with "The Stork Club" printed on them. Much nicer.

No one came for quite a while, but that was fine—no one was bossing me around or constantly asking me what I was doing. I can only imagine how any of the grown-ups would have reacted to a line like "I'm parking cars." Then, in the distance, the sound of a car. I didn't bother to hide the cigarette, though when Jane and the three Haywards—Brooke, Bridget, and Bill—piled out, I did hide the background fantasy about being a parking-lot attendant. Jane and the gang were very interested in the smoking thing. No problem—I ran back to the house again and got some full cigarettes and more Stork Club holders and very professionally demonstrated how to smoke them. Everyone picked up the method right away.

We didn't pay much attention when our mother's masseuse drove by but continued to march around, puffing away. Then—major rain on our parade—the masseuse passed on the observation that there were five children having a smoke-a-thon in the driveway, and Mother wasn't amused. The Hayward children were banned from 600 Tigertail for a month. Maybe it was two months. I thought that was very unfair—they were just following along. Jane and I were sent to our rooms, and we waited for our fate.

Our mother smoked Pall Malls, "Pell Mells" in the argot of the time, the *loooong* ones. We were made to smoke a pack each. Jane was first, and took her punishment without a whimper. I got very sick to my stomach and had the dry heaves. Jane made me feel so much better, though.

"You really smoked them? I only pretended to!" How sweet . . .

. . .

I don't dream about flying the Electrolux anymore, but from time to time I do dream about riding my bike to Brentwood Town and Country School, Hooray!, where I started school again in January of 1948. I really did make that ride, in real time. I was almost eight, and I'm not sure why I was allowed to do such a thing, but I do remember our housekeeper driving the Ford Woody slowly alongside me as I pedaled away. The ride back was fine except when we began to go up the long road to 600. Thankfully, I was allowed to put my bike in the station wagon halfway up the hill. I never asked to ride to school again.

Brentwood was anything but regular, but for those who attended the school during my time, it was the best education available, and it had its special perks. Each of the younger students had an older student as an overseer during whole-school activities such as the opening ceremonies. My guardian was named Mary, and she was beautiful to me. She was much taller than I, and as I stood in front of her, the back of my head pressed against her stomach, I would tilt my head up and see her sweet smiling face looking down at me, framed by her young breasts pushing out under her sweater. I had no real sexual understanding other than boys and girls were different and together they made babies when they were older. But there was no doubt in my mind that I wanted to lie beside Mary and put my head between those beckoning breasts, snuggling into the soft sweater. I wanted to be held and snuggled by all the older girls. Except for my sisters. Yuuuck . . .

In early '48, the family went on a skiing vacation to Sun Valley, in Idaho. We had felt real snow only twice before, once at Big Bear, a skiing spot near Los Angeles, and once when, in a freak of nature, it had snowed at 600 Tigertail. The snow hadn't lasted more than a few minutes, but it was the real thing, covering everything. Before that, we had only seen the snow on Mount Baldy from our house. It was in the days when we could see Catalina Island from the front lawn and turn to the east and see the snow-covered San Gabriel Mountains. Clearly, believe it or not. And, on Christmas morning, we would bound downstairs and stop in wonderment as we stared at the incredible Christmas tree filled with beautiful ornaments, tinsel, garlands, colored lights, and snow. Our Christmas tree, unlike the Haywards' or any of our friend's families', had snow filling every bough, making them droop just like the snow-covered trees we had seen in *National Geographic*. The surprise of the tree, which had stood barren for the few days before the holiday, had been bestowed by Father Christmas overnight. It was an incredible icon of everything Christmas trees were supposed to be, more exciting than the expectation of our unopened presents. It was magic, the best present of all, rendered so by our dad.

While we were living at 600 Tigertail, my parents had a few parties for their friends, and sometimes I was allowed to stay awake and spend a little time with the adults. It was on one of these occasions that I met Nat King Cole. I loved his name and sat next to him on the piano bench, watching him play. His voice was so beautiful. He asked me if I could play the piano and I told him no. I explained that I was left-handed and the piano was very right-handed. I told him that I was made to play the piano along with my sisters, but it was something I just couldn't understand. I'd been made to play at a recital, too, and it was a complete disaster. I was nervous about the stage and audience, and less than halfway into my piece I ran off the stage in tears. The piece I was playing was "Ladybug, Ladybug," and when I hit "Fly away home, your house is on fire and your children will burn!" I couldn't handle the thought and ran off the stage.

Nat laughed and showed me how to play "Cow-Cow Boogie." He explained that it was a left-handed song. He was so nice, and let me sip from his drink, and didn't talk down to me. I decided I loved him. None of the adults seemed to notice he was dark black, almost purple, so I figured that there must be lots of purple people, and they must be the nicest people on Earth.

At another party Jimmy Stewart was the snazz of the group in a white dinner jacket. Dad told Jimmy he had something special to show him, and Jimmy was all for seeing it, whatever it was. Dad pulled out a "special" fountain pen, and in the process of the demonstration, squirted ink all over Stewart's dinner jacket. Jimmy got quite upset, as did everyone else on his behalf, but within minutes, the ink had disappeared from the jacket. Dad showed me for the first time that under all that silence there was a little boy lurking, just waiting to pull a trick. It may have been that Dad and Jimmy had planned the whole caper. It didn't matter; it was the thrill of the evening, and I got to watch it.

. . .

All of us knew that something was up in the spring of 1948. Pan probably understood more than Jane or I, but the changes were very evident to all three of us. I didn't have a clue that we were all about to leave our paradise for a very different journey to the East. 600 Tigertail had such a permanence for us. We had each chosen the wallpaper for our bedrooms, the colors, the furniture. The house had been built specially for all of us. Large shade trees and already-bearing fruit trees had been planted, and the guy wires that had held them in place, while they took root, had been long gone. Who would ever leave a place like 600 Tigertail? I would learn, later in the life, what a great stage play was and why an actor, a dedicated actor, would give up anything to play a great role onstage, on Broadway. That is the true sex of the acting profession, and my father's play was *Mister Roberts*.

I think that it was during this time that I ran away from home. Something strange was going down, and I was determined to stop it or leave it behind.

I spent the night on a neighbor's back lawn refusing to come into their house for shelter. I was prepared to find my own shelter. I didn't need grown-ups' approval. I was on my way. On my own. I held the image and strength of E. B. White's *Stuart Little* before me as my guide to freedom, my Bible. If Stuart, a mouse born into a normal family, could have a normal and participatory life, then it was entirely possible that I too could be a part of a family, be accepted and strike out on my own to find my destiny. I worshiped Stuart. I never told a soul about my thing with Stuart. I read and reread *Stuart Little,* touching the words and soaking up the emotions. Before *Stuart Little* I'd buried myself in another guide to struggle, *Paddle to the Sea.*

Paddle to the Sea is a picture-and-word book about a young Native American boy, who, during a long winter in the Canadian Rockies, carves a model of a birch-bark canoe with an Indian figure holding a paddle from a piece of pine. As spring approaches, the model is finished, painted, and fitted with a lead ballast to keep it upright and a tin rudder to keep it headed forward. On the bottom of the canoe, the young boy carves "Please put me back in the water, I am Paddle to the Sea." The boy places the little carving on a bank of snow. The snow starts to melt, carrying its water and Paddle to a rivulet, to a brook, to a stream, to a river, to Lake Superior. On his journey, Paddle has harrowing experiences. He endures many events over which he has no control, like the things all of us see when we are very young.

chapter *Two*

*M*oving a family, uprooting and relocating, no matter how close or great a distance, is one of the most stressful things in life. I don't remember a thing about our move to Connecticut. I remember leaving Tigertail. I remember being very upset that we were leaving our cat. I cried a lot—that's all.

The new house, a rental in Greenwich, was called the Count Palenclar House. It had a small apple orchard in the front, and lovely grounds, with large trees all around and a four-car garage. There was a carriage garage, too, and an elevator. I had never been in a private house that had an elevator. I've long forgotten how many times I rode up and down in that thing. There was a large walk-in safe in the basement, and after a prolonged struggle I eventually managed to crack it. It was full of ledgers and files and . . . checks! I had never seen a canceled check before, so it took some time to figure out that they were useless. Until I understood this, I figured my sisters and I would be rich, if I could find someone to trade the checks for cash.

Eventually, a few of our belongings were in our new house, and we had some sense of ourselves. Mother was gone a lot, though I didn't know why or where. At our new country mansion, things were changing in ways in which I had no experience, and over which I had no control. I felt that Jane and I had been sent into exile from our Paradise, hauled along on some unspoken crusade of our parents.

There were no orange groves, no avocado trees, no fresh vegetables, and an even more bewildering silence at our supper table and "family" gatherings, gatherings that really meant the few of us were in the same room, usually by chance. (The darkness and damp of the woods and swamp was carried on in the house with its musky attic-like atmosphere. Jane felt the same way.) I had my bicycle. I could get away, be on my own, and I kept away from the house as much as possible, and took my dog Buz, a Dalmatian, with me.

Buz was my protector, and we explored. There was so many foreign things that lived in these woods. Trees I had never seen before, all kinds of strange plants, birds, and animals. Skunk cabbage, swamps, parasitic vines choking giant trees. The dense trees seemed so much older and unfriendlier than the oaks and pines that surrounded the magical land of Oz that I knew as the real world, and from which I had so abruptly been exiled. I never felt afraid while discovering these dark new worlds. When Buz caught scent of another animal, he would back up next to me, raise his hackles and start to growl in a very low, rumbling way. Whatever was lurking would scurry away. I learned to watch out for copperhead snakes.

The change from our bucolic and magical life in the place of endless summer to the fall and winter of the New England countryside caused more than a loss of innocence. Jane and I both felt the strain that crept into our everyday life. Having to find and make new friends, forge bonds with young people of an entirely different social order, and be subjected to a culture quite alien to us was very confusing. Jane immersed herself in the fine skills of horsemanship and, in a slight competition with our older sister, was determined to be Mistress of the Fox Hounds.

I, having no such skills, tried my best to be accepted by my peers. I tried to find the way to new friends, but I was unaware of the consequences of my parentage. We'd never been so close to cliques and social divisions based on race, religion, and family background. Greenwich's opinion of actors was reminiscent of a law that remains on the books in England, despite Sir Richard, Dame Edith, Sir Alec, and such: actors, tinkers, and mendicants can be arrested on sight. To the insular town blue bloods, the Fondas were white trash, despite or because of the fact that we had better manners than the people in Greenwich—thanks to our mother—and an appreciation of all people—thanks to our father. In Greenwich I first heard the words "kike" and "nigger." I had no idea what they meant, but when I came home one day and asked Dad about "kike," he reacted as if I had invented the word. He railed at me without explaining the problem, telling me to never use that word again. When I asked him what "nigger" meant, he went ballistic but still did not explain. So I went to my friend, a boy who had run away through the fields after the other students taunted and called him a kike. He said the word was used as an insult to Jews. I asked him what a Jew was. He thought I was joking. The East had many terrible secrets to reveal to me.

When Mother applied for my entrance to the Brunswick School, an all-male elementary school in Greenwich, the Brentwood Town and Country School, sent along grade reports and letters recommending that I repeat the third grade, as I had not completed the full year, and the teachers at BT&CS were not sure that I was ready for the fourth grade. My mother somehow convinced them I was, and I entered the fourth grade at Brunswick School in the fall of 1948. I also entered the very different weather of New England.

My new school was not at all like BT&CS, Hooray!. We had to wear uniforms. No more cowboy boots, no more blue jeans. My first tie. And when I suggested that we all would have a better time if we recited the Salutation to the Dawn, I was made to face the wall and be silent for a half hour. Although bigotry and racism were rampant in Greenwich, the Brunswick School kept a fairly tight lid on these disgusting practices, and gave its students a good education.

But I was taunted by the other kids at school all the time. It was the first time I had to deal with being Henry Fonda's son. I had no idea what that meant. Who was Henry Fonda, anyway? Wasn't everyone somebody's son or daughter? And, of course, there was my incredible skinniness. I was an easy target.

I had a fixation on one of my teachers, Miss Stephenson. She was my fourth-grade teacher and my homeroom head, and she was kind and patient with me. She encouraged my artistic drive, and when I was being bullied, she would stop the action. I used to daydream often that my own mother would die, and my father would marry Miss Stephenson. I never considered the consequences. Mother was inexplicably absent so much, and there was all the stress that is part of moving, the alienation of a new social standard, and the dread I felt for Dad's terrible silences, so I slipped into my daydream world for comfort and hope. It wasn't that Miss Stephenson was kinder to me than Mother. When my mother was there she was very kind and loving to me, very generous with her time. She did all the things that one could wish for in a mother, but at these critical moments she was losing herself and I was losing her. No one talked to Jane or me about what was happening; we had to make up for the bewilderment somehow. Forty years later I was amazed and delighted to learn that Bill Hayward, who joined me at Brunswick that year, had the same reaction to Miss Stephenson, the same daydream, for many of the same reasons.

. . .

I spent as many days sick as I did wandering in the woods or attending Brunswick. In the winter of 1948, I came down with severe bronchial pneumonia and whooping cough. During the most serious bouts, when conjunctivitis set in, too, I would awake unable to open my eyes. They were glued shut by hardened discharge and had to be soaked with warm water to loosen the lids. It was scary and confusing. Pan was in college, Jane rarely spoke to me, and Dad was certain I was malingering. I remember my maternal grandmother sitting with me, but I have only brief memories of our mother. She was somewhere else, and when I asked about her, I was told many differing things. She was away on business. She was in California dealing with the Tigertail house. She, too, was sick, and in a hospital. I do know that a few times, while I was very sick, she was beside me. But time moves differently for a child with a high fever. These were strange and confusing times. Perhaps our father was in pain, knowing that the family was delaminating. I will never know.

Several times, while we lived in Greenwich, Dad took Jane and me fishing for flounder on Long Island Sound. It was fine and terrible at the same time. Flounder are bottom fish and very tasty, and we fished for them by baiting a weighted hook with a bloodworm and letting the bait sink to the bottom. The knowledge that the worms were hurt by the hook was too much for me, and I refused to bait my hook. This, predictably, made Dad very angry with me. When he looked away in disgust, Jane would quickly bait my hook for me and tell Dad that *I* had baited my hook, a practice that made these fishing trips possible. We would fish without the wrath of our father descending on both of us. There was never much conversation in the boat. But in

my hour of humiliation, Jane became my savior. And though she says
she hated me and treated me meanly, she was there for me at every
critcal moment. Sister and brother, brother and sister.

When the moving-into-the-new-house feeling had become a little
easier, Dad began to paint pictures. Not like the ones on the walls
and ceiling of the houses on Chadbourne and Tigertail, but real, on-
an-easel, paintings. He used pastels, a very difficult medium. His
work was so beautiful, so precise. He did many pastels over the next
year. One day he came home with something new, a paint that could
be applied to glass or ceramics. The first thing he painted on was an
ashtray. He painted ashes, used matches, and squashed cigarette butts
on the inside of the little white bowl. When he had finished, the ashtray looked as if it had all this stuff *really* in it.

He was in New York City, several days later, when the maid was
cleaning the house. She picked up the ashtray and wiped it with her
ammonia cloth. She looked at it, and seeing that it still had ashes in
it, she gave it another, stronger wipe. It was then that she knew something was wrong. She quickly put the bowl down, looked around to
see if she had been noticed, and went on cleaning. I was terrified.
The ashtray was ruined, and I was sure I would be blamed.

When Dad came back to Connecticut, I wanted to hide, but at the
same time, I was fascinated about his reaction. He looked at the tray
and became angry. He looked at me, and I caved in and told him the
maid had done it. I had tears welling in my eyes. He stared at the
bowl and then began to laugh. For him it was the best compliment
about his work. But I was only eight, and I didn't understand why he
wasn't mad at me or the maid. But I did like the laughing Dad.

. . .

Just as Jane and I were getting used to our new house and sur-
roundings, there was talk of moving to a different place. We had
made new friends and often played with our old comrades, the Hayward children, who had moved east and joined us, so to speak, in
Greenwich. Maggie Hayward had married twice after she and Dad
were divorced. Her second husband was the director Willie Wyler.
Soon after their divorce, she married Leland Hayward, who had been
her agent when she married Dad. Dad's agent, too. For that matter,
Leland was the agent for the cream of the crop of new stars. His

clients included Jimmy Stewart, Katharine Hepburn, Humphrey Bogart, Mary Martin, Gary Cooper, Lauren Bacall, and many others.
When he sold his company—along with his client list—to Lew Wasserman and Jules Stein, MCA became the biggest and best agency in
the business. MCA stood for Music Corporation of America—starting
out as a musical act booking agency, based in Chicago. But Leland
Hayward was much more than an agent. He was an entrepreneur in
the most elegant sense of the term. He was an extremely successful
producer of big Broadway shows, including *South Pacific,* a film producer, an airline owner and innovator, and a good friend to all his
clients. It was with Leland that Maggie had her three children—our
three best childhood friends.

They lived in a beautiful house that had a pond, sweeping lawns,
and many weeping willows. Shortly after they moved east—Leland
was producing *Mister Roberts* and *South Pacific*—Maggie and Leland
separated. It seemed as if both our families were delaminating at the
same time. But our relationships had no dependency on our parents.

Hide-and-seek. Cowboys and Indians. Swimming in the ponds. Exploring. Jane and Pan told me to be careful of the snapping turtles, as
they might snap my little peepee off. I didn't swim very much after
that, though pools seemed safe enough. I loved to row the Haywards'
little boat around their pond. Bridget, on whom I had a major crush,
would sit in the stern with an umbrella, pretending it was a parasol.
We imagined we were rowing on some lazy English river, on a balmy,
sunny day, and spoke to each other in the best English accents we
could muster. The Haywards had a new stepfather whom we liked,
Kenneth Wagg, an Englishman. It was the first time I was faced with
a split family—unaware of the disaster unfolding in my own family.
Brooke, Bridget, and Bill still formed the nucleus that Jane and I knew
as "the Haywards," but there was an added something. Not quite a
tension, but close.

We visited them many times, staying overnight often. We put on
plays to amuse ourselves and their governess and their mother, Margaret Sullavan. She was a very likable and dreamy woman, in my
mind. When we all still lived in California, she would take us for
drives in her Chrysler Town and Country convertible, with the top
down. It was a very classy car with a wooden trunk lid and doors. It
must have been a wonderful sight: a gaggle of kids all blond and
laughing, except for Brooke, who had beautiful, shiny dark hair.

Whenever the family Fonda moved, so did they. Oddly, though, I don't remember them coming to our house many times, and when we moved to our second house, we moved farther away from them.

As stressful as the move east had been, I was actually pleased to be moving to the next house. Its newness masked the unknown darkness that was enveloping the first house. It had two ponds and many acres, with a long driveway. On the way to the Boomer House, as it was called, we drove past a house that resembled a very small castle. It, too, had a pond, and there were five swans that floated on it. There were willows and birches and all kinds of wildlife, but the swans were a real centerpiece. They were also very scary. They chased me and Buz every time we walked by the pond. At one point, I was selling packets of flower seeds and had to pass by the swan pond to get to neighboring houses, and Buz and I had to run our collective asses to make the public road before the swans bit us.

One might wonder why I was selling seed packets. On the back of one of my comics, there was an opportunity to get a Daisy BB gun if I sold a certain number of seed packets. So I sent away for the kit and dutifully went to as many neighboring homes as possible to get orders until my grandmother found out and forbade the BB gun. No BB gun and many apologies to the people who had signed up for the seeds. I am quite sure that they ordered their packets out of pity for me.

My father's parents, William and Herberta Fonda, had died before Jane and I were born, but our mother's mother, Sophie Seymour, moved east when Mother was away so much and became our visible guardian. She had joined us while we were still at the Count's place and moved with us to the Boomer House. She brought our housekeeper from Tigertail with her, so the whole thing made me a bit happier. I liked Katie very much. She was an American of Japanese descent, and the family hired her immediately after the end of World War II. Katie's presence was a small thing, but it meant a great deal to me.

. . .

By the time we moved to the Boomer House, California's fresh food had been replaced by Spam and tongue. One of my jobs was to knead the margarine in its plastic bag. These bags were ten- by six-inch pillows of white margarine, with a small sack of coloring in the middle that was to be broken and kneaded through the entire pillow until the white substance looked like butter. When I asked why it was necessary to waste time with this meaningless procedure, harmony fled the house. "Because you are supposed to!" my father snapped. "It's your job and you *will* do it!" Even then, I knew it was a superfluous act, with no end result, no better-tasting food.

But I am losing the point. Why were we eating Spam? Why were we eating tongue? It wasn't as if we were poor. We were living in mansions; Dad was working in a major hit play on Broadway. What was the purpose? Out of whack priorities? I took to writing "I hate the East!" on the walls, and in time I had learned more expressive terms, like "Fuck the East!" There was no way to deny that I was the author of these little proclamations. No one else in the family was short enough to scrawl such infantile hieroglyphics so close to the floor.

I was doing only so-so at school. I didn't like playing sports, and I was so thin that soccer and football matches maimed me. Things began to lose all sense.

The summer of 1949 was camp time for me, and a disaster. I'd write home on pieces of birch bark. "Dear Mom and Dad, How are you I am fine the weather is fine goodbye." Along with twelve other campers, I came down with a terrible fever, and because it was at the height of the polio scare we were sent to a hospital. The food at the hospital was better than camp food or even our home food, a small blessing.

. . .

One afternoon that fall, as Jane, Pan, and I got into Bunny Abry's Bentley (Bunny was Pan's fiancé), the girls said the word "divorce." I knew that it was a bad word, but I didn't understand how it applied to us. There were strong words at home, and even stronger silences. All the adults had short fuses. No one spoke further about divorce, but the cat was out of the bag. We spent many forced, silent dinners with Grandmother at the head of the table, Mother crying into her plate, and none of us knowing what to do. I always wondered what I had done wrong this time.

Our mother went away again, to a hospital, we were told, for an operation. Grandmother kept an eye on us, and Aunt Marjorie, Mother's sister, joined her to help oversee the house. The odds were getting worse. Five women and one-third of a man, six to one when

Mother's secretary was there. I learned to play canasta in preparation for adult life. Things were too far away for my bike to make a difference, but Buz and I continued exploring. The ponds froze over, and we all ice-skated. We saw the Haywards more often, Grandma having forgotten or having decided to ignore the smoking incident. It was more important that Jane and I had friends. When we skated on untested ice, I thought about falling through, and wondered if snapping turtles were active in the winter.

Mother came home for Christmas, and she seemed all right to me. Dad came only for Christmas Eve and Christmas Day. Snow was on the tree, but tension was all over the place. At the time, I had no idea what was happening, though I learned later that Mom *did* have an operation early that fall, something to do with her kidneys. But shortly after Christmas, she went away again, and we were told she was back at the hospital for further tests. I got little notes every now and then, but she didn't say where she was, or when she was coming home. She always signed them "Love, Mummie," with a little smiling face drawn nearby.

(from Greenwich, Connecticut, to Watson Webb, late fall, 1949)

Dearest Wat Wat—
. . . I know you understand why I didn't see you when you were here. It was a physical impossibility for me to see anyone at that time.
The shock of Hank wanting to remarry was almost too much for me— and too soon after my immense operation. Had it been a year instead of four months my nerves would have been in better shape for the blow. Since he has told me he hasn't been happy during our thirteen years of marriage all I can say is I wish him great happiness in this new marriage. I am sad for my children. If it wasn't for them you know where I'd tell him to go—I'd tell him to have his head examined. I am feeling better—and when it's over no doubt I'll be healthier and happier. Thank you again, dear Wat, for your note and thought of us . . . Have a wonderful Christmas . . .

Love and xxxes,
Frances

I received a copy of this letter from my godfather, Watson Webb, two years ago. It was the first time I had any insight to the timing of the events that were going on in 1949, and the first time I had a broader picture of the disintegrating family during that same period.

The family was sluffing away, week by week, and though I couldn't articulate what was happening, it did seem as though we were being left behind. Each adult was saying that *they* were in charge, but clearly none of them had a clue, and all of them lacked the moral and physical authority and strength of character of our parents. Dad stayed in New York City most of the time, and Pan was gone, too. Jane was moody and easily angered and kept to herself more. We stopped sledding, stopped doing much of anything that might be considered "fun."

Spring came, but it wasn't like any other spring. I don't remember how often Mother or Dad visited, but in early April, around the time of her forty-second birthday, on April 7, Mother came home one afternoon. Jane says she kept me in her bedroom when Mother was calling out for us, but I see Mother in the library, fragrant with perfume, smiling and telling me she'd be home for good in one week. I see her giving me a small note saying the usual things, with the same little smiling face at the bottom, though perhaps later I confused a note she'd already sent to me with a real memory.

A riding club and stables were within walking distance of Boomer House, and Jane and I took riding lessons after school most days. Or rather, Jane practiced and I took lessons, mostly for jumping. The next Friday afternoon, Jane was already at the stables when I got home from school. Only Katie was at the house, and when I asked where everyone was, she told me that they had gone to visit my mother at the hospital. I asked Katie if everything was all right. She wasn't sure, but she seemed very nervous. I had to get to my riding lesson, so I knelt at the side of the couch in the living room and prayed to Jesus that he wouldn't let anything bad happen to Mother. After the prayer I walked to the stables, sure that all was fine.

God, I hated the riding lessons. Jane was leaving when I arrived, having had a good practice, but after my tenth jump I was thrown from the horse. I landed flat on my back, knocking the breath out of me. I wiped my horse down and shuffled back to the house.

The house sat on a hill facing east, and the dirt driveway gave way to asphalt near some thick evergreens a hundred yards from the loop in front of the house. As I rounded the evergreens, I noticed many cars parked at the front, and when I entered the house, I entered another world. Marjorie and her husband, Monty, Katie, and Mother's secretary sat in the library. They were all familiar faces, but today they were all staring at the floor, all so still, and when I walked toward them they told me to go through the closed doors into the living room. I opened the doors and saw Jane, Grandma, and Dad sitting on the couches. Jane was on Dad's lap. I went to Grandma, and she told me that Mother was dead. She had died of a heart attack, in a hospital.

It was Friday, April 14. Jesus had failed me. Jesus had let me down. Jesus forgot my prayer about Mother. I was too young to know that little in life was fair. Jane, who later said she shed no tears, went to sit on Grandma's lap and I went to Dad's. Everyone was crying, even Jane. I never asked Jesus for anything ever again.

Later, alone in my room, a dreadful thought settled in my heart. After daydreaming that Mother would die so that Dad could marry Miss Stephenson so many times, it had come true. I had wished it so hard, I made it happen. I was horrified. It was only a dream. It wasn't supposed to *happen*. I didn't mean to dream her *dead*.

chapter $\mathcal{T}$hree

April 20

Dear Mr. Everett—

Mrs. Seymour and I want you to know how much we appreciate your kind help and understanding during these first critical days with Peter. You must realize as well as we do how successful your efforts were because he has come through it beautifully.

Sincerely and gratefully yours,
Henry Fonda

$\mathcal{I}$ can't remember much from this period; perhaps, having lost all context, I lost my ability to remember. My father's letter to Mr. Everett, Brunswick School's principal, written a week after my mother's death, infers that period of desolation was over. One week later? It took at least twenty-five years for life to begin to be put right. No one ever talked about Mom. No one seemed to miss her. It was almost as if she had never lived, and I couldn't understand it. Jane and I had not been at a funeral or service for her; I didn't know where she was buried. One doesn't necessarily take ten- and twelve-year-old children to any funeral, but usually they'll attend their mother's.

Later that year I ran away from school. The other boys had been pushing me around, taunting me about being a sissy and saying weird things about my mother. Fuck them. I hit the road, and when cars passed by, I hid in the bushes. I didn't see our station wagon coming from the other direction, and when Grandma made a U-turn, I took off through the fields. I didn't want to see anybody, especially anybody from the family. But Grandma's tears—at the time it never occurred to me that she'd lost a daughter—were too much for me, and I came back to her. She said I didn't have to explain a thing to her.

Everyone else in the family seemed to have a handle on the whole thing. Every time I got a handle on it, mine broke. Pan, now essentially an orphan, fled to art school in Europe. She occasionally sent me letters and snapshots, and I wrote back to her care of an American bank in Paris. Even Jane went on with her life, seemingly unaffected, though she never said a thing. I stopped trusting grown-ups, and I stopped trusting my family. There wasn't a whole lot of *me* I could trust. I trusted Buz, but he knew nothing; he could only sense what was happening to the family.

Dad only had one day of the week off from *Mister Roberts*, and whenever he visited I tried to please him, but my intentions never seemed to pan out. One work project I was assigned to was the fixing of the potholes in the dirt part of the driveway. I got very hot and hungry during my chain-gang job one day, and when I spied an apple tree close by, I ate about a dozen green apples. By dinnertime I had a horrible stomachache. Dad thought I was just trying to get out of eating my meal, but someone came to my rescue and explained. Dad said that should teach me a lesson about eating apples that were not ripe. I would have appreciated a warning.

· · ·

During the summer of 1950 Dad announced that we'd take a long drive together, just the two of us. This was a first, though in 1947, Jane and I had joined Dad, John Wayne, and Ward Bond for a day drive in the Duke's cream-colored Cadillac convertible, riding with the top down on red leather seats. We'd gone to the set of *Fort Apache,* director John Ford's version of Custer's Last Stand, which was being shot in Bishop, California. Dad played the part of Colonel Thursday, an unsmiling, bitter, strict hard-ass. When people ask me what it was like growing up as Henry Fonda's son, I ask them if they have seen *Fort Apache*.

So there I was, on the dusty trail with Colonel Thursday in the summer of 1950, in our Ford Woody. On the road with the Duke, there had been laughter from the men and a certain giddiness for me and Jane. On the road alone with Dad there were hours of silence. I was afraid to talk. I didn't want to do *anything* to make him mad or annoyed. Even a ten-year-old recognizes that a ten-year-old can be very annoying. We were going fishing, which meant that Buz couldn't come. I needed Buz at that time, more than anyone in the family understood.

We drove to Island Pond, Vermont, to visit an old war buddy of

Dad's, "Killer" Ken Dyer. Killer had a cottage on the south side of the lake, and we all went fishing right away. The men talked about war things, and I patiently waited for a fish to take my lure. At one point I thought I felt something, but the men told me I was mistaken. When they were ready to go back to shore, and as I began to reel in my line, there was a definite weight on it. Dad quickly pointed out that my line was wrapped around one of the oars, and that was why I felt a tug. He made it sound as if I had wrapped the line around the oar on purpose. God, life was grand. I tried to ignore him and struggled away, finally bringing a pike, big by my standards, into the boat. The pike was the first and only fish caught on Island Pond that trip. It was late in the day, so the fish was put in a bucket of water. Killer was delighted for me, but Dad was silent, though he said he'd take a photograph of me holding the fish the next morning.

That night, the meal was mulligan stew. I'd never had it before, and it tasted great. I sat at the table with the men, listening to their stories. Dad was called "Fearless" Fonda. I think it had something to do with a comic-strip character named Fearless Fosdick. Killer and Fearless finished their stew and two bottles of Jack Daniel's, and while they were snorting away about their past glories, I went out to check on my fish, still safe in its bucket. I must have gone outside twenty times that night to be sure the fish was still there.

The next morning was a bitch for Killer and Fearless, and a lesson for me about Jack Daniel's, the first time I heard the word hangover. It was almost noon by the time Dad was ready, or able, to take the photograph, but I put my fish back on the hook and held it proudly, as if I'd just caught it. I still have the photograph of me and the fish that Dad said wasn't there. The long night and following morning in the bucket had given the pike's body an unreal bend, so that it looks like a long, thick J which Dad had to try very hard to straighten out. My jeans are belted just under my arms, and it's the jeans that are the best part of the picture. The picture, in color, has faded quite a bit, but my memories are as sharp as a razor.

Dad and I drove on to a fishing camp on a lake near the Canadian border. We went fishing in the early morning for brook trout and caught several, which we ate for breakfast. Dad's knees and toes had been giving him a hard time—it hurt him to walk, and hurt him to sit—so I fooled around the cabin while he rested. The next day he had so much pain he couldn't come with me, so off I went with the guide, and Dad hobbled back to our cabin. I caught a five-pound lake trout, and I was ecstatic when we arrived back at the camp. Dad was very proud of me and when I insisted that we eat it, since I had killed it, he went to elaborate lengths to be sure that we had it for dinner that evening. I learned later that we ate someone else's lake trout, because he was going to have mine stuffed as a surprise.

I'd spent more time with Dad on this trip than I had in years, and all I had learned about him was that he had a friend named Killer; that he was known, to some, as Fearless; and that he had something wrong with his knees and big toes, problems I inherited. I didn't like the air of mystery. I needed to know who was hiding inside him: the little boy, whooping it up, and holding on to an enormous kite for dear life; the little boy who painted ashes in the ashtray to fool the maid; the little boy who squirted disappearing ink on his best friend's white dinner jacket.

Nine or ten years later, while having dinner with my father in New York, I asked if he ever dreamed about flying—I have no idea why *that* was the question—and he told me about a dream of coming home on a date, walking into the foyer, asking his date to wait just a minute while he walked up the stairs, and, from the balcony, yelling down to her, "I bet you've never seen this!" then flying all around the house. It sounded like the way I felt when I dreamed about flying the Electrolux vacuum cleaner. I also dreamed I could fly by just springing into the air and swooping around, jumping out of a tree and soaring like a glider, and I'd had a dream habit of jumping off mantlepieces back at Tigertail, but I never jumped off a balcony.

After the fishing trip was over, we drove to visit Jane. She was at a camp, God knows where, that specialized in riding and other typical camp activities. She was glad to see Dad but indifferent about me. I think she was upset that she was sent to camp and didn't come on the fishing trip with us.

Dad had to be in Boston to see the London production of *Mister Roberts,* with John Forsythe in the leading role, before it went over-seas. He also wanted to meet some old friends—John Wayne, John Ford, Ward Bond, Josh Logan—for an all-day gathering. I liked to be around the Duke and Ward. They never said a word about my incred-ible skinniness, and showed me tricks and played with me, the way normal people play with kids. After Boston, Dad headed back to New

York City and dropped me off at the Boomer House. It was a relief to
see Buz and the woods again, though I dreaded the war diet of Spam.

The day the Korean War started, Jane and I and Dad and Grandma
were visiting friends in Greenwich, the Turbells. The adults stayed
apart from the kids and seemed to be having some sort of crisis. We
all inched closer, heard the dreaded words "going to war," crawled
back to our little part of the world, and wondered what was going to
become of us. We all knew about the A-bomb, and doom filled my
heart. We stayed for dinner, and not a word was spoken about any
war, but Dad and Grandma got plastered. Grandma, theoretically a
little less plastered, drove back to Boomer House. She was only a
little less bombed, and the drive made me forget about the war talk
and simply wonder if we were going to make Boomer.

.   .   .

One day, near the end of that summer, Dad drove me into the
city with him. I was to spend two nights and travel by train back to
Greenwich. We went to Jones Beach, on Long Island, and lay in the
sun with a beautiful young woman named Susan Blanchard. She was
stunning, and she and I had a grand time running on the sand. That
evening I got to pick the movie, and we went to see *Rocket to the
Moon*. Afterward I went back to Dad's apartment and slept in a bed
that pulled out from the couch.

The next day I tagged along with Dad as he did business and went
to the Alvin Theater, where he was performing in *Mister Roberts*. I'd
seen the play three or four times already, though I was still fascinated
by the sets, and climbed all over them as if they were my own special
jungle gym. Later that day the stage manager sent me across Shubert
Alley to the show *South Pacific*. It was the first musical I had ever
seen, and I was completely blown away. I had to go back to Dad's
apartment and bed instead of seeing the evening show, but the next
several times I came to the city to visit him I made a point of seeing
South Pacific again, and memorizing the lines and music.

On the second night in New York, while I waited in Dad's apartment for him to return home or for sleep to catch me, I resorted to
my old habit of looking through his accessories and keepsakes. This
time I picked up a gold heart with another heart pierced by an arrow
engraved on it. On the upper left of the heart within a heart, I saw an

"H" and below it on the lower right was an "S." I held the heart, staring at it for a long time.

I knew what it meant. I was confused and upset, but I didn't say a thing to Dad. When I got back to Greenwich, I went to Grandma's room and tearfully told her of my discovery. I said that it seemed to me that Dad and Susan were going to get married. Grandma told me that, yes, they were going to marry, and that I needed to have a mother, and that Susan would be a very good one for me. I ran to my room and cried for a long time. Susan *was* beautiful and fun and all the right things, but I wasn't sure about what it meant to us as a family. In hindsight, the kindest thing my grandmother ever did for me was to tell me that I needed a mother, and that I should be patient, and open-minded.

· · ·

I'd spent the previous two years begging for a BB gun, and earlier that fall, Dad had stunned me by giving me a .22, a real rifle, instead. He took me out to the fields and showed me how to shoot one properly, and in early January 1951, I took my .22 and joined Tony Abry, Bunny's younger brother, and Reed Armstrong, both young boys my age, and drove with the Abrys' chauffeur to the family's skeet and trap range to shoot. Reed brought plenty of ammunition and an antique .22 pistol, and we took turns shooting my rifle and Reed's pistol and a 410 ga. The pistol broke open at the breech, and the spent cartridge was ejected in the same way as breaking breech shotgun. After a fresh, single cartridge was inserted in the chamber, the pistol was closed by holding the barrel with one hand and closing the grip, or handle, to the barrel. This action automatically cocked the firing pin and the trigger, which lay upon a post without a safety guard.

After I fired the pistol once I had difficulty ejecting the spent cartridge. I used the ram from my rifle to push the spent casing out of the chamber, put a new shell into the chamber, and closed the breech, thereby making the gun "live" and ready to fire. I failed to close the grip and the barrel correctly, and instead flipped the barrel upward. The grip came loose in my hand as the pistol flipped around, and the unguarded trigger was pulled by accident, discharging the weapon right into my gut.

There was no pain—I think shock set in instantly—but the knowl-

edge that I had been shot in a very bad way was immediate. I ran
down to the station wagon, where the chauffeur was standing, and
yelled to him, and he pulled up the buckskin shirt I was wearing and
saw a small amount of blood trickling down my belly. The driver, a
black man, piled us into the car and headed for the nearest hospital,
but when he stopped to ask a traffic cop for specific directions, the
cop ignored us until I mustered the strength to swear at the bigoted
man, to tell him that I had been shot in the stomach and needed
emergency attention. We were directed to Ossining Hospital and sped
off again. Tony, Reed, and the driver tried to make me lie down on
the backseat, but I refused. I knew I was dying, and lying down
seemed like giving up. I told them that I didn't want to see Michael
(the first dog we'd had at Tigertail, who'd been put down) or my
mother in heaven. By the time we arrived at the hospital I was scared
and hallucinating. Ossining Hospital was a large brick building, but
when I looked at it I saw one big brick, floating above the ground,
not a likely place to have your life saved.

When the chauffeur picked me up in his arms, the brick became a
building, and he carried me into the admitting area. There wasn't
much blood oozing from the little bullet hole, but we knew that things
were bad. The admitting staff refused to deal with the black man, and
he was told to sit on one of the waiting room benches. After a few
moments, he carried me back to the main desk, telling them again
that I had received a gunshot in my stomach. He was told to sit back
down. When he became agitated and argued they called him a nigger,
and I joined the argument, at once, using every swear word I knew,
until a passing doctor actually lifted my shirt, immediately ordered
the staff to admit me, and went off in search of help and a gurney.
Even then, the nurses behind the counter, hating the fact that they
had to deal with the black man, made jokes about whether the chauffeur was a parent or guardian, and asked if my parents were or ever
had been members of the Communist Party. That put an end to the
chauffeur's admirable patience. When the emergency staff arrived, he
wouldn't turn me over until he was sure they were going to do their
best to save my life. God bless him.

They rolled me into an elevator, cut off my clothes, and propped
me up on my right side. They saw the bullet just under the skin over
my left kidney, remarked that it looked like a big bee sting, and told
me they were going to give me a shot for gangrene. I didn't feel a

thing, and I didn't know what gangrene was, but I hated shots. I was very aware of the tension in the room when they cut out the bee-sting bullet and blood began spurting all over. I heard someone wonder if it had pierced my heart, and other people speaking about the amount of blood that must be in my abdominal cavity. And I remember that the doctor in charge was talking on a phone, asking someone questions, while the other interns worked on me.

"Well, where did he go duck hunting?"

An unheard reply.

"Did he go with anyone else?"

Another pause.

"Mrs. Sweet, we have a bad gunshot wound here. Did he say when he was coming back?" I could sense everyone waiting.

"He is?"

Dr. Sweet chose that moment to arrive home from his duck hunt. Timing. The doctor on the phone apprised him of the situation—a pierced kidney, a possibly pierced heart, a massive amount of blood in the body cavity—and it may seem far-fetched that I can remember what was said so precisely, but I can.

My hallucinations were coming and going as I was wheeled up to an operating room. Different people were moving around me, trying to reassure me. I was dying, and knew it, but I clung to life harder than I had ever done anything. I was still on my side, still awake but losing ground. I could no longer lift my head but I kept my eyes open, fiercely; I thought if I closed them, I would never open them again.

Dr. Sweet arrived, but all I could see were his lower legs and his hunting boots with their laces all loose and open. An oxygen mask was stuck on my face, and the smell of the oxygen mixed with ether frightened me. I ripped the mask off my face, screaming that they were trying to kill me. I have no idea where I got the strength to rip the mask off, but as the nurses were putting it back on, I cried out for my grandma. One of the nurses said, "I'm right here," but I knew it was a nurse. Then I saw a gray swirling. And then I saw nothing.

Someone reached my grandmother with what had to be the most upsetting news since Mother died. She and Jane rushed to the hospital and waited in a special area near the operating room. After several hours, Dr. Charles Clark Sweet came to speak to them, his surgical gown covered with my blood, and told them that I had lost too much blood and that my heart had stopped beating three times. He said he had done all he could do to save my life. He was very upset. Jane, who told me later that she'd prayed to God and promised to stop being mean to me if He would let me live, says that she and my grandmother thought Dr. Sweet meant that I was already dead. For a few seconds, Grandma and Jane had to deal with that terrible feeling, until one of the interns stuck his head in the room and told the doctor that they had started my heart again with an injection of Adrenalin. Dr. Sweet quickly went back to the operating table.

If it had been Jane on the operating table, and I heard that she had died, I think I would have died, too. I really didn't have anyone else but Jane. She meant everything to me, and even though she has told me that she was always mean to me, I never thought it out of the ordinary or unloving—it was the way big sisters treated little brothers. She said that she was mean to me right away again after I pulled through. I don't think so. She has said some things that were hurtful to me over the past forty-plus years, but she has never been mean to me, and I would never have weathered our storm of abandonment without her.

I may not have loved Grandma as I loved Jane, but when I regained consciousness, the first words I spoke were the last words I'd spoken as I went under the ether. Now my grandmother *was* right there. I had been holding her hand so tightly her fingers were bruised. I remember Dr. Sweet coming in and explaining what had happened during the surgery. I had tubes going up my nose and back down my throat to my stomach. One tube was for feeding me, the other was to remove the bile from my stomach. The bullet had blown the tip of my liver off, tumbled through the top of my stomach, missed my lower heart and abdominal aorta only because my heart was contracting when the bullet tumbled by—timing—and smashed through the middle of my left kidney, coming to rest just beneath the skin on my back. There were shunts in my organs to drain them, and the incision on my stomach was five inches long and closed with dissolving stitches. My liver, stomach, and kidney had been wrapped with a brand-new gauze that also dissolved, a gauze created for soldiers fighting in Korea who received vital organ damage.

Part of the lucky timing of the accident was that Ossining Hospital, next door to Sing Sing prison, was one of the first places to have the gauze ready to roll for inmates who suffered stab wounds, and Charles Sweet, the prison doctor, was the only surgeon in the area who had expertise with puncture wounds. I think I was the first civilian to be treated with this new stuff.

When the public first learned about the accident, the news was broadcast over the ham waves. My father and Susan Blanchard were on their honeymoon on St. John, and the ham radio and Coast Guard reports only said I was involved in a shooting accident. Everyone in the family knew it was an accident, but somehow the story got worked around so that it was a possible suicide because of my mother's recent death. That stuck with me for quite a while. At the time, Dad knew nothing of the specifics, and he was worried sick as he made his way back to civilization and a telephone. I remember him sitting with me in the hospital room when he got back to the States, and though he said little, I know it must have been a terrible time for him.

Grandma told me that Buz began howling when I was first wounded and didn't stop until the tubes were removed from my nose and I was upgraded from critical to stable. For the intervening week no one was certain whether I was going to live or die, though I don't remember worrying. As soon as the tubes were removed from my throat, I asked for my harmonica and played it softly each night. I couldn't laugh or cough, what with all the stitches; and the dressings, anchored by adhesive tape that tore my skin, had to be changed twice a day. I was not a happy boy.

As I progressed I was allowed to scoot around in a wheelchair. When the days were warm I went out on a little patio and watched the prisoners in Sing Sing move from one building to another. On some Fridays, it was fry-day, usually in the late evening, and the lights of the hospital would dim and surge.

During my three-and-a-half-week stay at the hospital, I was given several things to help me pass the time. Dad came to the hospital with a fly-tying kit from Dan Bailey's Fly Shop in Livingston, Montana. He brought a large tuna hook for me to work with, as it was much easier to tie on a large scale. I tied a royal coachman as well as I could, and sent the enormous fly to Dan Bailey for his critique, once I was home. Weeks later I received a letter back from him, saying that the tying looked pretty good but the hook was far too big for any trout he knew of. Twenty-four years later I bought Dan Bailey's log house in the Paradise Valley, south of Livingston.

After I was released I had to mend at home until the draining tubes' openings healed. It was a very spooky thing to watch the tubes being slowly pulled from my body. It took two weeks for the holes to close, and while I finished my recuperation at Boomer House, a very nice policeman visited me several times, explained that he, too, had been shot in the abdomen, and showed me the many scars left by a .45 caliber Thompson submachine gun.

Four or five weeks later, I returned to the Brunswick School a few days after my eleventh birthday, and the cake brought to the classroom read "Happy Birthday to Lead-Belly Pete." Oddly enough, both Tony Abry and Reed Armstrong, the two boys with me when I shot myself, suffered accidental gunshot wounds later in their lives. Reed shot himself in the foot, but Tony's wound was to his head—the bullet arched around the inside of his skull without damaging his brain.

. . .

As the end of the school year neared, Jane and I were told that we would be spending the summer with our father and new stepmother in California, in Los Angeles, on the beach. Dad would be finishing the national road tour of *Mister Roberts*. After a long flight from New York, as we drove to our hotel on the beach, I couldn't see enough of the place that had been our paradise—familiar buildings, palm trees, warm, clear light. Ocean House was a grand mansion, built by William Randolph Hearst for Marion Davies years before. It had a beach club, an Olympic-size pool, and marble everywhere. Dad and Susan had a suite with its own private terrace. The warm air and smell of the ocean were a tonic for me and Jane, and we were happy as clams. Our rooms had been servants' quarters, and we shared a bathroom, but they were the best rooms we'd had in three years.

At dinner I began to feel nauseous, and I knew I was going to get sick, so I asked to be excused. I think the excitement of being with Dad again and the adventure of the plane trip with Jane just got to me, but Dad's look of disgust made me feel like the biggest disappointment in his life. I went to my room and heaved. After I had rested for a while, I felt much better, and I went exploring.

Unfortunately, Dad saw me, and accused me of being a liar—he said that had I really been sick, I wouldn't be running around the marble pool and dance floor, and suggested that I'd only said I was sick to avoid having to finish my meal. He told me to stay in my room until breakfast.

Despite this rocky start, being back in Southern California was like being let out of jail. Even though I was skinny and had a large purple scar on my stomach, I was out on the beach as soon as I was released from my room. After our second all-the-doo-da-day in the sun, Jane and I were as red as anybody could get, painfully sunburned. We helped each other by peeling large areas of skin and rubbing whatever soothing lotion Susan would bring us over the hard-to-reach parts of each other's bodies. The pain barely dented our happiness, though we took it a little slower with the sun and surf until we had a bit of a tan going.

After a few weeks in Los Angeles, I missed Buz. I'd watch dogs playing on the beach and wish he could be there with me. My allowance was twenty-five cents a week, but I'd crawl under the slatted floor of the refreshment bar at the Sand and Sea Club and sift through the sand, finding dimes, quarters, nickels, and even half dollars, enough to call back east and ask about Buz.

Jane remembers me *always* on the pay phone in the lobby that summer, calling Grandma and crying or whining. And, yes, I was on the phone in the lobby, and, yes, I was crying. It took several calls and all the change I could sift from the sand to find out how my dog was. At first Grandma said Buz was staying with Katie, who'd moved to her own place. After three more calls trying to get Katie's telephone number, the truth came out. While I was playing in the surf and sun, while I was blissfully watching the moon dance in the waves, while I was having the happiest time I'd had since we'd left California three years earlier, Buz had been put down. Behind my sunburned back, Buz had been destroyed. And so was I when I found out.

They told me that there had been no place for Buz anymore, that Jane and I would be joining Dad and Susan in New York City soon, and that the city was no place for a dog. There were other explanations, all of them bullshit, all of them boiling down to the fact that everyone else considered my beloved dog an inconvenience. Adults in my family were not to be trusted anymore. I never kissed my grandmother again. I hated all those who were part of this insidious plot. My Dad. They killed my dog. *Goddammit*. He was only six.

Deep down, a child can probably hold on to a righteous grudge for much longer than an adult, but they're also more prone to distraction. The sun, sand, and surf were too much for my depression, and in spite of the dirty deed I continued to soak up the precious atmosphere that would too soon be lost. Dad brought a pie pan to the beach on one of his days off. He showed me how to throw it with a spin and make it float like a flying saucer, the original Frisbee. He would play catch with me until his toes became too painful. With the right spin, the pan made large curves as it floated to me and was easy to catch. When Dad wasn't there, I could flick it into the wind and it would return to me. It was a redeeming thing, and I stopped hating him for allowing Buz to be killed, at least while we played pie pan. But in my room, at night, I wept for my dog, and cursed those who took him from me. I tried to tell myself that Dad probably wasn't even aware of the dirty deed.

Some nights, there were large parties and dances given at Ocean House. Jane and I would come down from our rooms and go to one of the empty halls adjoining the party and dance together, spinning around in our own peculiar waltz. I enjoyed those moments of pretending to be grown-ups at a grand ball, dancing away without rules or embarrassment or criticism. The way *we* danced was the way dancing was done. My sister wanted me to be with her, and I got to pretend I was a young, attractive man waltzing with a lady of the court.

Susan was largely responsible for the fact that we danced at all. She laughed, she told jokes, sang songs, rejoiced in the pursuit of happiness, and allowed us to be children along with the child in herself. Dad was performing in *Mister Roberts,* and even after a three-year run he played each night as if he were just opening on Broadway. This gave Jane and me plenty of time to get to know Susan, and we adored her. She was as free of rules as a dream or a wish. She was magic, and she made me feel loved and important. She was our stepmother, but she was also like an older sister, especially in Pan's absence.

Susan almost made us forget that, with the summer's end, we'd be sent back to Greenwich, to the dreaded East; it seemed we wouldn't be living with them in the city right away, after all, which to me meant that Buz might at least have had a few more years to live. When the time arrived, Jane and I came down with bad colds. One would think we planned our illnesses to stay in Los Angeles a little longer, which was not the case. But it was important that we not have these colds

when we boarded the plane. So we both had to visit the doctor and
get shots. Neither of us liked that part. After the shots, we were told
that we would be fine in time for the flights. No one told us to stay in
bed or even inside or even out of the ocean. And there we were, in
the rain, with our floating mats, catching the last waves we might ever
see. The shit hit the fan.

"What in the name of God are you two doing? I can't believe you
let them do this, Susan!"

Susan, of course, knew nothing. She had been inside, packing us
up, on this rainy day. During the entire summer at Ocean House,
Susan was a prisoner of her own inabilities. She didn't know how to
drive. Other than a very few taxi rides to wherever, she stayed at the
beach with us. I didn't know that was why she was with us so much
until she told me in 1994. She said she was too embarrassed to say
anything to any of us. I think I'll stick with my version: she didn't go
anywhere because she wanted to be with us. By the next summer,
she had learned to drive, though in a tentative fashion.

.   .   .

Back we went, after our thrilling summer, to the sullen, restrictive
atmosphere of New England and the Boomer House. The shooting
accident had put a serious dent in my GPA, and I would have to
repeat sixth grade. I was going to a *new* school, with all the uncertainty that implied, and not only a new school but a boarding school,
Fay School, the oldest in the United States. This was not a good sign;
after all, the Barton School for Boys had been a boarding school. Jane,
also with Susan's help, went off to Emma Willard. Jane had graduated
from the Greenwich Academy and having a much better scholastic
record than I, began the ninth grade there.

Name tags had to be sewn onto all my clothing, and even that
little event spooked me. On several occasions, Grandmother, the dog
killer, drove me to a house that had supposedly been designed by
Mother, who must have been in a bad mood the day she dreamed up
the place. The house sure did make me wonder about her. It was very
modern, at the end of a cul-de-sac, and was stained a gray-green.
There wasn't a speck of warm color in the entire structure, but it was
better than the Boomer House and the sadness of Buz. It was the
house I would be coming home to on my vacations from Fay School,

my new boarding school. Jane liked the new house. For her it represented a solid and more secure place than the rented rambling mansions we had stumbled through. She recently told me that she needed
the security of a place that was "ours" and not rented.

I took the train alone to Boston and was met by a bus, along with
several other boys. No one spoke. I think we were all stunned by the
rejection we felt from our parents. One could tell the new boys from
the old. The veterans filed into Fay with sullen but determined faces,
but those of us who were new milled about, some quietly crying, all
feeling abandoned.

It took a long time for me to get accustomed to the idea that no
one wanted to have me at home, even though "home" didn't really
exist. Many nights I quietly cried myself to sleep, thinking about Buz
and abandonment. And the other boys began to taunt me a few
weeks into the program, which probably enabled them to forget their
own problems. When I was sitting by myself, feeling down, they'd
speak about me as if I couldn't hear, saying things like, He's feeling
sorry for himself because his mother jumped out a window, or, sometimes, He's such a crybaby because his mother shot herself. I thought
these little assholes were crazed—Mother had died of a heart attack.
But always, in the back of my mind, I knew that something was
wrong. I just couldn't put my finger on it, and I didn't know what
questions to ask.

After Thanksgiving break, Judy Rankin, the pretty daughter of the
assistant headmaster, invited me to her parents' quarters to make
brownies with her. I thought that was a terrific idea. She was nice to
me and we laughed as we made the little cakes. The other boys were
jealous of the budding relationship, and teased me about being a
sissy, making cookies with a girl, accused me of playing with dolls.
There were no dolls around when I was with Judy. At least they
slowed down on the mother stuff, and I liked being with Judy, very
much. She let me kiss her cheek, and I invited her to kiss mine. Judy
and I would hold hands when no one was looking. At Fay, I didn't
have to empty sand from my sheets as I had at Barton School. I passed
my room inspections most of the time, and because I got good grades,
I was allowed to study there. Whenever I did, I'd find a cookie or
brownie and a little note from Judy under my pillow.

Judy lent my life a little mystery. The older boys made fun of me
for entirely different reasons than my classmates had. They knew

more about girls, and they were outright jealous that Judy fancied me. One day, while her parents were away, she let me into her apartment and we kissed for a long time. I had to get back to my alcove before anyone could see me. It was dangerous, but very exciting, and back in my room I remembered the few kisses Bridget Hayward and I had exchanged. Both girls were pretty and gentle and smiled at me with the same sort of secret look in their eyes. I didn't have any money, so I couldn't buy Judy a Christmas present, but I wrote her a note saying I would be thinking of her on Christmas morning.

Coming back to the unforgiving house on Martendale Drive in Greenwich for holidays with our grandmother was not at all jolly. We had our old dining room table from Tigertail and some of our other familiar furniture, but the new house's layout was bizarre and depressing to me. My only bedroom window ran along the upper wall, parallel to the ceiling. It didn't open, and I had to stand on a chair on my bed to see out. At Tigertail, I'd had four windows and a paned door that led out to my own little porch. In the new family house, I lived in a cell. There was no bedroom for Dad and Susan, and I don't recall them ever spending a night in Greenwich.

One day, I was rummaging through some of the boxes from Boomer House and found a pair of Mother's gold earrings and pocketed them at once. Mother didn't have pierced ears and used spring-loaded clips. I tried the earrings on but they hurt after a while, and I couldn't understand why anyone would want to cause such hurt. Maybe women lacked nerves in their earlobes. Anyway, I went out and buried them in a secret place. I have no idea what the plan was. Perhaps there was no plan; perhaps I was trying to bury my mother. I never told a soul.

Without Buz, I roamed the place in a moody way. There was a waterfall just in the back edge of our property. It was intriguing but dark and heavily wooded, and it felt like an evil place. I wandered around the nearby estates, sneaking up to other houses like Jane and I had done in California, sometimes getting found out and running like mad to escape. I ran fast as I could, through woods and clearings, and I never got caught, but I was becoming a troubled child. I began to break windows of nearby mansions and greenhouses for no real reason. Something had really pissed me off, and I was doing my best to become a juvenile delinquent. It was then that I should have been sent to the Barton School for Boys. The police easily traced the van-

dalism to me and to a friend, and we were made aware, along with
our households and the neighborhood, of our descent into antisocial
behavior. Truthfully, I didn't give a shit.

Christmas was as grim as the year before. No snow on the tree. No
Dad to make things special. Just Grandma and her live-in daughter
and alcoholic son-in-law. Susan and Dad did come up on Christmas
Day, but it was about as much fun as the forced, silent dinners at
Boomer House, when Mother would cry. Later, I learned that Susan
was indignant with Dad, and demanded to know why we were staying with relatives and not with our father. Her instincts were right on
target, and Dad finally made the decision to take Jane and me back
to the city to live with them. She saved us.

Jane says *she* was the first one to ask Susan if she could call her
Mom. It hardly matters; without communicating with each other, we
wanted the same thing at the same time: someone to look up to, to
count on, to keep secrets with, to love in a familial way. Susan
Blanchard Fonda was twenty-four years old when she accepted the
mantle of "Mom," a mantle not easily granted or accepted. She was
only ten years older than Jane and twelve years older than I, closer in
age to us than to our father, twenty-three years her senior. She is a
wonderful person, and I am still the lucky recipient of her grace and
individuality. From time to time, Mom2, as I refer to her in this book,
still acts like my mother, treating me as if I were her twelve-year-old
son. I think it's a riot, and I love her for it; after all, she has been my
mother for more than forty years.

At Fay School, in the spring of 1952, Susan came to see me on
Founders Day weekend, the first time anyone had come to visit.
There was a dance, and I got to give her flowers and show off my
beautiful stepmother. She stayed for the whole weekend, and it made
my year. Not long after, I wrote her a letter asking if I could call
her Mom. I put the question in a postscript, ending the letter with
"Remember that I love you"; "good luck" written next to a drawing
of a four-leaf clover; a drawing of a baseball glove and a smiling face
wearing a ball cap with a backward "F" on it; "Love + xxxxxxxxxx-
xooooooooooo and all that sort of stuff"; "Pete"; a drawing of two
elephants (Susan loved elephants); and, finally, "P.S. Would you mind
if I called you Mom? I would like to very much."

I hated writing letters to "Dear Dad and Sue." It didn't sound right
and it didn't look right. Bless the dog killer for letting me have a

"Mom," for telling me that I needed to have a mother when I came home with the news that I feared Dad was going to marry Susan. Grandma could have been bitter about Susan, but she never said an unkind word, and so I passed from juvenile delinquency to a young person in search of truth. This earnestness, this willingness to be open again, was the hardest thing I could have done, but with the unbending support of Mom2, I survived and worked through the maze of minotaurs and false exits.

. . .

When school let out that spring, Jane and I joined Dad and Susan in an apartment on Forty-eighth Street and Third Avenue, 223 East Forty-eighth. Frank Lloyd Wright lived next door, and seeing him—black-caped, with a black hat and beautiful white hair—was a special thing, the big-gun aura visible to me even at twelve.

Dad obviously felt imposed on, but I felt we were, maybe, going to be a family again. I loved to be with Susan, and I explored the place as was my wont. In the library, Dad had his collection of records and a nice phonograph. I discovered Les Paul and Mary Ford, big-band jazz, and one album I couldn't understand. When I asked what the lyrics meant, Dad told me it was double-talk, not apparently worried that some of the dirtiest, funniest stuff I'd ever heard was hidden within the innocuous cover lyrics.

After only a few weeks in Manhattan we went out to Lloyds Neck, on Long Island, where Dad had rented a little three-bedroom shack. One could call it a cottage, but it really was a shack, though infinitely more pleasant than any of the Greenwich houses. I wondered if we were going to start eating Spam again.

Dad tried very hard to be with me. Whenever he had a day off, we played catch with a baseball. I helped him try to make a sandy beach between our little front yard and the tidal pools with their swamplike clumps of sea grass. He rigged up a large sifter with a screen, and we shoveled the coarse rocklike stuff onto the sifter, allowing the finer material to be separated. We never got much done, but the idea was great.

The house came with its own large oak dory and heavy oak oars. When the tide was in, I used all my strength to push the old dory out into the tidal pools, and spent hours rowing through the little islets of sea grass, following one channel into another. I got lost many times, but always found my way back. These little ventures made me feel more secure about myself. But when Dad finally got to the summer break for the show he was doing, *Point of No Return*, he had a grand surprise for me, a small sailboat called a catboat. It was fourteen feet long, dark green on the outside and varnished on the inside, with a tiller, a centerboard, a mast at the very bow, and no jib. I named the boat *Bali Ha'i* because of my love for the musical *South Pacific,* and because Mom2's stepfather was Oscar Hammerstein II, who wrote the lyrics and book for the musical.

Dad taught me how to sail that boat all around Cold Spring Harbor. It was glorious. I was only allowed to sail when he was with me (a smart idea), and I awaited each lesson eagerly. We kept it moored at the Lloyds Neck Beach Club, and sometimes I would swim out to it, climb on board, and pretend to be sailing in the South Pacific. I didn't abandon the old oak dory, which remained my private vehicle for adventure. I still rowed and pushed it through the maze of channels and islets. On a few occasions, Jane joined me in these grand explorations.

I had a plantar wart on the ball of my right foot that made bicycling and even walking painful. Dad acted as if I'd created the wart on purpose, but it was keeping me from life. So, one night with a bottle of "medicine" that "froze" the wart, I began to dig the thing out. It took hours, but finally I'd dug and tweezed every last black root out of a larger-than-expected hole. I was proud that I'd withstood the pain and removed the damn wart, and when Dad came back from the city, several days later, I showed him the almost healed hole. He told me warts were all in the mind, and could be thought away, ignoring the fact I'd tried "thinking" it away without results before resorting to minor but bloody surgery.

Dad usually had strange reactions to colds, cuts, and minor ailments, and often acted as if we had these maladies because we were not doing things properly, as if they were caused by some sort of sin in our soul. It must have been due to the whisperings of Christian Scientist influences in his youth. I have tried to go beyond the whisperings and find some fabric in the unspoken past, but I have never been able to penetrate the Fonda family silence about that time in their lives.

That summer Jane visited a friend who lived on Lake Erie. She only spent a few days away, but it seemed like forever to me. When she returned, Dad took me out to the tip of Long Island for a fishing weekend, more big time with the big boys. As we left the shack, Jane was lying on the couch in the front room. She'd been diving in Lake Erie and had hit her head on the bottom, and she said her back hurt and it was difficult to move, even difficult to lie down. Dad treated her with his standard contempt, pointed out that she shouldn't have been diving into the lake, shook his head, and hauled me off on another long, silent drive.

But we were going fishing for tuna and the mood began to change as we neared Montauk that evening. The next morning, we were up before the sun and on our way to the fishing grounds. I often wondered why people called these places—the ocean, with no earth in sight—fishing "grounds." We were skunked the first day, but up at dawn again on the second, listening to the skipper promise us better luck. We trolled around for hours. The men talked fishing while I kept quiet, which was hard for me to do because I ached to jabber away. Suddenly we were smack in the middle of a school of tuna, and both Dad and I had tuna on our lines in the churning water off the stern on the boat. The captain yelled down to Dad to let his line out quickly, and then pull hard with the rod. Dad did that, and the front half of a nice-sized tuna came flying out of the water, the hook still in its mouth. More churning water off the stern, and the captain told me to do the same as Dad. I released the brake on my reel, the line peeled off, and I remembered the kite in the north forty. The skipper told me to let it run, whatever "it" was, and when the line stopped stripping off the reel, he told me to give it a big yank. Dad helped, and suddenly a huge fish jumped clear of the water, shaking its head violently back and forth.

At first, Dad thought we had a marlin and was very excited, but the skipper said it was a mako shark, a fish considered a game fish because of its water-breaking fighting abilities. I didn't care what it was. The thing outweighed me by over a hundred pounds and I was going to bring it in. Hot damn! It was the longest forty-five minutes of my life, but finally the fish, fighting like mad, was gaffed and hauled up the side. I was in heaven and then some. The wire leader was bent and zigzagged in the serrated mouth of the shark, and the skipper and his mate talked about how lucky it was that they had changed my leader from normal tuna rigging to piano wire. I simply stood at the side of the boat staring at this monster fish that had just brought me through a major rite of passage, a big, fighting, deep-sea fish successfully boated by me, and boated by me in front of Dad.

When we arrived back at the docks, people gathered to look at our prize. As the belly of the shark was opened, we could see the fairly large tuna that had become its unwitting bait, and the back half of the tuna that Dad had hooked up. God, there were a lot of teeth in that shark's head. The skipper hacked out one for me as sort of a talisman of the event. Dad had filmed most of the fighting with his 16mm movie camera, proof of my large step into his world.

When we got back to the shack, Jane was gone. Susan had taken her to the hospital, and we learned Jane hadn't felt well because she'd broken her back. Even the great shark event couldn't shake my disgust for Dad's earlier indifference to my sister's suffering. I wanted to go back and get another fang from that toothy monster to give to Jane. I felt terrible for her, and it took a lot of explaining from Mom2 that her broken back was going to mend just fine, and she would be able to dance and do all the things she could do before.

Jane was fourteen and had been planning on her first big dance with real boys, not her brother, and she was devastated that she might not get to go. She'd been fitted with a cast from her crotch to her neck, and still wore it when she left the hospital. Mom2 was resourceful, though, and she went to a maternity store and found a pretty dress that could easily fit over the cast, and Jane went to the dance looking great. She was the talk of the party, and the memory of this small triumph still gives me pleasure. Dad did everything he could to make life easier for her, after his silly behavior when she was moaning on the couch. He'd moan, too, if his back had been broken. I saw what his knees and toes had done to his "dance" in Vermont, a few years earlier.

As the summer drifted by, I went fishing with Dad three more times. Dad bought a fiberglass skiff, a fairly new thing in 1952, and a five-and-a-half horsepower Evinrude outboard engine, and we'd look for striped bass right off Lloyds Neck. Dad and I would get up at three-thirty or four in the morning, depending on the tides, and motor around the land's end to the rocky shores. I had no problem, that summer, with putting bloodworms on our lures. The last morning we fished together, I caught two ten-pound-plus stripers. Dad took a picture of me holding both fish in front of the shack, and it was all I could do to hang on to them. He had the picture framed and hung on the wall of his bathroom, beside those of his other treasured moments, right next to photos of himself, Duke Wayne, and John Ford holding on to their marlin, and many other pictures that were windows to his past. The picture of me and the stripers is lost.

. . .

We had our 1950 Ford Woody, while we stayed at that shack for the summer of 1952, and Mom2 had learned to drive. She took us to many movies, letting us out of the car at the ticket counter and telling us to save a seat for her while she parked. She didn't know how to parallel park and didn't want us to know, she recently told me, so she would drive around looking for a place she could pull into without backing up. I wondered why I would see her driving past the entrance to the movie house several times with a very concentrated look on her face.

Dad had a black 1952 Mercury that he used to commute to the theater. We had no television or radio in the shack, so sometimes I would climb into the Merc and listen to whatever music I could find. Jane joined me a few times. But the last time I lay on those smooth red leather seats, listening to big-band music pumping out of New York, I forgot to turn the radio off. I wandered into the house for a soda and got sidetracked. Bad boy, Peter. No power to the engine of the Mercury. Even though we had jumper cables, I was banished from the cars, sent back to *Bali Ha'i* and to the oak dory and my imagination, my search for a place in life, which was fine by me.

And back to Fay, a new grade and Judy. This time, I was one of the "old" boys, and my heart went out to the clump of new boys, teary-eyed and bewildered, gathered at the school entrance. But I was in seventh grade and had the geography of the place down—because the location of my new dorm made reaching Judy's quarters awkward, we found a new place to hide together, under the Field House. We'd huddle together in the low light, hugging and kissing. It wasn't that I was in love with Judy or she with me, but we could trust one another. We explored the beginnings of boy-girl relationships without the pressure to "see how far we could go." Nothing *had* to be delivered. Judy was right there at the right time with the right response.

. . .

Dad was on the road with *The Caine Mutiny Court Martial,* so I spent Thanksgiving with the family of a schoolmate. Everyone talked to each other and encouraged explanation and description. Stories were shared, and even the youngest child had his full say, without adults losing interest in youthful wordings. The dinner was revolutionary for me, an eye-opener.

Jane and I joined Mom2 and Dad in Detroit for Christmas in 1952, where he was traveling with *The Caine Mutiny.* Our Christmas tree that year was a very small tree that sat on top of a table in the suite. There was snow on Christmas morning, and we were like a family, though Dad was still strict and aloof. On that Christmas Eve, Jane was initiated into the snow-making magic. One evening, on our way to dinner, he made Mom2 go back upstairs and put on lipstick. I thought she looked perfect, but maybe he felt she looked too young. Their age difference was embarrassing to him, and he was always aware of the young men who followed us when we were out in public. He'd always say something withering like, "Christ! They probably think you're one of my daughters." They were hurtful things to say to anyone, and Mom2 always gave it her very best; Dad also neglected to consider the young men might have been following Jane.

It was a very strange holiday, and it was over quickly, with Jane and me on our way back to boarding school within a few days. But at least it was *our* Christmas, our first as a "family" for too many years. When we were sent back to purgatory, I felt confident that the rest of our lives would be in harmony.

. . .

Only sixth-formers at Fay, boys about to graduate, had private rooms, and the rest of us slept in alcoves, small areas with curtains for doors and walls that did not go all the way to the ceiling. If our grades were in good standing we were allowed to study in this semi-privacy, and I often took advantage of this opportunity.

One day in the spring of 1953, I went to my alcove to read and to see if I had any mail, which was distributed and left on our beds each day. I had only one letter, but I knew how to "go through my mail" with only one letter, and one was better than none. My mail usually came from Mom2, but this envelope was a bit different. The handwriting looked familiar, not like Mom2's, but definitely like a mother's. It looked, in fact, very much like my mother's, *exactly* like my mother's. Confused and agitated, I tore the envelope open and looked closely at the letter. It started out in exactly the same way my mother had once written me, and I skipped, horrified, to the end at once. And, oh my god, it was from my mother. I'd known that something wasn't right about her death, and here was the proof—somewhere in the world, my real mother was alive and had written me a letter. She'd signed it just as she always had—"Love and hugs, Mummie"—with a little smiling face.

I'd been lied to again. I went completely nuts. I cried in a way that was only partly human, and impossible to describe. Several people had come running and were trying to calm me. I remained hysterical, refusing any offer of help, every explanation. How could anybody explain this horror? *No no no no no no no no no!* They held me down, and bit by bit I began to understand their words. They were telling me that it wasn't a letter from my mother, it wasn't even a letter to me. It was for Peter Teuscher, who had the alcove next to mine. It was all an accident, a total accident.

But deep inside me, something had snapped and fallen into chaos. After that, the taunting about my mother stopped. The next time I was with Judy Rankin, all I wanted to do was hold her tightly. Neither of us ever said a thing about the letter or my mother, but she knew I was in distress. She didn't go away, and she didn't leave me. We were two children holding on to each other, in the dirt, under a building.

. . .

When school let out that spring we returned to Lloyds Neck for our third summer with Mom2 and Dad, a rare continuum, though we rented a different house. This summer I had more freedom, and I made it my duty to patrol the entire area on bikes with Victor Miller, a friend from my dory days the summer before. We were very proprietary, and considered the *Bali Ha'i* our yacht. That summer, also, Judy Rankin visited friends nearby for a few days, and everyone watched us, all the time, a lesson in the relative privacy of school.

Dad continued to guide me through the correct procedures of sailing, and by the end of the summer of 1953, we handled the boat perfectly, the only way Dad could do it, and not a bad way to handle life. Jibing, tacking, coming about, center board up and down. We sanded the entire hull, repainted it, and put a fresh coat or three of varnish on the inside, the mast, and the boom. Of all the catboats I've seen, I've always thought the *Bali Ha'i* was the prettiest. We also fooled around in the fiberglass skiff with its five-and-a-half horse-power Evinrude, speeding it up on a plane in a snap. Shit, we had our own navy, power and sail. The skiff and the cat were moored at the beach club, and I remember endless days of boat bumming.

On one beautifully boring day, I took the *Bali Ha'i* out for a sail. I headed north, out of Cold Spring Harbor. As I neared the Sound, the wind shifted, blowing in from the south. I instantly realized that I was in deep shit. If I headed out toward the Sound, I might end up in Connecticut, if I was still floating. I came about as fast as I could and began tacking back in the direction of the Beach Club, which was several miles south, tacking back and forth against the wind *and* current.

After an hour I had only made a half-mile headway, and I was definitely getting worried. But I didn't want to panic, and I kept trying. As I tacked near the causeway that led to Lloyds Neck, Dad happened to drive by and understood my problem immediately. He drove back to the club, got the skiff, and came out to tow me back. I was certain I would be flogged or at the least be dragged back to the house on a rope tied to the rear bumper. But he said nothing, other than to ask if I was all right. The lesson was learned and needed no punctuation.

When the summer ended, the family—it actually felt like a family again by then—went back to the city. No more apartment, no more rentals. We'd bought a house with a feeling of permanence, a five-story brownstone at 151 East Seventy-fourth Street. I had my own room, my own space in my father's house, for the first time in years.

Much of the feeling of permanence, and of family, was due to the fact that my father and Mom2 adopted a little newborn girl named Amy that fall. When I was in New York on vacation I'd try to keep Amy quiet while my father napped before performances of *The Caine Mutiny*. She thought I was very funny, so I thought she was wonderful.

That Christmas I was initiated into the secret society of snow-on-the-tree makers. One large pail, a box of Ivory soap flakes, an egg beater, water, and plenty of time and energy. I've tried other soaps, but they don't work. The trick was in the ingredients' proportions, but in the end two pailfuls were plenty for the tree. Dad and I whipped the soap until it stood like cake frosting, then draped it on the branches with our hands. The foam hardens and stays on the boughs and shrinks just a little, so it appears that it has snowed on the tree the day before. I watched Dad very carefully, did exactly as he did, and when we were finished, the tree looked as if it *had* been snowed on. It was great maggage.

I went back to Fay School on a private high of self-esteem and security. We lived together again, and with my sailing escapade I had shown courage to myself—most importantly—and to my Dad. Tough to beat that.

This, my last year at Fay, was different. I was still a good student—I graduated near the top of my class—but the summer's courage was a new trick in my bag, and it stayed there. My times with Judy were different, too, and we hit a solid level of eroticism at Saturday night movies in the back of the gym. Everyone else watched the movie. At least I think they did, though I'm fairly sure my best friend, Jimmy Gibson, sworn to secrecy, was checking us out.

In an all-boy boarding school, some of the boys naturally had to play the female roles in plays, and when we performed *The Pirates of Penzance* I played one of the fair maidens, much to my chagrin. After the humiliation of the cast photograph—which I realized would last forever in the school's archive—I decided I would never play in the female chorus of *anything* again. Judy lent irony to my vicious nickname, "Fairy Fonda," but enough was enough.

While in New York for Christmas, I'd seen the Broadway production of *Stalag 17*, a comedy about a German POW camp, which I thought was very funny. Immediately after I returned to Fay, I sat down and wrote a play about life in a boys' boarding school, and called it *Stalag 17 and a ½*. As I'd written eight parts but only had five friends, I ended up exercising the prerogative of the playwright and playing all three extra roles. The plot centered on bitching about the guards and smuggling chewing gum, comic books, and explosives to the prisoners. The play was only thirty-three minutes long, but those thirty-three minutes were jam-packed with sight gags. The boys loved it, and finally, at thirteen, I was a success with my peers.

When the next school play was mounted—Shakespeare's *Twelfth Night*—I played Sir Andrew Aguecheek. And for the season finale, we performed Gilbert and Sullivan's *The Mikado*. I took the role of the Lord High Executioner, and succeeded in demolishing my frilly little girl image.

. . .

I had one strange encounter regarding grades and my study habits. After lunch, in the spring of my last year, I was summoned to the headmaster's office. He asked me if my ears were burning, as he had been talking about me. He then asked how I'd done on my math exam. I said I hadn't seen the test results so I didn't know. He asked me how I thought I had done, if I expected I'd done well. I never expected to have done well on anything, so I was surprised by the question and began to wonder what was going on.

Apparently, I'd answered a question about graphs that I could not have answered given what I had been taught. The implication was that I had somehow cheated on the test, and as no one else in the class could have answered the question, either, I couldn't have taken the answer from someone else's paper. The math teacher and headmaster assumed that I had seen the test in advance. I was outraged. The test had been an achievement test, so my plan had been to concentrate on the questions. When I came to the graph question, I applied the logic of what I did know about graphs—we'd covered them in an introductory way—and plotted the curves as well as I could, too well for the school's mind-set.

I'd never done anything really bad at the school. I refused to answer roll call while my name was pronounced "Fonder" and sat at the right-handed desk chairs sideways to help my left-handedness. The masters all asked me to sit facing the front, and I always replied that I would as soon as I had finished taking down whatever notes had to be written. The teachers were annoyed, but in both instances I had a point. And I had not cheated on the test, though I'm sure the headmaster and math teacher believed I *had* cheated and couldn't figure out how. When I left Fay, my name was Peter Fonda, and I had honors. No one came to my graduation. And though I knew I'd caused a flutter in her bloom, I kissed Judy for the last time, got on a bus, and returned to the city alone. Like *Paddle to the Sea*, I was on the move.

chapter *Four*

*O*ur sense of continuity was strengthened in the summer of 1954, when Jane and I joined Amy, Mom2, and Dad at Ocean House in Santa Monica again. During our second stay—about four weeks, before we went on to Hawaii—we were the only guests; perhaps the hotel was going out of business. It was a comedy of the absurd: a full kitchen staff, the dining room open every night, the same grand parties with great big-band music for the small family Fonda. Though we were three years older, Jane and I still danced our free-form style a few times. In the lobby it was as if everything were normal, with a coterie of receptionists and bellhops, though I only made one phone call from the lobby pay phone that last stay. I phoned my friend Jimmy Gibson, a fellow Fay School graduate, back in Maine. All was fine on the Eastern Front.

Jane and I had the same rooms as in 1951, and I think Dad and Mom2 took a large, balconied corner suite, with a master bedroom and a twin bedroom for Amy. The Sand and Sea Club was still there, thriving. Ward Bond came by in his 1954 Corvette. He'd visited Tigertail years before in his new Studebaker, the first car to blow my mind; the Corvette was the second. Cars generally seemed more interesting in California than they had in Connecticut. The club's swimming instructor had an MG TC and took me for rides up and down the Pacific Coast Highway. One day we drove to the Barton School for Boys. He was as amazed as Aunt Harriet had been. "Your parents sent you here?"

I had a job at the club as a beach boy, which meant that I helped people with their canvas chairs and umbrellas. The hardest part of my job that year was not the planting of the umbrella—difficult in the best of times because of my slight physique—but the incredibly hot sand on my tenderfoot, eastern, socks-and-shoes feet. I'd ask patrons where they would prefer to sit, and after they'd point to a spot I'd take several steps back and launch myself in the direction of the beach as fast as I could, carrying only the umbrella. Ten feet from my target I'd leap into the air and stake the sand as if it were Dracula's heart. Then I'd return for the chairs and run them out to the umbrella.

For my absolutely hysterical pole-planting, I received gracious tips. I was truly thankful, but usually in a hurry to reach the wading pool, where people could rinse their feet on their way to the food counter, with my burnt soles. I continued to augment my cash flow by retrieving the coins that fell through the slats in the food and beverage area at the Sand and Sea Club.

My Sand and Sea Club work was a real job. I had to get a Social Security card—an SS card, as I prefer to call it—and fill out my first set of dickhead government papers. Thankfully, Mom2 was with me—we went by taxi—and calmed me down when I raved about giving the feds *anything*. I was making less than minimum wage, plus tips, and I had to give the government money. At fourteen, the injustice of the situation seemed incredible. Today, knowing that SS will be broke and unable to pay me back when I am eligible, I think I should sue the feds for loss of income.

As the time got closer to the trip to Hawaii, I could hardly stand the anticipation. I got my paycheck from the club and Mom2 took me to a music store, where I bought a beautiful harmonica with everything I'd earned, all of $19.75. Dad told me I was wasteful, spending all my money on that one harmonica. I didn't care. It was what I had been working for, so it made perfect sense to me. I don't think Dad knew I could play the instrument, but I'd learned "Old Black Joe" at Tigertail.

When we said our good-byes to Ocean House, we headed for San Francisco, where we'd catch the Matson Lines' S.S. *Lurine* for Hawaii. Leland Hayward was in San Francisco opening the musical *Peter Pan,* and Brooke, Bridget, and Bill were there with him. We all saw the show, starring Mary Martin, and when I got backstage to pay my respects, I asked Mary, whom I'd met while she was starring in *South Pacific*, if she would sing "Bali Ha'i." Everyone else was embarrassed by my request, but Mary sang the song for me. I was almost in tears and told her that I was on my way to Bali Ha'i. Everybody laughed, but Mary said she understood me perfectly.

Bill and I rooted around town, got lost in Chinatown, and had a wonderful time. I remember seeing him way down on the dock with his father and sisters, waving good-bye to us. A Hawaiian band was playing and everyone was throwing paper streamers as we pulled away.

Jane and I stayed up very late drinking champagne with all the adults, who told us that the ship was beyond the long arm of the law, and we could be served. Dad never liked parties, and he and Mom2 had Amy, so they stayed in their suite.

On that magical morning when we were told we might first see the islands, I went to the bow of the ship and watched for land. There were a few clouds ahead, and we were told that the islands were in the clouds. When I saw the top of an island poking through, my heart nearly leapt from my chest and tears rolled down my cheeks. Was this *my* Bali Ha'i? The clouds lifted and "my special island" rose from the blue and green. I knew that it was the island of Oahu, but it was special to me in a very private way, not so much a place but a symbol. Ever since Mom2 had come into our lives things happened in special ways. We had smiling and laughter, dancing and jokes. There was an us, and there was the possibility of life.

We arrived at the dock just in front of the Aloha Tower and were surrounded by bands and dancers and pretty women giving flowers to everyone. The fragrance of the whole place was unbelievable. And, then, there was Waikiki Beach, Diamond Head, surfers, outrigger canoes, and only three hotels. The whole summer was every wish come true. Dad was able to stay with us long enough to learn to surf and enjoy the whole thing that was Waikiki in 1954, before he left for Midway to begin filming John Ford's version of *Mister Roberts*.

I made a little money helping Hawaiian women string frangipani and other beautiful flowers into leis, the garlands of flowers that men and women gave to each other on any occasion. At night in the cottage, I fell asleep to the sound of the surf and the music of Hawaiian steel guitars, and the swarm of smells that never let me forget we were all growing. Nothing in life stood still on this island. The experi-

ence was so fantastic, I forgot to worry about my personal little nightmare, and when I woke in the morning frightened by the dream, the
sounds and smells took me out of the past, putting me right in the
middle of life.

The big true Hawaiian Beach Boys (we referred to them in caps)
were not to be messed with. They had a reputation as being tough
and mean (and, boy, they sure as shit could be), but they watched
out over me, and taught me, a skinny haole, what I needed to know
to survive in the surf (plus a little of what I'd need to survive on the
street). I'd eat three or four peanut-butter-banana-and-honey sandwiches for lunch, and Blah James or Panama would make me lie on
the beach for half an hour or so. No wanna get da cramps, brah. After
waiting for an appropriate amount of time, they would pull me out to
the bigger surf by placing one of their feet on the front of my board
while they paddled their own, switching off from time to time to
spread the task, looking back at me and laughing. Hey, Toothpick,
you shaka? No problem, Toothpick, we take care of you. I was brown
as a coconut with a shock of blond hair; I probably looked as much
like a toothpick as I did a boy.

They taught me how to play the ukulele, and no one told me I was
holding it wrong. Four strings upside down and backward weren't
too much to handle. They taught me songs to sing with my clear high
voice. They liked the high notes especially. And at night, when they
left the beach to screw around with honky sailors downtown, I joined
new friends around a fire on the beach in front of our bungalow and
played the uke, and we would all sing. When my fingers were hurting
too much, I would pull out the harmonica and continue playing. I got
every penny's worth out of that harmonica.

I had a real girlfriend, and we sat on the beach for hours at night
necking, listening to the music floating out from the clubs on the Ala
Moana, letting the smells of life cover us. She was sweet and good to
me. When she held my head to her breast, I could hear her heart, like
the life I felt beating from the island. I was very sad when she and her
cute younger sister had to go, and went to the airport with Dad the
day they left; he was meeting the inbound Ward Bond, and I was
saying my good-byes. Wardo asked me why I was long in the face,
and I told him about my girlfriend and her sister. He joked with me
in a compassionate way and snuck a shot of whiskey to me. Wardo
said that a man with a sad heart needed a shot of great whiskey. Years

earlier, at our breakfast table on Tigertail, Wardo would take a glass of freshly squeezed orange juice, down it, and let out a satisfied *"Aaaahh!"*

The ritual had thrilled me at the time, and it still did. I grabbed the whiskey and did the same thing, but my "satisfied" *Aaaaaahh!* was more like the scream of someone whose throat is being cauterized.

When I got back to the hotel I decided to have a few more shots to help my sorrow. I don't remember the sorrow, so *that* part must have worked, but it sure messed up my paddle-tennis game. Jane kept asking me why I was laughing so hard. I had no valid explanation. I went right to sleep that night, though the next day I woke frightened by my dream. It was several days before the magic of the island took the fear of the morning away.

The year before, the tough playwright at Fay, I'd started smoking cigarettes. I'd felt that they made me look older, though I looked like a very stupid nine-year-old. That summer in *paradisio,* I looked like a ten-year-old with a drinking and smoking habit. What fools we children can be in our illogical pursuit of age.

I slept on the beach several nights, but one night was truly rare. It was moonless yet so clear, the stars gave enough light to see the details of the shore, the buildings, and the trees. Every time I think about this night, I wish Jane had been beside me, perhaps as a witness, certainly as the person closest to me. The surf and the sound and smells of the island faded slowly, as if someone had turned down the volume. At first I thought I was falling asleep, but I wasn't afraid of the dream, and lay there wondering if I was sleeping with my eyes open. I heard a door close somewhere behind me, and then a strange sound. A poi dog, walking along the beach, came up to me, wagging its tail and sniffing my body. I reached out and touched the dog. It moved away at first, but then came back and allowed me to wipe its eyes. It licked my hand and walked off down the beach toward the Ala Moana. I thought this was the strangest dream, as it seemed so real.

The sounds of lizards chirping and the wind in the palms were pure and clean. A fiddler crab ran over my foot and made me sit up quickly. I wasn't asleep at all. I could hear the noise of people, but it was muted, while all the sounds of the creatures and the water were sharp and clear. I looked back at "civilization," a word I had not really understood earlier in the life, and fully comprehended it at that moment as something different than what I had been taught.

The things around me were all in motion. The trees, the sand, the plumeria bushes, the whole island, were in motion, growing closer to me, picking me up and moving me along next to the ocean, clumps of phosphorescent plankton, curling waves glowing like long strands of muted, green light. I felt as if I were lying on a patch of sand in the sky, and I could see the land everywhere, even under the oceans, moving. I was a part of the living planet for the first time, and I kept as still as I could, trying not to disturb the moment. I could hear the planet breathing and found myself breathing in the same rhythm, very slowly, very evenly. I was overjoyed, and wept.

That night made my entire life change. The poi dog came back up the beach, walking right up to me, licking my face, and licking the salt from my tears, then walking on. I heard a motorcycle accelerate up the Ala Moana, out toward Diamond Head. The softness of the breathing life all around me and the sweet smells of the flowers swirled in my head, and I fell fast asleep. When I awoke with the dawn, I had no fear. The dreaded dream never came that night. I could see the tracks of the dog, both coming and going, and for a moment I did not want to go back inside our cottage. I wanted, instead, to walk out into the ocean and not come back.

I learned, that summer, that all that had been described to me as civilization, or civilized, was not. Nothing that had been created by man really qualified. The things not even considered in the running— trees and bushes and flowers—were the only civilization. Laughing lizards and fiddler crabs versus pavement and silverware.

. . .

Some things that mankind had dreamed up were at least fun. Jane, who was sixteen, had boyfriends who could drive, and we therefore had more freedom than Mom2, with whom our father was astoundingly restrictive. One hot August afternoon, Jane and I and several young men went driving up toward the Pali, the spine of Oahu that divided the east and north side of the island from the west. There was a special place on the west side that had a long ditch plunging down a ravine, with clear water pools fed from rain-forest waterfalls nearby. The idea was to wait for one of the constantly passing rain squalls to muddy up the ditch, grab one of the abundant taro leaves, so large they looked like elephant ears, and cut loose down the ditch, riding the leaf like a shovel. Ten minutes up the hill and a dazzling twenty-second plunge down the muddy ditch; much laughing and much mud.

Sometimes we'd lose control and pop right out of the ditch, tumbling over the spongy but bruising slope. I knew that the older boys would have rather not taken me along, but Jane insisted, and I had a blast. By the end of the afternoon we were all mud-packed, so we headed to the pools to wash off before returning the car to Honest John's Rentals.

Halfway to old Honest's, we belatedly realized that the inside of the Chevy convertible was full of mud. This would never do. We found a hose that appeared to be somewhat public, and hastily rinsed the hell out of the car. We drove around until the Chevy had dried a little, then beat the overcharge for the rental by minutes. I think Old Honest knew exactly what had been going on, as we were not the first young people to go to the mud slide in one of his cars. He never said a word.

Our summer ended much too quickly for me. Even today I can feel each moment, as if it were happening right now: the sand between my toes, the warm Pacific waters, the fragrance of every plant and tree, that extraordinary night on the beach.

. . .

I was on my way to a new school that fall, another step on the Ivy League road, a prep school named Westminster, in Simsbury, Connecticut, close by the Farmington River. This time, in preparing for the unknown, I had a picture of a real girlfriend, who had let me caress her breasts, and even one of her cute sister, inscribed to me. I never told my schoolmates that they were sisters, so I had *two* girlfriends, in their minds. I also had an ally in Mom2. She always made the right clothes choices and encouraged me to look "cool." Before, I had only thought of getting by, and I knew nothing about cool. Mom2 knew most of the great jazz musicians and "hip" people and was able to draw a perfect line between "hip" and "prep." Dressing as if I knew what I was doing helped me at Westminster.

I can't say that my entire prep school experience was terrible. Not terrific, either, but I had some fun. I had some good teachers, but my education was only partly made up of French, Spanish, biology, chemistry, English, Latin, math, mechanical drawing, geology, and lit. Although I took all those courses and kept good grades, I could have done a lot better had I not been so lazy. I learned that I desperately wanted to play music and sing, that the other boys were jealous of me, and that even the faculty were resentful of what they perceived as a privileged and enviable heritage. Little did *they* know.

They had major rules at Westminster, and major penalties. One evening, I was taken to a special room by the sixth-formers, and I was grilled about smoking on campus. I denied that I'd lit up, and the Storm Troopers produced a pack of cigarettes that they had found in my overcoat. I had never smoked on campus or done anything against the rules at Westminster, precisely because I preferred to avoid the school's unofficial enforcers, the sixth-form boys.

Never mind the idea that midget brownshirts had rifled through my coat. I was paddled twenty times for smoking on campus and had to carry a log around for a week because I'd had the cigs in my pocket. I accepted the fact that I should not have had the cigarettes on the campus and never again made that mistake, but the twenty whacks were given in a way that was more than punishment. Westminster had substituted real authority for abstract authority, and delegated its dirty work, and I was the brunt of the abstract, fanned by the heat of a "You-think-you're-somebody-special-don't-you?" sentiment. I understood the difference between abstract and real authority and had—long before Westminster—watched the practice of punishing "undeserved" privilege with disgust. At fourteen, I'd begun to realize what "Henry Fonda's son" meant in the small social environment of a private boarding school. Most of the other boys were born to prominent families in business or government, but none of the boys stemmed from an identity so great as to be monumental. Each boy came from a small community where his family held an exalted position, but none of them came from the entire country, where the high position had no social or monetary meaning, where the reverence, the daydream of Everyman, covered the economic graph. This doesn't mean that Dad did anything wrong, or held the sword of jealousy to my neck. He was a working man who had the distinction of doing the best job that could be done, and doing it so well, in such a romantic medium, that much of society paid homage. But I suffered for his luck. I was never upset with Dad for being Henry Fonda. I was upset with him for not being Dad.

. . .

We headed for Rome in the summer of 1955, where Dad was to film *War and Peace*. Dad, Mom2, Amy, Jane, and I flew overseas on a Boeing Stratocruiser, on the same flight as Marlon Brando and Dean Martin, who were on their way to Europe to make *The Young Lions*. Brando—Bud—was almost like family; his mother, Dorothy, had been the first person to suggest acting to my father, decades earlier in Omaha, Nebraska. Jane and I had seen *Viva Zapata!* the summer before, when Mom2 had taken us and had difficulty convincing the ticket seller that she was old enough to be our stepmother. She was only twenty-six and looked much younger. Once we made it into the theater, the beautiful Brando on the screen pointed to a new set of possibilities in life, a different set of rules, morals, and images.

I went down to the Stratocruiser lounge area and listened to Brando tell stories while Martin gave me beers. It was a long flight, and after many beers, I fell asleep dreaming about ancient Rome and Mexican rebels. In those days, I wore a tie and jacket whenever I traveled. But even in my tie and jacket, sneaking cigarettes and beers, I felt like a newly whelped pup around Brando.

In Rome, we stayed at an enormous villa just off Via Appia Antica. The Villa Uscida had its own vegetable and fruit farm and a natural mineral water pool (director Franco Zeffirelli now owns the place, minus the farm). The production company provided a car and driver for the family, Mario and his Fiat Familiari 1100. I was fifteen and into anything that had an engine and wheels. Dad also rented a Fiat 600, but Mom2, with her inadequate driving experience and Amy to take care of, was still like a prisoner. We were given complimentary memberships to a club for American diplomats, military attachés, and other employees of foreign embassies, and this was where we met most of that summer's friends, including one of Jane's boyfriends, Romano Gigioli. What a name! He played water polo. I kept my eye on *him*.

When Mom2 could find a sitter for Amy, she'd take us to Saint Peter's and the Sistine Chapel at the Vatican. We climbed the stairs to the top of the basilica and stepped out onto a small balcony overlooking the grand design. It was truly magnificent. All I could say was,

Man oh Manischewitz, part of a little jingle for a kosher wine in New York, and one of the tunes running through my head that summer. I didn't mean to make a joke—didn't know what a joke it was—but I almost put Mom2 to her knees with laughter.

Most of the time we stayed near the villa, though this was a delight, not a hardship. I'd liked my Latin teacher at Westminster, and he'd given me a list of places to check out. I'd had four years of Latin, so I was familiar with Cicero and Catullus and most Roman history, and I was fired up to discover the Appian Way, running north to Rome and south to Naples only a few yards from the villa. When things were boring or tense at the villa, I took long walks on that road, following deep ruts cut by wheels centuries earlier; ogling crumbling tombs and tall pines that had been growing before the time of Caesar. The pines still dropped cones to the ground, and the cones still produced pine nuts for any number of fine dishes. Closer to the walls of the city there were small trattorias where one could buy a beer or some wine and cigarettes with brand names like Cowboy and Western Riders. And when I made it inside the city I loved crawling around the Forum and the Colosseum. When I stood where Cicero and Catullus had debated, I heard their words in my head. The years of Latin had paid off.

I discovered that the Villa Uscida had its own wine cellar, catacombs filled with old, dusty bottles. Narrow steps carved in the side of the villa's artesian well spiraled down into the darkness, with passages leading to chambers of wine opening off the steps. There was no electricity, and I used to count the seconds it took before a dropped pebble hit the water at the bottom. Not having fear of heights or falling, but respecting the danger, I spent hours exploring my stash, slowing crawling down the steps, leaving candles and matches in each room. I didn't tell Dad of my discovery; he didn't know the wine existed, and if he found out he'd have put down a perfectly reasonable rule forbidding any further forays.

The embassy kids threw small parties several times that summer, and I wallowed in them. I knew how to kiss very well, and won impromptu contests where girls would line up to be kissed and give ratings. And I always had Cowboy cigarettes and, thanks to the ancient well, a bottle of wine. They could have been two- or three-thousand-dollar bottles. I had no way of knowing, but they came in handy.

One morning, while I sat at the table eating my breakfast—an Italian breakfast of coffee and milk and hard bread with marmalade—Mom2, obviously upset, with a tear-swollen face, came down to the table, sat next to me, and told me she was leaving Dad. I was devastated and burst into tears, begging her not to leave us. I could not believe this was happening. She cried along with me and tried to explain. As we were talking, Dad walked through the house on his way to the pool and gave me the most withering look ever, as if I were a traitor.

Mom2 went up to their room to pack. I sat at the table, heartbroken and stunned, trying to put the world back into a semblance of reality. Although I understood the words she had used and the reasons she gave, I could not make my brain accept the information. I wasn't sobbing, but I couldn't stop the tears, and sat there for many minutes, frozen with helplessness. Jane, I thought. Oh my god, Jane. She didn't know. I didn't want to be the bearer of this terrible news, but someone had to tell her. I couldn't let her walk out into the main room and step unprepared on this emotional land mine.

I went to Jane's room, knocked softly, and went in. She was just waking, stretching and yawning, with a look of pure delight on her beautiful face. I didn't know how to start and just sat there on her bed, rocked to my core, speechless as Jane began to tell me that she'd had her first sexual experience the night before. Her language was poetic and her face rapt, as if in a trance. She spoke of how two bodies holding each other grew sweaty with the passion, of how their stomachs made a funny sound when they pulled away. She put her hands together, pressing her palms tightly, then pulling them apart quickly, making a sucking noise.

I was astounded. The family had just gone thermonuclear at the breakfast table, and she was doing this thing with her hands.

"Jane, uh, oh fuck, Jane, Mom's leaving Dad!"

"Oh, Peter, I knew that long ago. This summer was their swan song."

I had heard that phrase before. It hadn't made sense to me before, and certainly didn't that morning. I'd been around swans. They were mean fuckers, and certainly never sang while they chased me and Buz.

I ran to my room and locked myself in, closed the big shutters outside my window, and tried to shut out all that had just happened.

I grabbed a bottle of the musty red wine from the tombs that I had hidden in my closet, filled my water glass, and downed the entire thing, then poured a second glass, drank it, and crawled back into bed. I didn't give a shit about many things for a long time. I heard Mom2's feet crunching back and forth in the driveway as she loaded her bags and Amy into the car, then listened to the car tires crunching down the drive, crunching away the family. I drank another glass of wine and hid my head under my pillow.

In less than three hours all my dreams were shattered. My life had disintegrated, and the "happy" family had been hollowed out by a mean old man. I didn't forgive him for a long time. I simply stopped thinking about Susan and, as much as I could, about him. Jane, seventeen, and with a better grip on life, was surprised by my devastation. She must have assumed that I also knew that the bomb would soon drop.

I don't have a clear memory of the next few days. Perhaps it was the wine. I did wake up later on that heart-of-darkness day and puke my guts out, and that was definitely the wine. Dad left for a location in the north and Jane and I stayed at the marble mausoleum alone, while I made many trips to the well. I know I visited the set on location once, but I'm not sure where. I completely ignored the memory of that day and the sadness. It was the only way to survive. But the fallout from my own little Hiroshima hung around for a long time.

The next clear memory I have is of a small party at the villa. Five or six friends of Jane's came for an evening visit. I was allowed to join them, because I was the one who could get the wine. They conversed about many things, finally coming to rest on "family finesse"— whatever that meant. The words "Mother's suicide" fell like deadly little bombs from Jane's mouth. Here came *my* Nagasaki. She'd thought that I knew, but this was the first time *anything* had been said about the real death of Mother. Five years of believing in a heart attack were vaporized in twenty seconds of emotional nuking. I met Jane's appalled, comprehending eyes and ran back to my room and more wine.

After those two deadly moments of truth, the rest of the summer washed by. I knew how to sublimate. Instead of the loving girl I wanted and needed, I was seduced by the wife of a military attaché. It wasn't tender, it was sex, a lesson learned. It was about her desire to seduce a young boy, a fifteen-year-old whose pubic hairs were barely visible, but she took me away for many hours, and I'm grateful for that. Being with a woman certainly changed the way I thought about being with a girl.

Dad took me to the Tivoli fountains and to Villa Adriana, Hadrian's Villa, to explore, and gave me several lurching driving lessons in the Fiat 600. My father gave precise instructions about the clutch and accelerator but said nothing about my mother's death or Mom2. When I asked the answer was, "Keep your mind on driving, son."

There was really no point in asking. I think I'd been so happy with Mom2 and had invested so much emotion that I'd lacked even the slightest awareness that things were rocky with her and Dad. When she began to explain the reasons that day, all the little things flashed through my mind. She'd had to lock her real self up, hide the young woman, and try to fathom the long silences. He didn't like parties. Though he was a very graceful man, he felt awkward when he danced. If you've ever seen *My Darling Clementine,* you know exactly what I mean.

I'm a girl, she'd said. I want to dance, I want to tell jokes and laugh. I want to have secrets with the man I love, I want to have intimacy, I want to go to a grand ball and dance all night. I want to sing. She was twenty-seven years old, and she'd given us four years of her life. He was a great actor, with a dazzling smile to pull from his trunk, but we all wanted what was in his heart, and he couldn't give it. Susan wanted him to be a little boy, to play with her little girl. I was just a little boy myself, and she was helping me to be a man. She said, "You've got to understand, Peter, I need to be loved. I need to be courted." I understood, but I needed to be needed, by anyone. I'd always ended my letters to her with "Don't forget to remember that I love you." Hours after our bright new life crunched away down the gravel drive, I wondered if she had forgotten, though I knew even at the time that it was a selfish thought. That day was the end of our family. Susan had been our last chance. I paddled on.

When we left Rome, I cried, and the song, "Arrivederci Roma," was theoretically the catalyst for the tears. I've wondered since why I was sad to leave the blast site, though I did—and do—love the city.

chapter *Five*

$\mathscr{I}$ returned to school a changed young man. I hadn't given a shit about many things since Mom2 had left us, and going back to Westminster didn't help. I brought my Latin teacher a little piece of ancient Rome, a small marble head I'd found in the fields at the villa.

That year, some of the student body had a new idea of entertainment. Friends from the outside sent us canned rum cake, as if we were inmates of Sing Sing. We drained each cake and bolted the rum, a tedious process but one that helped day-to-day boredom. But one night of raiding, post-rum, brought me face-to-face with the Bad One, the nightmare. While throwing a dormmate's bed out the second-floor window, someone goosed me in the ass, and it blew my mind. I was repulsed and able to articulate, for the first time, what I felt about the dream, the nightmare, in real terms: *Don't touch my ass*. I later used this declaration in disputes with the FBI, U.S. Customs and Treasury, and, more ironically, the Army draft.

I sang with the school choir. I was good enough for glee club, though not for madrigals. We had dances with girls' boarding schools, some at Westminster and some on the road. At one of the school dances that year, I stumbled onto the blessed fact that young women got horny, just like young men and older women. I was dancing with a real cutie, whom I'll call Nancy Fellings, when she pressed herself into me in an unmistakable manner, and let me know that it was for me only. Great. We snuck away to find some privacy, and discovered it in a deep doorway, in the shadows, where we kissed and grabbed each other. She let my hands explore her entire body—a beautiful one—while we kissed and pushed ourselves hard against each other. I knew and wanted more, but the place was wrong, and it wasn't offered. I needed to be needed, to give and be given to, not to take. Taking was easy; giving was the emotion, the cake. We had to get back to the dance soon, but in our own way we had some touch.

Life was a blur, though not a particularly happy one. That Christmas I insisted Mom2 come to the town house, but that hardly helped the collective mood.

. . .

What was left of the family went to Hyannis Port, on Cape Cod, for the summer of 1956. The house we rented was backed up against the Kennedy compound. My father and I watched the 1956 Democratic Convention there, and over the summer I met Jack, Robert, and Ted, though I didn't know at the time how lucky I was. Dad bought a Sailfish, a large, thick surfboard with a mast, sail, centerboard, and a rudder and tiller. He was both producing and acting in *Twelve Angry Men* in New York, and his sister, Aunt Harriet, came from Nebraska to be our guardian for the summer. She was very patient with us and taught me how to drive so that I could get my first license. I was sixteen and looked ten. When I chauffeured her around in our station wagon, having to sit on pillows to see over the wheel, I'd ask her to duck down in the backseat, so that my girlfriends would think I was driving around without a chaperon. Bless her, she did duck, and I got my license, though I was stopped many times by cops who, understandably, thought I was too young.

When he was home, Dad roamed the house sounding like a broken record, saying that letting me drive a car was like putting a deadly weapon in the hands of a child. It was more or less the same line he'd used on Mom2, and he failed to see the further irony in the gift of the .22, six years earlier. Harriet stuck up for me, and from time to time I was allowed to borrow the black '56 T-bird, two tops and a Continental kit.

I'd sail around the bay on the Sailfish, and on calmer days I'd sail out into the Atlantic. Being on that little board was soothing for me. I became relatively expert, and it gave me time for reflection. I decided that I wanted to be an Olympic medalist in sailing, but Dad was not about to sponsor me. When Dad finished *Twelve Angry Men*, he joined us with Amy and a nurse. He would take the Sailfish out and lie on the board, letting the sail luff up into the wind. I wanted to take the boat sailing, but he wanted to get away and just float around. When I asked him what he was doing, he told me he was working on the title sequence for the movie (he was the producer of the film, also). What could I say? He'd bought the boat. But he couldn't float in the little bay and drive the Bird at the same time, so off I'd zoom, taking girls for a ride, cruising for shakes and fries.

After a few weeks in our new summer place, Jane decided she would like to work as an apprentice at the Dennis Playhouse nearby. I know she had a crush on a young man from Yale who was working there as a stage manager and apprentice actor. James Franciscus, her secret love, would later become a big movie and TV star. Her first appearance on stage was without dialogue, but the entire audience was drawn to her. Later that summer she did the ingenue in *The Male Animal* with Dad in the lead. She was great. Dad was very impressed, but he only confided it to Harriet. I was slightly jealous, until I realized that I could use the Sailfish while he was rehearsing with Jane and the cast.

For a few days, Dad had his new romance visit us. We both took an instant dislike to each other. I was justified, as history will show. She was a flaky bitch.

When the summer ended we packed up the station wagon, loaded the boat on the roof, and headed back to the city. I had a reprieve, though: before I went back to Westminster, I joined my best friend, Jimmy Gibson, at his family's summer house in York Harbor, Maine, for a week and a half. In daylight hours we drove about in a Pontiac Super Chief station wagon, straight eight and lots of beans. We poked a billion holes in the muffler with ice picks and cruised the coast. At night, Jimmy and I would wait for his parents to go to bed, then sneak out with as many beers as we could fit in our shirts, making our way to the house of one of the local beauties. We always knew when one young woman planned to stay at another's house, and they became our target. We called ourselves the Alpine Climbers Club.

We were grand conspirators in the pursuit of happiness. The quest was basically harmless except for the dreaded possibility of accidental pregnancy—the only kind in those days, really—and it never happened to us. We were antiparents, antirules, propleasure, hundred-pound sybarites.

The trick to our night raids was climbing to the bedroom windows of our unindicted coconspirators. Our fearless approach and bold deeds made up handily for the skinny geekiness we both thought would be our fate for life. Beer, wine, and two slightly insane, fearless young men were always welcome at a pretty young woman's window. Sometimes third-floor windows were hard to get to, but we were members of the ACC, defying the moral impossibility of entering a girl's bedroom. The goal of the ACC was no more complex than ejaculation, any way possible, but most of the time the dreaded blue-balls syndrome made our retreats especially painful and adrenaline-filled, a mixture of lower-body agony and terror.

Our biggest fear was that Mrs. Chandling, mother of one of our favorite targets, would awake and hear us on the roof climbing into or out of Marie's bedroom. I know the Chandling's Labrador saw me, but we were friends. One time, having trashed the trellis, our only way out was to drop from the little bit of eaves that overhung the kitchen windows. Getting to the little roof was a snap; staying on the thing was a trick. Selecting the moment of "letting go," according to whether or not Mrs. Chandling would see us, was hit or miss. We found ourselves in that position twice, in "Wake up, little Susie, wake up!" situations. It always seemed to be worth the sensation of falling asleep next to someone.

On one night-raider episode, we drove the improved exhaust Pontiac Super Chief to Minni Alston's so that I might make an exquisite plea for passionate favors. Minni lived in a one-story rambling house, which made bedroom access a snap. I was only supposed to be *en casa* for a moment, but Minni always made a moment seem like a nanosecond for a man thirsting for pleasure. While we planned our next encounter, Minni's grandmother woke and shuffled through the house, using the bathroom, getting a drink of water, and finally opening Minni's door and peering inside her room. This put our ballistic passion under the bed, literally. I lay on the floor, looking up at the slats, as quiet as I could. But there was some giggling, and though Minni's grandma was elderly, she was not stupid. She knew that her granddaughter was a fox, and there were many hounds about. In my fervor, my absolute desperation for dangerous sex, I tried to get Minni under the bed with me and totally forgot about Jimmy in the Pontiac, engine off. Grandmother was up and about for a long while, though without ever calling Minni's bluff, which meant that *I* was in and out of Minni's bed like a rabbit. Jimmy, frustrated, came to Minni's window asking where the hell I was, and Minni explained that I was under the bed. This made no sense to Jimmy—I should either be in bed with Minni, or in the car with him. After many "shushes" I escaped and we were on our way, the Super Chief rapping its low exhaust like a true race car.

I made several visits to Maine before the ACC was disbanded two years later. Our record of thirty-eight missions and no interceptions stands as a model for future seekers of the Holy Grail.

. . .

Back at Bataan for fifth form, my junior year, I had yet another new dorm and another new roommate. The fall semester passed without disaster, and life seemed promising. I took many trips to an all-girl school that was only three miles away, the Ethel Walker School. We had dances; Nancy Fellings and I enjoyed seeing each other again. My grades, though spotty, were still good enough to allow study in my room instead of study hall. I'd made varsity soccer.

. . .

My sophomore year, our headmaster had asked my dad to provide me with an allowance. He'd suggested that it was time to teach me how to live in the real world of checks and balances, so I got a dollar and a half per week to put in the school bank and draw on with special checks. A buck and a half was not a great deal of money, even in those days, and though we got an extra fifty cents if our grades were good, I had to do what I could to supplement my meager stash.

Dad—whose previous concept of a high allowance was twenty-five cents—was dragged against all his might to this idea. He'd never felt that an allowance was something I was owed. The fall 1956 semester at Westminster I got fairly high grades, so the headmaster, Francis Keyes, gave me the fifty-cent bonus. I had to use this to save for a Christmas ski trip, but the money—augmented by whatever I could cadge from Mom2 (whom I saw whenever possible during holiday breaks) or win at cards—also paid for milk, bread, and peanut butter.

. . .

As fall turned into winter, the year took on a very different smell to it, and a not-so-good feeling filled the air both at home and at school. Because of the lunacy of the later part of the year, I'm not sure how reliable my linear memory is, but I am quite accurate about the actual events, and I doubt recounting them will make the Westminster School happy.

I knew that something was in the works when I visited Dad in Florida on Thanksgiving break. He was shooting *The Wrong Man,* and when going through his personals, as usual, I found a telegram: *Love love love love love love love love love love to my Angelo.* Pretty heady stuff, and it came from Italy. This must have been the same Italian woman who had visited my father briefly in Hyannis Port that summer, though the woman Dad was seeing in Florida was not from Italy. I wanted to make love to Dad's leading lady, Vera Miles. Fat chance. We were staying at the Fountainbleau, and I went out into the sun as soon as I hit the ground. I fell asleep on my right side, by the pool, which made me lobster red on my left side and boarding school white on my right.

Coming home to Seventy-fourth Street for Christmas in 1956, I must have arrived a bit earlier than expected. I walked up the staircase to the second floor, and there in the library was a stereo phonograph all set up in the middle of the room. It was quite separate from the built-in system that was Dad's. It was plugged in, so I took out a record and played it. The sound was great and the machine was portable.

Minutes later, Dad came down from his study and fumed at me for using the machine. "You just can't keep your hands off anything, can you?" It turned out that the stereo was my Christmas present, but it wasn't wrapped, and I didn't understand his anger. He could have said anything, and I would have never guessed it was for me. It would have been an even greater surprise to have opened it later as one of my presents.

That Christmas, I tried to insist on Mom2's presence again, refusing to be a part of the divorce, but it was too much to ask of her. Amy came for the holiday, but I missed Susan terribly, and left the Seventy-fourth Street house as soon as I could, driving off to Stowe, Vermont, with a friend, to ski away my problems with life. I was angry and wanted to be on my own. I simply announced to Dad that I was going, rather than asking for permission; I felt that he'd abdicated the role of Permitter, and he didn't bother to argue. The Christmas before, Mom2 had taken me to the best ski shop in the city and bought me good skis, poles, and boots. The rest of my ski outfit was Army surplus.

We stayed at a youth hostel, the women on one floor and the men on another. One evening, my friend and I went to the year-round Stowe drive-in to see *Invasion of the Body Snatchers*. I had a date, a young woman who'd approached me in the lift line named Garrie Gosner. Man oh Manischewitz. A few months later, in mid-April, I claimed on a fishing license (which I signed P.H. Fonda) that I was five foot nine and 120 pounds, a flat-out lie by two inches and five pounds. My front lock of hair was peroxided, and my skin was orange from carrot juice, the current fad at Westminster. I had never been hit on before, and Garrie showed me the little moves that count. All she had to do was run her fingers very lightly on the top of my upper legs, and I hit orbit. I had to find *Invasion of the Body Snatchers* playing somewhere else in the world before I could say I had seen the picture, or shall I say motion picture. I'll never forget her, even though I have had to change her name in this book.

That fall and winter I also developed an enormous crush on the wife of one of the masters. It was actually more of an obsession than a crush—I lusted after her, flirted with her at every opportunity, and let her know as subtly as possible. At dances I'd ask her onto the floor as many times as I could without making my ardor obvious. I told her, as we were dancing once, that I watched her sometimes. I told her I thought she was the most beautiful woman I had ever seen. It made her blush, but she didn't discourage me. She was reluctant to give me a photo of herself, though, so I took one with a borrowed camera and kept it in my wallet. She was petite, with dark, short hair, a perfect nose, and a perfect figure. And I was a little puppy.

The sixth-formers made as much fun of me as possible about my crush on the master's wife. One afternoon, I was stopped by one of these little fascists, who said something very bad about me and her. A woman whom I lusted after, whose grace I worshiped, whose honor I was committed to uphold, was being belittled by a savage, and without thinking, I hit the asshole as hard as I could in his sternum. I hit him so hard, he fell to the ground, gasping for air and not getting any. He was much bigger than I was, and I was amazed at the power I'd called up when I was pushed too hard. It was the first time I had ever struck another person. The rest of the sixth form made it their cause to get back at me, though none of them wanted to confront me directly, but my life at Westminster was going bad faster than I could have imagined possible.

One evening, while I was studying in my room, Mr. Lamont, who was the master for the west end of the corridor, summoned me to his apartment. Lamont was the head of the English and drama departments. He had a gimpy right leg, which had ruined his aspirations of becoming a Shakespearean actor. That evening he was drunk and began to dress me down for being repeatedly late for chapel. I admitted that I had, indeed, been late to many chapel services, and explained that it was mostly because I was making peanut-butter-and-jelly sandwiches, as the food was so bad from the school kitchen and I was trying to gain weight. Lamont was stumbling about with a drink in his hand. The volume of the confrontation rose, and I kept up my side, yelling in his face. Everyone could hear the argument—only sixth-formers were allowed the privacy of closed doors, and the door to the master's apartment was open. Lamont railed at me, saying that I was part of a community, and I should follow community rules or leave. Fair enough, until Lamont stepped over the big line and called my father a son of a bitch. I think the literal quote was that "anyone who's been married four times is a no-good son of a bitch."

Although my dad had not yet married his fourth wife, Afdera Franchetti, the Italian of the love letter and the visit to Hyannis Port, he'd driven up to Westminster a few weeks earlier in the T-bird to take me to dinner and tell me he intended to. The press had made the romance common knowledge. Lamont's remarks had nothing to do with school stuff, with my grades, or my attitude. A jealous man, a frustrated actor, was taking his wrath out on an innocent party. I responded by telling Lamont to shut the fuck up, and he screamed back that my father was a lousy actor, and I shouldn't feel above the rest of the world because I was his son. I called him a scumbag and hit him as hard as I could in the face. Lamont went down like a sack of shit, but I was too far gone to step out of the thing. I jumped on him and began to smash him in the face over and over, screaming that he had no right to call my father *anything,* and that he could count on my absence from chapel whenever I felt like it. The next thing I knew Jake Nolde—*my* corridor master—was pulling me off Lamont. I didn't want to stop; I wanted to mark the old fat fart for life. Nolde took me to his apartment and tried to calm me down. He asked me if I could use a drink, poured me a glass of vodka—a gesture that was well beyond unusual—and made me take deep breaths. After I had calmed down, I went back to my room and considered the events.

To cull me out for punishment would mean exposing Lamont as an abusive drunk, an embarrassment for the school, but the master had lost whatever authority he thought he had over me. As I continued classes, I inevitably crossed paths with this sack of shit, and once passed him and the head of the math and chemistry departments, Mr. Gow. I said good morning to Mr. Gow, as was required by school etiquette, but I said fuck you to Lamont.

My language to Lamont was unacceptable, but rather than openly reprimanding me, some of the faculty began to show me some of the ways they could make my life hell. Shit, my life was already hell, but those cloistered assholes had no way of understanding that, and I seriously doubt that it would have made a difference. I began to get papers back with the answers changed and marked wrong. When I began to do my assignments in ink, they still came back with the answers changed and marked failing. I resorted to proving my performance with my correct workbooks.

In early March of 1957, at the end of winter term, I went to New York for my father's fourth wedding, astounded that he wanted me to be his best man. I thought that the Italian was a total airhead and was after Dad's money and reputation. Afdera called herself a baroness. She wasn't, though her father (he *was* a baron, but it was only a lifetime title) had been the preeminent archaeologist for Italy in the North African colonies, the man who discovered several ancient Roman cities in the always encroaching desert. Afdera dreamed of gaining the spotlight in European aristocracy by marrying a world-renowned actor, but my father, though aristocratic, would never consider himself a part of any simpleminded aristocracy. He was completely a man of democracy, the epitome of the the great American Everyman, the man who stood the tallest among the living idols for representative democracy. He was an Eagle Scout and a Scout Master, the only honors I can remember him respecting, and I'm proud of his duty-bound affection for the ideals of Jefferson, Adams, Monroe, Franklin, and Lincoln. I am equally enraged that the United States State Department yanked his passport, branding him a communist sympathizer during the House Un-American Activities Committee commie witch hunt. They must not have seen *My Darling Clementine* or *Mister Roberts*. I cannot think of another person who stood so fast for representative democracy, though in later years I saw his voter registration application from when he was twenty-one. He was a registered Republican. Far out. But I am sure that he was so registered because of his devotion to the principles of President Abraham Lincoln.

When he enlisted in the Navy he was determined to be a simple "gob," an ordinary seaman, but the Navy learned of his scouting past and shipped him off to Officer Training School. When he kissed me good-bye on that strange night at Tigertail, he was Henry J. Fonda, lieutenant, junior grade. When he returned he was a lieutenant, senior grade, with honors, a Presidential Citation, and a Bronze Star for bravery in action.

The day before the wedding to the Italian, I told this very different Captain America about the problems that were mounting fast at Westminster. I was very distressed while telling Dad these things, honestly worried about school and my senior year. He was more sympathetic than usual, in that he asked me what I wanted him to do. Should he take me out of the school? Hell, I wanted Wyatt Earp to ride into town and bring things back to normal. He said he would write the school a letter. Well, a letter from Young Mr. Lincoln might make a difference. So I made it through the wedding and went back to school to face the music, waiting for the letter from Mister Roberts to make its mark.

While I waited, things only got worse. I continued to treat Lamont like a sack of shit while being quite courteous to the rest of the faculty. It was a bad move on my part but I was fighting for my sanity. Everything began to compress as each day passed, and the wanted poster from Marshal Earp never showed. A couple of weeks later the entire fifth form gathered in the study hall one night and listed the things I had done to disrupt the school. I'd called Lamont a fuckhead and had hit him, I was disrespectful of the school's rules, and so on. No matter that everyone on the corridor had heard how the fight started—they were going to kick me out of the fifth form by a vote. The only people who stood up for me were the school's token black person, Booker Bradshaw, the token Jew, and three other fellow "misfits," as the class referred to them.

Having been rejected by my form, a man without a country, I lost my room study privileges and had to stick to my desk during study hall. Over the last two years' worth of study halls I'd always joined in when the other students wanted to mess with the study-hall master via spitball fights, eraser throws, and other diversions. Those shenanigans were conspiratorial, but now I was into very personal disruptions. One day I took an earphone, ran the wire conspicuously over my desk and into the inkwell, and, as I studied my Latin, pretended to be listening to music as I tapped out a rhythm. I watched the study-hall prefect, a sixth-former, sneaking up on me to bust me. When he pounced, he grabbed the earpiece and flipped open my desk to find . . . nothing. No radio. Just an unspoken fuck you. He saved face by telling the school that I did have a radio, and they accepted his version.

Even though I was reported for such incidents, not much could be done to me. I was already a nonperson, expelled from my form, not a part of the system. But the bells were tolling for me. My emotional wires were starting to fry under the pressure of ostracism and degradation, and as no word came to me about a letter from Tom Joad, I felt fully abandoned.

I decided to seek help through the doctor who visited the school infirmary three times a week. On the first visit, when the doctor asked me what I was there for, I coughed out one or two words and then broke down sobbing, completely unable to tell him what was happening to me. He broke two pills in half and told me to take one half in the morning, before breakfast, and the other half two hours after supper. And so I did. Two days later, I met with him again. He asked me what I was so troubled by, and I sputtered out three or four words and then broke down sobbing again, unable to make words that would give a hint to my inner collapse. The doctor then gave me four pills and higher dosage directions: two pills before breakfast and two pills two hours after supper. Two days later, when I tried to express myself, I made it to six words before total collapse, and was given six pills, the extra two for lunchtime. After two days of this therapy, I was able to vomit out the basic dynamic of my problems, and the doctor recommended that I stay on the last dosage and report to him in three days. When that third day arrived, I was able to tell him what was going on in my mind-heart-soul for three minutes before I began weeping and was unable to continue. The doctor doubled the dosage to eight mystery pills a day: two before breakfast, two before lunch, two before supper, and two at bedtime.

Within a few days I was as calm and as oblivious to the world as a frontal-lobotomy victim, and I was finally able to tell the doctor what was happening to me.

Because of the pills, I went from being a member of the tennis team to ball boy, and even then I had to be reminded that I was supposed to get the balls off the clay courts after any play. I was calm, yes, but I was disintegrating rapidly, and I knew it. The doctor told me to stay on the last pill regime, but I did communicate with one of the masters, my English lit teacher. We'd had an essay assignment, and in mine I detailed the things that were happening to me on campus: my papers for math had their answers changed, but the supporting worksheet still showed the right answer; my fight with Mr. Lamont; the general faculty conspiracy against me; the sixth-form scheme; my fellow classmates' actions against me. The medication made it easy for me to write, and I turned in what was essentially a long letter. The English master seemed to be truly unaware of the events, and the essay blew his mind. He invited me to have tea with him in his living room, and told me that the things I had written were quite serious. When I brought some of my math papers to him to prove my story it made him nervous. I told him about my conversation with my father and the letter he had said he would write that never came.

The master advised me to try as hard as I could to keep a low profile and stay away from Lamont. He also suggested that I speak with the headmaster, Mr. Keyes, and explained that he could do nothing about my problem other that make himself available to me if I needed someone to talk to. He was straight with me, and at least there was one teacher who now had the full picture. He was perhaps the coolest teacher on the campus, inviting certain students to his cottage to listen to records of Dylan Thomas and other poets reading their works, and he took me and another student fly-fishing twice. I liked him very much, and I loved his dog, a yellow Labrador named Pogo.

The medication kept me functioning, and it didn't really screw me up; I simply didn't care about anything. Bad things continued to happen but I didn't get as emotional, or non compos mentis. But the reality didn't fade with the medication, and my internal suffering grew each day. Finally, in desperation, I decided to go to the headmaster, and one night in early May, in the middle of study hall, I got up from my desk and left the hall. The prefect in charge that evening shouted at me to return to my desk at once or he would report me. Report me to whom and for what, I wondered, muttering my standard fuck you as I left the room. I walked quickly across the campus to the main building and Mr. Keyes's office.

I was blown away when I walked into his office. A classmate sat there, and looked embarrassed when I entered the room. Keyes told me that they had been talking about me and what was going on. I was astounded—someone was sticking up for me? My fellow classmate was excused, and I was left alone with the headmaster. I told him everything that had happened, as calmly as possible but still with tears. Keyes acted quite surprised. He already had my school records open on his desk, and after I had covered the problem completely, he said it might be better if I were to leave the school. He emphasized that he was not kicking me out, that it was all up to me. He noted that my grades were good, that I already had enough credits to graduate though I hadn't yet finished my junior year. I had been working on the school magazine as an illustrator and contributor and my work was good. He seemed so calm. He apologized for Lamont's conduct and asked me what I wanted to do.

It all seemed too smooth, too fast. I said I wanted to leave the school honorably. Keyes guaranteed that I could leave without any mention of the mess and that I could keep all my credits. He asked if I would be returning to New York. I didn't know what to say—my father was in Europe on his fourth honeymoon, leaving only two Italian servants, Giuseppe and Fidalma, at the Seventy-fourth Street house. I would be alone. Keyes suggested that maybe I should call my sister and ask her to come and take me home. He had the phone number at Vassar in front of him and dialed it, asking to speak to Jane. When she came on the line, he introduced himself and asked if she could come to Westminster as quickly as possible to take me home. Where was that? I wondered. What did "home" mean, really? Jane asked to speak with me. When she asked me what was going on, I began to cry. All I could say was please come, Jane, I need you.

I hung up the phone and stood in front of Keyes, blinking back my tears. He became a little uneasy with me just standing there and asked if I would like some tea. I said I wanted to go to my room and pack. He agreed, shook my hand, and apologized again. I ran like a madman back to my room.

When I got to my room, I closed the door and sat on my bunk with my head in my hands. My roommate, Peter Hobson, was nervous about the closed door. I told him not to worry. Nothing more could happen to me at this place. I went up to the storage room, just off the art department area. I'd made a secret copy of the storage room key at the beginning of the year and went there now to grab my bags and my secret stash of cigarettes and bottle of vodka. Back in our room I actually locked the door this time, sat down on my bed, took out the vodka, and fired up a cig. I took a couple of my special pills and washed them down with the vodka. I offered him a drink and a cig, but he declined, not quite understanding and truly unnerved. When the sixth-form brownshirts started pounding on the door and yelling, I at first told them to fuck off, then unlocked and opened the door. The youth corps bowled me right over as they blasted into our room, but I got up, took a pull on the vodka, a puff on my cigarette and sat down on my bed. They went ballistic; I sat there, serenely anarchic. They told me to stand up, drop the bottle and the cig, and answer their questions. I told them, with more passion than even I knew I had, to fuck off. I picked up an old split fungo bat I used for stickball and told them to get out of my sight or I would pound the shit out of them and *then* call Mr. Keyes. They retreated slightly but kept screaming, so I took the fungo bat and pounded a grand slam on my footlocker. I felt such a deep rage, such a desire to take these scumbags out, that I had no fear. I told them that I was departing the place tomorrow, that they had no jurisdiction over me, and that I would call Mr. Keyes *and* the police and have them arrested for assault. Assault. *I* was the one with the fungo, but I was going to charge them with assault. The performance was too much for them and they ran from the room, yelling that they were going to "get this taken care of." Dickheads.

Once they left the building, Peter Hobson asked if he could have a pull on the bottle and a puff. Are you really not part of this system? he asked. Count on it, I said as I locked the door again.

The next day, when Jane arrived, no one could find me. She

walked around the quad, looking, and saw a large bush with four or five dogs poking their heads into it. She told me that she knew I was in the bush, and I was. The dogs ran free, but I had nowhere to go.

Jane took me to the train, and we headed for the town house in Manhattan. I was fairly calm, having taken the last of my pills beore we left.

"God! You remind me of Holden Caulfield, Peter."

"Umm-hunn."

"Are you all right?"

"Unh-unh."

"What will happen now? I mean, do you need help? Why did this all happen?"

"I don't know, Jane. I can't seem to talk about it, can't talk about it without coming unsnapped. What I told you, that's as far, as far . . . I think I'm going crazy."

"It's all right, Peter. It will be . . . everything will be okay, but I can't stay in the city very long. What are you going to do?"

Soon after we got to New York, Jane had to get back to Vassar. Dad was in Europe with the Italian, and Mom2 had moved to Paris. Jane called Dad's business manager, and it was decided that I would go to Omaha and stay with Aunt Harriet. By the time I got on a plane and arrived in Nebraska, I was five days gone, five days without the pills, without a fix. But I was very naive, and didn't know what I was in for. Three years later I learned that I'd been on phenobarbital, the hardest and most painful drug to withdraw from, worse than heroin, nicotine, anything. I *was* unhinged, but not bound for the bin.

In 1989, while looking at my file at Westminster, I found a letter from my father to Keyes, saying that he was quite concerned. It was dated the day before his wedding to the Italian, the same day he'd made the promise to me. Wyatt had come to rescue me, after all, and I'd spent those years thinking he'd abandoned me. Keyes had received the letter a month and a half before our special meeting. I paddled on.

chapter *Six*

I can see myself as I arrived at Aunt Harriet's. I was thinking, most of the time, that I was going crazy. The Menninger Clinic was just downriver from Omaha, actually downwind, in Topeka, Kansas. Bill Hayward had been packed off to Menninger's a year earlier, and he wasn't crazy. I'd seen him in Manhattan the day before his parents had had the net thrown, conned an old, semiretired psychiatrist into committing their son and shipped him out of town on Bill Paley's private DC3. Billy had seemed perfectly sane to me, though he'd told me he was on his way to Florida to marry a girl. I completely understood his desire to get laid, but he was only fifteen at the time, and marriage seemed an extreme step.

Bill had been sent to the Menninger Clinic because he needed to be needed, and I worried about being next. On the second day at Aunt Harriet's, I began to have severe stomachaches, cramps, and convulsions unlike anything I'd suffered before. I knew it wasn't some bug or common sickness, and forty minutes into the attack I was bent together, knees clenched to my chest, in even worse pain. Then I was terrified, sure, finally, that I was going crazy. I'd heard about how anxiety attacks could wrack a body, and I tried to keep from screaming aloud by holding a pillow doubled over my face. I hid in my closet, not wanting to be found in this state. Aunt Harriet had gone to meet with some friends, so she wasn't there to see my agony. Twenty minutes later, the pain disappeared; ten minutes after that, I was sweating like mad and chilled. The sweats and chills lasted less than a half hour, and when they were over I sat on my bed, baffled and frightened, my body feeling as if nothing had ever gone wrong.

These attacks continued for three days. I lost a few pounds from my bouts in the closet. The cramps and convulsions faded away slowly. I was never discovered in crisis, and after a little more than a week I felt normal. Harriet may have thought my sudden departures for my room at the onset of an attack were a part of the nervous condition that had led to my being kicked out of school. I did my best to explain that I was *not* kicked out of Westminster, and Harriet never overtly doubted my word or patronized me, but my reputation as a difficult young man had preceded me.

Harriet and Uncle Jack, a.k.a. John B. Peacock, were fabulous to me. Uncle Jack was a very distinguished-looking man, with great manners, great humor, and a great heart. He was a gourmand and a fine interior decorator who had a trunkful of stories and jokes. He looked like a colonel in some grand army, so I called him "Colonel." Neither pushed me about the events that had brought me to their home, and both concentrated on making me feel good in every way. It was the best therapy that I could have had. I ate lunch and din-ner—as much or as little food as I wanted—with both of them every day, and was allowed to sleep in and eat breakfast on my own time. Such leniency was mind-boggling, and I loved them for it.

I spent almost three weeks with Jack and Harriet before I finally had to deal with my real life. Harriet was very calm and practical when she brought up my future. You must go back to high school and finish it, she told me. I refused to even consider such a thing and said firmly that I had no intention of going back to *any* school. The thought of it made me very angry, and the anger made me feel like I was going to have one of my "attacks," so that I walked away from the first two conversations. What a brat I must have been.

But Harriet persisted. We both knew my father would not support me financially, so I must begin to look for a job. She made me ac-knowledge this simple truth. Harriet felt I should take a battery of aptitude tests to find out what I might be good at, rather than just pumping gas. I agreed again. My 1947 fantasy of being a parking-lot attendant had been discarded long ago, and though I didn't like the idea of a test, I couldn't argue with Harriet's logic.

She had an acquaintance, the dean of the liberal arts department at Omaha University and a practicing psychologist, who agreed to evaluate me through a two-week program. Each day I went to Dean Thompson's office and took a batch of "personal aptitude tests," most of which were totally ludicrous. One of the first tests gave away the system. A young student teacher arrived at the office, acting very businesslike and showing as much disdain for me as possible. The young man carried a clipboard and a stopwatch, and explained that he was going to say a word, start the watch, and see how long it took me to define the word. He ran me through the word test, and left.

On the last two days, I was given three multiple-choice, general knowledge tests. The puzzling thing was that the top of the page on all three, the part of the tests that explained their point, had been cut off.

The next morning Harriet came into my room early, quite upset. She was angry with me but didn't say what it was all about, and simply told me to get dressed and report to Dean Thompson's office immediately. And so I did, with all my hackles up. My trigger was set before he even accused me of cheating.

Dean Thompson said I *had* to have cheated: no one was expected to answer all the questions of the last tests correctly. It seemed he'd given me the entrance exams to Omaha University, the University of California, and Stanford, and they covered some subjects I had never learned in class. But I'd always gleaned stray information by reading the entries surrounding the assigned topic in reference books and encyclopedias, and I'd spent a good deal of time at Fay and Westminster wandering through the library, pulling down various books.

"You mean I got all the answers right?"

"Almost all of them."

I started to laugh hysterically through my tears of rage, and tried to explain my theory of test-taking.

"You mean you *guessed* the answers?" Dean Thompson croaked. When he realized I'd blasted the curves sky-high with some simple linguistic deductions he smiled, having decided I would, in fact, go far.

• • •

A week or so later, I learned that I would be spending three months on the Côte d'Azur in the south of France with Jane, Dad, Afdera, and Giuseppe and Fidalma, my stepmother's servants. This last was especially great news—Afdera, I'm sure, thought of them as her personal slaves, but I thought they were wonderful people. They spoke very little English, and I spoke a little more Italian, remembered from Rome in 1955, so we were able to communicate.

Harriet, who had—and has—much more patience than I ever did, suggested that I take a short tutorial in Italian as a gesture to my father's fourth wife. I distrusted Afdera, to put it mildly, but Harriet had a valid point, so, for my father's sake, as well as Giuseppe's and Fidalma's, I was tutored in Italian in preparation for my summer in France. This wasn't quite as strange as it sounds, for I already knew enough French to get along.

When I wasn't taking Italian lessons, Harriet or Jack would drive me out to the country club, where I could swim, bag rays, and play tennis.

The confrontation with Dean Thompson and resultant Big News— that I wasn't a mental midget, or insane—had made me a much happier person.

Harriet had arranged that my father come to Omaha to meet Dean Thompson, and my cousin Douw Fonda, only a few years Dad's junior, was in town on business and was there at Harriet and Jack's house when Dad arrived. I sat on the staircase waiting for Dean Thompson and listening to Dad and Douw on the couch in the living room. They were discussing how many pieces of toilet paper were proper for anyone to use. In a lifetime of bizarre conversations, this was one of the strangest I've ever heard, and Harriet later told me she was furious with the two of them. Neither of them knew what was going to happen, so they carried on with sharing this useless information. The correct amount of toilet paper was a very safe area for the two men.

Anyway, that was the tone on the afternoon of the Annunciation. When Dean Thompson arrived, he saw me on the stairs, and smiled and winked as he went into the living room. He had no way of knowing that three pieces of toilet paper was the correct amount, but after the necessary introductions, he got right to the point. He told Dad that he had spent two weeks testing me with a variety of examinations, and in his opinion, I should be studying at the sophomore level in college. He told Dad that I was a genius and could excel in *anything* I tried.

Dad was not ready to hear those words. "What!? What the hell has he been telling you?"

"Mr. Fonda, I want to enroll your son at the university in freshman and certain sophomore classes, while he completes two required courses at a local private school. He already has enough credits to graduate, he only needs to take those two required courses, and I believe he will do just fine."

"I can't believe what I'm hearing!"

I could tell by his voice that Dad was dumbfounded. Aunt Harriet told him that she and Jack had met with Dean Thompson and were very pleased by the news and *he* should be, too. After all, Dr. Thompson was the dean and a practicing psychologist. She said I would stay with her and Jack, and they both were happy to have me. They had, in fact, already settled on this with Dean Thompson, who weighed in again, saying that the stable environment at the Peacocks' was something I needed. From my post on the stairway I agreed heartily, and silently.

"I just can't believe it. What kind of tests?"

"Achievement, aptitude, IQ, everything necessary. Now you must make sure that he knows you're very proud about all this. He needs as much encouragement as he can get."

"Hank, you must see the wisdom in Dean Thompson's plan," Aunt Harriet said.

"I don't want to burden you and Jack with him."

"We *want* to have him here with us."

God bless Aunt Harriet. I began to cry when I faced him. I was so worried that he might take the idea in the wrong way, and I didn't want to hurt him by making him feel I was rejecting him. Funny how a mind can bounce around. So it was agreed upon that I would stay with Jack and Harriet, while graduating from high school and attending college. Though given the skepticism that was in Dad's voice and eyes, my dream of gettig Dad's T-bird to drive at college as a reward for being smart faded quickly.

. . .

I finished the Italian sessions and joined Jane, Dad, and Afdera in New York, en route to Europe. We stayed in Paris for a week or so at the Hotel Lotti, where Jane and I had adjoining rooms in the upper part of the hotel, in the back like the servants' quarters at Ocean House. I wondered if tucking us into the background was an emerging pattern; really, it had been the pattern all along, back to the days when the Hayward kids had been provided with their own, very separate, quarters.

Mom2 was living in Paris in the summer of 1957, and Jane and I took advantage of the coincidence and spent several lunches and afternoons with her. It was great to see Susan again. She was studying art in Paris.

The morning after one of those days with Mom2, I awoke and heard Dad yelling at Jane through the closed door that separated our rooms. I went to the door and heard him asking Jane how we could be so thoughtless as to see Susan while he was here in Paris with Afdera, his "bride" of four or five months. As if we could give a shit by now about Afdera. I flung the door open and screamed at him that *we* hadn't divorced Susan, he had, and we would see her whenever we wanted to, and to *never* yell at my sister about that or anything else . . .

Oh my god, what have I done, I thought. I was standing in the doorway with a towel around my waist, 118 pounds of rage, screaming new rules to my father. He could have whipped my ass with one hand tied, but he just looked at me in amazement, turned around, and left. Afdera acted hurt when she was around us for the next few days; such sulking generally involved her walking more like a duck than usual, or slurping her food especially noisily. Dad fell for the act and bought her a small purse made of woven gold.

With most of the week on my own, I went to the Louvre and several museums and galleries, all of them astounding. But one day, on my way to the Louvre, I was undone by the sight of a young French woman wearing a knit dress with no underwear, and I decided to go to the rue du Saint-Honoré, where the prostitutes worked. It had been too long for me, and the dreaded buildup had reached critical mass. I lucked out and found a young woman who took the edge off with a marvelous, multiple performance, one that left me relaxed and carefree for the next few days.

One morning, Dad announced to me that we were going shopping. Just the fact the *we* were going shopping was amazing. We took a taxi and drove up the Champs-Élysées, around the Arc de Triomphe and

down the other side. On the way up we passed brasseries and bou-
tiques, while the other side featured auto dealers, mechanics, and
electrical shops. We stopped in front of a Porsche dealer and got out
of the taxi. I couldn't believe my luck, but when we paraded into the
showroom we marched right past the Porsches. The next batch of
cars were Karmann Ghias. I'd heard of them, but never seen one
before. I thought the coupes were kind of neat, but we marched right
past them, too, and only stopped at the very back of the showroom
in front of a little gray car that looked like a bug. It had no chrome,
radio, or gas gauge and the owner's manual was written in French
and German, but it was going to be *my* car.

My father seemed slightly annoyed by the look on my face. "I
know you want me to let you have the T-bird, but I don't want you
to look like a spoiled child. I want you to be just like any regular
young man." (In less than five seconds, I had gone from being a
"child" to a "regular young man.")

The little car was a Volkswagen. Once I was back in Omaha, where
no one had *ever* seen a VW, I went to a movie, and when I came out
the car had been put up on the sidewalk by frat rats. For a "regular
young man" I stuck out like a very sore thumb. Everyone at O.U. had
expected me to be driving a Ferrari or some other fancy car. I
would—I thought—have been just perfect in the Bird, but instead I
got a lot of jeering and jokes. Where's the engine in that thing? Does
it come with pedals? In the long run, it was the best car for me. On a
twenty-dollar-a-week allowance, I could go ten miles on a dime's
worth of gas.

But I couldn't drive it that summer. Aunt Harriet and her daughter,
Jayne, who were also on vacation in Europe, borrowed it and drove
all over the place in my new car. I didn't get to drive it until I flew
back to the States with Harriet and my cousin, and we all declared the
VW on our customs list. In those days one could bring in five hundred
dollars of merchandise without paying any duty. The Bug had cost
eleven hundred and fifty dollars; we split it three ways and still had a
quota surplus for other buys. Though I never mentioned the five Italian switchblades I hauled through customs.

· · ·

We took the train from Paris to Nice. I felt rather sophisticated having a sleeping suite; the Orient Express played heavy on my mind as

we pulled out of the station. The next morning, as we neared Nice, Dad stopped by my suite to wake me for breakfast.

"Smoking before breakfast?" He snapped at me. "I don't believe it!" Maybe he'd forgotten that he smoked whenever he wanted, and I had been smoking for four years. I was becoming aware that he could only converse by way of criticism. The incident was a small one, but indicative of the time we spent together during that period.

We arrived in Nice after breakfast, and trundled off in two taxis for our new home of the moment on Cap Ferrat, Villa Tanit, a beautiful house overlooking the bay at Villefranche sur Mere. Across the bay was a tiny chapel built for the fishermen of the region and frescoed by Jean Cocteau. Pablo Picasso had a villa on the tip of the cape, and there was a summer school for fortunate Swedes smack-dab in the middle. Many blond beauties *and* Carl Gustaf, the now reigning king of Sweden. When my friend Jimmy Gibson joined our traveling circus several weeks later, he, Carl, and I made up a predictable triumvirate, young men in pursuit of happiness, set loose in a holding tank of young, lusting Swedes.

Shortly after Jimmy joined us at the villa, we all took off for Spain to see the running of the bulls festival in Pamplona, a ritual and place made famous by Ernest Hemingway in *Death in the Afternoon*. Dad rented a Nash Ambassador, a peculiar-looking car, for the drive. None of the European cars—in the price range Dad was prepared to pay— were big enough to carry five people in comfort, so off we rolled in the Nash, Dad and Afdera in the front, Jane, Jimmy, and myself in the back. There was a jump seat that folded out from the back of the front seat, so the three of us weren't cramped side by side (the Nash was broad in the front and narrow in the back). Each of the three of us took turns catnapping on the jump seat when we weren't singing songs or playing road games.

We stopped in Antibes for a rest, and as we walked down a boulevard with a center of old shade trees we saw Jean Cocteau sitting at a table outside a café. He recognized Dad, and the two men greeted each other with Afdera translating. Both Jane and I knew some French from school, but I was too awestruck to say anything but, "Bonjour, monsieur." I'd studied about him, seen some of his art, and would later put his maxims to use in films, but here he was in the flesh, part of a very special coterie that included Picasso, Spanish filmmaker Luis Buñuel and Salvador Dalí.

Something went very wrong with the Nash in Arles. It was evening by the time we found a mechanic who would work on the car, and it was precisely the darkness that revealed the problem, a cracked block *and* cylinder. In the squalid, dark cubicle that was the mechanic's garage, Jimmy and I saw the flash of the ignited cylinder through the crack in the block. A Nash Ambassador block wasn't an easy find even in the United States in 1957. Heavy anger from Dad, who didn't want to hear from Jimmy or me about how to fix the crack temporarily. But we got the mechanic to weld up the crack as well as possible, and spent the night in Arles.

The next afternoon, we left for the Pyrenees and the Spanish border in the midst of a darkening storm. My father, refusing to explain his reasoning, crossed the mountains by the most obscure roads, narrow ones without guardrails and long drops off the outside lane, our lane. In the rain and fog, little white painted boulders with kilometer markings were our only indication of the edge of the road. As we neared the border, Afdera became agitated, jabbering something about her passport. I think she was having a new passport made with a younger birth date (a passport lift, in Eurotrash parlance) and was without papers. This, it turned out, was why we had to take the road seldom traveled. Dad grew even angrier and we were in agreement with him.

Leaving Afdera and Jane in the car at the border crossing, Dad and Jimmy and I went into the small room that was the guards' quarters.

"Meester Enri Fonda, sí?" None of us could believe it, including the guard himself. "Jou are Meester Enri Fonda, thee movie star, sí?"

"Sí." Dad was embarrassed.

The head guard—the film buff—went to the back of the offices and returned with a bottle of brandy and some cigars. He very proudly gave these favors to Dad, and asked us to have some Fundador and a smoke with him. The cigars were terrible. The brandy was only marginally better. Jimmy and I pulled out two packs of American cigarettes and gave them to the man. He was very happy, and we were stamped and on our way after Dad gave him an autograph. Hard to figure how a person stuck in such a remote place could be a film buff. They certainly didn't have television.

The road through the Spanish Pyrenees was just as narrow as the French roads had been, and the darkness of the storm made the drive an anxious one. As we came out of the mountains, the storm lifted and we arrived in Pamplona with a beautiful afternoon sky. There was no room for Jimmy and myself at Dad's hotel, so we were sent to a posada, several blocks away. As soon as we had put our bags in our room, we went out to the street. We ran into several young Americans, some of whom treated us to beers, which was greatly appreciated. Jimmy and I had some money, but we weren't flush. We found a store with some cheap red wine, bought three bottles and a corkscrew, and went on the prowl. Jimmy and I promenaded around the square again and again, stopping from time to time to dance and exchange slugs from our wine bottles with other young revelers. Several of them spit out our wine as if it were gasoline, and while they coughed and gagged we bolted as much of their superior wine as possible. We went into a bar, ran up a huge tab and ran out, and later almost got arrested for it until a new friend pleaded for us in Spanish. By the time we got back to our posada, joined by Jane's boyfriend from our Hyannis Port summer, James Franciscus, our heads were spinning from all the booze.

I lasted about forty seconds on my bed, which began to whirl the moment I lay down. I barely made it to the window before heaving everything in my guts out and down to the ground, without leaving a trace in our room. The purging process seemed endless and made an insane amount of noise, and I remember angry shouts from other windows.

In the morning, we looked out the window and realized that I had carpet-bombed the interior courtyard. We reached the street without detection and hurried to the starting point of the Pamplona race—the famous running of the bulls—pausing just long enough for some hair of the dog.

The bulls were about to be loosed, and once at the starting position, I decided to keep on running. So did Jimmy. Behind us we heard the sound of thundering hooves and the blood-filled screams of men as they were trampled. The white pants and shirt and red sash I was wearing—a costume I'd acquired in a cigarette trade the night before, and a requirement for those men mad enough to think they could actually beat the beasts to the arena—were soaked with that morning's red wine, so that it appeared as if I had been gored already, even though I was leading the pack. When we had made the interior of the arena—an absolute miracle—the bulls were removed from the ring, and cows with horns stampeded out into the bewildering morning sun. How I managed to stay alive remains a mystery.

We left the ring as soon as possible and headed for the posada. My tongue felt as if a live Gila monster had a firm grip on it. We discovered our belongings out in the street in front of the building, ejected by a very irate landlady, and when we found Dad and gave him our sob story, he was quite angry. I don't blame him; he probably didn't think much of my wine-dyed outfit. You'll have to find a room on your own, son. I give up, he said.

This presented a very new trick for the now very old dog that had possessed me since the early hours of that painful day. Jimmy and I excitedly tried to tell him about running with the bulls, but my side of the story sounded like I was speaking with a mouth full of Ping-Pong balls; it was hard to sound convincing with a goddamn Gila monster gripping my tongue. Later, in *his* biography, Dad said he proudly watched as Jimmy and I ran in front of the bulls, being among the first to enter the ring.

Franciscus gathered some extra pesos. We went to a florist, bought the finest bunch of flowers in Pamplona, and then went to a wine and liquor shop, where we bought the best brandy in the store. We humbly offered these gifts to our landlady and begged on our knees for her forgiveness. She relented and we were allowed back to our room, where I flopped down on my bed and gratefully passed out.

That afternoon was the first bullfight, and after our nap we joined Dad and the rest at the hotel, where Franciscus now had a room of his own. I wondered about that for a nanosecond or two until the truth popped into my head—my charming stepmother, the *stronza*, didn't want us around. Jimmy and I were a distraction to her limelight parade. But she couldn't get away with the same treatment for Jane, though later she wrote, in her own pitiful autobiography, that we were both spoiled brats and she couldn't stand us.

The family walked to the arena while Afdera bitched about how bad Jimmy and I were. We had excellent seats in the shaded part of the ring. Across the ring were the cheaper seats, and, of course, all the people we had partied with the night before.

"Why are those people yelling and waving at you?" Dad asked.

"Oh, no, Mr. Fonda, they just recognized *you*," Jimmy said.

"Then why would they be yelling at you two?"

"Well, they, uh . . ." Sure enough, we could hear, "*Himmy!
Himmy!*" and, "*Peteer! Hey, Peteer.*"

"People we met last night, Dad."

After the third bullfight, I began rooting for the bulls. One matador
let his bull leave the ring alive, much to the thrill of the spectators.
But the picadors, whose job it was to thrust long pikes into the shoulders of the bull again and again, had done too much damage already,
and I'm afraid the poor bull was wasted. We met Ordoñez, Luis Mi-
guel Domenguin, and other matadors and watched their elaborate
costume preparations. They drove around in cartoon Rolls-Royce-
like, enormous, ornate, old-fashioned limos. Another world. Jane reminded me that we *did* meet and had lunch with Ernest Hemingway.
How could I forget . . . too hung-over.

I felt relief when we left Spain. I can't even remember the drive
back to Nice.

. . .

Once back at the villa, Jimmy and I began looking for a place that
would rent us a Vespa, an Italian motor scooter. Dad approached *full*
"Colonel Thursday" when we broached the subject. He called Jimmy's father and tried to persuade him that it was not a good idea, but
to Dad's dismay, Jimmy's father thought it was the perfect vehicle for
the two of us, and sent the money we needed for the rental.

For my father the Vespa was a bitter pill. For the two of us it was
our ticket to the Swedes, or a table at an outdoor bandshell in Beau-
lieu, with Fats Domino playing, or the casinos in Monte Carlo and all
the bars in Villefranche sur Mere. We became very well acquainted
with the Swedish summer school, and had the girls and Carl Gustaf
down to the villa as often as we could.

Dad had arranged for the Sailfish to be shipped to the villa, but it
was a real trick to launch the thing from the rocky shore. We took it
sailing as much as possible, and one day we took two friends from
Pamplona sailing across the bay at Villefranche to the seawalk on the
the opposite shore. There was a small mistral cutting into the bay,
which would normally mean a wind from the north blowing offshore.
The locals seemed to call *every* storm a mistral, and our crossing was
relatively exciting. With four of us aboard, the hollow body was almost submerged, but we cut across the bay at a very fast clip, eating

a lot of seawater and growing wet and cold. When we made the relative calm of the waterfront, wasted from the crossing, we secured the boat and went to the nearest bar. We only had a certain number of francs, just enough to buy us all a round of, yes, Fundador, and a bowl of sugar lumps. This was my idea of a quick sugar boost to warm us and fuel us for the next move. We all knew what was in store for us on the return leg. A little closer on the wind, a little more of the hull submerged, a lot of tension on the mast.

The mistral was picking up, and we sailed as high as we could. We knew we had to tack twice—at the least—to make our bit of surge and rock landing. As we approached closer on a starboard tack, we all saw Dad. Rather, we all saw *Henry Fonda* standing on the bluff overlooking the bay, his arms folded over his chest at full challenge, daring us to blow it. We made the first tack and stayed close on the wind. This meant we were going into the storm, really submerging the hull and getting soaked and cold. We made the second tack and began to beat to our area at the villa's little landing spot, difficult to reach at the best of times.

The force of the mistral and the weight of the submerged hull and its passengers were too much for the little vessel. The mast snapped and left us foundering as we were forced by the rough seas upon the rocks. Dad shook his head and turned away, but Franciscus, who had been watching next to him, clambered down to the rocky shore and helped us save the hull and sail *and* our own butts.

The boom was fine, but Jimmy and I had to fix the mast out of our own pockets. Fair enough, but our own pockets were pretty bare. His dad came to our rescue again, wiring us the needed funds, and we had a new mast made in the nearby fishing village. Dad was disgusted by the episode and refused to talk to us.

. . .

When Jimmy left, I was pretty much on my own. Jane was in her own social whirl, and Dad and Afdera went to dinners and other social functions often. This was not Dad's style, and I could sense his frustration. But every time they went out, they would give me some francs, so that I could eat in a brasserie in Villefranche. Giuseppe and Fidalma, on the other hand, would always make enough hand-rolled, delicious pasta for me when they made their own supper, and I saved all the dinner money and spent it on after-hours pursuits.

After Franciscus left, Ted Kennedy came by several times trying to hit on Jane. All the junior officers from the *Newport News,* the flagship of the Sixth Fleet anchored in the bay, also came, ostensibly to pay their respects to Mr. Roberts (Dad was invited to have dinner with the captain and several admirals), but possibly to get a closer look at his daughter. Jane actually swam all the way out to the ship and was invited aboard.

Greta Garbo came by, took off her bathing suit, and went swimming, but she left her rubber swim cap on. Stavros Niarchos sailed in on his four-masted, black-hulled schooner, and dropped anchor in the bay; on board the ship he had a very good collection of Picassos he'd bought from Edward G. Robinson. Gianni Agnelli, the owner of Fiat, gave Dad a special Fiat with wicker seats and a striped canopy. There were lunches on Onassis's *Christina*, named after his daughter.

Pan, whom we had last seen outside the wall of the villa in Rome, in 1955, spent a few days with us, I think while Dad and Afdera were away. One rainy Sunday, she and Jane had a great giggle on me by sending me out to find some Tampax. I rode around on my bicycle searching for a store that was open, and when I found one, I tried to shake off my embarrassment by announcing loudly, in English, that both of my sisters were having their periods and needed Tampax. Of course the only word that the druggist understood was "Tampax." He looked at me rather strangely, so I repeated myself, even louder, the classic tourist trying to make himself understood through noise. That theory defies logic, but what can you expect from good old white trash America.

.   .   .

I left Europe from Paris with Aunt Harriet, my cousin Jayne, and the Volkswagen papers. They flew on to Omaha, while I stayed in New York and took advantage of the time alone at our house on Seventy-fourth Street to visit friends.

One afternoon I drove Mom2 and a friend named Roscoe Lee Brown up to see Edna St. Vincent Millay's bucolic, simple farm in upstate New York. As we drove back to the city, we were stopped by the state police. It was night and the T-bird's top was up, so the sup-

posed problem wasn't my youthful looks, but having too many people in the front seat (there was no backseat in the Bird, and the front
seats were designed to handle a third passenger). And then the officer
noticed that we had a black person as a passenger. He decided that I
was too young, that we were deviates, and that he was going to take
the matter to the top. I told him that there was no reason to require
Roscoe to show an identity card or driver's license, and this made the
trooper go bananas. No one was going to tell him what he could or
couldn't do. I stuck to my guns, and we were hauled off, without
having been charged with anything, to a justice of the peace. I demanded we be released, at once, asked that the judge recognize
Susan Blanchard as a legal guardian, and suggested that any questions regarding our friend and fellow passenger were racist and con-
stitutionally illegal. I was not sotto voce. My license was legal, and we
were on our way. Maybe my mission in life is to ferret out pockets of
abstract authority and crush them.

Roscoe, Mom2, and I drove around the city during the next few
days, visiting jazz clubs and singing old gospel songs that Roscoe
taught us while we cruised in the Bird with the top down. I'd met and
heard the cream of the modern jazz movement through Mom2 since
the divorce. Dad had no way to control what I did with her, and I
didn't tell him. I met Jerry Mulligan, Max Roach, Sonny Rollins, Charlie
Parker, Thelonious Monk, Joe Williams, John Lewis, Count Basie,
Dizzy Gillespie, Milt Jackson, Chet Baker, and many others. Listening
to them play was fabulous. Getting to hang out with them was even
better. One of them would sneak me a rum-and-Coke at whatever
club we were hanging. Years later, when the Henry Fonda Theater in
Los Angeles was opened as a memorial to Dad, many people came
up on the stage to say a few words. Joe Williams said that he remembered more about having Cuban Cokes with me in small clubs than
he did about Dad.

Mom2 helped me get ready for my next adventure by taking me
shopping for the clothes I'd need at college in Omaha, starting my
library with some great books, and helping me pack up my stereo and
other personal things. She basically did what mothers are supposed to
do; I of course thought it was extraordinary. And I flew off to my new
home, where Harriet had made one of her upstairs rooms into "my"
room. She'd had a large Japanese print of a Siamese cat framed and
hung on the wall, and bought a large chair and a study desk along

with a highboy and nice wooden hangers for my closet. She'd had the ceiling painted flat black at my wishful-beatnik request.

I was going to live in the city of my paternal grandparents, where my father had been raised. I saw pictures of family outings, but I could not elicit further storytelling.

Perhaps some of this reticence was the way of things in an older time, but I doubt it. I think that my family had a peculiar bent to privacy, and the strictness with which Harriet and Dad and Aunt Jayne (who lived in Pasadena) had been brought up prevented them from getting close to their own children, or to their own inner selves. One of the few things I learned from Harriet and Jack about my paternal grandparents was that Herberta Jaynes Fonda, my grandmother, had been a Christian Scientist, and therefore followed teachings that ascribed sickness to some inner failing or sin. It was an astounding religion for a family with no talent or desire for insightfulness to choose.

Such deafening privacy extended to my mother's family, of course. All I know of my maternal grandparents—and they were both alive until I was in my late twenties—is that my grandfather was a debilitated (and debilitating) alcoholic, who would come home some nights completely blasted, and mow the lawns, stumbling around and screaming invectives at the injustices of civilized people. My grandmother was patient to a fault with him, as she was with us during the years of our mother's gradual disappearance.

The elder Fondas would also be classified as dysfunctional these days, but for different reasons, and though I know little about any of my grandparents, I doubt I would believe a story told me by any remaining elder from either side. Too much time has passed, with too much opportunity to revise and sanitize the truth, and I hardly want to bother Harriet with my questions, now that she's in her nineties. My own father's autobiography, as told to someone else, was full of so much sanitation that it had little base in reality, but this is hardly surprising—Dad was never one to open up. Jane told me she wished he had written it himself, but though I agree that the result might have come a little closer to the truth, I'd stress "little." Dad was too shy, too intensely private, to truly expose the part of his history that mattered to him. I, on the other hand, am even more the "little brother with the big mouth," as *Time* magazine once dubbed me. "You wear it like a hat, Peter," Jane has said.

Thank God for Harriet's and Jack's patience and their efforts. I was living with a family who had fun, despite their bred-in-the-bone reticence. And I will never forget the love and patience the Colonel gave to me. When Jack laughed, it was like seeing Santa. Even when he was empty-handed he seemed to be carrying a large sack of presents each evening when he returned, elegant and handsome, from work. I don't know if he knew how deeply I was touched when he blew a large tapioca ball at me during supper one night. He handled it like a spitball, curling up the sides of his tongue and letting go.

Harriet was—still is—also quite beautiful, and both she and Jack managed to care about me and have a sense of humor at the same time. They were not about to pack up and split. Many years later, when she was eighty-seven, Harriet told me how she felt about my struggles. She referred to the words Dr. Thompson had used to describe me. He'd said, very seriously, "Peter can do anything he wants and do it well," Harriet remembered. "It must have been terribly difficult for you, having been told that so many times, Peter, and not knowing what you wanted to do."

I never thought of it like that. I was confused and very angry. But that could cause some confusion, I guess, being told you can do *anything* at the same time that you were being told you were a disappointment.

· · ·

The private school where I finished high school with chemistry and American history, Brownell Hall, was only a few minutes from Harriet and Jack's house, and Omaha University was only a few minutes farther south. My Volkswagen was still on the way, so I borrowed Harriet's car to get to both schools at first.

Brownell Hall was also an all-girl boarding and day school. God works his magic in strange and mysterious ways. The social habits of the Omaha young seemed behind what I'd dealt with on the East Coast. At first, I felt there was a sophistication gap, but this opinion only lasted as long as it took me to realize that any lack of sophistication was entirely mine. The kids in Omaha were just a hair different than the kids in the rest of the country, but they were more moral. Their "rules for engagement"—to use the military term—were laced thoroughly with the very morality that our generation would reject completely in less than a decade. They loved Elvis; they loved rock and roll; they loved to party; they sneaked booze to every function we had; they were into fooling with parental "authority," though not as radically as I; and they were just as desperately into "petting," though on a slightly different moral launching pad.

One had to be "going with" someone to pass into the kissing stage of a relationship. "Going with someone" was a territorial thing. Sex was a passionate thing, a gift given with love and shared without guilt. It was a necessity.

Adjusting to midwestern sensibilities was more difficult than I had expected, and at first I stayed with the girls from Brownell Hall. When my VW Bug arrived, I was happening with the Brownies. They loved to ride around in the funny little car, and we'd pack in as many bodies as possible and cruise drive-ins and other hangouts.

However, on most of my "dates" with individual girls, the young woman would sit as close to the passenger door as possible. I'd follow another couple in another car to whatever place or party, and their silhouettes were almost always pasted together. I'd check my pits, and they'd be fine, check my breath and find it sweet, so I couldn't understand why the girls I was with were so indifferent to me. I later learned that they were determined to show that they were not impressed that I was Henry Fonda's son.

But I never spoke of my dad or the things I had done and the places I'd been in the Big World. I never thought that I was special in any way. I tried asking my dates about what they were up to, what interests they had, what they had in mind for their lives. The normal response was "I don't know," whether or not the particular girl seemed to be an airhead. Kissing was not part of the program. I opened car doors for them, helped them out, lit their cigarettes, attended to their wants as far as beverages or whatever, and never acted as if I expected anything in return. I walked them to their doors, always hoping for any small reward, and got none. On a rare occasion, I might be allowed a kiss on my cheek. I gradually believed this was a particularly midwestern moral standard, no touchy or kissy unless we were "going together." I was ready to do virtually anything just to get a kiss.

Whatever "sex" I was able to enjoy was with the nursing students at the med school. Aunt Harriet, sensing at least minimal activity, gave me the "facts of life" talk every young person was supposed to have at some point in their early years. It was hysterical, given what I had already experienced, but she was very serious about it. I had to keep in mind that she had raised two girls under the Junior League rules, and there was likely nothing in that rule book about what to say to a young man. I certainly wasn't going to quote the old saw: If you have a son, you only have to worry about one prick, but if you have a daughter you have to worry about all of them.

"Peter, you must stop dating those nurses. All they are after is your name and money."

I understood the name thing, but what money was she talking about? I couldn't even afford a radio. "You know what I mean" was the reply. I didn't, but there was no further explanation.

. . .

The house rules were that I be in my room, in bed, by ten o'clock on any school night, and eleven on Fridays and Saturdays. Harriet had raised two girls and that was the way it was done. I bargained my ass off until I pushed the Friday and Saturday time back to twelve. I also bought a set of headphones so I could listen to my music without Harriet knowing, when I was supposed to be in my room, studying, from eight to ten. When Harriet finally busted me, I was standing in the middle of my room, headphones firmly in place, conducting Copland's *Appalachian Spring,* swinging my arms toward the horns here or the strings there. I didn't even hear the door open.

"Have you finished your homework?"

"Oh, yes, yes." What a liar.

She didn't take the headphones away, but I stopped practicing for my career as a conductor of symphonic orchestras and sat at my desk doing my homework, or pretending to.

My first year at O.U. was fairly dull. The classes were behind those that I had taken at Fay in content and new material, and most of what I heard in my psych classes was so obvious that I wondered if I'd ever learn anything helpful about the problems I was having with my life. This was, after all, the main reason I signed up for psych. I hadn't dared say anything to Dean Thompson about my painful experiences upon my arrival in Omaha in the late spring of that same year, and I wanted to have some advance notice if the horror was going to repeat itself. Lacking any wisdom from my professors, my options were down to planning a quick escape to Mexico before anyone could throw a net over *me* like they did to Bill Hayward.

The summer of 1958, the family met in Malibu, at a house Dad had rented on the beach. It turned out to be the best house of all the places we stayed in during the entire "renting period," and for added continuity, Jimmy Gibson planned to spend the first few weeks with us.

Dad rented a new Ford station wagon and had the Bird driven out from New York. Jane, who'd had a bad experience driving on Cape Cod in 1956, did not want or like to drive, so Jimmy and I had wheels, sometimes the station wagon, sometimes the Bird. Robert Walker, Jr., who lived with his brother Michael at his mother's house two miles down the beach from us, had a '56 Austin Healey, and we had many good times. Lee and Paula Strasberg were renting a beach house on Santa Monica Beach, just a mile from the old Ocean House where Jane and I stayed in 1951 and 1954, and their son, Johnny, was happy to join us whenever he could. That made three beach houses, and three places to party; other friends, like Brooke Hayward and Jeffrey Gates, came to visit many times, as did Jack Hathaway. Giuseppe and Fidalma—the best part of the marriage of Dad and Afdera (perhaps the *only* good part)—were there as servants to Afdera and friends to me. My adopted sister Amy joined us with her nurse, Emilie Leiberher.

There was a fairly good surf off our beach, but I didn't have enough money to even rent a board, so inflatable canvas-covered mats were our surfing outfits. This wasn't a problem—Jane and I had become experts on them several years earlier. Playing in the surf and lying on the hot sand in the days, visiting friends at night: it was a fun summer, the kind of summer kids are supposed to have in an almost perfect world.

Bobby Walker threw a party with plenty of booze one night. I made a date with Alana Ladd, Alan's beautiful daughter. She was blond and buxom. It was a marvelous party. I spent most of my time necking with Alana, but I couldn't keep my eyes off Jimmy's blind date, someone Bobby and Michael had fixed him up with. She was unusual, with gorgeous eyes and a Mona Lisa smile.

Jimmy and I drove the two girls home in the Bird. Alana sat on Jimmy's glasses, by accident, as we crowded into the car. As soon as we were on our way back to the beach, I began to grill Jimmy about his date. Her name was Susan Brewer, and her mother was married to Noah Dietrich, Howard Hughes's right-hand man. Jimmy thought she was kind of a cold fish, but somehow I doubted that the girl I was fascinated by could be, though we had spoken only a few words.

Several weeks later, after Jimmy had returned to his summer place in Maine, I decided to add my house to the party circuit. On the day of the great event we made up the guest list at David O. Selznick's hillside Spanish mansion, where Bobby and Michael lived part of the time with their mother, Jennifer Jones, and Selznick, their stepfather. The Walker brothers and Bill Hayward had once surprised Jones and Selznick in a compromising position at the mansion, and the adults' response had been to build the boys a stilt house for their use alone, another extension of the Haywards' separate-house-for-the-children policy. But for most of us hosting such parties had to be guerrilla stuff, meaning no notice. Notice meant too much exposure, too much of a chance that parents would find out and impose their rules and, more than likely, their rejection of the whole idea. We knew, of course, when our different parents would be out at a late-night shindig. I don't remember where Henry and Afdera planned to be that night; I probably didn't give a shit, beyond the simple fact they'd be out.

I asked Bobby about the girl who'd gone out with Jimmy, Susan Brewer. I'd wanted to get to know this beautiful young woman who intrigued me. He gave me her number, I heard a wonderful "yes," and the planning went ahead. I called Giuseppe, told him about the party, and begged that he say nothing to Dad or anyone else. He simply asked what we wanted for food and drink. I suggested pizza, a large salad, red wine, some broiled Italian sausage, and a big plate of antipasti.

The party was a huge success. There was a large, low table in the living room, made of very thick pieces of mahogany, dovetailed and laminated together with many thick short legs. Cleared off, it was a perfect dancing platform, and so we all danced. Susan Brewer danced wonderfully, and we had a grand time. I kissed her and she returned the kiss with feeling. Lost in her eyes, but found in her kiss.

A few days later, Dad and I flew to Las Cruces—on the lower east coast of Baja California—in a small private plane, to fish for marlin and sailfish. It was extremely hot in August, and there were no other guests at the hacienda. Unlike the predawn trips we'd taken before, this time we got up around eight, had a nice breakfast, and set off at

a civilized hour. Before two o'clock, we had caught our limit of sailfish and marlin and headed back to the dock. Dad took a nap and I
went swimming in water that was as warm as the air. I dove for lobster, using a thick sock as a glove, and brought back five nice bugs.
We ate them for dinner that night.

The next day was a repeat of the first day, with fresh lobster again
for dinner. We flew on down to Cabo San Lucas and stayed at a resort
hotel still under partial construction, where we were the only guests.
It was so hot that I lay in a large fountain for as long as possible, and
slept soundly that night. By the end of the trip I'd caught enough
marlin and sailfish to last me a lifetime. Dad was proud of me—
though silently—and that made my summer.

. . .

When it was time to head back to school, Dad, in a move that was
quite out of character, asked me to drive the T-bird back to New York.
Johnny Strasberg volunteered to be my codriver and off we went. He
had a bag of pills that his sister, Susan, had given him to help keep
him awake. They were called "Dexies," but we never needed one.
We drove old Route 66 back to Saint Louis, and stopped at all the
goofy roadside attractions. It was hysterical. I especially remember a
sign that began to appear when we were just inside the Arizona border, and read WINSLOW, FOR MEN ONLY. Johnny and I were certain that it
was a billboard for a brothel, and stepped on it. It turned out to be a
clothing store for men.

We were not given much money for the drive. But we did get to
drive Route 66, the world's most famous highway, and made the drive
to New York in record time: seventy-three hours, with an E.T. of just
under four days. We ate some of the Dexies for the last leg, and
though they made us stay awake, the drive turned into a total grind.

I had just enough time to see Mom2 and go for a drive in the country before I headed back to Omaha. Earlier in the year, I had sold my
VW and bought an MG TF1500, but now I saw that the MG was a
liability in the winter and traded it in for the 1957 Ford Custom Tudor.
"Custom Tudor" meant no frills, no chrome, two doors, with three on
the column. But the Ford had a radio, and though I hated the look of
the car, it did have a nice large bench seat in front.

In those days, one's car was one's world. While we were in our cars, we were in our very own living rooms without parental control. One of the particularly good things about my living room, the Tudor, was its capacity. Eight of us could cram ourselves into its big American body, and as not everyone had a car, mine became a limousine. It was a perfect double dater, though I preferred to be alone with the ladies most of the time. The beatniks loved it. Everyone would kick in a buck for gas and oil, and we'd drive to coffeehouses and listen to poetry read to jazz or into North Omaha, the black district, and listen to all kinds of new music.

Some of my friends were not so sure about going to the black district for *any* reason, but their attitude was a mystery to me. One of only four or five stories my father told us about his family background was about the first time he witnessed true racism. My grandfather had taken his son to his print shop in Omaha and, from the upper windows, made him watch the lynching of a black man. Dad said he was frightened and disgusted by the experience, but his father had not spoken a word to him before, during, or after the terrible incident.

I had a favorite passenger that fall. The spring before, just after I'd bought the MG, I'd been fixed up with a blind date for a dance at Peony Park. When I picked up my date, I was speechless. She was absolutely gorgeous. Tall, strawberry blond, with a figure that shut down any other woman I had been with. She was intelligent, she loved the car, she thanked me when I opened the door for her. She asked me about my dreams about the future and told me about hers. We danced to Stan Kenton's big band orchestra. I was in ecstasy, feeling her body move with mine, seeing a smile that stopped my heart. She whispered in my ear that I was the best dancer she had ever been with.

She was considered a farm girl by the townie dorks, from a small town called Bennington where her family lived in a simple but large one-story farmhouse. I thought she was my own peerless Rita Hayworth. Her name was Jackie Grau. She was what I had fantasized about, and I fell madly in love. We took long walks on her family's farm, talking about the world. When I would bring her home after a date, we rolled around on the beautiful hardwood floors, kissing and caressing as if we were on a down-filled mattress. She let me explore her beauty and explored me in return. I was in the very heaven I thought I would never find. Her grace and beauty allowed me to

forget my anger and confusion about the life I saw ahead, whenever
we were together.

That summer, while I frolicked in Malibu, Jackie of course had
other dates. One night that fall, as I drove her home to her farm,
feeling close and protected, headlights from another car exploded in
my eyes when I turned into her driveway. Jackie yelped—it was some
frat boy with whom she had canceled a date to be with me. He took
it personally, and the duel was on. I backed out of her drive with the
wanna-be boyfriend right on my front bumper. I drove in reverse for
the next fifteen miles, sliding from one side of the country dirt road
to the other—evasive tactics to keep him behind me, so to speak.
Then, at an advantageous moment, I was able to spin around and
drive forward, still keeping him behind. He thought Jackie was his
property. Jackie was never *anyone's* property.

And thus we dueled back to the big city. My Ford was straining on
its engine mounts, and we could hear the fan blades cutting into the
radiator. Jackie's friend was driving an Olds Rocket 88, a much faster
car than my V8 salesman special Custom Tudor. Were it not for my
practicing with the Bug, he could have easily forced us off the road
and god knows into what. Overheating was just a kiss away. I was
standing on the horn, hoping to rouse a cop. No chance.

He fell back when we reached the lighted roads of the city, and it
took some fairly daring maneuvers to lose him. We made the safety
of Harriet and Jack's house and ran inside, where we fell together on
the couch in the living room, holding on to one another in passion
and fright. Unfortunately, our arrival roused the household, and the
Colonel, my cousin Douw, and Harriet all walked into the living
room. I suggested that Jackie stay the night—she could have my room
and I would sleep on the couch until I could drive her home in the
friendship of the daylight. I plotted, immediately, the move to my
bedroom, when everyone had returned to sleep.

Fat chance. The Colonel and Douw decided to drive her home in
a proper, moral manner. The only gift was the relative privacy of the
backseat. Douw and Jack kept their sleepy concentration on the road
ahead, giving the two of us the moments of privacy we needed.

Things faded away eventually. Jackie now lives in Arizona and has
two children of her own. She made me feel important, but she never
made me feel she needed me. The last time I saw her we passed each

other in cars and spoke briefly. She told me she was joining the Peace Corps, and the idea that she had volunteered made me feel great. All along I had felt she was a special person, an intelligent woman with grace and beauty. I told her I would always love her, wished her luck with her life, and watched her drive away.

chapter *Seven*

*M*y father had begun his stage career at the Omaha Community Playhouse, and while I lived in Omaha I appeared in several productions and worked backstage as a prop assistant, set painter, and sound-effects operator in the same building where my father had taken his first step onstage, more than thirty years earlier.

I was also as involved with the university's theater department as possible. I danced and sang in the chorus of *Guys and Dolls*. I received an award for best supporting actor for a role as a butler in another production. My opening line in the show was, "You screamed, sir?" During one performance, a chandelier accidentally broke loose and fell on the dinner table, startling the actors and audience. The leading man bellowed *"John!"* I came onstage and repeated, "You screamed, sir?" During an earlier performance of the same play at the Playhouse the disaster had been a grandfather clock, which, on its own whim, fell flat with a grand crash. That time I came onstage saying there was no need to scream, sir. Both times the audience roared with laughter.

Another time, on the stage at the university, I was cast as Elwood P. Dowd in the play *Harvey*. It is still a mystery to me why *I* was chosen to play the part of a seventy-eight-year-old man. I was nineteen and looked twelve. We only had three shows, but I studied like mad. Dad, without my knowing he intended to visit, came to the second performance, entering the audience when the house was going to black and hiding at the act breaks. Later, he surprised me, standing just outside the greenroom in the shadows and told me how much he had liked my performance. He was dressed in a tuxedo and had a scraggly beard he had grown for his TV drama series, *The Deputy*. He remarked that most younger actors, when playing much older characters, tended to wobble and wheeze far beyond the reality of the character. He said I made none of these mistakes, that I made him believe he watched a character named Elwood P. Dowd, a character that his best friend, Jimmy Stewart, had once owned on the Broadway stage almost a decade earlier. My heart leapt to my throat. What a compliment coming from my Dad *and* Henry Fonda.

Laurens van der Post suggests that there is no such thing as coincidence. As I was writing the paragraph above, my wife buzzed me in my office and told me to turn on *The Tonight Show*. There was Bridget Fonda talking about how she came to realize that she wanted to perform. To act. She was in high school, playing the part of Nurse Kelly in *Harvey,* and during one of the rehearsals, someone watching began to laugh at some piece of business she was doing. She realized that she could make somebody laugh, or perhaps cry, or maybe think.

It was *Harvey* that touched my soul and let me know that I was going to act, onstage, on Broadway. The night of our final dress, before our director, Dr. Clark, had given us our notes, I was pulled by something I can't describe to go for a walk in the rain with my costume still on. As I left the stage from the door in the back, I passed by one of my fellow actors sneaking a shot of whiskey. Egan, I told him, I am going to take my rabbit for a walk in the rain. Something profound was happening inside me, and a walk in the rain with my eight-foot rabbit seemed to be the best thing to do just then. I don't know why. But even more provocative, finally, was a performance of *Our Town*. I was playing the part of the drunken choirmaster, facing the choir and the audience from a raiser in the orchestra pit. A few lines into my routine I heard a loud whisper from the audience. It was two friends of Aunt Harriet's whispering, "Oh my god! He's drunk! Poor Harriet!" Such a rush, such sweet honey. The sex of the theater. When I got home, Harriet was waiting up for me.

"Peter, you're not going to believe this!" she said with a certain giddiness.

"Midge Sample called and told you I was drunk onstage."

"My god! How did you know?"

"I heard her whisper it, quite audibly."

"Oh dear, you're not upset by it, are you?"

"Are you kidding, Aunt Harriet? What a great compliment."

. . .

As I continued in school, I spent less time at my classes and more time hanging out with the beatniks. One spring afternoon, during philosophy class, I sat at the back of the room with my chair-desk in front of one of the windows. We were studying Francis Bacon and René Descartes. I leaned my head on the windowsill, looking up at the clear, blue midwestern sky. Far above us I could see the distinctive contrail of a B-52. I had been to the War Room at the Strategic Air Command, whose headquarters were twenty miles south of the campus. Something clicked in my eyes, like a flash on a camera. I sat bolt upright, raising my hand.

"Mr. Fonda." The teacher tried to sound incredibly bored. "You have not attended enough classes to be afforded a piece of our time, by way of a question."

By this time the room had filled with the usual light rumble as the B-52 flew overhead. "Sir, we are talking about philosophies that were suggested by men long dead." The rumble grew louder; the jet had already passed over the campus and most likely left the state. I raised my voice to be heard over the sound. "That plane flying over us right now is filled with enough H-bombs to obliterate China, a country that apparently does not exist according to our government, and on the side of that bomber is the insignia of the SAC. Below the shield is a ribboned motto, reading 'Peace Is Our Profession.' As none of us are about to be directly involved with something that was discussed over three hundred and eight years ago, and *all* of us could be directly entangled, within hours, in a thermo-nuclear war with a country that doesn't exist, in the minds of our leaders, we *should* be discussing the possible end of the world, and the philosophy of that motto and our government."

"Leave the class at once, Mr. Fonda!" Teacher was not amused.

I was on a roll. "I believe that we all should be excused from class, sir."

"Just you, Mr. Fonda, and make it quick!"

"How does the class feel about this, sir?"

"The class is going to feel much better when you are gone."

"You bet." I gathered my books and notes and began to leave. One by one the class also left their chairs and followed me out. Another blow for freedom, I thought.

"You were the one who froze up the parking meters that winter when you had the VW, weren't you?" one of the beatniks asked in a low and sensationally conspiratorial tone, referring to an incident when I rigged the school's parking meters so students could park for free.

"You bet."

"That's cool, man. Really cool. But the nuke thing was much better, man."

For me, the exchange with the teacher was not education, but performance. I knew that I was going to be an actor, a performer of ideas *and* nonsense.

As I look back at it all, my real lessons were being taught in the home I shared with Aunt Harriet and Uncle Jack. The lesson was learning to be a part of a family, playing cards with Harriet and Jack, and having supper in front of the television on Sundays.

Throughout the time I was in Omaha I heard very little from my father, or Jane. Perhaps they assumed, rightly, that aside from Christmas and summers and the *Harvey* parachute visit, I was best left alone with Harriet and Jack. But I told Harriet that I would *never* miss any graduation of *my* children, as my father had missed my honors graduation from Fay. That I'd at least call, send a present, *anything,* if I couldn't be with them for a birthday. That I would be there when my children needed me, would talk with them about life and the things that they felt were important, and give them love, demonstrate my love for them, hug and kiss them and leave no doubt about my commitment to them. I think I have done all of the above. But I am getting ahead of myself.

chapter *Eight*

*T*he realization that I was bound for the profession of a stage actor calmed me and gave me a sense of direction. A goal was in sight, though I knew it would take years of study and work to near it. But another powerful thing happened to me at roughly the same time. I met Eugene Francis McDonald III, and my relationship with him changed my life.

He was two years my junior and when he started classes in the fall of 1959, the local newspaper published his net worth as the heir to the company his father had founded, Zenith Radio Corporation. I found this offensive and so was glad to be asked to befriend him by Dean Thompson. He was solitary and needed to make friends and be understood, Dean Thompson said, and I was the best person for him to get to know, the one who was least likely to be impressed by his money or his background, to have preconceptions.

I'd met McDonald briefly before. Now I went to the administration offices, asked about his class schedule, and waited outside the appropriate classroom.

As the students piled out of the room, I spotted him and followed him down the corridor. I'd been told his nickname was "Stormy." I called out, "Stormy, remember me? I'm Peter Fonda, we met briefly—"

"Yeah! I know."

"If you don't have anything going on, maybe you'd like to have some coffee or something?"

We went to the cafeteria and got some coffee, and, just like me, he used a lot of sugar and cream. We sat and talked about everything we could fit into the time we had. He trusted me with his innermost thoughts and circumstances immediately, and I did the same. In less than forty-five minutes, it was as if we had known each other for the entirety of our lifetimes.

Stormy was my height but dark and well built, a little like a larger version of Montgomery Clift. He'd grown up in Chicago, and his father, "Commander" McDonald, had been world famous for his Zenith Trans-Oceanic battery-powered portable radio, and photos of American soldiers listening to the Trans-Oceanic for baseball scores constantly appeared in newspapers, newsreels, and magazines like *Life*. Legend has it that one New Year's Eve, in Chicago, when the Commander went to his office garage to get his car, he came upon five guys listening to the festivities that were already underway in New York City on a radio. The idea that men would listen to a radio bringing them the earlier midnight cheers and bands playing in a different time zone for a New Year's that had not yet happened in Chicago gave him the idea of the power of radio as a medium. The Zenith portable radio became a must in every house. Pan had one, and it was certainly the first portable I ever saw. He made the best and most expensive portable radios and, because of a close family member who suffered from a hearing loss, the best and least expensive hearing aids.

The Commander had died the year before, leaving Stormy in the hands of a legal guardian, Eugene Kinney. Kinney was a distant relation, but he had no problem overcharging the trust for everything he could get away with, including the milk Stormy drank and room and board in his large Chicago house. Stormy had to return soon for a trial: his father had divorced his mother early in Stormy's life, and kept sole custody of his son and daughter, but now the mother was trying to claim a third of the estate. He gave the story straight to me, without any twists, and I understood too well. I pointed out that, though it might be hard to accept, his mother was probably using him as a pawn. She'd been bought off in the divorce, had abandoned her children for money, and had given up the right to be considered a mother. She hadn't fought for him then, and now she was fighting only for money.

There were mysterious parts of Stormy's life that I let him unfold at his own pace. Many things were different about our relationships with our fathers, but there was much more that we shared in an innocent yet conspiratorial way.

I was concerned that he didn't get dragged down by his selfish mother, and told him what I knew about my mother, and her abandoning me so early. I told him that I was sure there was something more that was being kept from me, and that no one in the family would talk to me about it. He said maybe it was better that I didn't know; it was a long time before I told him about the day in 1953 when I opened a letter I thought was from my mother.

Stormy went up to Chicago anyway, and came back knowing that he *was* only being used. It angered him. It should have. But who, in the name of hell, was I to pass judgment? When we shook hands as he departed for Chicago, in the grasp was an energy that I cannot describe. I loved this man from the moment we met in the stairwell. I told him only a few of my family experiences at first, but he knew at once that we were in the same boat.

He was concerned about my past interfering with my present, and was remarkably good—at least then—at avoiding this problem himself. He wanted me to learn to laugh more. We often went to the drive-in movies in the Vette, just the two of us. I'm sure that many people imagined that we were homosexuals from the amount of time we spent together, but I never gave it a thought. I knew I wasn't and I was sure that Stormy wasn't. Other nights we spent at a local Texaco station with the Corvette up on the lift, and I learned a great deal about engines, camshafts, the whole works, all the car stuff I'd dreamed of as a younger boy.

We had a friend who worked the late shift at the station, so we had free access to the lifts and tools. We tuned exhausts, changed rear ends, tuned the fuel injection. We'd drag race all comers, and never lost, and every time we crossed the line, we cut those Buells loose. We cruised the local haunts with the Vette loping along in first gear. It was our calling card. Anyone into cars knew we were running a radical camshaft and were looking for a race. And *everyone* wanted to beat Stormy. He taught me how to drag, how to heat up the tires without moving the car and without letting the rear end dance too much. I became good at it. We felt that we were untouchable. We never took any money for our wins, even though the races all started out with a wager.

Brownell Hall was putting on *Stagedoor,* and they needed to have two male actors. It was a gas. Stormy was very cute and very funny, and all the girls loved him.

Harriet and Jack had him over for supper many times. They liked him, too, and they knew I needed the friendship. During one supper at Jack and Harriet's, Stormy pulled out a cigarette at the end of the meal.

"My goodness, Stormy, I didn't realize that you smoked."

"I took up smoking a few months ago to stop sucking my thumb," Stormy calmly replied.

"Oh, Stormy, stop it," Harriet said, thinking he was being outrageous.

"No, really, and it worked." I hadn't known about his thumb-sucking, but I believed him totally. He told me later that quitting was a major breakthrough for him. His honesty and forthrightness were an inspiration for me.

. . .

My sisters faded into the gray void, the running story of our family, all of us scattered and creating our own new selves. I'd heard, by way of Harriet, that Jane had gone to Paris to study, or perhaps to play. Harriet said she was rumored to be in the company of a notorious playboy.

Dad forced Jane back to the States, and during Christmas vacation in 1959, we gathered at the house on Seventy-fourth Street. Afdera's gremlin presence ensured the family mood was just as murky as ever. We saw Amy and Mom2 briefly, but Grandma Seymour was in California, and Pan was in Europe, having last visited in 1958.

When I returned to Omaha in January of 1960, I was shedding the old skin of a grievous life and taking life in my own hands. I wanted to say good-bye to the dark, silent, booby-trapped thing that had been my "family."

A little later that spring, Harriet woke me one Saturday morning with a news clipping about Bill Hayward. Isn't that your friend, she asked? The AP article, from Ames, Iowa, said that William L. Hayward, son of the famous producer and entrepreneur, Leland Hayward, was marrying a local Ames girl in Topeka, Kansas. I was out of bed and on the phone to the paper in Ames in a split second, and I was told the wedding was happening that evening. I started calling every hotel and motel in Topeka asking for Leland, and when I finally found him I said I wanted to come down. He arranged and paid for the entire trip, which included a charter flight from Kansas City to Topeka—the only way I could make the wedding in time—and checked me into the same motel with Brooke and Bridget.

Bill was dressed in the uniform of an 82nd Airborne paratrooper, and it blew both of our minds that I was there. He had told the doctors at Menninger's that he wanted to join the 82nd, and he was going to marry his shrink's sister. They took that to mean he was fit to resume normal life and let him out after four long years and the hospital record for escape attempts. Bill and his bride left right after the service, and I went to the motel with Bridget and Brooke. We celebrated with champagne and whatever other alcohol we could find, and stayed up late, talking about all the time that had passed since we last were together. I kept hoping that Brooke would go to sleep after the champagne, and I would be left with Bridget. The color of her eyes was a mysterious blue, shivering blue, silver blue. I loved her.

·   ·   ·

When the semester ended, Stormy headed off to his island in Ontario. I had no intention of returning to college that fall, and hoped to get into a summer-stock theater group that summer. The Omaha Community Playhouse didn't offer a session, and at Harriet's suggestion Dad gave me the $350 needed to join the group at the Cecilwood Theater in Fishkill, New York, under the well-respected guidance of Lonnie and Irmadene Chapman and Kurt Conway. As an apprentice, I built and painted flats, and worked on props, lighting, sound, and building and striking sets. Apprentices helped the other actors run lines, ushered and cleaned the theater, and listened to the professional actors, hoping to glean any trick or technique. It was work I had done before, but this was just an hour from New York City and Broadway. And, from time to time, apprentices got to play in a featured role. Just being in a supporting ensemble was a treat.

All the apprentices stayed in a large old house. Irmadene made all our meals and was a wonderful den mother. I had a large room, with no roommates, on the top floor. Large room, only one person? Party Room. I had driven from Omaha with my conga drum and jazz records and stereo in the '57 Ford, and we'd add pots and pans for jam sessions. We talked about our hopes and the very hard reality of getting a role on or off Broadway. We drank wine, lit candles, and smoked, thinking ourselves sophisticated. Candles. Cigarettes. We listened to the soundtrack from a movie about James Dean over and over, even though we had never seen the film.

The theater ran a new play every week, with the next play in rehearsals while the current one was in performance. Mondays were dark, almost—two rehearsals for the next play were held, with a dress rehearsal Tuesday afternoon, hours before opening night.

Of the many jobs each of us had to do every show, getting the props was the most fun. The theater had a truck; I had a large trunk in the Custom Tudor, a driver's license, and insurance. I was sent out many times to pick up a couch or table and chairs and such. But every time there was something to pick up at a place called Craig House, someone else was sent. At first, it meant nothing to me. But when the pattern became clear, I wondered why, and when I asked, I was told there was nothing strange. Kurt Conway snickered and said I was a very paranoid kid. Something was fishy in Fishkill.

When the last performance was over on Sunday, the sets were broken down, or "struck," in stage parlance, and the new sets were built before dawn and Monday's rehearsals. The apprentices were split into a strike gang and a build gang, and we all worked into the early hours of the morning, when the lights were hung while the props and the set changes were rehearsed and the actors studied their blocking. The morning stuff was done by the strike gang, who had had a bit more sleep. By afternoon, everybody was in action.

We looked forward to the time off, when we could sit in my room and smoke, drink wine, listen to music, and fall asleep for eight good ones. Many times, guys and gals would fall out right on the floor, exhausted. The more maternal young women made sure everyone got back to their own beds.

On the weekend of the Fourth of July, I was on the build gang, and while waiting for the sets to be struck, I drove to the little town's pizza hangout and had some beers. The owner of the local diner, a man with whom I'd chatted all summer, sat down next to me at the bar. After a moment or two he spoke.

"I knew your mother."

"You did?" I was surprised.

"Yep. I'd see her from time to time, you know."

"No, I don't know. What do you mean?"

He pulled out his wallet and removed a yellowed newspaper clipping. Carefully unfolding it, he put it in front of me. My eyes were perfect in those days, and I saw the same photograph of her that had been in the *New York Times* for my birth announcement, but the copy was very different. *Frances Seymour Fonda, wife of the actor, Henry Fonda, committed suicide yesterday morning at the Craig House, a posh asylum in Beacon, New York.*

I was stunned. I sat there for two or three minutes, speechless. He said other words to me, but I couldn't hear him. It was the fourth time my mother had died in ten years. A heart attack in 1950. In 1953, she was reborn for a few agonizing minutes, when I read the letter that was meant for Peter Teuscher, and died again. In 1955, in Rome, she became a suicide. In 1960, she died in an insane asylum on the Hudson River.

I already knew there was no heaven, but this stupid man made it quite clear that there was no god. Later, I wondered what on earth had led him to carry that clipping in his wallet for a decade.

I left the place and sped off to the theater, my tires making a wailing and moaning sound that was close to the noise banging around in my head. I fishtailed into the parking lot at the front of the theater and banged through the main doors, striding down the aisle and sitting in a chair. Everyone else knew. Knew *everything*! But not me. I felt as if I were going to explode into fragments of someone else's imagination, but I was very quiet. Rage can take on an almost peaceful countenance.

Someone must have called from the bar, because Irmadene came quickly into the theater and hurried up to me. She was very concerned and apologetic. She told me that they didn't know what to do about the whole thing; she told me that they didn't want me to get upset. Lonnie came up, too, and I could tell he felt very bad. Neither of them could have possibly known that no one in my family had *ever* told me the truth. I explained to them that, in the ten years that had passed since my mother's death, *no one* had been honest with me.

I was berserk. I drove toward the Hudson River as I exited the grove of big beautiful elms that stood tall against the world of non-theater people—civilians as I call them now. I knew which way to go. I sped up to ninety miles per hour as ten years of anger and bewilderment twisted around in my brain pan, and stopped just about two hundred yards before the driveway to the asylum, suddenly imagining what might happen when I rolled in there, so late at night, and demanded to know what had happened to my mother. *This guy is nuts. Get the net!* I truly felt that they would grab me and stick me away.

I whipped the Ford around and headed back to the theater, tires still screaming and heart just as twisted as when I'd left the bar. I was doing ninety as I approached the straight stretch that passed the theater. Directly across from the grove of elms was a large open field, and as it was the Fourth of July weekend, there was a big fair going on in the field. Suddenly a '55 Mercury sedan pulled out of the fair and onto the two-lane highway. They had no idea that an actor from hell was bearing down on them at a high rate of speed. I knew I was in deep trouble right away. The Ford was light, and when I tapped the brakes the entire car started to float. I kept hitting the brakes and the car kept floating, its tires moaning. I was headed right for the rear end of a Merc full of people, twenty yards away and still going sixty. I pulled into the left lane to the astonishment of the guys in the Merc, who saw a car perpendicular to them, in a full drift, passing them at sixty into a line of three or four oncoming cars. I pulled the emergency brake out all the way and stood on the main brakes. As a result my car bounced off the left rear quarter panel of the much heavier Merc, spun around, and came to a stop facing the direction I had come from, right beside the trees.

The Merc had been knocked off the road, and the driver of the Merc—a mad, *very* mad, volunteer fireman—came across the street. He yanked me through the window and threw me down on the pavement. A beating was inevitable, so I went into a full craze, not a real stretch that night. I screamed nonsequitur filth and lunged at the man on all fours, trying to bite his leg. He realized—belatedly—that he'd driven into a nightmare, and instead of kicking me, he desperately tried to get his leg away from my foaming mouth. By this time, Lonnie and several others had come through the grove of trees and pulled us apart. I kept swearing and trying for his leg, and Lonnie made him get back into his car, yelling at him to let me alone.

We all went to a justice of the peace, with me still simmering invisibly, and Lonnie and Irmadene did their best to explain to the judge that I was unbalanced because of what I'd learned that night. In the end, I was ticketed for crossing the double yellow line and made to pay for the repair of the other man's car. When we got back, I checked my Custom Tudor. Not a scratch, but the Mercury's left rear quarter panel and rear fender were demolished. I went up to my room and didn't come out for a day and a half, much, I'm sure, to everyone's relief.

My father was in Los Angeles working on a television series; I don't remember where Jane was that summer, but in 1962 I read an interview she'd given to *Colliers*. I learned—death number five—that our mother had killed herself by cutting her throat from ear to ear with a razor, one she'd apparently secreted behind a photo of her children during her last visit home.

. . .

The summer rolled on, all of us trying to act as if nothing had happened. *Amazing Grace,* a new play by Studs Terkel, was going to have its first performance at the theater, and the privilege of having an original play to perform was more than a treat. There was a young male supporting role up for grabs in the play, and all the young male actors were studying very hard for the part. I won the role.

The challenge of mounting a new play is a great thing for a stock company: the roles have never been done, and there's no prior performance to be judged by; *Hamlet* gets harder all the time. The chances that some New York theatrical agents would attend—and discover us—were high. And it worked—Stark Hazeltine, from MCA, the preeminent agency in the country, asked to represent me. It was the first original play, other than my own, that I had done, and the work was double trouble, as there was some rewriting going on while we rehearsed. I've never been more consistently careful in my life, but I did one incredibly stupid, irresponsible thing during that period

at Cecilwood. I drove one of the other actors into New York for a
meeting, which gave me a chance to do my own errands, call Stormy
on my father's phone, and leave with a bottle of Seventy-fourth Street
wine or vodka. We gave ourselves just enough time to get back, and
halfway there, the fuel pump quit on the Tudor. We were stranded on
a highway with no telephone anywhere near us, damned few pas-
sersby, and a matinee due to begin in an hour. A tow truck retrieved
us in time, but it was very unprofessional.

Near the end of the summer-stock season, Mom2 called to tell me
that Occi had died. Sad news for the whole world of theater, too:
Oscar Hammerstein II, my step-grandfather who had been so good to
me, who had given the world some of its finest lyrics, had died of
cancer much too soon in his gift-filled life. I went out to the grove and
sat against a tree and recalled the days at his farm in Bucks County,
Pennsylvania, playing cutthroat croquet with Stevie Sondheim and
others; watching Occi walk around his second-story porch as he
thought of the words to some of our greatest songs. *Here I am, your
special island.* I lay my head back against the tree, looking up at its
protecting arms that spread out across the sky, and I cried from the
depths of my soul. *Bali Ha'i may call you . . . Come away, Come
away.* I will miss him as long as I miss *anything.*

Happy talk, keep talkin' happy talk. I paddled on.

· · ·

At the end of August, after the last show was struck, I packed up
the Custom Tudor and left the group. Lonnie and Irmadene gave me
a hug and a kiss good-bye. I drove to New York, parked the Ford in
the garage with the '56 Bird, and left to help Stormy finish his summer
at his island.

Stormy's island was Pardsay Crag, on McGregor Bay in Ontario: a
twenty-acre glaciated chunk of granite with many beautiful fir and
pine trees, a huge main lodge, three smaller log buildings, a dock that
could handle an eighty foot boat, and a boat house with winter storage for eight smaller boats.

Stormy picked me up in Sudbury, and we drove to Whitefish Falls.
On my journey to his island, he gave me a tour of the area. There
were many islands, some with tricky passages, some with summer
cottages and log cabins and huge lodges. The Crosley family lodge,

the Carnation family retreat; a world-famous brain surgeon on one island and a private yacht haven across the bay. There were many younger people, party people, up for the summer, and they all waited for Stormy to arrive on his barge—used to bring fuel and other supplies to his island—and would go out in the bay at night for music and dancing and beers.

I spent two wonderful weeks there, then flew on to New York and the house on Seventy-fourth Street to retrieve the Ford. Next I went on up to Jimmy Gibson's summer place to goof around with him and our lady friends. Jimmy had a friend who was headed west and volunteered to be a codriver for me in the Tudor. We made it to Omaha in two days. I packed up all my clothes and belongings, sold the Ford, and flew back to New York to begin the search of all new actors—a job on the stage or, possibly, any kind of job. Leaving Harriet was very emotional for me.

I stayed at the Seventy-fourth Street house, which provided me with a bed and good food to eat, at the bitter price of living with Afdera. At Jane's suggestion, I enrolled in a modern-dance class, taught by a young man named Timmy Everett, to learn how the body moves, and how to make it move the way one wants. Bobby Walker, in New York to try his luck, stayed on the Lower East Side and took the class, too. The dance routines were hysterical, mostly because we were forced to watch ourselves in a mirror. While the rest of us were doing our best with a routine, I would see Bobby in the back, out there on a different trip. He was dancing, all right, but he was hearing a totally different drummer, on a count of his own. I took advantage of my relationship with Lee Strasberg to ask about auditioning for the Actors Studio, and to get some great eats from Paula Strasberg, who was still convinced I might waste away.

After six or seven sessions with Lee, he told me that it would be destructive for me to take part in the Studio's routine. He said that he had been watching me, in a way, for two years, when I would come over to his house for an afternoon gathering and some food, and noticed that I would always end up in his library reading some book about acting or drama. Lee said that the main thing taught at the Studio was being able to get in touch with one's inner self, and that my inner self was always about to burst through my skin. I had to learn to walk away from it all, learn to not act. Just be. He suggested that I see a psychiatrist. He felt that in order to use all the turmoil that was boiling just under my skin, I had to deal with the root of the turmoil. After the eighth session I actually asked him how much he would charge for treatment, and he loved the comment. "Well, you *do* pretend to be a psychiatrist, Lee," Paula said.

Most of the group I hung with had very little money—I was getting twenty dollars a week as assistance, thanks to Dad—so we all went to Horn and Hardart for food from a coin-operated, glassed-over wall of cubicles: sandwiches, mashed potatoes and gravy, hot meals or cold ones. The overhead at this restaurant was pretty low and the prices followed suit. We would sit there for hours looking over the call sheets for what was being staged in the city. I was fortunate—I had an agent, Stark Hazeltine and MCA—and I asked to be put up for as many plays as possible, even if I wasn't right for the part. I would read most of the plays that I found at Lee's. One was an oddball piece by a young playwright named Arthur Kopit, called *Oh, Dad, Poor Dad, Mama's Hung You in the Closet, and I'm Feeling So Sad*. I felt I was perfect for the part of the unbalanced young man. José Quintero was directing the play and I begged Stark to put me up for the role.

I got a reading. I'd been getting inside this character for several weeks and had the words down cold. I could concentrate on the advice Lee had given me: Don't act, just be. The young man in the play was as out of whack as I, so I felt that I could come up with some pretty intense stuff.

I went out on the stage for Mr. Quintero and listened to questions emerge from the blackness of the theater. I sat on the edge of the stage and answered each one as if I had been doing this kind of thing since I was born. I then got up and did the scene with as much nonacting as I could. I went through all these different emotions as if I were naturally schizophrenic.

Well, uh, that was very different, uh, Mr. Fonda. Thank you very much, was the statement from the black. I laughed and said, no, no thank *you* very much, and left the stage. I didn't get the part, but I still feel I could have blown the socks off the character.

One evening, Stark took me to a musical, *Tenderloin*. It wasn't bad, but it wasn't great. We had some dinner after, and Stark asked me what I was doing about an acting class. I told him about Lee, but said I needed to find a real class with other actors and scenes to do and someone to direct them. He promised to make some calls and help me find the right place. Bridget Hayward was supposed to have come to the theater with Stark and me that night, but I had been unable to reach her. I had called Tony Montgomery, one of her boyfriends, and asked if he had seen her or heard from her that day. He hadn't. I was worried and so was he. She suffered from a mild case of epilepsy. I went home, gave the signal to the alarm system, and went upstairs. Dad was sitting in the library looking very drawn and bewildered, and he had a drink in his hand. Very uncharacteristically, he asked me if I'd like a drink.

Something was up. I wondered what the hell Afdera had told him this time, but he told me to sit down. I was sure he was going to kick me out. Bridget has committed suicide, he told me. My heart began to race. I had great trouble breathing.

I looked at my watch. It was thirty minutes into the next day, and my very special Bridget, my very secret love was dead. There was nothing I could do. I couldn't even drink the scotch in my glass. I was weeping without any noise, afraid to look at my father. I heard him say, "Poor Leland." I got up, looked at him with tears streaming down my face, and said, "Poor Leland? Poor Bridget," and went up to my room. Now I understand his pain for his friend—Bridget was past feeling, but my father was a father, and the worst thing that can happen to a parent is to have a child die.

I was in a haze for a long time, stunned. Bridget's mother and my father's first wife, Margaret Sullavan, whom I adored, had killed herself ten months earlier. Suicide was happening far too often around me. I didn't return Stark's phone calls. I forgot about the acting schools. I stayed in my room for several days and only came out, finally, to go to the funeral, where I sat in the very back, next to Slim Keith Hawkes—Bridget's stepmother—so that no one else could see that I was crying.

· · ·

Dad was in the city rehearsing *The Critic's Choice*, and I was given the job of helping him run his lines. At first, when he would be late with his line, I would feed him the cue again or feed him the first few words of his line, just as I'd learned in Omaha and Fishkill. But Dad was a different kind of fish, and when I began to feed him the first few words, he'd snap at me. *I know the line, son!* Eventually, I realized that he knew the entire play, that he could have memorized the

phone book if it had been necessary. The long pauses after I had read
the preceding line were the moments of creating the character, when
he would visualize the moment, and how he was going to move or
stand, and the reasons behind every movement or stillness. He went
to his death refusing to admit that he was, essentially, a method actor.

As soon as I had figured out *his* method, I went to Lee at once and
excitedly told him what I had learned. Lee told me that that was what
I *had to* learn. He was right.

Meanwhile, life with Afdera was a constant source of embarrassment and annoyance to the family. She lived like a pig, and she was
always yelling at Fidalma and Giuseppe. They worked very hard
keeping the house, narrow but five floors high and with a huge basement, squeaky clean. It was a bitch to keep clean; most places are, in
New York City, and Afdera would leave the master bedroom a total
mess, with wigs, clothes, and underwear on every surface. I behaved
like a boy scout in comparison. She would stand in the middle of the
room and scream for Fidalma, who had to run up two flights of stairs
to understand what she wanted.

When Dad left the city for the out-of-town tryouts, I was left with
the bitch. I began to stay away for days at a time, coming back to do
my laundry and cadge some free food. I felt I was abandoning Giuseppe and Fidalma, but I think they understood. I stayed with Norm
Sample, a friend from Omaha, many nights. He had an old Zenith
television with a circular screen about four inches across. Instead of
rugs, we laid out a thick layer of cockroach powder almost wall to
wall. I cleared a path from the cot I slept on to the bathroom. I somehow felt that running to the toilet in bare feet on the powder was
more dangerous than coexisting with the roaches. The pad was right
above the printing shops for the *New York Times*, and the morning
printing, at four, was a wake-up call we were never ready for.

We roamed Greenwich Village, checking on the jazz joints and coffeehouses. I caught Bob Dylan that fall, and through my connections
with the great jazz men, we had an entrée to some other cool stuff.
Bobby Walker joined us many times. We would always go to the San
Remo Bar, where I would usually sit at the jukebox and pretend to
play the piano on the selection keys. People would drop money in
my empty glass on their way out. Many times we'd find Bobby Duvall,
the actor of the time, and hang out at his pad. I lapped up his words
of advice like a kitten laps up milk.

Things went from bad to terrible at the Seventy-fourth Street house. Afdera was telling Dad that I wasn't doing anything about finding a job, that I was having girls over to the house, that Giuseppe and Fidalma were going to quit if they had to keep on cleaning up my party messes, that I was being rude to her—you can make up the rest of what she said and not even come close to the full story she laid out for Dad, who was still in out-of-town tryouts.

One evening, while Afdera was visiting Dad on the road, I had a party at the house (the only one I ever had) and invited all my friends along with Jimmy's friends. Bobby came with his conga and I played the vibes. Giuseppe and Fidalma made a special meal for us. Homemade everything; most of my friends were low in the pocket, so the free meal was a full bonus. I doubt that they knew how good the food was, but they ate everything on the table and were happy as hell to be there.

Despite such nights, daily life and Bridget's death and the revelation of the asylum had put me into a full tailspin. When I'd asked my father about Craig House he stonewalled me again, and suddenly the entire world crashed on my shoulders. I couldn't make any decisions, and found it hard even to leave the house. When I did break the invisible barrier that kept me trapped, I wandered the streets in a fog.

Just at this time, I auditioned for a play that Stark had set up for me, *Blood, Sweat and Stanley Poole.* When I walked onto the stage and began to read, I was told that I was wrong for the part, too skinny. They were looking for a Bobby Morse type of actor, they said, and there was certainly no likeness between myself and Robert Morse. I told the black emptiness that I knew Bobby and offered them his phone number. I was dismissed and headed back to limboland.

I was short of breath most of the time, and I was afraid to talk to anyone. I spoke Italian with Giuseppe and Fidalma. They told me to see a doctor. I didn't know one and couldn't afford one anyway. I started to panic for no apparent reason. I called Uncle Jack, and it was very difficult to talk to him. He asked me if I was all right. I said no. Perhaps the fact I'd made the call spoke for itself. He sent me the money for a ticket to Omaha, and I fled New York.

I stayed with Aunt Harriet and Uncle Jack while I had sessions with Dean Thompson, who sent me to Chicago to be thoroughly checked up by his brother. The only thing physically weird about me was my blood sugar, which fluctuated rapidly. When I came back, I was put on a special diet. Dean Thompson had me waking up at six each morning, walking for a half hour, and, upon returning, writing down all the things that I thought about on the walk. After breakfast, I rested for one hour while I continued to make notes about my thoughts. Then I went to Dean Thompson's home and spent a three-hour session with him, went back to Harriet's for lunch, and returned to the doctor's for the second session. This continued for a month, then tapered off to Mondays, Wednesdays, and Fridays.

The rest of the time I spent with Stormy. Harriet was concerned that I was interfering with my therapy when I was with Stormy, but the elixir of his company was as good for me as the sessions with the doctor. He'd taken flying lessons and we went up together as much as possible, flying every type of fixed-wing aircraft we could get our hands on. Often, too, I'd act as radio operator. I understood the lingo and had a knack for it.

· · ·

That Christmas at Seventy-fourth Street, Jane brought along another friend. At the table, Afdera mentioned that she and Dad had been married almost three years. "Feels more like seven," Dad replied. It went right over the *stronza*'s head, but I smelled the rat.

Jane asked me to stay with her one night at her apartment in Manhattan. She was going out with Timmy Everett, the dance instructor. I thought he was a flake, and her request was almost a plea, though she pointed out it would allow me a night away from Afdera. She put me in her bed while she and Timmy stayed in her living room on a foldout couch, and a couple of hours later I awakened to a loud argument. I rushed into the apartment's kitchen and found Everett with a butcher knife stuck in his hand, having pinned himself to a cutting board in a fit of pique. He was screaming, but he was a screamer anyway. I yanked the kitchen knife out of his hand and rushed to Jane's closet to find a nylon stocking, which I wrapped tightly around his arm as a tourniquet, using a pen for a twister, and called Bellevue for assistance with my free hand.

Jane freaked. Bellevue's primary fame was in dealing with insane people, and once you were in there it was hard to get out. Exactly, I responded. That's where this little motherfucker was going for a very long time, as far as I was concerned. I felt Jane had wanted me to spend that night with her to witness this Napoleonic creep in action. My job, as her only brother, was to get it all straight, and Bellevue was the perfect solution. But Jane begged me out of it and hauled Timmy off to a different hospital.

. . .

Back in Omaha, I was still in therapy with Dean Thompson, but I had regained control of my life and no longer felt like a Future Member of Menninger's. Norm Sample's father had sold me a Falcon, not a hot car at all but a car, and another example of my increasing freedom.

One afternoon, Harriet called me at Stormy's and told me in a worried tone that my father had just called, and she needed to talk to me at once. The very tone of her voice made me want to say no, but back I went, finding her in her breakfast room, very upset. Sit down, she said. Your father is divorcing Afdera, and he is very concerned that you'll be upset by another divorce.

"Upset?" I said. "That's the best news I've heard all year." I asked her if she was all right. She said she was fine, a little bewildered by my euphoria. I told her I had to get back to Stormy to tell him the good news. A week later, I sat at my typewriter and wrote a long letter to my dad. I told him that I loved him very much, no matter the strained life we all lived, and I would continue to love him no matter who he was married to or how many times. I never heard back, but one of his agents said to me that he was quite moved by the letter.

I learned, as I approached my twenty-first birthday, that I would be inheriting some money from my mother's estate, just under $500,000. I could be independent now, keep myself fed and housed until I could get a break in the theater. I believed totally that I would get onstage one day and never look back, and this would give me the time to learn and the way to pay for it.

Once I knew what "your money" had meant, back when Aunt Harriet had warned me about the nurses and my name, Stormy and I plotted what car I should get. I went to the Chevrolet dealer and ordered a silver 1961 Corvette with a black interior and convertible top. A huge engine and a four-speed transmission were all part of the $4,000 deal. A week after I turned twenty-one, the car arrived. We changed the exhaust manifold and had four pipes turned and tuned into two for each side of the big V8. I put on the least restrictive mufflers I could find and I was ready. I had to be careful when I was accelerating because of the noise, but the car was fast, and as soon as I had insurance, I headed east for New York.

chapter *Nine*

I had a grand time hosting my own welcome back party at Horn and Hardart. I took Laurie Peters—who was playing the ingenue in *The Sound of Music*—out to dinner after the show several times, and when I'd pick her up I'd park right behind Mary Martin's 1936 Rolls-Royce. Mary would pull away so royally, waving good-night to me, and Laurie and I would blast away sounding like a rocket lifting off.

At dinner one evening, Jimmy Gibson told me he had been waiting for his date at Sarah Lawrence when a guy came up to the desk and asked about Susan Brewer. I had been trying to find her since our first date in Malibu. Bobby Walker always seemed to draw a blank about where she lived.

I called Sarah Lawrence immediately.

"Hello?"

"This is Peter Fonda, Susan."

"I was just thinking about you. That's amazing!" she said.

"That's a *sign,*" I replied.

I asked her out right then. She had classes. How about the week-end? She was going to Princeton for a weekend date. I'll drive you down there. Oh, no, I'll take the train. No, come on, I'll drive you; anyway, I have to take my car out for a higher-speed drive than the city allows. I have to blow the carbon out. It wouldn't be out of your way? Hell no. It's just barely enough road time, and I'm on my way to Vineland to watch a friend race formula cars. Well, okay. And she told me when to pick her up. I was a nervous wreck, but I was also thinking of what her date would think when she arrived in my car.

She was waiting outside when I arrived at Sarah Lawrence. I asked if I was late, and she said no, but she could hear me coming for several minutes. We laughed and were off in a neck-snapping millisecond, with me doing everything possible to be the total antithesis of an East Coast Ivy Leaguer, including taking her for a gourmet lunch at a turnpike restaurant.

She was prettier, more exotic than I'd remembered, and she'd matured. I hadn't, but I felt triumphant as I roared up the long tree-lined drive to Princeton University. That car made some noise, but it looked great. Nebraska plates, beautiful paint, real wire wheels with knock-off hubs, and the four exhaust pipes tuned to perfection. High-class white trash.

I saw her as many times as I could, picking her up after classes and bringing her back by midnight. Rules. Sometimes we spent the hours talking at Jane's apartment on Fifty-ninth Street, while Susan cooked a simple meal. We kissed, but that was all.

Jane having just finished her first film, *Tall Story,* and in rehearsals for the play *There Was a Little Girl,* stayed with friends, giving Dad her apartment when he left Afdera. He was working on Broadway in *Critic's Choice,* and not necessarily happy to see me drive into town in a new, expensive—in his thought pattern—sports car. Then again, he didn't have much to be happy about, period: Afdera took her time vacating the Seventy-fourth Street house, and when she finally exited she did it with typical style, taking all their belongings, ripping out two fireplaces, and pulling out window frames so that she could abscond with Jane's bed. Dad, to do him credit, was very strong about this last assault, and made her give everything back.

But in the meantime, we were stuck with each other. I tended to park the car right in front of the apartment, so he couldn't miss it. As Susan and I would arrive at the apartment, Dad would be on his way out to the play, and when it was time to return her to the world of rules, he was just coming home. He gave us some pretty cold looks, and eventually pulled me aside and said I was embarrassing him. I didn't understand and asked him to explain. He said that it was quite obvious: we waited until he left, would come to the apartment and, uh, *you know*. No, I said, I don't know. Have sex, he said. I wish, I told him, but all we do is talk.

He didn't believe me, but I couldn't have cared less. I was twenty-one and not under *anyone's* authority. As long as you're staying in this apartment, you'll follow my rules, he said. It's Jane's apartment, I said, and there are no rules here between you and me. He was very upset, but I was angry at his assumption. I asked him if he had noticed my car, he stormed into the bedroom. I walked down to my fast car and roared off to pick up Susan.

As we spent more time together, I began to tell Susan all about my life, or what I knew of it. The process took more than one evening. We'd have drinks (she liked brandy Alexanders; I had scotch and water), and we'd talk, or rather I talked. All the gory details and the fun ones. Finally, as we sat on cushions on the living room floor, she asked me why I was telling her all this stuff.

"I want to marry you, and you'd better understand what you're getting into." Wow! Where did that come from? Right from my heart. It never occurred to me that I was presuming she'd want to.

I took her back to the rules, endured more nasty looks from Dad, and after a month in the city left for Omaha. I missed Stormy, and I had to get back to my therapy. Susan and I promised to write often, and I had her send her letters to Stormy's, because the mail was delivered there three or four hours earlier than at Harriet's. At first, Harriet thought I was hiding something from her, but when I explained the timing, she said, Peter, you must be in love. Yes, I am, I admitted. Does she love you? I don't know, I admitted. I guess I'll find out. Harriet gave me a hug, and I went to my therapy.

About two weeks later, while I was at one of my sessions, Stark Hazeltine called from New York. The producers wanted me to read for *Blood, Sweat and Stanley Poole* a second time.

I told him that they wanted a Bobby Morse kind of look and had turned me down. "Look, Stark, I haven't gained an ounce since they last saw me, so I don't think they'll change their minds. Besides, I've got my therapy and . . ."

"They'll pay for you to fly back, first class."

"Pay my way back?"

"Yes. Of course. Round trip." As if I should have known. There was much I had to learn about the "business," but the free ride back meant I could see Susan and be next to her.

"I'm on my way, Stark." And I was. The day after I got there, I went to the reading. I did it several times, and in between I could hear low murmurs, out in the big darkness. Finally, they said I had the role, thanked me for flying back on such short notice, and I said, "No, no thank *you* very much."

I took off to rent a car so I could see Susan, which had been my real reason for coming east. We left Sarah Lawrence as soon as she could get away, and I drove around talking my head off and looking for a place to spend the night with her. She was not having any part of that, so I drove around looking for a place to park privately. The weather was turning bad, and lo and behold, I found myself in front of the Cecilwood Theater. Just as the clouds let loose a torrent of rain, we pulled under the budding elms. We necked passionately and for a long time, having to break for breath and composure. The music on the radio was just right, and yes, Aunt Harriet, I was falling in love.

"You know, Peter, we would have beautiful children," Susan said.

God! I thought the boys were supposed to hand out the lines. I got her back to Sarah Lawrence just before she would be found out, and one of her classmates let her in through a side door. I drove around for hours singing "Oh, What a Beautiful Morning," over and over. When I got back to the apartment, I ran in and packed my bag to leave for Omaha. Dad came flying out of the bedroom.

"Where in the name of hell have you been all night?" he demanded.

"Out necking in a parking lot in Fishkill." I was almost out the door when I turned back. "I got the part! See ya."

• • •

I knew that I was on my way, what with the play and all, so I wanted to do something nice for Harriet. I bought her a movable dishwasher that could plug right into her sink and convinced Dad to go half and half with me on a new car for her. In 1959, he'd given her a Fiat 600. I told Dad that the 600 hadn't been much of a Nebraska car, and this time we bought her a metallic gold Corvair Spyder coupe, the hot one.

Susan and I had made plans to meet in Omaha in June on her way back to Beverly Hills. I was excited for her to meet Stormy, and Harriet had given her blessing to the visit. By the time she arrived, I was in full battle plan. She was to sleep in the guest room, and its wall backed up to my wall. When we said goodnight, I told her that if she wanted to see me, she could knock on our common wall. The night was extraordinary in every way. As a storm outside began to give the elms and atmosphere at Izzard Street and Happy Hollow Boulevard a new voice, Susan knocked. When we came to know each other in the biblical way, there was—literally—thunder crashing and lightning flashing.

Susan stayed four days, and Stormy flew down from Chicago to meet her. I had coached her to say, "Well, if it isn't everyday, run-of-the-mill, wishy-washy, dime-a-dozen Stormy," a phrase he'd used, from time to time, when referring to himself. It was important to me that they meet and like each other. But when Stormy stepped off the plane, he totally blew my mind. He was dressed in tight, yellow-and-black plaid pedal pushers. He had a box of Kleenex and was constantly blowing his nose due to hay fever. His socks were short, thereby showing his black hairy legs. After a moment, I realized he was being as outrageous as possible. He knew he was going to meet Susan for the first time, and was going for maximum. Susan, of course, didn't know any of this and went right up to him to say the magic lines. Aren't you everyday, run-of-the-mill, wishy-washy, dime-a-dozen Stormy? Nope, he said, and walked right by her. She was very upset, sure that he was a completely rude, deeply strange nerd, and found it hard to understand why I was so fond of him. We all went to the country club to swim and catch some sun, and Stormy demonstrated that he was not a total fool by waiting on her hand and foot.

Susan went on to California while Stormy and I goofed off in Omaha, which was hard for him because of his crazed hay fever. He was going to meet up with Roger Dunbier in Arizona or New Mexico and take a Volkswagen bus to Mexico, so we decided to drive my Vette out to California and pay a visit to Susan and her sister, Ruth. My rehearsals didn't start until August, so I had time on my side. We drove to L.A., spelling each other at the wheel with the top down for the entire trip. We got very cold, very wet, very hot and dry, and very tired by the time we cruised into the large stone courtyard at Susan's in the early morning darkness. We waited to see if the sound of the car had awakened anybody. No luck. We didn't know where her bedroom was, so we went down to the pool and fell asleep on the lounge chairs. We were aroused in the morning by the sound of the girls giggling as they looked down at us from the patio above. Stormy stayed for a few days and then left for Mexico. I stayed until I had to drive back to Manhattan.

Susan's father had left very early in her life, and when her mother, Mary Sweet, married Noah Dietrich, he became her father. Noah adored Susan and her sister, Ruth, and he was known as Pappy. My own life was wonderfully enhanced by knowing him. Noah's house was spectacular, a large Spanish Mediterranean villa with many rooms and a separate guest house, which I stayed in that summer. Every night that she would have me, I met Susan in one of the villa's rooms and made love to her. I had already told her that I wanted to marry her, but I constantly asked her if she needed me. Loving me was never as important as needing me; perhaps I felt that if someone needed me, they wouldn't leave. Love had certainly failed to ensure this in the past. It must have been a puzzlement to Susan, and she was never sure how to answer.

Susan had two stepbrothers, John and Tony Dietrich, and I got to know Tony very well. When I had to leave for the East Coast, Tony was my copilot. We crossed Nevada and Utah on our way to Grand Junction, Colorado, a nine-hundred-mile run in those days, on highway U.S. 6. Every time we stopped in Nevada, I played the slots and won big. Tony figured we paid for our beer and burgers from the winnings, and maybe several tankfuls of gas. We stopped for a day in Omaha to visit Harriet, then zoomed on to New York.

Tony flew back to California and I began rehearsals for *Blood, Sweat and Stanley Poole*. Part of the role required that I learn the entire manual of arms, including the Queen Anne Salute, for an M1 Garand rifle. It had to be perfect, and when done onstage, the drill was made more daring by adding a real bayonet to the routine, which came at the end of the play and was part of the proof of my character's outcome. I thought of the dance routines I had studied, but it took much more concentration.

I was onstage for all but the first three minutes. My character, Robert Oglethorpe, makes his entrance stage left, coming to attention just slightly left of center. While Darren McGavin strides around me, I remove several hundred connected paper clips, some melting chocolate bars, and a copy of Toynbee's *A Study of History*—a very hefty book—from beneath my army shirt. I played a recruit who cannot do the bayonet drill in basic training, and my character folds completely when called upon to charge a dummy with a fixed bayonet rifle, yelling, "Kill! Kill! Kill!" So Oglethorpe is sent to the quartermaster (McGavin) to help organize the stores, where the quartermaster learns he is a genius. He gives Oglethorpe the task of teaching a group of master sergeants some fundamentals so they can pass an aptitude test and remain in the Army until they can retire with full benefits. The camp commander tries to stop the sessions in many cruel and funny ways, but in the end, when challenged to prove that he can master his own fears, Oglethorpe does the entire drill routine with a fixed bayonet. A *real* fixed bayonet.

I began my performance utterly terrified, and at the end of the third act, while performing the drill, I owned the stage.

I was immersed in the show and our rehearsals but managed to call Susan every day and every night. Susan was planning on spending the year studying in Europe. I had felt from the moment I was on my own, that I would not last in life if I had to be alone. I didn't think I'd make it to thirty.

But as my professional career began, my possible aloneness loomed ever darker. I stayed at the Seventy-fourth Street house while I was rehearsing, which was a real blessing for me, because in the divorce with Afdera my father got custody of Fidalma and Giuseppe. When people say to me that I've gotten my break as an actor because I was Henry Fonda's son, they're partially right. As Henry Fonda's son, I got to stay at his house, eat great food, and not try to figure out how to survive in New York City on ninety dollars a week.

By the time we were ready to take the play for its out-of-town tryouts, Susan had agreed to marry me, and a great weight was lifted from my heart. She insisted that she only wanted a simple gold band, but Stormy and I had a different plan. We took Susan and Pinkie, as Ruth was called, to Mario Buccilatti's jewelry store. I had long admired his craftsmanship, and Gianni Bulgari, a close friend of Pan's, had recommended Buccilatti. I had gone there with Stormy many days earlier and looked at his wedding selection. When the four of us arrived at the shop, Susan had no idea what was in store. I knew that I wanted his simple but very elegant man's gold band, but played ignorant as rings were brought out for the future Mrs. Fonda to ponder, over her objections. Then the ring I had admired the most was displayed for her. It was a wide band with yellow gold as its border, filigreed and Florentine white gold as the main body, and a lattice-work of perfect diamonds setting off the center stone, a ruby. Ruby was Susan's birth stone. She glowed when she saw it. It was one of a kind, and she couldn't refuse.

Four days after I had opened on Broadway at the Morosco Theater, I married Susan Jane Brewer at Saint Bartholomew's. Stormy was my best man, and Jimmy Gibson was my head usher. It was the last time I would be with Jane, Pan, and Amy at the same moment, and I insisted that Susan Blanchard be at the wedding, along with Grandma Seymour, Jack, and Harriet. My entire family thought I was out of my mind getting married just as I started my career, but Noah Dietrich pointed out to Dad that as both of them had been married so many times, who were they to pass any judgment? Bless Noah. Jane very generously let the two of us stay at her apartment rent-free, a great wedding present. Pan gave us a full silver service beautifully engraved with the letter *F*. Dad didn't know what to do until much later.

After the play had opened, my pay had been raised to $290 a week. I was astounded. They would pay me that much money to do something that I loved? During the vows, when it came to "for richer or poorer," both Susan and I began to laugh. And at the moment when I was supposed to put the ring on Susan's hand, Stormy pretended to get the ring stuck on his little finger. The moment was a perfect equalizer.

Our reception, at the Pierre Hotel, was grand. Mary Dietrich had done a fabulous job putting the event together, and she and Noah had spared nothing for the apple of their hearts. All I had to do before the wedding was remind everyone that I was about to open on Broadway and couldn't be distracted. I was prevented from wearing my black cowboy boots. I accepted this limitation reluctantly, and the only pair of black shoes I owned had a hole in the sole. How perfect, I thought.

. . .

During the out-of-town tryouts before the wedding, I'd learned many things quickly. Constant change is the whole point to tryouts, and sometimes we had to go on without true rehearsals. One learns to listen very carefully to the other actors and not just remember cues. I learned to take my nervous energy and turn it around with a form of yoga, really a trick I'd been taught for long-range target shooting. I took long deep breaths and exhaled slowly while shaking the length of my body in a loose manner, and just before my entrance I took three more deep breaths and blew them out quickly. The result was my body stayed loose, and my mind concentrated on my character.

But on opening night at the Morosco, when all the big-time critics were in the audience, no help was found from my little method. I'd be the one-too-many-Fondas, the proverbial third man on a match, and they'd be waiting for me to screw it up. Fortunately, as I've mentioned, my character was *supposed* to be terrified, and by the show's finale—the rifle routine—I felt as if I *did* own the stage. At the opening-night party, when the papers came in, I'd gotten outstanding reviews. Walter Kerr said that even my eyeballs looked terrified.

Use it, wrote Stanislavski. Be it, he advised. I did.

. . .

After the reviews, the producers wanted to put my name above the title next to Darren McGavin's. I felt that I should stay in the featured category, if only so that it would be easier for me to take another supporting role in the next play. I preferred learning as a character actor to being burned as an above-the-title sitting duck. I did, however, accept a raise in pay.

But something was going wrong deep inside. Several times Susan found me in the living room, banging my head on the floor, and I was unaware of how I had gotten there or what I was doing. I had enormous mood swings that I could not explain. She called Stormy and asked him what he thought. He had never seen me like that, and wasn't much help. I tried to analyze these bouts as best I could. I recognized that I felt trapped living in an apartment with people living above me, below me, next door on either side. At the theater some nights, I would pound the walls of my dressing room until my hands ached and bled from the knuckles. That seemed to put me back in focus for the performance, and I couldn't put on my makeup until I was focused. My understudy, Jimmy Caan, befriended me and tried to discourage my method of release, but as soon as I was onstage, I was fine.

One evening, though, something happened onstage that really

scared me. It was a scene with me and the older master sergeants, and I was teaching them some basic chemistry, and I forgot all my lines. In the theater, when one actor "goes up," it is the responsibility of the other actors to get him or her back on track. I didn't realize I had gone up until the scene was finished and the curtain fell. I didn't even know where I *was*, until I saw the curtain. I was mortified and apologized profusely to my fellow actors. I wondered why they hadn't tried to bring me back to the scene, and Robert Weil asked me what the hell I was talking about. I'd done the scene letter-perfect, my best job yet.

I was baffled and sat on the couch at the apartment going over the experience until the next morning, until I finally realized I'd been *so* into my character that I had forgotten I was on a stage, in a play, reading lines, hitting certain positions, the whole thing. And as I understood what had happened, I began to cry with such deep relief. The thing that had happened was what most actors strive for each performance. Suddenly, one isn't "acting," one simply *is*. A very scary place to be, the first time. Every now and then, I get the rush, and realize I've done the job. My daughter, Bridget, has given me the words to describe the process. She says that good actors are pathological liars, men and women who *believe* the things they say as they say them.

I think Bridget is right, but for Susan, the life and strangeness must have been a strain, even in the beginning. At Caan's suggestion, I joined the other actors who were working on shows in town at certain night spots for an after-show drink. I met George C. Scott in Downy's. I went bowling with Albert Finney and James Earl Jones. It made me feel more attached. Sometimes Susan would join me, but I don't think she really liked being around actors and other performers, even though she had done some theater herself. It's a very selfish life. I usually didn't get to sleep until three or four hours after I got back to the apartment, and then I'd sleep until noon.

One afternoon, my agency called and asked if I was interested in doing a *Naked City*, a popular TV series. I pointed out that I was performing in eight shows a week and didn't see where there was time for that sort of thing. They'll work around your schedule, I was told. I wondered how they could do that, especially with matinees on Wednesdays and Saturdays. They'll pay you one thousand dollars, Monique James told me. I said I'd do it.

I was a naive young man, completely lacking an overview of the profession and lacking advice from my professional family. Moss Hart had said, "Speak your first lines clearly, and the audience will be sure they hear you, even if you mumble the rest of the show, but if you mumble your first lines, the audience will be certain that they *can't* hear you no matter how clearly you speak the rest of your lines." Sort of like, put your best foot forward; first impressions. He was absolutely right about the psychology of the audience, but I needed more advice than this.

The *Naked City* episode also starred Jo Van Fleet and a young actor named Martin Sheen. George Voskovec was one of the top-line supporting actors, and the show was directed by Elliot Silverstein. One of the show's leading regulars took a liking to me at once, and we spent our hurry-up-and-wait time talking about the proposed film *PT109,* a true war film about our president, John F. Kennedy. He and Kennedy were at Annapolis as young cadets, and he felt that I had the perfect look to play the role. I thought I was much too young-looking, but he was persistent, even phoning some pal at Warner Bros. to gush about how much I resembled JFK, and how like him I was in my smile, mannerisms.

Shooting around my schedule meant that I had about four hours of sleep after the play, and then I had to fly around town to get to the set of that particular day's location.

Before the show closed, fellow actor Bobby Weil gave me a book to read. He said that after working with me for four months, he was sure I was going to become a major actor and more than likely a producer, and I should read this book and try with all my energy to make it into a motion picture. It was Howard Fast's *Conceived in Liberty.*

Susan and I entertained occasionally, but we didn't know a lot of people in Manhattan, and she was alone for much of the time. After the *Naked City* stint, we moved out of the city to a bed-and-breakfast hotel upstate on the river. I commuted to the city, and my head-banging tapered off. The inn was old-fashioned and almost like a honeymoon getaway. We weren't making love nearly as much as I needed, but I laid that off to the frenetic energy of the theater and my own puzzling moodiness.

As soon as the show closed in January, Susan and I drove up river to Craig House. We both felt that it might be good for me to find out what had really happened to my mother. Get it out in the open. We spent the evening there; we saw the large pipe organ that our escort said my mother liked to play; I heard a lot of nice things about her, and we ended up playing pool with the man. I learned nothing new or revealing about Mother, regardless of my questions. I had gone right to the heart of the matter and found myself as stonewalled as ever.

Susan and I packed up our new car, a Facel Vega HK500, and headed west to Omaha, to spend a few days visiting Harriet and Jack and Stormy and John Haeberlin, Stormy's friend. We celebrated my twenty-second birthday, and I had my wisdom teeth pulled. When I had recovered, Susan and I were on our way to Hollywood.

The weather got better as we dropped south to catch up to U.S. Highway 66, the *only* way to travel to L.A. As we drove through the deserts of California at night, a rainstorm was passing to the east. We stopped and spent ten or fifteen minutes standing outside the car smelling the fabulous freshness of the desert after a rain. As we looked back east we saw a moon rainbow. All the colors of the spectrum were there, but in muted tones with a gray wash over them. I had never seen one before and neither had Susan. She spelled me driving, while I slept in the backseat. We wanted to make it to Los Angeles without stopping anymore. We wanted to be somewhere that was more like home.

When we first arrived, we stayed with Noah and Mary Dietrich. We were lucky that they lived in a large villa, so it wasn't like moving back in with the parents, in their apartment. We stayed in Ruth's room, large and comfortable, but it had twin beds, a very definite disadvantage.

A terrible fire had burned much of western Bel Air and Brentwood a few months earlier, destroying my first paradise lost and my grandmother's house, a canyon away. I'd taken Susan to see Tigertail the year before, and now, as soon as we arrived from New York, we went to see the site. But my sorrow was something that I couldn't share. I was numbed. Only the foundation, the stone fireplaces and chimneys, the tennis court, and the pool were left. Some of the grand old oaks had insisted on surviving. I drove to Grandma's and shuffled through the ashes. I tried to buy the burnt-down Tigertail place with the remaining moneys from my inheritance. Fat chance. Seventeen houses stand where 600 Tigertail rambled and rolled, seventeen rather big houses with not much property dividing them. I paddled on.

. . .

My first encounter with a major studio was very enlightening. The call from my fellow actor in *Naked City* had made an impression, and Warner Bros. called me to screen-test for the role of JFK in *PT109*. I met with Bryan Foy, once one of the Seven Little Foys, a vaudeville troupe, and now the producer of record for the project. My heart sank a little when I saw his office. It was littered with photos of the president *and* the coconut, the very one that had been set adrift by Lt. John F. Kennedy in the hope of reaching helping hands. What I saw was just surface stuff, nothing any deeper than a newspaper idea of the story. I asked if the motion picture was going to get into the real story. Foy looked at me as if I were from a different planet. What exactly did I mean, "real story?" I got into the PT boats and their history in the war—not one had sunk an enemy ship, and many were sunk by our own patrol bombers. The entire effort was for naught, but the men who served aboard these plywood coffins did so with great bravery, and the men of *PT109*, led to safety by their captain, showed as much commitment as any soldiers in the war. War is insane, I told Mr. Foy, and nothing seemed more insane within the concept of war than the PT boats, yet human bravery rose out of this insanity, and one man led his crew to safety through shark- and enemy-infested waters. Commitment to a higher cause despite the insanity of the mission.

Mr. Foy asked me to leave his office, muttering something about New York actors. The screen test went ahead regardless, and I was sent to learn how to speak like an Irish Catholic from Boston, how to say Fond*er* instead of Fond*a,* the very name I refused to respond to during Fay School roll calls, ten years earlier. I studied the subtleties under the guidance of a man named Dean Hargrove, and halfway through the lessons I put the question of the accent to him. I didn't want to sound like a nightclub act. The story wasn't about a Boston man reacting with bravery to an impossible situation, but about a man, any man, responding to duty without regard to his own safety.

It was about a common man who turned out to be very uncommon; a story about my father, if you will.

Dean agreed with me about the accent, but he was hired by Warner Bros. and did not wish to upset his career. During the screen testing, there were many reporters from the world press there to interview me. I thought that it was insane to have newspapermen on the set for a screen test. I'd never heard of a press stunt like that, and I was greatly offended.

The final confrontation took place on a soundstage rigged with a dock, water, and a real jungle mound of dense foliage. I was supposed to walk down the ramp to the dock with the coconut in hand and using *the* cane, while spouting lines in bad Bostonian. I agreed to do the scene, but I refused to do the accent—I did not want a stand-up's JFK routine as my first screen test. Much loud discussion ensued. Foy shouted that *somebody* should tell my father about this. Where do you think I'm getting my *advice*? I shouted back. While Foy was on the phone to my agents, I went to the director, Raoul Walsh, who I'd come to know well during the first hard week of testing. Walsh had shot my father's first screen test. He was a fabulous person who wore a patch over one eye, like John Ford, drank vodka-and-orange-juice from a pitcher and told stories about working with Errol Flynn and other great action-adventure actors.

I asked Raoul, who agreed with my reservations but had no control of the situation if there was anything like an actor shooting "under protest," and he told me to talk to the cameraman. The cameraman told me the procedure, and I told him to be ready. He was thrilled. Foy, looking smug, said that my agents were on the phone, and my agents, who were employees of the studio, told me I *had* to read the lines with the accent. The scene was done, the cameraman did his thing, and I gave it my very best in the accent for that single scene.

At the end of the next day, I heard Hargrove's account of what went on when Jack Warner watched the dailies (in those days, studio heads watched *all* the studio's dailies). When the footage from *PT109* came up on-screen, Warner leaned closer to the screen and took careful notice. All was quiet, until the cane, coconut, and accent scene rolled. Only a few seconds into it, Warner shouted to back up the film. When he watched it again, he noticed the slate, the piece of wood and blackboard with the clappers that identified the scene, the production, the producer, the director, and the cameraman and take number.

"What does that fucking slate say?" he demanded.

"Where?" someone asked.

"There, dammit!"

"The slate is upside down, sir."

"I can fucking see that, you idiot! What does it say on the bottom?"

"Ah, well. 'Under Protest, Actor,' sir."

"What the fuck does that mean?" Warner was going ballistic.

"It means the actor did the scene under protest," Dean Hargrove said from the back of the room.

"That silly son of a bitch! He'll never work in *this* town. Never! I'll squash him like a little bug. That smug little asshole!"

God had spoken. The next day, the *Daily Variety* and *The Hollywood Reporter* ran front-page notices about the entire affair: Fonda Flunks Screen Test! The trades had never before announced that an actor had failed a screen test, on the front page or back. I had arrived, in a manner of speaking.

Cliff Robertson eventually landed the role, and he did it without an accent.

The next thing the agency wanted me to go for was *The Virginian*, a TV series based on the original motion picture. I was wrong for that, too, but I was saved by the stage—a role in *Under the Yum-Yum Tree* was offered to me for a three-week spring run in Mineola, Long Island. Back to basic stock, but this time I was paid: $2,500 a week plus a deluxe room at a nearby motel and a Mercedes Benz for the run. Margaret O'Brien and Hugh Marlowe were the other leads. The comedy is about a young couple—not married, but on their way—and the man who lives across the hall, who puts the moves on the young woman.

While I was working the play on Long Island, Susan continued to look for a house of our own. It was extremely kind of Noah and Mary to let us stay with them at the villa, but we needed our own place. When I got back from Mineola, she took me immediately to a house nestled in a hidden canyon in the hills above Sunset Boulevard. It had been the pool and tennis-court house for Myrna Loy and Arthur Hornblow's estate, and it was perfect. Their former house was on a ridge, just east of the pool house with its 250,000-gallon pool and full-sized tennis court, walled on two sides and high fenced on the others.

Tall old pines lined the northern part of the property, and carob trees and tall sycamores bordered the rest. All this was on just under two acres in the middle of Los Angeles, yet the property seemed like a place by itself. The asking price was $100,000. I had three Treasury E Bonds that were due and had to be moved, and for $33,000 down and twenty-five years at 6 percent (thanks to Noah's influence), paying $490, I felt I could earn the payments easily. It was one of the smartest things I've done in my life. We had our own place, in which to grow a family and to live quietly and privately.

chapter *Ten*

*T*he summer of 1962 was a season of television work, especially on the "anthology" shows, which featured a new guest star every episode. These hour shows were the best proving grounds for a young actor. One could learn about the camera without the great pressure of a full-length feature, and the pay was good, usually around seven to eleven thousand dollars for seven days. Then, in the late summer, I landed my first feature film role, *Tammy and the Doctor*, with Sandra Dee, Macdonald Carey, Beulah Bondi, and Adam West. I played the doctor.

The movie was to feature Tammy's first kiss in the series written around that character, and when the time came for the first kissing scene, everyone on the set became very intent, with much press and security hanging around. I got along swell with Sandy, and I had been practicing kissing for ten years. To the regulars on the soundstage at Universal Studios it was a big moment, but to me it was just a kiss.

I kept teasing Sandy about the Big Moment, but as we rehearsed, every time we came to the kissing part, the rehearsal was stopped. When we were finally ready to film it, the entire soundstage took on a somber but intense attitude. *Roll camera! Quiet, please! Speed! Marker! And . . . action!*

She was a good kisser, and we both got into it. *CUT! Cut!* The director came up to us and pulled me aside.

"You can't open your mouth when you kiss her, Peter," said Harry Keller.

"What? I can't open my mouth?"

"Right," he said, and walked back to the camera. I pondered the command. It made no sense.

Quiet please! Roll camera, roll sound! Marker . . . CUT!

"Peter, come over here," Harry said, and repeated the no-open-mouth bit. I was baffled. How does one kiss for real and *not*? Made no sense. So Sandy and I decided to give the next take a real biggie, and on action, we put ourselves totally into a passionate kiss. Well, that blew everyone's mind but ours. Another lecture, and the "code" was finally explained to me. Wow. I was back in Omaha in the mid-fifties. Open-mouth was a cardinal sin; in those days the studio mentality offered bedroom scenes in which the actors had to keep one foot on the floor at all times, whether or not the audience could actually see the feet.

On the next take, we kissed with our mouths closed.

"Perfect," said Harry Keller. "Print that one."

As soon as the camera was cut, Sandy and I went into a two-minute passionate kiss, to the profound shock of the set. I wondered about the mental stability of the motion-picture industry.

Mac Carey and I had our own fun. During a heart operation on Tammy's grandmother (Beulah Bondi), the camera never traveled below our upper chests, so we uttered surgical mumbo jumbo while clipping hemostats to each other's surgical gowns.

The best thing that came out of the movie was the invitation to come to Las Vegas and watch Bobby Darin, Sandy's husband, perform at the Tropicana Hotel Casino. Susan and I went for the weekend and were given a grand each to spend at the tables and comped at all the shows. I was awed by the performance of the backup musician, Jim McGuinn. He played an acoustic twelve-string Martin guitar with a flourish that I had never heard. His expression hardly changed as his fingers danced on the neck of that exquisite instrument, but the music had such emotion. Bobby, wisely, stepped back out of the light and let McGuinn have the moment. Later, McGuinn and his wife joined us at a table, while we were insulted, hysterically, by Don Rickles. Sandy and I and Susan played at the blackjack tables on our one-thousand-dollar-a-night comp, and many people gathered around us to watch, which is exactly why we were given the grand. An unknown singer named Tom Jones opened for Bobby.

. . .

That fall, I landed a role in Carl Foreman's *The Victors*, a film about the Second World War to be shot on location in Italy, France, and England, with interior work done at Shepperton Studios in London. Its theme was simple—war is hell, war is hell, war is hell and war is hell—but it was chock full of cameos and supporting actors with marquee names, including George Peppard, Eli Wallach, Jeanne Moreau, George Hamilton, Albert Finney, Vince Edwards, James Mitchum, and myself.

I reported for work in England in late October and spent the next several weeks waiting to start my part. Susan and I rented a flat from Wolf Mankiewicz on the top floor of a brand-new—actually not quite finished—building very close to Piccadilly Circus and Harrods. We were the only tenants, and we froze most of the time. Milk was delivered each morning, and the run to the bottom floor to retrieve it before it froze was a nightmare. There was no heat in the bathroom, and the law in London forbade electric heaters, something to do with electrocuting oneself in the bath. The towel racks were heated, however. It made no sense. We went to an appliance store to buy a heater and an extension cord only to learn that the appliance had to be installed by a licensed electrician, apparently to ensure that the heater couldn't be placed in the bathroom. I went to the electricians on the set and had them make a series of extension cords, bought two more heaters, and had the flat at least livable.

After a month and a half, I had to get out of the country. Susan had friends living in the suburbs, and she opted to stay in the Big Gray. I flew to the Bahamas, rented a Triumph, and soaked up the warmth. After a week of diving and sun, I felt ready to take on London and Carl Foreman. But on my first day of shooting, Carl took me aside.

"Now, I want you to understand, Peter, that here, on my set, you are just another actor. Being Henry Fonda's son doesn't mean a thing. So you must not think of yourself as special."

He said all of this with his eyes closed. He had no idea how close he came to being knocked flat by me. But the closed eyes bit saved his little pompous ass.

"Fascinating," I said. "Absolutely fascinating."

His eyes popped open. "What? What did you say?"

"I said it's fascinating the way you talk to me with your eyes closed and your head tilted back."

"Did you understand what I just said to you, young man?" He was snapping now but his eyes were closed again, chin in the air, a perfect target.

"Yes, Carl, I did. And if you say one more word to me about it, I'll pop you so hard in the sternum, you won't be able to stand up straight for a week."

His jaw was slack and I left him in the stairwell. Another blow to abstract authority. The film was overdirected, and it showed, but Carl's out-of-nowhere rant was piddling demagoguery compared to what happened soon afterward.

One afternoon I was hanging out on the set of a bar in France, chatting with Peppard and Eli Wallach, when three actors in costume came onto the set. It was all wrong—they were wearing modern uniforms, and we all knew how much of a stickler Carl was for the right everything. I mentioned it to Peppard and ventured a guess that wardrobe was pulling a joke on him, and we all had a chuckle, knowing that Carl would have a shit fit when he saw them. These extras were really full of themselves, too, strutting around as if they were the real thing. And wouldn't you know it, they came strutting right up to me.

"Are you Peter Henry Fonda?"

"No, I'm Jane. Are you Dick and Spot and Goofy?"

"You're under arrest. You will come with us, now."

"I'm what? Under what? Are you fucking kidding me? "

They made a move to grab me, and I jumped at them. "Who the fuck are you?"

"U.S. Military Command Europe, and we are putting you under arrest for evading the draft."

"The fuck you are!" I was right in their faces, and all the other actors surrounded them, taunting them. "This is British property, you have no authority, and I'm not a part of the U.S. Military, so you can't touch me. Not one finger!" I was screaming, and the production manager, first assistant director, and my fellow actors pushed them out of the soundstage. It seemed that as part of the Selective Service system I was supposed to have informed the draft board before I left the country. I'd received my draft card when I turned eighteen; as far as I was concerned, it meant I was able to be served in New York, and have 3.2 beer in Colorado. I never related the card to some actual U.S. government boogie. I never thought of it, period. After this run-in I had to speak to some three-star in Brussels and promise to report to a draft center as soon as I returned to the States, but the close encounter really spooked me.

Susan and I moved to the Carlton Towers just after New Year's. It was heaven compared to Wolf's flat, and pretty soon all the other American actors moved there. The hotel had room service and a very good kitchen, and it was warm. Jim Mitchum, Robert's oldest son, whom I'd known for years, moved in, too; we'd spent a good chunk of our free time colonizing London together. One evening, he told me he was getting some very good bhang, and asked if I would care for some.

"Bhang?" I had no idea what he meant.

"Yeah, man, some great fucking bhang!"

I looked at him blankly.

Mitchum stared at me with those marvelous hooded eyes, just like Big Bob's. "Bhang, man. Pot, grass. You know, *marijuana*!"

Ahh, marijuana. "Of course, man. I've just never heard it called bhang." I had never heard it called grass, either. I knew nothing about it, but Mitchum's father had, after all, been a Hollywood pot pioneer.

Mitchum told me he'd phone me when we got back to the hotel. On my way home from the studio, I had the driver stop at a tobacco shop where I bought a little corncob pipe. It looked like a toy, but it would do. Then, filled with excitement and wonder, I awaited the momentous appointment in my room. Susan was skeptical about the outlaw threshold, but I assured her that bhang was harmless—I'd done it many times and, no, it didn't lead to heroin.

The wait seemed to last forever, and I jumped when the phone rang.

"Come on down, man."

My heart was racing. Mitchum handed me an envelope folded lengthwise. "Have you ever smoked shit before, Fonda?

Another new name for it! "Oh, no, I've ah, sure, man. I've done it many times."

Mitchum's eyes looked more hooded than usual. It was a long, awkward moment. I couldn't lose face.

"It's got to be cleaned, man. But it's real good shit."

"Cleaned?"

More of the hooded stare. "Yeah. Cleaned. You know, seeds and stems. Are you sure you've done this before?"

"Oh! Sure. Ah, it's, ah, I mean it's always been cleaned before." What the fuck did he mean? Cleaned?

"Come on, Fonda, you never did it, did you?"

"Sure, man, I just never, uh . . ."

"Call me in an hour. Okay, pal?" The hoods had turned into a Chinese effect. If I'd really known my bhang, I would have understood that Mitchum had already indulged. I had a lot to learn about the world of reefer madness, such as the fact that one doesn't clean grass with the tweezers from a Swiss Army knife, as I did the first time I entered the forbidden zone.

After carefully removing every seed and stem, I stuffed a small amount into the corncob souvenir and fired it up. Susan looked dubious.

"Like this, darling," I showed her how to take a puff from the pipe. Like I knew what *I* was doing. "Sip it as if it were a hot spoon of soup."

She tried, but although she smoked cigarettes, she was not ready for the herb. "No, no, like this," I said as I sucked more smoke from the pipe.

Twenty-two or so "like thises" later, I was bombed, and I was a happy boy. Susan, although she had tried to do the thing, was *not* a happy girl. She had coughed her lungs out, and this was the sole effect from the bhang, pot, grass, marijuana.

I ordered everything I thought I might possibly want to eat from the room-service menu. When the waiter came with the food, I was in the bed with the covers pulled up tight. Susan signed for the food, and I began to devour it. I finished the entire meal and deep in my skinny, stoned-as-a-monkey inner self I decided that I had found the magic potion. I *knew* the way to gain weight and make my father proud of me.

The next morning, I forgot all about the dreaded herb and room service and went on with my job. When we finally left gray, polluted London I was just happy to have finished my role without blasting the shit out of Foreman, who'd ended up shoring up my sanity, after the incident with the Army, by making an appointment for me with the father of Anna Freud.

Upon our return to the States, I reported to an induction center in downtown Los Angeles for my physical. I gathered the requested medical reports and drove off to my destiny on Broadway and Eighth, for a different moment on a different Broadway with a different group of "critics" waiting to nail me.

A written test came first, and I was stopped up short by one of the questions: Has anyone in your family committed suicide? If so, state how and where in the space provided. Another question asked if I'd had any major surgery and why. Whoever was going to be reading *my* test would be in for a big surprise. After the testing, we all went to a gymlike dressing room and were made to strip, locking our things in a cage and taking the key with us. We were given a folder of papers and told to follow a yellow line on the floor. The line lead us through all sorts of alcoves, where we were tested for eyesight, flat feet, and so on. When we all were undressing, I looked about the room, embarrassed by my skinniness, but what I saw astounded me. Compared to most of the other guys, I looked like a body builder. I was too naive to realize that they had all been taking massive doses of speed and not eating for weeks prior to the testing.

Things came to a head during the examination for hemorrhoids, the famous "bend over and spread 'em" part. The man in the white coat told us that he was a graduate of Harvard Med, as if this information might make the process more important or dignified. I raised my hand to ask a question. He said, "Yes?" but I motioned for him to come closer, right up to me, his face close to mine.

"If you touch my ass, I'll kick your teeth into the back of your head."

He backed up and went around the room saying the famous words, while I stood still, planning how I would put my left foot into his mouth. When he came to me, I did not bend over, but looked him straight in the eyes. He took my sheaf of papers, scribbled something on them with a red pencil, handed them back to me, and moved on to the next poor bastard.

We walked through a series of rooms in a certain order and were made to keep that order for the entire process. The young man in front of me had a right leg that was as skinny as my right arm. He was not going to be in the Army, that was obvious, but he was put through the routine as if he were going to be drafted the next week. I talked back to anyone who gave me an order. I told them I was a civilian, not part of their system, and if they wanted me to do something, ask me, don't order me. At the next station, a Marine major took us one by one into his office, and ridiculed the fellow with the thin-as-bone right leg. All of us were close enough to overhear the derision, and I was next in line. When the boy with the bad leg was dismissed, I refused to enter the office, and called the major a sadistic, commie, faggot asshole loud enough to be heard by everybody. I wanted to make the man come out from his desk and take a punch at me. I ventured that he had won his rank by sucking some general's dick. The major bolted from his desk and rushed me, but he never fully came through the door, and instead grabbed my papers from my hand. Noticing the red pencil remarks, he ordered me to report to room 10. I told him I didn't follow orders, and before I would move from the line, he would have to ask me politely. He was very red in his face and he sputtered around his office, finally asking me to please report to room 10.

Room 10 was the psychiatrist's. He asked me to please sit down while he went over my papers. He noticed I was an actor and asked me if I was acting then. I told him that I was unemployed at the time, though I knew he meant if I was acting for him and the others at the induction center. Looking at the reports from Ossining Hospital, he asked me if I had tried to commit suicide. I told him that it had been an accident.

"So far, then, your mother's been the only suicide," he said.

I got up, spit in his face, and stomped out the door. I followed the painted line right out of the building and crossed the street to the lot where I had parked my '63 Corvette. As I approached the lot, I realized that the keys were with my clothes in the locker. I turned around and headed back to the building. Just then a Marine sergeant came running up to me carrying an overcoat. I told him not to touch me, that I was a civilian, and he told me that I would be arrested for indecent exposure, and to not be a fool. And I truly hadn't realized I was naked.

I dressed and waited on a bench while they decided what to do with me. Finally, someone asked me if I wanted to eat lunch there or go on home. I went home. Later, I received my draft status in the mail. 1 Y. This meant that I could be checked each year to see if I was suitable for service. The letter said I was incompatible with the Army.

Now, there's an understatement. I tore the card up, sent it to the president, and never heard another thing about the draft.

. . .

Looking back from the vantage point of my fifty-seven years on the planet, I've learned that I overreacted to abuse of authority. I don't blame my dad for my uncontrolled behavior, but I do realize it was a reaction to his always being critical of Jane and myself when we did something wrong in our early years. There was plenty of criticism but no praise for our accomplishments as children.

As an adult, no longer having to accept or answer to abstract authority, as you will see, I would go over the top and out of control. I didn't understand it, and no one around me understood. I was a tinderbox in a furnace. When I found out I was unfairly accused, something kicked in and I would lose control. By 1989, when I started my medication therapy, I could look back at my outrageous behavior with embarrassment. This does not mean I accept abstract authority. I've just learned to keep control of my temper and mouth.

. . .

In the late winter of 1962 I read a book called *Lilith* and decided to try to buy the property. My agents learned that the book had been optioned by Robert Rossen, the famous director of *The Hustler* and *All the King's Men*. I thought that purchasing, developing, and casting a director and actors and finding the funds was a possibility well within my grasp. But such was not the case.

A script had been written, and my agents obtained a copy. After reading it, they suggested that I try for the role of Vincent Bruce, the leading male role. I was totally wrong for the part and insisted that they submit me for the role of Warren Evachevski. They were planning to make me Disney's next young leading man, and they refused. I took a plane to New York and went at once to Rossen's office, unannounced. He was a short man with a gruff countenance, a bulldog. I told him I was the actor for the role, and he looked at me from behind his cluttered desk.

He gave me the once-over and snorted, "You're not Jewish!"

I reached across his desk and took the glasses from his face, putting them on my own.

"Now am I Jewish enough, Mr. Rossen?"

"You're supposed to be, ah . . ."

"In the script, I ask Vincent Bruce if he thinks I'm Jewish, telling him that my uncle was a Catholic priest, sir."

"I know that!" he snapped. "I wrote the damn thing!"

We spoke for a few more minutes, and then he asked me where I was staying. I told him that I would be staying at my father's until I heard from him about the part, one way or the other.

I sat at Dad's library phone and leafed through one of my childhood books, *Call It Courage*. I began to read it again, maybe for the tenth time, and the ringing of the phone brought me back to my older childhood. It was Rossen; I had the part.

Filming was scheduled for five or six weeks starting in early May, in Maryland. Susan and I drove across the country in the Vette. On a rainy night in Columbus, Ohio, staying at a motel with roaches crawling the wall, Bridget was conceived. I felt it. I really did. It never occurred to me that we would have a son, and Susan knew it, too. When we were sure she was pregnant, we only thought of girls' names. We tried Jennifer. We tried Bridget. I thought of Bridget Jennifer, suggesting that, when she was older, she could choose whichever name she liked best. I remembered Susan's words, that stormy night in Fishkill, two years earlier. We would have beautiful children, she had said.

. . .

During rehearsals, Bob Rossen asked us all to visit the local asylum and observe the mentally unbalanced in the zoo, as it were. I refused. Bob insisted. I told him that I was never going to go inside an asylum, because I was sure that they would not let me out. He sensed that I was quite serious, and I agreed to attend a meeting with various doctors along with the other actors, which seemed to satisfy him. But during the rest of the movie he would sometimes watch me for hours.

After shooting began, Bob came to my room and told me that if I didn't sign a five-picture contract he would replace me. I was astounded—after all, I'd already signed a contract, and the movie had begun—and I quickly bargained for my life. When the thing was settled, I had agreed to a six-year, multiple-picture contract. According to Bob, Columbia had demanded the multiyear contract, and to protect me from being forced to play in junk films, Robert Rossen would have the right to refuse the movie for me.

After we had wrapped the Maryland location, the company moved to Locust Valley, Long Island, where we would complete the filming. Soon after we got settled in our new motel room, Susan had very bad morning sickness. There seemed to be nothing that could help her, so she made me a large platter of Jell-O and flew back to California and our increasingly cozy house. Rossen told me he was keeping me on the shoot longer than I had expected, so that I could earn more money and stay close to him. We had an odd love-hate relationship, but he was always the Super Chief. The crew took a liking to me and saw to it that I had the best dressing room and the best attention. I was treated like a prince, and I thought about Carl Foreman's speech to me that afternoon in London, the year before. Rossen asked me about Foreman, and I said I thought he had overdirected the film and *acted* more like a dictator than a director. I sensed that there was some bad blood between the two directors. Bob asked me how I thought a director should act, and I said I thought a director should act like an axle of a big, spoked wheel, giving support to all the spokes that kept the rim in line.

"That's a tall order. When did you come to that conclusion?"

"As soon as I watched Harry Keller direct *Tammy and the Doctor*," I said. I hadn't seen Keller do a thing that might pass for direction. "And I think I can learn to be a great cameraman, especially after I finish watching Eugen Shuftan work this film."

Eugen Shuftan was a French cinematographer who was considered the best in black-and-white. I made friends with Joe Coffey, the camera operator, and constantly asked why each decision was made. He was nice enough to answer every question. I was working with the cream of the crop, and I knew it.

My next film, *The Young Lovers,* was lined up, but we needed to cast a strong leading lady. There was a three-week pause in the filming of my part in *Lilith,* and I wanted to fly to the West Coast to screen-test some candidates, but Bob wouldn't let me go. He said that I was one of the best performers he had, and he couldn't afford to lose me in an airplane crash; he used insurance as an excuse. Although it was a compliment, I really needed to be with Sam Goldwyn, Jr., the director and son of the living legend, on the search. Sam said not to worry, that he would fly back to New York and read some actresses with me. I wanted Katharine Ross, a young and exciting actress I had watched work over at Universal Studios. Sam wasn't sure, and I knew the only way to convince him was to test with her on film. But Bob had cut that idea in the heart.

I went out and bought a motorcycle, A BMW R27. I rode it to the set, and in between shots I rode it around the soundstage, always passing close to Bob and laughing about insurance. It was a pretty civilized bike, but it *was* a motorcycle. I rode into his room—which was right next to mine—during his production meetings, and took my time turning it around. He never said a thing, but the others were very upset with me. It didn't matter—I took my direction from the Super Chief.

One day, Warren Beatty and I had dialogue scene, shot from a long dolly pulling in front of us. As we walked past another actor, the man asked Warren if he had read Dostoyevsky's *Crime and Punishment*. Warren answered, "Half of it." I thought this was hysterical—Warren always cut his lines in half. He also had a tendency to mumble his lines or speak them so softly that I could not hear him, and now, when he muttered some lines that I couldn't hear, I did as I had learned and asked him what he had said.

Rossen yelled for a cut, and asked me why in the hell I had said that. I told him that it seemed natural, and if an actor was listening to another character and not just making his cues, he or she should respond in a very real way. I wasn't doing it to amuse or ridicule *anyone*. I did it to keep the scene real, and if I couldn't hear Warren, then most likely the sound mixer couldn't.

The sound guys nodded, but Bob bellowed that he and he alone would decide if things could be heard. I asked him what he had just said, as if I hadn't heard it. He threw the towel he kept around his neck and demanded to know who was running the show. We all answered, "You are, Super Chief."

That took the edge off the encounter, but Bob told me not to fuck with him. I said I wouldn't as long as he didn't fuck with me. When he yelled at me, asking me just when it was he had fucked with me, I reminded him that his refusal to let me fly to Los Angeles had cost me the actress I wanted for my next picture. He harrumphed a bit and called for another take.

I had a few months after *Lilith* and before I started *The Young Lovers,* so after I had some time with Susan in L.A., and some screen tests with Sam, I went back to New York to visit Rossen and Aram Avakian in the editing room for *Lilith.* Even though I had given Bob such a hard time during the shoot, he had invited me to watch the editing process, allowing me to have a huge and important lesson in the early part of my career. I knew that I would be doing much more than acting during my motion picture career, and interning an editing process with a great director and editor was quite a privilege.

. . .

The Young Lovers was also shot in black-and-white. I think the idea was that serious films were in black-and-white, and I'm not convinced that the idea had true merit—I think it's more accurate to say Sam Goldwyn, Jr., hoped to bestow seriousness on the movie by using black-and-white. We had a small budget and not a lot of rehearsal. Big mistake. I love Sam, always will, but I think he was just a little bit stuck in the morals of the fifties. The movie was about young people caught between their parents' ideals and their own realization that the morals of the previous generation did not fit contemporary problems. It also touched on the reality of unwanted pregnancy and the stigma of abortion. And although the movie dealt with the draft, the draft it portrayed had nothing to do with the terror and doubt and moral uncertainty of the current war. The story had been written before we knew what was in store for us ten thousand miles away, and could only get as close as the Korean War (funny, isn't it, that our government still calls it the Korean conflict). One might find these words of mine irreverent, given my own handling of the draft. I was lucky—the Army, by that time, did not want people who might ask why, or at least people who might have an audience if they asked.

The Young Lovers never addressed the real problems of its audience, and therefore was never a big success.

. . .

After the film wrapped, George Peppard invited me to go on a five-day elk hunt with him in Dillon, Montana. Unbeknownst to me, George and Dad, who were close friends, had decided I should go on a hunting trip to make a "man" out of me. George told me to bring an accurate long-range rifle. I had a left-handed bolt Winchester 270, with which I was very accurate, but George insisted that I find a higher power. A 300 Magnum, he suggested; most shots at an elk would be over three hundred yards. Noah told me to take his Holland and Holland 300 Magnum, and said he'd shot African geese at four hundred yards with it. I figured that any rifle that could whack a goose at that distance was probably just right. This was my first big-game hunt, not counting whitetail, but I did have a dictum: Never shoot antlers. You can't eat them.

George (accompanied by his favorite bourbon) and I flew to Butte on the first Monday of the season and rented a car for the drive down to Dillon. The next morning we were off to the national forest boundary with our guides and an International Scout pickup.

I was the first to encounter an elk, in a high meadow. There was a small copse of aspen about forty yards away from me, and a huge bull elk stood up and looked at me. I stayed perfectly still, watching this magnificent beast, listening to George whispering loudly to shoot it. I raised the rifle without chambering a round; I had no intention of shooting a bull, but I wanted to get a better look at its rack. When it turned and walked away, I heard a cartridge being chambered and turned and shouted not to shoot it.

Peppard came stumbling out of the trees, truly pissed off.

"Why didn't you shoot it?"

"I don't eat horns."

"You don't eat horns? What the fuck does that mean?"

"The meat of the male of most large game doesn't taste as good as the female, so I don't shoot horns."

"Well, I could have shot it until you yelled, you fool!"

If he'd shot it, he would have ruined the meat—the bullet would have splintered up its backbone and wrecked the straps. But no matter what I said, George wouldn't let it go.

"We come to Montana to hunt elk, first day out we see a trophy bull, and you won't shoot it because 'I don't shoot horns'?"

"That's right, George, I don't *eat* horns!"

"Well, Mr. Gourmet Hunter, you could cut the fucking horns off, you know! The next bull you flush up, you better hit the deck, because *I'm going to shoot it*!"

"You bet."

"Hell! I bet you were afraid to shoot it. You were afraid to shoot it! I can't believe it. You chickenshit sonovabitch!"

"I didn't even chamber a round, George; I had no intention of shooting it." And I walked back into the trees.

George was on my case for the next four days. At the end of each day, we went to a local bar, but George always brought along his sipping whiskey. In the back of one bar, there was a gaming table for poker (legal in Montana), mostly five-card stud. First card down and the next four up. The next night, after our meal, I went to the table in the back and took a seat.

"You old enough?" one of the ranchers asked.

"You bet.

"Then it's your deal."

When I returned to the front bar, George was in his cups. I flashed him the $176 I had won.

"Oh, Jesus! Man, you can't do that. You better give that back!"

"There are four other guys in there that tried very hard to get it back already."

"Those are hard men back there, and they won't take kindly to some little chickenshit asshole from L.A., Fonda!"

"That's great! *Now* they know my *name*."

On the last day of the hunt, Peppard was still on my ass about the first day. Not that he'd had any luck. I spooked a cow moose—rather, it spooked me—five yards away, and it looked at me and trotted off through the trees. My heart was pounding. I had never been that close to such a big animal in the wild. I told George about it at lunch.

"Why didn't you shoot it? *It* didn't have horns!"

"It wasn't an elk, George. I don't want to eat moose, I want to eat elk."

"Hell! I bet you haven't ever fired that rifle, have you?"

"Nope."

"That's it. Fuck if that isn't it! You're afraid to shoot that gun!"

"Rifle, George. Remember what Carl taught us? 'This is your rifle and this is your gun—' "

"You're afraid to shoot, aren't you? Why don't you just up and admit it? You're afraid to shoot *anything*!"

He was getting to me. I stood up, grabbed a number ten can that had been full of peaches minutes before, walked over to an embankment, and laid the can up against it. I took out my Smith & Wesson model 39 double action automatic, flicked off the safety, and pointed it at the can, which was fifteen feet away.

"Do you see the can, George?"

"I—"

"Keep your eyes on it." And I pulled the trigger, looking at the leaping can for the first two rounds. Then, still firing, I looked at Peppard. "Are you keeping your eyes on it, George?"

Eight rounds of Police Vels. One of the startled guides jumped up and got the can.

"Eight entry holes!" he said. "All eight in the can." He was impressed. But not George. Or at least he wasn't going to admit it.

"That was just a can, Fonda; you're afraid to *kill* anything!"

George declined to try his luck on the can, pointing out that I had most likely scared away all the game in a three-mile area. As we drove back from the forest toward Dillon, I was standing in the short bed of the Scout with one of the guides, and George was riding in the cab. The sun was just setting, and a few minutes later I spotted five cow elk, feeding in a lower field down the hill from us about six hundred yards away. I pounded on the roof and said to stop the truck.

"And if you can't stop your heart, get out of the car." I needed to brace myself, and didn't want anyone to move.

"What?"

"If you can't stop breathing or your heart beating, get out of the truck." I said all this while I took off my down jacket, rolled it up into a ball, grabbed the front of the leather sling, and cranked one up. I took three sharp and deep breaths and blew them out fast. Then I took one deep breath and let it out slowly, as I put the crosshairs two inches above my target. I had been watching all five cows as they ate. When elk—or any grazing game—are feeding, there is a pattern to their moves. So much time down getting the grass, so much time up chewing and checking things out. I took the one I guessed was dry that season, and put the hairs two inches above its head. I had set the trigger already, and as the cow came up to chew and check, I touched the trigger. There was a tremendous blast, and I was knocked backward. As I reached over to open the right-handed bolt with my left hand and crank a fresh round up, I pulled the rifle down on my jacket and grabbed on to the front of the sling, blowing breaths and scoping the remaining four elk. All four were standing up still as could be, wondering what the fuck had just happened.

This one was George's, so I didn't try to guess whether it was dry or not. Trigger set and *BOOM*! As I regained my footing, chambered another round, and got my scope back on the cows, my target was loping away slowly to the right. I led it by a little less than a foot and *BOOM*. But she had dropped dead before my last bullet got to her.

My ears were ringing so loud, I couldn't sense my heart, which was pounding like mad. And I didn't say a thing about my left shoulder, which felt like a circus tent peg. Why ruin a perfect scene? To George Peppard, I was the most amazing shooter he had ever seen. To the guides, I was a pretty good shot. To me, I was a fool to have wasted the entire clip of the pistol. I would have at least put a 9mm bullet in each ear, as plugs.

On that last day, when I learned about George and Dad's "man-plan" for me, I said, "Being a man means providing food for one's family. *That's* why a man hunts, George."

. . .

We flew home from Pocatello, Idaho, the next morning. Both of us had to pack and leave for London and the command performance of *The Victors*. We met the queen, Prince Philip, Princess Margaret, and the Queen Mother. George Hamilton was there along with most of the rest of the cast. The two Georges and I stayed at the Dorchester. Hamilton felt we didn't have good color on our faces, so he and I found a sun lamp. When we arrived at the gala, we looked like lobsters, and as we were passing the press corps, someone asked where we had gotten our color. The miracles of modern electricity, George shouted back. That was cool, I thought, not worrying about copping to the lamps.

After London, we headed for New York and the U.S. premiere. I stayed at the Seventy-fourth Street house and began to be very depressed again. I called Peppard, told him I was in deep trouble and slipping fast, and he came to the house at once. He gave me some sedatives and sat in a high-backed chair next to the bed until I was safely asleep. When I awoke the next day, he was still in the chair, snoozing. He had stayed the night to be sure I wasn't going to go over the edge.

When we left New York, George and I joined Lew Wasserman and the top brass from MCA on a Pan Am flight. Bored with the suits, I flirted with the stewardesses and reflected on my depression.

In Los Angeles, as I walked down the long corridor to the baggage claim and taxis, people passed by me with averted eyes. No one was talking. I retrieved my own bags; the sky caps I usually joked with were nowhere in sight, and I felt as if I were in an *Outer Limits* episode. Finally, someone checked to see if I needed any help, and I asked what was going on at the airport.

"You haven't heard?"

"I've been on a nonstop from New York. I haven't heard a thing."

"President Kennedy has been assassinated."

The man began to cry softly as he moved away. I was suddenly and totally detached from reality. I sat down on my bags and tried to find words that would carry me on. None were forthcoming.

"Mr. Fonda? Are these all your bags, sir?" A driver patted my shoulder.

"Yes, I, uh, yeah, this is all of them."

It was hard to look him in the eye. When I was in the limo and under way, I began to cry. I felt shock and sadness, but mostly I felt embarrassment. This kind of thing doesn't happen in the United States, I thought. It can't be true. But the radio in the limousine was bringing in all the details, over and over.

At home, Susan and I sat glued to the television, wanting more news, more detail. I screamed at the TV. It was a conspiracy, I was sure. It strengthened my inner anarchy and somehow cost me my citizenship. When we *saw* Jack Ruby kill Oswald I didn't cheer, and I didn't feel avenged. I felt that the government had set *that* up, too.

· · ·

A few weeks later I was out one afternoon checking for a place to do a paint job on one of our cars. Somehow, Susan found me at one of the paint shops by phone and told me that Peppard had called, sounding funny, and said that God hates a loser. That was all he said, but she told me she didn't feel right about it. The tone of her voice made me feel that something was bad. So I sped up to his house off Hutton Drive.

I found him sitting in his den, quite drunk, with an almost empty bottle of his favorite bourbon and a .45 on the table beside him. There were five bullet holes in the baseboard. I pulled out a cigarette and lit up, offering one to George, and we sat there for a while smoking. He was rambling on about his girlfriend in Manhattan, Elizabeth Ashley, and another actor, James Farentino. He was going to kill himself.

Suicide was my thorniest subject. I became a totally different person once that cat was out of its bag.

"Well, George, how many rounds are left?"

"Two."

"Fine. Okay. Let's finish it off proper." I took a pull from his bottle, picked up the pistol, and put the safety on. "I'll do myself, and then you do yourself, okay? I mean, I'll take the first round, but you have to promise that you'll do the last one. And do it proper, George. It would be terrible if you fucked it up."

It was the exact opposite of his approach toward me just weeks earlier in New York, but it snapped him around. He looked at me, slack-jawed, sobered up a bit, and began to talk *me* out of committing suicide. I unloaded the pistol and told him to get showered and dressed. I'd take him to the airport and he could fly back and straighten the mess out. After I'd gotten him into the shower and made a reservation for him on the red-eye, I sat there thinking the whole thing out, and the doorbell rang. It was a uniformed cop, who said he'd been called by Mr. Peppard's psychiatrist and warned that there was gunplay and suicide talk. He said that some of the neighbors had called in reports of gunshots. I told him that Mr. Peppard was upstairs showering and sobering up, and that I was driving him to the airport to catch a plane to New York. He's going to be fine; there's nothing to worry about, I said. The policeman asked me who I was, and I said James Farentino. He wrote it down and left.

I got George into my Mercedes gull wing and stuffed his bags in the back and on his lap. He complained about the car and the lack of room, so I felt that he had come around a bit, but when he was extricating himself from the car, I noticed he was carrying the .45 in a shoulder holster. I knew it didn't have any bullets in it, as I had carefully hidden them; he must have grabbed it while I was using the toilet. But he was off in the crowd picking up his ticket, and I wanted to get home. Susan was a bit frightened when I explained the story. I was shaking from head to toe, and took a long hot shower.

·   ·   ·

Our Christmas was full of baby things. Susan looked great when she was pregnant, but she didn't think so. As near as we could figure, the baby was due at the end of January. Stormy said that if she was born on his birthday, the twenty-eighth, he would give her a fifty-thousand-dollar bond for college. I told him that it was too much, so he made it a ten-thousand-dollar bond.

I killed time working out with a personal trainer Dad had turned me on to, and we had many tennis days. Dad only played once, but over the years everyone from John Calley to Jack Nicholson, Bob Rafelson to Norman Jewison came by. On Sunday, the twenty-sixth of January, we had a big doubles match arranged, and almost midway into the first match I was at the net. My partner served a beaut and his counterpart made a good effort to return the serve, but the return came floating high and slow over the net, offering me a slam dunk. I drifted back to put the ball away, tripped, and rolled over on my right ankle. There was excruciating pain for ten or fifteen seconds, then nothing. No pain. I assumed I'd pinched a nerve, got back up, and continued the match for eighteen more games. My side won and we were all back in the living room having lemonade when one of the players noticed that my right ankle was the size of a grapefruit. I looked down on it, and the throbbing kicked in.

As evening came, Susan started having cramps, and I immediately started timing them. She insisted that it was only gas and we finished our dinner. By ten, the gas was cramping every five minutes, so I called our obstetrician over the objections of Susan. Dr. Krohn said that most women want to think the same thing. It's only gas.

Into the Riviera, and off to Cedars of Lebanon. I'd made several practice runs at different times of the day, searching out the fastest route. I used my left foot to accelerate and brake, with my right foot propped up on the open glove box to lessen the throbbing pain. I have no idea what I'd had in mind when installing racing gear in a Buick Riviera, but it was a fast car, and we were there in a shot. I used an umbrella as a cane and gimped through the hospital doors, while Susan—understandably—waddled. I stayed with her until my cologne was too much for her—this had never come up before—and then went to the "fathers'" room for the Long Wait, where Michael Walker and Bill Karp, a friend of Susan's sister, Ruth, came to join me. We played gin while the nurses tried to work on my right ankle. At 3:45 A.M. of January 27, 1964, Dr. Krohn came to the room and told me he had just delivered the most beautiful baby girl he had ever seen. Great! I replied, then turned to Bill and said, Gin! I'd schneidered him.

I struggled into the required white smock and hobbled out into the hall with the help of the none-too-stable umbrella. Susan was being brought out of the delivery room on a gurney, and next to her was a small clear plastic cradle with Bridget wriggling around. I limped closer. Ten toes, ten fingers, all the right stuff, I was thrilled, but how could they tell she was the most *anything*?

By the time Bridget came home, I was in a cast, having managed to tear up most of the ligaments in my ankle by continuing to play and walk after the initial injury. Stormy came up to see his godchild and hang out, and arrived with a five-foot female boa constrictor he called Lolita Ya Ya. He put it in our pool, and it swam like a champ. When Dad came over to pay his respects, he was more interested in Lolita than Bridget, and told us about a time on John Ford's *Araner* when he found a boa under a refrigerator in Mexico. While he was telling us the story, Lolita slithered up his coat sleeve and out at his collar. Dad deadpanned, not seeming to know that a snake was crawling all over him. He had his longtime friend, Magnum photographer John Swope, come over to the house to photograph Bridget and Susan.

I was just a month shy of my twenty-fourth birthday when Bridget was born. When my son Justin was twenty-four, I was thankful that he'd been loved enough, wanted enough, to not feel the need to create his own family by then.

. . .

My first job in 1964 was a guest spot on the television series *The New Breed*. Soon after I did an *Alfred Hitchcock Hour,* playing a Tennessee hillbilly who scares a man to death by shaving him very close, as revenge for the death of his father. I had to have a Tennessee accent, so I went to Dean Hargrove, my would-be *PT109* coach. He was precise enough to know the difference between a Tennessee accent and a plain old southern accent and I was determined to do the best job possible for $11,000.

Twelve O'Clock High had a standard five-day shoot, and on one weekend off, we had a big tennis tournament. I had finished my matches and after sitting in the sun and swimming and having a few margaritas, I decided to take a spin on my Triumph. I took off under the influence, wearing just my bathing suit and a pair of loafers. As I drove up Hidden Valley Drive, an oncoming car took the corner on my side of the road, and as I dodged it, I hit a speed bump and lost control. I bounced along the asphalt, bunched up like a ball, trying to keep my face and head up. I got up, picked up my motorcycle, and drove it back to the house.

From the front, I looked perfect, but as I turned my back to enter the house, all my friends gasped. My back looked like ground meat. I went into the shower to clean out the wounds, and exploded out again the moment the water sprayed against my raw back. My left side had been ripped open at my hip bone. Susan had called the Beverly Hills Emergency Clinic and told them we were on our way. Three of my tennis buddies came along to help, and I bit into the dash of the Riviera to keep from screaming as the car moved. Susan is a good driver, so she wasted no time. We ran a few stop signs and one red light. We picked up a cop after the red light but we kept on moving. Susan drove right up to the entrance, and as I scrambled out of the car with the towel around my waist, trying to keep it off the deep wound on my left hip, I yelled invectives at the cop.

After cleaning and stitches and convincing the cop that the emergency had been real, with the help of Demerol we drove carefully home. I had to go back to the clinic early Monday, and when I finally reached someone from the production to let them know I'd be late, I emphasized that there were no injuries to my face. Our director, Don Taylor, a very energetic person, was so happy when he finally saw me that he threw his arms around me and gave me a big bear hug. I think the tears that spurted from my eyes and the distorted expression on my face let him know that my back was rejecting the rest of my body. He offered me a pain pill, told me they'd be ready for me in about an hour, and gave me a big pat on the back.

More apologies. A few minutes later, Jill Haworth, playing my romantic interest—a nurse—in the episode, came in with some tea and pills and tenderness. But the pain killers didn't dent me—I still couldn't bend enough to fit through the hatch into the nose of the B-17. We shot that scene later.

· · ·

One month after Bridget was born, on the twenty-ninth of February, Stormy married Virginia "Pookie" Baker in Las Vegas. I'd flown in from L.A., joining John Haeberlin, Marianne, Stormy's sister and her husband, and Roger Dunbier. Stormy had first met Pookie in Omaha, while we were playing the two male roles in *Stagedoor* at Brownell Hall.

Two months after the wedding she left him, and he was devastated. I offered to spend time with him on his island that summer; after my accident, plastered with dressings, I wasn't going to be doing too much swimming in the Pacific or the pool. Hot-rodding around an island in boats without getting wet would be a challenge, too, but I felt Stormy needed trustworthy love, and I was his best friend. I wanted Susan to come along with Bridget, but she felt that it would be difficult. If Marianne had been there with her children, I would have insisted.

Stormy picked me up in Detroit and we drove to Port Huron, where his thirty-one-foot Bertram was being fitted with new Chrysler 413 hp engines. The boat was called *Mizpah*, and it was the perfect lake boat. We dropped the new engines in the boat and powered through Lake Huron toward Mackinac Island, and Stormy's island home.

We had a wonderful time that summer. Better sound equipment, better barge parties. That year, Stormy had a utility drag boat, easily capable of turning over 127 miles per hour in a quarter mile, a very fast traveling experience. It was an excellent ski boat, and Stormy was an expert water-skier. I was thrilled when I was fully healed and able to get wet and goof in the water.

As soon as we were firmly planted on the island, we began to experiment with some pot we'd brought along. Stormy got some cigarette papers and a rolling machine and we smoked the first joint in the afternoon on the long front porch, looking out over the bay. In less than an hour, and though we'd just had lunch, we were devouring everything we could find in the kitchen. We planted some of the seeds, figuring that if it was called weed, growing it couldn't be too complicated. Our evening meals were riotous—it seemed there was never enough food. But we were laughing so hard, we couldn't explain our laughter to Bill, the caretaker, or his wife. No, we didn't need more food, we needed more time to roll around on the floor or laugh so hard we cried.

Partway through my two-month stay, I had to go to New York for

four days to do some publicity for *The Young Lovers*. I invited Stormy
to come with me. Our friend John Haeberlin (who didn't smoke cigarettes, and had a difficult time inhaling) had joined us with Basil,
Stormy's short-hair Saint Bernard, and so there was someone at the
island to keep an eye on the toys while we were gone.

While we were in New York, Stormy and I stayed at the house on
Seventy-fourth Street, and he tagged along on my interviews to see
what it was like. He flirted with the young models when I did a two-
day photo shoot for *Mademoiselle,* and at the end we took the photographer, models and fashion coordinator, Darlene DeSedle, to dinner. Darlene was a very hip young woman, tall and lean like an
Egyptian queen. She had some dynamite grass, and Stormy and I
went back uptown with a renewed stash. He and the pretty girl he'd
talked into coming along were staying in the master bedroom, and I
was in Jane's room, one floor above. Just as I was slipping off to
sleep, I heard some funny noises from the room below, definitely not
lovemaking sounds, and there was a lot of laughter. I went on down.
Stormy was walking around the room in his shorts, lifting his legs up
in an exaggerated way and laughing so hard he was squeaking. To
him, the floor felt like it was made of sponge, and in *his* mind, he was
bouncing around as he walked. The girl he was with was worried,
but I was happy as pie. He had really been tagged by the grass, and
he wasn't worried or paranoid. He and the girl went back to the island
while I finished my interviews.

Before I left, I went to Darlene's and cadged some more grass. She
and I sat in her apartment smoking joints—I was picking up the lingo
very fast—and listening to a record of music from India. It was called
"ragas," and the musicians were Ravi Shankar, playing a sitar, and Ali
Akbar-Khan playing drums called tabla. I had never heard anything
like it, and it was perfect for a stoned person.

I was sorry to see the end of the summer, but the *Mizpah* had to
get back to Chicago, and I had to get back to my family. I had spent
way too much time there, but I was fully healed from my motorcycle
accident, and the time helped me get loose of some pent-up childish-
ness without hurting myself or anyone else.

· · ·

As soon as I returned to Los Angeles I completed the missing
Twelve O'Clock High scene, but the phone wasn't ringing off the hook

with other offers. Several times I joined other actors in the park at the bottom of Coldwater Canyon to play touch football. Many of those times we played Elvis and his entourage. We were all aware that the other guys with El were bodyguards and might not have the idea of touch football and protecting the King in separate categories. Presley always wore eye makeup and a helmet with a face protector. Regardless, we were all just a bunch of guys playing touch football.

I began to seek projects on my own. I had read *Conceived in Liberty,* the book about the winter at Valley Forge that Bobby Weil had given me in 1962. Now I went after it with some gusto, never thinking that I would not be allowed to get the film going because I was so young, and I was an actor, in the eyes of the studios, and they didn't like to deal with young actors who have a dream for a production. I flew to New York and met with Howard Fast. I thought that it was the perfect film to record the Revolutionary War. There were some beautiful parts for any number of great character actors, and I had passion for it. Still do.

But no one would listen to me. Oh, they took meetings with me in their offices, but it was out of courtesy for Henry's son. When I mentioned it to Dad, he nodded and made no comment. During the summer—and many times before—Stormy and I had talked at length about our mutual dream of forming our own production company, buying books and scripts and developing them into motion pictures. I had him convinced that continuing an education at Arizona State was a waste of time. Our plan was that he would come to L.A., enroll at the USC film school, and learn all about production.

His out-of-touch guardian, Eugene Kinney, said that *all* colleges in California were hotbeds of Communism, and did his best to discourage Stormy, while at the same time telling him that he was a loser and amounted to nothing. Great counseling. But Stormy listened, and headed back to Arizona for school that fall. As many times as I went there to visit him, Stormy would come to L.A. to see us, usually staying in Pappy's guest house. He and Susan's sister, Ruth, were close friends.

. . .

Work was hard to find throughout 1964. I loved to work. Hell, I *needed* to work, but whatever sadness this might have caused in me

seemed secondary to what was happening to Stormy. All the fun and
pranks could not mask the depression. His divorce and the constant
harping from Kinney were wearing him down, and he was increasingly moody and self-doubting. I thought of different things to suggest to him that might broaden his scope and put his life in a more
positive mode.

Darlene was going on a shoot for *Vogue* in North Africa and the
Canary Islands, and she thought it might be a good change for
Stormy. He, having actual camera savvy and knowing how to develop
negatives and print photos, could be helpful, and after the shoot, she
would take him through Europe on a small tour. He thought it
sounded great, so we put it all together. They left for the Canary Islands with Stormy in a positive mood. He called, many times, from
different parts of Africa and Europe, and he always sounded great.

When he returned, he came by ship from Naples. I went east to
meet him. He was in fine spirits. He was full of stories about Europe
and the differences between cultures, having become a full American
chauvinist, which I took as another good sign. We rented a Lincoln
Continental and drove out to see the World's Fair on Long Island, and
on the way back to the city, Stormy fired up a joint of Darlene's grass,
which we smoked while we crawled along with the traffic. When we
hit the Midtown Tunnel, we were ripped. I thought I handled the car
perfectly, but as we neared the far side and the tunnel curved to the
right, the road seemed to bank heavily. I couldn't understand why the
car wasn't sliding into the right wall. Stormy and Darlene were chatting away, and I pointed out the problem. Darlene pointed out I was
so ripped I had forgotten that we had smoked *anything*. Reefer madness.

Bridget was only eleven months old for her first Christmas, but she
was a little bundle of beauty, and absolutely enchanted by the entire
ritual. The tree was wonderful, snowy, and full of presents, most of
which were for Bridget. Very few of *my* family members remembered
the first grandchild's first Christmas, certainly when compared with
the way that Noah and Mary showered their grandchild. Stormy came
for just two days, staying at the villa, and then went to Chicago, somewhat reluctantly. He didn't have a real Christmas, except for his time
with his sister.

Nineteen sixty-five showed little sign of improvement in the work
area, but I did my best to keep it from getting me down. My father

was always in a funk after *any* film or play had finished its run. No one is going to call, he would say. I couldn't believe then that Henry Fonda was worried about where he would get his next job, but the point gradually hit home.

Stormy's moods were on the swing again soon after Christmas. I decided that a fishing trip to the Big Island of Hawaii for an early birthday present and a getaway might do him some good. We had a great time swimming, fishing, and relaxing. We returned to the mainland ten days before his birthday and a week before Bridget's, but he quickly dropped into self-doubt.

Soon after we'd returned from Hawaii, things really started to come unsnapped. Stormy called constantly at night, and kept repeating that he felt his life was worthless, and that he had done nothing meaningful. He cried often, and he was alone, but when I'd offer to fly down he'd immediately calm down.

Stormy hit a low on a Tuesday in early February, and during the course of a five-hour call he talked about our best-friend pact, when we'd promised each other that when we were too old to contribute anymore, we'd take a plane and fly off over the ocean until we ran out of gas, an image that had always reminded me of the day my dad's glider had soared out to sea. I told him that I wasn't ready to take that flight, and neither was he, and the conversation ended when I told him I'd come down on an early morning flight, and be in Tucson by eight A.M.

He was heading out to a movie with some Tucson friends. Susan and I went to Bob Dossier's house for a party. Bob was an influential and classy producer, but the party was full of older types who were not at all in tune with the younger set. Mia Farrow and Stephanie Powers were at the party, also, and when I suggested that we all go to the Daisy, a local private discotheque, the girls were thrilled, and off we went. It was a good night at the Daisy, and I was with three of the most beautiful women in Hollywood. Hard to beat that, and I reveled in it. I got to dance with all three, and they *all* returned to my table. Tina Sinatra was at the next table, and she and Mia were in deep conversation about Mia's budding relationship with Frank, when, at 11:15, tears inexplicably spurted from my eyes and ran down my cheeks. It freaked me out, but Susan put her arm around me and said, "It's Stormy, isn't it?"

I knew at once that it *was*. Once back at home, I called Stormy immediately, and got his answering service. I left messages, and tried John Haeberlin and other friends with no contact, though I called late into the night. I didn't take the morning flight, or even the noon flight. I kept calling. I finally hooked up with Haeberlin, who said that he and Stormy and a few friends had gone to the drive-in to see *Mondo Pazzo,* a bizarre downbeat movie about the crazy—*pazzo*—world and the inhumanity that man brings upon his fellow men. Stormy had left for home at ten-thirty.

I told John to drive over to Stormy's house. As I prepared to take the late flight, sure the worst had happened to the man I loved most, I asked Susan to call one more time. As I was adjusting my tie and suit—I had never gone to visit in formal attire—I heard her talk on the phone. It's Stormy, my brain said with relief, and then I heard Susan say, "You'd better speak with my husband." She handed me the phone, saying that it was the sheriff.

"He's dead, isn't he?" I said.

"Who is this?"

"Peter Fonda. He killed himself, didn't he?"

"Why would you think that?"

"I know it, Sheriff. He killed himself at twelve-fifteen this morning. Do you want me to identify the body?"

"Are you in Tucson?"

"No. I'm on my way, though."

I told the sheriff the flight I was taking, and he said that he would have the mortician pick me up.

In Tucson, I was told that he was in his house with all the windows and doors locked from the inside, and that he had shot himself in the head.

"The barrel was in his left hand, wasn't it?"

"Why, yes. We had to break his fingers to get the gun. How do you know this?" There was no accusation in the mortician's voice.

"I can *see* it," I said. "He put one bullet in the pistol, cocked it with his right hand, and, grabbing the barrel with his left hand, put it to the back of his head and pulled the trigger with his right thumb." I said this with complete calm, but with a broken heart. I was curious why he wasn't at the morgue. The mortician said the family had wanted to avoid the morgue; there wasn't much doubt that it had been a suicide.

I identified him and went to a motel, where I drank a bottle of champagne and smoked a doobie in his honor and fell asleep, crying. I had a key to the house, but I couldn't go there. I knew that he thought I was coming on the morning flight, and that he intended to have me discover his body. Could I have . . . ? I think so today, but perhaps it's just my ego—no amount of baby-sitting could have kept Stormy on Earth if he couldn't enjoy the stay.

The next few days were almost abstract. The sheriff asked me to come to the house, so I did, and brought John and another friend with me. I saw the bathroom where he had died, with the bath still full of bloody water. He had tried to cut his wrists, and finding that too slow or ineffective, went for a gun. I followed the trail of blood from the bathroom to the shelf of drawers where he kept some of his father's gun collection. He had taken a pistol from these drawers, returned to the bathroom, and loading it with the wrong ammunition, fired it for proof. The bullet was a smaller caliber, and plopped out of the barrel. The pistol was there on the vanity with a spent cartridge, but the bullet was never found. The blood tracks went back out of the bathroom, into his bedroom, where he took his Colt single-action .22 Magnum, loaded it with one bullet, and returned to the bathroom. This time he cocked the pistol, and, grabbing it by the barrel with his left hand and the butt facing forward, placed the barrel to the back of his head and pulled the trigger with his right thumb. He didn't want to mess up his face, hadn't wanted me—or anyone else—to have to handle that. The sheriff was curious, but I had no explanation for the accuracy of my earlier vision. I hadn't known which gun he had used, until I saw the bloody tracks to his bedroom closet on his second trip out of the bathroom, and the empty Colt holster.

Susan joined me, and she and John accompanied me on the flight to Chicago with Stormy's body two days later. We had a wake at the Drake Hotel, and after a private service, we buried him next to his father in a mausoleum at the Queen of Heaven Catholic Cemetery. His friend, photographer Fred Neimann, brought up the back of the funeral procession in his bright red convertible, which I thought was appropriate.

Marianne, Stormy's sister, had said that it wasn't wise to go back to Tucson for the coroner's inquest. I felt it was my duty to see that he wasn't trivialized or made a mockery by those people. Had I been in an ordered state of mind, and had she reminded me, with conviction that he's been buried in a Catholic cemetery, I would have understood. But I was too far gone to pick up on anything short of absolute clarity. After a lifetime spent learning of my mother's successive deaths, I was in no mood for any more mysteries.

So I went off to Tucson to defend my friend, not knowing that the county attorney, Norman Green, had been instructed by Stormy's former guardian, Eugene Kinney, to be sure that a nonsuicide was reached by the coroner's jury. Somehow, seeing the stark photos of him on the bathroom floor was harder than identifying him in the flesh. Joyce Shank, a naive young girlfriend of Stormy's, testified at the inquest that Stormy "had a friendship of emotional love for Peter," a relationship she was "not capable of understanding." That led to speculation that we were homosexual lovers, thereby adding all kinds of possiblities of a probable murder. John, Joyce, and I were given lie detector tests—mine was done in Los Angeles—by the sheriff's department, and each of us displayed no guilty knowledge of how or why he died. Tucson Sheriff Burr had not told County Attorney Green that the testing had been done; the mess had turned territorial. "As far as I'm concerned, the tests don't mean a thing," Green insisted, trying to keep the murder charges looming against me and John. Nothing came of any of it, but Kinney got a passable verdict: Eugene Francis McDonald III was determined to have died in the presence of person or persons unknown.

A little later, John and I packed up the things Stormy had left me— all of his personal property—and hauled them up to L.A., along with Stormy's Saint Bernard. Basil stayed with us for over a year before John could find a place to live where he could keep him. He was a kind dog, and Bridget loved him almost as much as Basil loved our pool. Basil loved all the neighbors' pools, too, and sometimes I'd hear shouts from around our private little canyon—"Hey! Hey! Get out of there, dammit!"—that I'm sure Stormy would have enjoyed.

chapter *Eleven*

I discovered some time ago that my need to sing a song, tell a tale, paint a picture, write a poem, act a part—to be heard—was too impatient and long-buried an urge to be declared in a "normal" way. I think I put a damper on the need for as long as I could, and only really stepped up to the plate when my best friend took his own life, when it was almost too late for me, too. But "almost" is really only good in hand grenades or thermonukes, so in 1965 I pulled the pin, let the spoon drop, and watched my life come apart, blown full from the core, and gather above my head in a kaleidoscopic pattern.

In 1965, my best friend shot himself in the head; Dad married his fifth wife, Shirlee; Pan married Franco Corrias; Jane married Roger Vadim; and Watts burned to the ground. I took acid, met the Beatles, took acid with the Beatles, wrote a screenplay with Denny Lee Hopper and Don Sherman and found love again.

Among the personal effects that the misdemeanor outlaw left to me was a big Gibson twelve-string acoustic guitar. I'd met the Byrds, by then, and I'd listened very carefully to the beautiful music that came from McGuinn's twelve-string Rickenbacker. He, of course, was right-handed, playing a right-handed guitar; I was left-handed, and could never play like him even if I were right-handed. This didn't stop me. In the aftermath of Stormy's death, incredibly wounded, I picked up

his Gibson and played it with a vengeance, night and day. Blood from
my fingers dried on the neck of that beautiful instrument, and as I
bled I cried. One of the songs that McGuinn played beautifully was
Bob Dylan's "The Chimes of Freedom," and I played it over and over,
trying to emulate McGuinn's style. One afternoon by my pool, stoned
and lost, my left hand suddenly began to find the strings, and I was
blown away. I kept at it for twenty or thirty minutes, singing the lyrics
over and over, before I fucked up on a chord.

"I'm sorry."

Owen Orr, a friend, was with me. My cheeks were marbled with
tears, and he told me to keep playing, to not stop.

I played like a desperado. I sang my heart. I sang my life. I sang
for Stormy. And, after a while, I sang for all of us. I had the blood of
that song, the blood of the life in my throat, and I could make you
believe I knew what I was doing. The sun had set when I stopped
playing, out by my pool. I looked at Owen.

"Whew. That was great, man."

"Whew," I replied softly.

The next day, my arm was immobile, misshapen from the elbow
down. My muscles looked like golf balls under my skin, and I couldn't
play for four days. But I knew a big answer, or, rather, I began to
understand the question, began to have a way to articulate myself. I
knew that if I was going to find my spot, I had to stop playing the
roles that Hollywood was offering. I had to do something quite different.

The knowledge that something had to give didn't necessarily make
life happier. I grasped at anything. Susan and I went to the Bahamas
and Antigua, chasing the sun and fleeing the depths. It must have
been very hard for Susan, but I was too self-immersed to think about
the real world. I was trying my best not to get caught in the happenings and succumb to them. I felt very suicidal, and only the thought
of Bridget, and the essence of her that lived deep inside me, kept my
hand from the gun.

After we returned, I bounced around the walls of my confusion,
unable to express my desperation, and inner depression. I hadn't
been asked on an audition in months, and though we still had savings
I went to my father to ask for a $20,000 loan, trying to buy the time I
needed to straighten out my life without feeling further burdened by
my lack of work. Maybe I simply wanted sympathy. Whatever; he

refused. When I left his rented shack, I took the pistol that had been given me by Stormy, and that I had given to Dad as a gift of love for his birthday in 1964. I felt that he did not want to be a part of my life in *any* way that demanded a personal commitment, and I wanted everything that was a part of Stormy. I never gave it back and feel no guilt about it. It was Tom Mix's personal six-shooter. A 44-40 caliber pistol. It was the pistol Mix took on his hip when he toured Central and South America with his famous circus.

. . .

Jane had a party at the beach house she and Vadim had rented at Malibu, for the Fourth of July, and I arranged for the Byrds to play. She had been doing *They Shoot Horses, Don't They?*

"Can't you get them to turn it down?" my father, who was standing right beside me, yelled with his hands cupped around his mouth.

Of course I couldn't. At the break, the band and I went up on Bobby Walker's roof and shared the moment. We were free! God bless grass! God bless us all, each and every one. We were so innocent. Even David Crosby was innocent. We were so angry, so full of hope.

. . .

My sister Pan asked me to come to her wedding in Rome. How could I say no? She was my godmother, and she'd asked me to give her away. I was the only member of the Fonda family in contact with her. She wasn't in touch with Jane. Something was bad between them. Susan couldn't come—we really could not afford it. The trip to the Caribbean had run us too close to the empty mark. So I went to Rome. I was shooting in the dark, but at least I wasn't shooting myself.

Pan and Franco Corrias were married in the offices of the mayor of Rome. It was a simple ceremony, but full-dress. I had to wear a morning suit with tails. I was so happy for her; Franco was a kind man and he adored her, and that loomed large in my personality ratings. Pan had been studying art in Europe since she was nineteen. Franco gave her roots, something that had been torn away when she was orphaned by the death of our mother. She was supported by the will of her father, George Brokaw, and drew away from the society that had been our mother's inner circle. Twenty-five years later, they were married in the Catholic Church, an act of reaffirming their love on their anniversary.

I stayed at a villa owned by Franco's parents. It was outside the city on a large golf course and very beautiful, with a pool. I rented a Fiat 500, and when I wasn't bagging rays by the pool, I would drive into Rome to check on the haps, testing my memory of the city. Sometimes I would drive on the Via Appia Antica, south of Rome, and pass Ground Zero, the site of the family meltdown in 1955. Sometimes I would drive into the city, park in the Piazza del Popolo, and walk around.

So there I was in Rome for Pan's wedding, and what do you know, there was my marijuana mentor, Mr. Jim Mitchum, walking down the street toward me. He was in Rome looking for work. One afternoon, a few days later, he called me and suggested that we attend some film award gala. Said there might be some chicks. I agreed and picked him up with the Fiat 500.

It was a tiny car, not much bigger than a normal refrigerator, with a little canvas sunroof that folded back. At that time, I was six feet two inches tall, and weighed about 137 pounds. I *just* fit into the Fiat. Mitchum, several inches taller, 200 pounds and very well built, shoehorned himself into the car and off we went. We looked like something from a circus, a tiny car with two tall gringos, listing slightly to the right.

Before the award party, we did a number. So *many* names for that herb! Though the ceremony was very Italian, we located no girls, and headed to the next promising site, an outdoor nightclub.

"Come on, Pancho, you *know* there will be girls!"

Naturally, he was Cisco. He *had* to be Cisco. Can you imagine 1965 Italian rock and roll? Neither could the Italians. Strike two. Back into the *cinquecento*, doobie number two, and we were on our way. *La dolce vita*.

"Where the fuck are we?"

"How the hell should I know?"

"It's *your* fucking car!"

We got completely, predictably lost within the walls of ancient Rome. Time to twist up another one. We had been driving for what seemed to be hours. The streets can be very narrow in old Roma. I remember driving down a lot of marble stairs. *Bouncity bounce . . .*

The Spanish Steps? Naww . . . We were both shouting exact instructions at each other and managed to put the Fiat down a street that was not much wider than the car itself and was blocked by three ancient marble posts.

I explained to Jim that if I could see the stars, I would know which direction to go, but we couldn't open the doors. Just getting the sunroof open was a major struggle. I squeezed out of the top, climbed over the hood, and stumbled through the marble posts that added to the *en cage* effect. As I walked out into the square in front of us, I looked back at the car. Cisco was trapped. The car looked like it had been molded around him. He couldn't get out through the roof; I wasn't even sure I could get back *in*. I fell to the ground in hysterics.

"Not very funny, Fonda!" Though constrained by Italian metal, he was laughing just as hard as I was.

I pulled myself together and began to scan the skies. The stars were no help, but history was. I found myself standing in the Piazza Navona, one of the oldest squares in Rome, and immediately knew exactly where I was.

Getting back into the 500 was a whole other movie. Jim fished a roach from the ashtray and we sat there sobbing with laughter, unable to do a thing. Finally, I put the little Fiat in reverse and carefully backed out of the trap.

"This is the last time I'm going to take you dancing, man!" He snorted.

"Hey, man! It's not my fault. I'm left-handed and it's a right-handed car!"

"Oh, that's a fine excuse, Pancho."

. . .

Mitchum didn't waste any time before he fell into the role of tutor again.

"Fonda, you got no style." He was right. I had two good double-breasted, custom-tailored suits and some nifty shoes, but I didn't have a single good shirt. I was so slender, with long arms and a thin neck, that it was hard to find a good shirt.

"Hard to find? Shit, Fonda, you get them made, you silly fuck. You go to Battistoni's and have them take your measurements."

I thought "silly fuck" was a bit presumptuous, but I agreed to meet

him for lunch. When I arrived at the restaurant, I found that David
Niven, Jr., had come, too, and I joined the other Sons Of. Mitchum
and Niven were seated on one side of the table with their backs to a
low room divider that had a planter along its top. They could not see
the entry, and I could only see the heads of people as they came into
the room. Mitchum was acting more like a grandma than a pothead.
He made me show Niven the inserts on my shirtsleeves that Susan
had sewn perfectly. They were about two inches wide, but *did* make
the shirtsleeves fit my arms. I wasn't very interested in the demonstration of my lack of style, so I watched the bodiless heads that floated
above the plants. Jim told David that *he* might benefit from a visit to
Battistoni's, but David declined, explaining that he had a date with
his girlfriend, who was doing a fashion shoot for *Vogue,* and that was
style enough for him.

My eyes were drawn to a stunning head, floating over the plants.
And soon the head joined a long, perfect body, and then came another head and body, a bit shorter. That was David's date, and we all
rose as they kissed lightly. It was Marisa Berenson, and she was beautiful, but I was locked in on the tall one, who had stopped to chat
with some people at another table. She was perfect. I leaned forward
to Jim.

"Who's got the tall one?"

"Ha! Oh boy! No way, Fonda. No fucking way!"

One thing I admired about Jim was his confidence on my behalf.
We all rose again, and David introduced me to Vera Von Lehndorff—
Verushka—*the* top model in the world and numero uno for *Vogue.*

I quickly asked her if she was free for dinner, but she said that she
was on a shoot and had to be up early the next day. She had a sensa-
tional low voice that was much more addicting than Mitchum's weed
(my vocabulary had continued to grow). I explained to her that I was
an actor and understood about getting up early, but everyone needed
to eat dinner. She laughed and I completely forgot about the others. I
really didn't hear their polite laughter at me. Didn't care.

When David and the girls left for the *Vogue* shoot, my fashion coordinator hauled me off to change my style. I did, however, learn where
the girls were staying.

Pan and her husband, Franco, had left on their honeymoon, and
Franco's parents had gone for a summer vacation. I was alone at the
villa with one maid, no food, and an incredible desire for Vera. My

need for love took over. I called the hotel as soon as I thought the girls were finished with the photo session. I connected, almost, and persevered for two more calls. Each time I explained to Vera that I was alone at the villa, there was no food, I had to come into town anyway and would be eating alone unless she would accept my offer. The third time, she relented, more out of exhaustion than from a real desire to go out for dinner.

I arrived *multo pronto* at her hotel and waited anxiously. Every passionate love song I knew tumbled through my brain. And suddenly, she was there. She wore a yellow knit dress that left no doubt about her six-foot two-inch perfect body. I was sure everyone in the lobby saw what a nervous wreck I was. She was a bit surprised by the tiny Fiat, with Stormy's Gibson guitar taking up the entire back.

Vera suggested a restaurant and we had no problem finding a place to park—one of the car's fortes. After dinner, she said, "Let's go someplace." I almost fainted.

We went to the Borghese Gardens, a beautiful park outside the walls of old Rome. On this particular night, the lights in the gardens were not working, which I found very Italian. We groped around in the dark until we could hear a fountain and stumbled onto a bench. I began to play the Gibson for her and sang every song I knew. Sometime during "The Chimes of Freedom," she put her hand on my face and softly said, "Come with me, Peetah."

For the next few days, I barely saw the outside world. The two models had a suite of rooms in the hotel. The room with the twin beds was Vera's and my love nest, while David and Marisa used the large pull-out bed in the couch in the living room. They were together before we were and had dibs on the big bed, so Vera and I had to use the little, tiny, itty-bitty twin beds for our amusement. These beds were not quite long enough for *our* long bodies and not nearly wide enough for two midgets to sleep side by side. We were constantly falling off the bed, but we refused to sleep separately. We didn't care, at least at first, and would weave our bodies together and hold each other tightly as we slept.

One night, as we clung to each other on what now seemed like the narrow side of a two-by-four, we heard our sedate neighbors go into the living room. Although there was a funny side to the falling-off-the-bed routine, I thought that Vera and I should be granted at least one night in the magic castle. We've got to streak them, I told

Verushka. We smoked one and giggled through our plans of the big surprise show. The living room had a large French window directly opposite the foldout bed, with a curtain that could close off the little semicircle seat beneath the window from the rest of the room. I opened the door slowly and peeped into the room from the hallway. A small bedside lamp was lit, and I could see David and Marisa lying next to each other with their hands folded on their chests. At first I thought that I was being set up, that the three of them were making a big joke for me. *Naaaahhh* . . . Vera and I burst into their room, flicking off the light as we passed, and jumped behind the closed curtain. We heard a lot of "what thes," and then, having put ourselves into an absolutely ridiculous position, we opened the curtain. *Ta da* . . .

They'd turned the lights back on, so we were all quite visible to one another, and they lay motionless in the bed and looked at us as if we were lunatics. We quickly changed our position behind the curtain and did the *Ta da* again. Nothing. Vera and I were laughing like lunatics, but not a sound from David and Marisa. Nada. *Niente*. We closed the show out of town, and ran for our torture chamber. I threw both mattresses on the floor, and that is how we spent the rest of our nights at the hotel, still managing to fall off the mattresses every night.

Vera had to go to Milan, and I had to go to Sicily, but we promised to meet in Paris. I didn't want to leave her. After a few days in Sicily, I left for Paris and my second stolen moment with Vera.

She was staying at a typical little hotel on the Left Bank with many of the other models, but her preeminence meant that she bagged the best room. This time we had a great big bed, a huge bath, and a balcony that opened onto the rooftops of central Paris. We gamboled around the city while Peter Beard photographed her. At night, we'd go out to eat and then to a club to dance, and I remember seeing Sean Flynn, Errol's son, with George Hamilton at Castelle's, where he was having dinner, the last time I'd see him before he disappeared in Vietnam or Cambodia on a shoot.

But I had to get back to my home, to my wife and our daughter. I lost so much that year. Vera and I were both in tears when we said good-bye at the airport. She had given herself to me unconditionally, and we had shared a passion that I had never felt before. She wanted to be with me. She made me feel I was needed, answered my questions the way I'd always wanted them to be answered.

During the eleven-hour flight to L.A., I had plenty of time to con-sider the consequences of my affair. Though I didn't feel guilty, I was trying to put the feelings of love I had for Vera in perspective with the feelings of responsibility and love I had for Susan and Bridget. With Susan, I had a home and a family, a place that was a comfort to me most of the time, a place where I could be myself, a place with a certain kind of privacy that I needed. But the passion that had been given me by Vera was not something I had at home.

I never said a word about it, and home and hearth took hold of my heart in a strong way. I didn't want to repeat the failed-marriage syndrome that was such a burden for Dad, and for his children. I saw Vera only three times in the next six years, but those few times were always passionate moments. We wrote many letters. She sent hers to the American Express office in the Beverly Hilton Hotel, and they all gave me a wonderful rush when I read them.

In 1971, after I had sailed to Maui, I arranged to meet her in New York for a few days. I knew, as did she, that it would be the last time, the farewell bash. She had remained the top model in the world, and I had sailed the wide Pacific. I reserved a beautiful suite at the Re-gency with great discretion, ordered several tubs of caviar, the best Russian vodka in blocks of ice, and other decadent goodies. I didn't want room service to disturb us, but neither did I want to want for anything. Soft terry-cloth robes, flowers, the best pot, a stereo system up and running. Only Bill Hayward knew where in the world we were, or why.

Vera had been met at the airport by a limo and was waiting for me in the suite. Everything was perfect. The caviar, the vodka, Verushka—perfect. We toasted with Dom, smoked a joint, teased each other, deliciously. Perfect . . .

When the phone rang, I stared at it in confusion. The fucking phone was definitely not supposed to ring. Vera suggested that it might be room service, and I told her that room service had been taken care of, well in advance. The phone continued ringing. We looked at each other in bewilderment. *Ring . . . ring . . . ring.* I answered reluctantly.

"Peter, it's Jane."

I was stoned and bewildered. "Yeah? What's up?"

"Well, I'm here with Vadim and Warren and Julie and I . . . uh well, you know, do you have any, uhh, any . . ."

"Any grass?"

"Yeah."

Jane loves to cut to the chase. "What is it that you need?" I was undone. Nobody knew where we were—except Haywire. I looked at Vera and thought of passion and privacy lost.

"Well, could we . . . uhm . . . could we come up and—"

"Jane, where are you?"

"We're in the lobby."

"Just a second." I turned to Vera and told her what was up. We both agreed to take them in.

To this day, I wonder how she found me. I never asked Haywire. She doesn't remember that night, but I'll never forget it. They came up to our suite. I had rolled a couple of joints and we passed them around. We all toasted to our collective good fortune with the champagne and talked stoned talk. Jane didn't participate. Warren and Julie were amazed at how good the pot was, though Vadim said he didn't feel a thing. Of course, he never admitted to "feeling a thing," even when he, Bill Hayward, a friend, and I had taken mescaline one evening at Jane's farm outside of Paris.

After a while, Vadim said they had to be going, but Jane had fallen asleep on one of the couches and couldn't be budged. She was exhausted. I mean, she was face down and out.

"Zhane . . . Zhane, you muz wake up. Your bruhzaire wants to be alone . . . Zhay-ain. Zhay-ain . . . *Rien affaire,* Peetair."

Our other guests left. Vera and I went to the bedroom and made love for quite a long time. It was like being back in Rome, but the bed was five times bigger. When we rested, enjoying a lull, I was on my back as Vera lay on top of me. I kissed her left shoulder with my eyes closed, then opened them and saw Jane standing in the doorway, leaning against the jamb. I whispered very softly into Vera's ear that I was going to roll over while holding her tightly. She murmured yes, and when I was lying on top of her I whispered to her to slowly look over my left shoulder. I felt her body become rigid for a moment, then I rolled us back over to my favorite position. We made love again.

After a while, I got up, pulled on a bathrobe, and went into the living room. Jane was back on the couch, face down. Same position. I gently shook her and said she had to get up and go, now. She woke up and asked where everyone else was. I had a car and driver on standby, and I said she could go wherever she wanted, but that Vera and I wanted to be alone.

. . .

Early in 1989, I shot another movie with Jim Mitchum, this one in the Philippines, and then headed to Berlin, where I worked for a second time with Liv Ullmann. I headed back to the States in March, and spent several days in New York meeting with publishing houses, working on the best deal for writing this autobiography. Naturally, one of the stories I used as a taste was the Mitchum Factor: bhang, Battistoni, and Verushka. After the last meeting, I went to dinner with my wife, Becky, and Chosei and Suzy Funahara, the Japanese producer of the Philippines movie and his wife. Following a feast of *shabu shabu,* the four of us looked for a club in which to celebrate, and ended up at the Canal Street Bar, where we ordered Dom Perignon. The atmosphere at the club was perfect, and we were all in a wonderful mood.

One rude thing I always do when I am in public is scan: I look at interesting faces as if I were casting a movie. And this is what I did at the Canal Street Bar, where most of the people were artist types. There was a party of around ten people at a nearby table, and as I watched the types I fixed on one particular person, a girl who looked to be in her late twenties. I could see only her left profile, but her hair was ash blond and straight and she had a beautiful forehead. I studied her, holding my right hand over my right eye, framing her the way a camera sees life, through one eye. I continued to look at this interesting woman, covering my eye as if it were going to fall out of my head, not constantly but often enough to be noticed by several of the birthday bunch. I eventually pointed her out to the others at our table, and said that she looked like she could be Verushka's daughter. Becky and Suzy Funahara, who said that Verushka was her idol, agreed; Chosei said, "Very sixties." As I looked over again, the twenty-five-year-old Verushka clone suddenly turned and smiled at me. I was very embarrassed and quickly turned away.

As we neared the end of our second bottle of Dom I could sense the birthday bunch leaving, but I was not about to be caught staring a second time. Suzy Funahara said the girl was coming toward our table. I thought she was joking but Becky said, "She is, darling. And she's looking right at you!"

"Come on, you guys!" I was embarrassed enough, and kept my eyes on my champagne glass.

But Becky wasn't teasing. I turned and saw that the woman was indeed coming directly at *me*. I stood up as she drew near, and I looked into her eyes, dumbstruck.

"Vera?" I squeaked dryly.

"Peetah?" The wonderful deep voice and the rest of her had hardly changed in the twenty-five years since we'd had the affair I'd spent the last two days recounting.

A couple of nights later I took her out to dinner. I had to ensure that she would not mind if I wrote about our affair, and asked her about the last time we'd seen each other, at the Regency in 1971. I needed to know if I had been hallucinating.

Vera laughed. "You mean about Jane standing in the doorway?"

> *In a world of steel-eyed death*
> *and men who were fighting to be warm,*
> *Come in, she said,*
> *I'll give ya shelter from the storm.*
> —Bob Dylan

chapter *Twelve*

*I*n August, after I'd been home for a few weeks, Jane asked us to fly with her to Las Vegas for her wedding to French director Roger Vadim. We joined several friends, including Brooke Hayward and her husband, Dennis Hopper, on a chartered plane, and as we left Los Angeles, we could see smoke. Watts was starting to burn. I brought the Gibson twelve-string and sang at Jane's wedding. I sang Donovan's "Colors," emphasizing the last verse by singing it three times: *Freedom is a word I rarely use without thinking of the times when I been low.*

The next day, back at my house as the riots kicked in, I began to consider the idea of taking lysergic acid diethylamide—LSD. A doctor in London in 1963 had suggested I look into it for help with my manic depression, and said it altered the chemistry of the brain. I was interested in the suggestion that it could help me understand my mind—after Stormy's suicide, anything was worth investigating. I arranged to take the drug with three friends, renting a house within walking distance of my own for the "trip," as the session was called. I took five hundred micrograms of the original liquid from Sandoz Laboratory in Switzerland and lay down on a couch. Within forty minutes, I was hallucinating like mad, and it was beautiful. I never felt worried or fearful as I watched the world as I knew it change completely.

I walked back to my home, looked at the cars that were parked all over, and realized that I was obsessed with possessions. I had a Buick Riviera, a Chevrolet station wagon, a Jaguar XKE coupe, two motorcycles, a fifteen-foot utility drag boat, and a set-to-race Corvette Stingray. I got into the Riv, started it up, and slowly drove out my driveway. The steering wheel was continually collapsing in my hands, and the dash was rusting and falling into my lap. As I drove through the tall eucalyptus grove that filled the bottom our canyon, the trees began to fall down in front of the car, and the roadway was erupting like many volcanoes at each speed bump.

I pulled the car over, got out, went back to the rented house, and crawled into a linen closet, folding myself up so that I could fit on a shelf. I liked it there in the darkness, where my visions weren't compounded by external stimuli. In the dark, all scrunched up, I felt an unbelievable pain and ecstasy. I looked down at my belly and saw Bridget emerging as a perfect one-year-old child. Colors swirled around her. She led me out of the closet and out to the backyard, like Tinkerbell from *Peter Pan*. She brought me to Basil, and when the dog and I were on all fours, she flew away. I spent some time crawling around with Basil, but the ground was undulating, and a frog came out of a hole. It looked like a giant slimy boulder, but its eyes gave it away, and Basil chased it back down its hole. To him it was just a frog. I was curious that while all else around me seemed in a constant changing state, Basil looked quite the same as he always had. I crawled into the kitchen and found an oatmeal cookie. I knew what it was, but it looked like a mound of live worms and grubs, and moved about in my hand. I ate it at once, crunching the worms and grubs as I chewed it.

Back outside, I saw a shower of colorful bands of light emanating from the sky. I studied the thing from which the light was coming, and for a second I could see that it was a plane, and the colorful lights were the sound of its motors. As soon as I perceived this, the colors stopped and it became an ordinary airplane. The thick brush and shrubs on the side of a hill were gracefully swaying back and forth as if they were supple underwater plants, moving back and forth with the gentle surge.

Everything was different and everything was the same. Everything was everything. After my trips, I had a firmer grip on the realities that I faced and a fuller understanding of life and our place in it.

The Beatles came to L.A. and stayed on Benedict Canyon in a stilt house. I was asked to come over and play with the lads, as Derek Taylor, their publicist and road manager, called them, and I drove over in my Jag. I had been instructed to give a password to the police who were guarding the house, but the reasons for such protection only sank in when I came to a bend in the road just below their rented house and saw that the entire wall of the canyon was filled with screaming young people. What a scene; they pounced and pounded on my aluminum-bodied XKE.

As soon as I was in the house, David Crosby gave me "my" dose of LSD. I hadn't quite prepared for it, but what the hell. During the trip, we decided to go out on the deck and brave the storm of screaming teenagers. Once we had established a beachhead on our own property, the screaming seemed to quiet down. Actually, I'm quite sure that it continued nonstop, but we all stopped hearing it.

George was having a rough time. Apparently, he had been dosed before without knowing it and had a hellish experience. He said that he thought he was dying. I tried to calm him and let him understand that it was his own brain putting fear in his thoughts and trying to keep a control on the uncontrollable, just as impossible a task as controlling dying. I told George that I knew what it was like to be dead, and that everything would be all right. He wasn't so sure, understandably, and as I was telling him the story of my own death on the operating table in Ossining, John Lennon came over to where we were seated.

"Who put all that crap in your head?" he asked angrily. "You're making me feel like I've never been born!"

This was how the song "She Said She Said" came to life. John didn't like the role he'd assigned me—Trip Guide. We watched Jane's *Cat Ballou* that evening, too, and John had had enough of Fondas. Roger McGuinn—in those days known as Jim McGuinn—worked hard and fast to make things smooth. With Paul's help he got John to forget the incident and go on with the trip. We ended up in a sunken tub in the master bathroom—no water—while everyone played and sang. McGuinn and Harrison played their electric twelve-strings with no amplification, but the hard surfaces of the bath acted as a booster for the sound. George played some Bach riffs that blew my mind. At one point I went to the kitchen for something to drink and ran into Peggy Lipton, whom I knew, sitting in the living room looking lost.

"I don't know why I'm here," she said.

I went back to the boys and told them there was a pretty blond sitting in the living room. Someone asked if I was tripping, and I said, no, I sniffed her crotch and she was definitely a blond. Paul went to be the host. As it turned out, he was the only one who wasn't on LSD.

.   .   .

Later that year, Dennis Hopper and Ted Markland and Joe Steck, a lawyer who had just produced *Waterhole Number Nine* came to visit me. The conversation turned to independent filmmaking, and I said I wanted to make a movie about a man looking for love. After going through many funny episodes parodying our culture—huge Marlboro packs rolling like tumbleweed; the White Knight marauding through a dirty football field, only to be revealed as Sonny Liston—he discovers that he was in love with love all along.

Hopper jumped off the couch and began pacing around the room, saying that *everyone* talked about making a movie, but no one was willing to go through with it. When I suggested that *we* go through with it, and Hopper asked who was going to pay for the script, I said that it was my idea, and I would pay for it.

Within a few days, we'd found a stand-up comedian, Don Sherman, who volunteered to join us as a comedy and writing guide. He was paid as a full writer, as was Hopper. I didn't pay myself, but I did form the Pando Company, named for the Latin verb meaning to spread out, to stretch out; to show, tell, or relate; to publish; to bend in the wind like a reed or a bough. And when used with the word *capilli*—hair—it means disheveled. It was a perfect name for my production company.

I rented a small house in Sherman Oaks and put Stormy's beds, organ, and other furnishings in the house, along with John Haeberlin and Basil. John was working as my assistant in many ways, both of us still numb about Stormy, though we spent little time talking about it. Dennis, Don, a secretary, and I came to work every morning at nine-thirty and finished at five-thirty. The secretary took everything down in shorthand, and the next day, I would start off by reading aloud what had been written up to that point before we plunged on. We were always laughing hysterically when I finished the reading and up to speed for the next section, and the ongoing feeling made me set aside my grief and bewilderment.

We finished the script by mid-December. On the last day, I read the entire screenplay from beginning to end, pausing to wipe the tears of laughter from my eyes so I could *see* the page. Hopper wanted to call the work *The Ying and the Yang*. I explained that the word was and had been *Yin,* no *g,* but he insisted that it sounded better with the *g.* "It's a balance, man, you know what I mean?" said Dennis. "Two four-letter words, man." I told him that it wasn't a two-word concept, it was yin-yang. Inseparable, negative-positive, each interdependent.

We settled the issue by putting the *g* in parentheses: *The Yin(g) and the Yang.* When I had finished the last read, I turned to Hopper and acknowledged that he had undone what the great Buddhists had struggled to keep together for centuries. I had spent a lot of cash on the project and didn't want to spoil it with useless argument. We decided to shoot the movie in 16mm Panavision anamorphic, and planned to take the project to New York, less apathetic than in L.A., after the holidays. We wanted $450,000.

Near the end of the year, Roger Corman asked me to meet with him. I showed up in his office with my increasingly long hair, some very bizarre glasses that Brian Jones had given me, and a gold badge from the Office of Naval Intelligence, one that had been Commander McDonald's. Roger told me that he wanted to make a movie about the Hells Angels without making a statement. I thought that it was an interesting idea, but that making a movie about anything as controversial as the Hells Angels was in itself a statement.

It was all vague, and I left his office looking for work. By this time, things were becoming edgy at home. When I wasn't writing the script with Hopper, I was hanging out with rock groups, and I was gone so often that Susan became angry with me. She was very sweet to my friends and usually cooked for whomever I brought home, but she didn't like the life or the scene that completely energized me. She often said hurtful things in front of others about my playing and singing, and sometimes she would put me down as I played at home alone. I got away by going out to the front drive, getting into the Impala wagon—a muscle car for which Carrol Shelby built the wheels and tires—and singing my heart out. No one else told me to shut up. She wasn't that way in the beginning. We used to sing Everly Brothers' songs while I played my guitar. We did it often while we were in London for *The Victors*.

One night in late October, just as Susan and I had finished making love, I realized that she had gone for a baby. It wasn't something she said, but I understood that she had conceived. It was a very similar feeling to the one I'd had in Columbus, Ohio, when Bridget was conceived, only it was much stronger. When I asked Susan about it, she said that I was being cynical. I did a little math and figured out that the baby was due in late July 1966. I teased Susan about having a child that would be a Leo. Too much water in the family? Need some more fire, a little Leo just like you? This angered her, and I countered that the making of a baby was a two-person job and wondered why she had kept me in the dark. She had no answer, and we didn't discuss it, like that, again.

After New Year's, Dennis and I headed east to Manhattan to find our fortunes. I had arranged a two-bedroom suite in a hotel Sam· Goldwyn, Jr., had stayed in 1963 while we read actresses for *The Young Lovers*. The hotel was being torn down while we stayed there, so there was no room service, and the rates were *very* reasonable. I liked the irony. We had thirty copies of the script with us and a passion about the project to equal our passion for our possible futures. We were on our way. We were going to make our own pictures. We had a script, and we had energy, and we simply needed money. I was spending plenty and not bringing much in, but I never said a thing to Dennis. I didn't want him to think about anything other than the making of the film.

Through Hopper I met the powers behind the Pop Art movement. I met Claes Oldenburg and was privileged to watch him work. We hung out with Andy Warhol's ménage—there was a strange brew— and were introduced to Van Wolf, an entrepreneur who was into the film business, and who loved the script. We met Huntington Hartford, who told us he'd give us the money if I could levitate, and we drove around town in limos with Bill Blass and some top fashion models. We joined up with Mick Jagger several times, and sabotaged the dress code in Armando Orsini's formal dining room when Mick, Jean Shrimpton, and some other glitterati piled out of one limo and Bill Blass, myself, Dennis, and some more glamour rolled out of another. It was an unstoppable wave of high-profile performers. We had custom-tailored suits and turtleneck sweaters, and we looked sharp. Orsini's dress code changed after that evening. I liked Mick a lot. He had a fabulous aura of energy. He had interesting things to say and a

view of American society that was refreshing. I would meet Mick
again in the life.

When we weren't promoting our script, we went to parties and
promoted ourselves. We drove out to Stony Brook at the invitation of
Billy and Tommy Hitchcock and gave a reading for them. The focal
point for the group was Tim Leary, so I have no idea what they heard
while I read, but Dennis and I were laughing hard enough for the
whole bunch. We spent evenings with Larry Rivers and hung out with
Henry Geldseler and Robert Rauschenberg. At the unveiling of one of
Rauschenberg's commissioned pieces, a mechanical wonder some
old gal had paid over three hundred thousand for, we joined many
high-fashion models, a small rock band, and a slew of hotshot pho-
tographers. The big moment came when Robert plugged the metal
performance art piece into the wall. This wondrous collection of
gears, form, and substance began to whirl and within ten minutes had
collapsed on itself.

One night at Van Wolf's wild apartment, there was a party for the
cream of the city's artists and high rollers. Among the guests were
Salvador Dalí, his mistress and her very young girlfriend, the ubiqui-
tous Hunt Hartford, Bob Rauschenberg, Warhol, and Nico. Dalí's mistress told me she was a witch, and with her long black hair she could
have fooled most people. I told her that I was a witch, too, and whispered into her young girlfriend's long, black hair—I couldn't see her
ear—to watch a certain young man who was sitting about twenty feet
away. I whispered that he didn't smoke cigarettes, but that I would
make him reach over to the coffee table in front of us, and take a
cigarette and smoke it. I concentrated on him intensely, and in less
than three minutes, he reached for the pack, helped himself to a
Camel, and fired it up. The young man was Bobby Walker. When the
ladies complained that he was a friend and in on the trick, I pointed
out I hadn't started the conversation, or said anything to him. I hadn't
even known he was coming to the party. When I called out to him
over the noise of the chatter and asked him what he was doing, he
was totally surprised to realize that he was smoking, and put out the
cigarette.

We spent the rest of our time meeting with potential backers, some
arranged by Van Wolf. Van's apartment was being painted by some
blissed-out hippie to look like the miasma of an acid trip, and we met

the financial types at the Seventy-fourth Street house, where we'd moved after the hotel began to tear up the floor below us.

One evening, Dennis and I took Walter Hopps to dinner and invited Darlene DeSedle to accompany us. Walter had been head curator of the Pasadena Art Museum, and was on his way to his new posting as the head curator of the National Gallery in D.C., and he was a very down-to-earth man, not a bit like Hopper or me. We were to meet at Darlene's apartment on Fifty-seventh Street, and when I arrived a little late I walked into another world.

I'd been excited to show Dennis the full moon, but Dennis had something startling to show me. Walter was sitting on Darlene's couch teary-eyed, and Hopper, trying to explain, was like a bull in a small room. It seemed that Walter and Dennis were having coffee and talking art. Walter noticed a wooden oil-painted panel on the wall and commented that it was a very good reproduction of a panel from the Merode altarpiece, the fourteenth-century triptych by an unidentified Flemish master, commonly called the *Annunciation* or the *Second Chance*, which hung in the Cloisters, the Metropolitan's monastery museum in Manhattan. The thing that makes the piece so provocative in the history of art is that all other Annunciation paintings of the period showed three shafts of gold already touching Mary's belly and the archangel Gabriel telling her what has happened. In the Merode altarpiece, the shafts of gold have not yet reached Mary's belly; she has just finished the Old Testament, put it aside, washed her hands, and picked up the New Testament, cradling it in a clean cloth. The candle beside her has just been blown out by the coming of the seed and the presence of the archangel, the glow from the wick still there, and her eyes are just about to make contact with Michael's. It was an interpretation of the moment *before* the Annunciation, as groundbreaking as Picasso's movement from formal art to cubism and abstraction.

Darlene, on her way from her kitchen to her bathroom, told Dennis and Walter that it was the original, and that her father had bought it from Parke-Bernet as the original in 1935. Walter took the panel from the wall and began to study it closely. On Darlene's next trip to the kitchen—she was getting ready to go out on the town in a very small apartment—Walter asked her if she had the other two panels. "Yes," she said, "they're in the closet."

By the time I arrived, Walter had all three panels on the floor in front of him, and he was undone—the panels could possibly *be* original. The wood was correct for the period, and there were some differences in the piece as compared to the "original" up in the Cloisters; this during the time when many old masters that had been bought by the art museums were turning out to be fakes. The Merode altarpiece had been missing for three hundred years, hence the reasonable doubt that it was the original that hung at the Cloisters.

The full implication did not sink in until Walter estimated the price of the original at eight million dollars, and Darlene said, as she passed back and forth, that if the panels were original she would sell them and give us the money we needed to produce the film. We went out to a very tense dinner. Darlene and I had smoked a number in her bathroom before we left, as the other two were unable to do anything but consider their potential art-circle bomb.

The next day, I made an appointment to meet with several scholars at Columbia School of Art. More perfect coincidence—the school was housed in the mansion my mother had shared with Pan's father, George Brokaw. It took up most of the block on the upper east side, on Fifth Avenue. We carefully put the three pieces in pillowcases and, arriving at the Brokaw Mansion, boldly walked into the Den of Perfect Knowledge.

I played it very straight and cool, and after introductions walked about the place, pretending I had once played in these halls, trying to buy time and suss out their position before we answered queries. When we were finally brought to a basement studio, we were met with derision by the young Turks in charge, who looked at the three panels and remarked that the style was correct and the wood was of the right age, but the "original" didn't have this or that. In between they mocked my long hair and Dennis's manic belief. The Napoleonic furrow on Dennis's brow was getting deep. Then, a small, elderly man came into the room, and began to speak French to himself in an awestruck way, coming close to tears. The young Turks kept pointing out inconsistencies—notably a figure of a man on the left panel—but he shut them down thoroughly, and continued his rapture.

It seemed that he was the head curator for the Louvre, at Columbia on sabbatical, and when he tested the white paint for its content and declared that it might very well *be* the original, none of the Turks dared to question him. They asked to keep the painting for a few days to further study the paint and x-ray the panels, to "find the snow," the old Frenchman added, a reference that seemed to baffle even the Turks; there was no snow on the version of the triptych at the Cloisters *or* in Darlene's.

Dennis became very paranoid and pulled me aside.

"Man, don't you get it, man? They're going to keep the painting, man, and when they find out it's the original, they'll keep the real one and give us back the counterfeit one, man."

We put the three panels back in the pillowcases and left for Darlene's. We didn't feel let down at all. Darlene said there was a man in Brazil who would pay big bucks for *any* old masters, when the possibility was strong that the "original" was a fake, and that she could still help us with the movie. We thanked her profusely for her generosity, but said we'd find the money somehow without taking her father's gift from her. The movie never got made.

. . .

Dennis and I had to go back to L.A., but Dalí made me promise to return on February 23—my birthday—and take part in a large Happening at Lincoln Center. Van Wolf gave us a going-away party, and halfway into it, I got a call from my agent, Jack Gilardi. Corman was going to shoot his Hells Angels movie in March, and wanted me to play the second male lead, with George Chakiris as the lead. There were only fifty-some pages written so far, but Corman wanted an answer. Two weeks' work for ten thousand dollars. The pages were sent, and I accepted the role, even though my character would be dead for three-quarters of the movie. I needed the work and the money.

When I returned for the Dalí performance, I brought a Burns electric twelve-string with me and an Ampex reel to reel. My plan for the Happening with Dalí was to record, direct to the Ampex, free-form music inspired by what I saw actually happening on the stage, monitoring my music with headphones, a completely closed system. I had a major hassle with the stage unions to get electricity to the Ampex, but I finally prevailed. After watching the pandemonium of the preparations, I decided that I wouldn't use a take-up reel, thereby allowing the tape to end up in a chaotic pile that would fit the mood of the night.

Dalí had a giant, clear plastic ball onstage that was held in shape by a fan-driven air hose. Behind the ball and up on a screen, he projected the Luis Buñuel movies *L'âge d'or* and *Un chien andalou* (codirected by Dalí), while the performance was underway. The Happening was packed and utterly chaotic, but at the end I walked up to Dalí on the stage and handed him the huge jumble of unspooled tape, which I had gathered and held tenderly so as not to crease the stuff. He kept me beside him for my twenty-sixth birthday surprise: three people carried an enormous birthday cake onto the stage. Meanwhile, the giant plastic ball had been painted from the inside by Dalí and some others during the event, mostly by flinging paint all around it. Sometimes Dalí would take a brush, fixed to the end of a long pole, and put some strokes here and there.

I flew back to L.A. to prepare for the Corman film. The title, *The Wild Angels,* should have been warning enough. I was lounging in bed one morning, three or four weeks before the film was to start, when I got a call from Roger Corman, who said he was having a little difficulty.

"George can't ride a Harley, and you want me to do the role, right, Roger?"

He was amazed that I knew the problem. "Why, yes. That's exactly the problem."

It was as if I had had the conversation before. "I'll do it, Roger, but you'll have to change the name of the character. Jack Black is too predictable, man. I want to be called Heavenly Blues. My real name can be Henry, but everyone calls me Heavenly."

"Well, Peter, I, uh, why Heavenly Blues?"

"Because a few hundred Heavenly Blue or Pearly Gates morning glory seeds, ground up and swallowed with a very small amount of water, will give one a hallucinogenic experience. And I want my tank painted with Heavenly Blue morning glories."

I got the name but not the paint job. Too bad. Nancy Sinatra was the leading female, and we were already friends. I had gone to her house many times for actor-restaurateur Nicki Blair's Italian dinners. Other members of the cast included Bruce Dern (playing the role I had originally accepted, the Loser), Michael J. Pollard, Diane Ladd, and Buck Taylor, as well as several members of the actual Hells Angels, who gave me insight to what a brother does for a brother in the biker world. They also gave me grass that had been soaked in opium, ineffective but given to me as an acceptance token.

During the first days we shot a half-day, half-night at a hospital in Culver City, and I had been practicing riding my motorcycle while the camera wasn't rolling. It suddenly dawned on me that this was the hospital where my maternal grandfather, Eugene Ford Seymour, had died three weeks earlier. When I'm shooting a film, I tend to remove myself from the normal world. There is nothing normal about making a motion picture, so the separation is healthy. But he was the first person I'd seen in the process of death, and when I went to say good-bye to him, sitting next to his bed, I became aware that he wanted to die right then. He was very frail, and at first, I didn't think he could tell I was there, but when I took his hand he opened his eyes. I put my face right above him, and he whispered my name.

"I'm going to die soon," he rasped. I asked him if he was afraid. He said he was afraid he *wouldn't* die soon. I felt bad that he was alone, even though his aloneness was a result of his own thoughtless life. After he died, I asked the doctors at the hospital if anyone had been with him, and the no they gave me brought me back to Stormy, Bridget Hayward, and my mother, all alone.

I didn't know him well, but I knew that he had drunk himself out of a respectable law practice and judgship. And by this time in my life I knew that he had, through his alcoholism, messed up my mother and her brothers and sister. As I grew older, I would find out a few things that happened to my parents in part because of *their* parents.

When Roger found out that all this had happened recently, he asked if I would feel better not staying at the location. I thought that was a nice thing for him to have offered, but I had removed myself from that other world and had few bad feelings about those past moments. But I used it, and let it give me a different, inexplicable edge.

Several amusing things happened during the shoot, while we were on location outside Palm Springs. We had to ride to Mecca, down near Indio, to retrieve Bruce Dern's stolen motorcycle, and I found it interesting that we rode east to Mecca from the oil fields along the coast to bust up a Latino gang. On our lunch break, a few of us took off in my muscle-car station wagon, the Impala with the darkened windows, to smoke a bowl. As we roared across the desert, we ran right through the set of another movie, a big war picture called *Tobruk* being shot by Roger's brother, Gene. We blasted past some poor third assistant director trying to control traffic, and found ourselves in the midst of a large tank battle. Once we learned that it was Roger's brother who was directing, we blasted back through the battle, hanging our asses and Nazi-decorated costumes out the windows as we screamed obscenities at the actors playing the Brits.

We got back to our set just in time for lunch, but halfway through lunch break, five troop carriers and two armored vehicles from the *Tobruk* set surrounded our set and kidnapped me, driving off into the desert. I loved it, but our first assistant director was very concerned that I would not be returned and, totally unaware of Gene Corman's presence in the desert a few miles away, sent the Hells Angels to retrieve me.

During the shooting of the last scenes in a graveyard for the Loser's burial, Roger had set up a long dolly shot for me and Nancy Sinatra. Nancy is a petite woman, and I am a tall man, so Roger had two choices: build a ramp for Nancy, or dig a trench for me. I think that Roger didn't want to embarrass Nancy by making her walk on a platform, but the time and effort it took to dig the trench was probably more awkward for her.

After the trench was completed, we rehearsed the scene a few times. The shot started out as a wide two-shot and dollied closer to the two of us for our more intimate dialogue. It was necessary for me to start out walking normally with Nancy and, as the camera came closer, begin to bend down until I was in the trench, and then I had to straighten up slowly to make the shot work. We call the crouching part a "Groucho," for the comic way Groucho Marx would sometimes walk. I had to go from a half Groucho to a full stance to make the balance, and it was hard to keep a straight face. Several times in rehearsal, Nancy and I fell to the ground, holding each other and laughing our heads off.

While we were shooting up in Idyllwild, Nancy and I split a duplex log cabin. I stayed in my half with John Haeberlin, who was still working as my assistant, but before we turned out the lights, Nancy and I would sing songs as I played my new Guild twelve-string. Father Frank visited the set and the cabin. I assured him that nothing bad would happen to Nancy, as Haeberlin and I were right on the other side of the wall, but her dad knew he didn't have to worry. Nancy could take care of herself very well, and she'd earned the respect of the entire company. Hell, she could have taken care of herself, Frankie Jr., Tina, Nancy Sr., *and* Frank!

One of my best experiences on the shoot was working with Bruce

Dern, whose work I'd admired for some time. His persona was unique, and he filled his moments beautifully. He wasn't into smoking *anything,* nor did he know about bikers, and though I provided him with a pair of glasses and some of the dialect, he did all the rest. I think he played the Loser much better than I could have. Diane Ladd was a delight, too, and Peter Bogdanovich worked on the film as a second-unit director. I flirted with his beautiful wife, Polly Platt, every chance I could. When the film finished, I went back to L.A.

· · ·

I had to let the house in Sherman Oaks go once the script was done, though John Haeberlin and I stayed on for a bit, playing guitars and Stormy's organ and taking my last trip on LSD. At the end of my acid trip, I reluctantly answered an insistent telephone. It was John Lear, who loved flying rock groups to their gigs. He wanted to take us on a flight. It was quite a trip. I'd met John on a flight to Pensacola with Jim McGuinn and the Byrds in late 1965. Gene Clark hadn't wanted to fly on the Learjet, so I had the extra seat. We stopped at Sheppard Air Force Base in Wichita Falls to refuel, and the band and I went out and smoked one, sitting under the wing of a C130 gunship. When we took off, John climbed to forty-four thousand feet like a rocket. The full-throttle ride and the grass made everyone sleepy except for me and McGuinn, who were sitting right up next to the cockpit watching the altimeter spin. John was taking hits from his oxygen mask and turned to us, saying, watch this. McGuinn had a cup of coffee and I was holding a 7-UP. John put the jet into a fairly tight roll, corkscrewing through the thin air over Texas. Not a drop spilled from McGuinn's or my beverage, but David Crosby woke up in a panic.

· · ·

The Wild Angels was slated to open the Venice Film Festival in August, and American International Pictures (AIP), the financing and distributing studio behind the picture, sent me to the event. The film was the highest-grossing film they'd ever made, and the festival was the perfect marketplace for a European audience. As I walked up the red-carpeted stairs to the main cinema, I was accompanied by Françoise Hardy, a French actress who had on the smallest miniskirt I had ever seen. The press went wild with speculation, and the paparazzi went wild with the skirt. When the screening was over, the audience was astounded and negative, but the press corps went wild again, and this time it had nothing to do with Françoise's skirt. Françoise left immediately, as she was making *Grand Prix*.

Jane tracked me down and asked me to spend twelve days in Saint-Tropez. She implied that she needed me to be with her. I joined Jane and Vadim at a little hotel on the beach, named Plage Tahiti. By day, we would either eat at the hotel's small restaurant on the beach, or speed down the coast in Vadim's Riva, a beautiful wooden speedboat that was old-fashioned in its lines but pure speed and plush, for dinner at someone's villa. By night we would go into the village of Saint-Tropez and eat at one of the places along the harbor, or at a restaurant owned by a friend of Vadim's, Jean Marie's.

The Italian prince, Dado Ruspoli, and his wife, Nancy; J. Paul Getty, Jr.; French actress Françoise D'Orleac; Christian Marquand, and many others came along to Jean Marie's on various nights. They had a custom at the restaurant most evenings. After the meal, one of the group would pick up a plate and smash it on the floor. Others soon followed, until all the crockery had been broken, at which time, Jean Marie would come out from the kitchen with *more* crockery and begin to smash it himself. I don't know how the man survived in the business, replacing plates every other night.

After the smashing meal, everyone would go to a local discotheque to dance. I remembered the nights at Ocean House, in Santa Monica, dancing with Jane, but this was quite different. Dado Ruspoli went after every young girl, leaving Nancy on her own, and this was a definite mistake. I danced with her all the time, except when I danced with Jane, and it was fun to flirt with her.

One night, I was down in the bar at Plage Tahiti having a cognac. It was windy and the surf was making a delightful symphony, with the wind taking the spray and wafting it ashore. Suddenly, the beach side doors burst open, and in with the storm came a mermaid. Her hair was light auburn, long and tousled as if it had just been done for a fashion shoot for hair products. She had large, dark eyes and an exquisite body, with long, perfect legs. She was amazing, absolutely amazing.

The French paid no attention to her. What frogs, I thought; not a prince among them. I offered her a cognac or whatever she would like. "I'll even leave you alone," I said, trying to be polite.

"I'll have a cognac," she answered in perfect English. "With you." She drank her cognac and left, after kissing me lightly on the cheek and telling me her name was Tahlita.

The wind had stopped as she disappeared out the front toward the hotel's terrazzo parking area. I went up to my room, smoked a joint, and tried to get to sleep.

The next day J. Paul Getty, Jr., showed up with his fiancée, Tahlita Pohl, to give me a ride to a lunch party. They had an MG TC with the top down, but no matter the conditions her hair was perfect, as was she. I took a picture of her looking back at me and Paul's smiling eyes, in focus, in the rearview mirror. I wanted a beer, or maybe a gallon of water or a sharp pin.

One evening, after a fabulous meal and more plate smashing, Vadim, Jane, and I were headed back to the Plage Tahiti in the Ferrari. As it was a two-passenger car, Jane sat on my lap. We began singing Everly Brothers songs, something we did often when we were together. I think Vadim became jealous, and suddenly he turned the wheel hard to the right, causing the sleek car to swerve. The beautiful handmade aluminum body caromed off a stacked rock wall on the left side of the road, ruining the left rear end. Vadim followed this with a hard turn to the left, smashing the other side of the rear. Jane and I stopped singing. She doesn't remember the incident, but I shall never forget it.

Another night, I had an incredible reading by a psychic who seemed to know a lot about my life and my need for unconditional love. Afterward, I went up to my room and smoked several bowls, played my guitar, and sang songs to people who could not hear. Susan didn't like my playing and often criticized it. I'm sure she was angry at me most of the time, as she had every right to be. I wanted unconditional love, but at that time I didn't know how to give it myself. I slept, and my demons came and raped me.

I stayed by myself the next day, and that night I stayed in my room, and pondered my life and how I was living it. I played and sang for a while, wrote poems, smoked pot. I wasn't depressed. I had been around and about with some of the most decadent types I'd ever met, lovely, charming, sensual, and outrageous. I was alone in the middle of a wild moment, but then I heard a light knock; it was Tahlita. She asked if I was all right and began to read the poems I had written. The only light at the table was provided by two candles, and she was close to them, reading with her head leaning against her arm. I took eight photos of her in black-and-white with one of my Nikons. She asked me if I would kiss her like I photographed her, and I leaned over the table and kissed her as simply and tenderly as I could. I sat back, embarrassed by wanting her as much as I wanted life at that moment.

I asked if she wanted to go swimming, and she said that was a wonderful idea. It was still and hot that evening. We walked out into the Mediterranean and swam in the warm waters, swimming closer to each other until we were facing. She asked me if I was happy with my life. I told her I didn't know, and asked her if she was happy with hers. She didn't know, either.

We ended up on the beach, but sand is sand, and we showered and ran up to my room. We made love in the most tender ways, and we made love in full abandon. After a while she asked me where Jane and Vadim were. I said I had no idea, and that I only wanted to be with *her*. We made love, and after, she asked about Jane, Paul, and Vadim again. We had been together for a long time, so I agreed to help her find Paul and the others. With towels wrapped around us, we went out to the walkway. She began to knock on some doors, calling out softly. I stayed right next to her. I wasn't ready to let her go. She was someone's fiancée, and I was someone's husband and father, but the shelter she gave was all I cared about.

After we found the others, I drew her back out of the door and held her tightly. Tahlita took me into the room and made Paul and Vadim—Jane wasn't there—watch us make love. She wouldn't let either man touch her. She said she only wanted me, right then, right there. I was amazed, but once we got into it, I didn't give a rat's ass about the others, though I wondered what Jane would think.

Jane, Vadim, and I were going to Venice that next morning, because Jane had a film that was closing the festival. The stay had been like a big wheel of fortune that spun for twelve days, and every time it stopped it landed on greatness, extremes of sex, weirdness, kindness, outrageousness, moments beyond time. I thought about Stormy and wished he could have lived it. We stuffed ourselves into the now modified Ferrari. It was a complete circus. Not only was the car made for just two passengers, it was not made for luggage, period. Little brother had to share the sardine back with my twelve-string in its case, my camera bag, and *all* our luggage. And off we sped to Nice and the flight to Venice.

Jane and Vadim's film did very well at the festival. She had shot two versions, French and English, shooting one right after the other: *La curée* or *The End of the Game.* We sat with François Truffaut and Jean-Luc Godard, and it was exciting to listen to their comments and visions about the new cinema.

After the festival, Jane and Vadim went to Jane's farm, just west of Paris, and I headed for a small hotel I knew about in the city. But when I arrived, the only accommodation was a dark suite in the lowest part of the hotel. The windows were half below the sidewalk and had solid metal shutters. I kept them closed, feeling like the phantom of the opera.

I joined Dado, Nancy, and some of their friends for a dinner at the best Vietnamese restaurant in Paris. The meal was fabulous, and Nancy was flirting with me very intensely. As dinner came to its stuffed-gut end, Dado suggested that several of us go to a friend's apartment and smoke some opium. The apartment proved to be very large and beautifully decorated, not at all what I expected for an opium den, but the ceremony was spectacular. We went to a front room that had large silk-covered pillows set in a circle. There was an oblong cut-crystal vase with a wick and some liquid, and an eighteen-inch-long ceramic tube, inlaid with gold and silver wire and Chinese designs and closed at one end by an ornate silver cap. The bowl part of the pipe was separate, but it, too, was ornate, with gold and silver wire.

A man brought a vial of black liquid with the thickness of motor oil and inserted a long silver wire, which, when withdrawn from the vial, was coated lightly with the dark liquid, the opium. The chef, as he was called, held the wire over the flame from the candlelike vase and wick, and as the opium heated up, it thickened and bubbled up on the wire. The chef then took the bowl and, holding it over the flame upside down, twirled the wire and its gooey opium all around the inside of the bowl. At a specific moment, the pipe was held over the bubbling bowl as the bowl was fitted into a hole in the pipe, all the while the wire was being rubbed around the bowl over the flame.

The pipe was held out to one of us, bowl still over the flame, and we took long pulls on the smoking opium. I have a large lung capacity, and therefore finished my bowl and asked for a second. I was obliged, and watched closely by the others. I finished the second bowl and a third after the others had taken their turns.

We all lay on our pillows, and no one said a thing. A light cough here or there and nothing else. I looked over at Nancy, who hadn't taken any opium. A little later I became very thirsty, and stood up to get a wet cloth. The others all muttered in negative ways about my getting up and walking, but I didn't feel incapacitated in any way and knew that though one was not supposed to drink anything after taking any kind of opiate, the wet cloth would do fine and not make me puke.

After an hour and no high, I looked at my watch and noticed it was nearing dawn. I had begun the evening thinking that another door of decadence would be opened to me. Not that I liked decadence for its own sake, but I was seeing doctors, dentists, lawyers, bankers, stockbrokers, and politicians getting high, having orgies, and generally doing the very things that the establishment put people like me in jails for doing.

I finally asked to call a taxi to take me back to my dungeon, and Dado and Nancy said they wanted to leave, too. As we rode to my hotel, we talked about the experience. They were both very interested that I had never done these things before. I told them that I had had pot that was more effective than the opium.

When I climbed into bed and fell asleep as Paris was waking and walking right past my window, I felt that I would have a good long sleep. But I popped out of slumberland running from my nightmare and trying to tear my balls and ass off, itching like crazy with no idea where I was. I hadn't forgotten whom I was, and stumbled around the dark room, thinking I had the crabs (not realizing the itching was a reaction to the opiates), wondering what I would tell Susan and trying to remember suspect information from boarding school bull sessions. I scrubbed my crotch in the bidet—kill those little fuckers— went back to bed, and fell asleep at once.

I woke up around one-thirty in the afternoon, knowing where I was and not even remembering the crabs. When I joined Dado and Nancy for lunch at some brasserie, Dado had one of his young girl-friends with him, and I was pleased, thinking I could be with Nancy, remembering that Dado was going to Stuttgart to pick up a new Maserati and would be out of town for two days.

After our meal, we all went walking; Dado with his young girlfriend and Nancy with me. It was pretty bizarre, but everything that happened in those few weeks was bizarre.

"Too bad you have to go to Stuttgart to pick up your car, Dado."

Dado laughed. "What are you talking about, Peter?"

"Your new Maserati, Dado. Last night you told me you had to go to Stuttgart to pick it up." I was positive.

"I'm not buying a new Maserati, Peter, and I certainly wouldn't be going to Stuttgart to buy an Italian car." He chuckled.

Bewildered by my statement, I slowed down a bit and told Nancy that I was certain he had told me he was going out of town to buy a car, and I had been planning on my good fortune of being alone with her. She assured me that he had no such plans, and she couldn't be alone with me.

I was stunned. When we parted, I sat at another brasserie and tried to rethink my life. I rewound my mind and carefully sorted through the memory banks. Bit by bit, I began to put things into a clear chronology. *That's* what they mean by pipe dreams, I thought. The opium had put wishes into play. This also meant I didn't have crabs—I'd forgotten about this standard side effect—and I was pretty sure that my other memory, about saving my father from a house full of acid-crazed hippies, wasn't a matter for future concern, either. Yep. Took him out of an insane house he had been lured into and ran him down some streets until I was sure he was safe. I liked the thought that at least I would try to save my father if he ever got into trouble, though; it meant I loved him.

That afternoon, the hotel put me into a normal suite, out of the dungeon and into the light. I went out for an early dinner and came right back to my room, did some phone surfing, and found Vera in Morocco. I woke up late the next morning, had some eggs, and took a shower. When I came out of the bathroom, I found Nancy in my bed. Things were surprising me at every turn. She said she would make love to me, but I couldn't come inside her. I said in that case I'd better make it last for a long time. But at the crucial moment we couldn't pull apart. *Trop tard*, I said. Too late.

On my flight back to reality, I once again pondered my unfaithful ways. My adultery would be called womanizing today. But at the time, the affairs bolstered my lack of confidence. The fact that beautiful women wanted to be with me made me feel successful, took me from the darkness of my bewildering family and the disdain of my father. I still felt amazed that beautiful women wanted to make love with me, but man, you don't turn your back on the kind of affection I got from the women I was with. Perhaps I was as decadent as the others. I felt no guilt, but I couldn't understand why my life with Susan wasn't as passionate. Maybe I wasn't sexually right for her, good enough to please her. I didn't know. But I know I loved her.

. . .

When I'd given up the lease on the Sherman Oaks house, I searched for a small place to put a darkroom, as part of my deal with American International Pictures. I'd begun supplementing my income by photographing up-and-coming rock groups and head shots for actors' portfolios. I found a place among a little colony of single-story manufacturing businesses, an eighteen-by-eighteen-foot brick building that had been part of a chemical business. The walls were two feet thick. God knows why the eighteen-foot cube of brick was implosion-proof, but it had a bathroom with a sink and toilet, cold water only, and I ran the water plumbing to the darkroom I con-structed inside the brick cube. There was plenty of space left and I let my friends use it for whatever, at any hour. Bobby Walker used the darkroom and drier for making his own prints, and I developed my own straight black-and-white stuff, saving color and speeded-up film for a professional place out in Santa Monica. I found some old couches at rummage sales and chairs, and McGuinn and Crosby put in a Movieola to edit sixteen-millimeter film. Gram Parsons put in a few amps, and when he'd stop by late at night we'd sing Buddy Holly tunes. I could play my guitar there and not feel embarrassed; I needed to feel the acceptance of real musicians for my own musical desires.

It became a hangout for all types. Susan visited me sometimes, but she didn't like the scene as I did, never had, and couldn't be expected to start liking it now: she was pregnant with our second child. But sometimes we enjoyed ourselves at the same time, in the same place: One evening, we went to a party given by producer Frank McCarthy and Rupert Allen, my publicist. Rock Hudson was at the party also, and we ate hors d'oeuvres as I listened to Rock tell hilarious dirt. I'd popped a cherry tomato in my mouth and when he reached a punch line, I bit down, laughing and squirting the entire inside all over Rock's exquisite tan cashmere blazer. I was mortified.

Later at the party Susan Strasberg, her boyfriend, Chris Jones, and Rudolf Nureyev wanted to come over to our place to "try" some marijuana and listen to hip music. When we got back to our place, I turned on the tennis court lights, always a great effect. I had taken down the net, reasoning that competition screwed up my ankle in 1964; by removing the net, I took competition out of the picture. We burned two bombers and I went out on the court to demonstrate a trick with Basil. I jumped on my skateboard with a stick, and Basil took the stick in his mouth and ran full blast around the court, pulling me. Rudy wanted to try, and I figured that a man of his ability could balance on anything.

He was on the skateboard for less than a minute before it flew out from under him, tossing him up in the air and right down on his wrists and butt. Susan remembers that she had never seen anybody go so high in the air before *faw-down-go-boom*. I saw the Royal Ballet Company coming after me with knives—he was scheduled to dance the next night at the Hollywood Bowl with Margot Fonteyn in *Romeo and Juliet*. Susan and I went to the ballet for that performance, and it was flawless.

While I was setting up my darkroom, John Haeberlin found a nice place with a large yard, front and back, which was ideal for Basil. It was way out in Tarzana, but the price was too good to moan about the travel time. Once John was moved in he had trouble getting a phone. He didn't have any established credit, so I had the phone put in my name. I stored all my files and script notes in boxes plus two of my guitars in his garage.

The place was quite overgrown, and a bunch of us helped clear the weeds, water the lawn, and spruce the whole place up. John planted two pot bushes—skinny, barren, pathetic plants—that he had raised in a bathroom with a three-hundred-watt bulb. The Tarzana pad was a kind of hippie safe house, and among our friends from all over, it was a crash pad. It was too far away for me to hang out there, so I played my guitar and sang in the station wagon.

In early June, while John and I were at my house, Cass Elliot and her boyfriend called and told me that the Tarzana house was being busted (Cass had been crashing there). John and I thought it was a joke at first. Then a pal, Alan Pariser, called with advice about an attorney. Yikes! Everyone in town seemed to know that the Tarzana crib was going down. I called the attorney Alan had suggested, Harry Weiss, and he told me to get out of town at once. The cops would put me in the middle of the thing, he said.

Susan was angry, and said it was bound to happen given the crowd I was running with. John and I jumped into the Super Wagon and headed for Palm Springs and a loving friend, Barbara Orbach. We hung there for a few days, but I had to go to New York to promote the special screening of *The Wild Angels*. Harry said that there were no warrants for me—yet—but there was for John. We decided to both go to New York, but it had to be unnoticed.

I called around Palm Springs looking for a small plane to charter. By the most incredible coincidence, the son of my babyhood doctor, a friend of mine whom I hadn't seen for years, Johnny Sands, had a small Cessna. I left the station wagon in Barbara's garage, and we met at the airport and flew to LAX, where we landed at one of the private terminals and were met by a plain black Ford sedan and driven to the outside stairs of our flight to New York. Harry's boogie was smooth. We were never seen in the airport complex, our tickets were in the black sedan, and off we flew to the city.

AIP provided us with a huge suite at the Drake Hotel, a famous old New York hotel with eighteen-foot ceilings and a walk-in closet as big as a normal room at a present-day motel. The Byrds were in town. We had a dinner for them and some of the other actors in the AIP tour—champagne, caviar, pheasant—and then we all went into the walk-in closet and got high.

The night of the special screening for six hundred exhibitors, Dad's fifth wife, Shirlee, and John Springer, Dad's publicist, joined Haeberlin and me at the theater (Dad was busy performing in *Generation*). I was interviewed by the Armed Forces Radio Show. The first question the man asked me was why I was called Heavenly Blues, and I gave him the same answer that I'd given Corman months before. I was thrilled when the interview ran, because I had friends in Vietnam, and I wanted them to know that I was still out there fighting the self-sanctified establishment.

I dropped Shirlee, John, and Haeberlin off at Lincoln Center, where an after-theater dinner had been arranged by AIP, and went on to the theater where Dad was playing to pick him up and take him back to Lincoln Center. He had no idea how outrageous the film was, so he was not expecting the response we got as we walked into the dining room. The room became silent, and as we walked to our table, almost everyone began to hiss at me. I didn't give a shit, but Dad was slightly undone. The film was full of violence, sex, drugs, and Nazi paraphernalia. There was something to offend everyone. When we were nearing our table, a group of Canadian exhibitors, sitting at two tables, stood up and gave me a good round of applause. They told Dad to be proud of me, and they said to not even listen to the hissing—which was still going on—they were going to exhibit the film and make a lot of money.

No one there knew about the Big Bust back in la-la land. When John and I flew back to L.A., Harry Weiss had arranged for our pickup. The same privacy, and the same plain black car, but this time we drove immediately to the Van Nuys courthouse and appeared before a judge for arraignment on charges of possession of nine pounds of marijuana. It was the first time I heard what the charges were. Nine pounds? We pleaded not guilty and were bound over to Los Angeles Superior Court for trial, free on our own recognizance.

The arraignment was a bit of theater of the absurd. At least an hour went into what to call the nine pounds. I thought "bullshit" would be accurate; I'd never seen nine pounds of grass in my life. It turned out that John had been saving seeds for a long time, and they'd weighed the seeds *and* the glass jars they were kept in. Other than the jars of seeds, there was one small ice bag, about an eighth full, but that was Cass's stash. We *all* called it Ice Bag, as it was delivered to our houses by the pound in insulated bags, the kind one uses for ice cream, by the son of a former chairman of the Joint Chiefs of Staff, General Earle G. Wheeler. David Wheeler drove a Porsche 904 Grand Prix monocoupe, a *loud* car that was built only for Grand Prix racing.

Anyway, after much haggling, it was agreed that the pot was going to be referred to as a "green, leafy substance resembling oregano." A woman who'd been at the house when the coppers descended offered testimony that John and I had been there every day, and we had been smoking a green leafy substance resembling oregano. Between her testimony, the phone listing, the boxes of files, and the guitars with my name on the cases, the trial become publicly known as *The State v. Fonda et al.* Harry had been right. Los Angeles County District Attorney Evelle J. Younger decided to make me an example and show that the System was equal in its enforcement of the law.

Just as the movie opened country wide, the headlines ripped across the country: FONDA ARRESTED ON DOPE CHARGE. Younger people who were being denied and disenfranchised made me their hero, the brand-new rebel with a pocketful of cause. I went on a nationwide promotion for the film, and found crowds of cheering youths. Sam Arkoff and Jim Nicholson, the heads of the studio, realized the publicity was a great boost for the film. *The Wild Angels* cost $362,000 to make and earned over $20 million in film rentals. Of the five posters that showed me in character, one sold over 16 million copies in the United States alone, with over 30 million total sold throughout the world. The poster that sold the most showed me on a Springer Harley-Davidson holding a "roach" to my lips.

· · ·

Our son was the bright moment in the darkness of the reefer madness in which the conservative press and the police blanketed me. I was sitting in Corman's office at Fox one late afternoon, talking about our next project, when Susan called and told me that her water had broken. She had insisted on painting the back hall to prepare for our second child, and I believe that it induced her early labor. I rushed home, so nervous I didn't realize how early the baby was coming, and stayed at the hospital until Susan told me to go home and wait. Our baby boy was born at 5:08 on the morning of July 9, 1966. He was three weeks early, dark orange in color, and wrinkled. The doctors told me that, as with most premature babies, he had a slight respiratory problem but he was coming through it just fine.

When I was allowed to see Susan, I told her that instead of a little Leo, she had borne a double Cancer. Twice the water! It had been a very long labor, and Susan was not in the mind for funny stuff. She told me to get out, and I went back to the viewing window and fell in love with my son. It took us a long time to name him, but we finally settled for Justin de Villers Fonda, de Villers from my mother's side of the family, a bit of a tribute for her, but mostly for my sister Pan.

Among the flowers sent to Susan was a giant brandy snifter filled with white spider mums and a card that said "Congratulations on the birth of your son, love Pussy." Susan wanted to know who the hell Pussy was. An Italian friend of mine from Miami, I answered. I wonder how he found out? *He?* she said. What man would be called

Pussy? I reassured Susan by saying that this man was a big capo, a man I'd met on my *Victors* trip to Miami, and he could be called anything he wanted, but she didn't believe me for a long time. I thought it was the nicest thing for Pussy to do.

A month before the trial began, the rock scene and hippie followers had taken over the sidewalks on Sunset Strip. The shop owners up on the strip had gone to great lengths to stop the "gangs of roaming delinquents" from walking along the Strip, which starts at Crescent Heights and goes west to Doheney Boulevard. It was a big promenade for the young people, a chance to gather in a certain spot and show each other solidarity. To the mighty moral establishment, holding on to hard-won ideals, change of any sort was as scary as the imminent possibility of a nuclear war with the Soviet Union, and the hippies and flower children were perceived as a commie-backed plot against everything they had arranged as the "proper way to do things." The shop owners along the Strip had been complaining to the police for a year about the young people wandering along the Strip.

I had been doing some filming of the scene. The Pacific Cinerama Dome had taken a corner of a parking lot on Sunset and turned it into a bleak little burned-out display for the movie *The Battle of the Bulge,* complete with stubs of trees and tanks and cement gun emplacements. I decided on a small guerrilla antiwar film called *the battle of the battle of the bulge,* and first filmed the marquee, complete with my father's name as one of the stars. Next, as I stood with an Arriflex 16mm movie camera across the street on a tripod, a VW bus pulled into frame, disgorged eight young men and women armed with stuffed toy rabbits and rolls of crepe paper streamers and paper flowers who climbed the chain-link fence. They stuffed the flowers down the barrels of the guns, put the rabbits in the tanks and pillboxes and festooned the lifeless trees with the colorful crepe paper. I was in no way trying to belittle the brave men who had endured the real battle, but I was deeply offended by the lack of concern, shown in the display, for our brothers and sisters fighting a war based on the values and morals of the old establishment.

The assistant theater manager tried to stop us, but to no avail. I just yelled about my First Amendment rights, while Haeberlin kept him away from the camera. As we were loading up the equipment, ABC News arrived in their station wagon, asking what had been going on.

John and I had kept on filming the assistant manager as he laboriously climbed the fence and tried to remove the decorations. The news team didn't recognize me, so I told them that there was an apparent battle of the battle of the Bulge. Say, aren't you—and I was gone in a throaty roar of the Impala station wagon. My cast had departed as quickly as they had come.

A demonstration one weekend clogged the Strip, and the resulting arrests only served to heighten the tension and up the ante. The next weekend, I went down to the Strip with two Nikons and David Crosby and Brandon de Wilde, both carrying their own cameras. Just as we came to the corner of Laurel and Sunset, Susan's mother and sister were making a right turn. They had come to watch the conflagration, just like the tourists who drive around Beverly Hills and Bel Air looking for stars' homes. I warned them that things could get pretty hairy; we had learned from moles that there was going to be a large contingent of sheriff's deputies ready to pounce.

As David, Brandon, and I passed the Chateau Marmont, we could see the buses from the sheriff's department parked up along a fairly hidden road. I knew at once that the main confrontation would be at that area, just west of the line of jurisdiction between the LAPD and the West Hollywood sheriff's station. And that was what happened. Kids came running from the western part of the Strip and ran right into the LAPD at Crescent Heights. The weekend before the young people had burned an LAPD bus that had arrived to take them away. Until then the big question had been, why are they arresting us? This weekend, everybody knew the answer: for being kids. I stood with my back to a lamppost snapping shots of the police cracking the heads of young people, while David and Brandon scooted down an alley. Suddenly, I was grabbed by deputies and pummeled by nightsticks. They were trying to break my cameras, and they were also doing a good job on my body. I was finally cuffed, photographed with a placard that read "1A," and thrown on one of the buses. Do you think they knew what they were up to? Count on it. I saw Bob Denver, the actor from *Gilligan's Island,* and banged my cuffed hands against the bus window until I got his attention. He was astounded that I was on the bus. I yelled to him, asking him to get hold of someone to help me out of this mess.

When we reached the West Hollywood station, we were led to a booking area and told to take off our watches, rings, and other valuables. There were so many kids that things were not in total control; I didn't turn over anything before we were all thrown into a holding tank, packed in like sardines. I took out one of my cameras with a wide-angle lens and black-and-white film and snapped away, holding the camera over my head. Those who saw what I was doing cheered me on. A little later, we sang Dylan songs and huffed and puffed, saying we were going to blow their house down.

Once we were in larger cells, I began to counsel the others. I suggested that they demand a jury trial and a public defender. Each time the cops came to take someone new for questioning they yelled at me to stop talking to the others. I, of course, told them to go fuck themselves and continued to counsel and snap away. When it was my turn, the others hid my cameras, ring, and watch.

I was not cooperative. The charge was loitering. Shit, no one I saw was loitering; they were all running for their lives, being chased by sheriff's recruits much younger than I, whose faces were filled with complete terror. God knows what they had been briefed about. Once I heard the loitering charge, I went for the gusto. I had enough money for bail, but the cops, in their best authorive voices, said we were all going down to L.A. County Jail, where we'd have to talk to the main dickheads.

But when I was asked to speak with the captain, I was certain that it was not a chat about my group counseling. I was told I was going to be released and given a lecture on public ethics. I responded that my public ethics were in great shape, but their gestapo actions would make for great press.

By that time Jay Bernstein, my publicist, had already raised a major stink. They delayed my release, and that made him even angrier. Jay arrived with a Saturday *Los Angeles Times* that had a picture of me in a suit and tie, and an article by Kevin Thomas about what I was up to in my career, and how I'd become a cult hero. I'd mentioned to Kevin that I would be up on the street photographing the "riots," and Jay used this to put more freedom-of-the-press fear in their hearts. What they stalled for was timing: they wanted to be sure I was seen leaving like a privileged person while my brothers and sisters were being loaded onto buses for the trip downtown in cuffs, waist chains, and foot chains. All that protection for 127 people who had been loitering.

I jumped into Jay's metallic blue Jaguar sedan and never looked back. Jay began to counsel me about the fact that I'd be on trial in

Superior Court in a matter of weeks for the phony pot bust. Susan
was very upset that I had gotten myself into trouble just when I was
defending myself against the bust, so it was not a happy or comforting
house I came home to. I didn't expect it to be. I went out to the station
wagon with a joint and sang my blues.

Noah was angry about the whole thing, though, and told me to
take photos of my bruises to show to Sheriff Peter Pitches, who only
gave me a personal warning to shut up, as I had enough trouble down
in Superior Court. I responded that the two incidents had nothing to
do with each other, unless the 1A card at the bus on the Strip was an
indication that I was being set up to look like a hooligan.

Before the trial started, I was down at the beach at Bobby and Ellie
Walker's playing my guitar and singing for Ellie. A few days earlier,
we had gone to a party in Beverly Hills to meet and listen to a new
band from South Africa led by Hugh Masekela, a truly great trumpeter
and a scholar at the Juilliard School, and Stu Levine. Hughie was married to Miriam Makeba, a wonderful singer who was best known for
her "click" song, a way of singing that is native to South Africa. They
were there for lunch, too, and while Hughie was down on the beach
with his band, I was up in the house playing and singing for Ellie,
who was making food for everyone.

Larry Spector, a business advisor who was not only working to
help Dennis and me with *The Yin(g) and the Yang* but was also helping Hughie get established in the community, came up to the house
to ask Ellie something, and wondered what station we were listening
to. Although I had been friends with Spector, he didn't know that I
was into playing and singing, and he was impressed enough to call
Hughie up to the house to listen. I sang four or five songs, Ellie sang
some harmony, and Hughie wanted to hear more. I agreed to come
to his house and spend an afternoon singing for him. I was secretly in
ecstasy that a *real* musician wanted to hear more. When I got home, I
was in full peacock form, although I didn't say a thing about it to
Susan.

I began to play almost every afternoon for Hughie and his band.
Everyone got into it. I had always thought that my count was so bad
I couldn't get away with playing with real musicians, but the Africans
kept looking at me with amazement when I would stop playing, ex-
cusing myself for losing the beat. Little did I know that I was right on
the count they were used to, and Hughie reminded me that Dylan

couldn't count for shit. After two weeks, Hughie wanted to put some
tracks down. We arranged some studio time and in less than four
days, we had put down sixteen tracks. Crosby and McGuinn came to
the sessions and added their licks. It was one of the nicest compliments that I had ever received, second only to Vera's reaction in the
Borghese Gardens, so many nights before. By the time I had to go to
trial, I had an album of songs completed and was working on a single.

The trial lasted for three weeks, spread out over two months.
Fonda et al. was covered by the press of the world. Hughie and his
entire band watched for several days. Susan came four or five times,
but she had our four-month-old son to care for. At least she knew it
wasn't my pot or my bust. My father showed up to testify that my
residence was in Beverly Hills, not Tarzana. In *his* "auto" biography,
he writes that he came to the court and didn't like the way I was
acting on the stand; that after the morning session, he had a talk with
me and "straightened" me out; that when I returned to the stand I
was a little obedient puppy. He claimed that we had lunch, and that
he said I was dressed "crazy enough for them to believe you *are* on
drugs." I wore a custom-tailored, double-breasted suit, a Battistoni
shirt, Hermés tie, and fine black leather shoes, so I guess we *do* see
what we want to see. I didn't change a thing about my attitude to the
judge, the prosecutor, or the jury.

It was a farce. Not my house. Not my name on the lease. Never
stayed there for more than a few hours. Only my name on the phone
as a guarantor, and the boxes of files and guitars in the garage. By
law I could not testify that I was smoking marijuana. I was not a
forensic chemist or a narcotics officer. By law I could not testify
whether the clear liquid in any glass was gin, water, vodka, or sulfuric
acid. I had to remind the judge and prosecutor of that fact of court.
Dad thought that I was "playing the thing for laughs," but I was playing it for my freedom. I knew the judge, Mark Brandler, wanted me. I
knew that the D.A., Evelle Younger, wanted my ass.

As we broke for lunch one day, a narcotics officer said that he was
sure I had paid the woman—the one who'd testified at the arraignment, and who'd now dropped out of sight—$50,000 to disappear. I
shot back in full voice that had I $50,000 I would have bought the
case off, or at the least, him. I was determined not to show any courtesy to the judge or prosecutor. I showed courtesy to the court by
wearing my best suits every day and keeping my mouth shut at the

outrageous accusations being brought against me. Possession of *nine* pounds? Shit, we had sent one of our production assistants with a suitcase to buy some pot in southern Arizona because we were *out*.

When the jury brought back their decision in my part of the charge, they were ten to two for not guilty. When polled for their vote, the two for conviction had hard opinions. One, a full Junior Leaguer, said that if Haeberlin was my assistant, why did I drive out to Tarzana to pick him up for work? My attorney reminded her that testimony had been provided that John's car was in the shop for repairs. Oh, she said. The second, who looked like Mrs. Santa Claus, said she voted for a guilty verdict because the other lady had. Our system of justice at work, though ten people apparently saw through the charade.

chapter *Thirteen*

*A*fter Christmas, Crosby and I headed to Cozumel to bag rays and work on the single for the album with Hughie. Croz only lasted two days before he became totally paranoid that Gram Parsons was going to run off with his girl in his absence. (Gram *did*.)

So much for loyalty. Alone on New Year's Eve, I photographed all the worldly possessions I'd brought along: my extra lenses, my stash and Bamboo roller, my passport, my extra camera body, my *papel engomado,* and pictures of Bridget and Justin. My reasons for life.

We'd flown as far as Mexico City in a British-built Comet. Croz and I smoked some shit, and I took photos of the sunset from our window with Croz in full, backlit silhouette and the layers of pot smoke hanging in the air. The plane did not have a good ventilation system.

I stayed on Cozumel for a few days after Crosby left, diving and relaxing on the beach, then flew to Mérida, rented a VW Bug and drove to some of the ruins of the Mayan civilization: Chichén Itzá, Uxmal, and Kabah. I spent a day at each place, photographing them and photographing myself by holding the camera at arm's length while I posed in places like the top of the main pyramid in Chichén Itzá.

I flew home after three days, cut the single for the album with Hugh, and prepared for filming *The Trip* for Roger Corman and AIP. Jack Nicholson had written the best script ever about taking hallucinogens. Instead of overlaying flashing strobes and swirling, black designs—the light shows and slide shows that attempted to portray an altered state—Jack used an ingenious editorial style to bombard the mind of the audience and still keep a story line running. Roger had no idea what a hallucination was, let alone how to show one, and I kept after him to trip himself so that he would know what was right and what was phony. He resisted.

Unfortunately, Roger didn't shoot Jack's original script. He felt it was too risky, too avant-garde. I felt that was exactly the point—if one was going to step out into an unknown arena, one should go for the gusto.

I *did* become the first actor in a non X-rated film to appear bare-assed, and there were some very far-out sex scenes at the end. We had rented a beach house out on Broad Beach, and the scene required me and Salli Sachse to be totally nude. There is something completely unnerving about filming a sexual scene while there are cameras and lights and sound and running techs, and Salli was getting nervous as we waited for the set to be readied. I tried to calm her down with brotherly jokes about a bed scene I had already shot with Susan Strasberg, during which I'd told Susan not to be offended if I became aroused while we were in bed together. Susan had a huge fear that someone was going to take photographs of her in the nude and sell them to the tabloids or *Playboy*. She'd actually spotted a photographer in the catwalks. Later, she went on to tell the press about my remarks. No problem.

Roger shot without sound so that he could talk us through the moves he wanted. We did many takes from many different angles. When the camera was stopped, someone put a sheet over us and we remained in the bed until the next shot. At one point, the camera was panning up and down our bodies, while Salli Sachse lay on top of me. The view was gorgeous and Mister Happy came to full attention just as that part of our bodies entered the frame. Salli went rigid, trapping Mister Happy. She also turned her furnace on, and her body temperature rose high and fast. I could hear the camera still running and was curious what Roger was doing. As a love scene, it was all over. Roger, I guess, was fascinated by the effect. I made everyone leave the room, while we got our senses back together. Roger told Salli not to cry, but Salli wasn't crying; I was laughing so hard that it shook both our bodies and the bed. It gave the appearance that Salli was sobbing, and my laughter was coming out in squeaks.

As we neared the end of filming, Roger let me come to the editing room and work on the last three reels with his editor. The nonsex footage had been shot by experimental filmmaker Dennis Jakob, who'd done his own editing. It was brilliant. I learned some more about the possibilities in the editorial process. Later, when I saw some of Bruce Conner's Super 8 movies, I realized that *anything* was possible, and I have yet to see anyone come close to his editorial achievements.

. . .

Before I promoted *The Trip,* I had cut the single and nixed the album. That was my right; it simply wasn't there. The A side of the single was Gram Parsons's "November Night" and the B side was Donovan's "Colors," the song I had sung at Jane's wedding, and the one that got radio play.

I regrouped and finally caught a good concept for another album. I decided to call it *Got to Get You into My Life* from the Lennon-McCartney song; the theme, naturally, would be I've got to get you into *my* life. And, as in the case of many albums of the late sixties, I planned secondary tracks going with people saying things like: I really love your sister's last movie; I think your father's one of the greatest, et cetera.

As I sat in my living room one afternoon, thinking about the content of the next album, Dennis Hopper dropped by and demanded that he be the director of the record. I told him that it was not a good idea—he didn't have musical count, and I didn't have enough of it to cover for him. He went ballistic and screamed at me that everyone was stealing his ideas and other unintelligible things. He was into a full rant, and I couldn't bear it. I grabbed an expendable Sony reel-to-reel tape recorder and, hefting it over my head, smashed it down on the hardwood parquet floor. It broke into several pieces. Dennis was speechless for a few seconds, and that was all I needed.

"When you can put this thing together, you can direct my album. You know about cameras, but you don't know about the inner workings of a sound studio and mixing board."

"What the fuck did you do? I can't talk to you. I mean, what the fuck did you just do, man?"

"I broke the machine on the floor, man, and as soon as you learn to put it back together, you can direct my album!"

"You're out of your fucking mind, man. I mean, you're really out of your fucking mind! I can't talk to you anymore. You're a fucking child, man! I can't believe this! You're out of your fucking mind, and I'm not going to talk to you anymore, man! You're acting like a fucking child, man!"

He walked out of the house, still screaming that I was a fucking child and that he was never going to talk to me again. I tried to calm him down, but he got into his old Land Rover and drove away. I was sorry I had offended him. Through Dennis, I had begun to understand so much more about the art of films, the art of literature, the art of painting. *Art.* He introduced me to the cream of contemporary art in all its forms. And I didn't pay any attention to his vow of silence.

Susan was curious about the Sony, but I decided that the matter was better left alone, and claimed I'd tripped and dropped the machine. It was the perfect lie—I stub my toes or screw up my ankles constantly—and even twenty-six years later, it was reasonable for her to send me this opening-night telegram when I directed a play: *Don't stub a toe, break a leg.*

. . .

I'd rented a Nagra, the best quarter-inch portable tape recorder made. It's used in filming because it is relatively small, battery-powered, and equipped with a synch system that allows sound to be added during editing. In mid-September 1967, I packed the Nagra with the rest of my stuff, kissed Susan and the children good-bye, and left for Toronto and a huge convention of motion picture exhibitors and distributors to promote Roger Corman's *The Trip*. On the first day of the convention, I was sitting at a table that was set up for the reps of AIP, wearing a custom-tailored, double-breasted suit, Battistoni shirt and tie, and no shoes or socks. I had the Nagra tape recorder over my left shoulder. The no-shoes-or-socks style was a ploy to have fun as I did each interview. There are only a few *different* questions asked at any of this kind of interview. Only one reporter asked about my bare feet, but *all* the reporters could not stop looking at them.

There was a long table at one side of the main hall on a raised platform where the VIPs and glitterati of the moment were seated. At the podium was a new boy on the block, Jack Valenti, who'd just been appointed as the head of the Motion Picture Association of America by LBJ. Hot damn! He actually started his speech with, "My friends, and you are my friends . . ." and went on to announce that "we" should stop making movies about "motorcycles, sex, and drugs, and make more motion pictures like *Doctor Doolittle,* which cost twenty-seven million dollars," all the time *staring* down at me, the star of a movie about taking LSD that featured insane sex.

At the end of *my* day, I went back to my room at the Lake Shore Motel and sat on my bed, contemplating the afternoon's lesson. *No more motorcycles, drugs, and sex.* As I pondered, I knocked off a couple of Heinies and a doob.

Dozens of eight-by-ten photos were spread out on the desk and dressers, each with a note attached saying I should autograph one to so-and-so who owned two hundred theaters, another to the wife of the man who supplied Good & Plenty to Manitoba, and so forth. I was stopped up short by a photo that showed me and Bruce Dern on a chopper on the cement walk on Venice Beach from *The Wild Angels.* It was definitely myself and Dernsy, but we were so small and backlit that anyone else would have had a hard time identifying the two tiny figures in the middle of the black-and-white glossy. In imagining who could have possibly chosen this particular photo to be autographed, I allowed myself to step into the moment, into the picture, into the dream. And into the calm of that dream leapt an understanding of the bigger question.

I understood immediately just what kind of motorcycle, sex, and drug movie I should make next. It would not be about one hundred Hells Angels on their way to a funeral. It would be about the Duke and Jeffrey Hunter looking for Natalie Wood. I would be the Duke and Hopper would be my Ward Bond; America would be our Natalie Wood. And after a long journey to the East across John Ford's America, what would become of us? We would be blasted to bits by narrow-minded, redneck poachers at dawn, just outside of Heaven, Florida, and the bed of their pickup would be full of ducks. *I mean really full of ducks.*

And first they would shoot Hopper and speed away, and I would turn back to help Hopper, and the poachers would say, "Maybe we should go back," and they would. And the audience in the theater would think they were coming back to help. The audience would *have* to think that they were coming back to help, then be forced to realize that the poachers were coming back to get rid of the witness, the youth of the world.

I was rolling. I had the ending, I worked out the beginning, sketched out the middle, and called Hoppe.

"That's great, man! Fucking great! What do you have in mind?"

"You direct, I'll produce, we'll both write and star in it!"

"You . . . ah . . . you want me to direct?"

"Fucking A, man!"

"Jesus! I'm sure glad you called me, man, 'cause I was never going to speak to you again, you know, man."

Sleep was out of the question. I showered and shaved and floated back to the room.

I flowed through the morning interviews that are a part of such a convention on the kind of high one can only get from a live, onstage performance. Throughout the promotional tour, I was asked if I was promoting the use of LSD. My answer was always that one could die from a penicillin dose, or one's life could be saved. Today no one ever knows *what* one is taking. The so-called designer drugs are mysteries. And if you don't *know* what you are taking or snorting or smoking, *don't take it.* That day, at the head table, "the son of what's-his-name and the brother of what's-her-face" (the way I was referred to in *The Yin(g) and the Yang*) was seated next to Jacqueline Bisset. There we were, smiling out at the crowd. She hissed at me through her devastating smile, without moving her lips.

" 'eter, how cungh you don't have any shooz or socks on?"

"Cuzz I'nn going to 'ut ih foot uhf your dress!"

"Stop that!" She slapped me on the arm.

"You know ats utt I going to do!"

She slapped me on the arm again. Now, if you haven't already imagined, *every* person was checking Jackie out. I could feel the interest energy pop up a few dozen decibels, and suddenly I heard ". . . and gentlemen, Mister Peter Fonda!"

" 'Scuse me, Jackie, that's me." I went up to the podium and was presented with a gold Zippo, the long kind, engraved, *P.F.* on the top, then, *Thank you, Peter, Canadian Motion Picture Industry, Sep-*

tember 27th, 1967. It was very nice. There I was in Toronto, with my very own gold Zippo.

"Thank you. I, uh, don't smoke . . . cigarettes."

A laugh worked its way through the audience. I went on to talk about the relationship between the filmmaker and the exhibitor and ended my short speech with, "The only time twenty-seven million dollars should be mentioned is in the box office, not the budget!" Twelve hundred people stood, applauded, and cheered me.

By the time I got home to Los Angeles, I was cooking. I immediately told Susan the concept: two bike jockeys want to escape their lot. They smuggle some white powder, sell it, and hit the road to retirement in Florida on two outrageous choppers. They are not allowed in any motel. They must camp out, and they talk about their dreams (what bikers actually did in 1968, around their campfires). They talk about what's happening. They meet America the Ugliful. They "Lenny and George" it at the end (go read *Of Mice and Men*), and are both waxed.

Susan's response was simple. "That's the corniest story I've ever heard."

• • •

After the 1967 convention in Toronto, and after Dennis and I had put a few more details into the story, I flew to France to work in a film with Jane that Vadim was directing, *Histoires Extraordinaire,* or *Spirits of the Dead*. It was early October, and when Jane came into Paris to see me during costume fittings, we went to the opening of *The Wild Angels* (*Les Ange Sauvage*). After the premiere, Jane went back to the location, as the filming of *Histoires* had already started, or restarted: the film had been temporarily halted for the filming of *Barbarella,* and now the company had regrouped to finish the production on the west coast of France, in a small Breton town called Roscoff. I wasn't needed on the set right away and stayed at Jane's farm outside of Paris.

I learned that Tahlita (by then married to Paul Getty) was not feeling well, so I called and drove into Paris to see her. She was very sad, and said she hadn't been out of her apartment for days. I hauled her to a late lunch, ordered Dom, and tried to make a small celebration. We talked about our lives, and she began to laugh a little at some of my stories. She begged me to write her a poem about the moment, and I obliged. We walked back to her place, window-shopping and laughing about the rude Parisians. We drove to Jane's farm and went walking until dark. After a simple dinner, we bathed in the huge bathtub and loved each other until we fell sound asleep.

We stayed together for three days, and then I knew I had to give her back to that other world. I would see her again in two months, and one more time, two years later, but never again as her lover. She committed suicide several years later, by a drug overdose. She was most beautiful, with a tender heart that needed true love.

. . .

I left the farm after a week and was driven to Roscoff, a fishing village with several hotels for summer vacationers. It was mid-October, and I had the town to myself. Some days I would go to the set to be with Jane and my fellow filmmakers, but most of the time I would sit at the window of my hotel room and watch the tides turn, waiting for my turn on the shoot. I spent roughly four hours a day working on the story of *Easy Rider* while watching the tides. As the tide went out, the little fishing boats were left stranded on their sides in the mud and sand of the harbor. As the tides returned, the boats would slowly right themselves, eventually floating and swinging on their anchors.

It was incredible to be sitting on the west coast of France thinking about this very American film that I hoped would blow the collective mind. I would dream of the sailboat I was going to buy and live on. I designed the bikes, the costumes, the helmet. It was during one of these sessions that I put the two riders into the Mardi Gras in New Orleans. I knew that there would be thousands of people on the streets, many dressed in outrageous costumes, partying throughout the night. Free background extras in wardrobe—I'd learned something from Corman. After the sessions, I'd write letters to Dennis telling him of the new ideas, firing him up. At noon I would walk into the village to eat at the only restaurant in town, a large dining room in a hotel occupied by most of the crew and a few cast members, and virtually deserted during shooting each day. Fresh lobster, fresh endive, good French wine, and very reasonable. And then, after a long lunch, back to the tides and the story.

June 30, 1940. Christening day for me and Jane. Pan is my godmother, sticking her tongue out in an early sisterly gesture of love.
J. Watson Webb

Mother with me at the house on Chadborne, 1940.
Harriman/Fonda Archives

Myself and Jane waiting for Dad to come
home on leave. 1944. *Fonda Family Archives*

Mother, Little Joe, Pan, Jane, and myself at 600 Tigertail in early 1945. *Fonda Archives*

Young and innocent, with a
Connecticut cat. Note my right pant
leg roll; I rode a bike. 1948.
Fonda Family Archives

The peerless Susan Blanchard, my first stepmother.
My Mom2 in this book. *Peter Fonda Archives*

The ritual: Dad asserts his authority in 1950.
Peter Fonda Archives

The varsity soccer team. Jimmy Gibson is second from left front row, I'm next to him third from left. 1953.

Here are Jack Peacock, Susan (Mom 2), me, and Harriet Peacock.
Peter Fonda Archives

Dad visited me on the set of "The Young Lovers" in the fall of 1963.
Fonda Archives

My friend Stormy. *Peter Fonda Archives*

October 8, 1961. Susan and I have become Mr. and Mrs. Peter Fonda.
AP/Wide World Photos

My daughter, Bridget, at three years old, 1967. Check
out those eyes. *Susan Brewer*

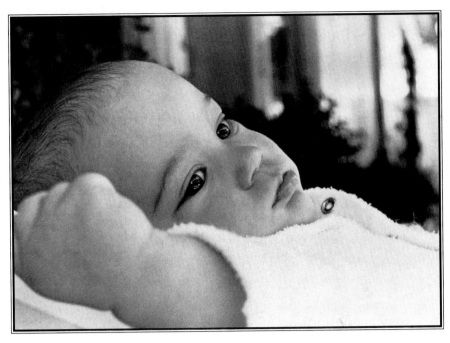

Justin de Villers Fonda in his first year. *Susan Brewer*

From a scene in *The Hired Hand* with Warren Oates, who became a close friend for the rest of his life. 1970. *Peter Sorel*

Tatoosh on the last leg of the Maui to Oahu Labor Day race. We are hauling ass on a close reach. Notice we have furled the mizzen sail. Thirteen knots, plus Waikiki is just ahead. 1974. *Peter Fonda Archives*

Dad at the wheel of *Tatoosh*. Kauai to stern. We sailed north until we lost sight of land. Summer of 1974. *Peter Fonda Archives*

Becky and Warren Oates at the Hennessey Cup Races just after finishing *Ninety-two in the Shade*. 1974. *Dan Gerber*

Becky and myself on the set of Jonathan Demme's *Fight Mad* in Arkansas, 1975. *Peter Riches*

Jane, me, and our dad in the mid-
Seventies. *Michael Dobo*

Thomas and Justin in Yellowstone Park.
Brothers in arms. 1976. *Becky Fonda*

My new family on our front lawn, 1977. *Peter Fonda Archives*

451-pound striped marlin. Landed aboard *Exact* in 1977. Owner and skipper David Hudson holds the marlin's fin, and first mate, Steve Elkins, stands right behind him. Many island needies ate well. *Peter Fonda Archives*

Cinematographer Michael Butler and myself setting up for a shot for *Wanda Nevada*, 1978. Michael's father was Oscar-winning cameraman Larry Butler. Michael shot *Ninety-two in the Shade, Wanda, and Dance of the Dwarves* with me. ©1979 *United Artists Corporation*

Dad, myself, and Brooke Shields on the set of *Wanda Nevada*. I got to direct and act with my father. The results were terrific. 1978. *©1979 United Artists Corporation*

With Becky's dad, Ned Crockett, in Kalamazoo. August 1981. *Dan Crockett*

Mr. Oates and myself after being honored at a film seminar on Western movies in Santa Fe, New Mexico, in 1981. *Lisa Law*

Justin, Thomas, and Becky, 1990. *Peter Fonda Archives*

The mighty Sting Fonda, father of my two current Labs and Bridget's two Labs. 1990. I call the photo "A boy, his dog, and his hog." A 1990 Fatboy presented to me by Harley-Davidson. *Paul Dix*

Jane and Ted's wedding at Avalon, in Florida. The happy couple, 1991. *Peter Fonda*

Eric Stoltz, Bridget, and myself at a Hollywood function, 1993. *Alan Berliner*

Bridget, Thomas and his wife Michelle, our two Labs, and Justin at our log house. Summer 1996. *Becky Fonda*

In my log house with Bill Hayward after the twentieth anniversary of Ride to the Ranch, 1997. We spent six days of great motorcycle cruising on the run from L.A. to Montana. *Becky Fonda*

During the making of *Ulee's Gold*. The director Victor Nunez, me, the DP Virgil Mirano, and the first assistant Gus Holzer. *MGM*

But I became bored with this bucolic life, and began heading to the set, where the food was terrific, and free. I had many great lunches with the famous British character actor James Robertson Justice. The production headquarters were in a very old castle, as were the dressing rooms, wardrobe, makeup, and even several sets. It was a true castle, spooky and kind of fun, with a moat, now dry, a drawbridge, and a very large courtyard. Sometimes I would get in costume, ready to shoot, but the shot would be put off, or the scene being shot would be apparently endless. I had already earned more in my per diem than I was paid for the gig.

And suddenly, parachuting right into the dream, was the wonderful, wacky-witted Terry Southern, the infamous novelist and screenwriter, the creator of such diverse imaginings as *Candy, The Magic Christian,* and *Red Dirt Marijuana, and Barbarella.* I was relaxing in my dressing room one afternoon, when I heard a harrumphing and the scuffle of shoes on the old granite staircase. He had come for a meeting with Jane and Vadim.

We were both very hungry and headed to the set to gobble. I was dressed like a German nobleman of the fourteenth century. Actors and writers and free food—we grabbed a bottle and loaded plates and sat down to some great talk. I told Terry what Dennis and I had come up with, a story that took quite a while.

"Just what are you and Den-Den going to do with it?"

"We want to find a writer to help us put it into script form."

"Well, I'm your man."

"Terry, your fee is the same as the budget, man."

"No, no, no. You don't get it! It's the most commercial story I have ever heard. And a real pip of an ending! I'm your man!"

And Terry was, certainly doing more than just putting an idea into script form. The first thing he did when we began working was give the story a proper title. He explained to me what "easy rider" meant. Perfect. This was going to be a humdinger. *Terry fucking Southern!* He'd come to Roscoff straight from Rome and a screening of *Barbarella* to help with the final editing stages, and now he was drawn into the fresh possibilities of our little low-budget motion picture.

At the end of the shooting day, Terry and I rode back to Roscoff with Vadim and Jane in the back of Vadim's Citroën D19S. Vadim was in close pursuit of the actor Serge Marquand, who was driving the same type of car, both of them traveling at over 110 mph. Vadim would come up right behind Serge and bump Serge's car with his bumper, as if to speed him up. Ah! The French! Terry and I were giggling about our new conspiracy and imminent death. Jane, trying to ignore the car antics, asked us what was so funny.

"Your brother has the most commercial story I've ever heard!"

"Both of you are stoned out of your minds." *Bump, bump, bump.*

"No, no, no, no, the best I've heard in a long time!"

"Hah! You're both ripped!" Jane can be persistent.

"No, no, no, you don't get it! Best ending I've ever heard!" *Bump, bump.*

"Are you serious?" She had a fixed smile on her face, and her eyes kept darting to the road ahead. "What are you, uh, how are you involved?"

"I'm going to help the boys write it!"

I was giggling away. A week or so later the car racing habit ended up with both Citroëns in the Roscoff harbor at low tide, sliding around in the muddy sand. Serge made it out of the harbor, but Vadim got stuck. Everyone piled out and tried to push Vadim's car along, but the muddy sand grew gooier and deeper, and the tide was headed in the wrong direction. I sacrificed two gold rings to the mud god as we feverishly tried to dig the car out, but the Atlantic was at the rear wheels before a farmer with a tractor took pity on us.

A little later, Jane, Vadim, Serge, his sister Carole, and I flew in a chartered Learjet to Rome, and I made a Super 8 movie of the trip. Our pilot was Bill Lear, Jr., John Lear's older brother. We saw the cut of *Barbarella* and all loved it. It was very funny. After a meeting with Dino De Laurentiis, we drove over to Dado and Nancy Ruspoli's place to see her new baby boy. Serge went off on a mission, and when he returned, he had a large fruitcake made with hash butter by expatriate American film director Tony Fouts. It looked as appetizing as any old fruitcake made by someone's grandmother.

Back to the Learjet and Roscoff, via Brest or Dinard, whichever had the least fog. Dinard was impossible, and we made a low pass over Brest. Some of the group were a little frightened about the fog. Serge, Carole, and I had eaten small chunks of the cake and were on the ride. We had picked up Vadim's editor and her husband, packed them into the little jet in Rome, and Serge was convincing her to try a piece of fruitcake. Bill Lear, innocent to the fruitcake's double nature, decided that we should land at Paris. We had little choice.

In Brest or Dinard, there had been no customs. In Paris, we had come from a foreign country, and we had to clear. We had no bags, as we didn't expect to stay overnight, but we did have a big, lovely fruitcake, and a partially eaten one at that. Serge never lost a beat.

"Would you like to 'ave a peece ov my granmuzzair's fruitcake?" He spoke the words just as I've typed them, making fun of the French accent when speaking English.

"*Ah, non, non, merci,*" they replied.

"Ah, but you must. Eet's from my granmuzzair!" Serge insisted, holding the mottled lump up to their faces. I tried not to laugh, virtually impossible given the circumstances.

"*Non, non, monsieur.*" They looked at him like he was a crazed man. Perhaps they'd had some of their own grandmother's fruitcake in their past.

So we waltzed right on through and called hotels for rooms and a dinner. We ended up at the Prince du Galles, a wonderfully decadent five-star hotel in the best part of Paris. At such short notice we had to take whatever rooms were available. The editor and her husband had a double, Carole and I shared a double, and Vadim, Jane, and Serge split a two-bedroom suite with a living room. We decided to have dinner for all sent up to the suite, as it had a large living room.

Everyone split for their rooms. Jane and I were delayed for a few moments because of our passports; we were, after all, U.S. citizens. On our way to the suite we were joined in the elevator by Orson Welles, who was smoking a cigar that looked like a baseball bat. The cake had yet to alter my visuals, but the cigar was the biggest I've ever seen. We shook hands as Orson smiled, grunted, and puffed away. When we got off the elevator, I told Jane that seeing Orson was a sign. Of what, she asked, and I fell to the floor in fits of laughter. I was still laughing when we got to the door.

We were dining in the Queen's Suite. Jane had placed our orders for dinner when we checked in, and during the waiting period, we all had a generous slice of fruitcake, except Jane, who detested fruitcake; even the editor and her husband wolfed their pieces down. When the food came, everything seemed normal. The seven of us sat at an elegant table, while four waiters attended to our needs. The appetizer and the rest of the courses were kept hot in several silver *réchaudes,* and the waiters stood against the wall waiting to serve, returning to their posts, throughout the meal, without making eye contact with us.

The appetizer kind of kicked in the full effect of the cake. We wondered about what the waiters might be thinking, and Serge, loudly and in his customs boogie mode, said that the waiters had no idea what was really going on. Then everyone began to roar. I think we were all close to puking during the entire meal. The waiters never cracked a smile. As there was no smoke or other residue to indicate that we were doing drugs, they must have concluded we were all very decadent people who had absolutely no table manners.

The next day, we were unable to find the editor and her husband. They were not in their room, not in the hotel, and, as far as anyone could figure, not in Paris. It was the first time either of them had experienced an altered state. I never learned of their fate. The rest of us took a train back to Roscoff, but no one touched granny's cake again until the wrap party, when our little group scarfed it and sat down to another fine meal. About a dozen people were inexplicably overcome by hysterical, fickle, and mysterious laughter. At one point, Jane made a squeaking noise and told me that Vadim's nickname for her was "Teeth." I told her not to worry; Susan called *me* "Gums." More hysterical laughter. I recall looking up from my meal and noticing that the tables were undulating like mad, but, as no food nor drink was spilled, I decided not to bring it to anyone's attention.

I finished the film, spent two days in Paris, saw Tahlita again, bought a gold Rolex watch as a present to myself for the story of *Easy Rider,* and flew to New York to meet with Terry. I flew Dennis in from Los Angeles, and, for the next five days, we all worked on the story.

One evening, I took Dennis, Rip Torn, Don Carpenter, Terry and his lady, Gail, and two of her friends out to dinner at a nearby restaurant. Rip had met with Hopper and me in L.A., before I left for France, and had agreed to do the part of the Texas lawyer. At dinner, a scuffle broke out between Dennis and Rip, who gripped each other's shirts and brandished butter knives. Terry and I broke up the fight, apologized to the owner, and slipped off into the night. I have no idea what started it, and perhaps didn't want to know.

The rest of the story meetings went smoothly, with only one dissenting moment. Hopper and Southern wanted the characters to go to a whorehouse. I felt that Captain America didn't need to buy sex—in this decade, it would come to him whenever he wanted it. I

was being stubborn, but Hoppe finally convinced me that we'd do it
for the lawyer, to fulfill his greatest wish. Hoppe told me that my job,
as an actor, was to get us out on the street, as soon as possible, back
to where the action was. I relented.

After two more sessions with the story, we were ready to put something down on paper. Terry suggested that I record myself telling the
story. I suggested that, as Den-Den was going to direct the movie, he
should be the one to tell the story. I wanted to hear what he wanted
to see. I went out and bought a small reel-to-reel Sony tape recorder
and made ready for the coming night and the Big Speak. Terry
brought along a young British director, Michael Cooper, so there
would be a new person to whom the tale could be told. We had a
few cognacs and sat down to the task. Dennis had the mike in his
hand and then put it down and stared at the machine. Sweat broke
out on his forehead, and the Napoleonic furrow deepened. I took the
mike and began to tell the story to Michael.

Forty minutes later, as I was wrapping it up, a strange noise slipped
from Terry's mouth. With cigarette ash all over his jacket lapels, Terry,
who had been in a trance, croaked, "Wait till you hear this ending,
my friend."

The tape was transcribed by Terry's secretary and edited down to
twenty-one pages. Dennis and I headed back to Los Angeles, and
after Christmas we showed the pages to Sam Arkoff and Jim Nicholson, the heads of AIP. They had some problems with the story, and
told us it was not possible to have two heroes smuggling hard narcotics, but that grass might be acceptable. I pointed out that they'd need
a tractor-trailer to haul the amount of grass it would take to come up
with a Florida retirement fund. Sam and Jim pondered that for a moment and then asked about hashish.

Hoppe and I knew we would have to find the money somewhere
else. We continued to negotiate with AIP and even agreed to have
Roger Corman as our executive producer, but there were still too
many restrictions. If Dennis fell three days behind, AIP could take the
movie. This was not something I was going to agree to.

Having no real deal and not very much help from my agents, we
decided to do another project in the interim, and came up with an
idea to shoot a film in four days. *The Queen* would star me, Dennis,
Rip Torn, and Michael McClure (a poet-playwright from San Francisco). We would each direct one day, and we would each be dressed

in white off-the-shoulder beaded evening gowns. We'd portray Mc-George Bundy, Dean Rusk, Robert McNamara, and Lyndon Johnson as they plotted JFK's assassination, and we'd do it all, including costumes, for $60,000.

Dennis, McClure, and I went to Bob Rafelson's office to pitch the idea in mid-January of 1968. During the pitch, a very tall, good-looking man with his leg in a cast came into Bob's office and sat down. Bob listened to our story, but we realized that *The Queen* was not going to fly with him. Jack Nicholson was writing and coproducing the movie *Head,* starring the Monkees, for Bob, and had basically quit acting. Dennis and Michael wandered into Jack's office to do a number. I stayed with Bob and the man in the cast.

"Have you met my partner, Bert Schneider? Bert, this is Peter Fonda."

Bert started to get up.

"No, no, please don't bother to get up." I was thinking about his leg in the cast.

"Nah! It don't bother me." And he pulled up a chair next to Bob.

"Well, how's the motorcycle movie coming along?" Bob asked. Rafelson had seen the pages when Dennis and I had first arrived back from New York. He'd loved the story and told us to ask for a million dollars. I had said that we were into a different thing, and wanted to do it all for under $500,000. Now I explained the AIP problems to him.

"How much do you want for the motorcycle thing?" Bert asked.

"Three hundred sixty thousand" I was winging it.

"Well, it's a lot easier to raise three hundred sixty than sixty. Is it a good story?"

"It's the most commercial story I've ever heard!" Bob said.

"Is it, now?"

"I, uh . . ." This was totally unexpected.

"I'm telling you, Bert, it's the most commercial story I've ever heard!" Bob repeated.

Bert eyed me. "Can you come to my house tonight and tell me the story?"

"You bet!"

I told Bert the story that night, and once again with a few friends of his present. I think the friends were part of Bert's brain trust. I gave Bert the Tape, which he sent off to a friend in New York—more brain trust approval. A few days later, I was in Bert's office while he was on the phone to some construction dude. He read the poor guy the riot act and assured him of unspeakable litigation for his shoddy workmanship. He then made a call to the New York friend, and put him on the speakerphone. The voice was effusive about the story. Bert asked me to bring Hopper to his office the next afternoon at two. I called Hoppe, and the implication made us both giddy.

I arrived fifteen minutes late. Dennis was already there and gave me a critical look, and I apologized for being late.

"Never apologize for being late!" Bert commanded. "What do you both want for this project?"

"What do *you* want, Bert? Executive producer or something?" I asked.

"No no no! I'm up to my ears with this project, *Head*."

I looked at Hoppe. "We want one-third of the picture." I said.

Dennis nodded in agreement.

"Fine. What do you need right now?"

"Forty thousand," I replied.

Bert wrote a check right then. Dennis and I went down to a little bar at Gower Street and Sunset Boulevard and had a drink to celebrate. Hoppe and I were under way with our first production, and we kept hugging each other in our jubilation.

chapter *Fourteen*

Life is cruel, life is a bust
You do what you do, you do what you must
You do what you must do, and you do it well . . .
—BOB DYLAN, "BUCKETS OF RAIN"

The Tape. God, these days it's almost like the Shroud. The Tape was the selling point. Bert Schneider bought the Tape, and we were under way. Bert told me never to write any story down again; just tell 'em the idea, he said. The Tape was lost, and it's too bad; I'd love to hear that special sound Terry made at the end again.

Bert Schneider and Bob Rafelson could easily afford to back *Easy Rider*. They'd invented the Monkees, and the Monkees had made them rich. Monkee money made *Easy Rider*.

We began true planning. In my eagerness with the story, I had forgotten the dates of Mardi Gras, and somehow, I thought the festival was toward the end of March instead of the last week of February, five weeks away. Larry Spector had become a part of the program just after we had written *The Yin(g) and the Yang*, in late 1965. He had office space in the best part of Beverly Hills and let us use it. We felt like we were two radical revolutionaries, camouflaged and invisible in the middle of the New York Stock Exchange. At that time—the mid-sixties—the people of Beverly Hills did not want to see blacks or hippies on their streets. They *still* would rather not.

But even though we had to pull a crew together quickly, we came up with the cream of underground filmmakers—Barry Feinstein, Baird Bryant, Peter Palafian, Les Blank, Alan Pariser, Seymour Cassel, Richard Rust. The exterior of the Mardi Gras was going to be shot in sixteen millimeter. We had four other cameras, besides Barry's Arriflex and a full set of lenses.

Before we went to New Orleans, we had to have some pages for a reference to make a schedule for the shooting days. I had help from the girlfriend of black activist Cliff Vaughs, who we'd hired to honcho the motorcycles we'd bought at auction, ironically from the Los Angeles Police Department. Cliff drove around L.A. in a restored '48 candy-apple red pickup with Mississippi plates and a white plaque on the tailgate that read Student Nonviolent Coordinating Committee, Jackson, Mississippi Chapter.

We worked late into every night with the pressure of the impending Mardi Gras. The only real secondary casting we had to nail down before New Orleans was for the roles of the two prostitutes, and Dennis really got into casting. He had chosen Karen Black to play his hooker, but we had a difference of opinion on the other part. Dennis had to leave for New Orleans to scout the locations, so he called and asked me to phone Billy Belasco, the agent for his choice to play my prostitute. I told him that I wanted Toni Basil to play the part. We'd both known her casually for years, and I'd gone out dancing with Toni and Annie Marshall at the rock bars, and watched her choreograph many rock shows. I'd seen her in one of Bruce Conner's movies, a wildly edited, mesmerizing striptease to a rock song that Toni had written and sung on the soundtrack. She was also choreographing the movie *Head* for Bob and Jack, so I saw her at their office. Bert agreed with me that Toni was perfect for the part, but we owed the first choice to Hopper, the director.

We argued, but Dennis continued to insist. I knew Billy Belasco; we'd played tennis on his court and mine, and I called him at home to offer the part to his client. Everyone was being offered scale, and Billy said he couldn't let his client do the part—which called for one week on location and one day in L.A.—at that price. I told him that scale was what everyone was going to get, but he apologized and declined the offer. Toni Basil would be playing "Mary."

Though the bikes were not ready, the cast and crew met at the Beverly Hills office on the Twenty-second of February and boarded a chartered bus for the airport. A lot of people and equipment, only an outline of the intent of the scenes that I had dictated to Cliff Vaugh's girlfriend, but no final cast, and no script. At 6:30 A.M., on February Twenty-third, a Friday, we all assembled in the parking lot of the airport motel in New Orleans after breakfast. It was very cold. We had a station wagon and Richard Rust's Clark-Cortez, the original motor home. Almost like a regular motion picture company. Almost.

Dennis started with a bang.

"This is *my* fucking movie, and *nobody* is going to take it away from me!" He screamed at the top of his voice, and he kept on screaming until he ran out of voice, two hours later. I looked at my watch many times in the interim. I was the producer, and we had permits to start shooting with the parades, but we had to be at the starting place to get in with the floats and people. Once the parades started we had no way to get into them or on the street with them, and the biggest and most important parades, the ones with the best costumes, were that day.

When Dennis finally lost his voice, we put him into a station wagon and we drove off, looking for a way to get in the parade process.

We began filming *Easy Rider* from the hip at about 11:30 in the morning. By the end of the day we were all exhausted, numbed by the pressure of the first "pep" talk, missed permits, and general confusion about what to shoot and where, what to say and how. The tension and disarray lent a very surreal look to the film, but at the time we were emotionally drained, communally confused. *His* fucking movie? *His* fucking movie? I'd been convinced it was our movie, our thing. All of us. *Everyone's* fucking movie—drivers, grips, makeup, and hair, greensmen, actors, electricians. There might be only one director, but everyone by virtue of sheer energy helps him put back the third dimension the camera takes away.

By the time I returned to the motel, I was greatly saddened, went to the room that I shared with Hopper, took a shower, burned one, and considered the day. Only then did I remember it was my birthday; I'd even been born on a Friday. I'd just turned twenty-eight. I went next door to Karen and Toni's room and told them. I played Karen's guitar for a while, sang a few tunes, and Toni and I shared the moment. Karen didn't smoke pot.

When we heard a ruckus in the outer walkway, I checked it out reluctantly. Dennis and Barry Feinstein, our main cinematographer, were having a serious struggle. Dennis was trying to take Barry's personal Arriflex-and-lens combo to shoot some shots of neon lights in the water reflections, as it was raining. Barry didn't cotton to that idea. He had endured the same morning as the rest of us, the day's shoot, the day's shot to the heart of us all, and now he had to endure Dennis kicking him. Barry had been a Golden Gloves champion, and how he was keeping his cool was beyond me. The fight spilled into Karen and Toni's room, and Dennis broke Karen's guitar over Barry before he picked up the TV set and threw it at him.

Somehow, we managed to pull Dennis off Barry and slow the thing down. I got Hoppe back to our room, made him smoke a doob—he'd been doing whites and wine all day—and I told him he needed to calm down. When he asked if I had any downers, I gave him a thousand milligrams of Placidyl, a heavy central nervous system drug, and listened while he wandered on. He spoke about the prime colors and how they were reflected on the outer wall of the motel, how they were reflecting on the rain-soaked streets he'd wanted to shoot. I understood, but I also understood Barry's point of view.

Dennis's speech became slower and slower, and he eventually went face down—*kaboom*—onto the coffee table. I picked him up, rolled him onto his bed, and began to take off his boots.

He sat upright, as if he had been struck by lightning.

"Don't ever take my boots off again!" Far out, I thought. On a thousand milligrams of Placidyl.

Then he fell right back down into his pillow. *Kaboom* again. I carefully put his boots back on and pulled up the bedcover. This is when I first learned that Dennis always slept with his boots—or whatever—and socks *on*.

I was a mess. Friday's child is loving and giving, but this was warping the envelope, and it put me in a total funk. I slouched around the walkway, listening to the rain and feeling the thing that rain was all about. As I neared our room, I noticed that the girls' door was open a crack. I knocked softly, and put my head into the room. A whisper.

"Peter?"

"Yeah . . . Toni?"

"Come here, Peter. Happy birthday . . ."

. . .

The next morning, in the parking lot, at 6:30, at the top of his lungs:

"This is *my* movie! Nobody is going to take away my fucking movie! You got it? This is *my* fucking movie . . ."

This time his voice gave out after only *one* hour, and we started

filming by nine-thirty. Dennis was two-for-two in the batshit department, transformed into a little fascist freak I'd only glimpsed before.
Each day was the same; each day was so different. Whenever I got
too spooked by it all, I would put my arms around Toni. Thank god
for her, and thank god for the whole crew. Several evenings into the
shooting, Barry and some others came to say they were only staying
with it because of me.

After the second day, Dennis began to demand that the exposed
film be given to him at the end of each shooting day. I imagine he
was worried that someone would take the film and not give it back.
The ongoing argument between Barry and Hopper about the possession of the negative culminated one evening when Barry brought all
the film cans down to the lobby and dumped them over Hopper's
head. Although Dennis was plastered, sitting in a large armchair he'd
staked out as his territory, he looked up and muttered that at least he
had his film.

Terry Southern was there, in absolute amazement at the whole
scene.

"What would Dad-Dad think?" he asked me one afternoon in Richard Rust's Clark-Cortez, as Den-Den and I were smoking a joint. He
wasn't asking about the pot. Later he told me he could not afford to
stay on as a coproducer for $350 a week plus expenses, *and* put up
with Herr Director's rules of the game. I understood, but I was doing
it for free.

One night, about four days into the shoot, most of the company
was in my room. Dennis was starting to get manic, and he was putting
it all on Karen. He had her in tears—not for the first time—humiliating
her in front of the company. It was part of his plan to prepare her for
the LSD scenes in the graveyard, and it worked, but it was extraordinarily rude. I would have humiliated her *privately*. As we began the
graveyard sequence the next day, things neared the breaking point.
Dennis was directing while acting in character, pulling from a bottle
of wine and popping speed. We staggered past the camera and collapsed at the foot of a very tall mausoleum. (In the delta of New
Orleans, the dead are buried above ground. Dig down three feet, and
you reach water.)

"We're going up for the last time," Dennis was saying. "Up for the
last time." Barry would pan up the tower of memories until he flared
out in the sun. Then he would start back on us, collapsed at the

tomb's base. After he had done enough takes, I brought out some foil-wrapped "LSD" (actually aspirin) and broke the tab into four pieces.

"What's that?" Karen asked.

"Heh, heh. Yeah!" Dennis hoarsed in. "What's that? Heh, heh."

"Just shut up and take it," I said.

"Umph, huhnn, yeah, just shut up and take it!" Dennis was into it. I passed the quarter tabs around, then grabbed Dennis's wine bottle, took a pull to wash down the tab, and passed the bottle down to Dennis. He had a sip and passed it to Karen. She asked again what she should do, and I took the tab and put it in her mouth. She took a pull from the bottle. Toni gave me a look, so I grabbed the wine back, put Toni's tab in her mouth, took a swig, and kissed her, filling her mouth with the wine. Very sensual. Perfect. All in response to Toni's look. She made it so personal, so something-between-us. What was going down was a kind of Holy Communion; we shared the Host and drank the Blood. Hoppe always quoted Jean Cocteau: 98 percent of true art was accident, 1 percent was logic, and 1 percent was intellect.

In the same sequence, Dennis asked me to get up on a statue and ask my mother why she abandoned me by suicide. I told him that simply because he had personal knowledge of my family's darkness-at-the-break-of-noon, he didn't have the right to make me take it so public. He kept insisting. I told him Captain America didn't have a mother or father; he sprang forth on the earth fully formed; he was just an idea. With tears streaming down his face, Dennis told me I *had* to speak to her. I kept insisting it didn't fit, that it was wrong, that it wasn't fair of him to ask me to do it. I finally demanded that he give me *one* good reason to do it.

" 'Cause I'm the *director!*" he shouted, wiping the tears from his cheeks.

I looked at him for a beat, then climbed up onto the lap of an Italian statue of liberty and began to ask questions I had never dreamed I'd voice. I wish even today that it wasn't in the final print, though Bert says I'm crazy to feel that way, that I don't realize how powerful it was. It embarrasses me, but at that moment, I found my-self getting into it, and not in a nice way.

Somewhere off-screen during this speech, I heard Dennis arguing with Barry about moving the camera. I looked down at this little mad-man yelling at the camera. I knew that Barry, through his telephoto lens, could tell I was going for the gusto, and he wasn't about to stop filming, and I became very angry. Hopper wanted me to go for it, and I was more than obliging him. He should have let it happen, but I think he was scared of the moment, and needed to get back control. I yelled down at Dennis to shut up. It's on the negative, and it's in the release print.

And it does work.

.   .   .

The filming in New Orleans was finished in six days. The company returned to Los Angeles on March 1, and I went to Bert Schneider with Bill Hayward, my associate producer and now partner, since Terry dropped out of his side of the producing team. I was upset by the happenings during Mardi Gras, and I didn't think we could complete the movie with Dennis in such a megalomaniac-like routine. Bill and I told Bert everything that had gone down, and I offered to give back the $40,000. Bert asked if I still wanted to make the movie, putting aside the Hopper question. Of course I did, but I felt that Dennis couldn't handle the fact that I was the producer and on the set all the time, that *I* had hired *him* to direct, and that *Easy Rider* wasn't his original idea. So . . . Bert told Dennis that I was stepping down as the producer, and he was going to produce the movie himself. No easy ride here.

A few days later Dennis and I flew to New York to write the script with Terry. The three of us sat on a couch in Terry's small office. We would all discuss a scene, then Hoppe would dictate to Terry's secretary, starting at the beginning and working our way through the story. This had been my intention in '67 when I asked him to record himself telling the story. And this is probably the genesis of his notion that he alone had written the screenplay. After this collaboration, the script still had to be put into a real screenplay structure with exterior (EXT), interior (INT), and other shooting directions inserted.

The day that Dr. Martin Luther King, Jr., was murdered, Dennis started in with the flying saucer stuff for the lawyer. He never explained, and it was several days before I got it. We were going to get the Establishment loaded and listen to what they had to say. An old term for lawyers is "mouthpiece," and the mouthpiece would do all the talking—until the first campfire with Jack Nicholson, all Dennis and I said was hippie jargon: Wow, man! Far out, man! Whew, man!

That's beautiful, man. Man, man! You know, man? So, this alcoholic lawyer—the Establishment—gets ripped and tells us all that everything is going to be fixed by people from Venus. This was perfectly absurd. People from Venus? It was as simplistic as the technocrats, who think that it will all be straightened out through as-of-yet-unknown technology. It certainly was the way we all felt about the Establishment then, and nothing has changed with today's political leaders, but at first, I was sure that Hopper had gone over the edge. The words that Jack spoke about the Venusians' way of life and their visitations to Earth were all lifted from a book that Hopper clung to during this part of the writing. It was only when I saw the scene in its context that I understood what he was up to.

As soon as we got back to L.A., Dennis completed the casting. Rip Torn hadn't been able to do the role of the lawyer for scale, and at first, Hopper resisted my notion of Nicholson taking over. He said that Jack was from New Jersey, and he wanted an actor who was a Texan, like Torn was. Finally Dennis relented, and a movie star was born. Jack had always been a good actor, but in the part of George Hanson he found his voice.

The old LAPD bikes were getting close to completion, with Dan Haggerty's help. I'd designed the extended and mildly raked front forks, helmet, sissy bar, and the tank, but the *forty-two degree* rake that was suggested by Cliff Vaughs was some piece of work. I began to ride one of mine as soon as it was ready. The first Captain America bike was the better of the two. They were all rebuilt panheads (a name given to them because of the look of their cylinder heads). We had one 1950, two '51s and a '52. Two bikes for me and two bikes for Dennis. The idea for the flag on my jacket came from a John Wayne movie, *Flying Tigers,* in which Wayne wears a jacket with the Chinese Nationalist flag sewn on the back, with Chinese characters printed below it saying "I am an American pilot fighting the Japanese, please give me assistance." I'd seen the film years earlier and thought the flag was a great icon, and now, in *Easy Rider,* I put the thought to work and had the U.S. flag sewn on my jacket.

As soon as I had the bike to go with the leathers, I began riding the L.A. freeway system. I was stopped every night by the police. They measured my handlebars, measured the height of the headlight, checked the taillights, the registration. They didn't touch the throttle. Once, when I didn't have any cash in my pockets, they wanted to arrest me for vagrancy, and I was actually taken, in handcuffs, to a station house to be booked. The booking sergeant recognized me and got rather hard on the arresting cops, who'd seen my license but were determined to hassle me. Though the flag was really at the root of each hassle, my nine-pound pot bust two years earlier didn't allow much leeway, and I was strip-searched. They didn't get to check my ass, though. One year after the release of the movie, *all* cops, throughout the country, had the flag on their uniforms, cars, anything they could put it on. The little victories.

After I'd mastered the freeway system, I began to take on the canyon arteries joining the Valley with Hollywood, West L.A., Beverly Hills, and Culver City. When I could navigate around the Laurel Canyon area with seeming ease (the operative word here is "seeming"), I was ready to put it on film. This time we were shooting with 35mm film, the big time. At Bert's request, we'd hired Paul Lewis as our line producer and production manager, and also hired the crew he'd been working with on a recent biker movie. Laszlo Kovacs was our new cinematographer.

We had a lot of scenes to cover in the L.A. area first, before we moved across America—the hippie commune in the Santa Monica Mountains, an entire billboard montage along Sunset Boulevard, a chase sequence of Dennis and myself smuggling drugs across the Mexican border, a scene at a doughnut shop trying to unload our "load." Dennis had a wonderful take on the Pop Art scene, and for this sequence we shot at a Winchell's Doughnut on Lincoln Boulevard in West Los Angeles. Across the street was an Oldsmobile dealer. We nailed a phone to a power pole, and as the camera moved around me while I talked to our off-screen dealer, the viewer saw a giant doughnut, eighteen feet in diameter, and then, across the street, a huge rocket outlined in neon. A rocket was one of Oldsmobile's symbols, and a 1954 Rocket 88 was a hot car for several years, even making it into an Everly Brothers song. The scene had nothing to do with doughnuts or cars, but the presence of these oversized neon and floodlighted pop icons lent a more-than-there-is-there feeling, the sort of feeling we wanted to lend to the entire film.

During this scene, a fight breaks out between Dennis, a midget, a very large man, and several other types. I leave the phone to help Dennis; we karate our way out of the mess; we leave the area to find refuge while we wait to make the connection. I had the notion that a drive-in movie would be a perfect place to hide, and suggested that we be watching a "beach" movie and smoking pot. After a while, the camera would zoom in on the screen, showing a surfer riding a wave, and then pull back out, revealing us asleep in our pickup, parked along the Pacific Coast Highway. Hoppe took this idea and pushed the envelope to a wonderfully different level—we'd be watching our own title sequence. We'd use the first Columbia Studios logo and montage that with all the other Columbia logos interspersed with our credits, and *then* zoom into the surfer, etc. Dennis also had us park next to a Cadillac with a man and woman inside. While we smoked a joint and watched our own credits, Dennis would became a voyeur, watching the couple in the Caddy. He'd try to get me to take a look, but I'd tell him I was into the movie. He'd insist and I'd glance over before returning to the movie.

Hopper worked scenes around like that effectively throughout the script. I had us joining a local high school band in a parade and getting thrown into jail for "parading without a permit"; an ACLU lawyer-type sees the arrest go down and comes to our rescue. Dennis put the lawyer in the jail with us, as a drunken local Brahmin.

We shot scenes explaining our identities and the background of the dream of making a big score and going to Florida to retire. At that time, Dennis and I both felt that retiring was a very real crime against the planet and the democratic process. I still feel that way. There's too much shit to be dealt with to even think about retirement. I heard Coretta Scott King say the same thing at a ceremony marking Martin Luther King's birthday, in 1995, but she didn't use the word "shit."

Dennis and I were young men, dissatisfied and disenfranchised, when we put *Easy Rider* together. We had lives to live that could contribute to our country, our cause. Dennis is a full Repo now; voted for Bush-Quayle. If anything, I've gone in the other direction, taking Jefferson's instructions to "alter or abolish it, and to institute new Government, . . ." as the best way of getting back to a representative democracy. Those scenes I've just described didn't make it into the final movie, but they were dropped for the sake of time, not because they didn't work.

In 1967, a year earlier, while landing at LAX in John Lear's Learjet 23, I saw a road running along the end of the runway aprons, where the planes turned to take off. I drove down there a few days later with my infant son, Justin, a friend, Skip Hamer, and my Super 8 camera.

It was a public road, and we stopped the station wagon, getting out to watch and film the planes landing right over our heads and feel the thundering sound of the ones taking off. I said, at the time, that this place would make a spectacular location for certain scenes in some movie.

It was impossible for a dialogue scene, but it would be perfect for a scene that was tense and self-explanatory. I took Hopper there and suggested that it would be just right for the scene of the drug sell. At that moment, a train passed running parallel to the road just fifty feet away. A mixed-media shot! To make even more of a point, the train was pulling flatcars with tanks and full-track armored personnel carriers on their way to Vietnam. Hoppe was delighted. When we shot there, trains went by with war equipment stacked on flatcars. We filmed them, but although we were both appalled by the actions of our government, we decided to leave the tanks out of the movie, as we were making a statement about our domestic society, not the war in Nam. Phil Spector, who played the buyer, saved us money by having his own Rolls-Royce and bodyguard, although he was terrified by the landing planes.

New Buffalo was the name of the hippie commune that was to be used just outside Taos, New Mexico, but a few weeks before we began filming in Los Angeles, it was burned to the ground by some disturbed locals. We had no time to find a new commune, so we built our own in the Santa Monica Mountains. What appeared to be deserts and endless vistas in the background were actually the smog and haze of Smell A. We cast all our likely looking friends as members of the commune, and even sent a few assistants to drive along Topanga Canyon and pick up appropriate extras. Susan agreed to be a hippie and brought Bridget and Justin as background kids.

One point of technical interest about the entire movie was particularly evident in the commune scene. There was a 360-degree inside-out pan around the commune members that ended with a prayer. Most first time directors try to do 360s. I did on *my* first film. During the shooting, there was a great deal of off-screen noise. Some of it was Justin, almost two, having a fit, but most were barnyard sounds from the chickens and goats we had placed around the area. When I was in Paris, France, in late 1969, overseeing the dubbing into French, the technicians were having a terrible time with the sound. Most European films were not shot with direct sound. Even in the United States, most of the background sound is mixed in later, creating a separate effects track. In the dubbing process, therefore, there are three separate soundtracks: dialogue, music, and effects. We didn't have a third track in *Easy Rider,* with the exception of two words from Dennis's character, a background wind and coyote sound, and a track of the crickets and cicadas (which we made on location) for a balance in the intercuts. As the camera pans inside-out during the prayer scene, the barnyard and crying sounds are what the soundman was hearing, at *that* moment. During the actual prayer, Justin was quiet, and the chickens and goats made their clucking and bleating in the moments that Bobby Walker *wasn't* speaking. Incredible luck, but very frustrating for the French, Italian, and German technicians. Bill Hayward and I were actually very pleased, and the Europeans were astounded at our ability to make a motion picture with a direct soundtrack that included all our sound effects.

After we finished the scenes that were shot in L.A., we prepared to go on the road, where my riding ability was going to be put to the big test. I'd mastered the tight turns of the canyons and felt completely confident at speed on the freeways, as evidenced by the shots of me and Hopper crossing the Colorado River, where I'm riding with my left leg crossed over the tank and my other leg, and my left arm relaxed in my lap, smiling and at perfect ease. We crossed the Colorado many times for different lenses or camera angles, riding slowly, at twenty-five to thirty miles per hour so as not to make the background a blur.

We began the ride in Needles, California. It was quite hot, and as long as we were moving, it was a pleasure to ride. But when we stopped to work out the next shots, my black leathers were like an oven, and I began to sweat. After a while, I took to riding my scoot up at seventy or eighty miles per hour when we stopped to reload the camera or plot the next shots. It cooled me *and* the bike down. We rode all day, stopping only when I forced Dennis to, so that we could all eat lunch.

We rode to Kingman, Arizona, but it was the equivalent of riding from Needles to Albuquerque, New Mexico, in number of miles ridden and filmed. By the time we got to Kingman, we were all thirsty and hot, so the plan was to gather at the little pool for a swim and some cocktails. As I pulled off my leathers in my room, however, I was blown away—even though I had soaked the pants earlier and worn them until they were dry, sweat had drawn the dye from the leather and turned my legs purple. In those days I was still very self-conscious about my skinniness; being seen poolside with legs that were both skinny *and* purple was too embarrassing to contemplate, so I showered, pulled on some clean jeans, and went to the bar.

We'd had a good day's shoot, and I was heady with the notion that the dream I'd had in Toronto was under way and on the road.

"Give me the largest, coldest beer you got."

The bartender brought out a giant, frosted mug of beer. I reached out for the mug and couldn't bend my arm. As casually as possible, I pretended the arm thing hadn't happened, reached with the other hand, and found I couldn't move that one, either. I'd been riding my chopper all day long, hanging on to handlebars, gripping that raked and extended front end at slow speed. I asked for a straw and pretended not to notice the other people in the bar. The script clerk had to feed me my supper that night.

From Kingman, we rode and filmed to Flagstaff, where we had our day off. We were staying at the All American Inn Motel, and our arrival was certainly noticed. We showered, did laundry, bought booze, and met in the lounge of the motel. There wasn't enough room in the regular bar to handle our whole cast and crew, so we went into an unoccupied dancing area and pulled together many little cocktail tables to form a circle. I put the banjo on my knee and we all partied to celebrate the break. I had my twelve-string Guild, and I began to play as the party sang along. Many drinks and songs later, a drunk from the bar came into the room and staggered into the middle of our circle. He began to call us commies, hippies, and pinkos, claiming war-hero status as he confronted each of us one at a time.

This did not go over well. Several of the crew stood up and retorted with their own service in Korea or tours in Vietnam. Our cinematographer, Laszlo Kovacs, still photographer Peter Sorel, and several other crew members stood and announced that they had stood up to the Soviet tanks in Hungary in 1958, but the drunk didn't give a shit for their patriotism or heroism, and let us know by stooping in front of each of us and giving us the finger. When he flipped Joyce King, our script clerk, three of our biggest crew members got up, lifted him by his belt and the back of his shirt, and put him outside the circle. We all stood and applauded, but as we all sat down again, the asshole pulled Joyce's chair out from under her. The cast and crew picked the idiot up and threw him into the regular bar. We then goose-stepped out of the building, telling everyone to get fucked, and circled up again in my room. Not because I had a larger room (I didn't) or because I had the guitar, but because I had the best dope. Many of the crew had never smoked pot, but that night was *all* about getting high. After that night, we became a Company, even Dennis, although his bodyguard, Virgil Frye, passed out in my bathroom, blocking the door.

For the next few days, Luke Askew, who had worked with Jane in *Hurry Sundown*, joined us, portraying the Hippie Hitchhiker. We did the famous scene at the Sacred Mountain Gas, where Dennis's Billy is very uptight at Captain A for having picked up the Stranger, let alone allowing him to see into the tank where our booty is stashed.

"Hey, man! Everything we ever dreamed of is in that teardrop gas tank, and you got a stranger over there pouring gasoline all over it, man. All he's got to do is turn and look into it, man, and he can see—"

"He won't know what it is, man. He won't know what it is. Don't worry, Billy. Everything is all right."

"I don't know, man, I don't—"

"I do, man. Everything's all right, Billy."

Nobody's that cool, and I still think it's a gas that I pulled it off. We'd always intended that the name of Dennis's character would be Bucky, but I'd found out, just before we shot this scene, that Marvel Comics was going to sue us for copyright infringement if we used the name. They held the copyrights for their classic comic *Captain America and Bucky*. Hoppe didn't know this, and when we shot the jail scene (and the bookless library in the whorehouse), he referred to himself as Bucky. A new name had to be looped in later.

We had had a fantastic ride through Sunset Crater National Monument. Our camera car was a 1968 Chevy convertible with partially deflated tires. We took out the backseat and put the camera, on standard legs, on a plywood floor ("standard legs" means a normal tripod for a 35mm camera). We used Vilmos Zsigmond's Angenieux zoom lens, and his blimp (a covering for the camera that muffles the noise of the motor, the shutter and the film moving through the gates) for the scenes that had dialogue. We were pulled over: a tourist had phoned the police saying that he had seen a motorcycle gang chasing a bunch of people in a convertible, and a machine gun was being used. The cops knew what was going on, but they thought we would get a kick knowing what the word was.

That evening, we rode way too fast on washboard dirt roads, trying to make the spot Dennis had scouted for the Monument Valley panorama–endless vista shot. The teardrop gas tank came loose, and I had to hold the fucking thing with one hand and control that bike with the other. We were late, anyway, and rushed. The film we were using was a brand-new raw stock—5247—from Eastman Kodak. In 1968 it was a prototype for the higher-speed Eastman 35mm motion picture raw stock. Laszlo shot under protest, doing film-speed tricks (we call it "pushing the stop" or "forcing the stop"), but we got that shot.

That evening, after we finished the sunset footage, we went into our second campfire, one of the truly improvised scenes in the movie. Luke Askew, Dennis, and I agreed on a rough structure for the scene. Our purpose was to do character stuff, very nonexpository. We were smoking very decent weed, and it all was beautiful for us, but the crew was stretched to the max with the scene. To them, it didn't make any sense, and after each take the actors went to the soundman, LeRoy Robbins, and listened to the dialogue. To us it made perfect sense, and wishing to give it more than one pass, we would say that it was beautiful, man, let's do another one. During one take I made a comment that I was seeing things flying all around. June bugs were going kamikaze at the light near the fire, and we all laughed at the stoned implications. I was sitting very close to the fire, and I said the smoke was really getting to me, using the double entendre on purpose. Luke laughed in character and mentioned that he noticed that I wasn't moving, which I found hysterical. I dropped character totally, and laughed with the joke on the set. But remembering Dennis's admonition about the Cocteau factor, I went with it and closed the scene as we had planned.

We wrapped that location and prepared to drive and shoot on our way to Taos, New Mexico. Jack had joined us, and we did a few days of riding shots. By the time we were shooting the opening of the movie in Taos, I had developed a bad cough, one the locals called miners' cough. Sabrina Scharf and Luana Anders had arrived for the hot springs scene, but the problem was that the location Dennis had scouted in May was under two feet of the Rio Grande's runoff in mid-June. We were shit out of luck.

Dennis decided to shoot in a small creek with extremely cold water. He'd found some petroglyphs and we filmed them in the background and foreground as the actors passed on their way to the "hot springs." The girls and I protested. I reminded Hoppe that we had been talking about hot springs, and this was hardly the image. He said we had no choice. The girls pointed out that with no springs to sit in they were much more exposed than they'd been led to believe would be the case, and they wanted to close the set. Dennis agreed and made everyone but Lazlo and the key grip, Tom Ramsey, go up the cliff and wait with the five-ton trucks. I continued to bitch about the icy waters, what with my cough, but we were pros, and we played hurt. At some point, Bert Schneider, who had come down to Taos to hang out with Dennis, Jack, and myself, peeked over the edge of the cliff and one of the girls spotted him. Dennis threw a shit fit for the women's sake, and the key grip, who was sporting a pistol for snakes (and maybe also for the women's sake), pulled the gun and fired it up at the cliff. My delirium deepened—we were shooting what was intended to be a sensual scene in frigid water, with no beautiful background, and our key had just shot at the executive producer. All but the petroglyphs and walk down the stream ended up on the editing room floor.

The next day we filmed the "buy" at a junkyard behind an old cantina, and I barely made it through the sequence, so I was sent to see a doctor. A moment or two after my white count had been taken, the doctor ordered me into the hospital, immediately—I had bronchial pneumonia, and did not know until much later how serious it was.

The crew came by to pay their last respects, bringing along my blender, some eggs, bananas, and a powdered protein mix. A few brought real medication. Several joints were secreted around the bed area, but for the most part I was knocked flat by the infection and lay on my side breathing from a machine that made a cool mist, and sounded as loud to me as my bike. I didn't even notice the cute candy stripers. I ate the numbers. The pot didn't do the bronchial part much good, but acted as a great equalizer, and made the entire hospital boogie go by without a worry.

While I was happily dying in the hospital, the Company filmed the hot-springs scene without me. Dennis had found an old, ruined building with hot springs, and Luana and Sabrina were much relieved.

They had to shoot whether I was there or not. We didn't have any money or time to spare, and they finished the Taos location as best as possible, knowing that we'd have to come back for my side of the scene.

On the morning of my fourth day in the hospital, the crew came and freed me, and we drove on to Las Vegas, New Mexico, where we shot the parading-without-a-permit parade and the exterior of the jail scene outside of the old fire department. We'd shot the interior of the jail scene in Taos, and if you ever watch the movie, you'll notice that something is not quite right with Captain America, perhaps a case of bronchial pneumonia kicking in.

There was something funny going on with Jack and Dennis. When I asked what was happening, Dennis told me that the two of them had gone to the grave of D. H. Lawrence and dropped acid. I tried to consider the trip an effort to share my near-death hospital experience, and when Jack toasted old D. H. I felt that the effort paid off.

We wrapped the Las Vegas location, shot some rides with Jack, and as the night came on, we drove to the location for the UFO scene and our campfire with the Establishment. Jack had been doing George Hanson for a week and had a good handle on the character. He studied the scene every day. There are photos of Jack sitting in a field with the script in his hands. He told me he was ready, and he must have told Hopper the same thing. I made sure that props had some very good pot, and Dennis went over the shots he wanted. He decided that he would shoot a ride in to establish the location, and there being a waxing gibbous moon, he had Laszlo pan down from the moon to Jack's helmet and slowly pull out to a two-shot master, with me rolling a single Zig-Zag paper doob. We were clean with the opening and closing lines and structure, and very explicit with the main body of the scene.

Dennis shot the wide two-shot, two wide singles of me and Jack, a close single of me, a wide single of himself, a close single of himself, a rising and sitting back down single, and all the time, on and off camera, I was dropping the dime on Jack, telling him to hold the hit in his lungs a little longer. Through every shot I kept giving Jack more of da kine, but we had not yet shot his close single of the UFO speech. I like to think that this was Hopper's intention, but, either way, Jack was getting very loaded.

With the camera on a single of Jack, Dennis sat to the left of the

camera, and I sat camera right, so that Jack's looks would correspond
with the geography of the master. Jack began his UFO speech. He was
letter-perfect, and very stoned, a pro. As we got deeper into the scene,
I began to feel a strange energy from the other side of the camera.
When I knew Jack was looking camera left at Dennis, I glanced to
that side and noticed Hopper stifling a laugh. I immediately had to
muffle my own laughter, and Jack just kept on rolling, but it became
increasingly difficult to keep control. Jack's speech and character
were doing just fine, but the absurdity of the speech's content was
almost too much to handle, even for The Pro. When Jack got to the
words, "meeting with people from all walks of life," it all went over
the edge. "To go up" means, in theatrical terms, to lose the line,
the thread of the thought. And when Jack came to that part of his
speech, the thread broke, and down came baby, cradle and all.

Dennis, choking back hysterics, called for a cut. "That was beautiful, man! Perfect, man. Okay, Laszlo? We'll do a print and a pickup."
This meant that we would start the scene again from the place it went
haywire.

"Oh no, Dennis! I'll do it from the top, man." Jack was striving for
perfection. But Dennis was on the move. The slate was prepared, the
amount of footage left in the magazine was noted, and Dennis called
for the camera to roll.

"Wait a moment, Dennis. I mean, I'll do it from the top! Okay?"

"Oh no, man! That was beautiful. Just perfect."

Jack almost came to tears, pleading to do the whole speech over,
but Dennis insisted on moving ahead, and the camera rolled, leaving
Jack in a big hole.

"Well, I mean . . . uh, where should I start?"

The camera was still rolling, but Dennis seemed calm. "Just start
where you lost it, Jack."

"Yes, well, uh, where. . . . Please, Dennis, let me—"

"Joyce, give Jack the line, okay?"

"Meeting with people from all walks . . ." Joyce was on top of it.
Pressure!

"Yes, I know, uh, listen, Den . . ."

"Action, Jack." Dennis was very sure of the situation. Jack wasn't.

"It . . . it . . . it would be a devastating blow to our antiquated
systems—so now the Venusians are meeting with people in all walks
of life in an advisory capacity."

The Pro. My take on that whole thing was that Den-Den *wanted* Jack to be stoned for real; that Jack's "going up" was part of really being stoned, forgetting what you were talking about, losing the thread, as it were. And the laugh was so genuine, so true to the grip of reefer madness. It worked so beautifully—when the scene was edited, Dennis left the moment just as it was shot, cutting from Jack's laugh to a close-up of a nonplussed Billy, one of Captain A shaking his head in stoned amazement, and then back to Jack, who started that part of his UFO rambling over, right where he left it. Ninety-eight percent accident, 1 percent logic, and 1 percent intellect. Right on target.

· · ·

We spent the night in a little town in northeastern New Mexico. There wasn't one motel that could handle the entire Company, so we had to spread out in three smaller ones. I ended up rooming with our assistant cameraman, Peter Heiser. It was late when we wrapped the campfire scene, so it was very late when we hit our rooms, and I found out what it was like to be the grunt of the camera department. We called Peter "Gort"—he had a neck that was almost as wide as his shoulders and a Mr. Universe physique, yet he would get under the lens, on top of the lens, all around the lens as if he were Alexander Gudonov.

On most of the rides Gort would pull focus, while Laszlo worked the zoom. The assistant cameraman had to fill out the camera reports for the done day, load the magazines for the next day's shoot, clean all the camera gear with compressed air tanks, pack the exposed negative in taped film cans, and then try to grab a few hours of sleep. The lessons learned proved to be very advantageous for me later, as a director, and even as an actor. My agents and advisors—the nonhip ones—have told me constantly that I hang out with the wrong group, and I wonder if they truly believe that the studio execs know how to make a movie. There's a phrase that's all wrong and sort of rude: Fuck 'em if they can't take a joke. Anyone paying attention will agree that the correct phrase is: I'm fucked if they can't take a joke. At least it's true when applied to me.

The next day we shot more rides with Jack, including the shot of the three of us pissing by the side of the road. We shot right up to the state line, but we didn't want to actually shoot in Texas (something to do with the conspiracy that assassinated JFK). So we drove on to Wichita Falls, Texas, where we stopped for the night, and planned to drive across the rest of the state without shooting and spend a night and day off in Shreveport, Louisiana.

Wichita Falls was in a "dry" county, but the motel had a private club that one could join for a price, and any kind of alcohol was available. I elected not to join the polyester parade, as did Dennis, and we both went to our rooms to unlax. I gave Dennis a couple of joints and soaked in a hot bath for a while, trying to figure out Hopper's schizophrenic love-hate thing with me.

The television was simmering in the background, and the pot was loosening up the tension in my bod. I glanced up at the tube for a brief moment, and in that split second, my life, my children's lives, the country's life, all our hopes, all our dreams, all gone. I heard Hopper fling his door open and scream into the night. I screamed with him and threw my door open, too.

"Oh, Christ! Oh, shit, man! What the fuck is going on?" Dennis was weeping.

"It's the beginning of the end, man." I tried to be as cool as Captain A. It wasn't working. We held on to each other for a while, weeping, as the TV simmered on and the pool of blood under our second chance grew bigger, Bobby Kennedy on the floor of the Ambassador Hotel's kitchen. Martin Luther King had been murdered while Dennis was creating the flying saucers scene. Everything was coming unsnapped.

It was a very somber drive across Texas. Several of us were in the Clark-Cortez, and we stopped at a roadside arts and crafts stand. After noticing our California plates, the woman running the stand told us to remember that Texas wasn't the only state where presidents were assassinated. She was sincere, and we were put back to square one. When we arrived in Shreveport, we tried to shake off the horrible sadness with a small party, but it didn't work. We went looking for a party, but that didn't work. We got blasted. No go.

After our day off, after our laundry was done, after our personal needs were met, after we'd let a little time go by, we started out for the restaurant in Morganza, Louisiana, riding and shooting our way toward the country witticisms scene. Dennis filmed us crossing every river he could find, including the Red River many times, and every type of bridge imaginable. Several of these bridges were riveted steel arches with wooden-planked beds. From time to time, we would cross one-lane bridges whose surface planks ran parallel to the length of the bridge. Most often these planks had gaps between them that were pure hell on my raked and extended front forks and skinny twenty-one-inch front wheel. As we were traveling slowly, it was even more squirrelly, and with Jack as baggage, the whole thing became impossible. Whenever the front end got railed, Jack clamped his thighs together. I have several cracked ribs that Jack could sign.

As soon as we had finished our filming of the bikes and bridges, Hopper, Jack, and I headed for the restaurant. We had a schedule to meet, and we were on a mission. Dennis had found the Morganza restaurant when he'd scouted earlier. It had a bank of booths along one wall with mirrors, and he designed the shot so that we would be seen in the mirrors as the camera dollied by the booths, catching the reaction of the customers to our entrance. Our advance man had arranged for six young girls and a number of men to be sitting in the booths.

When the three of us arrived at the restaurant, we were without the Company. The background players were expecting a movie crew, not three grungy bikers. They had absolutely no idea that we were the producer and the director, as well as the three main leads.

"I kin smell 'em! Kin yew smell 'em? I kin smell 'em!" A small group of men, gathered around a pop machine (one of the ones that opens like a trunk), were full of comments.

Dennis was immediately convinced that *they* should be the men in the booths. "Go ask them if they want to be in the film."

"You go ask them. *You're* the director."

"*You're* the producer, man—*you* ask them!"

We both went. As we approached them, the caravan of the Company pulled up in front of the building. Lighting equipment was being quickly unloaded from Foster Denker's five-ton. So as Hopper and I were talking with the men, a movie company *was* setting up.

"Listen, we're playing three really bad men. We've just raped a thirteen-year-old white girl outside of town. There is nothing you can say about us that would be too bad. If you would just say things like you were saying when we came in, it would be perfect."

"Is this really a movie thing?" one of them asked.

"Yeah, are you all from Hollywood 'n all?"

"Yep. You bet," I said.

"Can my mother see this movie?"

What a strange criterion for a grown man. "Of course. Of course she can, man." Dennis has his ways.

There was a real deputy sheriff with the group, and he asked if he could be in the scene. Bingo. Dennis showed Laszlo the camera set-ups, and we all broke for lunch. Some of the crew had discovered an empty room in the back with a dirt floor, a few tables, and a great jukebox. It had a much better selection than the one in the main room, so most of us decided to eat there. A short time later, we were told that we could not eat in this room—it was for blacks only. The undertone of the scene we were going to shoot became very clear.

Most of us sat outside the door to that back room and ate in the afternoon sun. We'd put several dollars into the jukebox, and we listened to those tunes as if they were the fucking National Anthem. We took the chance that the owners of the joint would not throw us all out and refuse permission to shoot there. Dennis was very worried about that, and I understood. There may have been other restaurants, and there was certainly a fucked attitude in this one, but there might not be another joint with mirrors behind the booths.

We were extraordinarily lucky when it came to the local people we worked with in Morganza. When Hayward Robillard (the man in the CAT hat) said, "You name it, Sheriff, I'll throw rocks at it," I knew that the rest of the players would work out just fine. And the young girls who flirted with Captain A, Billy, and George Hanson were perfect. Their raw innocence let them act embarrassed and interested at the same time. The set and scene were wrapped in four hours, a phenomenal speed considering the number of setups needed. There was the master bringing us to the table, the master dolly past the booths with us in the mirrors walking to the table, the individual booths, both sides of each booth, the three-shot of us at the table, loose singles of each of us, tight shots of each of us, and a wide shot of the woman behind the counter. Lighting us in the mirrors *and* the booths was a feat. The Company was sharp that day, and lots of days. Paul Lewis, Laszlo Kovacs, Aggie Aguilar, Mel Maxwell, Peter Heiser, LeRoy Robbins, Jaime Contreras, Tom Ramsey, Foster Denker—all of them were incredible.

As we departed the restaurant, my bike decided to show me an old trick. When I kicked the starter, it kicked back, right onto my damaged right ankle. Our head production assistant, delGado, had to cut the boot open on the inside seam to remove it that evening, but it was still painful. I played the George-gets-killed campfire scene without boots and in severe pain, though listening to Jack tell us what we (Captain A and Billy) were all about made me laugh despite the ankle and my cracked ribs.

The real deputy did not show up that evening for the beating scene, though everyone else did. Dennis decided to show only the legs of our attackers, and the scene was very effective. There had been no violence in the movie until that scene, a dramatic device that worked quite well.

After several days, we finished off that area with the ending. It was very hot, with 98 percent humidity. The weather had been perfect for shooting an outdoor on-the-road movie. Not one day of rain; not one postponement with the exception of my side of the "hot" springs scene. The day of the last scene was so hot it may as well have rained, but 98 percent humidity lent a perfect gloss to the moment. The intention of the stunt with Captain A's bike had been a clear vision in my mind ever since that wonderful night in Toronto. It was always the capper when I told the story to whomever. Dennis had the same vision. The motorcycle was supposed to cartwheel through the air in slow motion. We shot the stunt for Dennis getting smoked. Tex Hall doubled Dennis and did a perfect drop and slide. Next, we shot me coming back to Hoppe, turning that most difficult machine around, getting off the bike and running up to where he lay bleeding. I left the motor running in the long shot to save time and ankle, and simply ran back to the bike, jumped aboard, and popped rubber as I blasted away, going for help. I flipped the kickstand up between first and second, still popping rubber at each shift point.

Two guys came driving down the road and stopped to see what the commotion was. Cocteau's accidents, again; the men appeared as if we'd willed them to appear, and were all we could have asked for. They were pleased to be in a movie, and for fifty dollars they spent the next two hours of their lives driving back and forth for our camera. We loaded the shotgun with blood hits and drove by them with the camera in the Chevy as they fired at the lens. We had a large piece of Plexiglas to protect the lens, operator, and camera assistant. When the shotgun fired, the blood bag hit the Plexiglas and turned the whole frame red, a great editing device. Then we built a small ramp that was going to make the bike flip in a reverse somersault, front over back. Tex Hall rode the bike at speed up to the ramp, stepping off it just before the ramp. Tex had to leave the bike in a way that would not make it swerve or wobble, and he did his job well, but the ramp had other ideas. The motorcycle was so heavy, it flattened it.

We only had one chance at the stunt. We couldn't lose both Captain A bikes. We watched as the bike flew through the air after flattening the ramp, staying upright with one of its front forks and the front wheel askew, having been broken by the impact at the ramp. Later, when we were able to watch the effect in slow motion on the screen, I could see the exhaust spurting from the pipes as each cylinder fired. It was very eerie—a riderless motorcycle, most of its front end dangling like a useless arm, gliding through the air, crashing into the grass and exploding. We had rigged a charge near the gas tank and set it off by remote, and the result was much more powerful than a motorcycle somersaulting in slow motion would have been. It was as if the rider had been blown away without touching the bike. More "accidents."

We mounted the camera on a special helicopter mount as quickly as we could, and Laszlo shot the pull-away with the motorcycle burning on the ground below. One can see Hopper lying by the side of the road next to his bike, but unless one looks closely, Captain America's body is not part of the picture. I've always explained that Captain America was only a dream, so not having his body visible makes great sense. It *is* there, but was almost impossible to find/see in the days before video and the pause button.

. . .

When we'd finished shooting in Louisiana, the Company all headed back toward Taos to shoot my side of the hot springs. We were going to spend the night in Dallas, and I was in the Cortez with delGado, Joyce King, and Jack, driving over swamps and bayous on long, elevated roads. Dead cedar stumps, gray and covered with birds, poked up through the dark water and made the daylight part of the journey spectacular, but when night came, it was boring until we reached Carthage, Texas. On the far side of town we drove past an enormous drive-in movie theater with a marquee that featured a triple-header of biker films: *Glory Stompers* (Dennis's film), *Hells Angels on Wheels* (Jack's), and the main show, *The Wild Angels*.

Our laughter at such a coincidence was slightly hysterical, but what would happen next would literally blow our potted minds. We drove on out of the city and headed up a hill. The Cortez was not a fast vehicle, and it used a lot of gas; just outside Carthage, on the hill, we ran out. delGado cleverly backed the thing down the hill, with no power steering or brakes, to a gas station that we had passed, and lined it up with a slot of pumps without panic or embarrassment.

Everyone had used my credit cards during the production, and they had never been questioned. No one really knew what I looked like, exactly; they knew about Henry Fonda's son but weren't sure who he was. Tell you something? Anyway, I began to pump gas into the Cortez, and delGado took one of my gas cards into the office to pay. Within a minute, several cars filled with teenagers pulled up to some of the other pumps, and one was a convertible filled with pretty young girls. They got out and began to do the same as I was doing: getting gas. As I stood there pumping, one of the girls just *knew* that she knew me as "that" movie star—literally "that"—and began to scream as she held both hands over her mouth, hopping around, turning red, and from time to time looking back at some of her friends.

"You're . . . you're . . . omygod." She was now pointing at me with one hand, holding the other over her mouth, then her eyes and back to her mouth, starting to hop toward me. Two of her friends began to do the same.

"You're . . . omygod, you're . . . you're . . . Yes! Yes!"

"Omygod, you're right. He's, ah . . . you're . . ." The others were gaining ground, and the screams were getting louder.

Then, about twenty feet out, it came clear.

"You're . . . you're . . . omygod, you're Nancy Sinatra!"

Pay dirt!

"Omygod! Nancy . . . uh . . ."

Time for Mummie's little Petey-boy to haul freight. I made a dash for the Cortez. Jack, who had gone in to buy some junk food, saw me doing the dash and realized that the jig was up, though I'm sure he did not know exactly which jig or why. When the girls, now numbering six, saw Jack breaking toward the Cortez, they were sure *he* was somebody, too. They'd just seen him on the screen, but couldn't pin a name on him. Surely not Nancy. I held that distinction, and Jack and I both beat them to the motor home, but just barely. Arms began to tear out the screens to the open windows and reach inside, grasping for any kind of souvenir.

"You stayed in the paint too long, Fonda!" Jack snorted, as he wrestled a script away from the clawing hands. It would be a long time before I understood what he meant.

delGado had used the diversion to finish pumping gas, pay for it and sprint back into Fort Apache. We got the windows closed and started moving out while hands pummeled the side of the Cortez. Joyce King had been working at the table on her script notes and camera reports. When the attack came, she flung herself on top of her pages, guarding the vital organs of the script with her body. She was a brave girl. Jack lost several pages from his script, but we had effectively wrapped his part.

"This kind of thing happen a lot, Fonda?" Jack had no idea what was in store for him.

We were on our way again, but there was a different air to the cabin of the Cortez. We were quiet for a long time.

When we got to Dallas, it was raining very hard, a full Texas downpour. Jack left us for L.A. to do post on his movie *Head,* and I rented a Lincoln to drive the rest of the way. It made the ride to Taos a tad smoother. When we got to the hot springs, the water level had dropped a few feet, but once we established me in the doorway, it was not a problem to sell it as the same place and the same time. In the high shot and the shot from the doorway the first time, the audience sees legs, the tie between Luana, Sabrina, Dennis, and myself, but those are Laszlo's legs that Luana swims up to. We shot the reverse of Luana looking up at me, sitting in the door, and the legs became mine.

Cut, print, wrap that location and the road part of the movie. I drove the Lincoln nonstop from Taos to L.A. with Virgil Frye and Ray White. Somewhere outside of Vegas, Ray passed out some speed, one of the dumbest drugs ever invented, to keep us alert. When we arrived in the early morning my teeth felt like they were going to shatter, my neck was being torqued, and my mouth was very dry.

My homecoming to Susan and the children was like the return of Ulyesses to his island after the Helenic Wars. It felt as if I had been gone twenty years. But I knew that we had a Trojan Horse to put inside the walls of the studios.

We finished principal photography and came together for a wrap party at my house in Beverly Hills. I placed many umbrella-covered tables on my tennis court, but two or three times the number of guests we had expected showed. Most of the cast and crew brought along their families, and our lawns and the pool were wonderfully decorated with children playing in the warm summer afternoon. It looked like the Summer of Love being re-created in my yard. There were two straights that no one recognized, and I immediately thought they were police, there to bust our party. Our "Hit Squad" went right up to them, asked for their IDs, and found they were some of Bert's accountants. Yikes! I had forgotten to invite Bert and Bob. Oh! The shame, the shame!

A week after we wrapped, Tex Hall got married, and most of the cast and crew went to his new house for the reception. We brought him many bottles of champagne, a silver service, picture frames, the usual wedding stuff. A week and a half after the wedding, a biker gang came to his house in Simi Valley, tied up Tex and his bride, took all the champagne and silver and emptied his garage. Tex had eleven motorcycles in there, including the two "Billy" bikes and the one remaining Captain A motorcycle. No one knew about *Easy Rider* at that point. There'd been no publicity, no public relations person. We couldn't afford either.

So, the gang had no idea about the potential value of the movie bikes, and as is the case with most stolen vehicles, the bikes were undoubtedly dismantled and the parts scattered. But over the years, many people have claimed they had the original *Easy Rider* bike. No one does. There is no "original" Captain America motorcycle. One afternoon, several years ago, I noticed in *Hemmings Motor News* (a catalogue for cars) that "the original *Easy Rider* motorcycle" was for sale for $9,000. Dennis was the seller; he needed money for drugs. When Columbia realized that they had a major hit, they had two replica Captain A bikes built for theater lobby display.

Those two bikes ended up in one of the sheds on Hopper's place in Taos. He'd shown me the so-so replicas in the early seventies, and any aficionado would have seen the difference. The bikes were never made to actually run, but somehow Hoppe had fobbed them off. I've seen one of them since: its owner, who calls himself "Rodent," refuses to admit that his prize is a rip-off, and makes a tidy sum going about the country displaying the bike. He charges a fee to be photographed with the bike, but never lets anyone move it. The dissection and dispersal of the real bike was a fitting action. Somewhere out there many bikers could be riding with some little piece of the original: a fender, a wheel, something. I only wonder where the tank is.

A week or so after the theft, Dennis and I realized that we had forgotten to shoot the last campfire scene. In the script we had simply noted that the scene, written in a very abbreviated way, was to be about our having made it to Florida. We gathered the crew once again and went up into the Santa Monica Mountains, quite close to the location where we had built the hippie commune. We still had some of the raw stock left, which meant that we had the same emulsion numbers: at least the film would not have a different color balance. We also rented the Cortez. One more time. Going on up one more time.

Dennis and I sat in the Cortez discussing the scene.

"What do you think you should say?" Dennis asked.

"I just want to say 'We blew it, man.' "

"No, no, man. We've got to be more specific. We've got to say something about how we blew it, man."

"I don't think so. I feel that we should say very little."

"No, no, man, we've got to say something about blowing our heritage, man. You know what I mean, man?"

"I just want—"

"Listen, man, we've got to say that we've blown our heritage, you know, man, like when we went for the big bucks and the drugs, ya dig man?"

Our conference was a little more supercharged than I am describing now, nitrous-injected and explosive. I stuck to my proverbial guns.

"I want to do it like Warren Beatty, man."

"Like Warren Bea— what the fuck are you saying, man? Like Warren Beatty? What the fuck is that supposed to mean, man?"

"Well, Warren cuts all his lines in half and then mumbles the ones he *does* speak. I want—"

"What the . . . are you fucking kidding me, man? Warren Beatty?"

"I think we should say as little as—"

"You're talking like a fucking child. Shit, man!"

Where had I heard that before? " 'We blew it, man!' That's all I want to say, Dennis."

"I don't fucking believe this, man!"

The Napoleonic furrow became a canyon. Dennis had made me

say many lines that I didn't want to say during the shoot, but this was my last shot, and I hung on fiercely. We screamed at each other for another fifteen minutes until I said that we would say it both ways, first his and then mine. This is a terrible thing for a producer to suggest to a director. I told him that the crew had heard us yelling, it was getting dark, time to shoot and to give each other a hug and let's go down to the set. The crew will think we were just working it up like crazed method actors, I suggested.

"Yeah! Yeah, man! You're right, man." He threw his arms around me. "I love you, man, okay?" The canyon was deep, but he was making the effort.

"I love you, too. Now let's go on down there."

We went down to the set and took our positions in front of the camera. We had given the setup before we went up to the Cortez to work out the scene. I sat closer to the camera and stared at the fire with the most enigmatic look on my face. Inside my heart, I was finally exhausted, completely destroyed. At that moment I felt Dennis had taken our chance at making a successful movie, and therefore the chance to make another, and pissed it all away.

Dennis called for the camera to roll and then said his opening line. "We've done it. We've done it. We're rich, Wyatt. Yeah, man. Yeah."

"You know, Billy, we blew it."

He stammered along with all the words he just *had* to say.

"We blew it." I turned my flag to the camera, "Goodnight, man." As I turned my back on the scene, I could see the furrow going even deeper on his face. A full Grand Canyon. He turned his head and called for a cut.

"That was great, man. Just stay in the moment, man, that was beautiful." He had the camera move for a close-up on me (he shot all my close-ups with a 100mm lens). "Just keep the idea, man." And when the camera was ready, "Say the line again, man, just like you did, okay? Say it fifteen or sixteen times, okay, man? whenever you're ready, man."

We never shot it his way. Part of his genius was knowing that the moment was perfect, even if he hadn't agreed initially. In 1987 he said in an interview that I had never understood why he wanted me to read that line, *that* way. Give me a fucking break, Dennis.

Twenty-seven years later, Dennis tried to get me to sign a declaration that he and he alone wrote the screenplay for *Easy Rider*. One can imagine the love-hate relationship I've had with him all this time. Of course I wanted him to direct the film. I hired him! Who else had the passion? Of course I didn't think twice about his vow never to speak to me again. Of course I go to see all his work, and I call him to tell him how I liked it. Of course I go into his editing rooms, at his invitation, and watch his latest work being put together. Of course he wasn't the sole writer of the screenplay to *Easy Rider*. Of course he still thinks he was. Of course he thinks I cheated him. Of course I didn't. Not my way of life.

chapter *Fifteen*

$\mathcal{D}$ennis edited for twenty-two weeks. We had screenings every week, and even in its four-hour version with a SCENE MISSING sign that represented fifteen minutes, as Dennis would yell at each screening (the fifteen minutes was intended for fifteen hours' worth of 16mm footage from the streets of Mardi Gras), the viewers were blown away at the end. When Dennis had the movie down to two hours and forty-five minutes—still with the SCENE MISSING sign, which meant the film was three hours—and couldn't, or wouldn't, take it any lower, we sent him off to Taos with a mink coat for his girlfriend and a promise to let him cut the Mardi Gras footage. Don Cambren, the editor, went to work with Bert, Bob, Bill, Jack, and me to cut the slack, beautiful as it was, and change the balance. Within five or six weeks, we brought the film down to a more accessible length.

The movie had become an abstract tale about *Billy* and his pal, Captain America. With the agreement of Bert, Bob, Jack, and Bill Hayward, most of the dialogue that Dennis demanded I say in the first campfire with Jack was cut. The scene moved much more smoothly; and the looks I give Jack's character when he is asking about marijuana leading to "harder stuff," instead of words, make the point of the naive lawyer wanting to try it but concerned about the end results much more hip and honest. Jack polished all his scenes and cleaned them up beautifully with his editorial skills. We all worked very hard to make *Easy Rider* a visible and viable motion picture. Dennis's reaction? We'd ruined *his* movie.

Dad came to see a screening and afterward told me that he was worried for me. He knew I had all my eggs in this basket, and he doubted that *any* audience would get the film. Jane came with Vadim and Michelangelo Antonioni. Antonioni had a special yo-yo with him that had lights in its clear plastic body that lit up when it was spinning. I promptly broke the thing on my first attempt. After the screening, we all went to a bar not far from the studio. As we crossed the street to the bar, I spotted a ten-dollar bill in the gutter. I picked it up and told Jane that this was the first ten dollars of the ten million I was going to make from the movie. Michelangelo had a fierce nervous tick in his left shoulder. Famous for it. He sat dead still during the entire screening.

Dennis and I agreed that we should cut the film with music behind the rides to fill the track and lend emotion to the vision. We began by using music from our own record collections. It worked beyond anything we could have imagined, though some songs were finally too long. It was hard to cut out the ride with Bob Dylan's entire "The Gates of Eden." The music and film worked together perfectly, as did many of Dennis's lovely shots that spread the thread of the slim story. We had to keep the main story simple enough to let the allegory be felt, understood, or, at least, possible.

Even though we had intended to ultimately use Crosby, Stills & Nash, nothing could approach the music we laid in as a temp track. Crosby and the boys recognized that when they first viewed the rough cut. Our work was cut out for us—no one had ever used already popular tunes, staples of a rapidly unfolding history, as the entire soundtrack. We had to get to so many different artists, managers, and labels for permissions that it was a logistical nightmare. Bert Schneider was the master of this most difficult bit of business, and found the challenge invigorating.

The artists respected us, and we offered each one thousand dollars and the mechanicals (that portion of the film's income paid to the musicians who've played on the soundtrack) for the right to use their music. In most instances the offer was accepted readily, much to the dismay of their agents, labels, and managers, but the artists' take on the film was often fascinating. We had screened the film for Steppenwolf in a little room at Screen Gems. John Kay sat just in front of me wearing dark Ray·Ban Wayfarers. I kept wondering why he wouldn't take them off. When the screening was over, John turned to me and asked if the film was in color—he was profoundly color-blind. I told him it was. He said to show it to the Russians in black-and-white, said it would blow their little commie minds. Then, as his manager was trying to stop him from further commitment, he asked me if there was anything else he could do for us. We were using two Steppenwolf tunes as the opening songs: "The Pusher," by Hoyt Axton, and "Born to Be Wild," by Mars Bonfire. Just after we sell five pounds of white powder to the character played by Phil Spector, we drive off into the desert to fetch our scoots while the words "Goddamn the pusher-man" play over the scene. We meant to foreshadow the ending, but by using Hoyt's song over our bucolic drive to the desert hideout, most of the audience forgot its warning.

We had taken the film to New York City to show to the main executives at Columbia and to Bob Dylan. Dylan arrived for the screening with two Black Panthers and his manager, Fat Albert Grossman, and we rolled the film. When the lights came back up in the screening room, the Panthers were blown away. Dylan jumped up from his seat with his wife, Sarah, and hurried Hopper and me off to a private room as Fat Albert was trying to stop him. He told us the movie was fantastic, but we couldn't have his song "It's Alright Ma," and we should reshoot the ending—we should we have Captain America ram his bike into the pickup and make it explode.

I told him the whole idea was *not* to have any revenge, that we wanted the audience to leave the theater carrying the load with them, rather than being able to leave it behind like a half-empty box of popcorn. Everyone had to bring it on home. I told him that we wanted to hear the lyrics about questions without answers from his song "It's Alright Ma." Dylan said that the lyrics were redundant, that we had already said it all in the film, and that he hated his harmonica on the cut. I was flabbergasted and pointed out that any good fight was a combination of punches, but he wasn't going for of it. Dennis was just as disturbed. We wheedled, we coaxed. Finally, in desperation, I explained to him about the scene in the graveyard with me on the statue talking about my mother. I told him that I hadn't wanted to do that scene, but there it was in the film. That my name was Fonda, and that if I had something to hide, it was all over now. I told him that the scene embarrassed me, but it was still there in the film. I told him that my mother had slit her throat from ear to ear in an insane asylum, and that I needed to hear the lyrics about suicide remarks.

The part about my mother blew him away. Bob gave it up after that. We could have the first part of the song but not the last verses, the ones about questions in your nerves without answers. The *big* ones. He refused to budge, and asked what the ending meant to me. I wasn't prepared for that one. I told him that one could see the road that man built with the burning bike, that one could see what happened on that road, and then one could see the river, the road that god built. Dylan grabbed a piece of paper and wrote the lyrics to the "Ballad of Easy Rider":

> *The river flows*
> *It flows to the sea*
> *Wherever that river goes*
> *That's where I want to be*
> *Flow, river, flow*
> *Let your waters wash down*
> *Take me from this road*
> *to some other town*
> *Go river go*
> *Past the green shady tree*
> *Flow river flow*
> *Flow to the sea*

The lyrics were the total opposite of the ending that Hoppe and I felt was the capper, but Dylan said to have McGuinn put music to it and not to use his name. McGuinn managed to put a few lines in that gave an edge to the song. But I'm still an avid fan of his music, and we are friendly with each other when we meet. In 1994, I learned that one of the reasons he didn't want us to use "It's Alright Ma" was that he guessed the film's impact, and dreaded having to sing the song over and over again, endlessly, by popular demand. I understand his reasoning now. I have a friend who played on some of his early cuts, who said that Dylan came in to cut certain songs, did one take, went on to the next song, and so on, and then left the studio. I think you'd *have* to do it only once and only when you were ready.

Shortly after that episode, I was at a party at McGuinn's house in Malibu when a call came in for me. It was Robbie Robertson of The Band, and he'd just screened *Easy Rider*. I'd approached him the previous fall about doing the music for the film, but he'd made it very clear that he was not even going to talk to us, and only changed his mind, like many of the other bands, after he'd seen the movie. Now, though Robbie allowed that Dylan's tune "It's Alright Ma" was okay, he told me that the only music in the film that was really worth anything was "The Weight." He wanted to do the entire musical score. I explained that we were marrying the sound to the film in two days, and we had a date to show the film as the official U.S. entry at the Cannes Film Festival. Robbie didn't get the program, and insisted again. I was pleased that he felt so strongly about the film, but there wasn't a whole lot that could be done, and I reminded him of his refusal to even talk to us the previous fall. He still gave us permission to use "The Weight."

In New York, we all stayed at the Regency Hotel and took the film by refrigerator dollies to Columbia's New York City offices, which were only a few blocks away. In doing so, we passed right by the Le Roy Sanitarium, my birthplace, and as we walked by the entrance awning, I told Hoppe that this was where I'd been born. He wanted to go inside, right then, film canisters and all. The doorman, who wore a uniform with frayed gold trim and off-center epaulets and was the epitome of decay, refused to let us in. Hopper, typically, insisted, but the doorman refused again, saying that none of us could have possibly been born at this hospital. We all looked like radical hippies, with long hair, and Jack and I had full beards. When the Le Roy was torn down, a few years later, I wanted the giant Art Deco bronze doors to mount out in one of my fields or in the front lawn and call them the Doors to Perception. Maybe I'll find them someday.

We showed the film to all the Columbia executives *and* the man who approved the official entrants to the Cannes Film Festival. It was an incredible screening. The execs didn't understand the film at all, but the man from Cannes invited it to be the official entry from the United States. We returned to our rooms, feeling on top of the world.

• • •

We all arrived at Cannes at different times. Susan and I drove down from Paris. Things were strained between us, but we made our best efforts to accommodate each other. Jack and I were both sporting beards. I had rented the full-dress tunic, belt, sash, and hat of a Union Cavalry general from the Civil War, and wore this outfit to the dress premiere screening of *Easy Rider*. I answered queries by saying that as far as I was concerned, the United States was in a state of civil unrest, just on the verge of war.

We were feted aboard Sam Speigel's yacht *Malane*. We won the antifestival prize (a ritual begun during the demonstrations the year before) for best picture. The British movie *If* won the Gold Prize, the Palm d'Or. But no other movie at the festival, including *If*, was as talked about in the press or on the street as *Easy Rider,* and the Festival Committee created a new prize for the best film by a new director, so they could honor our little motion picture. I was delighted for Dennis. One of his lifetime dreams had come true. A film he had directed won a prize at Cannes.

When I was in Toronto to open the film, I was put into an enormous penthouse painted all white, with a white grand piano. I called Bert and told him I didn't need to stay in such splendor. It made me feel uneasy, and I didn't want all this opulence charged against the picture.

"Relax, Fonda, enjoy it. They'll charge it against the picture whether you stay in the room or in some girl's VW van."

I wanted to go to a small lake near Toronto to row a boat and shake off the stardom, but I was driven there in a limo. Under the circumstances it seemed out of place. When I arrived, there was only one boat left, the one I had reserved. It was the middle of July, very hot, and a young couple were walking away in disappointment. I called out to them, asking them if they would like to join me, and they happily accepted. When we were out in the lake, I asked them if they were cops. They were thrown a bit by that question. I wanted to smoke some pot, I explained. They pulled out a few joints, and we fired them up.

After floating around for a while, the tension slipped away from my body, my heart. They had no idea who I was. A great shout from the shore came floating out to us.

"They've landed on the moon," I said.

Later on, back in the white room, I sat patiently in front of the TV with my Nikon set at a sixtieth of a second to snap a photo of the first steps on the moon. I banged off twenty or more frames, then put down the camera and began to cry. Tears coursed my cheeks. I wept for my children. I wept for the loss of my generation's innocence. I wept for the loss of John Fitzgerald Kennedy, whose voice I couldn't get out of my head. One of his dreams that had become one of my dreams was happening. We, all of us on the planet, were making that first step on the surface of the moon, and that son of a bitch, Nixon, was going to take all the credit. That constipated, retentive crook was going to march out to the tune of "Hail to the Chief" and greet the astronauts.

Shit happens, I realized, but this shit was thrown right in the face of my whole generation. What did the little, low-budget motorcycle movie mean compared to all of the hurt that was going down? Vietnam, cops beating on kids. The Kent State murders had not yet happened, but somewhere in my crazed mind I knew they were coming. It wasn't enough that so many young men and women were dying for nothing in Vietnam; our out-of-whack government was going to kill us in our own front yards. Where were you, Thomas Jefferson, when we needed you most?

The film opened at the Beekman Theater in Manhattan on the fourteenth of July, 1969, with no TV or major print campaign, but two lines around the block for tickets. Bert had devised a scheme to get the word-of-mouth going around town even before we had won the prize at Cannes. I called each theater in which *Easy Rider* had opened, every night, to check on that day's box office gross. There wasn't a theater manager who wouldn't talk to me, and they were all pleased to have a record-breaking film in their house. I would ask them if they had a good print and sound, and they all told me they had never had a producer, director, or star call them and ask if the print was good.

In order to have the film shown on the screen in the United States we had to make a special arrangement with IATSE. The IA, as it's called, is the union that services (if that's the right term) the camera, sound, makeup, set design and dressing, props, *and* the projectionists. They wouldn't project the film, because it didn't have the IA seal. I called that unconstitutional and wanted to take it to the max. My lawyers, Susan, Bill Hayward, and myself met with Bert and Bob and Columbia's attorneys to discuss the problem, the crux of which was a contract I had signed with NABET (a competitive union that represented the guilds in television). I had promised to put *their* seal on the release prints, and now I was being told that we wouldn't be able to fulfill that promise. The lawyer who was representing Bert, Bob, and Columbia was Norma Zarkey. When we were introduced, she made a declaration that her son was one of the founders of SDS (Students for a Democratic Society), as if this was proof of her own liberal ideology. I didn't give a shit. All I could see was a force play to defraud NABET of its contractually guaranteed recognition. "Collusion" was the word I said most, and each time I used that word, the other side winced, and said no, no, no. But their signatures weren't on the contract. I claimed we were protected from secondary boycott by the U.S. Constitution. I brought Susan to the meeting, not only because she was a director of the Pando Company, but because I knew it would throw Bert off just a bit.

"You want to wave flags, Fonda, or do you want to make money?"

It only took me a few moments to make that decision. "Money, Bert. But I will call it a collusion that I am forced to enter into, when I speak to the press." I was pissed.

As it turned out, the movie did have some effect on our generational identity. From what I hear out in the world, it still does. And everything that was endured during the making of *Easy Rider* has been worth it, purely financially as well as in the way it influenced other movies from that point on. Bert's father, Abe Schneider, resigned as chairman of the board of Columbia, stating that if *Easy Rider* was the way the industry was going to go, he did not understand it and did not want to be a part of it. He told me he thought I was talking about him when we identified the antagonist. On the other hand, at the Cannes Film Festival, Serge Seminenco told me to call him direct the next time I was going to make a picture that cost so little and could make so much. We were sitting at a table with the heads of Columbia as he told me not to bother with them. That certainly didn't do too much for my chances to work at Columbia, though Serge was the financial entity for the studio, and the chief finance officer of the Bank of Boston.

There are so many people around the world who come up to me and tell me that *Easy Rider* changed their lives. Most of the long-distance riders I meet tell me that I started the whole thing. I didn't start it at all. I just put it on film.

Later that summer, the U.S. government invited me to fly to Washington, D.C., to answer a question—unspecified—that they felt was important to their understanding of my generation. The invitation came from the Health, Education, and Welfare Department (no longer known by that name). I was assured confidentiality, and they flew me first class round-trip from L.A. and gave me a suite at the Mayflower Hotel. They wanted to know everything I could tell them about cocaine and its use by the youth of the time. I was amazed. I'd only used it three or four times and didn't really know a thing, and asked why that was a big question. They told me that cocaine was going to be as prevalent as marijuana by 1974. Had I known that people like Oliver North, Reagan, and Bush would be running the games, I wouldn't have been so surprised.

The trade-off with HEW was simple. I'd answer their question and they, in turn, would answer any question I had.

"Who put the contract out on JFK?"

Silence. One of the ironies of the whole trip was that they flew me to D.C., first class, just when we were all pulling off the huge Peace March against the war in Vietnam. The main organizers of the demonstration were thrilled that I was there. *Easy Rider* had already become an anthem for the hippie generation, and in the eyes of the youth, I had become Captain America.

At home, however, things weren't so lofty. I forced myself to face the reality of my infidelities to my wife and our marriage. I knew that Susan's mother had told her to divorce me as soon as Bridget was born, and she really laid on that button when Justin was born. Late in 1968, Susan talked about divorce and it put me into a total panic. The fact that I lacked a relationship I clearly needed was not a valid excuse for my behavior. I feared the possible dissolution of the family I was responsible to and for, and I worried that I would end up like *my* father, in multiple marriages and with failed relationships with my own children. But I also needed the attention and sexuality—the unconditional love—I found with other women as much as I needed to have a family proper. I went to Jane and told her about my dilemma. Jane told me to ask Susan *why* she had married me. I did, and Susan didn't know how to answer.

During the summer of 1969, I went to England and Scotland to promote the film, though it hadn't been allowed to play in those markets yet, and I went to Paris to open the film in its original version.

While in Paris, I learned that Hilly Elkin's option for the rights to writer Kurt Vonnegut's novel *Cat's Cradle* had lapsed twelve days before. Providence was on my side. I had to fly to Boston to open the film there, so I phoned Kurt and made an appointment to meet him at his home on Cape Cod. To me, *Cat's Cradle* was the perfect book to put into motion picture form. The characters and the story were cinematic and could be easily translated to a script, and it was the best cynical look at our society and government I had read in a long time.

I finished my work in Boston, did my laundry, and headed down to Cape Cod. Kurt met me at the airport and we had some oysters, a delicious clam chowder, and several martinis. The sad news was that Elkins had renewed the option the day before I arrived. But, at Kurt's request, I stayed at his house for three days, enjoying his life. I tromped through the muddy sand in the marshes with the gang, as we hunted the prized steamer clams for a big barbecue. The house was full with Kurt's children and his late brother's children, and I stayed in the barn. After his brother and sister-in-law had died, Kurt took the whole bunch on as if they were his own. I admired that commitment. There was an old pedal organ in the barn, and I amused myself the first night there playing the organ *and* my guitar, despite my disappointment about losing the option. The kids came out to the barn to hang with me one at a time, and I wasn't sure about offering them any grass until *they* asked me if I wanted any LSD or mescaline. I advised them to wait for a better moment to alter their states. We burned a few bombers and they crept back to the main house, making me promise not to tell their dad. Of course not.

We went marsh tromping again and gathered enough clams for a real bake and, naturally, more martinis. At one point, Kurt invited me into his study, inscribed a copy of *Cat's Cradle,* and fished a joint out of his desk while asking me not to tell the children. What a wonderful family. After the bake with corn on the cob and some lobsters, we gathered in the living room and played music together. I played my guitar, Kurt played a clarinet and a saxophone, and the rest played any instrument they could find. It was the kind of life I wanted to have, the kind of life I *wished* I'd had, where acceptance and humor weren't limited to occasional games of hide the button and kite flying.

I flew back to L.A. for a moment with Susan and the children, then flew back to London in late September to open the film for real. It had taken a good deal of negotiating to get the movie approved for British release. We opened in a cinema on Piccadilly Circus and played twenty-four hours a day, with free showings from two A.M. to nine A.M. Kids came by rail from all over England to see the free screenings. The English press went wild, another coup for Bert.

Nancy Ruspoli came from Paris to attend the opening night with me. I insisted that we not arrive by limo to the affair, and it was arranged to bring us in by taxi and sweep us away by taxi at the end. The kids went wild. They didn't prevent me from walking through them to the cab, but once we were in the cab, they climbed all over it, as if they were trying to roll it over. Nancy was frightened, but I knew we were all right. They weren't trying to tip the car over.

One morning in London, I was awakened by a call from an old friend, Sue Barton, a top designer and former model. She had a script, and she wanted to give it to me personally. She stayed only a few moments, left the script after a passionate pitch, and was gone, back into the Big Gray. I had some interviews, radio and television appearances and the like, so I put the script in my flight bag and forgot about it.

Bill and I flew on to Paris the next day to begin the dubbing process. We fortunately had a real ace as our dubbing director, so things were quite smooth. Everyone in Paris wanted to have us out for dinner or a party. *Easy Rider* was making the most perfectly shaped wave, and I was in the curl. It was a very intoxicating feeling that had been building steadily since Toronto in 1967. It wasn't the adulation—fickle at best—it was the selfish feeling that a story I had put together, two years earlier, had made it to the world screen basically in the form and substance I had originally dreamed. Or, did I just dream this whole thing, Dennis?

Jane came in from her farm to have dinner with me and Bill and a couple of beauties, none of whom could touch her. She was proud of me and she glowed with her beauty. She asked me if I would mind if she stayed with me that night instead of trying to drive back to her farm. No problem. Uh. Well, umm. There was only one bed in my little suite at the Hotel Elizabeth. But I loved her and would do anything to please her. I needed her approval as much as I needed anything. Jane had always been just slightly below Dad on the need-of-approval scale, and as we were closer and more in touch with each other, her blessing was the more important one. She had a little over-night bag, and we shared the same bed in total comfort, brother and sister. I played my guitar, singing songs to her as she slept. I sang songs to both of us. Her ease of staying with me at that moment meant a lot to me. An almost family.

chapter *Sixteen*

$\mathcal{B}$ill and I finished the dubbing in Paris in a week. We had met a young Polish prince everyone called Stash, and we were all invited to come out to Jane's farm for the night, so Stash, Bill, and I drove there in Stash's 1969 Corvette T Top coupe. We had a plan: we would take a nighttime mescaline trip. The ride was fairly uncomfortable, as the car was intended to be a two-passenger vehicle, but Stash insisted we take his new toy. I remembered the ride to the airport in Nice after the wonderful Saint-Tropez summer of '66.

We arrived at the farm after Jane and Vadim had finished their dinner, and sat around talking for an hour or so. Then, talking was out of time. It was funny to watch everyone get to the moment of truth together in their own way. Just around midnight, after Jane had gone to bed, we took our dose and sat back waiting for the wonderful visual and emotional altered state. Mescaline is a smoother and more mellow hallucinogen than LSD. Everyone has their own metabolic rate, but eventually we were all blissed out on this extract of the mescal cactus. Vadim, typically, insisted that he felt nothing. I was stretched out on one of the fabulous rugs watching the fibers of my mind unravel and reform in amazing new ways.

After an hour or so, we decided to venture outside into the night. Actually, Bill had wandered out first and came back in a while—minutes were not part of the program—and asked Vadim how many cats were out in the front yard. One over the limit, Vadim replied, and we followed Bill back outside.

Since I had last been there, Jane had full trees planted with guy wires holding them in place until they had established their own root stability—a trick we had both learned from our Dad. Bill got messed up in the wires, which were almost invisible in the dark. The number of cats multiplied immediately in Bill's mind, and his dilemma made us all hysterical. I didn't see even one of the cats, but I knew they were there. Once we had figured out Bill's confusion, we went back inside and lay down on couches and rugs to continue our individual journeys into our inner selves. Our walk in the wires was quite compelling, though, and we eventually wandered back outside into the big dark. Bill got caught up in the wires right away, but didn't panic. As my eyes got acclimated to the dark, the light from the windows of the living room allowed me to see the wires. Occasionally, I saw a cat. We all stayed together in the area just outside the living room.

When the sky was getting much brighter, we went up to the large master bedroom, escaping the eyes of the farmhands and servants. I couldn't be stopped from going outside one last time, though, to watch the coming dawn. In the half light, I noticed a building that hadn't been there the night before, and I jumped back inside the house in fear. I peeked out several times before I was able to step back outside and look at the thing. A stable had been built on the western side of the grounds. It looked like it had been there from the get-go, but I hadn't seen it in '67. Jane later told me that she had it built and aged so it would look like an old structure. More lessons we had learned from our father and motion picture sets. And when the sun had risen well into the sky, Bill and I remembered that we had a flight to catch for our dubbing in Rome. We both grew increasingly nervous. Our bags were waiting back at the hotel in Paris, so it was necessary to return to the city before our flight. Time was suddenly thrust smack-dab into our altered state, and when one is truly "altered," time has no meaning.

Stash was now part of the team, and the three of us rocketed back to Paris. We all hustled to make our plane, just in time. Also aboard was Jean-Paul Belmondo. I had a conversation with him on our way to Rome, and I wondered if he was aware that his tweed jacket was coming undone very rapidly. It seemed to me that the material was flying off him and into the cabin, thread by thread. When we landed at Rome, the threads from Jean-Paul's jacket had regrouped.

Our dubbing room was just off the Piazza del Popolo, and everything went smoothly until Billy (Dennis) tells Captain America, "We ain't no traveling bureau," at the hippie commune. The Commandante, a seventy-two-year-old man in charge of the dubbing, said, quite definitively, that there were no double negatives in Italian. He had been forced on us by the Italian government, and had a bad attitude about our movie and us. I went down to the Piazza and found a young street kid who knew *only* double negatives and brought him into the dubbing room to demonstrate the double negative in Italian. The Commandante was furious, so I fired him. This action put a real bad wrinkle in the process and slowed us down a bit, but we were going to have the right kind of dubbed film or we wouldn't release it in *any* country. It also added an extra day to the process, which meant Bill had to go up to Munich without me and begin the arrangements for the German session, while I finished the work in Rome.

. . .

In the middle of the afternoon on Saturday, while finishing up in the dubbing room, I got a call from Bill in Munich.

"Peter . . . you've *got* to come up to Munich!"

"Well, I am coming up, Bill."

"No, Peter, you've *got* to come to Munich." He sounded a bit strange.

"Are you all right, Bill?"

"Yep."

"Well, I am coming up tomorrow, Bill."

"No, Peter, you've got to come up here."

"As soon as I finish the job down here, Willie."

"I'm going to hang up the phone, now, Peter."

"OK, Bill . . . uh . . ." He was gone. Very strange.

Bill met me at the plane in Munich with Dieter, our German interpreter. On the way to the hotel, Bill and Dieter were strangely quiet. They hustled me up to our suite, sat me down in the sitting room, and brought out a block of very black Afghani hash.

"You've got to come up to Munich, Peter."

"I'm here, Bill."

"So I see."

I went into my bedroom and placed a call to my agent. Direct dialing wasn't available in those days, so I had to wait for the call to be placed. I went back into the sitting room and smoked some of the hash. In less than two minutes I was ripped. I had no idea who I was. I was sitting someplace of which I had no knowledge, and looking at me across a low, narrow table were two people I had never seen before. Smiling at me. Nodding their heads and cackling at me. In the mysterious distance, I heard something ringing. The two strangers across the table didn't budge, so I went looking for the source of the ringing. I found an object that somehow seemed familiar. The phone. I picked up the phone and listened. . . .

"Peter? . . . This is Jack." Someone said, ". . . Peter? . . . This is Jack." Hmmm . . . I must be Peter . . . Jack . . . Jack . . . uh . . .

"Jack?" I croaked.

"Yes! You called me." Hmmm . . . I did? . . . Jack? . . . Oh! Yeah! Jack! Yeah . . . J a c k   N i c h o l s o n!

"Yeah, what's up . . . Jack?"

"Peter? Can you hear me all right ?"

"Sure. . . . Jack. . . ."

"It's Jack Gilardi, Peter." My agent and friend.

"Yeah, Jack, I can't talk right now, I'll call you back, later."

Now I had to find out who the two guys were in that other place. I mean, I must be Peter. . . . So . . . who the fuck were these other guys? I went looking for that other place and finally found these two grinning assholes, sitting on a couch.

"I'm Peter." Both of these fuckers started to howl with laughter.

"I'm Peter," I repeated.

"Yes . . . yes . . . of course you are." More laughter, now coming in on the shrieking level. I began to recognize one of the shrieks.

"Bill . . . ?"

"You bet!" Total collapse on the couch.

"Far out! We need some of this shit, Willie!"

"You bet!" I found out that the Germans call marijuana, "shit," and a joint, a "joint." What a great language.

During this time, I read the script *The Hired Hand,* and Bill and I decided that it would be our next movie. We were both taken by the fine writing and wonderful characters delivered by Alan Sharp. It was the first western I had read that showed the life of a woman in the

West of 1881. And not just that. It was the story of a man who had deserted his wife and infant daughter, leaving them to fend for themselves while he wanders the western lands with a friend and no purpose. *That* could describe me in a certain way. Great dialogue.

After we had finished the dubbing in Munich, we went back to Rome and a private screening of *Easy Rider* for our friends. Verushka came with her boyfriend, but he got pissed off at us for talking in an intimate way and roared away in his Ferarri, doing a bit of damage to the car as it bounced around on the curbs. Vera had bought him the car. Very Italian. The screening was a big success. We stayed at the Grand Hotel and visited Stash at the Villa Medici, which was under the guidance of Stash's father, the famous painter Balthus. After this, Haywire and I went back to the States. I had been away so much of the entire year selling, promoting, and working on the distribution of *Easy Rider,* that I hadn't had a chance to be with my kids. I thought a lot about my own father and his devotion to his work to the exclusion of many family things. Susan was obviously strained to the max, and our failing marriage was out of the closet and very much on the top of the daily life page.

I was unbelievably sad knowing that my family, started by Susan and myself, was breaking up. I felt despair, thinking that I would end up like my father, unable to have any semblance of a real family. I tried to make up for my extended absences by intense attention to Bridget and Justin, but it was a tale unable to be rewritten, at its core. There was no way they could understand my life and job—especially at that time in my career—and no way I could make up for the time already passed beneath my bridges. I *did* have a special relationship with Bridget that rose above normal, parent-child connections, but it couldn't repair the damage of my prolonged absences, and I hadn't had the time to develop that special thing with Justin. *So* much was happening in and to my life, and I wasn't able or willing to give up the journey. My sadness ran very deep in my heart, and I kept it to myself, except when I played my guitars and sang. I tried to talk to Jane about it, but I would always become too emotional and not able to speak. I paddled on.

When Hayward and I returned from Europe, we ran into Steppenwolf at the international building at JFK. Hayward's father, Leland, had some very heavy pull with the CIA, so Bill and I were taken from our plane in a very unusual way: we were escorted through the incoming customs building to a special area without having gone through customs. As we were walking through the actual hall where normal passengers have their bags inspected, the entire band from Steppenwolf was just arriving from an overseas gig. They spotted me and called out quite loudly, yelling about how much money the foreign mechanicals (that portion of the film's foreign income that is paid to musicians who have played on the soundtrack) had earned them. Kept us in excellent pot for the year, they shouted, right there in front of all the customs officials. I smiled as if I had never met them and had no idea what they could be talking about. Maybe Bill's father thought we might be carrying drugs and had arranged for the VIP treatment. Whatever. But we were both hip to the moves.

Once back in L.A., Bill and I put the full-court press on *The Hired Hand*. The script was not an easy sell, but the price was right. A $1.25 million "Peter Fonda" film right on top of the continuing and still stunning success of *Easy Rider* was too tempting to pass on. The only unknown factor was how much control I would be given. It was the first film I would direct, *and* I was also acting in it. The pressure was on.

We moved our offices down to Hollywood. A very unpretentious duplex on Seward Street, a quarter of a block north of Melrose. Our new digs had two flagpoles, one in front of each door. We put a large black flag on one and flew the flag of the United States of America, upside down, on the other. The black flag stood for anarchy, and the upside-down U.S. flag stood for the distress we all knew was infecting our country. Flying one's national flag upside down is the international distress signal at sea. We just applied it to everywhere.

We hired secretaries, bought IBM typewriters, filing cabinets, copying machines—all the normal goodies a production office should have. We also installed our own FM radio station that connected our vehicles and remote-locale shooting sets with the office.

Michael Cimino, when he first arrived from the East in his Rolls Corniche, used the couch as his office for a few months. We had phones *everywhere* and assigned him a number. Michael Gruskoff was a graduate of Pando University. One of the industry's best first assistant directors, production and unit production managers, David McGiffert, started out as a guerrilla first assistant director and overall filmmaker with me on a very different sci-fi flick, *Idaho Transfer*. Our secretaries were the tops. Everyone was hip, and the office was soon hand painted and collaged out in a most imaginative way. One felt comfortable at Pando. Unless one was a major studio exec.

We pressed on with *The Hired Hand,* demanding as much control as possible. We met with Ned Tanen at Universal, who bought the script. We had our budget and a green light, so we began casting the crew and actors. Warren Oates was my first and only choice, but his agent wanted much more than we could afford. I asked Laszlo Kovacs to shoot the film after he had completed Hopper's prophetic *The Last Movie,* but he was already taken by Paul Mazursky for *Alex In Wonderland.* Laszlo suggested Bill Zsigmond, whom he described as his mentor, and I hired him.

The budget was set, and we went on with our casting. Oates wanted fifty thousand dollars for the role, quite a bit more than we had budgeted for the part. Most of the parts were budgeted for multi-week SAG scale. I wasn't taking anything as the director, and Bill and I were going to split fifty thousand as a producing fee. We both agreed that Warren Oates was *the* actor for the role, and we gave up our fee so we could afford Mr. Oates. In other words, Bill and I were working for free. At least no one could question our commitment to the project. We finished the casting with the exception of the leading actress. For the part of Hannah, Jane had suggested Lee Grant. I loved Lee, but I wasn't as sure as I needed to be.

Christmastime! We had snow on the tree and tons of presents. It was Justin's third Christmas. There was an easy feeling about my future in the picture business, and we all joined together. Well, almost. Susan and I had drifted further apart. She no longer wanted to have sex with me, and though we shared the same bed, she kept to herself. It was very difficult for me, so I buried myself in the pile of children and toys. Children are very sensitive to high emotions, but I don't think Bridget or Justin were aware of the problem. I never fought with Susan; I rarely raised my voice.

I went to Hawaii, just after New Year's, to get a little distance from the preproduction of *The Hired Hand,* and to ready myself for the cameo I was going to do for Dennis Hopper's *The Last Movie.* I had done the same thing two weeks before I was to begin filming *Easy Rider,* but this time I brought Jane, her baby daughter, Vanessa, and a nanny with me. I liked the idea that I was bringing my sister with me for a vacation.

The beaches that scalloped their way along the southwestern coast of Maui were almost deserted in those days. Dirt roads were the only way to these fabulous beaches. I ran on the beaches and swam in the ocean all day. And I lay on the hot sand, rolling around to get an even tan, while I considered the different production problems I faced with *The Hired Hand* and of the character I was going to be playing. This particular prep time, I had the company of my sister, Jane, who shared my love of the sun and surf. She wanted to sunbathe in the nude, however, so I found myself checking out the kiave groves for Maui linemen who might be spying on Jane. I did actually have to chase one van away.

I knew that things were not very smooth between Jane and Vadim, and that their marriage was just about over. Jane had confided in me while we shook the outside world off in the sweet, peaceful tropics. She was not a happy girl, and I felt very protective of her. We had thatched cottages next to each other on the hotel grounds, and every night I came over to her wonderfully primitive hut and sang songs to and with her. She never criticized my singing or playing, so I could cut loose without fear of being put down. One evening, after taking a sleeping pill, I went to her cottage and sang songs as I drank a few glasses of wine. Next thing I knew, I slowly fell forward as I was playing, ending up with my forehead and my knees on the thatched rug, protecting the guitar with my body hunched over it. Jane didn't know about the pill and was understandably concerned by my actions. I smiled and laughed softly at my predicament.

"What do you want, Peter?" Her voice was full of concern. She helped me up and led me out of her shack and across the grass to mine.

"Watch out for that hose, Peter," she warned as she led me by my hand toward *my* hut. Oh, yes, the hose, I thought. *Wham!* I smacked my head on a low bending palm tree as I was watching the hose. I awoke the next morning in one of the two beds in my bedroom and looked over at Jane, who had slept in the other bed, making sure I was all right. Other than the scabbing scrapes on my forehead, I was feeling fine.

After my time in the sun, I was ready to make the pilgrimage with many comrades to Peru for Hopper's *The Last Movie*. I packed all my jeans and Wrangler shirts, all my athletic socks, two pair of cowboy boots, a half pound of very decent weed, and Tom Mix's 44-40 Colt Frontier Six-Shooter, along with a supply of small oxygen bottles, and bravely went where no man should have. No woman, either. Cuzco, Peru. Twelve thousand feet above sea level. Even though Lima is well inside the tropical zone, at twelve thousand feet the air is quite cold. I had a full sheepskin coat that kept me warm at all times. I slept in it. When I went through customs in Lima, I had Stormy's big, black leather Gucci suitcase, my valise, my twelve-string Guild guitar, and the Tom Mix stuck in my Levi's waist. One could not miss the 44-40 with its stag grips and Bar TM silver brand on the grips and back strap. No one wanted to check my things, and I was passed on through with the pistol in full view.

We changed planes and flew up to Cuzco. I had been telling all the cast members that they should be aware of the altitude and how it will make them very tired and light-headed. I had my small stash of oxygen, so I wasn't concerned for myself. We were all put up in different hotels in the city, which allowed a separation of the cast and crew, and therefore lessened the feeling of a company. But the way in which we were lodged kept us from feeling isolated. In my hotel, most of the cast that was part of the movie within the movie were put together. A smart move on Paul Lewis's part. Paul had been, if you recall, the production manager for *Easy Rider*. This main bunch at my hotel was: Michelle Phillips, Kris Kristofferson, Severn Darden, Ted Markland, Owen Orr, Jim Mitchum, Michael Greene, John Buck Wilkins, John Phillip Law, Dean Stockwell, Billy Gray, Russ Tamblyn, a fiery Latin American actress named Pupee Bocar, other eclectic actors and actresses, and myself.

All over Cuzco there were graffiti signs saying YANKEE GO HOME. There was also a festival of some sort that lasted most of our stay. The only result of the festival that I could see, was the constant barrage of water balloons directed at all gringos. I was never subjected to an attack, a result of my constant companion, Mister Mix, I guessed.

The Last Movie was about a movie company shooting on location in a primitive part of Peru, and what happens to the local people after they have been exposed to our totally different culture. A movie within a movie. It was also about some sort of gold find. Maybe an homage to *Treasure of the Sierra Madre*. The story, which was cowritten by Hopper and Stewart Stern, was the most original western I had ever read. At Dennis's request, I gave it to Dad. He had the same reaction. But he said he would never work in a film for Hopper, who was determined to direct it when it was made into a full script. I never told Dennis about my father's dislike for him, and when the story was part of a large interview by Rex Reed, I asked Rex not to include it. Rex was a gentleman about the whole interview, using my words as I said them and in their correct context, and not abusing the editorial process.

There was some delay in the main part of our shooting, so we filmed a few added scenes at a nearby ruin. We had been told what our parts were, but the scenes we shot had no connection to what we were told. I was playing the part of the young deputy; Michelle Phillips was the schoolteacher; Rod Cameron played the sheriff; Sam Fuller played the director of the inside movie. Don Gordon, Julie Adams, Tomas Milian, and Stella García played roles in the main movie. Dennis Hopper played the horse wrangler for the inside movie and the lead role in the real movie. Maybe "real movie" is an oxymoron.

It was a self-indulgent movie, but somewhere in all the footage there is a very good film, which we will never see. We shot for several nights filming the "wrap party" and indulging ourselves with many different substances. During the sequence, I got to perform with Kristofferson and John Buck Wilkins on film. We all sang and played guitars. After the long night shooting got bogged down, I went outside and sat in Dennis' pickup. Sylvia Miles came out and joined me, asking me what I was doing next. I told her about *The Hired Hand* and my vision. I had already cast Oates, but I was in a dilemma about the woman to play the lead. Even though it was a smaller role in lines and screen time, it was indeed the lead role. Sylvia told me to look at Verna Bloom. It was the most fortuitous advice.

Our main set was in a tiny village, Chincheros, up at fourteen thousand feet. The drive each morning was a movie in its own right. The roads were narrow and dangerous, often becoming a river of mud.

The set at Chincheros was just as I imagined it when I first read the script. Dennis's dream took full form at fourteen thousand feet with no electricity and no communications in a tiny village perched on the top of stepped sugarcane fields. Llamas roamed about free, colorfully dressed women watched us film, as they made alpaca and llama yarn in the manner that hasn't changed for two thousand years. The women waited patiently for our lunch breaks and scurried around picking up the empty pop bottles. They were amazed that we didn't keep them. I think they got more for their pop bottles than they did for the yarn.

There was a bar in Chincheros we called the Tome Coca-Cola Bar. No words were painted on the wall in which a small rectangular hole had been cut, or so it seemed. Just the Coke sign in Spanish at the top of the opening. Michelle Phillips asked me to go to the bar with her for a drink of the local white lightning, quinco. When we first entered the bar, I couldn't see a thing. Outside, everything was so bright, the wall with the hole was whiter that white. It took a long time for my eyes to get adjusted, and during that time Michelle ordered a bottle of Fanta and four shots of quinco. The Fanta was warm and the shots only came one at a time. Michelle bolted hers back and calmly chased it with the Fanta. When the next shot was brought to the table, I eyed it. The shot glass was a miniature beer mug, complete with a tiny little handle, and it wasn't a full shot. Not even near it. I picked up the thing and sniffed it.

"Big mistake, Peter. Don't smell it, *drink* it!" She laughed at me in a sultry way. Perfect for a dark bar in the mountains of Peru, shadowy figures beginning to appear in the background. I was in a movie within a movie within a movie. She was quite right. It smelled like Esso Extra, but I wasn't going to back out. So I shot mine back and went for the Fanta. The Fanta was a major part of the program for a novice like me. I threw that Fanta back as quickly as I could, forgetting completely that it was warm, and spewed it out all over the place. A dark chuckling slid out of the blackness like an asp. Michelle had already had her second shot, and by the time the tiny mug was put back in front of me, I was not going to repeat my Fanta fountain. I grabbed the little fucker, bolted it back—without smelling it—and gently sucked on the Fanta bottle. The next two shots were smooth as silk. And the 190 proof quinco added about two thousand feet to the altitude factor. After that, Michelle, myself, Ted Markland, Michael Greene, and sometimes Severn Darden paid our compliments to the Tome Coca-Cola Bar at least twice a day. The drive up the mountain with its near-death experiences each morning made the Tome Coca-Cola a must-visit place.

One afternoon as I lay out in the sun getting extremely tan, some of the other cast members asked if I wanted to watch the "bank" get blown up. I declined the invite, knowing that some major bad was going to happen. The horses were not Hollywood horses, and had not been trained to work with explosives. During the first week of shooting in Chincheros, we had no Hollywood rifles or pistols. They were being held up by the Peruvian government. So we did all the gun fights with wooden or rubber guns, and each time they needed a close up of someone firing a real pistol, they came to me and begged for Tom Mix. No need for Tom this afternoon. It was just a bank blowing up. I was very amused that the weaving women would have a real blast watching this antic. I heard the explosion and waited for the results.

Seemingly far away, I thought I could hear a horse crying and a lot of people yelling. Then the head stuntman and main horse wrangler found me and explained what had gone down. The bank blew up perfectly, and the horses "tied" to the hitching rail outside the bank broke and ran in fright. Unfortunately, one of them ran out of the village square and fell off a high wall—part of the narrow steppes— and had broken its back and shoulders. He asked me if he could use Tom with some of my real 44-40 ammo to kill the poor horse, whose screaming was making the deed imperative. It turned out to be the shot heard round the region.

Although there seemed to be no way of communication with the main base at Cuzco, it took less than an hour for two olive drab Hueys to come chopping into the small field on the far side of the village. They were sporting .50 cal's out of their doors, and three very short men with wide chests climbed down and took defensive positions. Finally, making his entrance, another small dude who was definitely Numero Uno came strutting out in a fearless forward position, his M16-wielding backup fanning out, slightly. The choppers kept their blades whirling. Numero Uno wanted to know who shot his horse. The stunt coordinator stepped up and took the blame. With what gun, Uno asked? I had already removed the remaining cartridges, and I handed it over to him. While the village priest translated, I told him that the pistol belonged to Tom Mix, a very famous cowboy and stunt-man, and that I had inherited the pistol. Commandante Uno knew exactly who Tom Mix was and asked if it really was Señor Mix's. I pointed out the silver brand markings on the matching stag grips and the back strap. Uno became very emotional.

"Tome Meex. Tome Meex. My horse was shot weeth the peestol of Tome Meex!" He said to his men in almost comical English. He stared at the pistol for a while, turning it over in his hands as if it were something holy. He noticed the caliber was 44-40, a nonmilitary weapon. "Tome Meex," he said aloud, but to himself. "My horse was shot weeth the peestol of Tome Meex!" And, tearing about the eyes, he handed it back to me, turned, and gave a signal to his men as they mounted up back into the Hueys. It took a long time getting the blades up to enough speed to take off at 14,000 feet, but they disappeared back down the valley. He gave the dead horse to the villagers. After that incident, all the Hollywood rifles and pistols were released to the production company. The law in the Southern Americas is: no military weapons or weapons that can fire military ammo. I think that is why Mix had that particular Colt made.

One night, Hopper rushed into our hotel full of paranoia and demanded that we give him all the drugs we had, right then, because the Federales were going to bust the entire cast and crew. He was like a frenzied preacher working a crowd. Eventually, he had everyone believing him and getting their stashes to give to him. Almost. I took a paper bag, crumpled it up several times to age it, put a stray sock in it, and brought it back to Dennis. Hopper knew that I wasn't into the blow, really, and said, "Thanks, man." He put everyone's stash in a duffle and disappeared into the night in his pickup. About twenty minutes later, everyone in the hotel realized that they would never see their stash again. The take was that Hopper wanted it all for himself. I know Dennis, and even at that time he would not have ripped off his friends. He may have made up the Fed stuff, but by the time he acted on it, he was in full belief that it could and would happen. Nobody got anything back, though. He said, later, that he couldn't remember where he hid it. I went to my room, finished off a large roach, and slept soundly, except for my nightmare.

Cuzco is an ancient city with a remarkable main square and a very beautiful church on one side. I, like many others, had my picture taken in front of the church. The method was very crude, but the results were excellent.

A few days after I had been photographed with some of the cast, I was eating at the main hotel where Dennis stayed. During the supper, an old man came looking for me. He showed me a very old but still in perfect condition photograph of my father and mother standing in front of the same church. I knew at once that I was in my mother's belly when the shot was taken. I had seen 16mm movies my father had taken while he and Mother were on a vacation there and other places in South America.

I was at a complete loss for words. I asked Tomas Milian to tell the old man that I would come to the square with some money to buy the photo the next day. I was without cash, and no one would give me any. Perhaps they were not aware of the significance of this piece of my true life. I never found the old man again, and whenever I think of that moment and the picture, I am sad not to have it. So little remains of my family's past, and I look always for evidence that shows the facts of my existence. The chance to have a picture of my parents while I was in the womb was almost unbelievable. But I saw the photo and will never forget it.

When our part of the film was finished, most of us were ready to fly back to the States. A day before we departed, Jim Mitchum received word from his father, Big Bob, that we were all going to be searched thoroughly when we returned to the United States. I had basically finished my stash (with the help of those who had given theirs away to Dennis), so I rolled up many numbers for the trip down to Lima and the fourteen-hour wait until our flight back home.

. . .

When I returned to LAX, Susan picked me up. We took the children up to Lake Arrowhead for a family reunion. The reunion was cut drastically short by the onslaught of amoebic dysentery, which had been hiding in my system since I drank the "pure" water at the airport lounge in Lima. I wanted to be with the children for a fun and private time, as I had been away for so long doing the work of a producer and star of *Easy Rider,* and I was about to take off for the making of *The Hired Hand.* All my children understand *now* what it takes to mount a motion picture and then promote it, but at the time it was very difficult for them to know why Daddy was away so often. I worked very hard at having a closer spiritual thing with Bridget and Justin, and recently I read in an interview with Bridget that she felt much more spiritually connected to me than her other friends did with their parents. But, for that moment, I was shot down by the dysentery. And Susan was not happy with me regardless of the incredibly fast dehydration.

I recalled vividly Justin's bout with dysentery several years earlier. I went to the hospital to see him (it was a very serious case) and was completely overcome by the sight of my little baby boy with an intravenous stuck in the bottom of his foot. I felt so helpless. He was pulled through by a nurse who gave him plain rice and tea. The wonders of modern medicine.

. . .

I began looking for a boat in the late fall of '69. During the start-up of production for *The Hired Hand,* I spent much time crawling over some of the finest sailing vessels in Southern California. Nothing was fitting into the plan I had for my life at sea—my life and my family's. My wife, daughter, and son, a small but excellent crew, and a first-class teacher to tutor our children. I wanted a life free of property lines and rapidly growing crime. My quip was: there is no such thing as *private* property. Don't pay your taxes and you will find out who *owns* your "private" property. Registered in the right state, the boat had no taxes. The only way the U.S. government could take my ship was by a declaration of martial law. I had lawyers who could give me a week's lead for that call. The feds could also take my yacht if I was busted carrying contraband. I wasn't worried.

While in San Francisco, I received a pamphlet about an eighty-two-foot wooden ketch named *Tatoosh* that was berthed in Seattle. I wasn't the least bit interested in a boat that large, and tried to beg off, but my broker was very enthusiastic in his evaluation of the vessel. I only looked at *Serena,* a ninety-foot schooner, and *Blackfin,* a seventy-two-foot open ocean racing ketch, as references. My partner, Bill Hayward, had sailed on *Serena* for a trans-Pacific race three years earlier. We both understood the out-of-touch reality of a ship with that much rigging. I went to Seattle to check *Tatoosh* out. It was much bigger than I had wanted, but the description of the yacht's construction was very intriguing. It had been logged in the cedar forests of Alaska, specifically for this vessel. A tree specialist had marked the trees to be logged, and when the logs arrived in Seattle, the same man came down to the waterway and checked out the logged timber. By simply looking at the end cuts, he was able to say what wood was right for the ship in its different construction modes.

When the wood was assigned, the Vic Francks Boat Yard milled the logs and prepared them for the construction of the ship. They had to build a foundry next to the yard for the bronze fittings. One could not go to a store and order the parts required for the construction of the ship; it was entirely custom built, and built like a Stradivarius. Nothing was spared in its building.

I was reluctant to board the vessel—its size, and the extra-large windows concerned me—but I was implored to come aboard and out of the rain by the cook, who had picked me up at the airport in the ship's van. I asked him about the very large windows that were on both sides of the main salon. I was concerned that a powerful wave might break the windows and thereby flood the hull with water, and asked how one could get the water out of the ship if such a thing might occur. He explained that the windows were bullet-proof, set into a two-and-a-half-inch stainless-steel frame built into the teak housing. Though I knew that major waves could easily take out most windows, I was curious about the interior of the hull and the jointer work. I was also glad to get out of the rain. Ah, Seattle.

When I crawled through the bilge, I was astounded by the bronze floors—sometimes called the knees. These are the fasteners that hold the keel and stem of the ship to the frames. They were quarter-inch bronze, and at their tallest, more than two feet high with holes cut out for the movement of air. In the constuction photographs, the hull, without its planking and deck, looked like the collected fossilized bones of a large dinosaur mounted in the Museum of Natural History. As I inspected the bilge, I found dry sawdust and carpenter's pencils. I realized that the hull had never really been worked. In other words, the ship had never seen its true hull speed; neither had it been really worked on the wind. The designed hull speed was 15.7 knots. While I owned the ship, I often went much faster than the hull speed.

The galley was so large, I eventually called it the kitchen. All of my sailing friends looked at me as if I didn't understand the true names for the various parts of a vessel. The galley had a freezer bigger than most airline first-class seats cubed out and a reefer of the same size. It had a vegetable crisper the same size as the reefer and freezer. One could keep vegetables fresh for ten or twelve days—a true luxury at sea on a sailing ship. There was a separate reefer for soft drinks and beer.

Belowdecks, one could see the true masts. They were Sitka spruce with the best grain one could dream for. An ashtray had been made from one of the deck plugs where the mast holes had been cut. Three inches of deck. One and a half inches of cedar marine plywood made for the boat and laminated to one and a half inches of teak. The teak top layer was routed out one half of an inch and filled with Thiakol that made the decks look like old-fashioned caulked decks and were very practical when one wanted to change head sails. The Thiakol gave one truly great purchase on the foredeck. This was one of the many little touches that made *Tatoosh* one of the finest wooden sailing ships *ever* built. The headroom throughout the ship was six foot eight inches. Cranston Boeing Pascal III had commissioned the ship. He was six foot five inches, and he didn't want to duck his head while he walked about below-decks. The part of Cranston's name that accounted for the spare-no-money construction of *Tatoosh* is Boeing. When I left the ship, I knew that this was the one.

My broker advised me to bargain for the price. Offer Mr. Pascal half, he suggested. Pascal was asking $500,000, and I was ready to pay him that amount. I understood the principle of bargaining, but I had only really practiced it at flea markets in Paris, the souks in Marrakech, or Rome. This ship was worth much more than a half a million dollars. My broker, however, said it was the way of doing business in the buying or selling of any boat. I was familiar with the process of buying a boat, the complete survey, the haul-out, the sea trials and so forth. But *Tatoosh* was a Stradivarius. Nevertheless, I put together a group of my friends who were more than aware of the proper workings of a well-found ship and flew them up to Seattle for the "negotiations." I brought along my friend Larry Hagman, who, though knowing nothing about the survey of a ship, was always a pleasure to have at any ceremony.

Before we boarded the plane in Los Angeles, I gave Hagman a very small, black aluminum Halliburton camera case, locked it, and told him not to let it out of his sight. John Calley, at the time production head of Warner Bros., sent his skipper, Gordie Krusen, along, also. And, of course, Bill Hayward. Hagman thought the case was full of drugs and wondered why no one was knocking at his door. The meeting was held in a conference room at our hotel. My face had a two-week-old beard—I was growing it for *The Hired Hand*. I looked like a complete vagrant wearing old—but clean—jeans and a denim shirt. I was introduced to Cranston, who, though more than a bit uncomfortable with my countenance, was a perfect gentleman.

I summoned Hagman to the room, and he arrived dressed like Engineer Bill, wearing a ten-gallon pure white Stetson. He had a genuine, big, old-fashioned mailman's leather bag across his shoulder, which was filled with cold champagne bottles and two silver goblets. He put the case in front of me, opened the champagne, filled the two goblets, placing one at my left and the other at Cranston's right, and waited until I dismissed him. Cranston kept a tight eye on Hagman. I could see that he thought he knew this stranger but couldn't quite place the face. It was a thrill to summon and dismiss Larry. He put his best "sahib" act on and left the room backing up, bowing, and doffing his big white hat. Cranston was amused but a little unsettled by the act. I could almost hear his frontal lobe asking . . . *Isn't that Major, uh, Tony . . . naw. I Dream of Genie* was still a big part of the collective American conscience.

I toasted Cranston, who then said his nickname was Boo. I explained that "boo" was a term that old black jazzbos used to describe marijuana. He laughed, asking if that was true. You bet, I told him and unlocked the case. As I listed the things I wanted to do on the sea trials and haul-out, I began placing thousand-dollar bills on the table between us. He could not see the inside of the case, but he didn't try. He never took his eyes off the cash. I had a hard time getting the one grand notes. I had to sign for each of them. I couldn't get *one* today. The five-hundred-dollar bills were not much easier. The bank probably thought I was on my way to make a very large drug buy. I could have cared less.

I continued to carefully place the thousand-dollar bills on the table. I considered my actions the true demonstration of the old phrase "decorating the mahogany." Each new thing I wanted to do on the survey was punctuated by one large one. After I had completed my list of sea trials and haul-out demands, I told Boo that if I liked the haul-out and sea trials I would give him $150,000 more in cash, as I turned the case around so he could see the remaining cash in five-hundred-dollar bills. But if I didn't like the sea trials or haul-out, he could keep the $50,000. His eyes pegged mine. "Excuse me," he said. Hookup, I thought. I don't think Boo had ever seen a thousand-dollar bill. I'm sure in most of his transactions he simply signed for them. "I can keep this money?" he repeated softly and dryly. "You bet," I said as I refilled our goblets.

We shook hands on the deal, and I brought the rest of my gang into the room to celebrate. More champagne and introductions all around. I introduced Hagman as Major Tony Nelson. A flicker of recognition passed across Boo's face. I never would have made such a grandstand move with all that cash had I not carefully crawled through the very dry bilge. I had just bought a Strad for $200,000: less than half the asking price.

We did the sea trials the next day, and I was delighted. It was like driving a Cadillac, and I invited Bill and Gordie to try the wheel. While Bill was at the helm, Gordie and I stood on the steeply canted fore-deck checking out the rigging. It was magnificent. The tall mainmast stood straight and true, and the shrouds were in tune like a fine guitar.

I accepted the sea trials, haul-out, and survey, gave the rest of the cash to Cranston Boeing Pascal III, and left to begin scouting for the filming of *The Hired Hand*. I arranged to have the ship delivered to Newport Beach, California, where a slip had been arranged on Lido Island. With a vessel as long and beamy as mine, it was hard to find a slip or end tie large enough. As it happened, I was berthed two slips down from John Wayne and his ship *The Wild Goose,* a 127-foot converted mine sweeper.

I had no time to visit the ship after I purchased it due to the de-mands of preproduction, so I asked Gordie if he would take charge of the delivery and learn as much as he could about the engine room, the emergency tiller, and other parts of the ship's operations. Al-though there were photographs of every stage of the building of the ship, there were no full hull plans and design detail, and Gordie's ability to glean schematics for the engine room complex and ship's wiring and plumbing design would be priceless. He accepted the job, with John Calley's approval, and went to Seattle to skipper the yacht down to Newport Beach.

Dennis Hopper had introduced me to Bruce Conner, a filmmaker from San Francisco. Bruce was the top gun in Super 8 with sound, but Bruce's work was not soiled by any desire to make features. He would come down to L.A. from time to time, and on some of those occasions he visited me at my home. We screened his movies and talked about our dreams. After watching his films—which I could do for hours—we often played music together. Bruce was a whiz on the harmonica, and we would play blues. After a while, he caught on to my peculiar rhythms, and we really had a good time. Once, Susan walked through the living room and stopped, asking us why we played the blues when we were obviously not feeling blue. Bruce told her that we were playing music, and that everyone had the blues. She said she thought we were just phonies and left the room.

In fairness, one has to put the previous five years into the mix. Since I decided that I had to change my career and the way I was living my life in the public eye and in my own heart in 1965, I had made radical moves that took me away from home for full days and late into many nights. The writing of *The Yin(g) and the Yang*; hanging with the top rock groups and musicians and absorbing the creative process of performing arts, going to New York City to look for funding, meeting the top artists in the Pop Art scene and other abstract art biggies, hanging with hip East Coast money, going off to Pasadena to see old prints of some of the top film directors in the world, or hitting three movies at a time in an art house in downtown L.A. and sitting up late at night with Dennis talking about *everything*. Things I felt were important fundamentals in *any* creative career. Things I now know must be a part of any artist's trunk. Susan must have felt abandoned, though she kept it to herself. She, admittedly, shunned the rock scene and wasn't into joining me on location, as she had before our beautiful children were born. We never fought; I refused. When she asked me why, I had no good answer. And though I always returned to her and our bed, I was very much distracted by my career and night moves. Maybe my distractions would have been mitigated had I not forgotten the little things. Flowers. Going out for dinner. A special bottle of champagne. A postcard from the road. The little things became a very big thing, eventually, and we rolled further apart. It all ended up costing me my family. It was a long time before I would get my family back.

chapter $\mathcal{S}$eventeen

$\mathcal{I}$ went up to Santa Fe, New Mexico, to meet Howard Koch, Jr. I went to interview him for my first assistant director on *The Hired Hand*. I liked him right away. He showed me how to make a steam bath in a Ramada Inn bathroom: take all the towels and paper products out, close the shower curtain, turn on the hot water for the shower, turn on the heat lamp, close the door, and wait fifteen minutes. It was a smashing success. We were in the room of two of the actresses in *Billy Jack*, which was being shot in the area. It was cold at seven thousand feet, so the steam bath–cum–sauna was a perfect touch. The ladies were perfect, too. Julie Webb, a dark-haired flower child, showed me how to make the Magic Fingers machine stay on indefinitely. Apparently, after five or six quarters in a row, this particular machine malfunctioned in the best of ways. The only thing that would stop it was housekeeping. They, naturally, would turn it off when they made up the room. I had them pass me fresh towels and linen through the door as I handed them the old stuff.

I had screened *Medium Cool*, Haskell Wexler's marvelous film, and, as described by Sylvia Miles, was astounded by the performance Verna Bloom gave. I arranged a meeting at the Seventy-fourth Street house, and I waited for her with my now fully bearded face and long-ish hair. She arrived dressed in tight black pants and a tight black sweater with a black hat. You can leave your hat on, I thought. She had the most outstanding figure I had seen in a long time. We spoke for a while. About her performance in *Medium Cool,* about my vision of *The Hired Hand.* She seemed a bit nervous from the top and finally asked me the big question that had been needling her: "Peter, do I have to take my clothes off on camera?" Wow! The thought excited me at once. I wanted her to take her clothes off right there, but I answered her that only *one person* took their clothes off in a Peter Fonda film, me. She seemed relaxed after that but a bit curious about my declaration. In one of the tawdry, phsycobabble biographies that was published many years later by Peter Collier, she is quoted as saying that my dad came to the house and my entire attitude changed to that of a frightened child, trying not to make him upset. Fat chance, Verna. I was making more money than Dad had made in his whole career, I was about to direct my first movie, and I had the self-esteem and ego needed to do that thing. I was no longer worried about what he thought about me. I looked at him as an actor I would like to direct in some motion picture. Anyway, he was out of town shooting a film. No matter. Verna can have her dream any way she wants. Her performance in *The Hired Hand* was outstanding. Magnificent. I will always be in her debt.

Universal was quite nervous when I hired Bruce Langhorne to score the movie. He had no track record in their world. In my world, he was a virtuoso on more than fifty stringed instruments, played the piano expertly, and was very capable on the drums and an array of percussion instruments. I had an entire orchestra in one man, and he was a good friend. I had his backyard shed made into a tiny recording studio.

Having completed the main casting, I prepared to scout locations. Bruce Conner had joined me as an advisor and coconspirator on the film. Alan Sharp had written one of the best western-realist scripts, the telling of the life in its everyday hardships and everyday joys. Sort of like Dad's *The Ox-bow Incident.* In fact, after my dad saw the movie many years later in a special screening, he said, "Now, *that's* my kind of western." Sadly, as of this moment, there is no print of this motion picture.

I returned to Santa Fe with Bill Zsigmond, art director Larry Paul, Bruce, and his girlfriend, Nastsha, and began driving the state, looking for the different sets or areas to shoot the many different scenes. During this stay in Santa Fe, Jane came to visit me. I was delighted.

She could stay only two days, but I was happy to see her. It gave me a sense of familial caring. Jane was full into her antiwar passion and feminism. She had left Vadim, left France, and moved back to America. She was paddling on, too.

We were driven all over the place. I brought a Baur Super 8 and shot every place that was unique or breathtaking, eventually deciding upon an abandoned old town, right next to a magnificent geological phenomenon: the core of an ancient volcano with its sides fallen away after millions of years of erosion, leaving the basalt inner core jutting up from the surface. It was called Cabezon.

To give my jeans the right look, I wore them during the entire location scout. Whenever we would stop for lunch or a beverage, I took out a nail file and worked away at the cuffs, the button-up fly, and the pockets. In this way, by the time I had finished aging them, they looked like they had been worn for years. I was a curiosity at the lunch stops as I sat there filing away at my crotch.

In a week and a half, we had seen all the places where I wanted to shoot. By this time, most of the main core of the Company was in Santa Fe. Sets were being built, permits were arranged, and Bill had managed to have the Santa Fe police make us both badge-carrying captains on the force. Bill could get the queen of England to grant him any wish. He has one of the most diplomatic and engaging personas one will ever meet. Can you imagine me as a captain of *any* police force?

The actors began to mosey in, and one morning Warren Oates rolled in. I didn't really register that he had been driving nonstop for fourteen hours. I directed him to get into my Blazer, and in less than five hours, took him on the entire tour of the many locations we had chosen.

The energy that was coursing through my body would be even more evident during the actual shoot. My father had always questioned how I could direct *and* act at the same time. Energy, concentration, and total dedication to the vision. One should never direct a film without a complete vision of the cinematic version of the story deeply set in one's heart.

My passion was so overpowering that I never felt at a loss as to what the next shot would be. It had become the very life that made me attack each new day without doubt and end it feeling victorious. Except for one. When we shot the opening of the film, we were on the west side of the Rio Grande. Most of the crew had been helicoptered in to the location. At the end of the day, when I called a wrap, we were choppered out. I drove out by crossing the river—I felt invincible in my specially set up Blazer. But among the last to leave the location was the head wrangler for the horses, a Teamster. He wanted to ride in the left front seat of the chopper. He was given the okay and, grabbing his hat on his head, he walked around the aircraft to board the helicopter. Everyone had been ordered to be very careful when boarding the chopper. Never walk around the tail boom and rear stabilizer. He did the forbidden out of excitement over the ride. He walked, head down, holding his hat on, right into the stabilizer rotor. He was dead instantly.

Having left by fording the river, I didn't learn of the tragedy until many hours later, back at the motel. I was completely demoralized. I often think of second assistant director John Poore, Bill Hayward, and the complete disaster that they had to overcome. When the tail rotor whacked the head wrangler, it lost a blade, and, as it is with all helicopters, the rotors did not stop at once but slowed down gradually. The out-of-balance tail rotor caused the entire tail boom to shake violently and break away from the rest of the chopper.

I called for a day off, but Dick Bruno—my head costumer, now an Academy Award winner—called me from the lobby several hours later and begged me to reconsider. We *must* continue shooting, he pleaded. It was the only way we would not be stopped by the tragedy. He was right. We gathered the next morning at the set, passed the hat around for the widow—the union was not very helpful, but the cast and crew were magnificently generous—said a prayer, and got back to work with a vengeance.

We started the film in the ghost town, and planned to shoot the first and last part of the film that was played out on its dirt street and crumbling buildings.

I had learned that Bill Zsigmond's real name was Vilmos. Three or four weeks into the shooting, I was driving home with Vilmos and our still photographer, Peter Sorel (he had been on *Easy Rider*) at the end of the day. Our normal procedure was to call a wrap for the day, wait until the bus and cars with the rest of the cast and crew had disappeared, and then take out Vilmos's own Arriflex, and with Peter helping Vilmos, shoot late evening shots of me walking around looking at the sky and thinking about the weather in character as Harry

Collings. On this particular drive back to Santa Fe, I was telling Vilmos about my vision for the next day, explaining the allegory and so forth.

"Jeezus Chrrist, Peeter, I don't need to know vhat za scene *means,* just vhere do you vant me to place za camera."

"But, Vilmos, if I explain the meaning of the scene to you, it might help you to give me suggestions."

"Peeter, just tell me vhere you vant za camera, I don't need . . ."

"Vilmos, what do you do with the other directors you've worked with?"

"Vhat uzzer directors?" I was shut down completely. If this guy was Laszlo Kovacs's mentor, I figured he had made a dozen films, but *The Hired Hand* was Vilmos's first feature film. His first film to be shot outside a soundstage. It was my first film to direct. Far out.

Susan came down with the kids by train, while we were still in Santa Fe. It was great to see my children. Made my heart glad. Susan stayed in a separate room. Things had not improved. But I was so into the shoot that during the day I was able to let it slide off my back. I had to take a sleeping pill and a joint with each dinner, though. I couldn't go to sleep on my own. On top of the constant nightmare, the great sadness I felt at the delaminating of my little family made my nights seem desolate. Until the pill, joint, and two beers kicked in. Then I could crash and get my eight hours and face the morning with its new challenges.

Verna was very dangerous all the time. I kept fantasizing about being with her.

Warren and Verna were so good, I felt the energy between them as I sat on a shooting stick next to the camera, while we shot the exterior back porch night scenes. This kind of relationship had never been played in a western. It was very cool. We had only one little problem. We had perfect sound—thanks to LeRoy Robbins and Jaime Contreras—and brilliant camera—thanks to Vilmos, but we could not control the ambient sound that was drifting through the cottonwoods out in the flats of the Santa Clara Indian Reservation, just near the joining of the Chama River and the Rio Grande. While we were shooting that great scene on the back porch, *Easy Rider* was playing at a local drive-in, some five miles away, just outside Española. Although it was cool down on the flats, at the drive-in, every convertible had its top down and all the speakers were cranked up to the max. That was the way we wanted the movie to be projected—big on the music score. Had to be, you know. But I never expected to be fighting one of my own movies' soundtracks whilst shooting another. The scene Mr. Oates and Verna were acting was very tender and subtle. Full of nuances and unspoken possibilities and "Don't Bogart That Joint, My Friend . . ."

Everyone took it with a great sense of humor, but I was fearful for my actors, who had to stay very focused and deliver the delicious lines Alan Sharp had written. We had many night scenes to shoot there, and *Easy Rider* played to packed parking for a full week. There must be *some* coincidences in the life. In the off-screen noise that would drift in from time to time, I was clocking major bucks, while in the movie under way, I was working for free, as I had in *Easy Rider*. Balances, I guess.

We finished the main location shots and moved to MGM's back lot for the town scenes. I flew the cast and crew from Santa Fe to L.A. in a chartered plane to save time in travel penalties and give them a full day's rest. Back Lot Three had the widest streets, and though Universal wanted us to use *their* western streets, MGM's was the only one that was built for realism. Streets in the old western towns were very wide. There had to be parking space for wagons and horses and still plenty of street for wagons and horses to pass each other in the middle.

An interesting joust with abstract authority went down in Back Lot Three. First day we rolled into the back lot, the guard at the gate stopped us *all* and wouldn't let us pass. I was four or five cars back, so I walked down to the guard and asked what was the problem. I was told that the other drivers weren't Teamsters and by union law could not drive a vehicle on the lot. Okeydokey. Let's take on the rule right in the face. The rules specifically state that the producer could cross *all* guild lines. The producer could turn the camera on or off, could move a prop, could hang a light, could mix sound, could drive a truck, could do anything he or she wanted on a union-controlled set. The guard had no idea who I was for a nanosecond. After shaking his hand and giving him my autograph as he babbled on about my dad, I told him that *all* the people in the cars in front of me and behind me were producers on the film. These days I notice the number of producers on any given motion picture. They put their names all over the opening credits. Not on my shoots, though, with this first exception. The guard had a list of the personnel to be allowed on the lot, and I told him that each driver was one of my producers. Bill joined me at that moment and allowed as that was the case, as frustrating as it was to have so many producers on a shoot. The guard had to let our core team drive onto the lot. I begged him not to let any of the extras get away with saying *they* were producers, though. He was totally buffaloed, but had no choice.

We finished the back lot scenes in a week and then headed out for our "ride-bys" back to New Mexico with a very short crew. At the end of the shoot, we all felt as if we were getting divorced from each other. Back in L.A., there were many days at the Hagmans' beach house. Many parades, each of us carrying some sort of flag. Hours of Frisbee. A time of families and togetherness. Almost.

Down at the slip in Newport Beach, I was preparing to haul the ship out of the water. We were waiting for a space to open at one of the few boat yards that could handle a hull like ours. One day, while fooling around on deck, I saw John Wayne going aboard his ship. I invited him to visit the *Tatoosh* whenever he had time. He came right over. I asked him aboard, and we went below. He marveled at the headroom and wondered about the rest of the ship.

"Mr. Wayne, the ship was . . ."

"Naw, none of that mister stuff. Why, I've known you since you came home from the hospital! Now, you call me Duke, like all my friends, and I'll call you Pete," he chuckled.

"Peter, if you don't mind . . . Duke."

"All right, mister, Peter it is."

I showed the Duke the rest of the ship, and he marveled at the construction and jointer work *and* the headroom throughout. He asked me for a drink of whiskey and ice, and I obliged. He peered out through the curtains closed over the huge windows as if to see if he was going to be caught having a cocktail. I told him that aboard my ship everything was private, and if he wanted a drink, he could certainly have one or two or however much he wanted. He laughed heartily, and then, looking around the main salon, spoke softly to me, saying that he understood about the whole marijuana thing, that it was all just publicity. And very effective, he added. God bless you, Duke.

I brought the ship up to our waiting end tie in Marina del Rey. For the special journey, I had Larry and Maj Hagman with their two children; Susan, Justin, and Bridget; Susan's stepbrother, his wife, and their three daughters; Bill Hayward and his girlfriend; and a special crew of three. We powered up to Point Vincente, then set our sails. We flew two jibs forward—called a double head rig—the enormous main sail and the mizzen. We sailed without the engine on right into Marina del Rey, coming into the marina with the wind abeam on the port as we headed to the far end, where we came about and sailed back to the harbor master's station, coming about again—a very complicated maneuver. The second time we came up into the wind—right in front of the Cal Yacht Club—I gave the command to drop *all* the sails. When all the sails were on the decks or booms, and the ship lay still in the water, I blew the air horn, and with an exaggerated movement pushed the starter button for the big Cat diesel—which fired up at once—and bowed to the snobs at the club. I had made a spectacular entrance into their world on the finest-built wooden ship in the world and with a very difficult maneuver, all under sail. Then I engaged the shaft and screw and powered to my end tie. I had arrived in the world of "yachting" as a sailor with a fine and able crew. Other skippers in the marina could probably do the same thing, but not the owners. I was paddling on, for sure.

．　．　．

The phenomenon of *Easy Rider* was an ongoing thing in the industry, and I was asked to appear on all the major talk shows. Back in New York for business, I agreed to do Dick Cavett's show. It was not the first show I had done with Dick, so I felt an easy relationship with him. Percy Foremen, the lawyer who had defended James Earl Ray, was also a guest. I was the first guest and Dick and I had some fun while I slipped in as many environmental zingers as I could. I liked to make people laugh and then hit them with a new bit of eco-disaster talk. Then Foreman strode on stage as if he was trying to be Duke Wayne. He and Dick talked for a while, until I could no longer sit still.

I asked him about the scenario he had put forth about James Earl not being part of a conspiracy. I wanted to know where Ray had gotten the money to have a false passport waiting for him in Canada. "Drug money," was Foreman's reply. I kept picking at him until I was able to make the lawyer say the forbidden.

"You know, you types are all alike!" he snapped. Whoa! He just blew his cover.

"What could you ever mean by that statement?"

"You hippies are all against the war, but none of you offer a way to end it!" He was getting in deeper, and becoming a great target.

"I wasn't aware that as an actor I am supposed to find a way to end the war, but now that you've mentioned it, let's check it out. I was brought up not to waste food. If I messed around in the vegetable garden, I was very aware that I had to eat whatever I pulled out of the ground. Now, in my view, we are wasting a lot of meat over in Vietnam. I mean, all those bodies going to waste." The audience was getting nervous. "If we are so civilized that we have a document called the Geneva Conventions of War, a document that forbids the use of a bayonet with a serrated back edge, a document that can be that specific about a knife at the end of a rifle, let's add another convention to the list. Whatever you kill you must eat!" The audience was a little disgusted, but this was coming right off the top. "Now, this will definitely put the clamps on the soldiers in the field. I mean, they'll be looking at that ground beef patty and wondering whether it was from the VC they had killed or the first sergeant they had fragged the night before, and they won't want to eat it. All those mothers back in Iowa who have dressed their sons for glory and declared that it is honorable to die for one's country, all those mothers will *never* send their sons out to be *eaten* for their country!" The audience squirmed, Dick put his head in his hands and shook it slowly. But he *knew* that was why he wanted me for his show. One can never know for sure if I'll stay in the bounds of broadcast dignity.

· · ·

During the editorial process on the *Hand,* I still had many things to do at the office on Seward. The business of a hit motion picture does not stop after the first wave of distribution. Several times, Bill had asked me to read a script he had found. Bill was very excited about the project. We can make it for a hundred and fifty thousand, he was always saying. I kept begging off, as I was in the thick of editing. Finally, as I was leaving Pando one night, Bill caught me in my Blazer and forced the script through the open window. "You've got to read this, Peter," he said. "It's just up your alley." And I drove home with it.

After our supper and after the kids had gone to sleep, Susan and I were in bed reading. I interrupted Susan's book and asked her to please read the script. We may not have been together as lovers, but I still loved her and respected her opinion. She assented and took the script. She asked what it was about, and I told her I didn't know. I pretended to be busy reading another book, but I kept a close peripheral eye on her reactions. She was deadpan. When she finished the script, she passed it over to me. I asked her what she thought, and she said to read it myself. I began reading the script called *Idaho Transfer* without any preconceptions. Bill had not said anything about the story or setting. Suddenly, Susan was in a fetal position, saying she had a great pain in her chest. I wondered about her heart, but she shook her head and said she was frightened. She was having an anxiety attack. I calmed her as best I could and dove into the script. An hour and a half later, I put the script down, got dressed, and, in the middle of the night, buried two automatic assault rifles I had bought for the boat and a small block of hash. The script had nothing to do with guns or drugs, but it had affected me in such an enormous way that I felt compelled to do what I did. It was *my* anxiety attack, delivered in a very different manner.

The story was about time travel, and the destruction of society as we know it. It was about a group of very young and brilliant scientists who are conducting experiments on material projection (disassembling an object in a kinetic way in one place and reassembling it in a different place). The project is interrupted by the government, stranding thirteen young scientists fifty-seven years in the future, where, as far as they know, there is no more human existence. The capper is the statement that we will use each other as fuel for our cars, for we will not give up driving automobiles.

Later, I dug up the guns and threw them in the ocean. They were stolen from an Army arsenal and could have caused me great trouble if they were found on the yacht.

I agreed to meet with the writer-director, Tom Matthiesen, the next afternoon. Bill had briefed me on the structure. Pando would finance and produce the movie, Matthiesen would direct his own script. He had a crew and cast—except for the main characters—all set up from Seattle, though some of the actors were from New York. Betsey Johnson had designed the costumes, but her company was too busy to make them, so Bruce Langhorne's girlfriend, Natalie Mucyn, found some generic, pastel tops that would work for all the actors, and she began to cut and sew the leather pants that were necessary for the lava landscape. They all were custom made for each actor. My little guerrilla movie company was on the move again.

I asked Matthiesen how much money he owed. What was his debt, to that moment? I wrote him a check for eight thousand plus change and told him that if he wanted to direct the movie—and it had been clearly written precisely for the screen—he must start right then, and he would be ready to start the film in April of '71. I was taking a very different path than my coconspirators on *Easy Rider*. The next Pando film would cost one-third of the budget of *Easy Rider*.

chapter *Eighteen*

*W*hile I was in the editing process of *The Hired Hand*, Maj Hagman honchoed the remodeling of the interior of the yacht. All the bunks were made for one person. Might have been fine for Cranston and his pals, but it was a major problem for young, sexually active people. At least they were six foot eight in length. I had all the after berths made into ample double beds. I had the settees in the main salon widened to three feet plus. All the berths, therefore, had to have new mattresses made, and the settees needed new upholstery. They had been a puce green vinyl that matched the cabin top. Maj suggested a burgundy mohair of theater plush.

A year or two later, *Rolling Stone* printed that the interior of the yacht was covered in velvet. What dorks. Velvet does not go with a seagoing sailing ship. Theater plush got its name because the material had to withstand the kind of abuse that seats in a theater faced every day.

I antagonized much of the hip press because of my perceived elitist move when I bought the ship. I was made to be a sellout to the "cause." What cause? *They* were the bunch that had become a commercial sellout to the establishment. I was a pirate. I was the owner and master of the finest wooden sailing ship *ever* made, and my word was LAW.

One of the most incredible things I discovered aboard was that when I slept, I had no nightmares. No tough dreams. Good, long sleeps. I was flabbergasted. I could hardly wait until the remodeling belowdecks was finished, so that I could sleep in my stateroom. Apparently, it did not matter if I was at sea or in the slip. I never slept aboard when the ship was out of the water.

I continued to edit *HH*, and began to get therapy from Sidney Prince, a friend and a good psychiatrist. Susan agreed to see him, too. We had been married for nine years. Susan was twenty-eight, I was thirty, Bridget was six, and Justin was four. It didn't seem to do anything for my happiness, but I was willing to try anything. Sometimes, we saw him together. I knew it was tough for her, also. When Thanksgiving came, the ship was ready to sail, and Susan, the children, their nanny-housekeeper, Maria, myself, and four other friends sailed to a little group of rocks and land off the southern tip of Ensenada Bay. Susan and I slept in separate beds in my cabin, and though this made me very sad, I didn't have my ghastly nightmare.

We had our turkey and all the trimmings plus a good amount of fine red wine, and then we took all the musical instruments I had brought aboard and paraded around the deck making a total pandemonium of the cove. We set off many large seal bombs to complete the havoc. The next day we explored the shoreline with two inflatable dinghies. It was fascinating, and Bridget and Justin were enthralled with the adventure. On the third day, the weather turned and came at us from the southeast, the only direction from which we had no protection. We powered over to the lee of the southern part of the bay off Ensenada, and spent the day in a rain-and-wind storm in the main salon playing board games.

When we arrived back at our tie-up in Marina del Rey, I didn't want to leave the ship, but we all drove home the next morning. Susan had not done well during the sail. She had motion sickness during the traveling but had felt okay at anchor. This was not a good sign, and I feared that it would pull us further apart. At least I had the film editing in which to bury myself. And I buried myself as deep as I could, staying up late into the night talking with my editor. Sometimes, Stephen Stills called me late in the night—he knew there was trouble in my home. Stephen had deep troubles himself, and we sat and talked, doing drugs and drinking. He would play each new song he had written, and I was always into live, personal performance.

I had a very interesting confrontation with my agents about their

supposed 10 percent of *Easy Rider*—a deal they didn't make or even
pay any attention to, so why should they think I owed them a piece
of something with which they had nothing to do? They thought that
they had an omnibus contract with me, which they didn't, but they
didn't know it. The agency I had been with was merged with another,
and the contracts were assigned to the new entity. They never bothered to read what my contractual deal was before the merger. They
just assumed I had, like all the other actors, signed an omnibus contract. This contract gave them the right to take 10 percent of *anything*
I did. I knew that they were not about to go find me directing jobs,
writing jobs, a recording deal, whatever. If I wrote a script and sold it
on my own, why should I pay anyone a percentage for doing nothing? No quid pro quo. They were furious. I left them in early '71 and
went over to a new agency headed up by Sandy Bresler, a friend, a
gentleman, and a great hardballer in negotiations. Jack Nicholson was
with them, and I liked the other guys in the office, too.

The editing crawled on into the winter, and I continued with the
psychiatrist. One afternoon, in the middle of a session, Susan called.
Sidney's secretary interrupted the session, saying it was an important
call. Susan said that the FBI had just been at the house looking for
me. When she said I was not home, they had replied that they knew
where I was, gave her a card, and left. I could tell that Susan was a bit
frightened by the whole thing. Who could blame her? I asked if they
were polite and she said, no, they were very intimidating. The children were upset. I asked her to tell me the name on the card, and she
did, and I told her not to worry too much, I would take care of whatever they were up to. When I asked Sidney if I could use his phone,
he was very into the thing. This was probably the most expensive
telephone call I ever made, as Sidney's clock was running.

When the FBI answered, I asked for Special Agent Dick Smith and,
far out, I got him. Boy did I get him. I was trying to crawl through the
phone and grab him by the throat, and he knew it. I called him the
most abusive things I could think of. I screamed at him. "If you knew
where the fuck I *was,* why didn't you come *there,* you Nazi fucking
cocksucking commie fucking prevert!!? And if you ever come to my
house and frighten my wife and children again, I'll step on your hemorrhoids fucking dick in the parking lot! You get that, you fucking
little commie shithead! And don't think for a second that I am not
fully aware of the federal laws about abusive fucking language to *any*

fucking federal agent. Ten thousand fucking dollars and ten fucking years in a federal pen! Now, if you want to see me, you can find me at my office in twenty fucking goddamn minutes, you little dicklicking Nazi faggot!" I am certain that there was much more abusive language than I have written here, but I think you get the drift of my attitude. Sidney Prince certainly did.

Of course, I knew I was in for a major deal with these agents, so the next call I made was to my top lawyer, Arthur Berman. I traced him to his lunch and gave him the general idea of the possible trouble I was in and begged him to get to Pando as fast as he could. I excused myself from Sidney's and drove back to my office. On the drive, I radioed in that the FBI was on its way and not to panic. I think I also said to maintain radio silence.

As I approached the office, I noticed a way-too-much-unmarked car. I mean, the damn thing stuck out like my VW Bug in Omaha in '57. There was a tall man in a suit and hat locking it up as I drove by and turned up Seward from Melrose. I pulled into the gravel parking lot, jumped out of the Blazer, and flew into the downstairs office. There was a younger agent gaping at my FM station and a huge copy machine that could be used to print all sorts of antigovernment leaflets. Just as he turned to notice me, the older one came striding into the office. I figured that the younger agent was Dick Smith, the recipient of my first barrage. At that moment, Arthur pulled up in his Porsche and entered the arena, as that was what it was going to be in a few short seconds. I was planning a real showstopper. Remember, I was long-haired and fully bearded.

If the government was going to take me down, it would have to be the abusive language law, and the way I looked at it, they didn't stand a chance. Oh, they could arrest me and all, but when it came to court, I was very willing to have the record read aloud as to the exact language I used. I counted on a jury of my peers to acquit me. And if they didn't, I would still make some pretty outrageous press putting me even higher on the old pedestal in my audience's mind. More ticket sales. For a very brief moment, I wondered if this could be about my tearing up my draft card, sending it to the president, and telling him to stuff it up his ass. I remembered that I had signed that note on my personal stationery, adding my left thumbprint at the bottom of the page. But my instincts told me it was not. I suggested that we go upstairs to my main office—actually, Bill's—and all the parties agreed. Now came the first breakdown of the Bureau's rule number one: always make the suspect precede you through any door, up or down any stairs. Arthur agreed and made calming sounds that it *was* the best place to conduct an interrogation. Up the stairs he went with agent Dick on his heels, and, as the older fart indicated for me to go ahead of him, I said, no no no, you must go first. These are quite steep and narrow stairs, and I wouldn't want some old geezer falling down, smashing my stained-glass Captain America window, and suing me. As he gazed at the window of the shield of the United States, I gently ushered him along in front of me. He had no idea he was dealing with a crazed director and followed my instructions, quite bewildered. As we climbed the stairs, he could not miss the poster of Nixon smoking a joint and saying, with bloodshot eyes, I want to make things perfectly clear.

After we all were seated in Bill's office, I asked them if they were carrying heat. They gave me a quizzical look. "Heat," I repeated. "You know, guns." They did not reply, so I whipped out the Buck knife, sticking out of my watch pocket on my 501's, opening it as I drew it out and placed it on the small table in front of me. "I could have cut you up in a second, you fools," I said. Arthur was frowning and shaking his head. "Just letting them know where it all stands," I told him, and, yes, I did realize I had pulled a weapon from my jeans. Then I cut loose with an even worse tirade of filth about their characters and their faggot boss.

After five minutes or so, I asked *them* just what they wanted to ask *me*! They asked me what I knew about Angela Davis, a Marxist teacher and fugitive from their law. I was astounded. This was what it was all about? I reached up to Bill's desk and punched the intercom on the phone. My head secretary, Mary, answered, "Yes, boss?" "Cancel the cheeseburgers, Mary, the jig is up." She said, "You got it." I looked up to the attic and yelled, "Hey, Angie, get your black ass down here now! It's all over, babe!" I waited two or three seconds, then asked them what the fuck I would be doing with a black Marxist. They were undone. "Haven't you dickheads read my interview in *Playboy*? Oh! Right! Of course, your faggot boss doesn't let you assholes read any tits-and-ass rags." I was getting into new territory now, but decided that I had laid out my agenda, just the way I wanted.

All this time, the giant American flag that was flying upside down on the pole nearest to Bill's office's side of the building was flapping in the wind and sliding off the front of the building, covering the windows of the office, turning the room into a soft blend of red and white. The agents were having a difficult time processing all the shit that was being dumped on them. I asked them if they had anything to say for themselves, like a scolding father. They stammered for a moment and then said they had to read me the federal law on harboring a fugitive. Man! They just couldn't give it up. Arthur interjected that he would stipulate that it was not necessary, but I chimed in that I had had *my* say, and now they should be allowed to have their say. They read me the law and looked at me, quite nonplussed. I yelled some idiotic filth at them and then said I *was* harboring fugitives from them. "My children," I growled at them. "And if you *ever* come on my property and frighten my children again, I will bite your dicks off!" Threats to a federal officer.

"Now, get the fuck out of my office. NOW!" Arthur was shaking his head and trying to stop me, but it was too late for that, and the agents got up and left. I picked up my knife, folded it into my pocket, and followed them downstairs. The younger agent walked back into the office with a ten-dollar bill asking if anyone had lost ten bucks in the gravel. Nobody claimed it, so he put it down on the table next to the couch saying to buy some dog food for the puppy of one of the girls. All of us stood up and applauded his gesture, saying *that* was the way to do life. The older fart stepped back in, grabbed the bill, and said if we wanted it, we knew where we could find it. All of us followed *him* out of the building booing and hissing him, telling him what a stupid fuck he was.

I now apologize to Agent Smith for my terrible behavior and ask him, if he were in my shoes, would he have done anything different? I never heard a thing from the FBI after that. I guess they figured that anyone who would go so far out to antagonize the system in such a personal way couldn't be hiding anything.

This was not the first time I locked horns with the government, and it wouldn't be the last.

Christmas came with snow on the tree, many, many presents for the children, and sadness in the bed. Just after New Year's, I flew to Yugoslavia with Hopper and Alexandro Jodorowsky, a South American filmmaker who had scored with a very interesting avant-garde western, *El Topo*. We were all invited to Belgrade for an international film festival. It was *Easy Rider's* first showing in the Eastern bloc. I relished the idea of *ER* in commie land. When we stepped off the plane, we were met by a young, well-dressed man who whispered to us that we should give him any drugs we had before we went through customs. I never carried pot with me on any international trips after my trip to Rome in '65—with the exception of Hopper's film in Peru. Hopper couldn't believe me, but we were both surprised by the suggestion.

"Come on, man. I mean, man, you've *got* to give him your dope!"

"I'm not holding, Hoppe."

"Don't be a fool, man. You dig, man, give him your stash!"

"I am not holding, man! I promise, Dennis."

"Well, I sure hope you're *not,* man, 'cause he's the man, man. You dig, man?"

"I'm clean, man, I promise." Which was the truth.

The festival was happening during the Slavic New Year celebration, on the thirteenth or fourteenth of January. I *was* clean, and we skipped right through customs. I kept remarking about the many men carrying machine guns, and Hoppe kept on telling me to shut up. We soon learned that in Yugoslavia, one could possess pot or hash, but one could not buy or sell it. As I walked in the streets of the city, thinking that no one would recognize me with my beard and long hair, young men came up to me saying, "Okay! *Easy Rider,* man," and passed fingers of hash to me. Far out. And both Dennis and I were assigned escorts. Female escorts. Mine was tall, beautiful, and the daughter of some biggie in the commie party. They were our personal translators . . . or something. This was a far-out country.

The hotel we stayed at had a gambling casino on its third floor. Yugoslavian citizens were not allowed to go there, but many people from England and other Western bloc countries came there by the hundreds. The mafiosi that ran the place were happy to tell us *all* about the scam. The hotel was right on the Danube River, and they said if they were raided, they could throw all the equipment right out the windows into the river. Hot air, I told myself. The whole thing was run by the state.

One time, I was called in my room and asked to come down to the casino at once; there was something wrong with Dennis. I went down immediately to rescue Hoppe. As I walked into the casino, two wise guys came up to me and said that Dennis was in big trouble, as he owed a lot of money to the casino. I didn't buy it for a second. I pulled out my wallet and flashed my badge—this time it was the Department of Defense badge, the one I wore in *Easy Rider*. Larry Hagman had given it to me just before we started shooting, saying that if I was going to be Captain America, I needed to have this badge. The wise guys weren't sure about the significance of the badge, so I explained that I was with the U.S. Department of Defense, and there wouldn't be any problem at all, or there would be the biggest problem they had ever seen.

They, of course, were putting a joke over on me, but they weren't thrilled with my response. I played the whole thing straight-faced. Deadly serious. I told them that there wasn't a problem, Dennis wasn't a gambler, and they shouldn't try to joke with me. I think they had some real worries that I might actually *be* with the DOD. One never knows. C'est on jamais.

Dennis and I were asked to talk on a major radio station, and we obliged. We spoke in English, slowly, and when we were asked what song we wanted to play for the youth of Yugoslavia, Dennis and I looked at each other and nodded, and I said CSN's "Teach Your Children." They played it, both DJs saying how cool it was. I was impressed that they even had the song, let alone understood its significance.

. . .

I was invited to lecture at the University of Hawaii's two campuses, one on Oahu and the other on the Big Island, at Hilo. A chance for some sun in the tropics. Bridget was attending Oakwood School in the first grade, and Justin was in kindergarten. It was a progressive school, and they didn't put up a fuss when we took the children with us. I wouldn't have gone without them.

I gave the two lectures, and toured the islands with the children, Susan, and our housekeeper-nanny, Maria. After the lecture at the campus on Hilo, we toured the Big Island. The volcano Kilauea Iki was erupting gloriously, and I wanted to get as close as possible to the vent. The flow was about to reach the eastern shore, or windward side, of the island. We rented a Toyota Land Cruiser, and using topo maps, I followed the different ways up the mountain. From time to time, we came upon blocked roads. I finally put the Land Cruiser in four-wheel drive and went around the blocks. As we came closer to the fiery crater, we could hear the deep hissing roar. Everyone else was not as keen as I to find the vent, but I had an intense desire to look down into the crater and see the blood of Mother Earth. I drove the car as close as I could, or at least as close as Susan, Maria, and the children would let me. No one else was interested in venturing out on the lava. The surface of an older flow was warm as I walked slowly out toward the great, glowing, and roaring hiss that was the main vent for this particular eruption. Suddenly Justin, who was then almost four years old, came bolting from the Land Cruiser, crying out to me not to go any farther. At first, I assured him that I was in no danger, but he kept coming closer to me, begging me tearfully not to go out any farther and to *please* come back to the car. In an instant, I recalled the incident with the Ford tractor and my dad, when I was six, and I turned back to the car, picking up Justin and carrying him with me. Everyone was thankful that I changed my mind. I was ashamed that I had so thoughtlessly frightened my children.

Life with Susan hadn't been as bad or strained as I may have insinuated, and although we were not together as a man and a woman—something I needed in a most desperate way—she was a very good mother to our beautiful children, a great cook, and an inventive homemaker. It was our lack of any conjugal contact and what it meant to me that was most frightening and sad.

The passion may have left our marriage, but *my* passion for my work had replaced the excitement lost. I lived almost every moment of my life to the fullest. And my anger became focused away from my father and mother and spread out upon humankind as a whole. How could we have fucked up the planet so badly and not cared? And not done everything we could to make it better?

We went to Maui and stayed at the Maui Liu. I introduced Susan and the children to the fabulous beaches near Kihei. I showed them where I went to prepare for my next role. Ray White, one of the mechanics on *Easy Rider*, joined us. During a short visit to Kaui and Hanalei Bay, I had come down with a mild flu, and Ray nursed me back with the help of Maria. It was windy and cold in Kaui, as it usually is in January, so as soon as I was better, we went home. And I dove back into the editing room and Langhorne's makeshift studio. I bought an eighteen-speed grand touring bicycle and was using it to go to my office. I had been influenced by the story in *Idaho Transfer*, and was trying to do my bit in the ecology department.

I woke up early one morning and felt like riding my superbike on Mulholland. The nightmare had given me a bad night, on top of everything else, and I felt that I could shake it off with a brisk ride. I left the bedroom through the sliding glass door onto the patio. As I jumped down from a three-foot wall to the cement walk by the guest bath, I landed on a bone that had been chewed to the size of a golf ball by Lothar, our German shepherd, spraining my left ankle badly. Actually, I knew that I had torn some ligaments, just as I had in '64, the day before Bridget was born. This time I crawled back to my bed and asked Susan to call Bob Rosenfeld, the man who had dealt with the right ankle seven years earlier. It was very painful. Someone from Pando came and drove me to the doctor.

Rosenfeld shook his head as he manipulated my left foot. He said that my ankle was as badly damaged as the right one had been and put me in a cast to stabilize it. I would be in the cast for four weeks or more. Major bummer. I had started making plans to sail to Hawaii, and this was going to be a big setback.

I went through four casts. The ligaments I had damaged kept on hemorrhaging, and the swelling ankle needed more room. One night, Reine Stewart, part of the guerrilla team of filmmakers, musicians, and friends, came by to visit me. She could see the pain in my face and asked if there was anything she could do. My pained-out mind said, yeah, fuck my brains out, but I asked if she would help me get down to my yacht. I wanted to be able to see the sky. She kissed me and said she would be right back. In forty minutes, she returned with Tom Matthiesen and his van. The two of them helped me to the van, stretched me out, and drove me to the marina. I was in my third cast by this time, but still in a lot of pain. I had to keep my left foot raised higher than my heart to stop the pain. I could use crutches, but the ankle was throbbing within minutes. Once at the slip, Reine and Tom helped me aboard. My friend John Haeberlin and his girlfriend, Virginia, were staying on the boat in my stateroom, so the four of them helped me maneuver up the boarding stairs and down into the main salon.

Tom went back to his little apartment at Pando, and Reine stayed on the boat. We all got stoned and listened to some music.

Reine and I have a very far-out connection, even though she is fourteen years younger than I. She was born at the Le Roy. It was the Le Roy Institute when she made her entrance on life's stage. It is like being born in the same taxicab with the same driver, fourteen years apart. I have since met two other people who have the same first address.

John and Virginia were ready to crash and went back to the stateroom. I wasn't ready to sleep yet. Reine, who had read my mind back at the house, took care of things, thank god, and I remember lying on the starboard settee, now nicely covered in burgundy mohair and big enough to sleep two people comfortably, with my left foot resting on the top of the seat back, well above my heart. Reine went home when I was fast asleep under one of Maj's comforters.

I went ahead with the voyage plan for Hawaii, and we all prepped for the occasion. I wasn't sure how I would deal with my messed up ankle, but I didn't give a rat's ass. I needed to be on my way. A very big part of the Paddle thing. Dad came down to the ship to see the operation. He had not been aboard before, and he was worried about the open ocean voyage we were going to make. I tried to calm his fears by telling him that we had Gordie Krusen with us as one of the navigators, but he was not familiar with Gordie or John Calley. Later, Dad never admitted that he had come on board before 1974. Even Shirlee insists that he didn't come aboard in '71 or anytime before the summer of '74. All of the cast and crew who made that wonderful voyage remember his being aboard that day.

He left us, not convinced that we would make it. He had a valid point, in a sense; looking for the Hawaiian Islands, over twenty-three hundred miles southwest of Los Angeles, was quite like looking for a needle in a haystack. Dad was into those types of euphemisms. If we were off course by two hundred miles, we might become lost at sea, having passed way south of the islands. My instincts were very sure about our ability.

We moved to the gas dock the day before we were going to leave and topped off the fuel and water tanks. Susan brought the children down to say bon voyage. I think she was worried, too. But I had to go. It was not a question for me, it was a command from my heart. I had, in a sense, been living for this moment since I was seven. Since I had read *Paddle to the Sea*.

With eleven people aboard, *Tatoosh* set sail for Maui at ten thirty, the morning of March 3, 1971, sailing down the slot between Catalina and San Clemente Island on a magnetic course of 180 degrees.

The cast on my ankle had been cut in half, and I was ordered to wear the back half bound to my leg by an Ace bandage whenever I was walking. On the second day, I threw the cast overboard and wore a simple elastic ankle support. We stood a British watch—four hours on the wheel and eight hours off—with two men to each watch. The last hour was always a bitch. I, of course, took the captain's watch: 0400 to 0800 in the morning and evening. On my watch, there were three men, including myself, because of my bad ankle. The last hour was still hell. Most of the guys stood their watches in foul-weather gear for the first six days. I shared my cabin with John and Virginia.

Our first visible sunset with no clouds was the evening of March ninth. On the twelfth, we had our first sunrise without clouds as the full moon was setting in the west. I filmed it, panning the camera from the full moon, slowly to the east, and just as the camera pulled the cockpit into frame, with everybody in total silhouette against the glorious morning sky banded in colors, the sun broke the surface. Everyone was on deck for the occasion. I cannot describe the feeling, though I am having it right now, as I write this. I had not only paddled to the sea, I was sailing its vastness. There is nothing in the world as awe-inspiring as a full canopy of stars at night, from horizon to horizon, leading to a full sky of blue in the day. Few people do what I did then and for the next fourteen years: sail a large sailboat over great expanses of ocean from needle to needle in the haystack of life, just for the pleasure of it.

On a hot, clear day in the tropics, with little wind, we put our largest rubber raft over the side, and six people took turns bathing in it. We had used almost half of our water supply, and orders were issued to use the remaining water only for drinking or cooking. This day, we felt sure enough to do this otherwise risky business. We were moving at five knots under sail, but most of the hull speed was due to the current. I rigged myself to the tow line and slid back to the Avon, helped aboard by my mates. Most times the people in the Avon raft pulled the boat up to the ship and changed bathers. We were all naked, and we were all in heaven, for a while.

With most of the hands in the raft, Gordie, myself, Tom Russo—my first mate—and Jill—his girlfriend and the ship's cook—stood the wheel and kept course. For some insane reason, Tom wanted to photograph the hull as it passed, from underwater. He jumped overboard from the bow with one of the ship's Nikkonos. In no time, we all saw that Tom was not going to make it to the rubber boat, and I ran back to the cleat holding the tow line and let it go.

We kept a tight eye on the raft, but faster than one could imagine, the rubber boat was lost from view. We made all the course changes in the best way we could, but one cannot be exact in this type of maneuver, and the sea was always changing, eliminating any point of reference. Once we were under power, we tried our best to retrace our course, but had little luck in spotting the rubber boat. We were all very fearful that we could very likely lose eight people at sea.

Finally, we spotted the Avon as we rode up on a swell, and they were on the top of a different swell. It took a long time to bring *Tatoosh* up to the rubber dinghy, as it kept on disappearing. Russo had found the raft and swum to it, being helped aboard by the others, during the twenty minutes it took us to bring the ship around and head back. They had watched the ship disappear swiftly to the west, growing fearful as the hundred-foot mainmast seemed to go down like a periscope.

No one said anything while we made the ship ready to continue on course. The lesson had been very keenly etched in all our brains. Gordie took some sun shots with the sextant and got us a fairly good line of position, and we got back to the course we needed.

Once we had been in the tropics and the steady trade winds for a while, everyone was in a great mood and the near catastrophe was put behind us. Our only problem was sailing directly downwind, as we had fallen off course too far to the south. But on Monday, March 16, at one-thirty in the morning, we sighted the light from Kauiki Head on the southeastern part of Maui. Thirteen days after we left Cat Harbor, we passed Kaanapali, on Maui's northwestern shore, at 0700, having traveled 2,351 miles on the finest-built wooden sailboat in the world.

I wrote, "Capt. Sextant lives!" in the log. Russo added, "Thank God." The only thing missing, and the real reason for which I had bought the ship, was my family, but I was filled with emotion and excitement, as was the rest of the cast and crew. I think that everyone was on deck soon after the light on Kauiki Head had been sighted and remained there until we dropped anchor. Well, actually, we didn't drop anchor for sure until many hours later.

We initially dropped the hook in the roadstead off Lahaina. A few minutes later, a surfer paddled alongside the ship, telling us that fourteen narcotics officers were waiting for us ashore. I was livid. We had just finished thirteen days of an incredible voyage, and there were narcs waiting to give me shit. Against the advice of Gordie and Tom, I tied the ship to the channel marker buoy for the entrance to Lahaina Harbor, an act that was forbidden by maritime law. We stayed there for an hour or so contemplating our next move. The tide was low, and therefore the entrance to the harbor was impassible, so we moved north and dropped anchor in the roadstead again. One quarter of a mile off the wall on Front Street, Lahaina.

We all took turns scoping the shore with our high-power binoculars. While in my stateroom, I told Russo to blow up the tires on the Studebaker, a forties-era bicycle that was strapped to the life lines on the starboard deck. I heard him clamoring around in the lazaret, which we referred to as the dive shop. I could see the bottom parts of the bike through my cabin ports and heard him hooking up a dive tank to the bike tires. I was looking out the porthole, as the tire exploded off the rim. I thought for a second and then reissued the order to *inflate* the tires. I gave very few "orders" on the ship, but felt that this definitely fit the criteria.

On the balcony of the Pioneer Inn, I could see the feds looking back at us through their binoculars. Within an hour, a twin-engine plane buzzed us several times, then dropped something into the water. I dispatched a rubber dinghy to retrieve the object, which had been wrapped in a roll of toilet paper that was streaming behind it as it fell. It was a vinegar bottle with a note inside. We broke the bottle and passed the note around. It said that our ship was a "big green boat, with narcotics police waiting to board" us. It told me to call my wife, each of my attorneys, and Bill Hayward, and listed the private phone numbers for each person. This was not a joke. I wondered about the "big green" thing and fumed about the reception committee.

Maj Hagman had made terry-cloth pullover robes for the yacht. She had done the same for each of her family members and each of my family. We had three of the cast and crew dress up in these hooded robes and paddle into the harbor with a paper bag with cans of Dinty Moore stew and "the stash" written in felt-tip pen on it. They put the bag on the loading dock and paddled down to the harbor master's office. It was manned by a friend. When they returned, they had a copy of a telegram sent to the Lahaina harbor master from the Marina del Rey harbor master, advising him to be on the lookout for a "ninety-foot sailboat with a white cabin top." It went on to say that we had $250,000 worth of cocaine, machine guns, and radicals aboard.

Think Tricky Dick was involved? I'll have to ask Deep Throat. We weighed anchor and I drove the ship up the channel to the sand bar, turned it on its own axis abeam of the Pioneer Inn, and shouted through a Mickey Mantle bullhorn, "We ain't got no cocaine, we ain't got no machine guns, but we can get radical real fast!" I turned the ship back out to the roadstead and dropped anchor for the third time. After that, I was spent by my anger and lack of sleep, and went back to my cabin, lying down in my bed.

I lay there for ten or fifteen minutes, trying to relax, when I heard the sound of an outboard motor approaching. I looked out my hull porthole and saw Bill Hayward, Morse Taylor, and Arthur Berman— two of my attorneys—in suits pulling up to the yacht. Man! This was really out of hand. I yelled up to the deck not to let them board with shoes on. I couldn't believe it. But it was not a dream. More like HELL IN THE PACIFIC! I slept a little while we waited for the tide.

The feds couldn't come out to do their dirty work without the co-operation of the U.S. Navy, but everyone else could. By the time the tide was right, we had been thoroughly briefed by the lawyers and had arranged for some assistance with the docking maneuver. I knew the ship could make it into the harbor, as I had a photo of it docked at the break wall, when Boo Pascal sailed it to Lahaina in the Victoria-to-Maui race years earlier. We were advised by the attorneys not to let an agent walk around the ship alone, and not to get into a confrontation with them. The latter part was said primarily for my benefit.

We entered the harbor with all hands naked except for the lawyers and Bill. If the federales wanted to fuck with us, we were going to *really* fuck with them.

By the time we tied up to the loading dock, the feds had all left. The talk around the harbor was that everyone in town was pointing at one or another agent and laughing and telling others, "There's one of them," until the feds—and probably a few locals—left town in disgrace. What a mess. If I hadn't been talking to my lawyers and partner, all of whom were in suits, I would think I had dreamed the whole thing. Jill assured me that I had not been dreaming. Bill and the boys stayed for a few days. We stayed at the loading dock for more than a week. Nobody wanted to tell us to leave.

I was down in the engine room one night, and Ray brought a
young woman down to the door. She gave me a bit of aluminum foil
and said it was from the people up on the mountain. There was a
brownish granular substance in the foil. No one wanted to try it at
first. The next afternoon, Ray tried to chop it up, but it stayed in its
peculiar granular form, so he made up a few lines on the library desk.
We all looked at each other and snorted the stuff up. Very bad idea.

Tom and I drove someone's Jeep over to Mala Wharf, an aging
cement dock that jutted out into the bight known as Mala. It had been
a loading dock for sugarcane, but it was basically condemned for any
real use. We walked out to the end and surveyed the bight as a possible anchorage for *Tatoosh*. It was protected from most Kona storms.
These major winds were called Kona winds because they blew up
from the Kona coast of the Big Island. Many boats had been blown
onto the reef off Lahaina by these winds. We didn't want to put the
ship in the way of disaster if there was another anchorage that would
suffice.

Tom and I agreed that it would be a fine spot for the yacht, but as
we turned from the end of the wharf, the world took on a whole new
look for me. I had snorted more of that shit than the rest, and whatever it was, it was messing with me in a serious way. The wharf was
undulating like a ribbon flapping in the wind. The holes in the surface
were opening and closing like big mouths. It wasn't pretty, and I
begged Tom to drive me back to the boat at once. I needed to be in
my sanctuary right away.

We drove back to the loading dock as fast as possible. Tom realized
that he would be on the same trip himself real soon. We made it back
in the nick. As I fled to the main salon, I noticed that others in the cast
and crew were coming to the same conclusion. We all ended up on
the main salon floor holding on to each other. At that moment, I
thought that we had been dosed by an undercover agent, and they
were sure to be boarding the ship at any time. We were all relieved
when the drug wore off. Lesson learned: if you don't know what it is,
don't do it.

Several sails needed to be repaired, so on my way back to the
mainland, I chartered a big twin Cessna to take me and the sails to
Oahu. We dragged the sail bags up to the loading area when the
plane arrived, and the cast and crew gave me big hugs as I left our

very special time zone. We had all done a grand thing in our crossing, and I doubt that any of us will ever forget it.

After dropping the sails off, I flew back to L.A. and dove back into the editing room again. I was pleased with how *Hired Hand* was coming along. I took care of office stuff, and spent some fine time with Bridget and Justin. I had to have a talk with one of Bridget's teachers and explain that *any way* Bridget wanted to draw an elephant was the right way. Let her be expressive now, I said; there will be plenty of time to learn the structure of drawing later, if she decides to become serious about painting. Justin and Bridget were such beautiful children, it was hard to let anyone outside the family try to mold them in whatever was the "approved method" of life. That was solely the duty of Susan and myself, and we both agreed that we would allow them certain freedoms of expression as children. They were both well behaved and had fine manners, and I had a very spiritual relationship with them. I told them that we would all be going to the yacht at the end of the summer for a tropical vacation.

After I had taken care of all the business at Pando, I flew back to the ship. It was hard for me to be away from it. The ship was my sanctuary, and I was determined to spend as much time aboard as I could. I also brought some boat stuff that was needed and not available quickly in Hawaii. I spent almost two weeks there, and every night was nightmare-free. I didn't quite understand why, but it really didn't matter.

When I returned to Los Angeles, I was right back into the editing room. Meanwhile, things were not right up in Seattle with *Idaho Transfer,* and I had to divide my attention. The start date was upon us, and things were coming unsnapped. Tom Matthiesen was starting to freeze up, and the whole group was looking for me to put things in order.

A meeting was called at Pando, and all my advisors and accountants suggested that I write the film off as an eighty-two-thousand-dollar loss. I was upset. I didn't get into the film to use it as a write-off for taxes. I believed in its reason and point so fervently, I refused to walk away from it. So I decided to direct the film myself. Matthiesen's script was so specific, I felt I knew what each shot was supposed to be.

I had not scouted any locations, but I had to finish casting the film. I needed the four top leads. During breakfast at a restaurant one morning, I watched the cashier deal with the customers. She was about nineteen, and had the right qualities to play the sister of the female lead. Bearded, long hair and all, I asked her if she had any experience onstage or on film. She laughed quite comfortably. I don't think she recognized me with all the hair. I gave her the copy of the script I was carrying and asked her to read it, then call me at my office. I wrote my name and number on the cover. Three hours later, she called me and told me she was blown away by the story. I asked her if she felt she could play the part of Isa, and she said sure. Her name was Caroline Hildebrand. I shaved my beard and had my hair trimmed. I felt it was better for me to look a bit more presentable for the casting sessions.

While at the bicycle shop, I watched Kevin Hearst, son of the owner, work on several bikes before he got to mine. I saw his intense concentration as he worked, and felt he would make a perfect Ronald, the nerdy scientist leading man. After listening to him talking, I offered him the role. But I was having a difficult time casting the lead role, Karen. She had to be in her late teens, and the total opposite of the rest of the scientist-type cast. I put the word out that I was casting the lead of a motion picture and gave a short description of the young woman. Many girls showed up. I finally asked Caroline to come and read with the other girls for me. She had such a low-pressure style that she was not a threat to the actors reading for the lead. I finally settled on an unknown named Kelley Bohanan. She had the stuff that was necessary for the part.

Keith Carradine, who had been hanging out at Pando, graciously joined the cast and played the role of Arthur, the brainy stud of the elite young scientific group. Having the full cast now, I sat with the director of photography, Bruce Logan. Bruce had emerged on the cameraman scene after doing the miniature and special-effects camera work for Stanley Kubrick's *2001: A Space Odyssey*. *Idaho Transfer* was going to be his first outdoor motion picture. Peter Riches ("PR") was our still photographer.

I began shooting the film in Arco, Idaho, on the vast lava flows where the story takes place in the script. We shot the last scenes of the film first (for which we needed overcast weather) in a hailstorm and its cold gray and white aftermath. We finished the entire wish list for the bad-weather scenes and headed on down the road to Mountain Home. Bruce and I were in heaven, because we had shot some of the most dramatic footage of the film from a let's-see-what-happens on a clear blue as blue morning. Kelley was riding with us in my Blazer, and felt good about the stressful ordeal. Complaining the entire afternoon, she had still performed her part perfectly. We took the next day off as a reward for our perseverance.

Lots of amusing and far-out things went on during the rest of the shoot. Two of the girls in the cast had complained about a Peeping Tom at their motel. Logan and I volunteered to stay the night with them and get rid of the problem. I'm sure we thought about playing with the girls, but it was a serious matter. We had a cop in his car hidden in the trees with one of our walkie-talkies. We had another walkie in the room with us. We made ourselves nice and comfy and burned a couple with the girls. After a few hours, we heard some scuffling outside the bathroom window. We keyed the cop on the walkie-talkie and he keyed back; then Logan and I snuck into the bathroom, finding a man half in and half out of the window. We grabbed him and radioed the cop, who pulled him back out the window and took him away. He turned out to be the son of a local politician, and everything was kept quiet. I liked it that way.

It was an extraordinarily right-wing town, and we were an extraordinarily weird bunch. But we kept all the production money in the local bank, which was owned by a wonderful older woman, who had a crush on the youngest male member of the cast. She pampered him and took care of business with us in a very friendly manner. A year or so later, a somewhat critical piece about me was published in the *Los Angeles Times*. A week later, she wrote to the columnist that she found me and my entire production company very polite and upstanding, and that the columnist must be talking about somebody else. I don't know how she found the article, but I will always be thankful for her support.

We went way over time and budget, and it was all my and Bill's cash. Marianne McDonald—Stormy's sister—lent me $250,000 to finish the postproduction. I paid her back. Most nights, I fell asleep while writing notes to the children and Susan. When I awoke in the morning, the notes were full of colored marker pen lines and squiggles, as was my body. And I could always count on the nightmare to make things even more twisted.

I met several guerrilla types during the shoot that would remain my loyal friends for a long time. My first assistant director was David

McGiffert. I knew nothing about his past experience, but each time I would turn around to ask the assistants to hold traffic or bring the set to order, I saw that he was one step ahead of me. It was very telepathic. Today, I look forward to the next time we will work together. He is now the most sought-after first assistant director in the industry, having worked on *Tootsie, Batman Returns, The Firm, The Fisher King, Rain Man, An Officer and a Gentleman, Absence of Malice,* and *Witness*. He became one of the Pando People, sleeping out in the back house. All the girls loved him. He was known as the short, cute guy. He was a lifesaver to me. John Fleckenstein came on as a temporary assistant camera for a few weeks. Seven years later he was my first operator on *Wanda Nevada*. On that shoot, he was known as Steadyfleck. His hand-held stuff was equal to a Steadicam, with no extra contraptions. Jim Lavin was one of the most inventive key grips I've ever seen. I was-am a very fortunate man to have met and learned from this grab-it-quick production team, and the many others I have worked with.

I was longing for the yacht, but striving for cinematographic perfection with the film. When I wrapped the principal photography, I chartered a Learjet to get me home as fast as possible.

I finished up whatever business I had in L.A., grabbed Susan and the kids, and flew to *Tatoosh*. Whew! I had surely missed the yacht during the long hot summer on the lava. We got to the ship two weeks before the Labor Day race from Black Rock at Kaanapali to the A buoy off the entrance to the Ala Wai yacht basin at Waikiki. I didn't even mention our sleeping together to Susan. I had done all I could about that and would never bring it up again on board my yacht. I just shut out any problems between Susan and me. I had learned that trick well, after thirty-one years of being Henry's son. I relaxed on the ship, took small tours to different beaches and different islands, went scuba diving, watched the humpback whales and the Maui girls. I was the owner and Master of the vessel, and I made the rules. I let no one dictate a thing to me, and those terrible nightmares were not allowed on board.

Justin and Bridget had a grand time. I geared as much of the daytime for their tastes and amusement as possible. Susan was pleasant and noncomplaining. Her motion sickness was not very bad at anchor or even on the excursions to other beaches and islands. Neither of us pushed the other. Ashore, there was a constant party. Shit, Lahaina was a constant party, and *Tatoosh* was becoming the flagship for the Lahaina Yacht Club. The wives of the local members and other Lahaina ladies made sure I was taken good care of. Make that great care of. We terrorized the club with mini firecrackers in the sugar bowls and creamers, gave great parties for the hip members, and passed the wealth around. For the next five or six years I was King of Lahaina.

When the race committee held the skipper's meeting, I realized the Establishment—this time in the form of the Hawaii Yacht Club—was not going to deal with me at all. They were rude, and they would pay for it. We packed the ship with expert sailors from the Southern Ocean Racing Circuit and other big races. I was put summarily in the Pacific Handicap Class; the last group of boats to be started in the race. I should have been in the A class, but we knew what we had, and they didn't. Race orders were announced aboard the day before. All hands had to be on board by two in the morning, and all hands had to be on deck at five A.M. Their condition was their own matter, but they must be ready to sail by five-thirty. No excuses were allowed. I went ashore to round up the strays at midnight and got delayed once or twice by a Lahaina beauty. By two, most hands were aboard. I had to drag several guys out of someone's bed and march them to the loading dock.

At four-thirty A.M., Russo put Little Richard on the tape deck at full throttle. We had a short meeting when all hands were on deck. I told them that we had been placed in a terrible starting class for the ship; I wasn't interested in winning; I was only interested in sailing the best course and maximizing the potential of the ship. Which meant winning. And off we went to the starting marks.

We dallied as the first classes started, watching their sails to see where the wind line was moving. Then, amidst a pile of little boats, we made ready for a Vanderbilt start. This required a very watchful eye on the committee boat's flags-and-balls signals from the yard of the committee boat and accurate timing on our part. Once we were sure of the timing of the start, we sailed back across the starting line for just so many minutes and seconds, coming about at the point we figured would put us on the line at the cannon or start. With all the little boats trying to edge up on the line, we counted on the right of way for the largest of the class. We crossed the line immediately after the cannon fired, and once across, put up our big red spinnaker. The spinnaker was tied with light yarn and filled with red, white, and blue confetti. The tying of the yarn was meant to keep the sail from open-ing too soon. In theory, the sail should reach the masthead, and with a simple jerk, the yarn will pop and the chute open up majestically and fully. It did that perfectly, and as soon as it popped, a huge cloud of red, white, and blue confetti drifted downwind from the sail.

Knowing the amount and direction of the trade winds as they passed through and down the Pailolo Channel, we made a perfect start and quickly over took most of the other classes before we passed the lee of Molokai at Laau Point. We passed the leeway to the east and south. Our spinnaker—we called it Big Red—had blown out ear-lier, and we were sailing wing-and-wing downwind, making good hull speed. We arrived at the finish line forty-five minutes before the next boat crossed. We had our whiskey staysail up—the canopy of sailcloth that kept the cockpit in the shade—and were having cock-tails as we watched the other boats cross the line, blowing our air horns to welcome them. When all boats were across the line, we motored into the yacht basin and anchored in the turning basin, but far enough north of it to allow the smaller boats to maneuver. We were not graced with a slip or end tie. For that matter, we were not even considered a part of the race. We had started last and finished forty-five minutes before the next boat, the *Robin,* a small but fast ketch that had started a half hour before us. When we went to the Hawaii Yacht Club for the race dinner and party, we noticed that our ship's name was not even on the blackboard. When we asked what our standing was, we were totally ignored. These sanctimonious jerks were not going to recognize our yacht. They never planned to. It was a decision made before the race began by the Hawaii Yacht Club race committee. I was furious. I was in a major pissing match with these assholes, who were jealous of my ship and our quite irregular crew.

As we left the club, having made every protest allowed, we wanted to shower off, but the showers had been closed, just as we ap-proached. I demanded that the showers be opened for my cast and crew, but the guard that had been placed at that area refused. I men-tioned something about kicking the doors down and taking our de-served showers. We had, after all, paid our entrance fee, and our yacht club had reciprocal guest amenities with this bullshit club. No dice. No showers. On our part, therefore, no mercy. I mentioned blowing down the shower doors with explosives as we left.

Some stuck-up woman was passing through the area and heard my explosives suggestion. When we were all back aboard, the ways were full of cops with flashing lights and major bullhorn authority. When they demanded we come back ashore and face whatever crap the yacht club was trying to put on us, we refused. We knew that they could not, by law, come out to our ship. I yelled that we had cops aboard and they saw no trouble, but we would be glad to give the cops ashore a *lot* of trouble. They bullhorned back, what cop? And David Hudson answered back that he was the harbor master at La-haina, he had not heard anything about blowing up the club, and he was advising the crew to stay aboard and shower on the yacht. Which we all did, right away. Abstract authority. Ground zero. No mercy.

Susan, Justin, Bridget, and I flew back to the mainland two days later, and I prepared for a European tour opening *The Hired Hand* with Warren Oates.

chapter *Nineteen*

The trip began in Stockholm. Oates was already there, and was quite used to seeing me seethe at authority. This time authority had reared its ugly head in the form of baggage destruction. U.S. citizens might not realize that the government will do whatever it can get away with. Sometimes it gets caught and has to apologize. In this case, it got caught and claimed it was all a mistake. Claimed my bags had gone to Argentina by mistake. Argentina!? It does not even sound like Stockholm! One wonders what the government could be thinking in delaying baggage and tearing it up. Literally. When the black leather Gucci bags got to me in Stockholm, they had been torn apart to see what could be hidden in the leather sides and beautiful lining These bags were part of the sad legacy left to me by Stormy's suicide. This space was only a third of an inch thick, 99 percent of that, leather. One could easily feel that there was nothing there. The agents from Sphincter Control had put it all back together by whip-stitching the torn seams with rawhide bootlace. What a class act! The Department of the Treasury was out to mess with my life in a very crude way. More about that later.

Even this rocket scientist routine of the treasury agents could not dim the eager anticipation I had for buying a 1971 300SEL 6.3 Daimler Benz on our way through Germany.

. . .

Well . . . the luggage finally arrived in my room at the hotel in
Stockholm with all my fresh clothes and stuff. Of course I was only
wearing Levi's pants and shirts in those days—maybe a few sportier
cowboy shirts for an evening occasion, but only things that I could
wash myself. Real down-to-earth guy, you know. Semihippie. Too
rich to be a real hippie. Thing is, I didn't remember that there were
no Laundromats in Europe. That could have turned into a real ugly
scene, but for the many young women who were only too happy to
give Captain America a hand . . . thank goodness.

Our adventure in Stockholm was enlightening for me. A good deal
of the time I was intensely interviewed by young, radical types who
assumed I was some sort of spokesman for all the disenfranchised
youth in the world. They waited for words of encouragement. Leader-
ship, I supposed. They were quite interested in how I lived my life.
Had I given up worldly things? (The U.S. government was giving me
a big hand with that one!) Was I going to dedicate my life to the
struggle they all saw as "our" struggle? They seemed pleased that I
chose to make a statement by only wearing Levi's, Wrangler shirts,
and cowboy boots. They either didn't hear what the reason was, or
refused to accept it. Simply telling them that I preferred to wash my
own clothes had to have a special meaning. For me it was simple
logic.

.   .   .

After four days of publicity and promotion in Stockholm for *The
Hired Hand,* Mr. Oates and I were ready to party a little. We had met
some fairly outrageous types, and were invited to a party at one couple's large flat. It began as a normal party with all of us talking politics,
motion pictures, how the young radicals were going to change the
system, sex, drugs, and rock and roll. Horny Warts had latched onto
a lovely Swede and was ready to club-hop. I found myself being challenged by a woman who was the editor of the local communist rag.
Her husband was a shaker in the Swedish Socialist Party, and the host
of the evening.

We all decided to join Oates and check out the Stockholm nightclub scene. The Swedes love jazz, and after four or five clubs, Warren
and I had met quite a few of the Swedish film and stage actors
and brought them along with us to the best jazz club in town.

Everyone was very generous to Oates and me, and we had yet to pay for a single drink. I decided that our turn was due, and I ordered up eight bottles of Dom Perignon. Very soon, I had to order another eight bottles. In two orders, I had repaid our hosts ten times over. Of course, we all smoked the best weed those Swedes had ever tried.

As the evening moved along and the gang began to get smaller, I became dangerously interested in the young journalist, and she was putting all the right moves on me. Oates whispered to me that he was going back to our two-bedroom suite with his date, and suggested that I might want to do the same. It sounded perfect to me, and I let my journalista know what the plan was with an intricate combination of body language, eye movement, and hand signals. I looked like one of the coaches in a baseball game giving the batter and runners the play options, but I got the idea across. It would have been easier to just say let's fuck, but I liked the more discrete intimacy. The journalista was delighted with the notion, but had a different place in mind. Walking through the lobby was not a smart thing for her to be seen doing, so she suggested we go to one of her girlfriend's apartments.

After we spent time at her girlfriend's place, we walked back to my hotel in top spirits as the sun began to light up the new day. We sang songs and danced in the morning sun on sidewalks, carefree, as one-night lovers often do. As we kissed goodnight (or rather good morning) in front of the hotel, I suddenly realized that the small bag I'd had with me was no longer part of my act, and I immediately freaked out. She told me with great confidence that there was nothing to be upset about. She said that the bag would be found and returned to me. Oates and I were scheduled to fly to Copenhagen that afternoon, and her confidence was not reassuring to me at all.

In the small bag were my passport, my driver's license, all the major credit cards, lots of cash, gold, coins, and several wristwatches. I quickly went to the concierge and explained my problem. He also told me that it would be found at whatever club I had left it and be returned to me. I was beside myself. I was sure that someone would find the bag, sell the passport, and run a quick scam with my credit cards. In a panic I called the U.S. Embassy and expressed my concern. I was told that I could apply for a new passport at the Embassy and that it would take only an hour to issue it. Relief! I knew that I should keep quiet about my fury with the U.S. Treasury, and thank god I could travel to the next destination.

Oates and I arrived at the hotel in Copenhagen shortly after sunset and, after a few handshakes and autographs, stretched out in our luxurious suite. I was a little baffled by the immediate recognition, as I looked like a crazed hippie with a full beard and dark glasses. Ornery and I fired up a doobie as he tried to calm my concerns about the lost purse. We both marveled at the new passport with its new photograph. The old one had a rather sedate photo with no beard. The new one had the beard, of course, long hair, and a crazed look in my eyes that gave proof of the sleepless night, sex, drugs, rock and roll, and utter paranoia.

Once the pot had worked its magic, we began to explore the massive suite. From experience I had known that it was almost impossible to take a nonregistered woman to one's room in a European hotel. The exception was if one had a suite. Having a two-bedroom suite was a total snap. Oates kept nodding in agreement with my theory of the suite system and I realized that, obviously, he was well versed in the European boogie of women-in-one's-room. Either that, or the pot was making every problem solvable. The phone rang us back to the foreign reality we both faced.

The concierge announced that a package had arrived before we had checked in and asked if I wished to have it delivered to the room. Apparently I had to sign some receipt for the item. I told him to send it on up. Horny and I wondered about the package. I guessed that, as I had to sign for it, it obviously wasn't drugs. As it turned out, it was better than drugs. It was my purse. Passport, cards, watches, and cash all as they were when I lost it. Absolute amazement. This incredible turn of events called for some special recognition. Up came the Dom and a tub of caviar. We rolled another one and thoroughly enjoyed this good fortune. I was completely amazed by this most honest citizenship displayed by the people of Stockholm, and I called my little journalista and apologized for doubting her understanding of the Swedish ethic. I swiftly began to plot different ways I could sell my original passport.

We joined a group of avant-garde filmmakers and actors for dinner and were told that the smoked salmon was loaded with saltpeter to lower the sex urges of the local citizenry. They talked about many other things, but I was caught up by the saltpeter theory in a major way. It seemed very unusual. They all might have been putting me on, but I was not going to take any chances.

Copenhagen turned out to be a just-business stop. No fun and games. Too much saltpeter. The avant-garde types were far too serious and intent on talking forever about the theory of filmmaking and looked strangely at me when I asked further about the saltpeter thing. All Oates and I wanted was a little hit-and-run. No big thing.

The failure of my first marriage weighed heavy on my heart and mind, even though it was mostly my fault. Yet a little touch could give me shelter from the storm.

Hamburg, West Germany, was our next stop. Lots of history and slivovitz. Too much slivovitz. Oates and I carried each other to our rooms several times. One of us would carry the other for twenty feet or so, and then both of us would crash in the hall, laughing hysterically. Then the other would take on the responsibility for the next twenty feet, and so on. Just a little touch would have been so much better for both of us. Hamburg was famous for its sexual proclivity, but it was all pay-per-view stuff and didn't fit into the program. Not that hit-and-run touch was elevated to a higher morality than loving a prostitute. But there sure was a lot better chance at romance.

After our tour in Hamburg was finished, we hopped a plane to Stuttgart. Two German TV crews stepped on board the same flight. They were packing their guns, and I was their target. They were very concerned that I was about to buy a 300SEL 6.3 Mercedes, and both news teams knew that was the only reason I was stopping in Stuttgart.

"Peter! This is the car of a burghermeister! You must not buy this kind of car!"

"I suppose that you feel I should buy a Citroën Deux-Chevaux," I snapped back.

"Yes! Yes! Absolutely!" Both teams were longhairs, young and radical.

"Why are you working for the fascist German media?" I replied. "Why aren't you working for some underground rag and shooting abstract German art films? Next thing, you'll be telling me what kind of bed I should sleep in . . . or what kind of film I should make, or what kind of dog I should own!" Hey! I was there to buy the fastest production sedan in the world.

Getting off the plane in Stuttgart was incredible. Mr. O, myself, and two news teams complete with 16mm sound cameras and lights. My hair was well down below my shoulders, and my beard was full and blond and red and brown; I was wearing jeans and a cowboy shirt and carrying saddlebags, with a skunkskin hat that still had a faint aroma jammed on my head.

A small group of men, all wearing dark suits and white shirts, were scanning the deplaning passengers. They looked like they were with IBM, but I knew that they were there for me. From their point of view, I was not the person they were waiting for. They were expecting an American burghermeister. By the name of Peter Vonda. That was how the papers were for the car. Their screwup, not mine. But it would prove to be a major problem for me later. Oates and I were singing, "Oh Lord, won't you buy me a Mercedes-Benz," and the news teams were grinding away as I came up to the four stooges. Now, you have to understand, the papers said Mr. Vonda. Und you know how dose Chermans are about your *paypahs.*

"I'm the one for the car." They looked past me, around me, over me. Not one bit of eye contact.

"Excuse me, boys," said Oates. "Do you all have a car for Mr. Fonda, here?" Oates, unlike me, looked very dapper, so they decided to respond to him.

"Vee haf a Daimler for a Mr. Vonda." They were all separated from each other at birth.

"That would be me," I said.

"You are Mr. Vonda?"

"Not really."

"Vell, deez paypahs are for a Mr. Vonda."

"Well, I have a bill of sale here for a 1971 6.3. Let's see if the numbers match." This was all getting too far out of hand, what with the TV cameras and the four stooges. I wanted to be out of there and on my way to Munich. I turned to the TV crews and asked them vat I should do next. They immediately turned the cameras on the stooges and explained that the car *was* for me. Didn't they recognize Peter Fonda? *Easy Rider?* Captain America? They took the bill of sale and my passport and huddled for a few seconds. Cameras grinding away. And after a while, they turned to me with utterly humorless faces.

"Here are your paypahs for za Daimler, Mr. Vonda." They were not going to give it up. Mr. O and I threw our bags into the trunk and sped off with the news crews in hot pursuit. However, I was at the wheel of the fastest four-door in za vorld!

In the car with us was the man who had dubbed my voice in German for *ER* two years earlier. A big blond Viking, laughing so hard there were tears in his eyes. He guided us on to the right autobahn for a quick sprint to Munich.

"I think you ought to slow it down a bit, pal!" Oates hissed. His lips were stuck to his gums in a fixed grin.

"Fuck, Horny, that's what this movie's all about." I bumped it up a few more miles per hour.

"I'd better smoke some shit, then." Oates knew what to do.

"Ja! Ja!" Said the Viking, and he produced a joint. The hip Germans had no problem with papers. They'd roll up a joint with them. The tour was finally getting into gear: 130 mph plus and smooth as a limousine. And mellow.

· · ·

We screened the film and did our press duties. I did my laundry. Three days later, Warren and I shot out of town on our way to Arnhem, the Netherlands. Just a few dikes away from Amsterdam, where the Family Fonda spent two hundred years in exile from Italy. It was in the afternoon, and we really had to skate. We blew off many Porsches, several Jags, and a Citroën-Maserati.

I spent my nonpromoting moments at the local Benz shop. We had discovered that the 6.3 used up a lot of oil. A quart every five hundred miles. I began calling the car "Janis," after the singer of the song we were singing when we picked it up in Stuttgart. And after the well-known drinking habit Janis Joplin had. I can't believe it had anything to do with the constant high-speed driving that was my natural choice. The car was an "executive-used" factory car and had already been broken in.

Next stop was Brussels. We had success there with the film. Oates had some touch, and as always, we were advised not to cross the border with France carrying any contraband. I continued to try and fathom Janis's drinking problem. I got a chance to do my laundry, and we were on the road again, booking it down to Paris.

Paris was something that Oates was constantly dreaming about. I figured that he must have met a cutie there at some earlier romp through Europe.

"Hey! Mister! Give me a five-klic warning before the border, okay?"

"Yeah, well if you'd slow it down a bit, I might be able to do that . . . Listen, you don't plan to just chuck all the shit out the window, do you?"

"Give me a better idea, Warren."

"Well, shit! I'm going to smoke as much as I can, Flyer." Oates called me The PF Flyer from time to time.

"You do that thing, mister, just remember the five-klic warning!"

"Well, if we pull off the road now, you can give me a few village names to look for."

"Age wins out over beauty once again, Oates. This is me pulling off the road." We dropped the speed and pulled off the road next to some beautiful old trees.

Soon the interior of the car was filled with smoke. I was under the hood checking the oil, and as I looked back at the car I could hardly see Oates. It was a very funny sight. And just then, the passenger door flew open, belching out a ton of smoke and a coughing, wheezing Worn Outs. He was laughing, or trying to laugh at the same time and fell to his knees.

"Greed raises its ugly head, Oates!"

"Well now, goddammit, Flyer, I just don't see throwing the rest of this shit out the window. It's just plain unfair!" He wheezed and coughed and sputtered his way through this speech, still on his knees.

"I don't think it's my high-speed approach to life that's going to take you out, Warren. It's dope-greed and cigarettes."

"No need to lecture me, Flyer!"

"Well, take a look at yourself, Warren. You're on your knees begging for some relief."

"And look at yourself, Fonda. You and your oil-addicted, fastest fucking four-door. Shit! You've got to stop every hour to check the goddamn oil!"

"That's precisely why I have to drive so fast . . . Got to make up for the downtime."

"Oh! That's terrific reasoning! Fucking brilliant, man!"

"Give yourself a few minutes, Ornery. You'll feel a whole lot better." I found the name of a town that was about six klics from the French border and made Oates repeat its name out loud several times to be sure he would remember it through the fog of the pot. I cracked one of the rear windows to let the smoke out of the interior and

cranked Janis up to a hundred. The higher speed would help evacu-
ate the purple haze.

We came into a little town square that was crammed with big
freight trucks and a bunch of burly men shouting at each other.

"What the hell do you suppose they're up to?" Warren asked.

"Looks like they're on strike or something." There was one lonely
policeman standing with his hands on his hips with all the truck drivers yelling at him. As the burghermeister Benz pulled up, he turned
to us and waved us on. We drove on out of the little village and I
wondered how anything got done in Europe. Someone was always
striking for something.

"Better start looking for our drop zone, mister."

"Better slow it down so I can *see* the fucking drop zone!"

"I never should have brought you along, mister; all you do is
gripe!" Of course, I never would have had any fun without Oates.
Never would have done the film without him. Never would have
done that trip without him. We loved being bad together, being good
together, being together. I miss him. I had many more movies to do
with him. Much more life. We did two more films before he coughed
up the Big One.

I began to notice a few French plates on some of the cars parked
along the road. I pointed this fact out to Oates as proof of our nearing
the border and the inevitable sacrifice of the sacred substance.

"Maybe we'll see some poor hippie and bring joy to his life."

"Maybe." But I was seeing more and more Frog plates and cars.

Soon, all I was seeing were French cars. "I don't like the looks of
this one bit."

"Of what?" Oates croaked.

"Too many Frog cars, man! I'm going to ask at the next town where
the border is." After a few more minutes of high speed, I brought
Janis to a dead stop along the road.

"What's up, Flyer?"

"Forget the drop zone, man. We went through the border back
where the trucks and cop were!"

"Maybe they have a secondary checkpoint down the road."

"This is not Mexico, Warren."

"You bet!"

"You bet."

"I wonder how we could have missed the whole thing?"

"Maybe we're stupid, Horny."

"Oh . . ."

Paris was looming large . . . we could see the top of the Eiffel Tower, and Oates seemed to take on a new persona.

"You holding out on me, Warren?"

"What do you mean, skipper?"

"Have you got some touch stashed in Paree, pal?"

"Are you kidding? This is the first time I've been to Gay Paree, man."

"How the fuck could you come to Europe and *not* see Paris?"

"First time I've ever been to Europe, Harry!" Harry was the name of my character in *The Hired Hand* and Arch was Warren's.

I began to understand why Oates was so upset with the high-speed run we were making. Every time I'd say, "look at that, man!" he would watch whatever sight I was speaking of rapidly disappearing in the rear window. I felt quite bad that I was so insensitive to not know this was a first for Warren. I immediately slowed Janis down and became as much of a tour guide as possible. I knew a good deal about Paris, and I showed Oates all the sights I could. He was very grateful and rewarded me with a case of Dom. Very generous.

We were in Paris for five days. Five days of fun and games. Except for the Cinematheque. An SRO house did not necessarily mean a good house. Or a friendly house. After the screening, we went on stage to do a Q and A. There were many comments on the number of dissolves and the slow pace of the film. I responded that things in 1881 did not move very fast. Days didn't pass much faster than the sun did across the sky. Riding a horse was not at all like driving a 6.3 on the Autoroute. Living life was a slow process. They were displeased with the film for all the wrong reasons.

It only hurt for a short time. For we had a case of Dom and some touch. No matter how slow the *Hand* was, most of the French press took time to tell me how much they liked the film and Mister Oates's performance. They raved about Verna Bloom, as well they should have.

Aside from the toads at the Cinematheque, the press gave us very high marks, and they printed all the thoughts I had on the mess the World was making for itself. Most of the angst that others of my generation had about the Vietnam War was not the way I chose to express my disgust with the policies of my government. I was very opposed to the war, but I chose to use it as the extreme example of the pollution that humans brought to their planet.

As always, others would approach me on the streets, in restaurants, anywhere, and pass grass or hash on to me. I never really had to take any stuff with me. Someone would always say to me, "Here! You must try some of mine!" In this way the French were as generous as everyone else. And so, after doing in Paris as the Parisians did, Mister O and I headed on down the road with renewed vigor and a fresh stash. Zurich was our next stop, and we were both in for a surprise.

There was a mutual friend of ours in Zurich: the strikingly beautiful Eurasian actress Greta Chi. We looked forward to seeing her again, as we knew she had her finger on the best-looking women in Switzerland, and we hoped for a grand party with the cream of the crop.

After the PR was done, Owatays (another name for my coconspirator) and I were ready to find Greta and have some fun.

We hooked up with Greta, and along with her boyfriend and two outstanding young women, we went to the boyfriend's villa just outside Zurich and had a party. His family was away (he was a little bit younger that the rest of us) and we had the run of the villa. In the basement, he had built a small discotheque with all the right equipment, and we partied there for a while. Naturally, I had my twelve-string and brought it along. When we weren't dancing to the disco tunes, I pulled out the guitar and played and sang a few songs. This activity settled the problem of who was going to be with me or Warts. The blond enjoyed Horny's dapperness, and the dark-haired beauty took a shine to me.

After a while, it was time to head back to the city and our hotel. Reluctantly, we gathered out in the driveway of the villa, and holding my new friend Alex, I asked her to come back to my suite. She said that it would not be allowed to bring her to the suite, but I insisted that it was fine, as we had a two-bedroom suite and that would make it all perfect. As we kissed out in the drive, she said that the rules were different in Switzerland, and we began to kiss quite passionately, forgetting the others.

I recall hearing Oates saying, "Lets get a move on, Flyer! It's getting late." But I was getting more and more passionate and she was reciprocating. I recall hearing the 6.3 fire up, but I was not able to break away from the wonderful moment. It was filled with romance!

Suddenly we were hit by something just below the knees. It

knocked us down, and I did my best to take the fall so that the passionate Alex would not hit the pavement. When we realized what had happened, we were both still holding each other. Only by this time, the differential of the 6.3 was just next to our heads. Someone was yelling at someone. Oates, in a move designed to get things rolling, had backed up over Alex and me. Fortunately, in trying to break the fall so that Alex would not be hurt, our legs and arms were tightly entwined and did not get crushed by the wheels. And, yes, I did say, "That was quite a kiss!" But I meant it.

I hollered up at Oates to put the car in "park" and pull the white knob that was just below the speedometer. Slowly, the hydraulic suspension raised the car four inches and put Alex and myself in a little less doom-impending position. I then told Oates to pull forward, slowly. With much asking if we were all right and directing the car forward, Alex and I continued our passion. Nothing was going to end this night early for either of us.

When we arrived at our hotel, I discovered that the girls were right. No dice. No guests in the suite.

Alex whispered to me that we should go to her apartment, and we took that option. It seemed that Mr. O had his act under control, so Alex, Janis, and I sped off to her nest.

"My boyfriend is a gangster," she said as we let ourselves into her place . . . Ahhhh-ha, dangerous love . . . I saw many photos of her gangster boyfriend. Sure enough, there was no doubt. He *was* definitely a gangster.

"Why on earth would a woman as beautiful and smart as you take up with a gangster?"

"It keeps the creeps away."

"Didn't stop me for a minute!"

"You're not a creep."

"Lots of guys aren't creeps."

"Lots of guys don't pick up a guitar and sing such beautiful songs to a woman like me. And even through all that silly hair on your face, I can see the sweetness in your eyes."

For the next several days, I came very close to shaving "all that silly hair" from my face.

Mr. O and I had both bought timepieces while in Switzerland. Mr. O was very frugal in a demented way and was determined to take advantage of the tax refund when exiting the country. Oates explained that one would never get ahead in the financial world if one didn't take advantage of every money-saving move.

It was getting late in the day as we approached the Swiss-Italian border. The border-check place was being rebuilt, so there was a bit of confusion. Very Italian. We pulled up to the border guard and presented or little tax refund slips. This was a major mistake. Although I spoke Italian, the border guard was not going to be fooled for a minute by these suspicious banditos. He took the papers into a little hut for some confab with his superiors. When he returned, he told us to pull the 6.3 over. We did. We waited for a long while. Too long.

A bit annoyed, I decided to make a dramatic move. I pulled out the little lever that raised the car four inches.

"What are you up to, Flyer?" Oates was in for a surprise. I pulled the Benz around the back of the building and out over the construction area. At a fairly fast speed, I whipped and dodged through the area and doubled back to the approach lanes. This time the same border guard came out to see us. Same guy, same car, same us. Only this time, when we were asked if we had anything to declare, I said no, and we were waved on through. We pumped the speed back to one hundred plus and hightailed it to Milan.

Oates and I did our thing with the press for the next two days.

We screened the film for a very dressy critics' group. It was called Circa de Stampa. Kind of like critics' circle. The audience was very eager to see the film, and the "circle" was headed by the local Catholic cardinal and the head of the local Communist Party. The evening was going fine until the third reel. It was out of focus on the screen. It wasn't shot out of focus. In fact, everything on the shoot was tack sharp. I waited for a few moments to see if the projectionist would refocus. As both projectors had been used for the first two reels and were in focus, I couldn't understand why it was suddenly out of focus. I finally went up to the booth. The projectionist said, over and over again, that it was the film, not the projector. I jumped on the lens and failed to get focus. It *was* the film, but, as I said, the camera neg was sharp as a tack.

This batch of five reels had been processed at the Technicolor Laboratory in London. There went my chance for a prize from the Circa de Stampa. You can count on the fact that I was very pissed off.

Oates and I left Milan the next day and headed for Rome. Ah,

Rome. We were blasting down the autostrada at blistering speeds. I was ranting like a madman about the focus fiasco, and Oates was feeling the same way. As both of us were ranting away, we shot across the Po River. The Fonda family had started, as a "family", in the Po River valley, south and east of Genoa, in the twelfth century. Air brakes, full flaps, hard stop. I explained to Oates what it was all about as we backed up to the bridge. We walked out over the river and looked down on its flowing waters. The water was not flowing . . . For that matter, it didn't really look like water. I took out an aluminum Italian coin and flipped it over my left shoulder telling O-wat-tays that it would bring good fortune. As the coin flipped through the air, Oates asked if the good fortune was for the river or us. When the coin landed in the river, it stayed flat on the surface. We watched as it oozed along slowly under the bridge, still on the surface. So much for the family seat.

We had arranged with my sister Pan to meet us at a certain exit, and we followed her to her villa in Porto Santo Stefano. It was great to see her and visit her beautiful country home. We got smashed on her home-pressed wine and sang songs. When she put her children to bed, before we had dinner, I watched as she put them in their pajamas. The cooing and cuddling, the smells, the tone of her voice . . . the everything of the moment . . . I was transported back to my own early childhood. I clearly heard the same sounds and cooing that our own mother made when she got Jane and me ready for bed. It was eerie. It was perfect. Oates and I blew a number and crashed soundly in the guest rooms for a long and needed sleep.

The film thing in Rome was a special screening of *The Hired Hand* for the David de Donatello committee. This is the Italian equivalent to the Oscars in the United States. The screening was set up in the best small theater in Rome, and I went in praying for a perfect print. My brother-in-law's father was on the committee, and I was hoping for a favorable reaction. I also wanted to make my sister proud of me. The lights dimmed and the film began. The beautiful opening sequence was greeted with many oohs and ahs. Things were going better than I could hope for . . . and then, along came the third reel, even more out of focus than it had been in Milan. Dammit! There went my chances at a good European prize for this fine film. I began to get really paranoid. Many phone calls to Technicolor London. Many threats. I think I suggested that having so many chemicals around was a potential disaster. I recall saying that the entire lab could suddenly become part of the atmosphere.

I spent the press interviews railing against the way the people of the world were destroying their planet. I didn't speak about the film. I was so embarrassed. It had been perceived that I had shot out of focus on purpose. An attempt to be artistically different. I had been betrayed by my own industry. There could be no other explanation. Universal Pictures and Technicolor had both claimed that the prints had been checked and were of the best quality. I *knew* that this had not been done. Had Columbia's extreme dislike for me, Bert Schneider, and *ER* been passed on to the other major studios?

I arranged for the 6.3 to be shipped from Rome to the United States, and, with a heavy heart, flew from Rome to London for the opening of *The Hired Hand*.

Just before Oates and I checked out of the hotel in Rome, we had a phone call from three women in Munich who wanted to meet us in London at the Dorchester. We arranged for a car to pick them up in London and left for the airport. I was full of anger and despair. The film was to be screened for the British press at nine o'clock the next morning, and I had no way of knowing if the print was okay. I was stunned that the screening was at 9:00 A.M. This is not a good time to view and critique *any* film. More paranoia.

When Mister Oates and I arrived at the Dorchester, I was in a froth. Oates suggested that I relax with the girls, while he went to screen the movie. He said it would be better for me. I looked at the girls and agreed. The four of us frolicked with caviar and champagne. We were disturbed by Mr. O, when he returned. Returned much too early, by my reckoning. He burst into the bedroom and asked me to come to his room for a moment. I asked him if he had watched the film at high speed, explaining that it was very difficult to check for focus at high speed. He told me to sit down, have a puff and a sip. His advice was not making me feel optimistic.

"Bubba Bear," he said, "it is no longer a question of focus. The entire third reel has been printed so light, that the only way I could tell that it was our movie was the soundtrack, which was perfect." Visions of conspiracy flooded my life.

After many conversations with Technicolor and Universal, I felt that we had come to an agreement (on threat of sure death and destruction). Thankfully, the screening was canceled (because of technical problems) and would be held the following afternoon. Fortunately, a new print was sent and it was perfect. Universal Pictures had done their very best to ruin the film's European release. But in Great Britain we were voted the "Best Film from Any Source" by Films and Filming for 1971. The little victories.

. . .

Oates and I returned to the States and continued life in a more normal fashion. Our Mr. Toad's Wild Ride had been an incredible journey, for sure, but we both had work to start or finish, as in my case. Time to get heavy into the editing process of *Idaho Transfer*. Referring to my sexual needs, Susan told me to get a girlfriend. There were many, but it didn't make my home any happier. I was so frightened about losing the children.

I poured myself into the editing, and when things got too strained, I would leave for a week on the ship. There were many scripts that came to the office. Only a few were interesting and demanded a new approach to filming. But independent money was always tight and full of many restrictions. By this time I'd joined the Director's Guild of America, and its lowest allowable fees and contingencies made it virtually impossible to direct a low-budget or experimental film. I had been snared by the Establishment, and they were not going to give me or any other young filmmaker the chance to broaden our abilities. Too much "by-the-book" and rules that had no real application to independent shooters.

One afternoon, I decided to pay an unannounced visit to my dad's place in Bel Air. My take was: if this is the family home, I should be able to come and go as I please, so long as it isn't in the middle of the night. I drove up to the house and saw some extra vehicles. Company. Undaunted, I walked around to the patio off the library and came upon my dad, his accountants, an attorney, and Shirlee in conference in the library. A conference about his future money management. I walked on in and sat in one of the chairs. I had interrupted their meeting, but played it as if nothing big was going down. I don't remember how the subject came up, but soon I was being reprimanded for my attitude about the consumption of pot. The "elders" were telling me that just because I didn't agree with the law, it wasn't right that I break it. Laws were laws for specific reasons. The gauntlet had been thrown at my feet. Not being one to cow to abstract law, I stepped right up to the plate.

"Hold on a moment, guys. Law is law in your eyes, and breaking it has no just reason. Now, in the State of California, there is a law that prohibits oral copulation, but you men see that law as moral and arbitrary and choose to ignore its existence."

"What is oral copulation, Peter?" Shirlee asked. Oh, thank you, thank you, thank you, Shirlee. What a perfect straight man you were.

"Oral copulation is when a woman sucks on a man's joint or vice versa. And these gentlemen find *that* a moral and arbitrary law that really has no meaning to their conduct. In other words, they choose to break that law because of their concept of it. Moral and arbitrary and not applicable to them. I find that the laws governing the use of marijuana are moral and arbitrary, and therefore hold no real weight in the rules and regulations of human conduct. I just suck on a different joint, Shirlee. It's that simple."

All the men stared at the ground, very embarrassed by the exposé of their own disregard for the "law."

"When you can see the same defiance of the state and its arbitrary rules that you all eagerly dream of breaking, you should see the same defiance that I practice." I got up and left the house, having scored so many points in the debate of right and wrong that I would never again hear about it.

In early February, I left for location to shoot *Two People* in Morocco with Susan. We were going to give our relationship a final chance. But things deteriorated during rehearsals to the point that we could not get it back. Susan left while I was out rehearsing, and when I came home, the room seemed like a mausoleum. I wanted to change rooms, but there were none available. Four days after she had gone, we started filming, and I celebrated my thirty-second birthday. Celebrate isn't really the word, but the company gave me a party. I spent the night with Lindsay Wagner. No sex, but I couldn't be alone. Being alone has always been a difficult thing for me. It was not a happy time off the set. But on the set was wonderful.

·   ·   ·

Four weeks into the filming, we were in Paris, shooting nights and sleeping during the day. I awoke in the middle of my "night" with my right big toe hurting so badly, it was as if a spike were being hammered into it. Out of nowhere. I had had no earlier indication that there was a problem with my toes, so I just lived with it. It wasn't constant, and it usually happened late in my sleep pattern. During this same time, I was awakened by a call from my sister Jane. I was kind of groggy from some pain pill a French doctor had prescribed for me, but I knew it was Jane, and I remember what she said. She told me that if she were Susan, she would stab me in the back with a big knife. I began to object, but remembered it was Jane, and there was no way to change her mind on the phone. I would have taken this comment from her very badly, but I knew she didn't realize the circumstances of the dissolution of the marriage. She never asked.

Recently, while we were going over some old family photos, we came across a picture of Susan and me at our wedding. Jane asked me why I had married so young. I told her I was madly in love and afraid to be alone. I never would have lasted if I had been alone at that time in the life. I would have lost it completely or committed suicide. Yes, I see, she said.

When I returned to L.A. in June of 1972, knowing I would have to be able to see the children during this sad period, I sent for the ship to return to Marina del Rey.

I wanted the boat back in Los Angeles, as I knew I would not be staying at the house, and needed my own nest and a place for the children to be with me in an easy way. A woman I had taken to Hawaii in January of that year came to stay with me on the yacht, and I was comforted by not being alone. The rest of the cast and crew didn't like her very much, but it took me a while to come to grips with my situation.

When the yacht came back to Marina del Rey, we got our old end tie. We also got a very bad reception. Feds were climbing all over the ship as soon as we tied up. The cast and crew on that voyage was all male. Thirteen guys. After fifteen days at sea, eating mostly Dinty Moore stew, the cast and crew were not a bunch to fuck with, but the feds hadn't figured that out. They were going through everyone's underwear and generally ransacking the ship. Poncho Pollack sat in the helmsman's seat telling them to suck his dick. Bill Crawford—"BC"—finally decided that the whole thing was absurd and went to the phone, saying he was going to call the lawyers. At the mention of the word, the coppers left at once. What a bunch of dickheads. They were obviously not kosher with their search, and did not want to deal with my attorneys. They were also probably trying to get back at us for the public humiliation they had suffered in their attempt to take me down in Lahaina the year before.

chapter Twenty

I spent the summer sailing in the Channel Islands, and finishing the editing of *Idaho Transfer*. Thanksgiving was spent with the children in the Channel Islands. It was a sad time for me, but I never let on to Bridget and Justin, who were now eight and six.

That fall, Jane married political activist Tom Hayden. I went to their wedding full of trepidation. Because of their activism and anti–Vietnam War policies (they had gone to North Vietnam, and Jane had been photographed smiling while sitting in an antiaircraft bunker surrounded by commies), I had received several phone threats at my office that the wedding would be stopped with physical harm to Jane. I would not let that happen, even though I dissaproved of the anti-U.S. propaganda with the photo and her broadcasts to the American troops that were just short of betraying her country. She was my sister. I arranged to have the house where the wedding was to take place surrounded by many of my friends, armed and ready to protect her from any attack. She was unaware of this, and when she reads this it may be the first time. I never trusted Tom. I always felt he used her and abused her. But it was her life, not mine, and I stood by her as they exchanged vows.

I had Christmas on the ship in the marina. The darkness of winter added to the darkness of my life. My girlfriend betrayed me badly. I should have kicked her off the ship. Maybe I was punishing myself for what I had done to my little family. Earlier in the year, after I had returned from filming *Two People*, I went to the house to explain to Bridget and Justin that I would not be living there anymore. It is the most difficult thing I have ever done. Justin grabbed my arm and bit into it, showing his anger and despair, pleading with me not to go. And though we kiss and hug hello each time we see one another, and we kiss and hug good-bye each time we part now, the pain of that whole time remains in my heart.

The children were told that I was leaving their mom for another woman. There wasn't "another woman"; I doubted there would be for a long time. I was leaving Susan because there was no more "us" in the marriage. We were unformed when we married, both needing something, and we didn't form together. But maintaining a life together for the sake of the children would have been an even greater mistake. At least we had these two beautiful children we put on the planet. Sometimes, at night, I would weep, begging for a way to mend the tear I had made in the cloth of their fairy-tale beginnings.

Papers for divorce were filed in the latter part of '72. I was thirty-two and Susan was thirty. On February 2, 1973, my attorneys advised me that Marvin Mitchelson was representing my wife, and he was going to come down to the boat and assess it. According to Mitchelson, I was hiding two million dollars from her. I shot right back saying that when he found it, I'd love to have half. He's doing time now, or maybe he's out. You, dear reader, get the point, I'm sure. I had offered Susan a very fair amount in alimony, plus three thousand a month in child support *and* all medical and dental expenses. Each time I went to pick up or drop off the children, my bitchy girlfriend gave me grief. She would sulk and wonder if I had had sex with Susan. Well, of course I wanted to—Susan is a very sexy woman—but it was not happening. And I was not about to let Mitchelson come on board *Tatoosh*.

On the morning of February 3, 1973, there was ice on the dock. I had started to quickly assemble a crew the day before, and we spent most of the day shopping at the Boys Market in the marina, stocking the ship. We sailed to San Diego, where we waited for some more cast and crew to join us, while Bob Eichelberger and I went to the Mexican Consulate to get papers for our voyage. Ike—as we all called him—was my first mate. I had met him while sailing in Hawaii.

As we left San Diego, we had eight people in the cast and crew.

Jeff Hooper was our naviguesser. Mike Malone, Poncho Pollack, Ike, Ray White, myself, Gail Herren—Ike's girlfriend and the ship's cook—and my girlfriend.

Our first stop was Scammons Lagoon, the first place the California gray whale comes to calve and mate. I am particularly interested in this whale, as there are no known fossils, and it is the only species of its family. Getting into the lagoon was difficult, but we finally made it. That night was very restless for all of us. The ship was booming like a big bass drum. We figured it was our anchor dragging over some rocks, so we arranged an anchor watch, using the lights from another ship in the lagoon and our perception of the shore as references.

The next morning, we dove on the anchor and found only sand. We had not moved at all during the night. Not even swung on our chain. Why the big booming, then? No quick answers. We watched the whales from the yacht and planned an adventure ashore. That night, the booming started again, and we were all on deck, bewildered. Suddenly there was a big whooshing sound just ahead of the bow. It was a whale blowing. The booming, we soon discovered, was the whales scratching themselves on our anchor chain. So cool.

The *next* morning, having slept well to the whales playing bass, we were approached by a brand-new baby gray, who was sticking his head out of the water, turning it from side to side to look at us. We all gathered at the boarding ladder and waved at it. Quickly, its mother came and grabbed it by its lateral fin and pulled it away. While we were diving on the anchor in the murky water, we noticed the outline of the ship as we rose to the surface. We did look a bit like a whale with two little babies behind it. The babies, of course, were our rubber dinghies.

We spent days out in the lagoon watching the whales mate, calve, and cavort. We got into the inflatable dinghies, and the whales came right up to us and slid beneath the little boats. Some of us jumped over the side to get pictures in the murky water; others stayed on the boats trying to get their assholes to loosen up. It was fairly intimidating to see an enormous creature fluking right before us.

Once, the people who were on the other vessel—it looked like a science vessel—came up to our yacht and demanded to know who had given us permission to come into the lagoon. They were quite jealous that the whales were playing about our ship and around our little boats and staying away from them. I came out of the main hatch sporting my two stainless-steel Smith & Wesson model 60 "Chiefs Special" .38s with consecutive serial numbers. They had been presented to me by Smith & Wesson

"I did," I said, "and I'm the captain of this ship, and my word is law. If you're going to complain, you should stop running your goddam one-ten generator all night and day. You idiots are disturbing the dance!"

"You can't talk to us like that!" they replied.

"The hell I can't!" I said with my best Duke Wayne voice, and they puttered away, never to bother us again.

I found many shells on the long curving beaches that were on the ocean side of the lagoon. Most of the shells were cockleshells; scalloplike. They had been pierced by some sea animal right at their hinges, and some of them had perfect holes surrounded by shell. I made cereal spoons and soup spoons for Bridget and Justin, using driftwood for the handles, wrapping them with multicolored thread, and varnishing them with many coats. A sort of Swiss Family Robinson thing. A definite lure for their little minds to come away with me on my magic ship of fools.

We continued on our way down the coast to Puerto Magdalena, where we tried to find a port captain to sign our papers. This was the law in Mexico. One must report to the port captain when one makes first landfall to get his *firma* on one's documents. Finally some old geezer wandered out of a hut, but he had no idea what the fuck we were talking about. No one had ever reported in at Puerto Magdalena before. But after we gave him some boxes of .22s and a *Playboy,* he gave us his *firma,* and we were off to the tropics: 23°26.5' north and south of the equator. We put a small boat ashore when we spotted a banana grove, and brought aboard two stalks, hanging them from the roll bar—the stainless-steel bar that went from side to side of the cockpit and had the boom crotch on its top. We were preparing for the tropic party in the Club Cho Cho, a.k.a. the cockpit. At 0100 hours, the log reads: *quackers, cognac, pot & Little Richard 23°26.5'!!!* I have always been a firm believer in an accurate log.

We stayed in Cabo San Lucas for two weeks, mending sails and other maintenance plus water sports. I flew to Los Angeles for three days, right after my thirty-third birthday. When I returned, we sailed to Mazatlán. We caught two mahimahi as we neared the mainland.

When we made the harbor at Mazatlán, we had a great fresh fish breakfast. We stayed in the harbor for several weeks. John Wayne was in the harbor aboard *Wild Goose*. We needed to repair some things on the Caterpillar, and he had the means aboard his ship. His skipper was very helpful.

His son, Ethan, came over to our yacht and went water-skiing and surfing behind our inflatable Pirelli motorboat. Ethan was on our ship so much, the Duke wanted to come aboard to see the cast and crew. By chance, I had found a pamphlet from the John Birch Society and brought it aboard. When I saw the Duke coming alongside *Tatoosh,* I placed the pamphlet on the chart table, in plain view. The Duke and I spent time walking from the forecastle to my stateroom as he told me more wonderful stories about the old days with Dad and the gang, and some pretty grisly ones about John Ford and his terrible alcoholism. On one pass by the chart table, he noticed the pamphlet, picked it up, and made a very agreeable sound, then went on walking and talking.

On several of my many trips to L.A., the Duke was on the same flight and asked me to sit with him. I enjoyed his company, and felt that he didn't have many people to gab to like he did with me. He liked the way I called my shipmates "the cast and crew." Very movie-set talk. I reminded him of the drive up to the location of the fort in *Fort Apache*. The color of his Caddy convertible with its leather seats. The set and all the dust and horses. The way Ward Bond would sigh a big "aahhh" after a tall glass of orange juice. The way the men all hung together. The clearing of the "south forty" and the fire-baked potatoes. He was amazed at my ability to remember all the little details. I think it gave him a touchstone to the times gone by and made them all childlike and full of wonder.

He was a fine man in my company. The great American hero as an aging man, and still full of the qualities that made the country adore him. Although he was of a very different political bent than I, somewhere deep in the childlike soul of all actors, we shared a little of the pirate in all men who travel the great waters. I will always remember his big wonderful self laughing as he remembered life. I think he was always ashamed of the way he treated Dad in the McCarthy days. He and Bond called Dad a pinko, which hurt Dad very much.

· · ·

I had to go to New York City on a press tour for *Two People*. While there, I bought two female Abyssinian cats. When I returned to Mazatlán, I had the cats and a bag full of cat food and other staples we needed. The cats were a big hit with the cast and crew, thank goodness. It is a great responsibility to take care of two animals aboard a ship, but everyone loved the two of them. They kept the ship free of flies at the expense of the fitted, wonderful curtains in the main salon. They could jump so far and fast as they chased the flies, bouncing off the windows and grabbing the flies in their paws and scarfing them right down.

After a maddening delay while the Mexician officials went through our papers, we finally sailed from Maztlán the next morning, cats and all, for San Blas.

There are a couple of good breaks off San Blas, and we hoped to get a little surfing in. I went into town and booked a suite at the best hotel. My girlfriend and I showered, and I arranged for the ship's laundry to be done. We cruised the main plaza and bought some fresh fruit and other goodies. We stood out quite a bit. Not many gringos came to town in those days. Most of the cast and crew stayed in the town. Last time I saw them they were playing dice in the plaza. I went back to the yacht, put up the whiskey staysail, and cazhed out in the warm afternoon.

For some inexplicable reason, I sat up off the cushions in the cockpit and scanned the shore. I saw two of the cast and crew waving frantically at the ship. Because of the shallow waters, we had anchored out quite a way. I jumped in one of the little boats and gunned it for the shore. The news was not good. Most of the men in the cast and crew had been jailed for gambling in the square. It was a totally bogus thing. The boys had been playing craps among themselves with tiny little dice they found at a *mercado* stall. Some locals wanted to play the game, but the locals had different rules than the boys. "Cheating!" was being yelled as the police approached, and the boys had been taken to jail. None of the locals suffered the same consequence, so I figured it had been a setup.

With my limited but useful knowledge of Spanish, and the help of Gail, I located an attorney who would take the case. She was very capable and agreed that it was most likely a setup. She could do nothing until after siesta time, so the girls and I grabbed the laundry and raced back to the ship with Jeff, the only mate that had been inside the jail and was allowed to leave.

I grabbed a wad of pesos and dollars, and we started to plan the breakout. I put together a sack of seal bombs and simulators, wire cutters and rope and dumped it in the shore boat. I felt that I should go back in, check out of the hotel, pay the attorney with extra for a grease job, and get out of town fast. The word was out that I was there, and I saw no reason to give the officials any other hook to put in us. Even though *Easy Rider* had not been allowed to play in Mexico—that would come six years later—I had done enough films that had played well in the country to be recognized. In that sense, I was an added target. Our plan was to break our mates out during a festival in the square that evening, if all else failed. I raced back in, did the business, and shot back to *Tatoosh*.

We knew that the top of the inner court of the jail was covered with a slightly thicker chicken wire than normal, but no one ever had gone out the top. It was an impossible climb, hence the rope, a nice thick long one, and the wire cutters. Poncho, Ray, Mike Malone, and Ike were the mates in the slammer. Jeff Hooper, I, and the four girls were on the outside. Jeff and Gail went back to see what could be done. If it required a breakout, I would go back with Jeff and get them out, while the gals stayed aboard.

As Jeff and Gail went back ashore, I weighed anchor. My girlfriend kept watch with the binocs. Finally, we spotted the gang as they ran down the beach to the speedy little inflatable boat. The lawyer had prevailed in a sense. She had bought a few minutes for an escape. As soon as they were on their way, five or six men ran down the beach after them. I could see the other guys asking for a boat. There were several pulled up on the sand. They made a connection and started out after our people. But they weren't nearly as fast. We made ready the boarding ladder, and picked them up as we were under way.

We sailed on down the coast to Puerto Vallarta, where we spent many days. We began a plan to sail from Puerto Vallarta to Maui in early June. We needed a few things from the States that couldn't be found in PV, so I phoned Bill Hayward and asked him to drive down to PV with some provisions. Thankfully, he agreed. We needed canned goods and other staples and . . . kitty litter. He was on his way. We also needed an extra hand or two for the crossing, as it would be a much longer one than we had ever done. I sent for John

Haeberlin, who was very willing to take the cruise, and a stuntwoman friend of mine had a boyfriend named Spookie, who would make up a full crew.

Bill arrived, finally, quite wired on blackbirds. His journey to PV was most incredible. He had all the things we needed stuffed into his '72 BMW 20002 tii. A small two-door coupe, but very fast. He was jacked up enough to tell us the details, as we tried to calm him down with some excellent pot, thanks to our local pals.

When Bill crossed the border at Mexicali, there were no problems. But twelve miles or so into Mexico, there was another checkpoint. This time Bill had to get out of the car and open the trunk. So far, no problem, thought Bill. In the trunk were our foodstuffs, canned goods, and three large bags of kitty litter. When asked what was in the large bags, Bill said kitty litter. This was not in the Spanish-to-English dictionary. One of the guards slit open a bag. Most of us know what kitty litter is, but not at this checkpoint. In those days, Mexican authorities made a big thing about stopping gringos from bringing drugs into their country. No one was *ever* bringing drugs into Mexico. We were getting our drugs *from* Mexico.

As Bill explained what kitty litter was for, the guards knew they had a hot one. In their Mexican minds, no one would put stuff in large sacks for cats to shit in and market it. They were sure they were onto a big drug haul, so they emptied Bill's trunk. When they came across a small black Halliburton case—the same one I had used in the purchase of the ship from Cranston Pascal—they demanded that he unlock it. It contained most of my best knife collection—around twenty thousand dollars' worth, an extra body for my Nikon F, and, for some forgotten reason, a clip to a Colt .25 caliber semiautomatic pistol. That did it. Where's the gun, they demanded. Bill, of course, had no idea. I remember, today, exactly where it was. In a shrink's office in Sherman Oaks, California. I was very suicidal and broke down during a session in which I was trying to learn how to stop smoking and eat more, and admitted that I was not very stable and gave him the gun. It had been Stormy's.

They took out the backseat and found two shotguns, two high-powered rifles, and a number of pistols, among them, Tom Mix. This is when the shit hits the fan, in Mexican law. They couldn't find the pistol that went with the clip, and that drove them crazy. While they were getting frantic about the missing pistol, Bill was figuring out who Mister Big was in the group. When he spotted the head guy, Bill went over to him and asked for a private moment while showing him the captain of the Santa Fe Police badge and official ID card.

Mister Big took Bill into his office, and they had a chat. Bill told the dude that he was very embarrassed about the weapons, as he knew it was against the law. He went on to explain that he always carried his weapons under the backseat to protect them, and he had simply forgot they were there; he really *was* on his way to PV to deliver some charts and foodstuffs to his friend, who was sailing to Hawaii in a few days; the stuff in the bags was really for cats to go to the bathroom, and there were two cats on board the yacht about to take a twenty-day sail to the islands who would need this special odor-eliminating granular litter. It was essential for the cats and the people on board. Mister Big ran a check on the badge and police ID. The answer came back that it was a real badge issued to William Hayward, who *was* a captain on the Santa Fe force. Bill had done his number like one cop talking to another. It worked. I will grant you reciprocation, Mister Big said, but he would have to hold the weapons until Bill returned— except for the knives—and let Bill go on his way. Far out. But when I thought of that word "reciprocation," I wondered how many Mexicans are running around with guns and badges in the United States.

When we left Puerto Vallarta, we had a cast and crew of nine people. Seven guys and two gals. But we didn't have enough water. We altered our sailing plan and charted a course for Cabo San Lucas, where we could get water right from the shore. The water in Baja California is sweet and pure right out of the ground, and the fellow who owned a restaurant-bar and trailer court had a very long hose. Really long. But a storm was building off the southern Mexico coast, and we had to leave sooner than we'd planned.

We left Cabo with less than six hundred gallons of water. Less than half our capacity. After Ike busted my girlfriend washing her hair— which was beautiful—he turned off the water to all the heads. I con-curred with his decision, and all hands were put on freshwater rations. We told the cast and crew that we had only three hundred gallons. Barely enough to get us to Hawaii. Sixteen days after we left Puerto Vallarta, we arrived off Kaanapali at noon.

During those sixteen days, I realized that I was in a ruinous rela-tionship. I was hiding aboard my own ship. My girlfriend made dis-paraging remarks about my smoking pot, even though she was loaded on pills quite often. I awoke to reality one afternoon, smoking a joint with John Haeberlin. I looked at John and said that I was owner and master of the vessel, but I was hiding from my girlfriend while I smoked a joint. It was bullshit. No kidding, agreed John. It was a destructive relationship. But I put off ending it.

As we approached the Big Island, I called the Coast Guard and informed them that I was a U.S.-documented vessel making landfall from Mexico. They requested that I report to the harbor at Kahului. I answered back that I was making landfall at Lahaina. They insisted on Kahului. As was my right, I told them I was picking up my mooring in the Lahaina Roadstead, and would await a customs officer before I let anyone ashore.

We waited for quite a while. But I figured on that. We were most concerned about the cats. Hawaiian law forbids animals to come ashore until they have been in quarantine for six weeks. Liberty and Shada were not going to spend six weeks in the care of some underpaid quasi-vet. These two fine Abyssinian cats were worth one thousand bucks a piece! Most times, when strangers came aboard, the cats would hide and check things out before they showed themselves.

After an hour and a half, a man came out on a small skiff and climbed aboard, very uncertain. He was a real customs agent, but he was very uncomfortable. We showed him all our passports and allowed him to check our reefers, freezer, and stowage, and said we had nothing to declare. As he was going over our papers and passports on the chart table, Liberty and Shada were racing around the decks, having freed themselves from my stateroom's head. The course of their grand prix took them right through the deadeyes that ringed the front of the main salon and, therefore, right in front of, around, and over the customs agent. He asked about the cats and I told him they had been on the boat before it left for the mainland, in '72, and would remain aboard for more than six weeks before we put the yacht in a slip or at a dock. He was satisfied with our declarations and papers, told us to dispose of the few remaining foodstuffs, and asked to be let off the vessel as soon as could be arranged. He was getting very seasick. Transportation was summoned at once.

While all this stuff was going on in Lahaina, Bill was going to get my guns back from the Mexican authorities. The boogie had been arranged by our favorite attorney, Arthur Berman. We had to pay ten thousand dollars to the Minister of the Interior, and sign official papers promising that we would never try to invade Mexico again. Far out!

After I had been in the islands for a month, I got a call from my agent to come to L.A. and meet about a movie with John Hough directing. The movie was basically a stunt film with cars, but the white trash character I was going to play was really great. I met with the director in a bar on Vine Street, just north of Hollywood Boulevard. After a successful meeting we went out to our cars, in a lot across the street. There were three men lagging quarters at a yellow line in the lot. I fished a quarter from my pocket and joined the game. When I left the game, I had three dollars in quarters and the director was thrilled with the character I was developing as we spoke.

While in L.A. to meet John Hough, I spent as much time as I could with Justin and Bridget. Whenever I was in L.A., I carried a pager with me that the children could use to reach me wherever I might be. The three of us were down near Marina del Rey in a rented car when the pager went off for the first and last time. I went to a phone and called for my message. It was Jane, and the number rang in her room at the hospital where she had just given birth to her son, Troy. I teased her that she had made the baby come early just to negate my prediction that it would be a boy, and it would be born on July 9.

Tatoosh was back in Lahaina and things were fairly cool. I had flown to L.A. to pick up Bridget and Justin, but they were gone. In Mexico, I was told. It was my visitation time with them, and I was not going to let it pass. I let Susan know that I was coming to Mexico City to pick up the children and I wanted them to be at the airport when I arrived. I knew it was one of Susan's mother's tricks, and there was no way I was letting it go. She reluctantly brought them to me, and we left for Hawaii.

We spent the rest of the summer having water sports on the yacht. We entered the Oahu–to–Hanalei Bay race in July. The sponsoring yacht clubs begrudgingly let us participate. It is an eighteen-hour race from the A buoy off the Ala Wai to Hanalei Bay, Kauai. We had done the race in '71. We raced well this time, and actually finished in the silver.

We repaired the damage to the sails and other rigging. There was always something to repair on the yacht, even if we were just at anchor. Especially if we were in a slip. At the time, we hadn't been able to get a large slip at the Ala Wai yacht basin, so when the yacht came back to the Ala Wai, we rafted up to the *Louise*, a seagoing tug that belonged to Peter Aerpoff, owner of the only small boatyard in the Ala Wai. Twice the privacy from the law. One must get permission from Aerpoff to board *his* boat, before one can ask to come aboard *Tatoosh*. After the repairs, we sailed on down to Lahaina for more water sports, softball, and water balloon fights. Bridget and Justin had a grand time. We prepared for the big Labor Day race. First, we signed up all the best sailors and surfers. This race was going to count heavy.

Since we had been doing this race, starting in the last group and crossing the line first, we had never been recognized. We knew all about the jealousies that run through the self-styled upper-crust yachtees and their clubs. The International Ocean Racing Association had refused to measure *Tatoosh,* and banned us to the Pacific Handicap Class. But we had shown that we were superior sailors, being the first to finish in all but one race. In recognition of the yacht's consistent performance, Louis Abrams, the winner of the first Trans Pac, donated his trophy to the Lahaina Yacht Club for the first mono-hull to finish the Labor Day race. Louis liked the spunk and perseverance of the cast and crew, and promised us that we would finish in the silver through the grant of the trophy. According to the rules of the IORA, we would have to start a day earlier to actually win the race. After we had won our first Abrams Cup, the Hawaii Yacht Club began to recognize us and our superior crews and yacht.

We finished the race and the summer fun. I had to return the children to their mother and prepare my next motion picture, *Dirty Mary Crazy Larry*. Someone had to pay for all the fun and toys.

I arrived in Stockton, California, in mid-September, and ensconced myself in the local Holiday Inn.

As I met the different members of the crew, I was warmly greeted. Our first assistant director, Ron Schwary, was a gas, as were the rest of the office crew. I met the second assistant, Steve Lim. I knew that this at least would be a fun shoot. There were two brothers from the electrical department who were young and energetic, and everyone was happy to be working with me. All the young new people in independent production anywhere were always saying how happy they were to know me. I was perceived as sort of a beacon in the dark for the young independents, though I never felt that I had the kind of expertise to be *any*body's leader or mentor. There had been independents long before I came into the business. It was more like my independence happened at a time when young filmmakers were working their butts off to make a standard B formula film, but had an avant-garde script in their back pockets that no one would finance.

I had met Adam Roarke, who was costarring in this movie, at one of the screenings we had to find an ace cameraman for *Easy Rider*. He sat at the back of the screening room and stayed aloof at the gathering for drinks afterward. We spoke three words. I thought he was one of those L.A. actors who wasn't going to like me at any cost.

When we met again on the set, it was like two dogs sniffing at each other's ass as they turned in a cautious circle. I knew we had to get a really big thing going to be able to put some characters together on the screen that would hold the story together in the theaters. It took us five minutes, and we were the best of buddies. We made silent oaths of brothers forever, and though we seldom saw one another after the filming, I was his silent friend for life. He died of a heart attack recently.

Some of the days were very hot, and the crew would bitch about it just a little. One afternoon, Adam and I were released early and went back to the hotel. As soon as the driver left, we jumped into my new 3.0 CS BMW and went to buy a bunch of balloons. We filled them all up and lugged them out to the front sign, in wastepaper baskets. When the bus with the crew slowed down to turn into the hotel, we let loose a barrage of water balloons in the open windows of the bus. It was a complete surprise to the crew, who took it very gracefully, but ambushed both of us later in the walkways, drenching us with water balloons of their own and anything else that would hold water.

At the end of the shoot, Adam and I had to do a retake on some shots. Adam seemed nervous the whole day, but he didn't know why, or he wouldn't tell me. When the shot was finished, I turned around to John Hough and asked him how he was going to cut the piece into the film. While I talked to John, a very large pie hit me right in the face, as did one to Adam. Suddenly, pies were flying at the two of us from every corner. At least fifty pies. After the pies came the deluge. A hundred or more water balloons. Adam and I were rolling in the dirt, laughing our hearts out. It was the nicest thing that our wonderful crew could have done. Drenched and covered with frosting and whipped cream, we tried to give a farewell hug to all our mates as they ran from us. We didn't take the dried cake and frosting off for quite awhile. We gloried in it all.

Not everything was fun during the shoot. I came back to my room after a shooting day and found my girlfriend curled up in bed, and my twelve-string guitar stabbed nineteen times with one of my Randalls. The knife was still in the guitar when I entered the room. I pulled it out, sat down on the edge of the bed, and played Stephen Stills's "Change Partners." It had a very different sound, that moment. My girlfriend mumbled to stop singing the song. I said to stop stabbing my guitar, and stop trying to fuck with my head.

Dirty Mary Crazy Larry was a big hit in the movie houses, outgrossing *ER,* for a while. People went four or five times to see it. I can only imagine that it was the impenetrable bond between Adam, Susan George, the lead actress, and me that caught the audience.

Five days after I finished shooting *DMCL,* I flew to Spain to start shooting my next film, *Open Season,* starring John Phillip Law, Richard Lynch, myself, and Bill Holden. I had a grand time shooting that film, also. My friend and Oscar-winning costume designer, Dick Bruno, helped me get costumed in two days, during my layover in Los Angeles. I spent as much time as possible with my children.

Thanksgiving, Christmas, and New Year's were spent in Madrid. Dad sent a telegram wishing me a merry Christmas and a happy New Year. It was the best present I received. My girlfriend was barred from the set because of her jealousy. I agreed.

When I was on my way back to L.A., I asked Maj Hagman to arrange a house on the beach for me and the children. She found one two houses down the beach from her fabulous place. It was like a family, as our children had grown up together. Bruce Langhorne stopped by several times, as did Roger McGuinn, and we sang and played for the kids. We had a second Christmas. I was so happy to be with them. As soon as I had to give them back, I left for the sanctuary of the yacht.

I flew back to L.A. to loop *DMCL* for five days—lots of interior car stuff—and returned to the yacht for further R and R. David Crosby was there with his beautiful John Alden schooner *Mayan,* and we went diving together off the southern part of Lanai. We went to a place the locals called Cathedrals. It was a long finger of lava that had an enormous cavern with holes to let the light stream in. One could sit on different shelves and relax with the view of many beautifully colored fish swimming in and out of the cavern. When we returned, everyone crashed on the sun-warmed decks. Later, Crosby played many songs for us. We visited him often on his yacht.

In early April, Bill Hayward, Ted Markland—one of the actors on *The Hired Hand*—and his girlfriend Debbie joined David Welker, Conrad Bagly, Bob Eichelberger, Gail Herren, my girlfriend, and me for a sail to the Big Island and a cruise down its western shore.

We stayed at Cook's Cove for several days. On a Saturday, a few kids came out to the cove in small speedboats to picnic and dive. All the people went diving except for one young woman. We, of course, had been eyeing her from the shade of the whiskey staysail in the cockpit. She swam out to the boat and pulled herself up onto the boarding ladder. She was very pretty. She asked nicely if she could come on board to look at the boat. I wanted her to, immediately, as did all the males aboard, but remembering that hell-hath-no was festering in my darkened stateroom, I had to tell the pretty that the yacht was my house, and it wouldn't be right for people to come walking through my house. What an idiot I was. All the guys agreed with that description.

I went up to the sail bags on the foredeck and crashed out in the sun. After a while, I heard some footsteps approaching and a shadow loomed over me.

"I suppose you wanted to fuck her!" It was my girlfriend. "Well? Did you? Did you want to fuck her?"

I looked up, shielding my eyes, and said, "You bet." I thought for a moment, then continued, "I am leaving tomorrow or the next day. I want you off the ship with all your belongings by next Thursday. I'll have a ticket waiting for you at the airport to take you back to the mainland. And I do not want to talk about it for even a second."

"You can't just, you know, just . . ."

"I could throw you off the boat right now, with all your stuff, and you could swim ashore and ask that girl if *she* wanted to fuck me. Not another word!" Did it! No pain, all gain. I felt fabulous. I was free from the daily moods and meanness. I was in charge of my life and my yacht.

From the ship's log:

Capt. Cookout to Eatenalive Kiluealohaha 12 April '74

Remarks: (in Ted's hand) *Capt. High recovering after Gail's Birthday Party. Took lobotomy pill—*

Fell out! Capt. America is looking good. Big party tonight!
(Aloha Party) YAHOO!
Benson and Murdock were caught doing sodomy in the
Foc'sle!

Bill, Ted, Debbie, and I flew out of Kailua Kona the next afternoon with a nice aloha from the cast and crew, minus one. We had to wait for our private plane to Honolulu for an hour at the landing field on the Parker Ranch. A *Hawaii Five-O* episode was being shot at the airport. And lo and behold, there was Leslie Nielsen, my friend from the *New Breed* days. One of the truly funny men in our business. We flew on to Honolulu and our flight back to the mainland. The farther I got from the destructive relationship with my ex-girlfriend, the better I felt.

I spent a week or so doing business in L.A. We had sold *Idaho Transfer* to Cinemation, and they were developing a release plan, but before I was going out to promote the film, I took the children back to the yacht for their spring break. We had fun and water sports.

Having the children with me aboard the yacht, sailing around in eighty-two-degree clear Pacific waters, was how I had pictured my life so many years earlier. It meant so much to me. I knew that they felt better about me without my ex-girlfriend. The yacht was more of a family thing for them. They didn't like her. Didn't trust her. I should have acted so much sooner, if only for their sakes.

We flew back to the mainland, and I went to work promoting *Idaho*. On the last leg of the tour, in Chapel Hill, North Carolina, during a live early morning television show, I noticed a young English professor from the nearby college eyeing me. I was paranoid at once, thinking he was gay and going to make a pass at me. Sure enough, at the end of the show he came up to me and handed me a small novel, saying that I was the only one who should make the book into a movie. He was not gay, but he was certain of his mission. A mission that would change my life completely. The novel was *Ninety-two in the Shade* by Thomas McGuane, and on the flight back to L.A., I read the book twice. I could have shot the movie using only the book, it was so visual and hysterically funny. As soon as I landed, I called Bill Hayward and told him to buy the rights, if it was possible. "I'm bringing the book to your house right away," I said, "but start the clock on getting the rights, now."

Bill read the book in three hours. I think he read it twice. He agreed with me, and we both knew we were onto something, if the rights were still available. We were really excited. Two days later, we learned that Elliott Kastner had the rights, but Bill encouraged me to chase the role. I had to return to the yacht, *molto pronto,* because it was coming out of the water for its yearly haulout. Much paint, varnish, sanding, and sweat. Before I left, I got McGuane's phone number in Montana. I knew that no one had been picked to direct or act, and McGuane was writing the script, so I decided to lobby Tom by phone.

Every night, after a hot day's work with paint and varnish, I went to a nearby pay phone and called Thomas McGuane. Most times, I forgot the three-hour difference in time zones. So at nine-thirty or ten, Hawaiian time, it was twelve-thirty or one in the morning in Montana. Each call was answered by a cheerful woman's voice, no matter the time.

Sometimes, the wonderfully bubbly voice told me he was at the guest house. I assumed the guest house was, probably, only a few hundred feet from the main house. Much later, I learned The Guest House was a motel in town. I called ten or fifteen times, sometimes reaching McGuane and sometimes not. I wasn't making a lot of headway with him, as I told him I was the right person for the part. Finally, after the fifteenth call, I decided to make a full break for the goal.

"Okay, Tom, maybe you don't like my on-screen style or even my way of acting, which is your prerogative, but if you don't cast Warren Oates in the part of Nichol Dance, you're a fool." Pretty heady remarks for a man wanting a job.

"Well, as a matter of fact, Oates is sitting across the table from me as we speak!" Tom laughed.

"Then, there it is, Tom. If there needs to be a sign about my being right for the role, you have just seen it." He agreed to meet me in L.A. before the part was cast. A hearing. That's all I wanted. A person-to-person hearing.

I knew that Dad, who was sixty-nine, living in Bel Air, and looking for work, was coming to Kauai to visit his good friend Jim Garner, who was filming on the Hanalei side. The cast and crew thought it would be a grand thing to take him sailing, something he had never done on *Tatoosh.* We sailed up to Kaui, leaving the Ala Wai before midnight, which put us on the north coast in the early afternoon. We sailed as close to shore as possible, and could see the movie company shooting. I hoped that Dad would look out to sea and get a glimpse of us sailing by. We pulled into Hanalei Bay and dove on our mooring.

I made contact with Dad and arranged to pick him up at the pier at a certain time. The yacht was spiffed, as we had just completed the haul-out and topsides, and we were all pretty buffed from the work. We picked up Dad, his wife, Shirlee, and Jim's wife, Lois, in the morning. Jim, who was a friend of mine, too, couldn't come because of the shoot, but he was at the pier to shake hands. I think he was concerned about Lois's safety, also. Lois and Shirlee were not thrilled with the idea of sailing out into the ocean, but they both insisted on coming. Lois was there for Shirlee's sake.

We had the sails rigged on the foredeck ready to go up. The mainsail was raised, and as soon as it was full, we let the mooring float go and fell off to port on a starboard tack, putting up the heavy genny as we moved. I thought that it would impress Dad to watch us sail this eighty-two-foot ship off the mooring without the Cat on. It showed confidence in our own abilities and a knowledge of the anchorage. Remember, Dad was an Eagle Scout *and* a Scoutmaster.

Tatoosh sailed out of the bay heading north on a starboard beam reach. The main was in its first reef and the mizzen was not used. This configuration was the easiest to handle and the most comfortable sailing. It was a pristine day. We sailed on this tack for several hours. Dad spent much of the time on the afterdeck watching the lures being let out and talking fishing with Ike and BC. I asked him several times if he would like to take the helm, but he shrugged me off.

Finally, I decided to make him take the wheel. I had been seated behind the wheel with my feet resting on the brass rim. The sails were balanced so well that I didn't really have to steer. Lois and Shirlee were both in the cockpit along with David Welker, and hadn't noticed that my hands were off the wheel. I got up and began to climb out of the cockpit, and Shirlee became very nervous. She asked me who's going to steer, and I told her that Dad was, as soon as I could get his attention.

I turned to Welker and issued one of the few commands I ever made, telling him *not* to touch the wheel. Shirlee was on the verge of hysterics. When I got to Dad, I told him that his wife was very afraid about no one at the helm and asked him to help me out by manning the wheel. Reluctantly, he went to the cockpit and took the helm.

Forty-five seconds later, he was in his element. We got an old CAT ball cap and presented it to him along with a can of beer. Perfect. He held the wheel and smiled so wide that it made me feel great.

Shirlee had been hinting that she felt seasick, and when I offered to help her with some compazine, Lois snapped that I was going to give her drugs. Of course. Compazine is a drug that is given to heart patients before they go under the knife. Its specific use is to remedy the urge to vomit. I had them in suppository form, so the recipient wouldn't chuck up the medication. Logic. But even with her husband at the helm, Shirlee insisted on the seasick thing. Dad was right there to see the game, but he didn't say a thing. When she became crazed, I suggested that we come about. Dad said that someone should man the helm, and I said that he *was* manning it very well and to come about on my command. Everyone stood their stations and I called to come about. Dad turned the wheel perfectly as we tacked the head-sail and main. The maneuver was first-rate, and when I asked him how it felt to man the helm during the tacking, he replied that it beat the shit out of steering a Destroyer. Shirlee stopped complaining as soon as we came about.

Kauai had disappeared from the horizon long before we tacked. I think that fact had something to do with Shirlee's problem. She had been a stewardess for years and had never complained about motion sickness. This was my one chance to share the wonder of *Tatoosh* with my dad, and she was putting a big wet blanket on it. Oh well. We sailed back on the same course. We had bagged one mahimahi, so the outing was otherwise complete. I took the helm as we approached the bay and sailed the ship right up to the mooring. BC picked it up just as the yacht stalled into the wind. The sails were dropped at once, and we all cheered. We had left the mooring under sail only and had picked it back up, six hours later, without turning on the engine. Dad noticed that, and I could feel his approval, though he said nothing. It didn't matter, you know. What a gas!

When *Tatoosh* sailed back to Lahaina on the fourteenth of June, 1974, I flew to L.A. to meet with McGuane. We met at the Beverly Hills Hotel for breakfast. This was not a part of my routine. I wasn't into business at the Beverly Hills Hotel. Tom and I had eggs Benedict, and he eyed my shortish hair, which I'd cut for the movie in Spain, as I eyed his long ponytail. I watched him carefully as we ate. He was interested in my sailing. He was a sailor, too, he said. I saw a look I knew very well in his eyes. After we finished our meeting, he was going to meet Sam Peckinpah as a possible director. I knew Sam well. We were friends, but I knew he might cast Kristofferson in the role. I had to blunt the force of the meeting quickly.

"Tom, do you want to direct the film?" I knew the answer before I asked. "Do you?"

"Well, yes. I do."

"If I tell you yes, you can direct, you'll get at least a mil and a half on my yes. But if I tell you yes, you have to promise me something."

"What would that be?" He asked.

"When you want to cut the camera on any scene, you have to promise me that you will count to ten, and, then, if you still want to cut the roll, do so."

"Why should I count to ten?"

"Because, when you've heard the actors finish speaking your words, you will think the scene is over and call for a cut. But if you count to ten, you will see what actors do with their characters. It might be a pause and turn, a beat, a look back, something . . . that is what actors do. The scene doesn't necessarily end with the last word out of an actor's mouth. It's talking *and* walking. That's what we do, and you must give us the chance to fill the moment." He gave me an odd look, but promised he would follow my suggestions. Had I looked a little deeper into his eyes, I would have seen his real desire. But I landed the part. The two of us had a similar funny take on the Establishment and our parents, I woud find out later.

I even had to lobby Warren Oates's agent, because we were basically working for nothing. It was Warren's daughter, Jennifer, who came to my rescue. Warren had been given a thriller script to take to me for the two of us. Warren wasn't really interested, but Jennifer said it was a very scary script. I read it, saw the possibilities, and asked for a large fee and piece of the profits. I also said that Warren had to have the same deal. It was his biggest paycheck to that point in his career. It helped both of us work for very little in *Ninety-two in the Shade,* as we knew that we were going to be employed right after we finished Tom's film. Always a pleasant thing for any actor.

Back to the tropics. I started to grow a beard as soon as I landed the job in *Ninety-two in the Shade.* I couldn't get the children until later in the summer, so it was day sailing and water sports aboard the yacht. It was also a summer of freedom for me in Lahaina. *All* the wives and girlfriends of my island pals were happy I was out of the darkness of my previous relationship. They encouraged me to have as much fun with the ladies as possible. It was a true summer of love.

I rode around the town on my eighteen-speed bike. Although it was a very expensive bicycle, I had aged it down incredibly—with the help of the salt water. It looked so ratty that no one would steal it. I often went to the houses of my Lahaina ladies and showered or just hung out.

One day, I went to shower at one of the homes and found that the ladies had been out in the cane fields picking the shade leaves off the pot plants that their old men had planted much earlier. The guys would start the plants in small containers, and when they were big enough, they would be replanted in the cane fields. Nobody could see them as they grew tall and healthy. At a certain time, the gals would go out to the fields and tend to the plants by picking off the shade leaves so the buds would grow bigger. The gals would come home with large garbage bags filled with shade leaves and reduce them to butter. The butter was used to make gingerbread man cookies. The gals gave me a gingerbread-man and advised me not to eat more than an arm or leg at a time.

The cookies tasted terrific, and I ate an arm and a head before I realized it. Later, as I biked back to town, I began to notice how narrow the streets were. Especially Front Street. I wondered how the tour buses could pass each other. Then, I started to wonder how cars could fit in this *really* narrow street. When I was rescued, I was leaning up against the side of the Maui Belle, holding my bike in my arms as if to keep out of the way of the murderous vehicles. I was rescued by one of the gals, who reminded me about the one-arm-at-a-time rule.

One night I was at a restaurant with the whole cast and crew. The hostess was an exotic and beautiful young woman. Tall, blond, perfectly slanted blue-green eyes and a knockout bod. I looked at her and told her I didn't have a leg to stand on. Upon which, I took one of my legs and kicked the other out from under myself, falling to the floor. A perfect pratfall. She blushed, and I melted. The other eight members of the cast and crew picked me up and carried me to our table. I was smitten. Word went out at once for further info on the girl. I could hardly eat.

David Welker had hooked up with a cute blond, and announced

that his date was the hostess's roommate. I asked her to invite her friend to the yacht for water sports the next day. The roommate told me she was with her boyfriend. I said bring him along, by all means. He wouldn't stand a chance on board, I figured—and I figured right. Two days later, he was gone, and she and I were inseparable. It was the talk of the fishy little sleeping village. Everyone was very happy for me.

I was even more happy. Her name was Martha, but everyone called her Martee. I chartered the yacht to some pretty hip Euro-trash types for a week, and stayed with Martee and her roommate. No problem. I was concerned about the charter, but distracted by Martee. It was the first time I had chartered the yacht. Rules of the road in chartering forbade me to be on board.

Martee's father sent her a telegram saying to keep away from me, because I was a commie. She knew I wasn't. I flew back to the mainland to pick up the children.

On August 17, I was back on my yacht, with my two beautiful children aboard. We set sail from the Ala Wai to Lahaina. When the children awakened, we were on our mooring in the roadstead. Our days were filled with water sports. We powered up to Kaanapali or down to Makena Beach. In the evenings, we watched the cat races. Our Abbysinians liked to frolic after dark, and would race each other around the decks. We could sit in the main salon with the sex lights on (this is what I called the indirect lighting in the main salon) and watch Shada and Liberty race around. Sometimes, late at night, I would hear the cats running on the decks. And sometimes I would hear a plop or two in the water. In the morning, we would find the two Abbys, looking like drowned rats, in one of the rubber gigs tied to the stern pulpit. They always had a pissed-off look, as if to say, why the fuck haven't you awakened earlier and taken us back on board? The Abbys loved to swim.

We went up to the top of Haleakala and drove to the Seven Sacred Pools. It was a *National Geographic* paradise vacation. We played softball games, and the kids of the Lahaina ladies came and picnicked with us, so Bridget and Justin could play with kids their own age.

I made a decision that Martee would not stay overnight. That was difficult, but I wanted the children to feel they had me to themselves. I watched how Martee was with them, and how they were with her. I was getting too serious about our relationship. She was quite a bit younger than I, but I saw by the way she treated the kids that she could be a good mother. I could also see that she was serious about me, and she wanted to have children of her own. This was a major problem for me. I had two perfect children already, and I did not want to have more. I needed to put the pieces of my own family back together. Needed to concentrate on Justin and Bridget, who were now eight and ten, and heal the wounds of the broken home. It would not be fair for me to ask Martee not to have children, but I wanted to be with her, all the time. We were good together. Had good times. Great sex. I was in a big dilemma.

The Labor Day race was coming up, and all the girls and boys who were, in one way or another, part of the cast and crew signed on for the race. We were going for the Louis Abrams Perpetual. The *big* silver. Conrad Bagly was a top-ranked sailor in the SORC, as were several other members of the cast and crew. We cadged the top guns who were in Maui. Some flew down from Oahu. To many, *Tatoosh* looked like a big motor sailer, but we unofficially held the fastest time from Lahaina to Ala Wai, beating even George Walker's *Flying Cloud*. Our crew included Bill Crawford (BC), David Hudson, Howard Cooney, Floyd Christenson, Jon Payne, Steve Elkins, Jay Lester, Steve Clark, Jamie Somers, and Annie Haley, a former top model for Vogue. David Welker, Barry Hilton, Poncho Pollack, Jeff Hooper, Annie Henderson, Betsey Cooney, Gail Herren, Diane Hudson, Jim Lindersmith, Samoan Tony, Billy Shaunerd, and many more completed the group.

We always had a large cast and crew for the Labor Day race, something no other boat would carry. Most skippers were into as light a crew and as few friends as possible. We needed many hands on the foredeck, changing foresails and handling the spinnaker, the running backstays, the main sheet, and the main halyard, the mizzen, the mizzen staysail, the four prototype Barient 30 winches on the after cabin trunk, the wheel and centerboard. We also had the wives and girl-friends or boyfriends of all the deck mates. Big Annie, as we called Annie Haley for her height, could take any deck position. She was a top Hawaiian canoe racer. We also put out four or five fishing lines on the race. When we caught fish, the ladies would make sashimi and serve it on the main cabin top. Had to have our instant protein hit. I had Martee come the day before and spend the prep night on the yacht with me. Lucky me. Actually, for this particular race, almost everyone was on the yacht by midnight.

Once again, we were handicapped in the Pacific Handicap Class. We started last. As we sailed by the committee boat to announce our boat, everyone in the cast and crew stood naked on the deck. Everyone except Justin, Bridget, and Martee. Little Richard and Jerry Lee Lewis on the speakers woke us in the early morning. I gave my usual prerace pep talk: An accurate log is essential, (we never logged a race) and we are not trying to beat anyone. We are all going to sail the ship to the A buoy off Ala Wai in the most efficient way possible. Which means we are going to beat every boat in the race!

We did. We picked up the Big Silver. Thanks to Louis Abrams and our incredible cast and crew.

When I left Martee, I felt terrible. I was falling for her, and I knew she was in love with me. I had not been able to tell her that our love was forever just out of reach. I couldn't have a new child. I needed to put all my efforts into mending the broken family I had created.

chapter *Twenty-one*

After the race, I had to return the children and get to work on *Ninety-two In The Shade.* I bought two more Abyssinian female kittens, for unexplainable reasons, and took them with me to Florida. The film's location was Key West. I had let my hair and beard grow long and, before I left, put a shit pile of henna tea in both. In other words, I had red hair and a flaming red beard. I drove the 3.0 BMW to Florida with the cats, a nonspill water dish, and a small litter box.

My ex-girlfriend, who had been a very good secretary, needed two more months working for the Pando Company in order to qualify for unemployment benefits, so I brought her down to Key West to cook for me and do the company's correspondence. I didn't object to a little sex, either, but it was a begrudging relationship. No problem for me. But most of the crew and cast of the film thought I was slightly out of balance, putting up with her trips. What did I care? I was dreaming of Martee and the impossibilities.

When I arrived, I was given directions to my half of a rented duplex, and told that everyone was meeting at the Bird Cage, a small local bar around the corner from my quarters. As I made my way to the Bird Cage, I passed some people on the street. With my flaming red hair and beard, I was not recognized. I entered the bar and began to meet the others in the company. I noticed Warren Oates at the bar with a tiny but exquisite blond woman. Warren was about to introduce us, but I heard that bubbling voice I had heard so many times when I called McGuane's ranch. This was Tom's wife, Becky. Warren introduced us, and she was just like the voice I had heard when I called McGuane. Becky was completely thrown off by my red hair and beard. She was very infectious. If one is around her for even a little time, one can't get her out of mind easily. And the more time one spends with her, the harder it is to think of anyone else.

My duplex was shared with the director of photography, Michael Butler, and his electrician, Don Wollack. We hit it off perfectly the first time we met. My ex-girlfriend was jealous of every friend I made, but, as I have said, I didn't care.

I buried myself in the motion picture. Tom McGuane, who was directing, had given me some very insightful advice about the part, but when it came time to shoot, he forgot our deal and cut short every scene. But by that time I was working for the director of photography, not Tom. I felt very frustrated by Tom's ignorance or indifference. I was not the director, and didn't want to battle with him. I should have.

Just before we began principal photography, Michael Butler had a party in his half of the duplex. My ex didn't want to be a part of the celebration, so I was alone. At one moment, Tom's wife was standing against the kitchen wall talking with her friends, and I, very much out of character, walked up to her and said, "I don't care what anybody says," and I kissed her, fully. After that outburst, I went back to my side of the house and played guitar. I have no idea where that move came from. It was very unusual for me.

The shoot went on, and I noticed that Tom wasn't paying close attention to his promise or duty. He was after every skirt in town. He was playing the part of the director, and not directing. I didn't realize that he wanted his name in lights.

The shoot wasn't miserable, but it wasn't fulfilling. I did get to know Michael Butler and his crew. They were a tight bunch, and worked faster than any crew I had ever seen. Johnny Black, the key from *Dirty Mary,* was the key dolly grip on *Ninety-two.*

Everyone who was a head on the shoot was looking for some Jamaican grass. I found a source in Miami. I had to cash a check, so Becky went with me to her bank. It was then that I noticed her name on her checks. Portia Crockett McGuane. She is Davy Crockett's great-

great-great-great-granddaughter. I immediately started calling her Portia.

Toward the end of the shoot, we had a scene to film on the water. We had to wait forty-five minutes. Some of the crew went swimming, some fished. I couldn't go in the water, as I had to be on film at any given moment. I grew bored and began to fool with the walkie-talkies. I imitated Miami airport approach control radio conversations.

"Miami approach, this is Delta five five, three five zero, heavy, with Bravo." No response. "Miami approach control, this is Delta five-five, three five zero, heavy with Bravo." No response. One last time, "Miami approach control, this is Delta flight fifty-five, thirty-five thousand feet, heavy with information Bravo, how copy, over?"

"Roger Delta fifty-five, turn right heading one eight zero, maintain two five zero, you are following the Tri Star." Bingo! I had hooked up with someone who knew the routine. I then became Air Cuba, defecting, and Air France, refusing to land at such an American white trash airport. It was a marvelous little radio exchange. But Tom McGuane, wanting all the attention, tried to get in on the gig. He was pitiful. He crashed. I picked up my transmitter and said, "Listen, McGuane, if you're not careful, I'm going to end up with your son *and* your wife!" I was speechless. I was mortified. I dropped the radio like a hot potato. Michael Butler, a few boats away, mouthed the words What are you saying? in shock, as did several other crew members. I couldn't say a thing. I was dumbfounded.

Several weeks earlier, many of us had gone off to an outer key to sunbathe. The adults decided to sun in the nude. Tom's son, Thomas, felt a little embarrassed, so I suggested we walk the beach and look for treasure. He was delighted.

During the shoot, I would drive by the McGuane residence and ring my Bermuda bell in the car or throw a firecracker into his driveway. Thomas always came running, and we went to the White Street pier to fly kites, or went to get some burgers. The first moment I saw Thomas, I knew he was a special person. A very bright person. It was like having my own son with me. After becoming his friend, I learned that he wanted an older brother. In his mind, I fit the bill, but I only acted like an eight-year-old. I told him about my son, Justin, who was fifty-one weeks older than Thomas. We shared many secrets.

On this day of nude sunbathing, I took him walking along the shore of Old Woman Key, looking for treasure. We found a bar of copper from some old generator that had washed ashore. "This is treasure," I told him. He was skeptical. I pointed out that pennies were made of copper, and pennies were money. He accepted the valuation, then looked at me and asked if I loved Justin more than him. "You little shit, how can you ask me something like that?" I said, and he smiled a devilish smile.

As we prepared to round the corner and face the adults. I told Thomas to sit on my shoulders, and we would walk past the adults, totally ignoring them. I told him not to look at them. To pretend they were not there, no matter what they might say, and stay on my shoulders as we walked on into the ocean. I said we would walk past the others, as if they were not there, and continue walking on into the water until we were both completely submerged. He was delighted with the notion, and so we did. As I walked by the others, I was thinking that I would show his mother how a father played with his son. For what reason, I'll never be sure. I had no thoughts of being with his mother, but obviously I was deeply into her. From the get-go, I had thought she was a gold mine.

After finishing the film, I flew back to L.A. with the cats, and David McGiffert—my first assistant on *Idaho*—flew down to Miami to drive my car back. I had to get to L.A. quickly, as I was going to Tokyo for a promotion and needed some time to see my children and catch up with things at Pando. I saw the children, and came down with the flu. Not from the children, though, probably from someone on the plane. On her birthday, I called Portia McGuane to wish her well. I received a letter from her thanking me for my work and help on the movie, before I left for Japan. There seemed to be something written between the lines, and I asked Peter Riches to look at it. He said it was a love letter. I went along with his thought and wondered why she had written it in that vein. I was delighted that she had, though.

Until recently, I thought she had written me that one letter. So did she. But I found four more letters while going through some files for this book.

While I was in Tokyo, I called her in London. I was watching a soccer game that was broadcast live from England. She was in London with Thomas, visiting Tom during the editing process. The actress Margot Kidder was with Tom, also, feigning pregnancy. A cheap trick, but one that would be my saving grace.

I returned to L.A. and a little beach house Maj Hagman had arranged for me to rent that Chirstmas. I got to see my children for Christmas. We spent Christmas Eve at Norton Simon and Jennifer Jones's beach house. Norton had a fondness for Justin. The entire Hollywood A-list was at the party. After they had all left, only family was there. Bobby Walker and his three children, Brooke Hayward and her brother, Bill and me and Bridget and Justin. I remember saying to Bill that marriage was not in the stars for me. I told him I figured that the rest of my life with women would be great sex and meaningless relationships. "You bet," he said. I yelped, "I didn't want to hear that." "Then you shouldn't have asked," he replied. That was early in the morning of December twenty-fifth. Justin was fast asleep in Norton's arms.

I could only have the children for a few days, because Susan and Bill Tennant, a former agent of mine and then an executive with Polygram, were going to get married and wanted the kids with them. They didn't get married, and I had only four days with Bridget and Justin. Another cheap trick. Martee, my girlfriend from Hawaii, came to the house often, thankfully. I finished whatever had to be done at Pando, and took off for San Antonio, Texas, to begin filming *Race with the Devil,* the thriller Oates had brought to me.

Less than a week into it, Warren told me that Tom and Becky were getting divorced. I ran to the constable who was assigned to our shoot. He was cool. I asked if I could use his highway radio phone, telling him I had a charge number. When I reached her, I told her that it was not a good thing to be alone right then. I told her to pack some warm clothes and come up to San Antonio. She accepted, and I went into full alert. I asked the constable which hotel was the finest in San Antonio and arranged for the best room. Then, with the help of the constable, his wife, and more than likely several other cops' wives, I bought every yellow rose in the city and surrounding area. They were all delivered to the suite, and I placed them on most of the flat surfaces in the room, the bathroom, in the drawers. The room was literally covered with yellow roses. A yellow rose means loyalty. Add that to the mix of the yellow rose of Texas, Davy and the Alamo, and my eight-year-old heart, and you might just get near to the feeling I had when the limo arrived on the set at night on the nineteenth of January.

After we wrapped, Portia and I rode back to the hotel with Warren in his motor home. We all called it the Roach Coach. We necked like two teenagers. When we got to the room, I felt like a virgin, not sure what to do. Things obviously worked out as they should have. I was fully blissed. Portia went someplace she had never been. The next day, I called Bill and told him that he had been wrong about my marriage prospects. He said I should tell myself that I was wrong. She stayed with me for a few days, then had to get back to her son. It was awful to see her go, but she promised to come back as soon as possible. At least before my birthday. I moved back to the Holiday Inn. She came back to me on Valentine's Day.

She told me that when she arrived the first time, she thought that the boys had stuck her with the swell suite once again. In the past, when her friends and Tom gathered, they would stay in a cheap hotel, book her into a fancy hotel, and charge the whole thing to her. She had all the money. Her grandfather, Lou Crockett, was one of the four founders of Upjohn Pharmaceuticals. The company was a very successful venture, making a big fortune for the founders and their families. Her friends weren't being rude to her; it was just the way they did things. Most of them were writers without much money. She had supported Tom while he was writing and hoping for success.

On my thirty-fifth birthday, Portia Rebecca Crockett gave me her childhood copy of *Stuart Little*. I wept like a baby. It took me quite a while to recover. I had never told *anyone* about my hero, Stuart. It was a deep secret. I was losing altitude rapidly. What kind of person gives a thirty-five-year-old man a children's book for his birthday? And how did she know my deep feelings about *Stuart Little*? I answered myself by saying: the person that you were meant to be with. The person you were born to be with. On the twenty-third of February, 1975, I buried my mother. There would be no more surprises about her life or death that would trouble my heart ever again. I hoped for the same to happen to my sisters.

Portia had to leave again, to take Thomas to his paternal grandfather's funeral. But she came back to me every chance she had. It must have been a little frightening for her, as I was constantly asking her to marry me. Jane told me to lighten up, give her a chance to find her own life. Well, that was exactly what I had in mind for Portia. We talked on the phone all the time, and I bought a small portable typewriter to write my thoughts and send my love in a more concrete way. She wrote me as many letters as I wrote her. Probably more. They are all little gems I have collected in our life.

Most of the shoot was at night, and night shoots are always difficult.

But Warren and I loved working together so much, we hardly noticed. We *did* have to tape signs on our doors that said, in Spanish and English, do not disturb before 4:30 P.M., during the night shooting. We would wrap by 5:00 A.M. or so, and take the drive back to the motel. Portia and I would make love and fall asleep in each other's arms every morning. By the way, she is four feet eleven inches tall, and I am six foot two and a half.

I had been to a gun show in San Antonio several weeks earlier, and had purchased many pistols and knives for my collection. They were stashed in my bedside table. One afternoon, the maids came knocking at two, saying loudly, "Maids! Maids! Maids!" This was why we put the signs up for the entire company, and it wasn't the first time they had ignored the signs. It pissed me off. I took one of Portia's cigarettes, lit it, took a firecracker, and, after igniting the fuse, flicked it out under the metal door. After the bang, I heard the maids laughing and scurrying down the hall. I got back in bed. Less than a minute later, they were back. "Maids! Maids!" Damn! I got up and wrapped two crackers together and flicked them under the door. BANG-BANG! Minutes later, there was a pounding on the door from a man claiming to be the manager. I got up and yelled at him through the door. I told him that my rooms had been paid for and they were, in a sense, my castle. And can't you read the sign on the door? If you pound on my door again, I'll come out and pound on you, asshole.

Sitting on the bed with Portia, I was probably not going to get back to sleep. Goddamn! And way off in the distance, I could hear some sirens.

"I think those are for you, darling."

"You bet."

Within minutes, there was a fierce banging on my door. "Open the door, this is the police!"

"Fuck off, assholes!" Pound! Pound! Pound! Pound! "Stop pounding on my door, dickheads!"

"Open the door, this is the police!" I got up and went to the bolted and chained door and peeped through the little optical device. There were five uniforms just outside the door with their guns drawn and cocked. The uniforms were an almost perfectly racially balanced bunch. A Mexican American, an Asian American, an African American, and two whites. I wondered why we all couldn't be just Americans. I think that was the point of the entire experiment, back in 1776.

Nevertheless, these idiots, with their guns at the ready, were seriously thinking they were going to be invited in.

"Go fuck yourselves, you fascist preverts!"

Pound! Pound!

"It's a metal door, assholes, and pounding on it will not insure your gaining entrance! Go away!" Becky was sitting on the bed with the sheet pulled around her. I opened the door with the chain still on and asked them what the fuck they were doing.

"Can't you read the sign?"

"Open the door, now!" I slammed it shut, and almost immediately they began hurling themselves against the door.

I screamed back, "I've got to take the chain off, dickheads!" They stopped throwing themselves at the door. I took the chain off and flung the door wide open. I was completely nude and well endowed after the passion with Portia. All the uniforms dropped their eyes and pistols, still cocked—they could have blown my feet off—and pushed their way through. The leader ordered me to put on my pants. I told him "no." He repeated the order. He had no idea that I didn't follow orders. I took film and stage direction, but no orders. "This is my room, and I'll decide what to do in it, you jerks. You put your guns away and I'll put my gun away!" I had been watching them case the room. One of the uniforms had opened the drawer with the pistols and quickly closed it. I have often wondered what he thought when he saw ten or twelve pistols in the bedside drawer.

Much yelling was going down. Stuff about getting a report of gun-shots at the motel. As they had put their guns away, I pulled on a pair of jeans and grabbed one of the little plastic glasses that was full of bullets and firecrackers. I pulled out a cracker and asked if this was what they were referring to. "You must have noticed all the little frag-ments of red paper outside my door!" Two plainclothes burst in from the other room with Warren's assistant, Bob Watkins, trying to keep them calm. They were carrying shotguns.

I explained in a very loud and threatening voice that the maids had ignored the sign, just as they had, and had awaked me two hours early. I was on a night shoot, I yelled, and certainly cops who had to go on night shifts from day shifts should understand why sleeping in the daytime was a difficult but necessary thing.

"Why haven't you talked to the manager?" one of the cops asked.

"We've been shooting nights for five weeks, now. Do you really think we haven't talked to the manager? Why do you think there are many rooms with signs in Spanish and English asking to not be disturbed until after four-thirty? What the fuck are you doing in my room?"

"We had a report that there had been gunshots in your room, and when we get a gunshot report from this part of town, we respond!"

"Gunshots! The man who called you knew they were small firecrackers. You just wanted to fuck with me. It isn't a state secret who lives in this set of rooms. A telephone call could have saved you a lot of trouble!"

They all left the rooms apologizing, and I took a shower. Everybody's pits went off during the battle. As I soaked in the shower, I wondered if Portia would be packing her bags. I mean, I certainly hadn't shown a great deal of what *she* might call control. In my mind, I was in control all the way. I wondered if she had ever been around this kind of confrontation. When I stepped back into the bedroom, she was still there. She opened her arms to me and hugged me, telling me to calm down and everything was going to be fine. We made love and went off to work together. I was told that a news team had arrived in the lobby, while the storm troopers were leaving. The head uniform advised them not to disturb me. A lesson *was* learned.

Our relationship was growing fast and taking deep root. I felt terrific about everything in life. I called the ship and told them to start preparing for an extended cruise in the South Pacific. They were thrilled. This was the call the entire cast and crew had been waiting for. Portia had agreed to take the sail with me. She said she had experience sailing and didn't get seasick. I wondered about how she might feel about spending two months on a yacht with seven people she had never met. It took only two days to fill the bill. David Hudson, the harbor master in Lahaina when *Tatoosh* made its famous first appearance under my flag, and a licensed captain and celestial navigator, and his wife, Diane; David Welker, our tried and true naviguesser; Robert Eichelberger, our fearless captain; BC, our sail master; Danny Johnson, our number one swabbie; Gail Herren, our chief cook. I knew all the hands except Danny. I also knew how cool Diane Hudson was, and that she and Portia would get along fabulously. Ike mailed me a chart of the Pacific Ocean that included the islands we were going to visit. The chart also had a squashed cockroach on it. I loved the personal touch. The chart was put up on the wall of my motel bedroom, right above the bed.

Of course, the movie was still being shot, and Oates and I continued to have a grand time. I spent my time waiting for the camera and typing letters to Portia.

We were back to day shoots or split days—noon to midnight. And the movie was coming to an end. Steve Lim remembered the pie fights and water balloons from *Dirty Crazy*, and we began to plan for the wrap shot. Oates wasn't real sure of the plan, but had no choice. He owed me.

After the first week of shooting, the director was replaced. A hatchet man from Twentieth Century-Fox flew to Texas to do the deed. Oates met with me in my room before we were going to meet with the producers. He made me promise not to become confrontational. I agreed. I also felt the director should have been replaced. We went to the producers' room and met with the man from Fox. Oates sat on a couch with a glass coffee table in front of him. I sat on the protruding air conditioner–heater. Out of the blue, Oates went ballistic.

"Well, I don't like this one bit. No sir, I surely don't like it!" He leaned forward and flipped the entire glass-and-metal coffee table, so that it landed back on its legs. It was a very dramatic move. I wasn't supposed to get mad, but Oates went for the wall. I think he felt that I had gone to the wall too many times and didn't need the heat that always followed.

A mutual friend, actor-director Jack Starrett—Hopper's second choice for the lawyer in *ER*—became our new director. It was a wise move. But Jack had no idea about my famous wrap shots. After more than six weeks of shooting, we were picking up all the extra shots we had missed or needed in the editing room.

The movie was about two friends who go for a vacation with their wives in a very long motor home, and the strange things that happen to them when they observe a satanic ritual killing of a young woman as a sacrifice. We had two of the motor homes. One for on-screen outside shots—called the hero motor home—and one for interior shots. The latter was the brunt of many company jokes. It had a scaffolding of aluminum pipes rigged around it to hold lights. The lights were so hot, the windows began to sag. We called it The Ring of Fire.

The wrap shot came with us in The Ring of Fire. Starrett was acting the part of a gas station attendant pumping gas into the Ring's gaping tank. We had hidden many pies and water balloons on board. Starrett didn't see it coming. I pied him as I ran around the back of the Ring, and Oates pied him when he turned around to look at the camera. Somehow, the crew had their own plan. They hurled water balloons at the Ring's windows, pushing them into the motor home. Oates, Lim, and I did our best from the motor home, but we were surrounded. The fight ended with all of us throwing pies, water balloons, and anything we could find at the Ring. We never wanted to see the damned thing again.

Portia was getting a new bed for her house in Key West, preparing for my arrival. A close friend, Dink Bruce, made rings for us from a sabadilla tree that grew in her backyard. I flew to L.A. and did whatever business had do be done at Pando. I told Martee about Portia and my intention to marry her, and said that there would always be love in my heart for her. That was a hard one. I took the red-eye to Miami and a charter to Key West. Portia picked me up at the airport and drove me to her home. I crawled into the new bed and fell asleep. When I awoke, hours later, there was a little button pin placed carefully on the table by the head of the bed. It showed two hands clasping and the words "We Welcome You" around the hands. It had been put there by Thomas. I was deeply moved by his thoughtfulness.

I flew back to L.A. to pick up Bridget and Justin and bring them back to Key West for Easter. When we arrived, Portia brought Thomas and a new car to the little airport to meet us. It was the first time my children had met the woman I was bound to marry, and I was praying like mad everything would go all right.

Justin and Thomas hit it off perfectly. We had put an extra bed in Thomas's room for Justin and a guest bed for Bridget in the screened front porch. It was nice and warm down in the Keys, and Portia's house was built perfectly for the tropical conditions there. Tall, screened windows were the theme throughout the house. An ingenious system of cypress shutters, when open, allowed the air to move through the house or closed to keep out the cold or wind and rain.

The new car was a 1955 Chevy Bel Aire station wagon, painted metallic blue. A perfect Conch car. "Conch" is the term that Key Westers use to describe themselves. They refer to their island as The Conch Republic. I'd had some time in island mentality, having ruled the roadstead off Lahaina for four years. I think the transmission was full of sawdust and thin oil, and there were many rust spots along the bottom of the body, but the car was perfect for our needs. The two dogs, three children, and all our swimming, fishing, and diving gear *and* the rubber boat, fit in with room to spare. No need to worry about the sand and dirt. Wash it out with a hose and continue on with life. And life was becoming something to continue on with a smile and a happy heart. I was seeing my chance to pull the family out of the ashes. The more time Bridget and Justin spent with Portia, the closer they felt to her. They could easily see she loved their father, madly, and their father loved Portia just as passionately. The emotion was infectious.

And so I lived the next few weeks, flying back and forth between Key West and L.A. Always returning on the red-eye.

. . .

Before I had finished *Race,* another movie was lined up for me. Its location was South Africa. I was dubious about the location but wanted to put a lot of cash in the bank before I went sailing to the South Pacific. Most of the shoot was in South-West Africa—now known as Namibia—and that intrigued me. Namibia was where Stanley Kubrick shot the opening plates for *2001: A Space Odyssey.* The oldest basement rock in the world was in the deserts of Namibia.

Back in Key West, I prepared for the next role. Like a fool, I had my hair permed and grew my beard back. I had bought a seventeen-foot Mako shallow draft fishing skiff with the biggest outboard engine I could find, and spent many days with Portia, sunning on the bone-fish flats or swimming through the mangroves. I was in constant touch with the yacht, growing more excited about the grand journey we would make after I finished the film in Africa. Although I was still having my nightmare, the great love and closeness I was given by Portia made the mornings easier and the nights. We both worked with each other in the most harmonious ways. It was as if we had known our "us" since we had known life.

Slowly, I learned the little pieces of Portia's past. Her father was a kind man and loving father. Portia's mother had abandoned her three children when Portia was two months old. Her father was a bit of a playboy, but doted on his children. When Portia was old enough, she became the female head of the house. Her first stepmother, Barb, was the true wicked witch of the north. But Portia was well grounded by her closeness to both her paternal and maternal grandparents. I envied her relationship with her grandparents, though I had been fortunate enough to have Occi Hammerstein as a grandfather image. The few years I had with him are always in my mind.

I reluctantly left Portia to begin filming *Diamond Mercenaries* in Namibia. She joined me two weeks later, arriving at the same time as O. J. Simpson, who was also acting in the film. The sight of the two of them walking in from the constant desert was very funny. He had no idea who she was, and, of course, she knew right away who he was. She knew he was going to be in the movie. Lost and confused in the dust of Windhoek, and dressed to the nines in Pierre Cardin, O. J. was rescued by my little wonder woman and taken to the plane that flew to Swakopmund, where we were all staying at the Hotel Das Hansa. Maud Adams was my romantic leading lady. She was great and joined in the conspiracy of fun-on-the-set.

At the end of each day, I came home to a hot bath, a glass of fine champagne, and the loving arms of my Bundle of Joy. (Portia uses only Joy perfume. She is quite small, therefore, my "bundle" of Joy.) After each bath, the tub had a deposit of fine sand at the bottom. No matter what one did, one *had* to deal with the sand. Even in Das Hansa.

The shoot was fairly uncomplicated and not very intelligent, but it put a lot of cash in my bank and allowed me to go sailing for two or three months. The producers still owe me over sixty thousand dollars. What's new in La-La Land?

We had one week of shooting in South Africa, just outside of Johannesburg. The company flew us to Jo'burg in a chartered 727. It was night when we arrived in Jo'burg, and we had to wait for our baggage due to the charter thing. O. J. needed to go to the men's room, so he and I went. Outside, a sign was posted saying WHITES ONLY. I suggested that we ignore the sign because, as U.S. citizens, we were neither black nor white. This concept from a fair-skinned person was not something O. J. had really heard before. I'm sure that all of his fair-skinned friends were trying to be black while they hung with him. I was being myself. In my mind, O. J. was a person who was born on the same day as my son.

In we went. There was a shoe shine inside the entrance. As we walked by, O. J. said, "How're ya doing, brother?" and the shoe shine recoiled. I told O. J. there were no brothers in South Africa, which puzzled him for a moment. I stood against the far wall with my left hand inside my jacket, as if I were carrying a piece. I acted like O. J.'s bodyguard. What a concept. He stood at a urinal trying to piss. After a moment, he said, "Damn, I sure wish I could take a piss." Most of the other men in the room were white Europeans, who knew who O. J. Simpson was. A moment of laughter and then silence. I told O. J. to forget it and follow me. We went upstairs to a room called "for nonwhite people." These fucking fascists were not even going to give a black person an identity. They were "non" people.

The room was empty. It was exactly like the one on the floor below. Same number of stalls and urinals, but no shoe shine, no attendants, nobody, except O. J. and me. And the room was immaculate. I don't think any nonwhite person had ever used the room. We both pissed and left the room. As we walked down the stairs, I saw five policemen running up the stairs. When one runs up or down stairs, one usually keeps ones' eyes on the next step. They ran right past us, turning around after they realized the perps had just passed them. O. J. and I walked calmly back down to the rest of our company. Therein lay the protection zone. As soon as we made it back to our group, the cops were hesitant about hassling us. We were in a protection zone: a movie company. The director was the authority, and I carried the mental pistol.

When the word was passed around about the trouble, the whole company stood, shoulder to shoulder, as a phalanx. There was no way *any*body could penetrate the company persona. We were left alone. The coppers were outflanked. Portia was not pleased with my defiance. She, rightly, saw the trouble that could befall us all.

Portia. Okay . . . My wife's mother is named Portia. I called her by that name, because I wanted her to know who was talking. Who knew how fabulous she was/is? But as I remember who and what her mother was in the realm of motherhood; as I glean, each year, the history of her past, I realize that her name is Becky. No matter my desire to be identified, it must remind her of the fact that she was abandoned by her mother, Portia, and I can relate to that. So, today, I call her Becky, and a hundred other sensual, sexual, or comical offshoots.

There is a mad, ironic twist to her mother's life. She, as of this writing, is alive and living in Pennsylvania. She has two daughters.

Becky has met one of them. The daughter heard that Becky's real first name was Portia and remarked that *her* mother was named Portia, also. Becky didn't say a thing. She learned that her mother's next two children were born on the same day as her oldest brother, Dan, and her own birthday. What I know of mothers and their children tells me that Becky's mother is bound to remember, on each of her other daughter's birthdays, when her first son and her first daughter were born. Becky's mother has never tried to contact her first children. Very twisted. I know that it affects both brothers.

Becky had to get back to Thomas, who was staying with his father and Margot Kidder in Montana. She bought a ranch adjacent to the ranch she had bought while she was with Tom. She wanted to be close enough to her ex, so her son would have easy access to his father. This kind of attitude is not prevalent in Hollywood. I thought about how unselfish she was. I realized that she wanted out of her first marriage so badly that she just walked away. No property settlement, no alimony, no child support. Just out of there, as fast as possible. Becky left Africa a week before we finished filming.

The last day of my shoot in Jo'burg was a pickup shot for me and O. J. We did the shot as fast as possible, ran to take a shower, and went straight to the airport. We had packed our bags before we went to the set. The assistant director drove us to the airport. Just before we got there, we went to a secluded place and burned one. It was a perfect burn. Great timing. Both of us crashed on the plane, as soon as we were airborne. We refueled in the Cape Verde Islands and flew on to New York. O. J. stayed in New York to do a Hertz commercial and I flew on to L.A. and then Honolulu. O. J. was a very affable guy. Fun to be with.

It was a very long flight for me, but I was quite anxious to get to the yacht. I could feel the excitement ripping through the cast and crew. Most of the gang had come aboard and stayed there while the yacht was prepped for the journey. I was very surprised to see that all the guys had shaved their beards and cut their hair shorter. They, of course, were in hysterics about my permed hair and full beard.

Right after Thomas's eighth birthday, Becky flew to Honolulu. We welcomed her at the airport with so many leis that she could barely stand, and whisked her to the ship. The afternoon of the Fourth of July, we set sail for Lahaina. Becky watched all the gang, determined to jump ship if she felt we were less than perfect sailors. Five or six miles into the Molokai Channel, on a port tack, the hull port blew out in Berger's cabin. We had to come about to a starboard tack, while the port was secured, and that was a tricky maneuver in the big waves, but it was done without a hitch, and we tacked back to port and our course to Lahaina. Ike and Gail's bed was soaked but the ship was perfect, and Becky understood.

There were many aloha parties for the cast and crew the day and night of the fifth. At one point, I had to go out to the ship to get some cash from the safe. Becky and Danny Johnson came with me. It was night, and there was a large glowing fire to the south. I called it to Danny's attention, and assumed it was the Navy doing practice bombing on Kahoolawe. He agreed, but there was something not quite right with our assumption. I kept watching the event and suddenly realized it was not a night bombing by the Navy. The glow looked more like a cane field burning. Before sugarcane is harvested, the fields are burned. Part of the process of making sugar. But there were no cane fields on Kahoolawe. There are no cane fields on the southwestern part of Maui. The information suddenly hit the mark. We were watching the eruption of Mauna Loa. The first in twenty-five years. Back on shore, everyone scoffed at my declaration. The next morning, the eruption was the big talk of the whole state.

On July sixth, we set sail for the South Pacific and the Marquesas Islands.

chapter *Twenty-two*

*W*e sailed *Tatoosh* through the lee of the Big Island, hoping to see more of Mother Nature's show. No show. When we cleared the south point of the island, we sailed as close on the wind as possible. The Marquesas Islands are southeast of the Hawaiian Islands, eight degrees south of the equator, and we had to make as much way east as we could. For ships sailing these routes, the phrase is "easting," or making east. The main point was to cross the equator as far east as possible and fall off the wind, picking up the South Pacific trades on our beam or aft of the beam. This is one of the most comfortable attitudes of sail. After so many days of sailing on the wind, we longed for the warmth and comfort of sailing off the wind.

Becky would wake at night, and finding me not beside her in our bed, she would get up and prepare hot chocolate for us while we stood watch. It was such a fabulous experience for me. Finally, with a soul mate, I was fulfilling my dreams from years before. I was sailing into the South Pacific with my love. All those shows of *South Pacific* I had watched were coming straight into my heart. The voyage was a song, a dance, a dream come true. Only the children were missing, and they were all too young to make this sail.

At night, the sounds of the hull slicing through the water and the rigging as it worked were music beyond the beautiful songs of the great musical I had watched again and again. I was happier than I had ever dreamed I could be. When I got off watch, at night, Becky would rub my feet with lotion to help me get to sleep. Many times, I awoke for my next watch with one foot feeling great and soft, while the other was still dry and cracked from the salt water. She would fall asleep as soon as I did, nestling up against me. Sometimes, we had to use leeboards. Leeboards are pieces of light plywood that fit into slots, thereby dividing the beds and keeping one body from rolling onto another. Becky was so small, she could sleep while lying athwartships in my oversized bed and not need the board. I never minded if she rolled into me.

When she got up on my watch at night, she would call out to me through the main hatch. She used many little nicknames for me. Peach pit. Tuna trousers. Wonderfully wacky names. The other guys tried to make fun of it, but nothing they could say made me defensive. Hudson would laugh a great warm huff of understanding. They were both Michiganders, as was Diane Hudson. Sometimes, she would come on deck at night and say, "Well, where is George (meaning our grass, which was a gift from George Walker)? Don't I get a little puff?"

We came upon an enormous blue whale, just north of the equator. It was sleeping on the surface. What a sight. The whale was as long as the yacht. It put the things of nature in a perfect perspective for all of us. Very awe-inspiring.

As soon as we crossed the equator, we slowly headed more south, picking up the southeast trades. Everyone was warmer and lying in the sun in the cockpit or on the foredeck. No bow spray. We all were playing a game we called Off Watch. The scoring of this game was incomprehensible, but we never let on. We even started a new game for the first to spot land. We all had cabin fever. Actually, I didn't. I was just getting relaxed. Just cutting loose all the years of frustration.

Fifteen days out from Lahaina, and everyone was poring over the main chart that David Welker had been plotting. Everyone knew we were getting close. We were also out of beer and onions.

Excitement was building, but I was feeling almost ambivalent about the landfall. Part of me didn't want to stop sailing. Eight other shipmates would never understand, so I kept it to myself.

At 1642, we have dropped anchor in Taio Hae, Nuku Hiva. All hands well—a twelve-porpoise aloha, a man overboard and incredible excitement from everyone . . . After five years,

HERE WE ARE!

chapter *Twenty-three*

Taio Hai is a beautiful, large, protected harbor. It has a fairly narrow passage between two tall walls of an old volcano crater that open up to an ample anchorage. There were only a few small boats when we arrived. We anchored in the middle of the circular bay. There had been much talk about a place in Taio Hai called Maurice's. He had propane. He had beer. He had his own small generator. His was the first so-called bar, with groceries and the little things sailors just off a long passage would want. He was the 7-Eleven of the northern Marquesas. The village was very small with a long cement pier that accommodated the pocket freighters that plied the islands for the copra or coconuts and brought different islanders from other ports in the archipelago or Tahiti. The only other modes of transportation were long, outrigger canoes with outboard engines. There was electricity in the day from a larger generator operated by the local French port authorities. We raised the yellow quarantine flag as is the law, and the cast and crew began inflating the rubber boats.

I asked to be hauled up the mainmast to repair the masthead running light. All the weather and sea spray had put it on the fritz. It needed to be dried and recaulked with silicon gel. I enjoyed the view of the harbor, and watched the cast and crew as they went ashore for their first steps on land in more than sixteen days at sea. I could hear them perfectly as they chattered and joked. I watched them land at the dock. I heard the ladies as they found the different things they would need. I watched them walk excitedly along the shore right up to the fabled Maurice's.

After completing the repair of the masthead light, I sat back and watched the breezes working around the big bowl of the harbor. It was very peaceful.

In a while, Becky came back with Ike, Welker, and Diane Hudson and begged me to join her ashore. I couldn't refuse. I joined them at Maurice's, and we all toasted our good fortune with the smallest bottles of Heineken and Vahini beer I had ever seen. Maurice also had many bottles of Portuguese red wine. We learned a lot about the island and its history. We all got completely plastered and carefully made our way back to the ship. We all crashed and slept soundly that night. No watches. No schedules.

The women washed the laundry in a large cement washing basin on the pier, while I presented myself with everyone's passport to the port captain the next day. His English was limited, as was my French, but he could say Zhane Fonda. Zee bruzaire of Zhane Fonda. I invited him and his family to visit the yacht when we pulled up to the pier to refill our water tanks. A young native boy befriended us and asked where we wanted to go. He would be happy to be our guide. His English was fairly good. He had several open sores on his legs, so I cleaned the lesions well and put tetracycline powder on them after making him promise not to get the wounds wet. I changed the bandage twice, heaping tetracycline into the sores. They healed quickly and we were feted, later, by his family.

We climbed up to some bamboo forests on the very same path that Herman Melville took when he landed here and jumped ship. The young boy was our guide. There were coconut trees everywhere, and the boy shimmied up one, cutting down the best coconuts. He showed us how to shuck the outer shell in a few seconds and expertly opened the nuts so we could all drink the milk and eat the spoon-meat, as the most tender was called. None of us could come even close to his dexterity.

We spent the next twenty-three days in the Marquesas visiting the other islands. Rumor was about that a cool dude was living on the north shore of Hiva Oa. We sailed to Ua Pou, Fatu Hutu, and Tahuata. We found the cool dude on Hiva Oa's north shore. He lived in a small cove with a large grove of coconut trees. We were greeted warmly—

apparently word had spread through the island chain—and a goat was cooked in a pit for a big luau. In his hut, the fellow had a refrigerator, but no electricity. There were photos of Cadillacs in frames. No roads. He had some da kine, though. He appreciated the boxes of .22s we gifted him with. Guns were strictly controlled, but most families had .22 rifles.

In his oasis, freshwater came pouring out of the side of the hill like water from a hose, cascading down to pools. We bathed in the pools and washed our clothes near the last pool on the rocks. Island style. The French painter, Paul Gauguin, was buried on the other side of the island. It was the main port for all the Marquesas Islands but still very primitive. When we were ready to leave for the Tuamotu Archipelago, we sailed back up to Nuku Hiva. The Tuamotus were very dangerous, as they were all atolls, eight to ten feet above water, at the most. Many ships and boats had wrecked on these atolls over the centuries. We were only interested in Rangiroa, the largest of the atolls. We wanted to arrive at a specific time at the only navigable passage into the lagoon. Tiputa Passage. We wanted to approach the atoll from a more northern position, so we could avoid some of the smaller and more dangerous atolls.

16 August 1200: Arrived at Tiputa Pass, Rangiroa.

Our intended time of arrival was 11:45. The importance of the timing was critical. We made our time in a mixture of sailing and motor-sailing, mostly sailing. I am very proud that we made our intended position, basically on time. Rangiroa has a radio beacon that helped us see our course at night, but it was David Welker's superb celestial navigation that put us at the place at the time. The time was slack tide. On that date the tide was slack at 11:46 A.M. Very important. Tiputa Pass was only ninety yards wide and ninety-five feet deep. When the lagoon was on the tidal change, a lot of water rushed in or out through the pass. One could not navigate a deep draft vessel through the pass while the tide changed. The currents were so extreme that *any* boat would have been put upon the rocks. Many had. We entered the lagoon at the perfect time, and picked our anchorage west of the pass, just offshore of a thatched roof hotel and bungalows. The hotel was serviced by a small airfield, but we didn't consider it civilization.

We spent eight days in the lagoon, snorkeling, scuba diving, and tripping on the incredible colors of the water and many fish. On one of our excursions, we were dropped off outside the lagoon a short time before the tide was going to be rushing in. The view was totally different. The sides of the atoll fell away to a shelf, barely visible, 150 feet below, then dropped off to more than 2,000 feet. I saw many sharks below us. Our dive master banged the metal butt of his knife on his dive tank, summoning us to pony up with him. We were wearing jet fins to help power us to the pass. The water was ripping along at over nine knots as the tide rose in the lagoon. One could get in the flow or sit on the sandy sides of the bottom and watch the others fly by like Superman. I don't know the reason the flow didn't really disturb the side, but the effect was fantastic.

The owner of the thatched roof hotel-bungalow was an arrogant Frenchman with absurd facial features. He treated Becky rudely. Bad move on his part. We left the atoll for Papeete, sooner than we had planned.

22 August 1200: Arrive Papeete

A true Tahiti tie-up, stern to the wall. Many people showed up to watch the yacht anchor. I went ashore as soon as possible with the telephone numbers for the different families of the rest of the cast and crew, so I could go to the post office and place calls back to the States. A young Chinese guy came to the harbor on his chrome-plated Harley-Davidson. He had built it in San Francisco and shipped it to Tahiti. He rode me to the post office on his chopper, waited for me, and took me to his family's restaurant, which was covered with posters from *Easy Rider, The Hired Hand,* and *The Wild Angels.* I signed many of them for him and went back to the yacht.

A crowd was still there. I had reached most of the people back in the States, and the cast and crew were very excited to get a party going. I think the entire voyage, and its release once we tied up in Papeete, was too much for all of us. We stayed on the yacht and crashed.

On the second morning, we were given a royal tour of the island by a troop of Tahitians. They arrived at the harbor in two open buses with buckets of punch at ten in the morning. By eleven, we were all snockered. We were fortunate to have lived through the tour. The

Tahitians were used to it, I suppose, as they kept on playing their guitar-ukulele crossbreeds and singing great local songs in perfect harmony. I tried to play the instruments, but it was hopeless.

Becky had to get back to Thomas. She had never been away from him for such a long time. I was so in love with her, she could do anything she wanted, though I didn't want to be away from her. After arranging for funds to be transferred to Papeete for the yacht and the cast and crew, I left for the States and *my* children.

I still get a little choked up when I tell the story about Paddle to the Sea. But I know I have made my journey and gone beyond. It remains to be seen what I do with the experience.

The Hagmans met me at the airport with Bridget and Justin and their own two children, Preston and Heidi. We went down to Mary Martin's desert hacienda for a few days. I was stalling so that Becky had time to get some necessary things for the new ranch before I came. I was aching for her.

The children and I flew up to Montana just before Labor Day. We had no idea what to expect. I had made an emotional and physical commitment to Becky and her life. And the same to Thomas. I had the very intense commitment to the yacht and my life aboard her, but I wanted to be with Becky. Live with her. I had proposed to her several times. I had kicked in a fairly large amount of cash to help her buy the ranch. As I said earlier, she had walked away from her first marriage without asking for a thing. The two pieces of property she and Tom owned had been bought with her money. She didn't want to have anything to do with him. But she wanted to buy this ranch so Thomas could have easy access to his father.

I found this commitment to her son's life most unselfish. It made a very big impression on me. I realized that I would have to move from my ship to the mountains of Montana, if our relationship was going to be as serious as I wanted. Hollywood divorces most always carried bitterness and vindictiveness along as lifetime baggage. This was a very unselfish person. A gold mine, indeed. I also realized that I would never get custody of my children as long as I was living on my yacht, but the thought of leaving the tropics *and* the ship was almost too much for me. Almost.

The ranch has a fabulous log cabin surrounded by tall, beautiful blue spruce trees, outbuildings for farm equipment and animals, a fine red barn and apple orchards, the original homestead house, and

a view that is·spectacular. It is on the northern end of the Paradise
Valley, a valley heading north out of Yankee Jim Canyon. The Yellowstone River snakes up the valley through Alan Spur Gap and heads
east at Livingston, a town of sixty-seven hundred people, to Billings
and on to join the Missouri River at Buford, North Dakota. Becky's
ranch was eight miles south of Livingston.

I had always daydreamed about living in a log house, and this one
was perfect. On the outside. The inside walls had been covered in
lath and plaster and didn't give the feeling of a log house at all. Behind the cabin, the property included a nice hill rising up almost one
thousand feet with junipers, bristle cone pines, and nesting golden
eagles. Whitetail and mule deer looked at us curiously as they grazed
in the hay fields in front of the buildings. A small ditch was running
with water through the upper orchard, behind the cabin through the
spruces, behind the homestead house, and out into the lower orchard. A larger creek ran through the middle of the entire ranch. The
hay fields were not in very good shape, as they had been neglected
by the previous owners. The ranch came with a 1962 Minneapolis-
Moline tractor and a 1952 Dodge Power Wagon with a dump bed
back. The '52 Dodge was a very serious four-wheel-drive vehicle. I
would find out that serious four-wheel-drive rigs were a necessity at
my new home. Paradise lost so many years ago was now paradise
found.

When we arrived, Bridget, Becky, and I went for a tour of the barns
and other out buildings. Justin and Thomas were off somewhere
being the brothers they both had wanted. When the girls and I
opened the big barn door, a large rattlesnake quickly coiled a few
feet away. I was carrying a .38 Special in my back pocket. I took the
pistol and shot the snake in the head. The ladies were impressed. I
was amazed. It's a snub-nosed revolver.

Thomas and Justin were almost lost in their new world. It was wonderful to see. I could feel the mending of two broken families, even
then. It would take some time.

I was off to shoot a film called *Fighting Mad* in Arkansas. Fortunately for me, it was written and directed by Jonathan Demme. I, of
course, wanted to call it *F*****G A!* Roger Corman was producing.
Scott Glen played my brother. I like Scott. Like his work. Jonathan
was amazing. He was so full of positive attitude, anything was possible. He never let on to any stress or pressure, and he was basically

working for free. Becky came down to visit as much as possible. Things were fairly difficult for her back in Montana. Tom was always pressuring her, and she had to make things happen on her own. I guess she had to have been doing that since she was a little girl.

On the way to the set one night, I told her that I didn't want more rejection in my life, and I would stop asking her to marry me, but I would live with her like a husband, take care of her for her life, and be a good father for her son. In a week and a half, we were married at Sheriff John Thomas's house, by Washington County Judge Val B. Lester. On November eleventh. Armistice Day. We spent our honeymoon night in the two-room "suite" at the Ramada Inn. Sheriff Thomas's house was in Sonora, Arkansas. When people ask where we were married, I tell them Sonora, leaving them to think Mexico.

I had to travel to other locations for a few days of shooting before the film wrapped, and Becky went back to the ranch to prepare for Thanksgiving. I would be bringing Bridget and Justin and my "step"-brother–executive producer–partner, Bill Hayward. I was wrapped from the film just in time to fly to L.A. and pick up my entourage, and in order to maximize my ground time with the children, we flew up to the ranch in Jimmy Walker's Learjet 23. When we arrived at Mission Field, east of Livingston, there was much snow on the ground and a lot of wind. It was hard to find the little airfield, and I could hear the tower talking to Jimmy about the wind and visibility. Jimmy suggested that we land at Bozeman, forty miles west, but I told him the pass was closed, and we couldn't get to the ranch, so he decided to give Mission Field a shot. We made our approach and were heading for the single runway while the wind was calmer. I was sitting on the left side of the jet and could see an enormous cloud of snow— called a ground blizzard—heading right for the runway at a ninety-degree angle. Jimmy could see it, too. But he is a very cool pilot and landed the jet at 210 knots—flying speed—putting the left gear down first. Smart. When we reached the little flight building, it would disappear from time to time due to the blizzard conditions. Winter in Livingston. Something new. Five days later, Jimmy flew us back to L.A.

For the next few months, I commuted between the ranch and Pando. Sometimes Becky would join me. We had a carpenter working on the cabin, and things were a bit disjointed. My friend and first assistant director, David McGiffert, and Bill drove a serious four-wheel-drive pickup and the two Abyssinian cats from the office up to the ranch. I was slowly getting the stuff of life in the mountains and snow together. I had become so centered on living in the tropics, it took me a while to get the program straight.

I met most of Becky's friends and found them very accepting of me. The novelist and poet Richard Brautigan lived just down the road, and novelist-screenwriter William Hjortsberg and his family were next door to Brautigan. Everyone called Hjortsberg Gatz. A great painter, novelist, and essayist, Russell Chatham, lived one creek south of us. Further down the valley, Terry McDonall, then editor of *Outside Magazine,* had a house on the Yellowstone. These were all friends of Becky's, and they were all very creative and fun to be with. I learned that while we were sailing, many male friends of Becky's got together in L.A. to approve or not of our being together. None of these men had been lovers; they just all perceived how unique and wonderful this fine woman was, and they didn't want her to go through another bad relationship. Fortunately, they all cast "yes" ballots about me. Although Big Tom, as everyone called Thomas's father, was at the same parties and gatherings as we were, there were no uneasy feelings or suspicions about Becky and me from these friends. They all knew the reasons for Tom and Becky's divorce.

Christmas was coming, and we prepared our little cabin for the children. The plan was to have Christmas and New Year's Eve at the ranch, then move down to Becky's house in Key West. I had to return the children before New Year's, but we all had a grand time and a white Christmas. There was snow on the tree. It wasn't Susan so much as her second husband, Bill Tennant, who made the most trouble for me as a parent. He was trying his best to compete with me, and that was a very bad idea. Bridget stayed loyal to her mother, but Justin pined for his life at the ranch with his brother and best friend. He loved his mother very much, but hated his stepfather. This problem continued for four years.

On the good side, both my children loved to come back to Key West for Easter. Becky, as she had done for years, brought both her dogs, Molly and Zip, *and* the new additions, the Abyssinians Tana and Red. Tana had been nailed by a wildcat at the ranch and gave birth to three kits in Key West. One was snatched by a neighbor. The other two became the first "children" of my new family. We named them Bob and Monty. Magnificent cats, but not pure Abby. They carried the best part of the Abyssinians. They were great hunters and very quiet pets.

My friends in Hawaii were invited to come on a special cruise in the Leeward Islands, those islands northwest of Tahiti, while *Tatoosh* was still in the South Pacific. The log reflects that everyone had a good time.

Bill Hayward and Larry Kubic joined Ike and the rest of the cast and crew in June to sail the yacht back to Hawaii. I bought a '76 Eldorado convertible and went to Houston to film *Futureworld*. Thomas and Justin joined me with Becky in tow. They were busted skateboarding in the long underground passage ways of the Johnson Space Center. Life was getting better all the time.

Summer was spent at the ranch with a few side trips to the yacht back in Lahaina. Justin and Bridget arrived at the ranch in August, and we all went ranching, fishing, hiking and touring Yellowstone Park. Summer at the ranch. And "someone" thought it was better to send my son to camp.

I was going to make *Outlaw Blues* for Warner Bros. in the fall, so Bruce Langhorne joined me at the ranch to begin working on the songs. I was going to do my own singing and playing, and I was stoked. I hated the song they had picked for the title tune, though. Bruce came with me and all the family to the ship at the end of August. Bruce and I worked on the songs, while Becky, Bridget, Thomas, and Justin played in the sun and toured the island. The Labor Day race was sailed and won, and I went to Austin, Texas, for *Outlaw Blues*. I had a blast doing the movie, but I still hated the Hall and Oates title tune.

Working with Susan Saint James was fun. It was like a conspiracy while we did our scenes. We developed moments for our scenes and didn't tell the director, who loved the way we filled them. Lots of chase scenes in boats and on motorcycles. Great toys. The stunts were very well done, and once again I got to do most of mine. So did Susan.

Susan had to leave before we finished the film, so she missed the grand finale. No water balloons. The last few days of filming were done at Huntsville Prison, the largest state prison in the country. Lots of interior hallway stuff. Cell scenes, exercise area. Matt Clark was in these sequences with me. I was never fearful of the interior shots. The cons were nice and polite to me, and the liaison with the prison officials was very helpful. Many scenes were filmed out in the work fields: my character picking cotton and so forth. And mainly me running my ass off for two days, being chased by the warden and his deputies and dogs, as I tried to make my many escape attempts. Running past the camera, away from the camera, into and over the camera, through trees, shrubs, and finally in a swamp. Caught.

On the last day, waiting for the cameras to be set up, I noticed the sound department, standing out in a field, looking down, bending down, and then straightening back up and looking around as if wondering who might be watching them. I ran over to them immediately, and discovered what I thought I would find. They were looking at mushrooms, and wondering if they were *the kind*. I accurately stated that they *were* the kind, as I reached down and picked them from old cow pies and popped them in my mouth. The boys were shocked at first. I explained that if the 'shrooms were growing out of the cow pies, they were the kind, and one didn't have to worry about being poisoned. I was amazed at the number of them around. We began picking them as fast as we could. Something about doing this kind of foolishness inside the control of a pretty big authority was interesting. Nothing abstract about Huntsville. You're there because you really fucked up in a major way.

Soon, the camera crews were watching us and came wandering over to check on the haps. Gobble, gobble. The effect of these 'shrooms was almost uncontrollable fits of laughter over the smallest, screwy things. One didn't stagger around and fall down. Matter of fact, the running was a lot more fun. I felt like I was running in slow motion. And after each time the director called, "Cut!" I would fall to the ground doubled up in laughter. Of course, when I fell down laughing my ass off, the sound department and much of the camera department fell down laughing about *me* falling down. I emphasize that the stone didn't effect our work or stamina. Rather, as many doctors say, laughter is the greatest medicine. Naturally, the drivers got into the fun. And, as the last shots were coming up, one of the Teamsters and Becky drove off to the nearby town to get some pies. *Yes! PIES!* I mean, why not? Got a tradition to keep going. At least a tradition on shoots that were fun and good.

When Becky and the driver came back, they were laughing so hard, there were tears coming down their cheeks. The pies were secreted around the equipment trucks and other places, ready for the big call. The wrap shot on the movie. The pies started flying before the words were out of the first AD's mouth. There was a particular person in the production department whom all of us hated, and she got the first and biggest barrage. Although many times whoever was about to let fly with a pie would collapse in hysteria, the pie ending up in his or her own face. Just imagine this huge pie fight going on inside a prison, while the field warden—who had been playing himself—watched in utter disbelief. Just perfect. I couldn't convince the director, Dick Heffron, to try a few 'shrooms, though. He said it was just as much fun for him to watch us. Dick had also shot *Futureworld,* and I liked him and his wife very much.

I wanted to get home quickly, so Jimmy Walker came to Hunstville and flew us back to L.A. in his jet, where Becky and I picked up the Eldo and drove up to the ranch by way of Jackson Hole, Grand Teton National Park, and Yellowstone National Park. It was a nice decompression for me. The children came up for Thanksgiving and all was well. The boys tormented Bridget—mostly Thomas—and she took it with grace. They all loved each other, but younger brothers have a penchant for teasing their older sister. Thomas had a huge crush on Bridget, so he was really on the button in the tormenting.

I had decided to pull the sticks out of *Tatoosh* and re-rig the whole ship. This was a major bit of business. We wanted to take the masts down to the wood and put on many coats of varnish. All the toggles and some turnbuckles had to be replaced. One doesn't go to a marine hardware store and order this stuff. Nobody carries these things at a store; they have to be made from scratch. Finally, when the work was finished, *Tatoosh* looked truly magnificent. I flew back to the mainland to finish the soundtrack for *Outlaw Blues.*

They had to have more time for the editing before I laid down the music tracks, so I went to Toronto, Ontario, to film *High Ballin',* a story I had put together with Larry Kubic.

The shoot in Canada was a difficult one, due mostly to the weather. A fierce flu didn't help me much, either. Basically, we didn't have a Christmas. Or New Year's. The life of an actor. Becky flew up with Thomas for the last week of shooting. Having even a little bit of the new family with me made me feel much better. As soon as we wrapped, the three of us jumped in Jimmy Walker's jet and flew to the ranch. The bitter cold at the ranch was not helping me gain back my health, so we left for Key West as soon as we could. Becky and I spent our days out on the water in my little fishing skiff. I healed and tanned and swam, snorkeled, and pretended to be back in the tropics. At Easter, Justin and Bridget joined us. I still had to do the singing vocals for *Outlaw Blues*. Other than that, I thought I would just take some time off.

Becky and I flew back to the yacht in late April for a cruise down to the Big Island from Lahaina, as she had not seen the Kona Coast.

We moved on down the Kona Coast to the Kona Surf Hotel. We got the great suite and had the laundry done; then we motored down to Cook's Monument.

We moved on down the coast to Okoe Bay, very near the south tip of the island. I went swimming and diving along the shore, and when I returned to the yacht, I found that Becky had made some fudge cake with the best grass I had. I was a little upset. It's like cooking with the finest Chateau Latoure. I pleaded with the rest of the gang to wait a little while after dinner to eat the dessert, but the fudge tasted so good that no one listened. Two hours later, I was watching the natives fishing by torchlight along the coast. I passed glass cigar tubes—that had once held my premier stash—full of ice-cold vodka and a splash of V8 juice to Ike and Jimmy Head up through the galley skylight. I had turned on the spreader lights to show the natives that we, too, could fish by light. One had to drink the little shooters at once. There was no way one could put the tubes down. Ike and Head were zoned out on the sail bags, laughing and trying to fish. Everyone was blasted by the fudge. I had rarely seen Ike so stoned. It was hysterical for everyone but Becky. She spent the next two days in our stateroom recovering.

Cruising with Becky was wonderful. She loved the yacht and sailing, and always had the cast and crew laughing. She was good medicine for me and the ship. We weren't sad leaving the yacht. We were healthy and happy together, looking forward to our ranch and knowing that we would be returning.

I flew to the yacht several times for a week or two during the recording sessions and other Pando business. It was always the greatest for me. Of course, they were the no-more-nightmare times, but there were so many of my friends whom I hadn't seen as often as I had before Becky was my life. I also bought a BMW 100RS motorcycle at the suggestion of Hayward. It was a fine motorcycle, very fast and smooth.

Negotiations for how much time I could have custody of Bridget and Justin were getting harder. I couldn't believe that Justin *had* to go to a summer camp, when we had something so much better at the ranch with his brother. It was the stepfather, just trying his hardest to mess with me. I was starting to hear stories about the way he treated the children. I was staying at a rented house in the West Hollywood hills. One afternoon, Bridget called me, crying. She needed some help with something, and I came running. I raced over to her mom's house in the Eldo and went to her room by the outside brick stairs. I was with her for some time doing my best to make her feel better and not to worry about her math too much.

While I was with her, stepfather dearest came home. I left by the same private entrance and drove off to work at the recording studio. The next thing I heard was some major threats about never coming to the house again without being asked. I blew up. I mean, really! My daughter was in tears and trouble, all alone, and I would come to her whenever she needed me and wherever she was. I will still do that thing as long as I live. From time to time, she would ask me to pick her up at school on the motorcycle. I gladly obliged, relishing those moments when I roared into her mom's place, ever the outlaw. In the same vein, I think she got a kick out of being picked up at school by her dad on a motorcycle. I was thrilled just to be asked. I was just as thrilled to have Justin with me for the weekend, though having the children for even a day was becoming a bitter fight with the step-fucker. I'm sure he was trying his very best to make things tough for me in the industry, and was probably succeeding from time to time.

Bill and I decided to ride our motorcycles to the ranch. We planned the trip to coincide with Justin's eleventh birthday. Our idea was to arrive at Justin's camp on his birthday and take him to dinner. I wanted the camp counselors to see his father, and I wanted the other boys to see that Justin's father would come to the camp for his birth-day. I wouldn't miss one of Thomas's birthdays, unless I was filming in another state.

We left Pando very early in the morning on July 9, riding up to Fresno on the back roads and then up to Justin's camp. We arrived there in the midafternoon. Justin's counselors said that he had some planned activities for that day, and they couldn't just let him go with me. I was there with Haywire on his motorcycle, John Haeberlin, John's girlfriend, Julie, and John Vincent, a sound mixer and genius on-set sound department, all three of whom were driving my Eldo convertible with a large cooler filled with fruit juices, sandwiches, and other goodies in the trunk. They were our chase car. Pretty classy. As the camp fascists tried to impose their rules on me, I put Justin on the back of my bike and we all went out for a birthday dinner.

We had brought along two two-meter shortwave radios, and I had one with me in the Eldo when I drove Justin back to the camp. We tried to keep in touch with the gang back at the hotel, but we weren't too successful. When we did make contact, Bill's voice sounded like Mickey Mouse. I must have sounded the same to him, but Justin and I were cracking up. Justin was pleased and happy that I came there. It was a complete surprise.

Bill and I got separated from the Eldo when we got off the freeway that first morning. The idea was not to ride on any freeway, but when we became lost from one another, Bill and I were worried about how to find them. By sheer luck, we met before we started up the mountains to Justin's camp. After that, Vincent would work out an exact route for the next day, and Bill put the instructions in a clear plastic map compartment on his tank bag. We went over Donner Pass and down into the Lake Tahoe area.

It was a marvelous ride, and we took our time, stopping at all kinds of strange places and hearing the talk of the real America. Some of these guys thought that Ronald Reagan was a leftist, because he was an actor and now governor of California, the hotbed of commies. The farther into the hinterlands we went on the ride, the more racist the rhetoric.

We got to the ranch after five days and not a drop of rain. Doing ninety miles an hour, I almost hit a cow in Idaho, after Haywire beeped his horn and spooked them. Almost hitting a cow is much worse than *any* ride in the rain. Thinking about it, I wonder who was more insane. Me doing ninety on a country road, or the radical right in the bar in Idaho? Me. Never go ninety on a country road. In any kind of vehicle.

After a wonderful August and Labor Day with all our children at the ranch, Becky and I went back to *Tatoosh* for a sail up to Hanalei Bay, on Kauai. I wanted Becky to see the islands as I had, on board our own private hotel. This visit was a bit different. Before we left the slip in the Ala Wai, a tall, beautiful woman named Mona came to the ship. She said she was a good friend of Hayward's girlfriend, Joanna;

she had come to Hawaii for a vacation but had been sick for a week; she knew we were sailing to Kauai and wanted to make the sail with us. I called Joanna, and she confirmed Mona's story. Joanna told me Mona was cool and she just wanted to get to Kauai. We invited her aboard.

We had other guests coming with us. Nyarie, Queen of the World, from Australia, a friend of a friend. Nyarie was a very striking woman, also. She was tall, very hip, with thick, strawberry blond hair and a great figure.

Becky, Nyarie, Mona, and I took the Whaler up the Hanalei River as far as we could. It was just a little bit like *African Queen*. As the guava trees became too thick to navigate through, we just picked guavas and pigged out. On that adventure, we renamed Mona. She became Wanda of the Jungle. There were many expeditions to the fields of the Hanalei flats for the prized mushrooms. As there hadn't been much rain, the pickings were slim but adequate.

I was pleasantly surprised to fine Graham and Susan Nash renting a house on the beach of this beautiful bay. I invited them out to the yacht for a little sail. They came out, but Susan was quite pregnant and the motion of the ship under sail was not helping her at all, so we returned to our anchorage.

The ladies asked for a mushroom salad, and we obliged. There is an interesting thing about the mushrooms: they are not effective for many days after one ingests them. For the record, one should wait at least five days before eating more 'shrooms. I find *that* a great equalizer. This hallucinogen is self-regulated.

Mona figured out that Graham Nash was Graham Nash. The next thing the Nashes saw was Mona doing her "yoga" exercises on their front lawn. She had been doing them on the foredeck. The exercises are like a full commercial for "come to me." Susan Nash was thrilled with the whole thing. Very pregnant. And Wanda of the Jungle was in her front yard splitting her legs and contorting her wonderful body.

A script, *Wanda Nevada,* had been sent to me that late summer, to read as a director and actor. I read it and was captivated. I knew I had to make this movie. When I went into the little village of Hanalei to phone my agents, I ran into two Asian Americans who had just returned from China. They both had seen *Futureworld* in Beijing and said I was a big hit in the mainland of China. The Chinese thought that the film was a story about real things in the United States Far out.

I arranged a meeting with the two young men who owned the script. We sailed back to Oahu, and Becky and I flew to the mainland. She went on to the ranch, and I went to San Francisco to meet with the young producers and drive down the coast a bit to meet Brooke Shields, their first choice for the title role. Brooke was wonderful. She had such presence, and seemed to understand what the camera was all about. Although I met with other young actresses, I think I had made up my mind when I met Brooke.

The first meeting with the producers was quite typical. I asked them if they had the money. They stammered a bit, and their "yes" was very qualified. What's new in independent filmmaking. I was very positive about the script, though, and I never doubted the movie would be made. I began to gear up.

We had Christmas at the ranch with all three children. We had lots of snow on the ground. The skiing was terrific. The snow is so dry in my corner of Montana, it is the best powder in the West. Justin and Thomas were becoming skilled skiers. It was great fun to watch the two of them play together, the slowly mending family.

chapter *Twenty-four*

$\mathscr{B}$ecky and I rented a house on Broadbeach, west of Malibu, to be able to have Bridget and Justin with us at Easter. I don't recall why, but it was the only way to have them for a week or so. Regardless of the reason, it turned into a most fortunate result. Thomas's father and his third wife, Laurie, were staying at the beach, also, and at an afternoon gathering, I ran into Michael Butler, the cinematographer on *Ninety-two in the Shade*. I'm not sure why Big Tom was there, but the meeting of Michael, again, was perfect. I gave him *Wanda Nevada* to read. I knew he had just been working for eighteen months on *Jaws 2* and probably wanted to rest, but I took the chance. He loved the script, too, and agreed to shoot it with me. He asked me immediately if I had the money. I laughed. I told him that I would get the money. We needed four million dollars. I needed to get on the phone.

With the help of Dennis Hackin, the writer, and Neal Dobrofsky, the producer, I got several inside numbers. I'm sure their lawyer, Gordon Stulberg, was a big help. Gordon had been at the helm of Twentieth Century Fox, when I made *Dirty Mary Crazy Larry*. The movie had made a lot of money for them. I called my dad and asked him if he would consider doing a cameo with me. He had already suffered two heart attacks and was not in the best of health, but it would take only one day to shoot his part. I offered him fifteen hundred dollars and said I would send his sides to him. "Sides" is the term used in the theater for the part of the script that has your lines and cues only. It was a way of saving money in summer stock by not having to make copies of the whole script. He bellowed at me, in a good-natured way, that I wasn't even born when that term was used. I guess he forgot all the plays at Omaha, my stint in stock at Fishkill, New York, and all the other stock theater I had done. Yes, he told me, he would do the part. *All right!*

On a Sunday afternoon, I called Bob Grossman at his home. He was the head of business affairs at NBC. He had the flu but took the call. I told him I had Brooke, Dad, and myself in this new movie, and I needed four mil to shoot it. He said he would do the deal and then asked me if I would send his sons some autographed pictures. You bet! We were in business.

Steve McQueen lived just down the way, and we visited him often. He and I would go to his garage and smoke da kine. The garage was full of antique motorcycles. Each time, he would tell me that I had screwed up motorcycling with *Easy Rider.* I never understood his reasoning. He told Becky that it was because so many people began riding motorcycles long distances. (McQueen had a crush on her.) Still didn't make sense to me. But Harley-Davidson was thrilled about the movie, I know that.

A week before I was to go location scouting with Butler, I was hit with the worst case of chicken pox. I was thirty-eight, and chicken pox in older people is very dangerous. My doctor told me not to go to a hospital but to get a hotel suite, and he would arrange for nurses around the clock. I moved at once to the L'Ermitage. The pox sores hadn't yet made their full appearance, so I skated past the front desk without them knowing that a highly contagious disease was going to be running its course in their wonderful hotel. I asked my doctor to be sure that the nurses were dressed in street clothes, so as not to give away the secret. I had Hayward do the scouting for me. He was going to be the executive producer, he knew my style, and I trusted him completely. Within hours, I was a mess.

There wasn't a part of my body that was clear of the very red sores, except the palms of my hands. My head and face were bloated with them. They were down my throat, in my stomach, and behind my eyeballs. Most of the time, I was semidelirious with a 104-degree temperature. I was there for fourteen days.

I wondered what else I didn't know about my youthful years in the disease department. I was particularly concerned about the mumps. No one knew what my medical history was. Mother was dead, and Dad never knew what was going on at home. Sickness was an embarrassment to him. More than likely because of his brush with Christian Science. He always called me a sickly child and hung the label of hypochondriac on me. That had been an unfair call. Even Jane called me that. Bill called me every day and said, "Don't scratch." I remembered a drug called temeril that was specifically designed to turn off the scratching urge from the brain. My doctor agreed, and with the help of the nurses, and temeril, I didn't scratch once.

While this was all going down, I learned that United Artists, to whom we had submitted the script, upon learning that we had the money, decided that they wanted to do the movie. Not just release it but finance it, also. I had to blow off Bob Grossman from NBC and felt terrible about it. He had been such a great supporter of the project and had really committed the funds. For me, I had been put in the position of backing up and suffering severe tire damage. UA's accounting department had agreed that the four million dollars was right in the ballpark. But as we drew near our start date, they pulled a million and a half from the budget. Dirty move, man. Really bad form. But we had no choice. They pulled one point five from the budget and had not removed a page. I decided to shoot a three point five budget no matter what they said, and I surely missed the extra five hundred thousand.

A week after Brooke Shields turned thirteen, we started principal photography on the film. Our first seven days were spent rafting down the Colorado River and shooting each day. It was hot and difficult. We did our best, which was a lot better than most crews ever do. The first night we spent on the river, we were still in Marble Canyon at the upper part of Grand Canyon National Park. The walls of this part of the canyon are almost vertical. As we all lay on the sand looking up, we could only see 10 or 12 percent of the night sky. I had moved my gear up with the camera crew and passed out L-tryptophane to help everyone get to sleep. This is a natural protein and one of the essential amino acids in the human system. Our makeup man was snoring so loudly, we all whispered about the different ways to drown or kill him. We were saved by Brooke's mother when she hit him in the face and told him to shut the fuck up. Man, what a trip. But he stopped his chain-saw-on-a-metal-post snore.

I awoke the next morning to find the river two feet away from my sleeping bag. The flow is controlled by the Glen Canyon Dam. I am not so sure that this control thing is doing right by the river. If the dam and its plan were put together by the U.S. Army Corps of Engineers, one can count on it not doing right by anything.

When we got to Phantom Ranch, we were hungry for a normal, flat bed. The ranch wasn't quite ready for us, which put us all in a marvelous mood. The production manager had not been on top of this very simple thing. We were in contact every day with the office. They knew where we were and what we needed at all times. I had put a communication package together for the shoot, and while we were down in the canyon, John Haeberlin drove a very serious four-wheel short-bed truck with an antenna booster to pick up our radio transmissions and talk back to us. The truck moved to different points of the south rim to maintain good reception.

We all helped unload the shooting equipment. All except for the snoring makeup man. He felt above it all, saying it was not his department. He was totally fucked from that moment on. That kind of attitude was forbidden by me. He must not have been listening to me at our final production meeting. "You're part of the team or you're out," I had said, specifying that particular phrase: "not my department." When the rest of us got to our bunkhouses, my group—mainly the camera crew—found his kit on one of the bunks. Realizing the disaster that might happen, we relocated his gear to another bunkhouse, and when he came back, we all told him he was really mixed up, and that his kit was probably next door. He might have been murdered in his sleep if he stayed with us.

I fired the production manager when we reached the top of the south rim and the El Tovar Hotel. I couldn't fire the makeup man without good cause. By union rules, that meant he had to have screwed up in his job.

By the time we were ready to shoot Dad's part, we were a tight team. He came a day early and stayed with the rest of the main company, up in Page, above the dam. The camera crew and I stayed at a small motel-like place called Marble Canyon. We called it Lost Your Marbles Canyon. The daily high was past 120 degrees and, by our reckoning, was unsuitable for normal people to work. But we were pros. It was so dry that one never really sweated. The sweat would evaporate quicker than it would show on our faces or bodies.

The morning of "the day," Michael Butler and I arrived at the set and were told at once that Henry Fonda was pissed. Everyone on the set was walking on eggshells. Michael and I went to the makeup trailer and found him grousing like mad about the beard that had been made for him. Made by the makeup man. He told us that we couldn't shoot any close-ups, because the beard looked so phony, and he was very right. But no one was going to tell me how to shoot them. Michael and I had a shared vision, and it was that vision that decided the day. Each day. The beard was very bad.

I told Dad that I had some ground-up licorice for him to chew on instead of real tobacco. The part called for a man spitting chewing tobacco out, and no one could tell if it was licorice. He defiantly refused, saying that Bill Cosby had given him some Red Man chewing tobacco, and *that* was what he was going to chew. Cosby had given me some of the same stuff before I left on my 1971 crossing to Maui. Michael and I took some of the licorice, chewed it up, and spit it at the beard. Dad was astounded. We went outside and got some dirt, returning and throwing it at the beard. When it looked ratty enough, we said the close-ups would be fine, but Dad still groused. Back outside, Butler and I fell to the ground, laughing. That was Henry Fonda we were spitting on and throwing dirt at. The tobacco caught him at the lunch break, and he passed out in his dressing room. I was concerned because of his heart, but the medic assured me it was the nicotine.

Dad left the next day and flew back to L.A. Becky accompanied him, and they both got to know each other much better. A week or so later, I got a letter from him. It was the third or fourth letter he ever sent me, not counting the letters he sent from the Pacific during the war. I was too young to understand those. This one was very different.

15 July 1978

Dear Son:
I started thinking about this letter flying home a week ago, but the crowded days have passed so quickly, I never seemed to get to it. I got up at six o'clock this morning before another dynamo day goes by. I felt so badly about the phoney makeup. I wanted you to know that I

fully understood if you found that you couldn't use the scene. It meant a lot to me that you asked me to participate, and I so wanted it to be meaningful to the picture . . . It would have been such a gas if it had worked . . . Anyway, I want you to know how proud I am of you. Your whole company so obviously worships you, and it's a beautiful thing to see. And I haven't seen it so often in 43 years that it doesn't impress me. And you're a very good director . . . You are a thoughtful man, and I love you.

Your Dad

Of course, I was in tears as I read this most wonderful letter, and I walked across the road to show the letter to Michael. He came to tears. I passed it around the company, as it was the company that deserved the credit for the work done. Not just me alone.

We worked very hard in quite difficult conditions. By ten o'clock, the temp usually hit 115 to 120-plus degrees. We had to carry all our equipment into the location from the closest road. We could use mules, but no vehicles. It is a national park, with strict rules. A seven-thirty in the morning call meant a nine-thirty on-the-set for rehearsals. Sometimes we wouldn't get going until ten or later, depending on how much set dressing was needed or whether we wanted to lay dolly tracks. All those different requirements took time to fill. A lot of carrying stuff over trailless terrain.

UA sent Chris Mankiewicz down to have a talk with me. They felt that I was doing a "country-club shoot" because of the start times, lunch breaks, and wrap time. I explained the whole thing about getting the equipment to the set each morning, the excessive heat, and the loss of energy by the early afternoon. Then I asked Chris if he had noticed the number of setups and pages shot each day. He hadn't. "Thirty to forty setups each day," I said, raising my voice. "What country-club shoot does that kind of work?" I asked. He had no answer, and I was pissed, as was Michael. Chris wondered what he should tell his boss, Andy Albeck. I told Chris to tell Andy that he had two point three million in the game, as of that time; he could look at the dailies and see what cards he had; if he didn't want to stay in the game, let me know as soon as possible, because none of us wanted to go back out there in those 127-degree days without being able to finish the film properly. I left the table poolside at the Page Holiday Inn, jumped on my motorcycle, and sped off, back to my own private Lost Your Marbles Canyon stone house.

We finished the film doing pickup shots and a few interiors we couldn't get on location, on a soundstage in L.A. True to form, a grand pie fight closed the day, and at one forty-five in the morning, the Teamster captain drove me, Bridget, who'd joined me to watch the shooting, Brooke, and Larry Gorden's daughter back to the L'Ermitage and my town house suite. We all walked through the lobby sometime after two A.M. I vaguely recall wondering what the people behind the desk were thinking. Here I was with three very young teenage girls going up to my suite. We got to the room and I fell down on the floor, spread-eagled, and let out a huge sigh. I told the girls that they must all sleep in one of the two king-sized beds, as I was going to sleep in the other. In the morning, they could go downstairs, pull out the bed in the couch, order breakfast, and watch television. They were all going roller-skating the next day.

As I sat in the living room, slowly decompressing, I heard the girls giggling and jumping back and forth from one bed to the other, finally breaking them. I burned one, and when they were asleep, I went up to bed myself. I went into the bathroom and almost fainted. The room was completely walled with mirrors. On every inch of the mirrors they had made lipstick kisses and written things like: "Thanks Peter, you were the best," "We'll sleep with you anytime," "We love you so much," and on and on. I repaired my bed as best I could without waking them and was sound asleep when they left to go skating.

When I returned to the room, later in the afternoon, the maids had left the mirrors decorated as they were. I wish I had photographed the bathroom, but I'll always have the memory. I love all my memories of *Wanda Nevada*.

I rented a house in the hills above Malibu, and installed a KEM Table, three Moviolas, film racks, and trim bins, to begin editing *Wanda*. Becky came down as much as possible. Justin came over and spent as many nights with me as the stepfather would allow. He was going through a difficult period at home, poor little guy. We edited with gusto, but each morning, I was awakened by the repeated sound of my father saying to me, "Reckon one of us got up a little late this morning. Know it weren't me!" It was the first line Dad—in the role of Dutch Gravelle—said to me in the movie. I thought it was hysterical that I had my Dad saying this particular sentence. It was as if he and I were in real life, and he was berating me for not having put the top back on the toothpaste tube. Just like he had done for years. Scott

Conrad, the editor, put that line on a loop of tape and would play it over and over, until I got up.

I had fun editing the film. There were so many little throw-away lines that were very funny. Dennis Hackin, the writer, has a real touch. Basically, I sat in the sitting room, until I heard a scene being played too many times. That was my cue to come to the Flight Deck and put my thoughts in. At a certain hour, Scott would light up a cigar and dabble for a while. The day of hard work was winding down. Sometimes, the sound editor and assistant editor would stay for supper. I told them I was making beef Stroganoff. What I was really doing was making noodles and putting Campbell's Chunky Beef Soup on top. Becky was very curious when the boys said I made a great Stroganoff.

All the children spent Christmas with us at the ranch. Nineteen seventy-eight was a heavy snowfall year. We were really snowed in. Alan Ray Carter, a neighboring rancher and friend, drove his small Caterpillar full metal track bulldozer across the fields, and we chained up our pickup truck, and Alan Ray pulled it back across the field, plowing a passage as he went. The snow drifted right back in less than an hour, worse than it was before the dozer plowed its way in and out. Justin and Thomas convinced Becky to buy a snowmobile— the one they insisted on was a racing machine, but what would Becky know—and they were flying around the fields in ecstasy. The ridge that was left from the bulldozer took on the look of a cresting wave and was very packed. The boys made a high-banked track by blasting along the face of the ridge with the snowmobile. We dubbed it the Tunnel of Love.

Becky and I had to walk out of the ranch through the fields for a mile and a half to the next ranch where the pickup was stashed and plugged in for the block heater. Zip and Molly ran in front of us, helping to break a trail. After walking so far in high snow, we had the flattest stomachs and tightest butts in the area when we finally could drive in and out. The wall of the Tunnel of Love was the last thing to melt on the road. It had been packed really hard after countless shooting the curl by the boys. It was so wonderful watching the boys. They loved each other fiercely.

Back down to Smell A and finishing the editing. During the last part of the process, Andy Albeck, UA's top suit, ordered 850 prints from Technicolor. I recognized the release program. Dump it in the

South with a cursory play date in the larger-city market. I had been tipped off by one of our insiders at Technicolor. I was pissed. Our rough-cut screening was a hit at UA. I called Albeck and asked him to sell the picture back to me. I offered him six million dollars for the three and a half million he had in it.

"Have you talked to Steven or David?" he asked. "They are the mavens in the company."

"Are you the head of the company, Andy? Because I only talk to the head of the company when I want to buy the film. I don't talk to mavens unless they are *my* mavens."

"But you must talk to David or Steven."

"Look, let me buy the film. You aren't thrilled with it, for whatever reasons, and I can sell it better without your negative attitude. Anyway, you'll be two point five ahead, and that will look good for you at the stockholders' meeting."

"You must talk to Steven or David."

"Listen, you little Nazi fuck, take the six in cash and give me back the film." I hung up. In a few minutes, the phone rang, and Becky told me *I'd* better answer it. I didn't, so she did. I could hear the screaming as she handed me the phone.

"Nobody *ever* hangs up on me! Nobody *ever* hangs up on me!" Albeck shouted.

"Here comes take two, Andy," and I hung up the phone again.

United Artists released the film, and it was well received during the previews. It got good reactions when I took it on the road for its openings. As I expected, the main release was in the thirteen southern states. It never was released in New York City.

In this case, it *was* something I said. And I regret it for all the others in the cast and crew who had put such great effort into the making of the movie. I have learned not to call the head of a studio a Nazi fuck or hang up on him or her. Dad called Darryl Zanuck much worse names, but I wasn't Henry Fonda.

I finished '79 out with a TV movie called *Hostage Tower* in Paris. Many things were interesting about the shoot. I got to work with Maud Adams again. I worked all over the Eiffel Tower; I even had to jump in the Seine River. Becky came over to Paris as soon as she could, and joined in the fun we all were having on the tower. Artist Russ Chatham came, too, and joined with musician Jimmy Buffett, and friends Guy de la Valdéne and Guy's brother-in-law, Christian, in an old-fashioned game shoot on Guy's property, outside the city. Guy had a castle—he is a French count—and the gang went shooting in the European method. I had to work, but Becky was escorted around Paris by this incredibly wonderful and eclectic group. Guy was one of Becky's old friends who had decided the fate of my love and life with Becky four years earlier, in L.A. Eventually, everyone had to go back home, including Becky.

Paris hadn't changed much since Oates and I rolled through in '71. Fart fart.

chapter Twenty-five

*C*hristmas at the ranch. Much snow all around, and great skiing. Bridget's sixteenth birthday was coming up in late January. I bought her a Mazda GLC for her birthday, and hid it in one of the outbuildings. She found it, but wasn't into driving in the snow. My plan was to drive it down to L.A. in January in time for her actual birthday. I looked at the little car—GLC as far as I could figure meant great little car—very Japanese—and remembered my dad buying me the Bug in '57. Bridget's car had a radio, heater, gas gauge, and the other necessary instruments, front-wheel drive, five-speed tranny, and plenty of space to trash out in the back. It also got really great gas mileage. It was her key to her own freedom, just as mine had been, so many years before.

I flew Ike up for a short stay in the freezing winter—just to remind him how much we both missed the tropics, and to enlist his help in driving the car back down to La-La Land. Whenever I was driving, Ike kept his eyes tightly closed. He didn't want to see death approaching, he explained, commenting on my driving style. We did have to start out the trip by parking the little car way out in my driveway, so we wouldn't get drifted in. We made Hickory Dickory Dock—Rick and Lynnette Berg's bayside house and dock in Newport Beach—before nightfall in a day and a half. Around eighteen hundred miles. Bridget's birthday car was well broken in by the time she got it in her hot little hands. A good thing in my book. Broken in properly, the car should be trouble-free in the engine department for quite a while.

I met the ship at the California Yacht Club in Marina del Rey with Bridget and her boyfriend, and took them sailing to the Channel Islands for a birthday cruise. We returned in three days and I took the kids home. When the cast and crew reboarded the yacht to take her back to Newport, they were jumped by DEA agents and pushed around with quite a bit of force. One of my men stated that he was going to call the lawyers and was pushed back down into the main salon and told he could call whomever he pleased after they—the DEA—were through with us. Those little fascist fucks. Had I been on board they would have had to shoot me to stop me from going to a phone. These intimidation attempts by the U.S. government agents were getting close to the boiling point for me. I had had enough of their shit. I looked forward to the time when they would try to take me down or put the intimidation moves on *me*. Little did I know.

No sign of work in the pipeline, so it was back to the ranch and skiing with Becky and Thomas. Justin had been making a lot of noise about how badly he was treated by his stepfather. He had called the child-abuse hot line, I was told. Angie Dickinson, a dear friend and neighbor of the Lime Orchard house, told me of a very frightening encounter with the man in the middle of the night. He had broken into another neighbor's house, trashed their kitchen, broken several windows and a glass door, and run down to Angie's, demanding that she let him in. He was cooked on cocaine and booze, and literally out of his mind.

The other neighbor corroborated the story. It wasn't the first time they had called me to warn me about the situation in the house with my children. When Justin would ask me to take him away from the madness, I told him that he had to be at least fourteen years old before a judge would listen to him, and that I didn't want to make it any harder on his mom, who must have been going through hell. I advised him that leaving his mother like that would make him feel guilty for the rest of his life that he had abandoned her. It was tough for me not to simply take him and let the shit hit the fan. I didn't want to let this monster abuse my son or my daughter. I was even pissed that he was bad to my ex. She didn't deserve bad treatment. Bridget never said a thing. She was very loyal to her mom.

Becky and I had been invited to Tokyo by Akira Kurosawa, the brilliant Japanese motion picture director, for a special screening of his latest film, *Kagemusha*. Francis Ford Coppola had put this event together. Arthur Penn, Sam Peckinpah, William Wyler, and James Coburn were some of the other invited guests. We brought Kurosawa a tooled leather belt from Montana with "Akira" tooled in the middle of the back. Kurosawa was a tall man with a forty-four-inch waist. He chuckled and proudly said that his sons couldn't take this belt from him.

The movie was magnificent. Francis Ford Coppola wanted the Japanese government to recognize that Kurosawa was a national treasure and help finance his movies. All of us who are independent filmmakers owe a great deal to Francis. Most of us have stolen some part of Kurosawa's work. It was a great honor for Becky and myself to meet this wonderful man. The event did have some hysterical moments, though.

On the night of the big screening, we all were waiting in the lobby of the Okura Hotel for Sam Peckinpah. No show. Jim Coburn and I bravely went upstairs to get Sam out of bed. We pounded on his door, hearing him rant and stumble around his suite. Sam came staggering out in his underwear, drunk as a skunk, and started dancing with Jim. Jim quickly twirled Sam over to me. He asked me if I thought we could get him dressed in time, as the door to his suite closed loudly behind us. No key. Coburn had a brilliant idea. You keep Sam moving and I'll get another key, he said, loping down the hall to the elevators. I didn't mind so much, but dancing with Sam in the hall was a very uneven happening.

A security man came around the corner and discovered us. He had no idea what to do. I told him what was going on and asked him if he could open the door. He looked at me blankly. I identified myself and repeated the question. Sam kept saying, "Yessir, he's Peer Fonna, allrigh, yessiree." The security man was joined by a maid and a hall man. They just stood there staring. Sam was becoming harder to keep standing, let alone moving around. I finally got him pressed up against a wall, holding him up with my hands under his arms, but when he would start to pass out, his arms went quite limp, and he slid down the wall. It took a great effort to get him back up on his feet and propped against the wall again. Jim returned just in time, and we both danced Sam back into his room. There was no way he could make the screening. Coburn and I straightened ourselves up and went back down to the lobby, telling all that Sam was having a bout of the squirts and couldn't leave the toilet.

The movie was extraordinary. A great epic of early Japanese history. A masterpiece by a true master. No wonder Francis put so much into showcasing it. At the reception afterward, we were introduced to the cast and other notables in the Japanese motion picture industry. Toshiro Mifune the Magnificent, and several of the top Japanese cinematographers—they have some really hotshot shooters over there. It was a treat and an honor.

Becky and I went skiing in Hokkaido for five days with some friends. When we returned to the States, we were delayed at U.S. Customs for three and a half hours, as this little worm of an agent went through all of Becky's things. He even stuck his fingers into her face creams, while he gave us the evil eye. My god! These people are very bad actors. I finally went up to him and told him that the whole thing was going to come apart when he tried to look up my ass. "I can if I want," he said with his best war face. I pointed out that he hadn't bothered to check our skis or poles or boots, and that if he wanted to try for the ass check he would die quickly. I added that I would more than likely die next, but he could *count* on dying first. I mused that it would most likely be hand to hand, as there were so many people around, and peppered my musings with many colorful invectives. I gave him the old ten-years-and-ten-thousand dollars shot. I guess that the Treasury Department or Justice Department hadn't checked with the U.S. Army about my ass thing. He finally told me to just get out of there. If we were being watched to see who blinked first, everyone could see that it wasn't me.

We returned to the ranch and prepared for the summer. To my utter amazement, Susan told Justin he could come up to the ranch and stay with me, while he went to high school. She was very brave to do that. It was the perfect thing to do, as Justin wanted desperately to live with us and his brother, but it must have been very hard for Susan. I think it made the difference in Justin's life. It took a lot of patience to turn him around from being negative to being positive about himself, but it would happen in the following years. Bless your brave heart, Susan.

Susan also told me that, as Bridget was now sixteen, I needed to spend some very special time with her. She was right, and I began to think about what kind of special time would be right. I make movies, and that's pretty special in the larger view of a working man in the world. But if one is not *in* the movie, one can get quite bored very fast. And then I was struck by my own special life. Forget motion pictures; I sailed a large yacht around the tropics of the Pacific just for the adventure. One-tenth of one-tenth of one-tenth of one-tenth of a percent of the people in the world do that. *That* was something special, for sure.

So I made plans with the cast and crew to sail to Maui with my precious daughter. They were all very stoked by the idea. *All* the casts and crews who had sailed with me loved Bridget. And Susan agreed. Fab. Take my darling one and do a grand crossing. The yacht was in prime condition.

The plan was to leave Newport in time to make the Labor Day race. Our cast and crew for this special voyage was Owen Minney, a.k.a. Count Noport; Jimmy Heuman, our naviguesser; Jeff Hudson, backup nav and expert deckhand, Ike and his new matie and chief cook, Debbie; Peter Pinkham; Michelle, our backup cook; Gary Nutzel; and Bridget, whom we all referred to as the Pearl of the Pacific. When we were all aboard, the cast and crew gave me the most wonderful gift. For *every* voyage we made, I was just another crew member. I stood my watch with my partner, or reefed sails, raised sails, worked the winches, rigged the spinnaker pole, fixed things that were broken, and pulled my own weight without claiming status and privilege as the owner and master. For this crossing, I was given the liberty to do as I pleased. I could stand a watch, any watch, or not. It was the first time on a long voyage that I could go "yachting." And I *loved* it. Of course, I couldn't help but stand a watch or help with the rigging. But it was incredible to laze out in a deck chair on the cabin top with full sails and warm days. I never expected such a gift of time. Time to do as I pleased, whenever I pleased.

When Becky and I were in Japan, earlier that year, Sony gave me two of their latest products: the Walkman. For all the sailing we had done, music during the late-night watches was one of the few things the cast and crew might complain about. With the Walkman and two headsets each, a watch team could listen to music without disturbing those who were sleeping. I brought both Walkmans along for the voyage with plenty of great tapes to add to our own collection. They were an instant hit.

A few days into the crossing, we found out about the only problem with the Walkman. The listeners would begin to sing along with the tapes. This in itself might not have been so bad, but very few of the men at the helm could carry a tune. The result was a sort of caterwauling from the cockpit. The more the watch liked the music, the louder they would "sing" along. The result was also hilarious. Truly hilarious. It was so much worse than loud Little Richard at 0230 hours that someone had to let the offender know. It all came down to a show-and-tell. Once Berger heard how another shipmate was so out of tune and yet so into it, he got the message.

All the way to Maui, we caught fish, sunned, and enjoyed ourselves. When we reached land, we were greeted royally. Many alohas and a big luau. We made ready for the Labor Day regatta. The race began at 0630 for *Tatoosh,* but we were becalmed in an unexpectedly large lee off Molokai and didn't get near finishing in the metal. It was fine, though, since the entire trip had been such a fabulous experience. We were a tight cast and crew after twelve days of sailing, fishing, singing along with Ry Cooder, and yachting. So we pulled into the channel at the Ala Wai, feeling just fine.

When we entered the turning basin in the Ala Wai and paraded down to the end of the way, many of the other boats, already tied up, greeted us with a full naked crew, bending over as we passed and mooning us. It was a perfect welcome. We returned the compliment with a barrage of water balloons as we turned around and paraded back to Club 780. My slip.

The special time that I needed to spend with my daughter was more special than I could have dreamed. She will always be the Pearl of my Pacific. And the cherry on the cake was my son, Justin, coming to live with us at the ranch and starting high school in Livingston. He was fourteen, and in deep league with his brother. They were a perfect duo, though Thomas had a year to go at Saint Mary's before he could join him. Justin got his first driver's license. In Montana, one can get a license on one's fourteenth birthday. It is a very traditional thing. All hands are needed at a farm or ranch, so there is someone who can drive a car or truck as the haying or cattle drives are under way, even if it is a fourteen-year-old. Justin was very proud.

Becky got a phone call at the end of the summer from her very best friend, Therese de la Valdéne, Guy's beautiful wife. Terry was quite concerned for her friend. She told Becky that I had another wife in L.A., and was bragging about her all the time. Becky was momentarily stunned. He *does*, Terry insisted. Everyone knows about her. Terry went on to say that my other wife's name was Portia. Terry didn't know. There's lots that I don't know.

· · ·

During the summer, Dad, now seventy-five, had been getting weaker, so I went down to L.A. often to see him. He was as crabby as ever, and not easy to be around when he felt weak. It wasn't a feeling he could deal with easily. But I was more stubborn, and I wouldn't let him take me down to his level. Sometimes, I took on the part of the father, remembering the times in Connecticut when I was so ill. I worried for him. I knew he could not stand to be around weakness. There hadn't been any work, so far, in '80, so I decided to write and direct a little home movie, as it were.

Dad and I had been on the phone one autumn afternoon, and the spirit was in me. "Dad, if I have enough ego to call myself an actor, writer, producer, and director, there is this little scene I am going to write and direct. And you're going to star in it."

"What are you talking about, son?"

"I'm really saying, 'Your clock is running, and there are no time-outs.' "

"Sometimes, I can't follow what the hell you're saying, Peter."

"Well, you watch a lot of sports, so you're familiar with the phrase 'the clock is running and there are no time-outs.' "

"Jesus, Peter, I can't keep up with your thought pattern. I don't understand what you're getting at."

"What I'm getting at is, your heart is not going to get better, and there is nothing you can do about it. Your clock is running, and there are no time-outs." I wasn't going to let him get away. "So I'm writing this scene and I'm going to direct this great actor in it—that's you, Dad—and the name of the scene is 'I Love You Very Much, Son.' " He sputtered for a moment then hung up the phone. A few days later, I called him and told him about the news at the ranch, how the apples were doing, how the boys were doing. Things one says to someone who doesn't do much talking during a phone conversation. "Conversation" is giving Dad too much of an active role, given the way that he normally played on the phone, in the kitchen, in his garden, or even as a captive in a car. Anyway, at the end of our "conversation" I said, "I love you very much, Dad." No preamble. Right to the quick. He sputtered again and hung up.

After five or six of these exchanges on the phone, and after I had said I loved him very much, he spat the words "Iloveyoutooson," into the phone. "No, no, no, Dad, you don't say the line as a response to something *I've* said. It has to come from your heart. It has to be an original idea that is not a repeated phrase. You have to fill its moment with your own reality. Now, we won't do the scene again, today, but think about what I've just said, okay? And I'll call you again in a few days. I love you very much, Dad." He said yes, and hung up.

Soon, he was beating me to the end of the telephone "conversation" with his very own, "I love you very much, son." With the distance and the plastic between us, I had given him a chance to ease into the scene. But I knew it would only count if we could do it looking down the barrels, person to person, live. I told him that there were some things I had to do in Smell A, and I would drop by for a visit, the next week. I had nothing really important to do in my business, but I had this very important thing to do with my dad.

A week later, having called first, I drove over to his house in the early afternoon. He was out of bed and walking around the lower floor with the aid of a walker. "I really hate this thing, son, but my cane doesn't work well on the tiles." He was embarrassed about his weakness, but he needn't have been in front of me. We went into the library-bar and he poured himself a shot of tequila with a beer back. I was astounded. I passed on the tequila but shared a beer with him.

He was more animated than usual, and spoke about the neighbors' complaints over his chickens. But there was no stalling about the reason I was there.

I could see that he was tiring, so I made the noise of have to go to some meeting. That relieved him a bit. I had taken the initiative to get to the end of the scene. We both walked slowly to the front door. Once outside, he took me by the shoulders. It was as if he were pushing me away, and at the same time drawing me close. Tears were streaming down his cheeks. Slowly and choking on the high-powered emotion, he said, "I love you very much, son. I want you to know that."

I hugged him so hard, I could feel the pacemaker in his chest. Tears streaming down my own cheeks, I told him I loved *him* very much and kissed him on his lips. Something we had never done before. I quickly drove off, stopping at a nearby park to have the good hard cry I needed. It had been done, and done with real emotions and originating feelings. Years of frustration fell off my heart like melting snow sliding off a roof.

We had a wonderful Christmas with great skiing. I had made some good cash endorsing some Japanese products, so the year wasn't a loss financially, but not working at my craft was very difficult. We had to sell the house in Key West in order to buy land butting up to the creek that flowed through my property from Big Tom. It was a forced move, but one we had to do to protect our ranch. For all I knew, Tom would sell the land to a developer, and we would be looking at a trailer park every morning. We got swizzed by him earlier into buying several hundred acres in the next county, so we had no choice. It was almost as if he was trying to bring us down, but I can't really believe it. And I don't care.

Nineteen eighty-one was looking much better. I was offered a role in a movie to be directed by Ted Kotcheff, *Split Image*. I would be costarring with James Woods, Brian Dennehy, Tatum O'Neal, Elizabeth Ashley, Michael O'Keefe and Peter Horton. I was playing the part of a cult leader, and felt I had a good grasp on the role.

Dad went into ICU at Cedars in West Hollywood and I flew in to be with him. When I arrived at the room, Dad was in bed with all sorts of tubes going into his body, and everyone in the room was very down and scared. I walked in and asked him, loudly, what the hell he was doing in this ICU room. "Are you trying to scare us all, or what? Oh! Wait a minute! I bet you've told these doctors you have some sort of heart problem, so you can get in here and get some drugs! That's it, isn't it?" I was saying all this as I made my way around his bed. "What kind of drugs are you taking, anyway?" I asked in a more conspiratorial tone as I looked at the IV bags that hung by his bed. "Whoa! What the hell is this stuff? I bet you don't even know! You just want to scare people and take drugs. I told you that if you wanted drugs, call me! Remember?" By this time I was around to the other side of his bed. Everyone in the room was shocked at my behavior, but I knew exactly what I was doing. I grabbed his head and kissed him fully on the lips. "I love you very much, Dad; you know that, don't you?"

"I do, son. Yes I do." And he gave me a big smile. The dourness of the room left, and family was together with Dad in his dying time. If any of them thought that he was going to be getting better, they hadn't been paying attention. Jane pulled me aside in the hall and asked me how I did that. How did I just walk in there and bustle about with all my voice, trying to be funny?

I told her that we didn't have much time left with him, and we had to get in all the love and closeness we had missed for years, as fast as we could, and on *our* terms. And being funny was great medicine. Now was not the time to tread lightly. Go for the gusto, I told her, there wouldn't be another time. I was thrilled to hear that Jane would come in, later, and just grab his feet and massage them. He had never let anyone touch his feet before. Maybe Shirlee.

Becky and I went down to Palm Beach, Florida, to visit Terry de la Valdéne. About a week into Palm Beach, Elizabeth Ashley called me and said, in a worried voice, that the shoot for *Split Image* was falling apart, and the crew kept asking about me and when was I coming. She believed that if I came a little early, it would help keep the crew from bolting. I had worked with many of the guys on camera and the electricians. I took her seriously, and prepared to go to Texas. Becky joined me once we were under way.

When I checked in with the production office, I was warmly greeted by the group. They handed me a call sheet without any comment. I thought that was weird, as I wasn't working for a week or so. The call sheet for that day listed those actors and scenes to be shot. It read: Tatum O'Neal travel to L.A. When I asked them if this was the first time she was told she was off the picture, they nodded. How terrible, I thought. What a low-rent thing to do. She had to be replaced, as she was a minor and couldn't do all the night stuff that was required. Still, I thought there was a better way to let her know. My opinion of Kotcheff dropped considerably. His on-set producer wasn't much better.

I spent two days with former president Jimmy Carter's sister, Maureen. She was the head of a religious cult that was nearby. After our meeting, she told me that *I* could "be good at this. Really good!" She was dying at the time, but was very pleasant, and helped me a lot with my character.

When the movie finished, Becky and I drove back to the ranch in the 6.9. The drive back helped me to leave the madness of the set behind.

I had another offer to do a film in Toronto with Oliver Reed. I accepted at once, as I wanted to work with this legendary actor. Reed and I got along well. After an evening of Cuba Libres, he took me on a tour of Toronto that I will never remember. I awoke, wearing my raincoat, lying on my bed. The twenty-five hundred dollars I had in my pocket was still there, thank goodness. The film was released on cable as *Spasm*. It may have had a theatrical release; it was definitely forgettable.

With my Japanese endorsements and the two films, the year was fiscally terrific, and we enjoyed a great Christmas. Dad was going to the hospital often now, and I flew in to be there each time. I wondered how he felt about his condition. He promised Shirlee he would stay alive until Halley's comet visited again, but that was not even close to possible.

One afternoon, sitting at his bedside at home, I was very moved to see and hear him making sounds as if to say no and shaking his head. He appeared to be asleep, and I took his hand in mine. He continued making the sounds and shaking his head from side to side. I was thinking that he wanted out. He squeezed my hand twice, and thinking he was acknowledging my presence, I asked him slowly if he wanted to die. He stopped making the sounds and shaking his head but didn't say anything. Once again I asked him if he wanted to die. I drew very near to his ear and whispered that if he wanted to die, I would do anything he asked. He turned his head slightly, touching my right cheek with his lips, then moved away back to his pillow. "No, no, no, no, no," he said. He went back to making the sounds and shaking his head.

I was very upset. Dad was now incontinent, and the little I did know of him made me aware that he couldn't abide not being able to take care of himself; he had no patience with malfunction or inability, where there had been such ability and perfect function before. I put his hand back on his chest, fixed the oxygen tube that was taped to his neck and face so it didn't fall away, and went to the kitchen. As I walked there slowly, I remembered the many times he would bat the tube away as if swatting a fly. It annoyed him. It was a constant reminder that he needed assistance to do the simple things. The father I knew couldn't bear the thought of someone else cleaning him up and bathing him, even if it was his wife, Shirlee. She must have loved him very much, as she never complained to anyone, and she was always the one that cleaned him and bathed him. I walked into the kitchen and sat at the table with Shirlee and Aunt Harriet. I told them that I thought he wanted to die now. That the dignity of his private life was gone, and that loss was too much for him to face each day, as his heart slowly failed. Harriet nodded as I described the moment just past. She had watched him do the same thing repeatedly, she said. Shirlee asked if he had said anything, and I told her he had said no four or five times quickly. We all fell silent.

"Please don't give up, Peter," Shirlee begged softly.

"*I* won't give up, but I think he might, and I don't want him to suffer the ending of his life in despair. I hope he has his dignity intact, right up to the last minute." Harriet nodded with big tears in her eyes. Shirlee sat grim-faced, but with an attitude of positiveness. I had to go. It had been a rough twenty or so minutes for me. It must have been incalculable for him.

. . .

I had accepted a role in a movie to be shot in the Philippines. It was a great character, and another chance to play a comic role: a drunken helicopter pilot with a run-down Huey, flying around the jungles of some equatorial country. Part of the deal was that I got to take my camera team. I didn't trust the director or producer, though the producer hadn't done anything really wrong. My camera team was Michael Butler, David Butler, Bobby Guthrie, Don Wollok, and Ray Ochoa. The all had been on *Wanda Nevada*, and we were a tight and fast group. Michael and I went with the production manager to scout the locations outside Manila. The producer met us there. The director missed the flight. We found out that the generator promised hadn't been in service since 1950; the sixty feet of dolly track only went together one way. There was no chance to add a curve or add a piece; the soundstages were so full of birds that a direct soundtrack was impossible, let alone an added bit of poop dropping in the middle of a scene. I was a bit discouraged, but Michael reminded me that if anyone could do it, we could do it better with less. We called ourselves Los Goddammits.

On our way back to the States, we cleared customs in Honolulu. I was the third person in line and presented my passport to the agent. For the first time, I noticed that the passport control agents were using small video monitors instead of the old books with names of undesirables and other state enemies. As I looked at the monitor, I could see my name, my federal ID number, my long-useless California driver's license and . . . wait a minute . . . what the fuck was that? It showed "narcotics violation boat." I said loudly, "What does that say?"

"You can't read that!" the agent said, quickly covering the screen with my papers and passport.

"The hell I can't. I helped pay for it!" And I shoved the papers away from the screen. I had to touch the agent to accomplish the move. Start counting: abusive language, pushing (assaulting) a fed . . . more than ten and ten. "What does that say, asshole?"

"You've had a narcotics violation on your boat!" he snapped back without thinking. At this moment, a tall silver-haired agent came over to us.

"What's going on here?" he demanded.

"What the fuck does that say?" I demanded back.

"Don't use that kind of language to me, young man!" Young man? Who was he kidding?

"Fuck you, mister. Fuck you and your ten and ten!"

"Ten and ten? What do you mean, ten and ten?"

"Ten years and ten thousand dollars for abusive language, dickhead! Now what the fuck is the meaning of this shit?" I demanded even louder, pointing to the video monitor.

"You've had a narcotics violation on your boat!" I stepped back for the dramatic moment.

"You and you, malicious libel and slander! And I've got over a hundred witnesses. Isn't it lucky for you fucking fascists that the government and its agents can't be charged with those crimes. If I had a fucking narcotics violation on my *vessel*—you see, "boat" is not a legal term—if I had a fucking narcotics violation on my vessel, who would own my yacht?"

"It would have been confiscated, and stop using that language!"

"Fuck you! This is totally fucking bogus! Let's go down to the Ala Wai and see who the fuck owns my ship, you slimy dickheads!" I screamed. The older man was really undone by my bombardment.

"Stop swearing at us," he said. "We're not the ones responsible for this information!"

"But you're the ones disseminating it, you stupid fuck, and I will *not* stop swearing at you or anybody until this is cleared up!" There! That set the playing field, I thought. The older man must have guessed there was a huge mistake. He went and got a paper with the letters TECS on it and gave it to me.

"This is who you have to straighten things out with! Now get out of here!"

"What the fuck does TECS mean?"

"Treasury Enforcement Communications System." God, how those bureaucratic assholes love their acronyms. The producer, Michael, and I went on down to my yacht to shower, shave, and use the phones. It was never too early to call my attorneys. I asked them to find out everything there was about TECS. I was pissed. And I would stay pissed for quite a long time.

.   .   .

Manila was so polluted and dirty and full of honking horns, police whistles, brownouts, and traffic, it was almost too much. Almost. The producer had arranged rooms at the best hotel in the city. It was right on the bay with a beautiful pool and very nice rooms. We were all grateful to him. A rough shoot is always made better with nice accommodations. These were terrific. We traveled each morning in the dark on our way to Los Baños, a rain forest two hours outside of Manila.

A strange thing happened during the shoot. Deborah Raffin, playing my female lead, and I were supposed to be pushing my dilapidated Huey out of its hangar.

Now, two people cannot push a Huey half an inch. But this is the movies and push we did, with the help of thirty-five Filipinos pulling on a large rope tied to the front and ten or twelve others pushing on the tail boom.

Deborah and I were both warned about the wheels that were clamped onto the Huey's skids, so we wouldn't get hurt by them. I heard "action," and the whole bunch of us moved this thing while Deborah and I did our lines.

Take one was good, but we wanted another, so here comes take two. This time I tried another approach, and as I was getting in real deep, the fucking wheels ran over my right foot. Very slowly. It hurt a lot. But after hopping around and yelling "fuck" for five minutes, I was ready for the next take. It was just at the end of my lines that the wheel ran over my foot for the second time. Watching the dailies later, it hurt to see my face on both takes. It hurt so much that we all were screaming with laughter. I was wearing dirty white sneakers, but one could see where the wheels ran over my right foot. Jesus, it hurt. But we went on and finished the scene. By this time, I was hardly able to walk.

The day's shooting was over, so the production manager, Mitch Gamson, took me to the main hospital in Manila. He found a wheelchair and pushed me around looking for someone to x-ray my foot. We found our man and explained what had happened. The hospital was experiencing a brownout, but the doctor was able to see that my foot looked like a small swim fin. He gave me a shot of Demerol, and by the time the power was back up, I wasn't in pain and the X-ray machine could do its magic. On the film, one could easily see the spreading of the metatarsal bones, but none of the bones were broken. I was lucky.

One afternoon, as I sat on the toilet in my suite, the phone rang. There was an extension right on the wall. I felt a cold, clammy chill come over me. I answered it.

"Duke, are you sitting down?" It was Becky.

"Yep." I was certain she was going to tell me my father had died.

"Warren's dead, darling."

"What? Oates?" I squeaked.

"Yes, sweetheart. I'm so sorry to tell you, but I thought it would be better to hear about it from me than a newspaper." She was right.

She explained the dirty thing to me, and I said I had to hang up. She understood. I flushed the toilet and immediately puked into it. Warren Oates was only fifty-two. I loved him dearly. We had done three films together and planned on many more.

He never had to die. He had stopped breathing because of an acute attack of emphysema. I'll always miss him. That evening, those who knew him on our shoot gathered in my suite. We had a small wake at sunset.

We were in the jungle near Los Baños, when word came by way of a ham radio operator that Dad had won the Best Actor Academy Award. The whole set erupted with joy. All the Filipinos loved my dad. I was certain that he would get it and only hoped he lived long enough to know. Though he had always said the award meant nothing to him, I felt that this time it was an exception.

The producer gave us five days off during Easter. As a goodwill gesture, he explained. The entire country shuts down for Easter; he had no choice. I took Bridget and Justin, who had flown in to visit me, to a resort. Bridget's hair was the color of an Eberhard-Faber No. 2 eraser. Dirty pink.

Becky came in a few days after the kids had left, to spend the rest of the shoot with me. We wrapped the film and flew to Hong Kong for a week's party. We all stayed at the Regent Hotel—one of the best in the world—and ate our little hearts out. The manager and his wife took a liking to us and arranged a different dinner each night.

One afternoon as we were cruising the streets, we came on a movie house that was going to play *Wanda Nevada*. This concept stunned me. We met the exhibitors and offered to cut the film down a bit if they'd like, but they wanted it just as it was. They had found it while they were in L.A. looking for product to exhibit. They were in the library at UA and saw the title and stars of the film. When they asked about it, they were told it wasn't very good, but they wanted to see it anyway. They bought the film for a two-week run for ten thousand dollars flat. It earned more than six hundred and fifty thousand dollars in profit for them in just one theater. As soon as the rest of the Golden Triangle (Japan, Singapore, and Indonesia) heard about it, they all wanted to show it. Suddenly, UA wanted 70 percent of the take, and asked for a fifty-thousand-dollar rental. That killed the deal. I wonder why UA would do a thing like that. Couldn't have been Andy Albeck and the "Nazi" phone call hang-up? . . . Naw. Not possible . . . is it?

After drinking all the '71 Dom pink in the hotel's cellar, I flew to Germany by the back door for my next film, and Becky and the rest flew home. I spent four weeks in Munich making *Peppermint Frieden,* a movie about the life of a young girl just after the Second World War. A German avant-garde film. I jetted back to the States by Concorde. I had to make Bridget's graduation. I had promised my children I wouldn't miss any of their graduations.

After the ceremony, Bridget and I were walking together, and she told me she wanted to be an actor. "Don't you *ever* say that again!" I said.

"But, Dad . . ."

"It's a verb, not a noun. Where are you going to study *acting*?"

"UCLA."

"Like hell. You're going to go to Princeton or Yale or . . ." I began to act as if I were having a nervous breakdown.

"Stop it, Dad! Everyone is looking!"

"I, uh uh hu, don't, un un, omygod, no you, uh, uh . . ."

"Pleeease stop it, Dad."

"If you're serious about *acting,* you should go to NYU. They have theater there. They have great acting schools and teachers. They have all the new, hip off-off-Broadway stuff. There's learning in them thar concrete and glass towers. New York University. Work in every student film. Get used to the camera. Get used to yourself being someone else. I love you more than words can say. Take my advice." My little girl. The Pearl of my Pacific. She certainly had presence and grace. All she needed was to work on her talent. She did.

Shirlee wouldn't let us come by for a second so Bridget's grandpa could see his first grandchild, who had just graduated from Westlake—two minutes from his house. He wasn't up to it, she told me. I learned later that he was visiting with someone else at the time, and wasn't even aware of her graduation, though he had been sent an announcement. That pissed me off so much. I knew it wasn't Dad who decided that. I should have just gone there, with my Pearl on my arm.

I flew to the ranch with Becky, made a videotape of the place with its new gravity-fed irrigation system and the beautiful apple blossoms to show to Dad, and we all flew to the yacht off Lahaina for a few weeks. I had a commercial to shoot in L.A. in early August, and needed the break. Before we left, I began researching TECS. I called my lawyers and let them know how angry I was about the whole narcotics-on-the-yacht affair. I suggested that a claim be put in for whatever shit the feds were up to by way of the Freedom of Information Act. I didn't have a lot of confidence about just how much "freedom" I would get in this bid, but I knew I had to do something drastic and confrontational. I knew I would get what I needed if I stayed in their face about this piece of garbage they were throwing around about me.

In the middle of the commercial shoot, I got a call from Shirlee saying Dad was in critical condition and back in ICU at Cedars. I went there that evening, and spent some time in the ICU. Jane came with her husband, Tom, and we all stood by Dad. I didn't do any funny stuff. I knew that the Big Bell was tolling.

Dad lay in his bed, very weak. At about ten o'clock, he opened his eyes and looked around the room. He stared at Shirlee, opening and closing alternate eyes as if to find focus. He looked over at his first-born, his daughter, and did the same thing. He looked at Tom and then he looked at me, pinning me with both of his beautiful blue eyes. "I love you so very much, son. I want you to know that." And he closed his eyes and lay his head back on the pillow. These were the last words he spoke before he died. There are not many sons who get to have that moment with their fathers. Everything that had gone so wrong for so long was wiped from the slate.

There are times when I still get angry with him for some omission or other meaningless thing, but those times are immediately pushed away as I hear my dad's last words ringing like the Chimes of Freedom in my heart.

The next morning, we all went right away to the hospital. Shirlee had phoned me early to say that Dad had died. It was August 12, 1982. We all got to the ICU about the same time. I kissed his cold forehead, angry that the nurses had not changed his face from the death grin. I tried, but to no avail. I pulled him back to the middle of the bed, touched him for the last time, and went to his house in Bel Air with Jane and Shirlee. It was a very upsetting thing for the two of them. I wasn't dancing a jig, but I wasn't surprised. I hoped that the peace I had found in my relationship with him would be felt by Jane.

He had specified in his will that he be cremated and his ashes be thrown out with the trash. He wanted no service, no memorials, no special attention. That sounded just like my father. Friends began to arrive at the house, bringing food and other things. A gathering was going to happen, no matter his will. It was the will of his friends, family, and wife, and he had no way to stop us all from coming together to share in his life and his death.

Jimmy Stewart came by and sat in the library, silently, for a long time. At the right moment for Jimmy, he said, "I remember the kites." He went on for a half hour, and no one made a sound.

Later in the evening, Jim Garner and his wife, Lois, came by to be with Shirlee during those frightening and suddenly empty first nights.

I had been staying at L'Ermitage, but moved into the gate house at the Bel Air villa to be with my sister and Shirlee. I was out in that place watching the video I had made for Dad. He never was well enough to watch it. I'm sure that everyone in the family was quite worried about me. I had been the one of the bunch to react the most emotionally to the tragedies that befell us all. It was the exact opposite for me. At least this time I was able to watch the entire passage of a parent or loved one. I had closure with my father. There was no mystery about his death. I was upset because he had been gathered much too early at age seventy-seven. If he had a healthy heart, he might still be alive and grousing about some injustice happening in the world; he might be still hugging me and kissing me on my lips with his fatherly love. But he isn't. And I don't feel abandoned by him anymore. And I don't feel incomplete.

Anyway, Jim Garner came out to the gate house to visit with me. He was so cool. He brought a silver cigarette case full of joints for me, and we talked. About Dad. About life and death. I'm sure he was concerned about me and whatever grief I might be having. The house was full of females. We were waxing as Jane came in.

"Peter, there's a problem."

"What kind of problem?"

"She wants him, but his will specified that he was to be thrown out with the trash after he was cremated."

"Sounds like him, the way he'd say it, I mean."

"But she wants his ashes, Peter. She's clinging on to whatever there is left of him." I certainly understood that.

"Okay. It's okay, Jane, she can have him." But somewhere I have this very different idea that I betrayed him. At that moment, I should have stood firm. Stood by his last will, and so forth. Prevailed with the family motto, persevered. But it was all Shirlee had left of the man she couldn't live without. And what difference did it mean to him? He dismissed his significance. Being kept by Shirlee was certainly better than being thrown out with the trash.

The next night was very similar: Garner and I out in the gate house, remembering. Jane came out to the house. "We've got another problem, Peter. She's got him under her bed."

"That's sick," I said.

"I know, but what are we going to do?"

"Get him out from under her bed." I had a plan. "Go back to the kitchen and get Shirlee and Lois to keep their attention centered on the table."

"What are you going to do?"

"I'm going to boost the house and get him."

I've often wondered what Garner thought about this two-part conversation. To me it was all hysterical. The way we referred to the ashes as "him." The whole idea of sneaking into the house to liberate him. Jane, who was much more undone by the death and this extended wake, brought me this bit of family news as if we were in some spiritual conspiracy. I like that thought. I think that's the way I'll remember this special moment. My sister and I trying to do right by our father's wishes and, at the same time, trying to make things as easy on Shirlee as possible.

Of course, I needed Jim's help in the caper. He was definitely in for the gig, but he wasn't quite sure what the gig was. As we were sneaking our way around the house to gain entrance, Jane came out, whispering loudly to me that everything was all right, she had taken him out from under her bed. "Where is he?" I asked. "I don't know," she said.

The whole reason that was given for getting his ashes was to scatter them on the Platte River, which runs through Grand Island, Nebraska, Dad's birthplace. Great idea. But Dad is lost somewhere in the Bel Air house. Why do I hear, ripping through my brain? *Oh, Dad, Poor Dad, Mama's Hung You in the Closet, and I'm Feeling So Sad,* a play by Arthur Kopit, which I read for in '60.

I finished the commercial and went back to the ranch, satisfied that I had parted with my father in a very pure way. I can still see Jane, in the early morning, sitting under one of his apple trees, holding on to it and softly crying. It touches my heart in such a sad way. My sister deserves to be a happy person. She has done so much for so many. She's done so much for me. I want to do something fine for her. If the family motto prevails, I will.

We took the children to the yacht for a few weeks and played in the sun. We all loved the times on the yacht, but I was spending more and more time at the ranch.

I went off to make a movie in Tokyo, right after the Labor Day race. The children had to be back in school. It was Justin's freshman year in high school.

I had a great time in Tokyo. With the generosity of the producer, I was put in the penthouse of the Keio Plaza. I did laps around the huge suite as part of my exercise. Becky joined me just before we left for a location on Saipan, one of the Northern Mariana Islands. We went to a Stevie Wonder concert in Yokohama. It was great, and Stevie invited me out onstage to sing with the group. I was thrilled.

Saipan was a perfect paradise for the two of us. It was getting colder in Tokyo, and both of us love to swim in the warm oceans. We had our seventh anniversary on the island. As usual, Becky had to get back to the ranch for the boys, but not before she had her fill of sun, sandy beaches, and a great tan. The people of the island were very nice to us and took us diving and fishing. The lagoon on the west shore was magnificent. We dove on old sunken World War II planes and tanks one could see clearly in the light, blue-green waters inside the coral reef.

A week after Becky had left, the hotel informed me that I had a telegram from her, which read: "Don't worry, the boat is fine and all the boys are okay. Much love, Bundle."

Don't worry . . . ? What the hell does she mean? I thought. My mind was racing. What happened to the yacht? What does it mean that the boys are all fine? The connection of the word "boys" was specifically put in the yacht's terms, not referring to our sons. When I was finally able to reach her at the ranch, all was explained.

An enormous hurricane had hit Hawaii. Becky's flight took her from Saipan to Guam to Honolulu, where she cleared customs and heard the concern all the island people had about the incoming storm. From Honolulu she flew to L.A., spent one night there, and flew on to the ranch. As soon as she got home, she called the ship. Ike answered the phone in utter disbelief. The phone jack and power outlet were both under several feet of water. The fact that the phone was ringing was a miracle.

More of a miracle was that Owen Minney, Poncho Pollack, and several other members of the cast and crew *happened* to be at Club 780 just before the storm hit. The waves and surges were coming over the breakwall as if it weren't there. Two feet of water, at the least, were flooding the parking lot. All hands were on deck manning the twin bow and stern lines and the spring lines. As the water rose, the men let the lines out just enough to keep the hull in its slip area. When the water receded, they took in the lines and kept the hull from hitting the cement dock or the two large cement pillars that framed our slip. It is very possible that the surging and breaking water could have put the yacht up onto the parking lot. Had that happened, there was no way to put the ship back into the water. The yacht was too big and heavy to lift by crane, even if the sticks were out. It would simply be on its side in the parking lot. A lost cause. Or a hamburger stand.

Timing was the magic thing. Owen had been in Tahiti, it had rained during his entire stay and he came back to Hawaii on his way home. Poncho had been on a charter out of Australia that was lost at sea for four weeks, and he had come back looking for shelter. Others just happened to be there at the right time.

We had a nice Christmas at the ranch, and then Justin and Bridget joined their mother. Thomas, Becky, and I drove to Sun Valley to ski and be with Jane and her children. Shirlee was staying there, too. It was her first Christmas without Dad. We had a good time there.

I remembered everything from so many years before. There were times when I looked at Jane, and she was only nine. Fortunately, no one else saw her that way.

chapter *Twenty-six*

*O*ther than a big show in Las Vegas for my Japanese benefactors in the commercial world and a nice, big bundle of cash, 1983 was a bad one. The actor's strike stiffed the two projects I had lined up. I have never understood how an actor can strike. From everything I learned about the gift through my father, an actor's strike is an oxymoron. But strike they did. I spent the summer at the ranch.

In midsummer, my Freedom of Information Act file arrived from the Treasury Enforcement Communication System. Almost all the information was blacked out. I was livid. What part of "freedom" doesn't the government understand? My name was spelled correctly, as were Ike's and BC's. The name of the ship was spelled correctly. My California driver's license—which had expired years earlier—was accurate, as was my Federal Identification Number. Most of the rest was blacked out. I fumed around my cabin for a few days. Things had been added to the pages by federal agents. They were all the codes and rules under which the feds could avoid fulfilling the rights that were granted by the Act.

On a sunny afternoon, several days later, I noticed the papers sitting in the sun on the dining room table. I saw that the blacked-out stuff was covered with a substance different from the paper. I took a small pen knife and, very gently and carefully, began to scrape the black substance from the paper. Soon, I saw a typewritten "e" and stopped further scraping. I called Anthony Pellicano, a high-powered private investigator friend, and explained the haps. I was hoping he could retrieve the rest of the document by some chemical means.

Anthony laughed in a delighted way. He explained that instead of sending me a photocopy, the boys at TECS simply had mailed the grease-penciled copy to me. Foolish boys. Anthony was able to retrieve everything: even the names of the different informants and other names of TECS agents. Bingo. The Big Bingo, for that matter.

The United States Department of the Treasury stated—not alleged—that I was manufacturing five pounds of coca paste a week from my "boat," smuggling marijuana from Hilo, on the Big Island, to Seattle, and generally trafficking in drugs. What dildos. Nobody smuggles *anything* from Hilo to the mainland. Everyone leaves from Kauai. And five pounds of coca paste? Do we all know what coca paste is? It's the base for the manufacturing of cocaine powder. In order to manufacture paste at a five-pound-per-week rate, I would have to gut the entire belowdecks area and buy another ship of at least the same size. I was definitely dealing with dangerously delinquent logic. The "information" came from a person trying to make a deal with the feds in San Diego to lessen his own downtime. His name is in the file, as are the names of all the local and federal agents and informants involved.

I quickly learned everything there was about TECS: how it was formed, whose idea it was. Normally, one would just be outraged, but in this case I had a great shot at suing the U.S. government for major bucks. Abuse of process. Not an easy case to make and win. But on my side of the case, I could demonstrate real monetary loss, *because* of their abuse of my due process.

When you want to take down the snake, go for its head. And I certainly knew how to hit the snake in the head, even with a snub-nosed revolver. Poor Peter Grimes. Little Petie Grimes was the head of TECS.

I called Mr. Grimes as soon as I had his number. He took the call! I don't think he even knew of the plot to brand me as a narcotics trafficker. He probably asked his secretary if it was the *real* Peter Fonda. It was. Hee hee. I threw every vituperative you have read in this book, and those that I dare not write, at him. I also gave him the ten-and-ten routine in an extraordinarily calm voice, then went back on the high board, blasting right through his fucking phone and biting his ear off. I probably suggested that he not start his car, and that he should keep his children locked up in his house. I was truly ballistic. This asshole was sitting at the head chair of the conference room, deciding to put this gross misinformation into the public collective knowledge. Now, *if* I *had* been running drugs, I would have quietly had the mess taken care of by my attorneys. **BUT I WASN'T!**

Weeks later, my attorneys called me and told me about the deal they had worked out with the government. I told them I might not be interested in a deal. They told me to get serious. Apparently, the government realized they had screwed up in a major way, and promised to clear my record, but I would have to understand that I would be treated like any other normal U.S. citizen. I had been trying to be treated like a regular citizen for a long time.

When I go through customs now, everyone is polite and friendly, asking me about how my life is, when am I going to make another *Easy Rider,* saying how beautiful my daughter is. I am not treated like the enemy. I declare everything, and the agents say that this or that isn't necessary, or whatever. They actually help me properly evaluate different items. We talk about the Braves and Jane and Ted. I hear you live on a ranch in Montana, they say. Nice things. And I, in turn, am very polite with them. No reason to be otherwise.

After all that, I was ready for a good sail, and we all went to the yacht. When the winds were forty-five knots plus in the Pailolo Channel, we went sailing, tacking back and forth between Maui and Molokai. Big waves, big winds, big boat, yes. I knew that I would have to sell the yacht, soon, though. I was getting older and all of my cast and crew were, too. We couldn't live the life we had created much longer. The men and women who made up the cast and crew needed to have something in their banks. They needed to have some security (oh, that dirty word), and I couldn't blame them.

No work brought much stress to my life. To offset the stress, we skied in the great "cold smoke." This is what we call the powder at Bridger Bowl, twenty-eight minutes from the ranch. When the wind blows, the fine, dry powder flies like smoke from the trees; it looks as if they are about to burst into flame. Everyone came for Christmas, and I wallowed in the family. My blessed family.

I got a good movie of the week with NBC, but it barely scratched the surface of my inner needs. However, with another commercial for the Japanese, the money was just fine. Or so I thought.

Justin was about to graduate from high school, while I was just finishing the movie of the week. The producers were very kind and let me fly to Montana for the ceremony. I rented the Learjet and flew up. I took Shirlee with me. Jane and I were doing our best to keep including her in the family haps. I was so proud of Justin. So happy I could be there for him. Shirlee promised him his grandfather's gold watch, when he graduated from college, and we flew back to L.A. I had to be on the set the next morning.

I was able to be with Bridget a few times, and that always made me forget the pressure and stress. My perfect Pearl. She was slaving away at NYU and studying with Anna Strasberg.

Jane and I tried many times to make a movie together, but it wasn't in the cards. We were both into the idea, but we couldn't come up with the right story. It wasn't because we were too picky. Several scripts were written, but they didn't turn on any of the studio heads we were close to. I could feel a strain in her life with Tom, but if she didn't say anything, I wasn't going to pry. I loved her very much and didn't feel she was being treated well by him. Regardless of the stress and pressure, Becky always made me feel that things were going to be all right. I loved our little cabin, and the two boys, inseparable, were a great stabilizer for me. I had to keep fighting, if only for them. I took one last sail on my beautiful yacht and sold her.

> *17 April, 1984 2245*
> *Tomorrow, we take on new owners. We do this reluctantly, sadly and, for myself, with a tremendous wound in my freedom and sovereignty. My hopes are that* Tatoosh *will be maintained well. She is the last great wooden ship built on this planet. So much passion passes from my direct access and control, it is hard to imagine. It is hard to imagine myself without* Tatoosh *or* Tatoosh *without me . . . I search all the horizons* Tatoosh *has shown me and wonder if anyone can understand this . . . I regret only that Justin and Thomas, my dear sons, never made a long crossing. I wanted so much for them to experience the thrill, discipline, and delight at sailing aboard the last great wooden sailboat . . . I've been so proud of her for the almost 100,000 miles she has sailed for me . . . I shall miss her and all who have joined with me in her great adventure. I wish all who will sail her know the peace, life, beauty, and excitement we have all loved so much. I wish them safe passages. God save this ship and all who sail upon her.*
> *Signed: Peter Fonda, owner and master. 1970 to 1984.*

I wondered what was going to happen with my nightmare, which *Tatoosh* had almost made me forget. Sure as the sun rises, baby, it came back with a vengeance. I was helpless against it.

In August, Becky gave me pick of the litter from a local Labrador breeder. It wasn't something I was really ready for. I hadn't had a dog since Buz. Lothar, the dog who'd lived with Susan and me, wasn't really mine. He came to the family when he was over a year old. He was magnificent, and he adored me, but he never entered *my* heart. I think I wouldn't let him. I think I knew that he would be taken away from me and didn't let him in. He was. Susan told me he had growled at Heidi Hagman in a very threatening way, so he was given to someone living in New Mexico while I was away working. I wasn't going to give anyone else the power to rip my heart out, and I let him go as if he were someone else's dog. But this new puppy was something quite different.

With great trepidation, I went to the litter and looked at all the pups. We already had a female black Lab that Thomas's dad had given him in 1980. Becky's pointer, Molly, had gone off to die while we were away, and though it broke her heart, she accepted the new pup as a mate for Zip. We called her Bridget, so we always had Bridget with us. Bridget—my Pearl—loved the idea, and the dog was beautiful, even though she chewed up everything that either of us had cherished. Zip loved her. He knew she was for him. He had been looking for Molly for weeks, and this little black beauty was his new love. Zip had come to the family by way of Jimmy Buffett, and Thomas's "Can I keep him?" was too much to ignore. Zip had died in Becky's arms, and we all felt the loss of this wonderful dog.

And now Thomas and I were at the new breeder's, looking at the two best males. One was called Naughty and the other was Nice. Thomas and I looked at each other and picked Naughty. He turned out to be the nicest and kindest dog any of us had ever known. He was magnificent, and Bridget knew he was her new consort. As he grew, so did my love for him. We called him Sting, because he looked like Sting, the very talented composer-singer from the group The Police. Years later, I was watching Sting, the singer, walking down the beach at the Hagmans', and noticed the regal way he stepped. My Sting walked with the same dignity.

The fly-fishing was great that year, and the skiing was tops, also. The work was not there. But my life, with few exceptions, was full of love.

By the beginning of '85, my right big toe was in need of surgery. The only thing I inherited from my dad was bad big toes. Not a dime;

just these very painful big toes. *Hallux rigidus.* I made arrangements for surgery in L.A. and prepared for it.

Before I had the surgery, there were more important things with which I had to deal. Because I wasn't paying close attention, certain pension plans were created by my money manager, and a great deal of money was put into these pensions. The idea was in my interest, if one calculated the amount of money I made each year as an ongoing feeding trough. Now I found out that I owed the government money. I had declared my taxes and made arrangements to pay the money due, but I was in debt to the U.S. government. I certainly wasn't happy about that. I had always played those confrontations as hard as I did, because I *knew* I was clean. But, suddenly, I was dirty in the eyes of the government. They had been subjected to my out-of-control-hair-trigger-explosive-device act for years, and now, I was in debt to the very same bureaucracy I was struggling so hard to defeat. What is a boy to do?

My accountants asked me to come down to Smell A and have an "interview" with the IRS. Whoa! A what? And I was sternly advised to keep my language nonconfrontational and expletive-free. All right, someone's taking this seriously. I met with IRS agents Joel Levitz and associate. I understood, right away, that it was a bogus deal. I sat in the smaller of the firms' conference rooms with my accounts manager and myself on one side of the table, and two IRS agents that looked like they were from five generations of incest. Seriously! Separated at birth! I hadn't denied my earnings of *any* year. I wasn't denying that I owed the government money, but I thought I had reached an agreement with them for payment plus interest. What were these guys up to? They each had a pile of papers by their side and would refer to them as they whispered in each other's ear, throwing looks at me from time to time. This was the intimidation phase of any government agent's move to make you feel you're about to be shot or jailed. They kept up the whispers-and-looks routine too long. I looked at my accounts manager and decided to take affirmative action.

"What the fuck do you guys want?" My accountant's nervous tick kicked into high gear. "I mean, I've flown down here for a conference with you, and all you can do is try to scare me with whispers and stares. What do you want?"

"We want to know what you've done with the undeclared money from all these movies you've been doing."

"What fucking movies?"

Agent Levitz picked up some of the papers by his side and showed me the source of his high-priced information. The first piece of evidence was a squib from the *National Enquirer*. The *Star* and the *Globe* were right behind.

"The *National Enquirer*? Are you, uh, man, I don't fucking believe this shit! This is where you get your inside information? I don't have to put up with this shit!"

"We can take your furniture, you know."

"Take my furniture? I'll send you the furniture, you dipshit! I'll send it all down to your office. It's all from Goodwill, you assholes. This is ridiculous. Get the fuck out of my face until you can come up with something better than the *National Enquirer*." I left before I got to the actual assaulting-a-federal-agent level of criminal behavior.

While I was flying back to the ranch, the IRS person in Bozeman raided my bank accounts in Livingston. That little maneuver was quickly put straight by my Livingston attorney. The person was pissed, though, and spread the word that she wanted my blue Benz. The 6.9. I thought of finding a wrecked blue Benz, having it cubed, and sticking it in her office.

We watched in seething anger as the IRS started a campaign to ruin us in our own community. We arranged a half-million-dollar loan on our ranch and paid the Feds. I didn't like having paper on the ranch, but I wasn't going to let the agents from Sphincter Control have *any* control of my life. I mean, life is a bitch, and then you have to kill somebody.

Back to L.A. The surgery was successful. Wendy Stark, a longtime dear friend, came by with a bottle of vodka for me. Hopper came by just to spend some time with me, and several other friends stopped in. I hadn't told anybody about the surgery, but word gets out in Hollywood. I was grateful that my friends came by. Becky couldn't be there, but we talked four or five times a day on the phone. I went to Thomas's graduation with my leg in a cast. I had been released from the hospital the day before.

I went back to the ranch with a banjo on my right leg. Seven weeks into the cast, I was getting very bored. On Sunday, June thirtieth, I jumped on my BMW bike, made specially for me, and rode down the valley to watch a friend jump out of a plane and sky-dive to the front lawn of Chico Hot Springs. My friend was successful in her skydiving. I was unsuccessful in my drive home.

I drove home, having had too many tequila shooters while playing pool. At twenty-eight miles per hour I had to dump the bike as I was caught in a large pool of water, overflowing the road due to a change in some hay farmer's water routine. My right leg hit the ground first. I destroyed my posterior cruciate ligament in my right knee, broke my back against a highway signpost, and broke my neck when my head hit an old broken piece of a culvert. Blasted the helmet off my head.

I was taken to our local hospital. They dropped me in the emergency room, and I remember Thomas wanting to take a swing at them because of it. As I sat strapped to a very straight wooden chairlike device, I heard the doctors commenting on the different broken bones in my body. Look at this, they would say. But when they came to my neck, the tone of their voices changed dramatically. They began to talk about my broken neck. As they did, I looked at my fingers and toes and wiggled them, trying to convince myself that there was nothing wrong with my neck. "Yes! Yes!" one of the doctors said. "There is a fracture here on the neck." "Wait a minute," said another doctor. "This is an old break. Very old." The radiologist, Bill Hunter, cautioned them about the older break. Doctor Bray turned to me and asked me if I'd had a trauma to my head when I was about six or seven years old. Bells and whistles went off in my brain.

"Yes. Now I know exactly what happened. Unreal. I was thrown out of a barn window by some older boys at the boarding school I was attending. I fell about twenty-five feet to the hard ground, landing on my chin and wrists." I felt as if the wind had been knocked out of me.

"Did you know you had broken your neck?"

"No. I was told that I had chipped my chin."

"Good God! Did anyone tell your parents?"

"No. My head and neck were wrapped in a major way; I was fed liquids through a hole in the bandages and had little slits, so I could see. I was there in the school infirmary for quite a while." I've always wondered why no one from my family came to visit me. I think the school kept everything very quiet. Maybe they thought they would be sued.

"It was a very bad break," Dr. Bray said. "Did you have any trouble with your arms or legs when you healed?"

"I'm still trying to process the first bit of news. I, uh, I don't remember. You mean, I broke my neck when I was six?"

"Exactly. You were a very lucky boy. Very lucky."

"You don't know the half of it, Doctor Bray. I *am* a very lucky boy." My mind was flashing through the entire episode. I remembered Aunt Harriet commenting about the dirt floors in the infirmary. Wow. I broke my neck back then. I was a bit stunned. Dr. Bray told me that the new break was a very small compression fracture and should heal quickly. The one on my sixth thoracic cost me about a half inch in my height.

I was put in a room and left to my own devices. Most of the time, I asked for pain relievers and Valium. I was getting referral pains in my chest and severe spasms. But hospital types don't like to be told what to do. I didn't give a rat's ass. I was in heavy pain. Becky came to the room and begged me to stop asking for heavier drugs. She said the hospital would think I was a druggie. I didn't give a shit; I wanted the pain to stop.

I was hooked up to a delivery system of pain relievers that allowed me to push a button every twelve minutes and add a precisely measured amount to the IV feeding me. It didn't put a dent in the pain, and I complained. Becky was still mad at me about my asking for something stronger. She was lecturing me as she stood by the bed. Suddenly, she disappeared, and I heard a few swear words break from her lips as she reappeared on the other side of the bed. She had slipped on something on the floor. We couldn't find the source until I pumped for pain, and the liquid squirted straight to the floor. Now Becky had something to say to the hospital types. She was furious. She became Danger Mouse—a nickname I use when she's on a mission. Nurse Ratshit (the head nurse) was banned from my room, and a working pump-for-pain device was hooked up. The drug was combined with something else, and I felt so much better within two hours.

I lay in my bed for two weeks, occasionally taken to a bathtub and given mild therapy, when they determined I was healing well. I missed my boys' birthday party—they held a double party instead of two parties a week apart. Thomas gave me all the details. Justin was so mad at me for being so stupid, he refused to visit.

I came home very carefully on the fifteenth of July. The rest of the summer was one of recovery for me. Things were pretty stretched between Becky and myself. She was, rightly, very angry with me for being so careless and forgetting of those who loved me when I rode my motorcycle under the influence of alcohol. But the tension was shattered by Sting, who cornered me as I sat on the toilet with my right leg in a serious brace. He started us both laughing until tears of relief were flowing from both our eyes. Becky forgave me my sins, and harmony came back to our cabin.

In December, I got a job directing a commercial for Citröen. The shoot was in Almería, Spain, and I got the agency to hire Bridget as the Citröen girl. They were looking for a new girl, and I happened to have some fabulous photos her mother had taken. They hired her at once, and we planned the shoot. At age twenty-one, it would be the first time she worked on camera as a professional. She would go back to NYU with three thousand dollars in her pocket for two days' work. I knew she needed the cash.

The French cameraman invited me to operate the camera for the first professional shot of my daughter. I was delighted, climbing up on the hood and getting on the camera.

I had photographed her many times, filmed her on our Super 8. But the flickering of the shutter on the Arriflex lent a different look to her. I was amazed. I was looking through the lens at someone I had never seen. She was pure magic. She did her bit of business three or four times, then looked at me through the lens saying an exasperated "Daad!" I suddenly regained my composure and cut the camera. I could see that we were going to get better light soon, so I told the cameraman to operate the second take. I apologized to Bridget for letting her just hang there. The light was right and I called for a roll. When the camera was at speed, I said, "Action." Bridget did her stuff, and we all watched in a kind of stupor. Another three or four times doing the same thing, and she said, "Daad!" "Oh!" I exclaimed, and the cameraman realized he, too, had fallen under this amazing spell. "I aim going to marree youah daughtair," he stated. Fat chance, I thought.

As Bridget was winging her way home, I received a very well-written script to start filming in January, a frontiersman-western type of action and human drama. And a very good salary. If I accepted the role, my salary would be put in escrow. These are the words that an actor in an independent film wants to hear. I called Becky on her birthday and told her the good news. I flew to New York to meet with the producers and director. I stopped by the house where Bridget and her friend Dana Kraft were staying. It was a house Dana's father bought and was fixing up. Dana and B lived in the upstairs part. As I walked into B's bedroom, I was very surprised to see how neat and clean it was, and praised Bridget. Then she opened her closet door. Things had been stuffed so tightly into the closet, that they flew out into the room. Within seconds, B's room looked as if a clothes tornado had struck the place. We both sat on her bed laughing our heads off. My darling Pearl.

Back to the ranch and a happy Christmas. I was still quite thin from my convalescence, and began growing my beard and lightly working out. Filming was to begin in the last two weeks of January.

Off I went to Dover, Tennessee. Everything looked right except for the weather. We needed snow—badly. Tennessee had been in a drought for the summer, and it looked like the same was coming for the winter. We shot lots of little scenes and pieces of bigger ones, basically shooting around the no-snow effect. It was very frustrating for the whole team. The New York producer had no idea of what any of this meant. She was just pissed that she wasn't getting the footage she was promised. It was then that I heard the bell toll.

One of the many tricks used by low-budget, independent film producers: shoot some of the fine action scenes with a little of the character scenes for the look and the talent first. Then take the footage to a distributor and pray to get the rest of the budget. In our case, the producer conned a man who owned forty thousand apartments in New York City into giving us the necessary start-shooting money. She promised that a distributor would cover his initial investments and line his pockets with prerelease money. Thank god my fee was in escrow.

We drove all over the hills of Tennessee, Kentucky, and North and South Carolina looking for snow. Not a chance. The director pulled us out of production, while he tried his best to make it all work. It is not a good feeling to have to stop shooting because of money.

Becky joined me and helped me keep calm in the midst of the unraveling. We had a break, so we flew to Palm Beach to visit her best friend, Terry de la Valdéne. I remember, several years earlier, staying with Terry as I prepared for *Split Image*. This time it was a moment of mercy. The two beautiful women did everything they could to make me feel necessary. Make me feel loved. And I do love these two wonderful ladies. They pampered me and made a fuss over me.

Becky and I rented a car and drove to Key West to stay with our dear friend Dink Bruce. I had known Dink as long as I had known Becky. Dink knew that things were getting really stretched thin, and he made us feel welcome and needed. Good friends are more important than money. It was nice to be with those who respect one's inner self. I would be coming back for shelter from the storm a little later.

I returned to the ranch. We took Bridget, Justin, and Thomas to Maui for Easter break. I rented a house right on the beach in Lahaina and a Mustang convertible for the kids, and borrowed a pickup from David Hudson. We all went fishing with David and did the beach thing. We were all happy to be back in Maui, but we missed *Tatoosh*.

We did have one major family moment. I had been consuming a lot of beer and smoking pot that had been a gift from the old gang. Mostly, I wanted to keep the deep worry about the movie and the paper on the ranch as far away as possible. But Bridget was seeing the thing for what it really was. As we all sat in the living room, she tearfully explained that she had seen this behavior from her stepfather, and she was worried for me that I might become a toss-away, that I'd become a beer-a-holic and pothead and let it all slip away.

I was stunned. I wouldn't have gone that route in my life, but I could see, clearly, how Bridget felt that way, and why she might think I would let it all slip away. It had taken so much patience and time to get the mending of all our lives under way, and letting it slide was not part of the life. But Bridget was right. I had all the symptoms. I promised her I would never let *anything* slip away. Seeing that I had worried her to the point of tears tore at my heart.

The year before, I had had the terrible accident on my motorcycle. She was as angry with me as Becky was. She had asked what would have happened if I had died. If she had never been able to have me as her father because of alcohol and thoughtlessness. I remembered saying to Bridget and Justin years earlier that I would always be there for them, even though I was leaving their mother. I felt ashamed.

Because it was done as a family, the confrontation was finished. It didn't require any more talking. Everything had been put on the table and had been dealt with. We all came closer together. I would need this togetherness soon.

Easter break was over and we all went back to the mainland.

Bridget went to NYU; Justin and Thomas went back to Montana State University; Becky and I had a few days together at the ranch. Then I flew to L.A., picked up the 6.9, and started out for Tennessee. As I was driving there, each night I stopped and checked in with Becky. Things were getting worse on the film. The producer was trying like mad to reach me. There was talk of my taking over as director. I said to Becky and Bill Esensten, my accountant, that they were to say they had not heard from me other than messages on the answering machines. I could smell the rat.

I got to the production office and felt like I was walking into a morgue. Everyone in the company looked like balloons that had been inflated for a long time, but had just been let go to sputter around the room and fall like wrinkled, old skin. I learned that my fee had not been put in escrow as promised by contract. The head of my talent agency in New York had a special relationship with the attorney for the producer, and had agreed that they would not have to put up all my money before the start of production. I had been fucked by my own agents. The director allowed me to fly to Key West, while the mess was being untangled. I stayed in close touch with the production office. I could be back in Dover before the start of the next day. I didn't want to be the excuse for stopping the production because I wasn't on the set. It was messy, all right.

Things never got resolved. I was allowed to go to Bridget's graduation from NYU. Allowed. Man, I would have gone even if I was not "allowed." I flew up to Newark, took a taxi to Washington Square, or at least as close as I could get. Four thousand people were there from all the different colleges that make up NYU. Then Speaker of the House, Tip O'Neill, was giving the graduation address. There were many Secret Service agents. I spotted Becky and the boys. A miracle. We didn't know where Pearl was.

I went to a tree and stood there watching the hordes of students in their gowns and robes. I grew disheartened, feeling that my Pearl would think I hadn't made it. About thirty feet away, I saw a hand that looked familiar, but no face to go with it. I saw badly bleached blond hair and a flash of a nose. That nose . . . but then I lost sight. I stood my ground. Then, suddenly, the hand, the hair, that nose all came together, and there was my precious one.

"How did you find me?" she asked.

"I think I was meant to find you."

After the ceremony, we went to a small bar and restaurant and sipped champagne; then I was gone. I had to be back on the non-set before six that evening. But I had made B's graduation, and anything else that might be thrown at me by the producer I could handle and throw back with deadly force.

I watched as the production came further and further unsnapped. I could sense the plan that was being hatched behind my back. The shots we *did* get were hinge shots. Everything was being done to keep my character in the story, but only as a hinge to a secondary story to be shot after I was finished. They couldn't afford me anymore. When the checks stopped, I stopped. I shaved off my beard and flew with Becky to Key West for a short rehabilitation of my soul.

After a week or so of soaking up the sun, we flew back to Dover, then drove back to the ranch in the 6.9. The production still owes me sixty-five thousand dollars.

I relaxed on the ranch, fly-fishing and doing my field work. I did my best to throw away the terrible feeling of the aborted film. My own private nightmare was kicking in much stronger than ever.

One evening, in the heat of an argument, I told Justin that I didn't think he really loved me or respected me. He came and sat next to me in the front room, sobbing, telling me that the reason he was with me was because he loved me so, and couldn't I tell that he re-spected me more than anyone. I put my arms around him and held him close. The stress in my life was not letting me see the overview of my family. My precious boy. My angry accusations had hurt his heart, the one place I wanted to protect the most.

I was offered a film in South Africa, and accepted it after checking with Hugh Masekela. It would start in mid-November and finish a few weeks after the first of January. The director was not ready to direct anything, but I needed the work, so I did my best, but everything that we worked on as actors was ignored. All the character background was dismissed. The filling of these moments didn't take up more screen time, and they made our characters real, but we were all disap-pointed. Jim Mitchum was with me in the film, and he was as dis-mayed as I. Another forgettable movie. The director wouldn't let me use the expression "M.O." "What means 'M.O.'?" he asked. "Modus operandi," I replied. "What means 'modus operandi'?" "The proce-dure by which one works," I explained. He wouldn't let me use the expression. I asked him if he had ever seen *Starsky and Hutch* on television. "Yes, yes, of course." "Well, they use the term all the time." "But you cannot!" he insisted. "No one will understand." I began to use the foulest language I could think of in my character's lines. It all flew over the director's head.

Back in Montana, before I left for Africa, Sting had been caught in an illegal baited coyote trap set twenty yards from my western property fence by a neighboring imbecile. It was the opening of big-game season, and we were always worried about our dogs. We were awakened early by a young hunter who was not a good shot, and had to chase a deer onto our property that he had wounded. I told him to clean up the guts after he dressed it, so that the Labs wouldn't get into them.

We were both worried, as we hadn't seen Sting. I called as loudly as possible and heard his bark from a distance. I ran down to our barn and sheds and heard him barking from the west. I jumped into the pickup and drove down to the paved road and back up toward our west forty on a cattle road. I found Sting with his right paw caught in the trap. I pulled the trap open and freed him. He ran to the pickup and jumped in with some blood coming from his paw. I jumped in after him, and then I saw the real damage. He had been trying to bite the trap off his paw, and had shattered all his canine teeth.

I drove like a maniac to the vet, whom Becky had called. His teeth were almost completely shattered, but a local dentist, who had Labs of his own, came quickly to the vet's. They put Sting under and worked as best as possible to grind smooth and fill the exposed roots. I sat and fumed. My baby Sting, just a little older than two, had, with his Labrador nose, found the baited trap and fallen prey to ignorance and savagery brought on by the idiot kid. This dickhead had set a trap illegally on land he did not own. We had lived on our ranch for twelve years, and most of our neighbors knew about our Labs. I had to leave, but at least I knew Sting would be all right. I was very pissed at the savages.

I joined Jane on an old-fashioned bus tour throughout California promoting the Clean Water Act with a group of other celebrities and a third bus full of press. We played charades and sang songs as we covered the state. I stayed with Jane and her children at her house in Santa Monica for the few days I had before my departure to Africa. You already know about the famous dinner, when I told Jane about my book.

I had an offer to do a European television four-hour special with Liv Ullmann. It was Alberto Moravia's *The Time of Indifference,* a classic written about Rome in 1929 and the lives of a family ruined by their business manager. I was asked to play the business manager. The chance to work with Liv was most fortunate for me. The director, Mauro Bolognini, and his cinematographer were like a chocolate roll at the end of a great Thanksgiving meal. I began work in mid-March, moving to an apartment with Becky for the twelve-week shoot. She had never been to Rome for much longer than time to catch the next plane.

We had spent a week with my sister Pan and her family at their seaside villa in Porto Santo Stefano in 1984, but now Becky could get to know the real Rome. We had a wonderful time there for those many weeks. Russell Chatham spent a few days with us. He is such a great painter, chef, and raconteur, each moment with him is a learning experience. Another friend made it possible for Chatham to get up on the scaffolding and watch the restoration of the Sistine Chapel.

Working with Liv is like doing a comedy of the world each day. She would arrive at seven in the morning looking like a twenty-year-old girl, totally gorgeous. And in two hours she was the matron of a decadent family. We were always playing practical jokes on each other and making up the most outrageous stories about our fellow actors. We got a five-week story going about each other's spouse that would have us sick to our stomachs with laughter that we *had* to contain. For us it was a motion picture, not something made for television.

When we arrived back at the ranch, another script was waiting for me. This is always nice for an actor. The new project was another one in Italy. This was a three-hour TV-special movie with a fascinating story. My character would have to age from thirty-six to forty-eight to seventy-eight. It was a science fiction film without the need of any special effects. It was the story of a man who is touched by some extraterrestrial being in the form of sound, and his quest to understand the meaning of the sound. *Suono.* The English title was *The Long Voyage.* More Rome for Becky. More work for me. More money to whack away at the paper on the ranch.

I drove Sting to a specialist on dogs' mouths and rebuilding broken teeth, in Ann Arbor, Michigan. The process took some time. First a cast of Sting's mouth was needed, then the time it would take to make gold teeth to fit over the shattered remains of his once perfect mouth. During that time, I visited my friend Dan Gerber in Fremont, Michigan. Dan had four female Labs that adored Sting, and I had fun staying with his family. He was up in Lake Leelanau visiting the writer Jim Harrison, but he came home just before I had to take Sting back to Ann Arbor and the fitting of his new gold teeth. I like Dan a lot. He is the heir to Gerber, the makers of baby food, and he used his money to start a publishing house, Sumac Press. It is very hard to be published as a poet, and thanks to Gerber we have Harrison's incredible poems. I think Jim is our finest American poet.

On the Fourth of July, I hosted a major live event from the Capitol Center in Washington, D.C. It was the last in a series of concerts that began in Kansas in late '85. In February of '86 we had a sold-out concert at the Forum, in L.A. The concert went on full blast for almost five hours, until the Forum pulled the plug. All these events were fund-raisers for Vietnam Vets. We called them Welcome Home. The first featured David Crosby, Stephen Stills, and Mike Finnigan; George Thorogood and the Destroyers; and John Fogerty and his band.

In the Kansas concert, we all gathered in the dressing rooms and talked about what song would be the best concert closer. Everyone said "Proud Mary." Everyone except Fogerty. He said he wouldn't be singing "Proud Mary" ever again. We were stunned. He said "Roll Over, Beethoven." We all moaned and said none of us knew all the lyrics. We weren't even sure that Chuck Berry remembered them. John said not to worry, his black backup singers would cover for us. All we had to do was move our lips. Far out. The concert was a total smash, and we somehow made it through "Roll Over," making the audience believe we all were right on the money. I say "we" because I was the MC and brought out each act. Of course I was going to sing! Couldn't stop me.

The big concert was on the Fourth, in '87. We had Crosby, Stills and Nash, Linda Ronstadt and James Ingram, Anita Baker, James Brown, Stevie Wonder, The Four Tops, John Fogerty, Whoopi Goldberg, Jon Voight, John Ritter, Richie Havens, Neil Diamond, Bonnie Raitt, Herbie Hancock, Neil Young, and so many more. HBO carried it live, with an 800 number for donations. It went over five hours, and it raised more than three and a half million dollars. All the 'Nam vets were let in free, and they went wild with emotion. I was helped out in the MC role—thank god—by Voight and Ritter. When Fogerty took the stage, he also took a moment to talk to the vets, both in the auditorium and on television. He was truly amazing. He spoke about things that had affected his career and certain bullheadedness that had been the result. He told the vets to write down all the things that they were carrying around in their hearts, that made them feel helpless or hopeless, angry or despaired, and put them in an envelope addressed to him and mail them away, get them out of their lives, stop looking back and forget about them forever. He then began the opening chords to "Change in the Weather," but stopped for a beat and went right into "Proud Mary" and all the other old hits he had stopped singing because of some bad things that had happened to certain parts of *his* life. It rocked the house. We were making history and, very belatedly, welcoming home all those men and women who had fought in that most terrible war.

After the concert, Becky, Thomas, Justin, and myself went down to Myrtle Beach, South Carolina, to visit Bridget on the set of *Shag,* a movie she was about to start. The ocean water was in the low eighties, and we all had so much fun. B was fabulous. We had dinner with her and the rest of her cast. Then, far too soon for me, we went back to the ranch. I wanted to spend the rest of my life swimming in those warm ocean waters. Warm ocean water is where I belong.

I spent the summer fly-fishing and relaxing, and left for Rome and filming *The Long Voyage* in early September, stopping for a few days in L.A. to see Jane. The afternoon I came to see her, I sensed something was quite different, but I didn't have a chance to ask what was up. Jane took me into her library and, shutting the door, sat next to me on the couch. She made me promise that I would spend five days with her, alone, within the next year. She was very emotional, as was I. She needed to talk about our childhood, she said. Needed to know about all the little details that I remembered, so she could try to put the crazy broken pieces of the puzzle of our early life together. We held each other tightly and cried softly. I promised I would spend the time with her. She said she needed to know, soon, and she was worried that something might happen to me before she could . . . and she broke down. We just held each other for a while, until we could gather ourselves up and go on with the day. I flew on to Italy, but I didn't forget what we had promised. Later that year, I learned that Jane and Tom were divorcing.

· · ·

We began the movie on location in L'Aquila, the capital of the region of Abruzzi. One afternoon, I was having some Polaroids taken of me with the seventy-eight-year-old makeup, and as I watched the picture develop, I was freaked out at the image ghosting in. I looked so much like Dad, it was spooky. I sent some of the photos of me in the older makeup to Jane. She was a bit spooked, too.

Becky and I were happy when we returned to Rome and our apartment on Via di Ripetta, a stone's throw away from Piazza del Popolo and a nice walk to the Spanish Steps, Via del Corso and Via Condotti. We both love Rome very much. I never worried about Becky and shopping in that most expensive city in Europe. She was much too small for the clothes. (I had forgotten about Maud Frizon shoes!) But Becky is always practical about her clothes. And she can have as many Maud Frizon shoes as she likes.

We finished the film and flew back to the ranch for the December skiing with the boys. We had a fun Christmas, but I was becoming more and more crazed by the money pressure, and my cute little nightmare was taking control of my days, too.

Trying to keep a happy home in my heart, I took a bunch of frequent-flier miles, and Becky and the boys and I flew to St. Thomas for spring break. It was a fabulous time for us all. We went sailing on a nice forty-five-foot racing sloop, diving and snorkeling. I felt much better about the life when we returned to the ranch, but I knew that the ice was getting thin.

A film was offered for June and July in Toronto. The part was very creepy, but good for the actor inside. I flew into T.O. and began to separate the life from the role. Although I use many parts of my life in each role, I must always have a small place for my most inner self. Stuart Little's matchbox bed. The director and producer were very committed to a great film noir, but two weeks into the shoot, the money stopped coming. Once again, my fee was to be put in escrow, and wasn't. I flew home, feeling as dry and deserted as the drought-filled land I crossed.

The great fire of '88 was under way when I returned to the ranch. The Park Service has had a policy in place for years: let it burn if it was started by nature. In this instance, the entire area had been in drought conditions for four years. All of us who were living in the area knew how bad the drought had been. The sky turned brown and stayed that way all summer. The fishing was so unnerving, everyone stayed home and worried about the fire, while more than half of the park burned.

A film that I had been talking to some producers about for two years was finally financed, and the money was put up *before* I signed the contract. At least I was going to work. This always lifted my spirits. The location was the Philippines, but the hotel was in the noisiest part of Manila and the pool was a dirty joke. We struggled through, though. Jim Mitchum came over for a cameo and we had a good time. Tia Carrere was my costar, and we made the best of everything.

I had been working out for the role, and I was in the best shape I'd been in since before the motorcycle accident. The good thing about working out is it becomes a habit. A good habit. It's only an hour, and one feels great. I looked great, and if the hours of the schedule threw my workout off, I made sure to take the time to do it. My gym was pretty primitive: a small set of weights and an inclined bench that could drop flat. I didn't use more than sixty-five pounds, but I did lunges and many reps slowly, adding a breathing pattern that maxed my muscle oxygen. I was very lucky to be the type that can come back fast. It had been years since I had done free weights, and the result was good. My gym was our bedroom and the sweat would come off me where I had the most fat. Jane would be proud of me, I thought. I wrote her many letter-poems on an old Hermes Rocket portable typewriter.

When the film was finished, Becky and I needed to find a place to get rid of the pollution and noise of Manila. I thought of the Maldives or the Seychelles, as I had another film with Liv Ullmann starting in a few weeks in Berlin. Fons Rademakers was directing. It was a good story entitled *The Rosegarden,* and I got to play with Liv. But the Maldives and all were far away, so Becky found a place off the Philippine island of Palawan. El Nido.

It was the most wonderful place I could have hoped for. Owned by the Philippines, it was run by the Japanese. Very primitive, very exclusive (only twenty people at a time), very clean but not too expensive. We spent ten days there enjoying the sun and surrounding little islands with pristine beaches, monitor lizards, and green sea turtles.

I returned to the ranch with Becky and prepared for my role in *The Rosegarden*. The week I spent at home was one of the coldest yet, but the warmth of El Nido and the love of my wife more than compensated. And off I flew to Berlin.

Rademakers is an Oscar-winning director and former actor. Working with him was very smooth. Liv is more than smooth. I played her rather thoughtless ex-husband, a German lawyer, with a Cherman accent. The one that came most easily for me was a Bavarian accent. I had played three different American accents, but this was my first foreign one. I thought I did well. Liv's husband, Donald, and Becky joined us, and we had many laughs.

We stayed at the International Hotel, and there was some high-ranking conference on the European economy taking place at the same time. The entire bunch became a little nervous one night, when more than one hundred bikers showed up to give me a cake and several dozen red roses. As it was February, the bikers were bundled and leathered up. There were all kinds of motorcycles in the group, but the pretty women rode Harley-Davidsons. They had come to pay their respects to Captain America on his fiftieth birthday. They were a year early, but the thought of their journey—some had driven two hundred miles—made it impossible to tell them I was only forty-nine.

The roses were so fine, they lasted a week. And the cake was very tasty. The prettiest of the women asked if I would ride on the back of her bike. "If you can kick it over, I'll be glad to take the ride," I told her. Off we went, leaving Becky to wonder if she'd ever see me again. We went around the area of the hotel for a few blocks and returned to a cheering bunch of bikers. I then signed their helmets and gas tanks. It was a fine birthday gift from fans in a foreign land who followed the idea of riding as a way of life. Like the characters in *Easy Rider*.

After we wrapped the film, Becky and I went down to Munich for a week to visit the friends I had made during *Peppermint Frieden* and take a drive in the Alps. After this, we flew to New York, and stayed at the Hagmans' apartment. I met with the top publishing houses to negotiate a book deal for my autobiography. It was done.

On those occasions when I had to go to L.A., I stayed with Jane. She surprised me one day with the news that she was going out with Ted Turner. She was not sure about the whole thing. I said, "Wait a minute, Jane, you don't understand! This is no run-of-the-mill businessman. This guy is a classic. Don't you know about the America's Cup?"

"No."

"He's been the greatest modern-day sailor in the world! Up until him, sailing was the domaine of a network of rich, upperclass men. Turner came along with none of the accouterments of the sport, and before they learned to take him seriously, he'd won the cup out from under them." And I explained CNN to her. She never was much of a TV viewer. This was the first date Jane had had in seventeen years, and she was utterly terrified. She wanted me to come down and be with her as the man of the house. A role I would gladly fill for her. I flew down immediately.

I had long admired him for his daring and his abilities behind the helm. I had seen his name often in reports about the Southern Ocean Racing Circuit. I had also been completely sucked into his television systems. We had put in a dish in '80, as we couldn't get clear television where we lived in the mountains. So Becky and I became fans of America's Team. The Atlanta Braves became our team. By the time Jane was going to dinner with him, he had captured the way news was delivered to the people and made the three networks start to scramble to catch up. They're still playing catch-up. So, I was going to meet this marvelous maverick soon.

As Jane got ready, I played one of my guitars, singing to her. The doorbell rang, and I opened it to welcome Ted. "Hi, Ted, I'm the brother," I told him. Jane called from her room that she was on her way down. Off they went into the night, and I hoped that he would be so charming that he would sweep her away. I knew that he wouldn't be using her. That he didn't need her money. That he wasn't about to be blown away by her exalted stardom or business success. Hell, I wanted the best for Jane. I had the best, and knew that everyone deserved to have a shot at the best.

Justin deVillers Fonda graduated from Montana State University on June 9, 1989, with his bachelor of science degree in film and television production. He was the first male Fonda to have graduated from college since the family arrived on this continent. We were all very pleased for him. I encouraged him to take a five-year term. The same with Thomas, who would be graduating the next spring. They lived together most of their college years. They skied together, rock climbed together, fished together. They were magnificent.

The summer was coming quickly, and Jane and I had the opportunity to spend those days together we had promised each other. She and Tom Hayden had separated some time ago, and Tom was not going to make it easy for my sister, although Jane had made life easy for Tom by supporting him and financing his various political campaigns. I flew to L.A. to meet with her in her house, and at her ranch in Santa Barbara. For me it was an amazing experience. Jane had never let me in so close to her heart and mind. This was not a conference; this was the sharing of those moments of our past that might help explain to both of us the actions of our parents and other things about our past that could be affecting the way we acted in *our* adult lives. There were many very personal insights to Jane that helped me understand her in ways not possible before.

Perhaps it is better that I didn't know some of these things earlier. I most certainly would have reacted strongly to those who might have caused her pain and doubt about her own life and inner values. In most cases, I have acted more strongly against those who have been harmful or hurtful to others than I have acted for myself.

At one point, having eaten a large bowl of pasta Jane served, and relaxing with her in the sun, I told her that sometimes I felt guilty when I thought about how quickly I tumbled to Mom2. Asked what I meant, I explained that I felt as if I had betrayed the bonds to our natural mother by loving Susan Blanchard so completely that I didn't even think about Mother. Jane stood up, walked for a few feet, then turned to me and said that I should *never* feel guilty about any of that. "We were abandoned and we were abused," she said with a great anger inside her. Had I not understood the circumstances we were in, at that moment, I would have thought she was angry at me. I didn't say anything in response, as I was too surprised by her words. I had thought, all these years, that *I* was the only one who felt that way. And I was not going to be the first to mention it anywhere. We had been discussing abuse and abandonment, but I was more circumventing than she. And from that time on, I have been able to deal more evenly with those moments that flash in my frontal lobes from the recesses of my main hard drives.

Jane recorded all of what we said. I think she needs to listen to some things several times to assimilate them. That she needs to attack her defenses strongly and continually to break through them. I envy her ability to defend her inner self. I tend to pull it all out, like turning a sock inside out and letting it shine in the sunlight. "You wear it like a hat, Peter," Jane has often told me. And she is right. But it is the only way I can deal with those same ghosts and stifled screams of the darkness from my childhood past. As I watch these things dance in front of me, I wish I could eliminate each one. But I realize they are, by this time, many of the very things I use as an actor or writer.

I joined Jane that summer while she took a fly-casting and fishing course at an Orvis casting school. I got rid of some bad casting habits I had picked up, and I got to spend these special days with my sister. During the casting lessons, one day Jane turned to me and said that I should call my memoirs *Don't Tell Dad*. I was pleased that she had been thinking about it in a good way. The last day of the school, Jane and I went fishing with Ted and a guide from the Orvis school on Ted's main ranch, just a few miles down the road. We fished Ted's Cherry Creek, a spring creek in the Madison drainage in the northwestern part of his ranch, The Flying D.

When we got to the creek, and were about to take our beats, Jane went walking through the water, and Ted told her not to walk through the water like an elephant. She shot him a look, and when she turned to keep on going, she slipped and fell right on her tail. "Gawd, Jane," Ted jokingly mocked, and I wondered who would ever think of talking to my sister that way. Ted was magnificent.

As we drove up to my cabins, I noticed a trike—a three-wheeled motorcycle—and wondered who of my biker friends was going to surprise me. It was Dennis Quaid. He stayed for supper, and we all sat on the front porch watching a lightning storm roll slowly through the valley. The moment was sparkling and electrifying. Something I'll never forget. It was just the right moment for Jane. We bonded well.

In the fall of '89, I drove through New England, visiting those places of my childhood for recollections for my book. I walked the school campuses and reminisced. I never had a problem finding my way to the schools or the houses in which we lived. I visited the houses where the Hayward children lived. I even visited the Craig House, where Mother died. A security guard tried to stop me from taking pictures: "You can't be photographing this place; it's private." I told him my mother had died there in 1950, and until his bosses came clean with me, I could do as I pleased.

That fall I found myself really on thin ice. Things were great between Becky and myself and the children, but something was slipping. Somewhere I was losing it in a way that I knew too well. I needed help. Stress was mounting in my heart, and my nightmare was pushing itself into every moment of my life, whenever I was questioning my worth. I went to my local doctor, and told him the whole story as fast as I could. I told him of the beginnings of my anal abuse nightmare when I was being checked for a tapeworm, and how it was becoming more destructive to me, and that I wanted to keep a strong heart for Becky and my children. He put me on a drug therapy of nortriptyline that seemed to be a waste. I took the therapy for the prescribed four weeks with no results. In my drug experimenting days, I would have stopped taking the pills after the second night if no results appeared. But for some inexplicable reason, I stayed with the program.

Somewhere into the sixth week, I awoke after having the most beautiful sleep I had ever had. Even on the yacht. My doctor whooped. "That's what we want to hear," he said. "Stay with the program." I advise anyone with the types of background "disorders" that might cause the trauma I had, to ask their doctor about chemical treatment. Drug therapy. It can help.

After driving around New England and visiting my Aunt Harriet in Omaha, I went to Munich for a children's benefit, then popped up to Berlin to watch The Wall come down. I was amazed. While I walked along the wall, I saw children and teenagers, women with long fur coats and students and young couples, all chipping away at the wall, which had become the most tagged wall of concrete in the world on the West Berlin side. I have several pieces of the wall I chipped out myself. When I got a few hundred yards away from the wall, I couldn't hear the babbling of human voices, only the many clinkings and chippings of so many little hammers. I sat down on the ground as if I had been hit in the sternum, and big tears rolled down my forty-nine-year-old cheeks. I was hearing, watching, feeling the Chimes of Freedom. It was a very heavy moment.

I walked around to the other side and marveled at its colorless, nongraffitied facade. Some of the East German guards asked for my autograph, as did many of the people who had come to peek at the West. Though many people were driving back and forth through the holes, many were still so surprised that they acted unsure. Once the autographing started, I wanted to get out of there. Go away by myself. I frantically searched for a sound technician. I wanted to record the sound of the clinking in stereo. I wanted to mix my own version of The Chimes. It was a Sunday, and no one was around.

Well, the sound remains in my head. I can call it up anytime. I wish I could share it with others, but maybe the sounds of freedom are different for each person. It comes from the same source, but is heard in many different ways. One of the things I cherish is the privilege of performing. It frees me, and maybe, just maybe, it might show someone the way to their own freedom. This is not the reason I need to perform. *That* need has no articulate expression; it comes from deep inside and flows out like a river of lava.

Close to Christmas, I was visited by the young Swiss director Nick Hayek. He flew to our ranch to meet with me about a very different kind of motion picture. I was taken by his script right away, and when I met him, I was taken by his enthusiasm, insight, and very quick mind. I gladly accepted the role. I had to be in Lucerne in early February, a nice birthday present.

I played the part of a nightclub juggler, but I never had to juggle. Instead, I had to pick up a top hat with my foot and flip it up onto my head while playing very drunk. Many empty bottles of Dom were scattered around the room.

My fiftieth birthday came in Zurich. Becky was with me; Thomas called me; Bridget faxed me saying, "Guess what, it's Kind Dog's birthday!"; and Justin was pulling focus somewhere. Justin has never been at ease when it comes to celebrations, except for his brother's wedding. I did wonder why I hadn't heard from Jane. I *always* call her on her birthday. I need to call her on her birthday. She would probably prefer that I didn't.

When we got to Milan, I noticed many posters announcing the performance of Hugh Masekela, and was lucky to have that night off. Becky and I went to a club in Milan, sat on the floor, and watched the show. Toward the end, Hughie spoke to the audience, introducing his band, and then he announced that I was in the audience and told them that I had given him everything he ever needed to know about Hollywood, twenty-five years earlier. It was a sweet gesture. After the show, we gathered for a while as the roadies were packing up, and reminisced about the life. We had both survived, and that was the anchor of our love for each other. The same big heart embraced me as it had twenty-five years ago. Continuity is a major thing for me.

Becky and I returned to our ranch, ready for the summer and, for me, writing this book. When I walked into the house, I spent many minutes loving my two dogs. After the love-a-thon with the pups, I went up to my office—formerly the bedroom of my sons—and saw a page in the fax bin. It had been there for quite a while, as it was slightly faded. I quickly grabbed it and read the most beautiful poem written and sent to me by my sister Jane on my fiftieth birthday. It brought me to tears at once. She hadn't forgotten. I tried to call her, but I couldn't keep my emotions under control. I think I gathered my wits as best I could and called her, taking deep breaths every two seconds as I forced the words from my heart, thanking her for her dear thoughts. A few days later, Thomas graduated from MSU with a B.A. in English lit. I am very proud of him. He makes some of the most beautiful straight and folding knives I have seen. Each one is made by hand from the beginning. No jig is used. One blade at a time. He makes his own steel in a small forge. This is his job in life, and he is becoming a master. The irony is that his degree is in English lit.

Justin and I went to Sturgis, South Dakota, in August 1990, for the fiftieth anniversary of the Motorcycle Classic, at the invitation of Harley-Davidson. The weeklong event was nothing less than terrific. George Thorogood and The Allman Brothers Band gave a tremendous concert, and I signed photographs for ten dollars each as a fundraiser for the Muscular Dystrophy Association. I rode up and down the main street of Sturgis, its sides lined with motorcycles and a row of bikes in the center, two deep. When I was recognized, people didn't hassle me for autographs; they just waved, yelled, took photos, and told me they were glad to see me there. Over five hundred thousand motorcyclists came to this little town for the fiftieth during a two-week period. It was a thrill to have been at this enormous party celebrating motorcycling and the lifestyle that the participants all shared. I saw bikes from the thirties on, hot custom jobs and some of the rattiest I'll ever see. Each one was beautiful in its own right. Each rider I met became emotional about meeting me at the Classic. "Man, you changed my whole way of life" was the most common statement told me. We had a great feast at the Bent Shoe Ranch at the invitation of the Hells Angels. There were motorcycle drags and oval track racing. Willie G. Davidson, his wife, Nancy, daughter, Karen, and son, Bill, hosted us at some of the events. Willie G. and Bill are Ugly, and so am I. Proud to be. We all belong to a motorcycle club called Ugly MC. A fine bunch of brothers.

Iraq invaded Kuwait during the event. I wandered into the living room where Justin was sleeping on the roll-out bed and thought about him fighting for his country in a war ten thousand miles away, remembering my feelings about the war in Vietnam. My worries about a world going mad were washed away with the sound of thousands of Harleys. We were both happy to get back to the mountains.

In the fall, Becky and I went to Köln for their first international film festival. Max Schell and I were the honored guests. A week of interviews. Many bottles of mineral water and apples, sunflower seeds, raisins, and at the end of the day, a bowl of fresh filberts and a decanter of great sherry in a plush suite. At the end of the week, I had a mild pain in my lower gut that I ascribed to rich German food, though I hadn't had any. Becky woke me early on the morning of our departure, very concerned. My body was so hot, it had awakened her. My lower gut was quite sore now, and we were worried. It was October third, German Unification Day. A big party for the German people. By pure luck, the hotel manager reached a friend of his who happened to be a gastroenterologist. He came up to the suite and checked me out. He could feel that my temperature was much too high: 105. He called his wife, who was also his assistant at his own clinic.

By the time I reached the clinic, I was failing. My white cell count was twenty-four thousand. At twenty-eight thou, oxygen is no longer delivered to the brain. But I knew what had to happen.

I was fifty and aware that I was in deep trouble, but I was becoming completely terrified. The doctor had to look into my colon. Even though I was given a shot to help me, the doctor had no way of really understanding what was going on in my head. A simple shot was not enough, and as I lay on my side in a fetal position, I reverted to my six-year-old self on that terrible morning in 1946 at Johns Hopkins. I cried like a frightened six-year-old, but begged to be killed before I was raped like a fifty-year-old. I pleaded with them to kill me. I was serious. Part of me knew that I had to be checked out, but part of me did not want to have *that* happen to me again.

I was put on a very serious but specific antibiotic and told to stay in bed, basically, for three days, and if the antibiotic worked and I was out of danger, I could fly back to my home. On the flight back, I wrote a song. Music and lyrics. I hummed the music into a little re-corder as I wrote the lyrics so I would remember it.

If I had been alone, or if Becky hadn't snuggled up to me as she

usually does, I would have died in my sleep. Septic toxic poisoning.
For three days I tried to conjure up an image of my mother to scream
and rail at and get rid of my humility resuffered, of the rape she had
ordered to find a tapeworm. My father escaped this rage, as he most
likely had no idea what was happening. More than likely, he was
trying *not* to know.

Even when I was back in the safety of our cabin in Montana, I was
living in dread of the certainty that I would have to have this procedure again, in a much more serious way. Great. My own private nightmare was now the daily happening. The doctor kept saying not to
worry, I wouldn't remember a thing. I replied that I had been raped
twice now, and I wouldn't stand for a third.

When the day came, Becky drove me to the clinic, trying to reassure me. I was led into the examination area and prepped for whatever drug was going to let me not experience the hurt or trauma.

The drugs did their thing, and I didn't suffer the trauma, but as I
was wheeled out of the examination room, I repeated every word the
doctor and I had said during the procedure. Never tell me I won't
remember, Doctor, unless you can guarantee it.

All the ground I had gained over the forty-four obsessing years and
lost during the past few months was given back to me. I still will not
consent to any other person having control over my mind or body. It
is not allowed, and severe physical damage will occur if someone
tries. But I had done one of the things I had wanted for most of my
thinking life. I had written a song. "The In Between." One more thing
that I have fulfilled in the life.

Christmas came, and the family had a grand time. No work, but
happiness always helps.

I spent most of '91 cranking away at the book and hoping for work
in motion pictures. I had paid off 80 percent of the paper on our
ranch, but the last twenty was just as hard on us as the entire thing
had been.

The Hagmans, Becky, and I decided to mate Sting with their beautiful female, Fida, after they had come to our ranch to see Sting. When
I first took Sting down to Malibu, Fida didn't come into heat, but I did.
And with Dennis Hackin, the man who had written *Wanda Nevada,* I
cowrote the story and the screenplay *Sons of Guns.* The creative process is so fantastic when one collaborates with someone very good.

The best way to describe *Sons of Guns* is a Gary Larson–style spaghetti western. I took Sting back to Montana.

On December 2, Larry called me and told me to get Sting down there at once. Fida was finally ready. I flew him down and they coupled right away, and I flew back to our ranch.

A few weeks after the successful coupling, we flew to Tallahassee, Florida, to be at Jane and Ted's wedding. It was on her birthday, December 21. Ted's plantation, Avalon, outside of Tallahassee, was the perfect spot. Knowing that the event was coming, I had been practicing Tony Arata's "The Dance" to sing to Ted and Jane on the big day. Becky and Justin told me it was too sad a song to sing at a wedding. I wondered about it for a while, and finally called Patrick Wayne, whose dad, the Duke, was in the video accompanying Garth Brooks's version of the song. Pat told me he thought the song was a celebration and, knowing a little of the things we had gone through in our lives, said it was the best song to sing for the occasion.

Unlike the other weddings, this was more personal to me. I totally approved of Ted, and I knew he had been through some pretty rough stuff in his youth, too. His dad had committed sucide when Ted was twenty-three. This time, I sang the song to the two of them in their bedroom right after the ceremony. It was hard for me to sing it. I was getting the emotions of the song tumbling through my heart as the words escaped my lips. I made it through fairly well, though, but had to leave the room, teary-eyed, as soon as I finished.

Troy gave his mother away, and he gave the best toast at the dinner afterward. He is such a great young man. I love him a lot. He is very gifted artistically, and could be a fine actor-painter like his grandpa.

· · ·

Fida whelped nine pups. Five males and four females, and it was quite an ordeal for her and us. Once all was done and well under way, Becky returned to the ranch and I stayed in Malibu for seven weeks as puppymeister. The strain of having me constantly at her house (even though I stayed in the guest house) was too much for Maj, and it almost ruined our relationship. But seven weeks later, I left with the pick of the litter. Bridget and her boyfriend, Eric Stoltz, took a female. My little Tuffy—as I called him—and I flew back to

Montana. Lake Speed. Great name for a dog. After the famous race car driver.

That fall, I did Love Ride 9 for the Muscular Dystrophy Association in California, and for the third year, met up with Dwight Yoakam, the outstanding country-rock-hillbilly singer and composer. This ride, Dwight asked me if I was interested in directing a play that he was producing. I told him I hadn't directed a stage play in twenty-five years. "Well, it's about time to do another one," he said, and asked for my address to send a script.

The next January, I was in Los Angeles holding readings for the parts in the play, *Southern Rapture,* a southern gothic allegory. After reading many actors for the male lead, I insisted that Dwight read for the role, at Sally Kirkland's urging. Sally was part of the cast, and she got some actors together to read the other parts. They all came to my hotel room, and I watched Dwight very carefully as he read his part. At first, I thought he was really slow with his lines, like Dad had been so many years earlier. But I quickly understood that Dwight was going over his lines for character and *then* giving me the reading. He was incredible. Even with his reluctance to play the role, he was better in his out-of-beat reading than *anyone* we had auditioned before.

I spent an unusual amount of time with the play at the table. I worked on timing and value before I let the actors learn the blocking on a taped floor. In his stage and video performances as a singer, Dwight was a minimalist, and a perfect one for his persona as a singer. Even though he danced in an extraordinary way, his moves were minimal yet incredibly suggestive. But in *Southern Rapture* he had to roam the stage like a tai chi artist. At first, he put up a small struggle with me at the beginning of each blocking rehearsal. As I would correct him or explain the moves to him, he would take down the blocking notes very slowly, giving me annoyed looks. But his blocking notes were the best of any of the other actors. The most precise, the most detailed. He was magnificent. He had done a little bit of stage work in high school, but none of us were ready for his very powerful stage presence, and his talent as a stage actor.

Dwight and I became very close and remain so today. Becky came down just before we opened and marveled at my calmness, as did Bridget. On their way to the opening night, B picked Becky up at the hotel and drove her to the theater. During the drive, B worried that I had fallen for this magnetic persona and lost sight of the true stuff of acting. She said she didn't have time to come to the opening-night party. She told Becky she would just sneak away after the curtain call. She also warned her that L.A. theater critics were notorious about giving bad reviews.

On the twenty-ninth of April, we opened. I sat way up in the back of the theater and watched as B and Becky went to their seats. I could see the concern on both their faces. The lights dimmed to black, and the play began. Within forty-five seconds, no one was watching Dwight Yoakam, the country singer, trying to act onstage. Everyone was watching Tommy Joe Blain, DY's character, do his thing. At the act break, I watched as Bridget and Becky went to the lobby. The looks on both their faces were perfectly calm. At the end of the show, the sold-out house applauded the actors, but the applause took on a different intensity when DY walked onstage for his bows. All the performances were great, but Dwight's was fabulous. There was only one thing he had to learn about stage acting. "Smile when you take your bow," I told him. "Even if they throw vegetables at you, smile. Smile because you know you'll have some food for the table."

The critics tore the play apart. It deserved it; it did not stand up as a literary piece, which all plays must do. The author refused to change a word. But there were six great characters, and six good actors who played them very well. This was the only reason to mount the play. Badja Djola, Sally Kirkland, Joe Unger, Vanessa Marcil, and Mark Kilburn, thanks to you all. The artistic energy that had to be used at full strength during the directing of the play was a great renaissance for my inner self.

I have since coached Dwight for a role—most times at one or two in the morning—in a movie several times. Or a reading for a part. I turned him on to my acting coach, Harold Guskin, whom B turned me and Jane on to. And Dwight has done very well. His is a special talent. He is a prodigy and a true friend. In his last role to this date, he played a venomous, mean-spirited bad guy. It was a Billy Bob Thorton screenplay, in which Billy Bob played the lead, produced the film, and directed it. Dwight was scary and wonderful, and has recieved some very well-deserved reviews.

That fall, I did a role in a two-hour special, *Heat of the Night,* and got to flex some more muscle. While I was considering the role—Carroll O'Connor offered me an outrageous amount of money—

Bridget called. I told her of the offer and she asked about the role. I told her.

"A throne, Dad? You get to sit on a real throne?"

"Yes. And I get to blow myself up with eight pounds of semtex!"

"Dad, anytime you're offered a role where you sit on a throne, take it!"

Thanks to my newfound energy and all the encouragement from Jane, I bought the paper on the ranch back from the bank. We had a great Christmas.

In January, 1994, I accepted a role in a very avant-garde film called *Nadja*. I got the chance for the part because Eric Stoltz, a great actor himself, suggested me. The part was as his uncle, who turns out to be his father, and Eric mentioned that we had similar facial features. I played Dr. Van Helsing, the man who stakes Dracula. I worked for low-budget scale as a Screen Actors Guild member. I didn't even know there was such a thing as low-budget scale. I thought that I had learned everything there was about scale acting from Roger Corman.

With plenty of frequent-flyer miles on Delta and a great apartment in New York that is Mom2's, I could afford to come to the city and do the part. I worked with Martin Donovan, who had taken the part that Eric was to have played but couldn't due to family commitments, and Elina Löwensohn, who played the title role to perfection and has one of the most dangerously attractive personas I have ever seen. Jared Harris played her twin brother; Suzy Amis, my niece-or-maybe-daughter; Galaxy Craze, Martin's wife; and Carl Geary, Nadja's driver and personal escort. Mary Sweeney and Amy Hobby produced for David Lynch. Other than the actors, everyone else worked for a very low flat rate. The cinematographer, Jim Denault, was outstanding, and we all loved the script by Michael Almereyda, our fearless director.

I had the best time I'd ever had acting in a movie. And after its release, I had the best reviews in a long time. It's as if I had found a new gear, and I intend to use it to its fullest.

Months later, on *The Tonight Show* with Jay Leno, Dennis Hopper said that he had fired Rip Torn from *Easy Rider,* because Rip had pulled a knife on him at some restaurant. The reader might recall that episode from a few chapters back. Hopper never fired Rip from the movie; I didn't ever hire him, because he needed more money than I could afford. The "knife" thing went down just as I have written. Rip got all bent because the Leno show made him look like he was fired for pulling a steak knife on Hopper, and he took Hopper to court. Hopper, to rectify in his own mind how and why this incident took place, made up a back story of hearing that Southern and I had not done any writing while he was out scouting locations. He said that he got furious, flew to New York, and burst upon us at this restaurant, and in his heated state of mind, told Rip that he was cutting the part way down if not out, and Rip then pulled the knife. Rip remembers that *he* disarmed Dennis, who had put a steak knife to Rip's throat, because of his military background.

This incident, which was quite different in its real time, took place more than twenty-five years ago. It seems to me absolutely insane that these grown men would put themselves in court over an ancient incident that didn't even happen the way it was described by Dennis. The most foolish thing, though, was the refusal by Dennis to go back on the Leno show and apologize for his misstatements. Rip would have dropped the whole thing if he had. He asked me to take that message to Dennis, and Dennis refused the chance.

On the twenty-third of July, 1994, Thomas married Michelle Wilken, a strikingly beautiful young woman from Bozeman, Montana. Justin was the best man, and Bridget was a bridesmaid. Justin made a fabulous toast at the dinner, and Bridget welcomed Michelle into the family. Michelle and Thomas had been together for several years, and we were all very happy. They all go camping, canoeing, rock climbing, skiing, and mountain biking together. Thomas and Justin often cook for their friends, finding it less expensive than eating at a restaurant. The two boys have become real chefs over the years. They cooked for sixty people at our ranch for a fund-raiser, even making all the hors d'oeuvres.

chapter Twenty-seven

Looking back on the memory of
The dance we shared, 'neath the stars above
For a moment everything was right,
How was I to know that you'd ever say goodbye;

And now, I'm glad I didn't know
The way it all would end, the way it all would go.
Our lives are better left to chance,
I could have missed the pain,
But I'd have had to miss
— TONY ARATA, "THE DANCE"

Late in February of '96, Sting Fonda could no longer function as a normal dog. He could not take care of himself. He had waited until I returned from a trip to the Yucatán. We put him down that very morning. Becky and I held his head in our laps, kissing him and stroking his head as he succumbed, first to the powerful tranquilizer. We told him what a wonderful dog he was. How good he had been. How much we loved him. This is the way he left us: feeling loved and cherished. Another little piece of my heart left when his life coughed from his magnificent body in a last spasm. I truly loved him, and he loved me back in the way that only great dogs do. Nobel Laureate Konrad Lorenz would have honored him with the phrase "rarest of the rare." It was painful for Becky and me, but we could not let him suffer the indignities of not being able to care for or defend himself just for the sake of our wanting him to live longer with us. I cried for a while and then decided that it was better to remember him as the great, intelligent, and loyal friend he was. This is how I manage to remember him without deep sorrow. He left me while I held him and loved him truly. He wasn't taken from me. He wasn't put down behind my back, in thoughtlessness. And my heart has grown much larger than it was when I was eleven. I could afford the loss and know that the missing piece would heal. I feel honored that I was the human that could share the magnificent life of this animal. Bridget and I have both a son and a daughter from the twenty pups he sired. They are beautiful and . . . there will never be another dog that can fill the place in our family's heart that was Sting's special domain.

•   •   •

In the last few years, I have had the opportunity to work with some of the more interesting people in motion pictures. I did a stint with John Carpenter and Kurt Russell in *Escape From L.A.* Allison Anders directed me in *Grace of My Heart,* and though my scene was cut from the film, my voice does play in an overlay. I loved working with Carpenter and Russell. They were a hoot. I look forward to working with them again soon. Allison was simply great. Funny and full of new ideas. She is best known for her films *Mi Vida Loca* and *Gas, Food, Lodging.* I hope I will be getting a call from her for *her* next film. I was critically acclaimed for my role as Dr. Van Helsing (of Dracula fame . . . Van stakes Drac in the original story) in Michael Almereyda's *Nadja.* Working for Michael was most unusual. We used several different mediums in the filming process: straight sixteen- and thirty-five millimeter black-and-white Eastman Kodak and a toy video camera from Fisher-Price: the PXL2000. The latter is known in the underground film world as "Pixelvision." I had such a great time working for nothing with Michael and his crew (who worked for less) for six weeks in New York City at night that, until the spring and early summer of '96, I would say I had the best time I have ever had during a film *or* play. The most satisfying experience as an actor. But, as of the first week in April through the last week of June '96, I *did* have the most exciting time ever on film or stage. *Ulee's Gold.*

I worked for Victor Nunez in *Ulee's Gold.* He was the director, the writer, the editor, the real producer, *and* the cameraman. The camera operator! Victor is so fiercely independent that in almost twenty years he has directed four films. *Gal Young'Un, A Flash of Green*—starring Ed Harris and Blair Brown—*Ruby in Paradise*— which brought Ashley Judd to the attention of Hollywood—and *Ulee's Gold.* While effusing about Victor in an interview, I was asked if he reminded me of myself. I answered that he reminded me of my goals. My ideals. I do not know what I will do if I work for a director with less integrity. He is the most generous director I have worked for and the most exacting. His crew is as devoted to him as the crew my father described in his letter about *Wanda Nevada* was to me. And it *is* a rare thing.

I love making movies. Real motion pictures. I love being as involved as possible. Maybe that's why I love to direct *and* act in the same film. After I read the script for *Ulee's Gold,* I sat very quietly trying to keep my emotions inside my body. This was *the* role for me. I *was* this man. The part of Ulee—short for Ulysses—demanded the kind of performance only actors like my father give. They must be played with the lightest touch. As a matter of fact, they must be played by being the part. I worked hard. Very hard. When we watched a rough cut, Becky could not see the wheels turning. Could not see me. She saw only Ulee. I was emancipated. Working for someone like Victor has done me a world of good. It reminds me that there are all kinds of deals in the business, and not all of them are bad. I forget that from time to time.

We moved from St. George Island, off the panhandle of northern Florida, to Orlando for the last week of shooting. Most of the Company was moping around with heads hung low. When I asked why they were all so down-in-the-dumps, I assumed Orlando was the reason. We had been staying at a motel on the island with the Gulf right outside our rooms. We had bonfires on the beach almost every Saturday and Sunday night for eight weeks, and now we were in the seediest part of Orlando. The Company told me that they were all feeling down because it was the last week of the shoot. I told them that I had just had the best sex ever as an actor and was not going to mope about it. My problem was: when would I get laid like that again?

I managed to keep the feeling rolling when I was voted Beekeeper of the Year by the Florida State Beekeepers Association. I flew down to Gainesville to accept the honor. It was not given lightly. It meant as much to them as it did to me. After the ceremony and a rolling party with those members of the Company who lived in the area, I went on up to Tallahassee and sat in with Victor as he was editing. Even taking only nine seconds out of the film was such a gas for me. Being part of the postproduction. A backdoor call from me to Van

Morrison resulted in the rights to use his most magnificent song, "Tupelo Honey." In the vernacular of the motion picture, Ulee's gold means tupelo honey.

. . .

Dennis Hopper is still insisting that he alone wrote the screenplay to *Easy Rider,* and has sued me for cheating him out of "millions and millions of dollars" during the twenty-seven years the film was released and royalties were paid to The Pando Company and Raybert Productions. It blows my mind. I "cheated him out of greed and hate" the suit claimed, as did Dennis on TV, radio, and print. Far out.

. . .

I have learned that it is all about forgiveness. I have learned to forgive my mother and father. Yes, I even forgive the dog-killer, Grandma Seymour. In the glow of hindsight, I can empathize with her today. She lost her youngest child, a girl, at age six. She lost my mother to suicide. I don't know that I could carry on with life as well as she, if *I* lost one of my children. And all those who hurt me deep in my heart. Yes. I think it's about forgiveness. And, most importantly, I have learned to forgive myself.

. . .

I am remembering an evening in late '69 or early '70. Dennis Hopper and I did a *David Frost Show* in L.A. The other guests were Nancy Sinatra, the Everly Brothers, and a few other young people in the industry. We were asked what was the main thing that concerned us. I suppose that the producers thought that we represented the disenfranchised youth. We all sat around on the carpet of the set. I said, with great passion, that I was worried about what water my children would drink and what air they would breathe. The questions were right, but the audience was not ready to even think about them. Today my children are all young adults, and I still worry about what they are going to drink and breathe. Today, the water part is beginning to sink in, but the air part still flies over most people's heads.

While everyone is buying their bottles of water, they haven't understood that they won't be able to buy air. Imagine if everybody on the planet took a breath at the same time. The possibility of everyone breathing in at the same time is real. Just understand that it's a possibility, and therefore it possibly exists. Understand that ten thousand persons are born every half a second, not to mention all the mammals, and the planet cannot produce enough oxygen to sustain the amount of people that will inhabit its surface in a few decades. Consumption is going rampant, and nobody cares. I know that nobody is getting out of the parking lot alive, and I have no problem with that. I am not exempt. But I do think we can keep the parking lot much cleaner.

Apathy has set in so deeply, and the bureaucracy that feeds on it is not going to give up an inch. When just a little over 30 percent of the electorate is exercising their democratic right to vote, we have already lost our representative democracy. Albert Einstein said, "The strength of the Constitution lies entirely in the determination of each citizen to defend it. Only if every single citizen feels duty bound to do his share in this defense are constitutional rights secure." As for myself, my parking ticket has been validated by the person who was born to do that thing. I am married to her. I will defend the Constitution with my life, but I will zealously defend, first, our unalienable rights to Life, Liberty, and the Pursuit of Happiness.

Jane asked me to be sure to give more details of our parents' background, so that others with broken and distorted childhoods like ours can understand their own lives better. I know what she means, but I don't have a lot to go on, and I do my best to stay away from the buzzword. Dysfunctio . . . you know. Our mother had a terribly alcoholic father, and her first husband was a major alcoholic, also. But I think her abandonment by our father was the match that lit her waiting fuse. I really don't have much more of her history. Most of the sealed lips have been gathered and are gone forever. I know that she made her marriage to our father happen, but she must have already been losing herself. In my own life, I watched her withdraw completely, but I have no real hard reason why she took her own life. It may have been in the letters that burned. I'll never know. And that doesn't matter anymore.

There are four or five stories about our father that have been repeated, and that is what we know. Generally, when asked about his parents, he would only say they were perfect. Mary Baker Eddy and

Christian Science play in the background, somewhere, but all I know is that she had some sort of influence on his parents, and "some sort" offers no explanation. Things happened to him that we will never know. He was never beaten. But something happened to him that made him very quiet, very shy, and he let those qualities define his personality. They were the makeup and costume that he wore in real life. Somewhere, he found it was easier to say nothing. Easier on his heart, I mean. I believe that he loved us both. Very much, I think. And it was that "very much" that was the hardest thing for him to show, let alone say. The deeper the emotion, the deeper he hid it. I say more about our father, because I know more about him. But I'll never know enough. And the forty-two years that was our mother's life, and the twelve years she was our mother, would never be enough to know about her.

To my eyes, we lived in a very special place. Our mother was meticulous about the way she kept her house. There was a place for everything and everything was in its place. In that matter, she and our father shared the same strict rules of engagement. Both perfectionists. Both extremely retentive. Yet the house they built, the farm on Tigertail, was the opposite of their inner selves. It was a paradise.

No sooner had we moved in, than our father left to fight for his country. I will never belittle his patriotism, but I often wonder if going to war was a way of keeping himself from the kind of commitment that a family with two very young children demands. He had a tremendous sense of humor that hardly anyone saw offstage or offscreen. He probably tried his very best to hide that, also. But now and then, he could not contain it, and it burst forth from him like a Roman candle. And like a Roman candle, it disappeared very quickly. But those of us who had seen it were in awe of it, and waited patiently or impatiently for the next show. We all learned not to let on to that thirsting no matter how hot the desert got. I only hoped to be around when it would burst forth again.

I think our mother loved us. Maybe very much. But we weren't enough to keep her with us for a natural life. Other than my daydream about my fourth-grade teacher, I have never felt that I let her down while she was with us. Only after she died and I, needing a mother, invested everything I had in Susan Blanchard, Mom2. Mother's early departure left us scarred. But we have the skills of a great plastic surgeon and can sculpt the scars away. Almost. I have stayed away from the details of my two other sisters for their privacy and our lack of connection, though Pan did her very best in the earlier years. She now has a daughter, Pilar, and her son, Alessandro. They are both beautiful and stand in their own light. Dear Amy is married and happy and the mother of twin girls, Rachel and Haley. She is a psychologist and has her own practice.

I knew I didn't *have* to pass along the same pains to my children. But I was born in a different time. A different idea. And not passing it on was much easier. Jane has told me that she despised me for a long time, but she took me along with her when she went searching for something we didn't even know. I was like a puppy, following her lead. She never kicked me away, so I kept on trying to puppy up with her. Over the years, I have drifted away from the rest of the family, but strangely, I seem to have drifted closer to her. Maybe because we have gone through so much that no one else can see but us. Like a drop of splattered quicksilver, we seem to have drawn ourselves back together. Though we have far too little time to *be* together.

I often think about the advice or commands that Jane has given me for all the years we have been sister and brother. Some of it was so on target, and some was a total mystery. I often wonder what she really meant when she would advise me or command me. I wondered what was in her mind, that she might say some of the things she did.

Right now, I can clearly see her standing at Vadim's Ferrari with its crumpled rear end that early Saint-Tropez morning in '66, when we were packing all the gear to go to the Venice Film Festival. Jane did all the talking. She organized as best she could—and she is the best—the impossibility of stuffing me into the car with all our things. And I can see so clearly those wondrous days of decadence that swept me away, for a moment, with Dado, Nancy, Tahlita, and Paul.

"Okay, Peter, put that bag in first, then . . . no, put your guitar in and then . . . Okay, first put the hanging bag in, then you get in on top of it, then we'll put the other bags on each side of you, and you hold on to the guitar so that the long end sticks out front. Okay?"

Once inside, with me tangled up in guitar and luggage in a space meant for a briefcase, we sped off to the airport. When we got on the Autoroute, Vadim pushed the needles up, and soon we were whip- ping along at 132 miles per hour. I could see the speedometer be- tween my guitar and Vadim's arm. But I was not about to say anything. I didn't want him to start trick driving at that speed. Nothing had been said after the packing instructions. For that matter, it was pretty intense in the cab of the car. It was almost as if none of us were breathing. Critical mass. And then, out of the confinement,

"Peter?"

"Hmmmm?"

"Don't tell Dad."